LIBRARY AND INFORMATION SCIENCE ANNUAL

VOLUME 3

1987

LIBRARY AND INFORMATION SCIENCE ANNUAL

VOLUME 3
1987

Bohdan S. Wynar EDITOR
Ann E. Prentice ASSOCIATE EDITOR

ASSISTANT EDITORS
Anna Grace Patterson
Sharon Kincaide

1987

LIBRARIES UNLIMITED
LITTLETON, COLORADO

Copyright © 1987 Libraries Unlimited, Inc.
All Rights Reserved
Printed in the United States of America

No part of this publication may be reproduced, stored in a retrieval system, or transmitted, in any form or by any means, electronic, mechanical, photocopying, recording, or otherwise, without the prior written permission of the publisher.

LIBRARIES UNLIMITED, INC.
P.O. Box 263
Littleton, Colorado 80160-0263

ISBN 0-87287-596-2
ISSN 8755-2108

Library and Information Science Annual (formerly *Library Science Annual*) is a companion volume to *American Reference Books Annual*.

Libraries Unlimited books are bound with Type II nonwoven material that meets and exceeds National Association of State Textbook Administrators' Type II nonwoven material specifications Class A through E.

Contents

Publications Cited................... vii
Introduction ix
Contributors xi

Part I
ESSAYS

Collection Development in Schools of
    Library and Information Science
    by Ann E. Prentice................... 3

The Oryx Press: Information, High-
    Technology, and Libraries
    by Dick DeBacher................. 13

CD-ROM in 1986 by Carol Tenopir........ 21

Microcomputer Hardware:
    Current Offerings and Trends
    by Myke Gluck..................... 26

School Library Media Program
    Research: Review of 1986
    by Daniel D. Barron................. 36

The Research Efforts of ALA and
    ALISE by Ron Powell and
    Sharon L. Baker................... 44

Part II
REVIEWS OF BOOKS

General Reference Works................. 51
    Bibliographies....................... 51
    Biographies......................... 53
    Dictionaries and Encyclopedias....... 55
    Directories......................... 58
    Handbooks and Yearbooks........... 61
    Periodicals and Serials............... 63
    Quotation Books.................... 64
Architecture 65
Automation in Libraries................. 66
    General Works..................... 66
    Reference Works................... 67
    Data Manipulation.................. 68
    Databases 68
    Networks and Networking........... 69
    Online Public Access Catalogs........ 72
    Online Searching................... 74
    Telecommunications 75
Careers............................... 76
Cataloging and Classification............ 78
    General Works..................... 78
    Cataloging-in-Publication............ 80
    Classification and Classification
        Schemes.................... 80
    Descriptive Cataloging.............. 83
    Special Materials and Problems....... 86
Children's Literature.................... 89
    Bibliographies...................... 89
    Biographies........................ 92
    Dictionaries........................ 93
    Directories......................... 94
    Handbooks 95
    Indexes 97
    Picture Books...................... 98
**Collection Development and
    Selection of Materials**................ 99
College and Research Libraries.......... 102
**Comparative and International
    Librarianship** 107
    General Works.................... 107
    Africa............................ 108
    Asia 108
    Australia 110
    Canada 111
    Europe........................... 111

Comparative and International Librarianship (*continued*)
    Great Britain.......................113
    Latin America......................114
Conservation...........................115
Copyright..............................116
Education..............................116
Festschriften...........................119
History.................................120
Indexing and Abstracting................122
Information Technology.................123
    General Works......................123
        Dictionaries...................123
        Handbooks and Yearbooks.......124
        Indexes and Abstracts..........125
        Monographs....................125
    Information Management............127
    Information Systems................128
    Information Theories...............129
    Technological Computing............130
        General Computing.............130
            General Works, 130; Dictionaries, 131; Directories, 133; Handbooks and Yearbooks, 134; Indexes, 135
        Microcomputing 135
            General Works, 135; Dictionaries, 136; Directories, 136; Handbooks, 140
Intellectual Freedom and Censorship......141
Interlibrary Loans.....................143
Law and Legislation....................143
Library Humor.........................144
Library Instruction....................144
Library Research......................147
Library Security.......................147
Management............................148
Nonbook Materials.....................152
Public Libraries.......................153
Public Relations.......................157
Public Services........................158
Publishing.............................159
Reference Services.....................160
Research Methods......................163

School Library Media Centers............164
    General Works.....................164
    Bibliographies.....................167
    Collections 167
    Media Skills and Programs..........170
    Microcomputer Use.................172
    Toys and Games...................174
Service to Disabled Users................175
Special Libraries and Collections.........175
    General Works.....................175
    Archival Collections................177
    Art Libraries......................178
    Government Publications...........180
    Law Libraries.....................184
    Medical Libraries..................185
    Museums.........................186
    National and Federal Libraries........187
    Newspaper Libraries................188
    Science and Technology Libraries.....189
    Serials 190
    State Libraries....................191
    Theological, Church, and
        Synagogue Libraries..........192
    Toy Libraries.....................194
    Women's Collections...............194
Technical Standards.....................194

Part III
REVIEWS OF PERIODICALS

National................................199
Subject-oriented........................208
Regional...............................219

Part IV
ABSTRACTS OF LIBRARY SCIENCE DISSERTATIONS
by Gail A. Schlachter

Introduction...........................229
Abstracts..............................230

Author/Title Index.................245
Subject Index......................259

Publications Cited

FORM OF CITATION	PUBLICATION TITLE
ARBA	American Reference Books Annual
BL	Booklist
C&RL	College & Research Libraries
Choice	Choice
CLJ	Canadian Library Journal
EL	Emergency Librarian
JAL	Journal of Academic Librarianship
LJ	Library Journal
RBB	Reference Books Bulletin
RQ	RQ
SLJ	School Library Journal
SLMQ	School Library Media Quarterly
VOYA	Voice of Youth Advocates
WLB	Wilson Library Bulletin

Introduction

With this volume, *Library Science Annual* changes its title to *Library and Information Science Annual* (*LISCA*). This change reflects our intention to expand the scope of this annual to include the closely related field of information science in more depth. The reader will note that there is a greater number of reviews on information science included this year, and we plan to include even more comprehensive coverage in volume 4. We hope that readers will appreciate the substantially enlarged scope of *LISCA*. In order to facilitate this expansion of materials included and the broadening of *LISCA*'s focus, Dr. Ann Prentice, Director of the Graduate School of Library and Information Science, University of Tennessee, has kindly agreed to assist us as our new associate editor.

LISCA volume 3 retains the same broad objectives of the first two volumes:

1. To review all English-language monographs and reference books in library science published in a year, not just selected or recommended titles. Volume 1 reviewed 253 titles, principally U.S., a few Canadian imprints, and some other imprints distributed in the United States. Volume 2, extending coverage of Canadian imprints, reviewed 305 titles. Volume 3, with even greater coverage of Canadian and British titles, reviews 382.

2. To evaluate systematically all English-language library science periodicals and indexing services. Each year, the editors of *LISCA* will select titles for review. Forty-two periodicals published in the United States and Canada were reviewed in volume 1, including some of national or regional interest and some that are subject-oriented. Volume 2 reviewed twenty-two titles and began coverage of library science databases with reviews of LIBRARY LITERATURE (WILSONLINE) and LIBRARY & INFORMATION SCIENCE ABSTRACTS (LISA). Volume 3 reviews 41 periodical titles.

3. To highlight research trends in library science by providing abstracts of the most significant doctoral dissertations produced in a year. For volume 1, Gail A. Schlachter contributed abstracts of 32 dissertations. For volume 2, she expanded coverage to 50 abstracts. Volume 3 contains 40 abstracts.

4. To report on the production and distribution of knowledge in library and information science through essays by prominent library educators, practitioners, and publishers. Specific areas will be emphasized in each volume. For example, volume 1 included several essays on library science publishing. Volume 2 featured several important articles on reviewing. Volume 3 begins with an informative discussion of collection development by our new associate editor, Ann Prentice. This year's essay on a library science publisher is from Oryx Press, and recounts that company's development since its founding in the early 1970s. In accordance with *LISCA*'s expanded coverage of information technology, volume 3 includes essays on computers by Carol Tenopir and Myke Gluck. Completing part 1 are two reports on research in the field, written by Daniel Barron and

the team of Ron Powell and Sharon Baker.

5. To attempt, over time, a permanent record of the intellectual activity in librarianship and to impose bibliographic control over the literature.

6. As was noted earlier, *LISCA* now covers more Canadian and British materials. In contrast to previous volumes that included foreign titles only if available from U.S. distributors, all Canadian titles known to the publisher are included here, as well as many British titles. We hope that next year this coverage will be complete for Canada and that we will be able to include many more British titles.

Certain categories of materials are not covered in *LISCA*. Those include specific periodical articles, publications of vanity presses, and certain in-house publications which are institution-specific. For the time being, limited distribution research reports, audiovisual materials, and some continuing education "kits" produced by ALA divisions or affiliates will not be covered.

REVIEWING POLICY

The editors of *Library and Information Science Annual* have applied the same rigorous reviewing standards that *American Reference Books Annual* is noted for. The *LISCA* staff keeps an up-to-date list of well-qualified library educators and practitioners so that books may be assigned for review appropriately. This year *LISCA* has used the services of 167 librarians and scholars at libraries and universities throughout the United States and Canada; their names are listed following this introduction. Reviews in *LISCA* are signed as a matter of editorial policy.

Standard instructions for *LISCA* reviewers, prepared by the editorial staff, are briefly summarized here: Reviewers should discuss the work and then provide well-documented critical comments, positive or negative. Such things as the usefulness of the given work; organization, execution, and pertinence of contents; prose style; format; availability of supplementary materials (e.g., indexes, appendices); and similarity to other works and/or previous editions are normally discussed. Reviewers are encouraged to note intended audience and/or level, but the review need not conclude with specific recommendations for purchase.

All the materials reviewed are given full bibliographic description, and citations to other review sources are given for books.

ARRANGEMENT

LISCA is arranged in four parts. Part 1 contains 6 essays contributed by authors well known in Canada and the United States, treating various library and information science publishing areas. Part 2, comprising reviews of 382 books, is arranged into subjects, including such areas as automation, cataloging, comparative and international librarianship, information technology, school library media centers, and special libraries and collections. Reviews of 41 periodicals, arranged under the headings National, Subject-oriented, and Regional, compose part 3. The fourth and final part has abstracts of 40 dissertations listed alphabetically by author's name.

AUDIENCE

We hope that all professional librarians will benefit from *Library and Information Science Annual*. It has been created with the needs of students and researchers, practitioners and library educators in mind. We believe that publishers and other information professionals will also find much of interest. We urge librarians to contribute their suggestions for improvement, and to support our efforts to create an outstanding annual review for librarians in the United States and internationally.

ACKNOWLEDGMENTS

In closing, we wish to express our gratitude to the many contributors without whose support this third volume of *LISCA* could not have been compiled. We would also like to thank the members of our staff who were instrumental in the preparation of *LISCA*: assistant editors Anna Grace Patterson and Sharon Kincaide, as well as Judy Gay Matthews and Carmel Huestis. Special recognition should be given to Debbie Burnham-Kidwell, who compiled the author/title and subject indexes.

Editorial Staff

Bohdan S. Wynar, Editor-in-Chief
Ann E. Prentice, Associate Editor
Anna Grace Patterson and Sharon Kincaide, Assistant Editors

Contributors

Donald C. Adcock, Director of Library Services, Glen Ellyn School District 41, Glen Ellyn, Ill.

Chris Albertson, City Librarian, Tyler Public Library, Tex.

Ann Allan, Assoc. Professor, School of Library Science, Kent State Univ., Ohio.

Walter C. Allen, Assoc. Professor, Graduate School of Library Science, University of Illinois, Urbana.

Mohammed M. Aman, Dean, School of Library Science, Univ. of Wisconsin, Milwaukee.

James D. Anderson, Assoc. Dean and Professor, School of Communication, Information, and Library Studies, Rutgers Univ., New Brunswick, N.J.

Susan B. Ardis, Head Librarian, Engineering Library, Univ. of Texas, Austin.

Sharon L. Baker, Asst. Professor, Dept. of Library Science/Educational Technology, Univ. of North Carolina, Greensboro.

Robert M. Ballard, Professor, School of Library and Information Science, North Carolina Central Univ., Durham.

Gary D. Barber, Coordinator, Reference Services, Daniel A. Reed Library, State Univ. of New York, Fredonia.

Curtiss Barefoot, Asst. Professor of Mathematics, New Mexico Institute of Mining and Technology, Socorro.

Daniel D. Barron, School Library Media Program Coordinator, College of Library and Information Science, Univ. of South Carolina, Columbia.

Susan S. Baughman, Univ. Librarian, Goddard Library, Clark Univ., Worcester, Mass.

Donna Toler Baumbach, Media Dept., Univ. of Central Florida, Orlando.

Ruth E. Bauner, Assoc. Professor and Education and Psychology Librarian, Morris Library, Southern Illinois Univ., Carbondale.

Carol Willsey Bell, Genealogist, Youngstown, Ohio.

Helen Carol Bennett, Reference Collection Coordinator, California State Univ., Northridge.

Linda Leveque Bennett, Director, Allen Parish Libraries, Oberlin, La.

Mary K. Biagini, Faculty, School of Library Science, Kent State Univ., Ohio.

Marjorie Bloss, Asst. Director, Technical Services and Automation, Paul V. Galvin Library, Illinois Institute of Technology, Chicago.

George S. Bobinski, Dean and Professor, School of Information and Library Studies, State Univ. of New York, Buffalo.

Judith M. Brugger, Serials Cataloger, City College, City Univ. of New York.

Robert H. Burger, Assoc. Professor of Library Administration, Univ. of Illinois, Urbana.

Lois Buttlar, Asst. to Director, Center for the Study of Ethnic Publications, School of Library Science, Kent State Univ., Ohio.

Greg Byerly, Reference Librarian, Kent State Univ. Libraries, Ohio.

Esther Jane Carrier, Reference Librarian, Lock Haven Univ. of Pennsylvania, Lock Haven.

Jack Carter, Reference Librarian, Los Alamos National Laboratory, N. Mex.

Joseph Cataio, Manager, Booklegger's Bookstore, Chicago, Ill.

Dianne B. Catlett, Lecturer, Dept. of Library Science, East Carolina Univ., Greenville, N.C.

G. A. Cevasco, Assoc. Professor of English, St. John's Univ., Jamaica, N.Y.

Frances Neel Cheney, Professor Emerita, Dept. of Library Science, George Peabody College for Teachers, Vanderbilt Univ., Nashville, Tenn.

Boyd Childress, Social Sciences Reference Librarian, Ralph B. Draughon Library, Auburn Univ., Ala.

Margaret E. Chisholm, Director, School of Librarianship, Univ. of Washington, Seattle.

Larry G. Chrisman, Visiting Lecturer, School of Library and Information Science, Univ. of South Florida, Tampa.

Thomas C. Clarie, Head Reference Librarian, Buley Library, Southern Connecticut State Univ., New Haven.

Harriette M. Cluxton, formerly Director of Medical Library Services, Illinois Masonic Medical Center, Chicago.

Gary R. Cocozzoli, Director of the Library, Lawrence Institute of Technology, Southfield, Mich.

John W. Collins, III, Librarian to the Faculty of Education, Monroe C. Gutman Library, Harvard Univ., Cambridge, Mass.

C. Donald Cook, Professor, Faculty of Library and Information Science, Univ. of Toronto, Ont.

M. Kathy Cook, Asst. Education/Psychology Librarian, Morris Library, Southern Illinois Univ., Carbondale.

Camille Côté, Assoc. Professor, Graduate School of Library Science, McGill Univ., Montreal, Que.

Brian E. Coutts, Coordinator of Collection Development, Helm-Cravens Library, Western Kentucky Univ., Bowling Green.

Milton H. Crouch, Asst. Director for Reader Services, Bailey/Howe Library, Univ. of Vermont, Burlington.

Lisa K. Dalton, Documents Librarian, Joyner Library, East Carolina Univ., Greenville, N.C.

Donald G. Davis, Jr., Professor, Graduate School of Library and Information Science, Univ. of Texas, Austin.

Dick DeBacher, Oryx Press, Phoenix, Ariz.

Anna L. DeMiller, Humanities/Social Sciences Librarian, Reference Dept., Colorado State Univ. Libraries, Ft. Collins.

Carol A. Doll, Asst. Professor, Davis College, Univ. of South Carolina, Columbia.

Judy Dyki, Library Director, Cranbrook Academy of Art, Bloomfield Hills, Mich.

G. Edward Evans, Librarian of Tozzer Library, Harvard Univ., Cambridge, Mass.

Joyce Duncan Falk, Data Service Coordinator and Reference Librarian, Univ. of California, Irvine.

Evan Ira Farber, Librarian, Lilly Library, Earlham College, Richmond, Ind.

Adele M. Fasick, Professor, Faculty of Library and Information Science, Univ. of Toronto, Ont.

Mary K. Fetzer, Documents/Reference Librarian, Rutgers Univ. Library, New Brunswick, N.J.

Susan J. Freiband, Consultant, Library and Information Services, Washington, D.C.

Ronald H. Fritze, Asst. Professor, Dept. of History, Lamar Univ., Beaumont, Tex.

Ahmad Gamaluddin, Professor, School of Library Science, Clarion State College, Pa.

Mary Ardeth Gaylord, Reference Librarian, Kent State Univ., Ohio.

Charlotte Georgi, Librarian for Management Bibliography, Univ. of California Graduate School of Management Library, Los Angeles.

Ray Gerke, Mercy College, Dobbs Ferry, N.Y.

Carolynn Germann, Reference Librarian, History Dept., Los Angeles Public Library, Calif.

Myke Gluck, Science and Technology Reference Librarian, East Carolina Univ., Greenville, N.C.

Suzanne K. Gray, formerly Coordinator of Science, Boston Public Library, Mass.

Laurel Grotzinger, Dean and Chief Research Officer, Graduate College, Western Michigan Univ., Kalamazoo.

Leonard Grundt, Professor, A. Holly Patterson Library, Nassau Community College, Garden City, N.Y.

Blaine H. Hall, Humanities Librarian, Harold B. Lee Library, Brigham Young Univ., Provo, Utah.

Marvin K. Harris, Professor of Entomology, Texas A & M Univ., College Station.

Thomas L. Hart, Professor, School of Library and Information Studies, Florida State Univ., Tallahassee.

Mark Y. Herring, Library Director, E. W. King Memorial Library, King College, Bristol, Tenn.

Joe A. Hewitt, Assoc. Univ. Librarian, Univ. of North Carolina, Chapel Hill.

Helen Howard, Director/Assoc. Professor, Graduate School of Library and Information Studies, McGill Univ., Montreal, Que.

Wendy Hu, Head, Serials Div., Kent State Univ. Libraries, Ohio.

William E. Hug, Professor, Dept. of Instructional Technology, Univ. of Georgia, Athens.

Janet R. Ivey, Automation Services Librarian, Boynton Beach City Library, Fla.

E. B. Jackson, Professor Emeritus, Graduate School of Library and Information Science, Univ. of Texas, Austin.

Joan W. Jensen, Head, Reference Dept., Univ. of Connecticut, Storrs.

Richard D. Johnson, Director of Libraries, James M. Milne Library, State Univ. College, Oneonta, N.Y.

Thomas A. Karel, Asst. Director for Public Services, Shadek-Fackenthal Library, Franklin and Marshall College, Lancaster, Pa.

Linda S. Keir, Reference Librarian, Univ. of Dayton, Ohio.

Dean H. Keller, Curator of Special Collections, Kent State Univ. Libraries, Ohio.

Sharon Kincaide, Staff, Libraries Unlimited, Inc.

Thomas G. Kirk, College Librarian, Hutchins Library, Berea College, Ky.

Alex Ladenson, Executive Director, Urban Libraries Council, Chicago, Ill.

Shirley Lambert, Staff, Libraries Unlimited, Inc.

Hwa-Wei Lee, Director of Libraries, Ohio Univ., Athens.

Catherine R. Loeb, Asst. to the Women's Studies Librarian-at-Large, Univ. of Wisconsin System, Madison.

David V. Loertscher, Staff, Libraries Unlimited, Inc.

Elisabeth Logan, Asst. Professor, School of Library and Information Studies, Florida State Univ., Tallahassee.

Sara R. Mack, Professor Emerita, Dept. of Library Science, Kutztown State College, Pa.

Margaret McKinley, Head, Serials Dept., Univ. Library, Univ. of California, Los Angeles.

Constance Mellott, Asst. Professor, School of Library Science, Kent State Univ., Ohio.

Connie Miller, Science Librarian, Univ. of Illinois, Chicago.

Jerome K. Miller, President, Copyright Information Services, Friday Harbor, Wash.

Joseph H. Morehead, Assoc. Professor, School of Library and Information Science, State Univ. of New York, Albany.

P. Grady Morein, Univ. Librarian, Univ. of Evansville, Ind.

Michael Ann Moskowitz, Library Director, Emerson College, Boston, Mass.

K. Mulliner, Asst. to the Director of Libraries, Ohio Univ. Library, Athens.

James M. Murray, Law Librarian and Asst. Professor, Gonzaga Univ. Law Library, Spokane, Wash.

Danuta A. Nitecki, Assoc. Director for Public Services, Univ. of Maryland Libraries, College Park.

Margaret Norden, Reference Librarian, Falk Library, Univ. of Pittsburgh, Pa.

O. Gene Norman, Head, Reference Dept., Indiana State Univ. Library, Terre Haute.

Judith E. H. Odiorne, Independent Library Consultant, Oxford, Conn.

Jeanne Osborn, formerly Professor, School of Library Science, Univ. of Iowa, Iowa City.

Larry N. Osborne, Asst. Professor, Graduate School of Library Studies, Univ. of Hawaii at Manoa, Honolulu.

Berniece M. Owen, Coordinator, Library Technical Services, Portland Community College, Oreg.

Joseph W. Palmer, Asst. Professor, School of Information and Library Studies, State Univ. of New York, Buffalo.

Miranda Lee Pao, Assoc. Professor, Case Western Reserve Univ., Cleveland, Ohio.

Jean Parker, Humanities Reference Librarian, Ralph Brown Draughon Library, Auburn Univ., Ala.

Maureen Pastine, Director of Libraries, Washington State Univ., Pullman.

Anna Grace Patterson, Staff, Libraries Unlimited, Inc.

Thomas H. Patterson, Head, Reference Dept., Fogler Library, Univ. of Maine, Orono.

Ann H. Paulsen, Staff, Libraries Unlimited, Inc.

Susan Perkins, Media Specialist, Northside Elementary School, Cairo, Ga.

Daniel F. Phelan, Media Librarian, Ryerson Polytechnical Institute, Toronto, Ont.

Dennis J. Phillips, Head Librarian, Allentown Campus, Pennsylvania State Univ., Fogelsville.

Edwin D. Posey, Engineering Librarian, Purdue Univ. Libraries, West Lafayette, Ind.

Ron Powell, Assoc. Professor, School of Library and Information Science, Univ. of Missouri, Columbia.

Ann E. Prentice, Director, Graduate School of Library and Information Science, Univ. of Tennessee, Knoxville.

Richard H. Quay, Social Science Librarian, Miami Univ. Libraries, Oxford, Ohio.

Hannelore B. Rader, Director, Library/Learning Center, Univ. of Wisconsin-Parkside, Kenosha.

Randall Rafferty, Asst. Professor and Humanities Reference Librarian, Mississippi State Univ. Library, Mississippi State.

Kristin Ramsdell, Asst. Librarian, Meyer Library, Stanford Univ., Calif.

Carol Rasmussen, Editor, National Center for Atmospheric Research, Boulder, Colo.

James Rice, Assoc. Professor, School of Library and Information Science, Univ. of Iowa, Iowa City.

Sandra A. Rietz, Professor of Education, Eastern Montana College, Billings.

Stan Rifkin, Director of Research and Development, Master Systems, McLean, Va.

Ilene F. Rockman, Assoc. Librarian, California Polytechnic State Univ., San Luis Obispo.

Antonio Rodriguez-Buckingham, Professor, School of Library Service, Univ. of Southern Mississippi, Hattiesburg.

JoAnn V. Rogers, Assoc. Professor, College of Library and Information Science, Univ. of Kentucky, Lexington.

Samuel Rothstein, Professor, School of Librarianship, Univ. of British Columbia, Vancouver.

Michael Rogers Rubin, Attorney, United States Dept. of Commerce, Washington, D.C.

Edmund F. SantaVicca, Humanities Bibliographer/Reference Librarian, Cleveland State Univ. Library, Ohio.

Robert W. Schaaf, Senior Specialist in U.N. and International Documents, Serial and Government Publications Div., Library of Congress, Washington, D.C.

Jay Schafer, Librarian, Design and Planning, Auraria Library, Denver, Colo.

Gail A. Schlachter, President, Reference Services Press, Los Angeles.

Isabel Schon, Professor, College of Education, Arizona State Univ., Tempe.

Anthony C. Schulzetenberg, Professor, Center for Information Media, St. Cloud State Univ., Minn.

LeRoy C. Schwarzkopf, formerly Government Documents Librarian, Univ. of Maryland, College Park.

Ravindra Nath Sharma, Asst. Director for Public Services, Univ. Libraries, Univ. of Wisconsin, Oshkosh.

Patricia Tipton Sharp, Asst. Professor of Library Science, Baylor Univ., Waco, Tex.

Gerald R. Shields, Assoc. Professor and Asst. Dean, School of Information and Library Studies, State Univ. of New York, Buffalo.

Marilyn L. Shontz, Chair, Library Science Dept., Shippensburg Univ., Pa.

Bruce A. Shuman, Assoc. Professor, Library Science Program, Wayne State Univ., Detroit, Mich.

Kari Sidles, Staff, Libraries Unlimited, Inc.

Stephanie C. Sigala, Head Librarian, Richardson Memorial Library, St. Louis Art Museum, Mo.

Robert Skinner, Music and Fine Arts Librarian, Southern Methodist Univ., Dallas, Tex.

Jeanne Somers, Asst. Director for Technical Services, Kent State Univ. Libraries, Ohio.

Barbara Sproat, Librarian, Denver Public Library, Colo.

Patricia A. Steele, Head, School of Library and Information Science Library, Indiana Univ., Bloomington.

James H. Sweetland, Asst. Professor, School of Library and Information Science, Univ. of Wisconsin, Milwaukee.

Steven L. Tanimoto, Assoc. Professor, Dept. of Computer Science, Univ. of Washington, Seattle.

Miriam H. Tees, Assoc. Professor, Graduate School of Library and Information Studies, McGill Univ., Montreal, Que.

Carol Tenopir, Asst. Professor, Graduate School of Library Studies, Univ. of Hawaii at Manoa, Honolulu.

Rebecca L. Thomas, Librarian, Shaker Heights City Schools, Ohio.

Andrew G. Torok, Asst. Professor, Northern Illinois Univ., DeKalb.

Joanne Troutner, Media Specialist, Klondike Junior High, West Lafayette, Ind.

Dean Tudor, Professor, School of Journalism, Ryerson Polytechnical Institute, Toronto, Ont.

Phyllis J. Van Orden, Professor and Assoc. Dean, School of Library Science, Florida State Univ., Tallahassee.

Sayre Van Young, Reference Librarian, Berkeley Public Library, Calif.

Carol J. Veitch, Librarian, Onslow County Public Library, Jacksonville, N.C.

Jean Weihs, Course Director, Library Techniques, Seneca College of Applied Arts and Technology, North York, Ont.

Bella Hass Weinberg, Assoc. Professor, Div. of Library and Information Science, St. John's Univ., Jamaica, N.Y.

Darlene E. Weingand, Asst. Professor, Univ. of Wisconsin, Madison.

Emily L. Werrell, Reference/Instructional Services Librarian, Northern Kentucky Univ., Highland Heights.

Lucille Whalen, Assoc. Dean and Professor, School of Library and Information Science, State Univ. of New York, Albany.

Patricia L. Whatley, Librarian, Marcos de Niza High School, Tempe, Ariz.

Wayne A. Wiegand, Assoc. Professor, School of Library and Information Studies, Univ. of Wisconsin, Madison.

Robert V. Williams, Assoc. Professor, College of Library and Information Science, Univ. of South Carolina, Columbia.

Wiley J. Williams, Professor Emeritus, School of Library Science, Kent State Univ., Ohio.

Nancy J. Williamson, Professor, Faculty of Library and Information Science, Univ. of Toronto, Ont.

Glenn R. Wittig, Asst. Professor, School of Library Service, Univ. of Southern Mississippi, Hattiesburg.

Lubomyr R. Wynar, Professor, School of Library Science, and Director, Program for the Study of Ethnic Publications in the United States, Kent State Univ., Ohio.

Virginia E. Yagello, Head, Chemistry, Perkins Observatory and Physics Libraries, Ohio State Univ., Columbus.

A. Neil Yerkey, Asst. Professor, School of Information and Library Studies, State Univ. of New York, Amherst.

Arthur P. Young, Dean of Libraries, Univ. of Rhode Island, Kingston.

Marie Zuk, Language Arts Coordinator, Carman-Ainsworth School District, Flint, Mich.

Part I
ESSAYS

Collection Development in Schools of Library and Information Science

Ann E. Prentice

BACKGROUND

Library collections in support of education for librarianship predate the formal opening of the School of Library Economy at Columbia University by Melvil Dewey in 1887. Several years before opening the school, Dewey had begun to collect materials he planned to use in the instructional program. The curriculum emphasis would be on practical training and materials were selected to support that objective. When the school was opened "materials for a special library were collected ... and all important forthcoming publications were to be added to this collection."[1] Duplicate copies of important and heavily used books were to be acquired so that students would not be prevented by cost or difficulty of access from reading them.

Concurrent with Dewey's collection of materials, the American Library Association (ALA) began collecting a "Bibliothecal Museum" which included "library catalogs, reports, application blanks, and models illustrating library methods, fittings and supplies."[2] This collection was located at Columbia University and when the school was moved to the State Library at Albany, New York, in 1889, the collection was moved with it and continued to support the instructional program. The collection continued to grow and to include all aspects of library science practice. In addition, there was also a practice cataloging collection. The 1911 fire at the State Library destroyed this collection, which had reached nearly ten thousand volumes. A collection in support of the school was rebuilt along the lines of the earlier collection, and although many of the lost items could never be replaced, the new collection was adequate to meet the needs of the instructional program.

The Library School of the New York Public Library opened in 1911 and the curriculum was supported by a collection of books in "technical or professional subjects, books needed for quick reference when there is not time to consult the reference department of the library and books needed (chiefly translations of foreign novels) for the course in fiction or for the study of criticism."[3] When the two schools were joined to become Columbia University's School of Library Service in 1927, their collections were combined and included works on library economy, practice collections, a historical collection of children's books, periodicals, and writings of alumni. By 1937, the collection had increased to some twenty-one thousand volumes and approximately two hundred periodicals. The collection development policy elements set forth by Dewey served as the base for this library, which has become the collection of record for library and information science.

Other schools in their early days were located in university libraries with the director of the library often serving as director of the school. In this configuration, the library served as a laboratory for the students. There was therefore no need for practice collections. Several schools began to develop their own collections, and by 1937 each of the accredited schools had its own collection.[4] Collection development policy followed the curriculum needs of the school. Practice collections in cataloging and reference plus a small professional collection were the norm in the separate collections. These two early approaches to the library and information science collection, the separate collection and the integrated collection, continue to serve as models.

Over the past century, materials needed to support the library and information science collection have developed from those that described the practice of librarianship to become multidisciplinary, and include information concerned with creation, recording, transmission, storage, retrieval, and use of information as well as the social and political environments in which the various information professions are practiced. The collections are developed in concert with the curriculum, support it and, to a degree, through this support determine the quality of the program in instruction.

Limited guidance in collection development was provided by standards for accreditation set forth by the American Library Association. The first standards for accreditation adopted in 1925 required "library facilities adequate for research." Subsequent standards stated "that the collection be judged in relation to the curriculum offered and that it be adequate in scope, size, content, and availability to support the goals and objectives of the school."[5]

During th 1960s and early 1970s there were several studies of library school libraries and their collection development. David Kaser's study of library school libraries was published in the *Journal of Education for Librarianship*.[6] Thirty-six schools responded to his questionnaire, twenty-nine of which had separate collections. There was wide variation in size of collection, availability, and materials expenditures. This article described collections and did not address collection development. A study by Kiewitt, Head of the Graduate School Library at the University of Indiana, was also published in the *Journal of Education for Librarianship* (in 1972),[7] and collected data from librarians and deans of accredited schools of library and information science to determine the need for a core reference collection and to identify the reference sources in the school's collection. She found that 85 percent of those responding favored a core reference collection, as it was convenient, allowed for heavy student use, and prevented interference with the reference activity of the university library. Some of those responding cited cost and duplication as limiting factors in student searching as negatives of practice collections.

In 1973 Finguson stated that accredited library schools should operate self-contained libraries as experimental libraries for the training of students.[8] He objected to the use of the university library as the information resource and access area for students and recommended that the library school collection be used more intensively.

ESTABLISHING GUIDELINES

As a means of gaining control over the literature of library and information science, a conference on the "Bibliographic Control of Library Science Literature" was held at the State University of New York at Albany in April 1968. Robert Lee of the Department of Librarianship at Kansas State Teachers' College set forth guidelines for the development of a library school library.[9] He recommended that there be a separate library science collection, as it was easier for students to use, it could be used as a laboratory, and it would keep students isolated. He also projected a reduction in photocopying costs. The objectives of the library were to support the curriculum in the following ways:

- Make a wide range of library literature available.
- Provide basic supplementary and research materials.
- Provide suitable space and facilities.
- Serve as a model of effective modern practice.
- Provide a climate to encourage reading and study.

The collection development policy to support the school's aims is controlled by a number of factors from outside the school. These include the relationship between the university library and the library school, student and faculty access to children's and young adult collections, access to campus audiovisual services, and the availability of funds and space. Levels of collecting within each area would depend on both program objectives and the overall university collection development policy. The selection policy should be based on the following assumptions concerning the selector:

- A thorough knowledge of the curriculum, course outlines, and needs of the library science community.
- An ability to stimulate and anticipate use of material.
- The intent to maintain a balanced collection to meet both general and special demand.
- An ability to recognize the merit, usefulness, and timeliness or permanence of an item.
- The experience necessary to understand and maintain quality.

In 1971 an institute on the "Role of the Library School Library in Education for Librarianship" was held at Emory University.[10] The emphasis of the discussions was on the role of the library science librarian in supporting the graduate program in library education. Cooperation among libraries on campus and among library and information science libraries was stressed.

Discussions continue among those responsible for library and information science collections as to the best ways to interact with faculty and other libraries and information sources on campus to develop collections that are supportive of teaching and research in the library and information science programs. Discussion groups within the American Library Association provide a forum for those concerned with collection development to deal with both the new and continuing issues important to providing quality collections and service.

REPRESENTATIVE COLLECTION DEVELOPMENT POLICIES

From the beginnings of library and information education, two collection development models have existed: the independent, self-contained collection allied to a university library, and the collection integrated into the university library. The collection development policies of three library and information science collections are presented here. They are the collection of record (Columbia University), a medium-sized separate collection (Emory University), and an integrated collection (Tennessee). Each supports the faculty and curriculum of an ALA-accredited program in library and information science and each is an integral part of the larger research library near where or in which it is housed.

Columbia University

A statement approved in 1977 by the Columbia University Libraries indicates that the purpose of a library's collection policy is

> to provide information about the materials likely to be available in or through the library to guide users and for other libraries to use when determining their own collection needs [and] ... to provide criteria and priorities for action within the library to guide those who select, process, preserve and weed the collection and those responsible for the funding and administration of these activities.[11]

The university library has the authority to establish and implement policies and to delegate them.

Three service groups are identified: the primary group consisting of faculty, students, and administration of the university; the secondary group consisting of reciprocal arrangements with other libraries; and a third group consisting of those needing service but who do not fit in the first two groups, such as alumni and independent researchers. Those materials collected provide the resource to support instruction and research within the institution and in cooperation with other institutions. Materials of general interest and for recreation are collected, but not extensively. The collection is balanced to support both graduate and undergraduate studies with "subject areas of outstanding strength ... sustained in quality." "Economy of storage and maintenance as well as convenience of use are considered when material is available, or might be preserved in alternate forms."[12]

Columbia University Library's policy includes five collection levels:

1. minimal; those materials out of scope in which only a few basic tools are purchased

2. basic; up to date general information to aid immediate understanding are purchased

3. instructional support

4. research materials; includes major source materials for dissertations and independent research

5. exhaustive; collection of everything possible.

The School of Library Service (SLS) as collection of record collects at level five. The collection development policy statement of the SLS library fits into the overall university policy. The 1984 statement covers in separate sections library and information science, children's literature, and graphic arts. Each section includes background information, a description of the collection, cooperative arrangements and related collections, criteria and guidelines for collection development, plus any special considerations. Index terms to be used are listed. The primary collection is library and information science, and supports instruction and research at the master's and doctoral levels, and as the collection of record "a great number of noncurriculum related materials are bought to support the present and future needs of national and international scholars."[13]

The library and information science collection consists of ninety-eight thousand volumes of monographs, periodicals, and pamphlets; approximately thirty-seven hundred microforms, most of which are dissertations and reports; some three thousand currently received serial titles; and some audiovisual materials. Materials acquired in the area of computer applications to information processing are coordinated with the Engineering Library, and those dealing with information processing are coordinated with the Business and Economics Library. Because it is the collection of record and one of the most comprehensive in the field, scholars from outside the university use the SLS library routinely. Columbia faculty and students find little need to use collections outside the library. All library and information science materials are collected in seventeen broad areas, with priority given to English and Western European languages. Material is acquired regardless of format.

The children's literature collection of some 12,500 items is primarily post-1950 American picturebooks and fiction and nonfiction for older children. The historical collection of approximately 10,000 books and 450 periodical titles dating from the eighteenth to the early twentieth centuries, with a heavy concentration in the late nineteenth century, is housed in the Rare Book and Manuscript Library. The SLS collection is supplemented by gifts, and no formal effort is made to collect beyond the addition of 500 to 700 review copies per year.

The Graphic Arts collection is based on the American Type Founders Company Library and Museum collection purchased in 1941. The original collection of sixteen thousand items is supplemented by gifts.

For a number of years SLS has had a reference laboratory collection to support instruction in the basic reference course. Its purpose is to provide current basic tools, but not to duplicate expensive titles held elsewhere or to build subject-related specializations.

Role of the Collection Development Officer

The collection development officer is responsible for monitoring the availability of new and out-of-print publications of research value and to initiate and coordinate selection decisions. The collection development officer or representative attends curriculum committee meetings and keeps current with research projects so that appropriate materials are available. There is active participation by faculty and library staff as well as input from RLG (Research Library Group) and other regional and national groups. Approval plans are used as backup for collection development. Firm orders are placed for nearly all items, including from three to four dozen periodicals in addition to faculty requests and recommendations. Figure 1 shows the SLS guidelines for information science collecting.

Subject Heading in Information Science	SLS Collecting Level
abstracting and indexing	3
automatic control	0
automatic indexing	3
data tapes	3
EDP—by subject	2
electrical digital computers	1
information services	3
information storage & retrieval— in subject libraries by subject	2
information theory—in subject libraries by subject	2
language data processing	2
machine translation	1
math linguistics	1
modulation theory	0
programming	0
programming languages	1
semantics	1
statistical theory	1
switching theory	0
telecommunications	0

Fig. 1. Guidelines for information science. From School of Library Science, Columbia University, "Collection Development Policy Statement" (26 October 1984).

There is also comprehensive coverage in other areas and comprehensive collecting of codes standards, classification schedules, thesauri, directories, bibliographies, and other reference tools. In 1986, a draft collection development policy for the university was presented. The guidelines drawn up in 1977 remain essentially the same.

Information policy has relevance to machine methods of information storage and retrieval, as well as to information services. As information science materials became increasingly important to various programs, the departmental libraries in 1977 divided collecting responsibilities according to what was seen as primary use (see figure 2).

Subject	Primary Library	Collection Levels of SLS
management science	Business	1
computer technology	Engineering/Computer Science	1
systems analysis	Business	1
linguistic analysis	Engineering/Math	1
indexing and abstracting	SLS	3

Fig. 2. Collecting responsibilities. From Columbia University Libraries, "Collection Development Policy Statement" (1977).

The SLS library also set up guidelines for levels of collecting in information science in 1977.

Weeding

In a collection of record, weeding is a minor concern. As teaching emphasis changes there may be weeding of duplicate materials. Reference tools replaced by new editions may be removed.

Emory University

Emory University's Division of Librarianship library had its beginning in the teaching collection of the training classes of the Carnegie Library of Atlanta in 1899.[14] In 1985, the library holdings consisted of 1,627,351 books and serials. Division of Library Management holdings were 35,505 volumes.

The collection development policy, revised in 1979, has as its purpose support of the master's program in librarianship. The primary users of the Division Library are the students and faculty within the Division. Materials are available on a limited basis to the university community and to Atlanta area librarians. As part of the Emory University Libraries, its holdings complement those of other university libraries and will ordinarily depend on them for the selection of materials that fall within their major subject areas. Because of the Division's limited size and budget, no attempt is made to build a collection inclusive of all areas of library and information science. Because of opportunities for cooperative agreements with other libraries, an extensive in-house collection is not seen as necessary.

In the selection of materials, the following criteria are of primary importance:

1. Appropriateness and importance to the collection.
2. Potential usefulness to the intended audience.
3. Relation to the existing collection.
4. Current and/or permanent value.
5. Scarcity of other materials on the subject.[15]

In addition, the following criteria will be considered when relevant to specific types of materials:

1. Reputation and qualifications of the author or creator.
2. Reputation of the publisher or producer.
3. Clarity and accuracy of presentation.
4. Appearance of the title in important bibliographies, lists, and indexes.
5. Attention of critics, reviewers, and the public.
6. Availability of materials elsewhere in the area.
7. Format.
8. Price.[16]

The Division's policy describes four levels of collection. Level one is coverage of graduate education for library and information science. Intensive coverage of all information on this subject in all formats published in English in the United States will be collected. Level two is coverage of Division curriculum. Course offerings are divided into seven major areas with the needs of each area indicated:

Administration — general materials in support of the curriculum plus materials specific to the Southeastern United States and Georgia will be collected.

Children's/Young Adult's Media — this limited collection is to reflect current and past trends.

History of Manuscripts, Books, and Libraries — the Division library will insure, alone or in combination with other campus libraries, that a basic collection on the "origin and evolution of the alphabet, manuscript production and illumination, the invention and evolution of printing; the history of the book trade, the history of book illustration and the history of libraries" be available.

- *Information Retrieval and Automation* — materials within the Division and university libraries are to be available at the depth necessary to support the curriculum.
- *Media Production and Services* — material will be selected to emphasize audiovisual media services and production design and technique. Guides to selection and utilization of hardware and software, receiving tools, and catalogs of basic nonprint collections will be collected. Material should not duplicate those available elsewhere in the university library.
- *Reference* — materials dealing with the reference process and on bibliographic control will be collected. With few exceptions, reference works will not be collected, as they are available in the university's other libraries.
- *Technical Services* — course relevant materials in cataloging and classification and collection development will be purchased.[17]

Level three is the core collection, materials that make up the foundations of the profession, provide examples of all phases of current practice, and suggest future developments. Included are recognized classics in the field, major texts if not duplicative, major current work on theory and practice of American librarianship, major research studies, publications of major library and information science associations, periodical literature with emphasis on English-language titles indexed in *Library Literature*, reference materials on library and information science that do not duplicate other campus holdings, and materials related to intellectual freedom and copyright. Level four covers supplementary subjects such as education, psychology, communication theory, and management. Other libraries will be relied on for materials in these areas unless they are of particular importance to the student understanding, receive heavy class use, or are not conveniently available elsewhere.

Format of material is secondary to content. Certain materials are purchased in microform, such as NTIS (National Technical Information Service) reports and dissertations. Paperbacks are selected if hardcover is not available and as second copies. Rare books are to be purchased only as examples for the curriculum in the history of books and printing and only if not available elsewhere on campus.

Weeding

Included in the policy are criteria for weeding, a listing of cooperative agreements and procedures for interlibrary loan, plus an intellectual freedom statement and procedure for policy review. There is also a collection statement for newsletters. Weeding is done on a continual basis by the Division librarian, with consultation from faculty according to the following criteria:

1. Provision of current information.
2. Duplication in the collection (e.g., once-popular works).
3. Relevance of content to current librarianship and the curriculum.
4. Future value for research and historical purposes.
5. Obsolescence created by later editions.
6. Physical condition.
7. Past use.
8. Inclusion in standard bibliographies.[18]

Materials related to the history of the Division and to the history of librarianship in Georgia will be kept for historical and research purposes. Similarly, materials directly related to librarianship and library service (including the subject of reading habits), as developed in the United States, will not be weeded. Only representative bibliographic control tools will be kept. From 1979 to 1981, the librarian with student assistance developed the guidelines for weeding the collection and conducted a thorough review of the collection, bringing the collection in line with the 1979 collection development policy. The result was a working collection relevant to the curriculum. An added benefit was expansion space within the library. "Specifically related to weeding is the need to identify the collection areas which require constant monitoring."[19]

Tennessee

The University of Tennessee Graduate School of Library and Information Science does not have a separate collection. Its resources are integrated into the larger library, as are those of most other units on campus. The purpose of the *Descriptive Guide to Development of the Collection*, prepared by a library task force in 1980 "is to identify each sector of the patron community, outline the scope of the library collection and the extent to which the library will seek to collect in specific disciplines."[20] The mission and scope of each of the units within the library system are defined and the integrated nature of their resources affirmed. A detailed statement for each existing course of study leading to a degree was prepared based on an intense review of the curriculum as outlined in the *Graduate Studies* and *General Catalog* of the university plus faculty perceptions of present and future levels of support needed in the disciplines.

Five levels of collecting have been identified:

A. *Comprehensive level.* A collection in which a library endeavors, so far as is reasonably possible, to include all significant works of recorded knowledge (publications, manuscripts, other forms), in all applicable languages, for a necessarily defined and limited field. This level of collecting intensity is that which maintains a "special collection"; the aim, if not the achievement, is exhaustiveness.

B. *Research level.* A collection which includes the major source materials required for dissertations and independent research, including materials containing research reporting, new findings, scientific experimental results, and other information useful to researchers. It also includes all important reference works and a wide selection of specialized monographs, as well as a very expensive collection of journals and major indexing and abstracting services in the field.

C. *Study level.* A collection which is adequate to support undergraduate or graduate course work, or sustained independent study; that is, which is adequate to maintain knowledge of a subject required for limited or generalized purposes, of less than research intensity. It includes a wide range of basic monographs, complete collections of the works of more important writers, selections from the works of secondary writers, a selection of representative journals, and the reference tools and fundamental bibliographical apparatus pertaining to the subject.

D. *Basic level.* A highly selective collection which serves to introduce and define the subject and to indicate the varieties of information available elsewhere. It includes major dictionaries and encyclopedias, selected editions of important works, historical surveys, important bibliographies, and a few major periodicals in the field.

E. *Minimal level.* A subject area which is out of scope for the library's collections, and in which few selections are made beyond very basic reference tools.[21]

The scope statement for library and information science identifies the purpose and emphasis of the library and information science collection, outlines parameters, and lists collecting levels. Its purpose is to support instruction and research leading to the MLS as well as the concomitant research and administrative needs of the faculty and staff of the Knoxville campus library system. Areas of concentration include administration, collection development, technical services, computer applications, government publications, reference, and bibliography. The Main Library is the principal collecting unit. The Science-Engineering Library collects material on computer design and theoretical problems of information retrieval. Figure 3 lists the collection parameters and collecting levels.

Within the overall university collection of 1,152,527 it is difficult to identify all of those titles that are specific to library and information science. The Z collection of 26,727 includes titles most specifically for library and information science. The collection development officer is assisted in selection by a liaison from the Graduate School of Library and Information Science and reviews the literature and coordinates faculty requests that are related to curriculum needs and interests. A second faculty member coordinates materials to support instruction in the juvenile collection.

Collection Parameters.

    Language: English is the primary language; reference and bibliographic materials are represented in most languages, although European languages are emphasized.

    Date of Publication: Current in-print materials; augmented with retrospective purchases of standard research and bibliographic titles.

    Chronological Coverage: Current developments, primarily.

    Geographical Coverage: Primarily U.S.; selective materials covering areas throughout the world.

    Format: Journals, monographs, microforms. Limited collection of pamphlets, primarily academic library annual reports, examples of newsletters, etc.

    Treatment: Graduate level texts and professional applications; publications of associations, including conference proceedings, directories, handbooks, etc.

Collecting Levels.

Administration	B
Collection Development	C
Technical Services	C
Computer Applications	C
Government Publications	C
Reference & Bibliography	C

Related Subject Statements. Juvenile Literature; Computer Science; Management.

LC Classes which define the subject. Z, QA75-76, TK7800-8300.

Fig. 3. Collection parameters and collecting levels. From *Descriptive Guide to Development of the Collections* (Knoxville, Tenn., The University of Tennessee Library, 1980), 27.

PROBLEMS AND ISSUES

As the field of library and information science becomes broader and therefore less defined, it becomes increasingly difficult to delineate what should and should not be collected. The same problems that are faced by researchers and practitioners are reflected in collecting the literature. Questions of what is included within the discipline of library and information science and how to develop interfaces with related disciplines continue to arise and the answers continue to change as the disciplines of information science, telecommunications, engineering, business, and others continue to enlarge and overlap.

One way to approach this problem of definition is to note what researchers research and what is reported and to be sensitive to what publishers publish. This awareness, plus a current knowledge of developments in curriculum, is basic to defining the discipline. A further means of defining the field which has not received sufficient attention is to monitor the development and implementation of information-related systems in business and industry. The information flow among academics and researchers has a long tradition. The flow of information between the nonacademic work place and the academic information base is not as smooth as it might be. As the work place becomes increasingly an information place, those in academia who develop state-of-the-art library and information science collections must develop and strengthen the information flow and its records.

Within the academic institution, defining what library and information science is creates its own problems. Is library and information science a discipline, an application, or both?

Where does communications as a discipline end and information transfer begin? When are expert systems an engineering interest and when are they an information interest? As the technology to provide storage and enhanced access to information continues to grow, these and related questions become even more complex.

As teaching methods change, attitudes toward laboratory collections change. Earlier favored by many faculty, the idea that one provided the student with the one hundred basic reference books which they would then learn to use has given way to different views. The library school as laboratory is a changing concept, and as it changes, so do collection policies. Many faculty have come to see the laboratory collection as an artificial one which does not reflect the larger world of information availability. It limits the student's initial exposure to a narrow group of materials and thus may limit the possible locations in which they seek desired information.

New ways of looking at collection development may well emerge as work on the RLG conspectus and other research in collection development continues. Libraries will identify and collect in areas that do not duplicate the collections of neighboring institutions in those areas and at those levels they might earlier have seen as necessary. The development of collection policies cooperatively with other institutions is now more possible because of the RLG conspectus studies and the increase in the number of university libraries now with operational online catalogs with dial access and the ease of identifying location of materials at other sites. The document delivery problem is still with us, but in geographically contiguous areas, it is less of a problem.

The primary purpose of the collection development policy is to provide materials in support of teaching and research. Although formats change and access mechanisms allow for cooperative development of collections, that purpose does not change. The questions of how one defines the field are asked in the classroom, the laboratory, and the library. The collection development policy responds to the answers that come from those who teach and do research, and results in a working collection that supports the discussion.

NOTES

[1] "Library School Libraries," in *Encyclopedia of Library and Information Science* (New York: Marcel Dekker, 1968-1983), vol. 16, 1.

[2] Columbia University, School of Library Services, *School of Library Economy of Columbia College, 1887-1889: Documents for a History* (New York: School of Library Service, Columbia University, 1937), 103-4.

[3] Darthula Wilcox, "The Library of the School of Library Service, Columbia University, New York City," Illinois University Library School, *Occasional Papers* 20 (April 1951): 1.

[4] Louis R. Wilson, "The American Library School Today," *Library Quarterly* 7 (January 1937): 215.

[5] American Library Association, Committee on Accreditation, *Standards for Accreditation, 1972, Adopted by the Council of the American Library Association*, June 27, 1972.

[6] David Kaser, "Library School Libraries," *Journal of Education for Librarianship* 5 (Summer 1964): 17-19.

[7] Eva Kiewitt, "Reference Collections of Accredited Library School Programs," *Journal of Education for Librarianship* 19 (Summer 1972): 19.

[8] Ronald L. Finguson, "The Library Science Library: A Necessary Duplication," *Journal of Education for Librarianship* 13 (Winter 1973): 93-97.

[9] Robert Lee, "The Special Collection in Librarianship," in *Conference on the Bibliographic Control of Library Science Literature, April 19-20, 1968* (Albany, N.Y.: State University of New York, 1968), 1-16.

[10] *Institute on the Role of the Library School Library in Education for Librarianship, May 2-4, 1971* (Atlanta, Ga.: Emory University Department of Librarianship, 1971), 1-46.

[11] Columbia University Libraries, "Collection Development Policy Statement" (New York: Columbia University, 1977).

[12] Ibid.

[13] School of Library Service, Columbia University, "Collection Development Policy Statement" (New York: Columbia University, 26 October 1984).

[14] June Lester Engle, "Weeding Library and Information Science Collections: An Experience Using Student Assistants," *Collection Building* 5 (Fall 1983): 25.

[15] Emory University, Division of Librarianship, "Library Collection Development Policy, Revised 1979" (Atlanta, Ga.: Emory University, Division of Librarianship, 1979).

[16] Ibid.

[17] Ibid.

[18] Ibid.

[19] Engle, "Weeding Library and Information Science Collections."

[20] *Descriptive Guide to Development of the Collections* (Knoxville, Tenn.: The University of Tennessee Library, 1980), 1.

[21] Ibid., iv.

The Oryx Press
Information, High-Technology, and Libraries©

Dick DeBacher

THE VISION TAKES SHAPE: 1960-1973

As one would expect of a privately held publishing company, The Oryx Press was shaped by and reflects the vision of its founder and owner, Phyllis B. Steckler. One can best appreciate what The Oryx Press is today by tracing how that vision evolved and was nurtured during the 1960s, the decade before the company's founding and a time when many of the technical systems that support contemporary information publishing were emerging. The idea for The Oryx Press occurred as Steckler recognized the value of employing and orchestrating the new publishing technologies that were in the air in the late 1960s, but that had not been fully applied to meet new market needs by the larger corporations for which she had worked.

Phyllis Steckler's publishing career began in 1954, right after graduation from Hunter College, with a job as an editorial assistant at the R. R. Bowker Company, then, as now, a remarkable training ground for library and information publishers. She worked for Anne J. Richter, who was her first mentor. Ten years later, Daniel Melcher, then president of Bowker (Steckler's second mentor and, like Richter, a major influence on her thinking), gave her the assignment of automating Bowker's huge bibliographic databases. She standardized the dozen or so separate bibliographies, working with an outside computer software firm to produce the first computerized bibliographic database and the first computer-typeset editions of the *Books in Print* family of publications.

In the early 1970s, at the information publishing divisions of Macmillan and Holt, Steckler participated in other exciting projects and activities with a handful of creative individuals such as Jeffrey Norton and Richard Kollin. But in each setting, she began to sense that the larger corporations were constrained by various factors (often quarterly balance sheets) from fully exploiting the unfolding potential of new technologies in the service of information publishing. Again and again, her high-tech information publishing career was put on hold or dropped altogether, lost in the shuffle of corporate takeovers and other larger forces. To take control of her future, Steckler decided to strike out on her own and build the type of company she had come to envision.

This company, which was to become The Oryx Press, consisted of three basic components: information, high technology, and libraries. From the outset, Steckler knew she wanted to publish information products in various media using the latest available technology, especially computers. At Bowker, she also had come to appreciate the special role that libraries play in the organization and distribution of information.

Library publishing comprises two basic elements: professional library literature (the "how-to" of librarianship) and the types of reference works specifically designed to help librarians meet the information needs of their patrons and clients more effectively. Steckler regarded these as complementary publishing

---

© 1987, The Oryx Press, 2214 N. Central at Encanto, Phoenix, AZ 85004-1483.

activities; both types of publications would serve the profession. She had watched John Berry establish a line of practical library science monographs at Bowker that enhanced the company's position in the library world. Publishing professional librarianship monographs, especially those addressing contemporary practical needs and written by the most creative minds in the field, could help place Steckler's young company in its own special relationship with the profession that would constitute its major market.

The strategy of Oryx Press, in a nutshell, was to use the latest technology to bring vital information to all kinds of libraries, quickly and at a fair price. The continuing value of this goal for the company is reflected in the mission statement recently adopted by its management as part of its strategic plan: "To achieve a continuous and sustained increase in the value of Oryx Press through the publication and dissemination of quality and essential information and reference products, in any medium, for libraries and professionals."

THE EARLY YEARS OF ORYX PRESS—1973-1976

Although not formally incorporated until after 1975, The Oryx Press traces its first activities to spring 1973. Phyllis Steckler began that year at Holt Information Publishing in New York, faced with the discouraging task of closing down an operation that had fallen out of corporate favor. One of her specific assignments was to sell off contracts and properties held by the information division of Holt. Among these was the contract to publish a *World Directory of Environmental Research Centers*, the data for which had been compiled by William K. Wilson, with whom Steckler would work on a number of key projects over the years.

Steckler bought the contract for this directory, worked with various vendors with whom she was familiar, produced camera-ready pages for the book (financed by a $3,000 consulting fee she had earned just after leaving Holt), and arranged to have it copublished and distributed by Bowker. This joint effort provided the seed money for Oryx Press, which had just been established in Phoenix, Arizona, where the Steckler family had relocated. Interestingly, the name for the company had been chosen earlier in New York from a list of possibilities drawn up by a learned acquaintance. Steckler sought something short, distinctive, and memorable. Oryx fit the bill, and it struck her as sad but appropriate that the oryx, a rare species of desert antelope native to the Middle East, was in danger of becoming extinct. High-tech information publishing seemed to face a similar fate based on her experience, and yet it had scarcely been born!

When the Stecklers arrived in Phoenix, they received a newcomer's package from the local Chamber of Commerce. Among the items included was a piece from the Phoenix Zoo describing its program to save the oryx from extinction by breeding a herd in captivity and then returning animals to their native habitat. This twist of fate dispelled any lingering doubts about the name of the company. It would be The Oryx Press, and the Stecklers became involved in supporting the project at the Phoenix Zoo.

In working with William K. Wilson on her first directory, Steckler learned of the grant information system he had developed at the State University of New York at Fredonia. Wilson was using an elaborate index card system to identify research grant programs from government, private, and foundation sources to collect and record information about the programs and to alert interested faculty members about the programs, application deadlines, and so on. Steckler, recognizing the potential of this resource, signed a contract with Wilson to computerize the information and to produce various publications from the database. This was the beginning of the GRANTS database, now the largest and most complete single source of information about such funding sources.

Working alone in Phoenix, Steckler reached an agreement with a local firm, Datagraphics (which for the times was doing some very advanced work with computer typesetting systems), to produce type for newsletters and directories that would be spun out of the GRANTS database. She wrote and designed the first Oryx Press promotional brochure announcing the publications available in the *Grant Information System*. If the product line was to be successful this brochure needed to generate enough subscription revenue to pay for the first typesetting and printing bills. It did, drawing 41 charter subscribers, and the first Oryx Press subscription products were published in April 1974.

Still working alone, Steckler proofed and edited the Grants publications, promoted and sold subscriptions, filled orders, kept her books by hand, and maintained her customer data on index cards. The customer base grew. Within a few years, the GRANTS database became accessible online through Dialog, and today several annual directories covering grants in various fields of endeavor are a permanent and growing part of the Oryx Press list.

In 1974 Steckler learned that one of her former employers, Macmillan, was planning to drop a major bibliographic resource that was no longer profitable: the print products derived from the National Agricultural Library's Agricola Database, the *Bibliography of Agriculture* (BOA). Knowing the value of this publication, Steckler sought to acquire it. She flew to Washington with Mike Fields of Datagraphics, conferred with NAL officials, and announced her intention to begin publishing the BOA in January 1975. She then visited the Macmillan offices in New York, and, as the newly announced BOA publisher, was given the subscribers' list.

Steckler returned to Phoenix and worked on a letter notifying subscribers of the change of ownership. Weeks of frantic work with Datagraphics followed. Hundreds of hours of programming, particularly on the subject index, were required to convert the data to a form compatible with the Datagraphics equipment. But the deadline was met, and the January 1975 issue was published on time.

Now the publisher of an internationally recognized bibliographic tool, The Oryx Press was formally incorporated in the state of Arizona on 1 February 1975, still with a staff of one but now capitalized at $11,000, the total amount of cash then in the checking account!

But by August of that year, Steckler found herself unable to keep up with the expanding operation. Overwhelmed by the stack of renewals from Faxon and Ebsco, she took the recommendation of a friend from the Jaques Cattell Press (then a Phoenix-based division of the Bowker Company) and hired Kaye Reed to do her bookkeeping. The first Oryx Press employee, Reed was eventually to become the first Director of Marketing and play a major role in the automation and growth of the company. At this early stage, though, the company was still a long way from being full automated. Steckler and Reed worked in the rear of Stuart Steckler's art gallery in Scottsdale, using a high school typewriter and an old adding machine. All mailings were labelled, tied, and sorted by hand on the floor of the gallery. There was nothing glamorous about it. It was hard work.

THE FIRST LIBRARY SCIENCE MONOGRAPHS FROM ORYX PRESS—1977

In 1976, Steckler held discussions with two friends from her Bowker days, Patricia Schuman and Jack Neal. The three shared an interest in publishing library science monographs modeled after the works they had seen published at Bowker. Schuman and Neal felt they could draw on their connections in the library world to sign up more manuscripts than they could publish themselves. At the 1976 SLA meeting in Denver, Steckler signed a three-year agreement for 14 books to be acquired by Neal-Schuman and published by The Oryx Press. Soon Oryx would be publishing both types of the library literature mentioned above.

Manuscripts for the first four Neal-Schuman books to be published by The Oryx Press arrived early in 1977. Putting all the company's limited resources to the task, all four books were edited, typeset, proofed, and printed and bound in only four months, just in time for the annual ALA Conference in Detroit early that summer. The first four librarianship titles from this joint effort were: *Expanding Media*, edited by Deirdre Boyle; *Approval Plans and Academic Libraries* by Kathleen McCullough, Edwin D. Posey, and Doyle C. Pickett; *Libraries in Post-Industrial Society*, edited by Leigh Estabrook; and *Library Acquisition Policies and Procedures*, edited by Elizabeth Futas. The idea for the last title was jointly conceived by Pat Schuman and Phyllis Steckler, who, as library publishers, had always wanted to have a guide to the acquisitions practices *actually* used by public and academic libraries. Now in a second edition, it is one of Oryx's all-time best-selling titles.

The plans for the new books reflected another key tenet of the evolving Oryx approach to publishing. Phyllis Steckler felt very strongly that the books and the promotional literature announcing them had to reflect a distinctive and memorable "look" that would mark them instantly as productions of The Oryx Press. Born in an art gallery, her firm has from the outset placed a special importance on design in everything it produced.

The book covers and their promotional brochures were designed by Henry Slesinger and Chris Yaranoff of Slesinger, Yaranoff & Associates of Phoenix. The distinctive look they imparted is retained today in the books and promotional literature produced by The Oryx Press. The books are easily recognized by the warm colors of their binding material against which the white sans serif stamping contrasts sharply on the front cover and spine. The bright colors and bold designs of the promotional literature have been retained and refined in the work produced today in-house by the Art Department under the direction of Linda Archer, who moved from Slesinger, Yaranoff & Associates to The Oryx Press in 1979. Coincidental to Archer's joining Oryx was the purchase of a computerized typesetter—a Mergenthaller Linoterm. The company, even at this early stage, had decided to typeset its monographs and promotional materials in-house.

ADD A DASH OF HIGH TECHNOLOGY

The publication and promotion of the early Neal-Schuman titles, the Grants publications, and the *Bibliography of Agriculture* began to attract other authors and manuscripts to Oryx Press. Before long Steckler and her small staff were once again awash in a flood of paper and clerical work. Two of the basic elements of Oryx Press were in place. Information products were being published. Links with libraries were established, and publications by and for librarians were being produced. By instinct and experience, Steckler knew it was time to turn to technology to cope with the overwhelming paperwork.

Coincidentally, a local software firm, Computing Information Services, Inc., was interested in working with Oryx Press in developing the first integrated minicomputer-based publishing program. Steckler was inclined toward the idea in principle and found the CIS approach particularly attractive since the program would be developed on an accessible, English-language Pick operating system. The Oryx Press in essence became a test site for this developing program which is still used by Oryx and by many other publishers throughout North America.

As they developed this system, the relationship between Oryx and CIS became very close. Barbara Flaxman, who joined the Oryx staff in 1978, and who serves today as Production Manager, left the firm for two years in the 1980s to work directly with CIS on the program. Other Oryx Press employees from this period, including Kaye Reed, were able to build new career opportunities from their experience in developing this pioneering program.

THE ERIC CONNECTION— 1979

The next crucial block in the Oryx Press foundation was put in place in 1979. Learning that the National Institute of Education was about to put out an RFP for the contract to publish *Current Index to Journals in Education* (CIJE), the journal indexing publication derived from the ERIC database, Steckler made another bold move on behalf of Oryx Press. She submitted a proposal describing the capabilities of her company. After a long period of review and evaluation, the contract was awarded to Oryx, and the first issue of CIJE published by The Oryx Press appeared in March 1979.

The new link with the prestigious ERIC database moved Oryx quickly to the forefront of publishers serving the information needs of education. In addition to the CIJE monthly index and semiannual cumulations, Oryx picked up ERIC's *Resources in Education* annual cumulation. Other ERIC cumulations on microfiche, the *Thesaurus of ERIC Descriptors*, and, later, other print products, would round out this new major product line. With it came a host of new editorial responsibilities and burdens.

To cope with these, Steckler hired Susan Slesinger in January 1979; she brought to the task a solid background in editing professional journals. Slesinger later became Managing Editor and today serves as Editorial Vice President, supervising a group of 15. The core of this group includes the staff developmental editors. Under Slesinger's guidance, this group has earned a well-deserved reputation for the creativity and painstaking care they bring to the task of converting manuscripts into polished books. Slesinger is assisted by Anne Thompson, now Assistant Managing Editor.

LIST BUILDING—1978-1979

Although the contract with Neal-Schuman ensured an early stream of quality books for Oryx Press, Steckler knew she would need to build her own sources for good manuscripts if her company were to continue to grow after the Neal-Schuman contract had expired. A number of measures enhanced the visibility of the new library publisher and attracted new projects to consider. Oryx began exhibiting regularly at ALA conferences beginning with the 1978 midwinter meeting. These appearances and the vigorous direct mail campaigns put forth for the first publications were very effective in putting Oryx on the map. Soon a network of friends and advisors was assembled and authors begat authors.

Doyle Pickett, then of the Baker and Taylor Company and a coauthor of one of the first four Oryx Press librarianship titles, introduced Phyllis Steckler to Jennifer Cargill and Brian Alley, then affiliated with Miami University's library. The relationship has been enduring and mutually rewarding. Cargill and Alley proved to be remarkably prolific and productive writers, editors, and manuscript scouts, and their contributions to the Oryx Press list, its growth, and its place in the library world have been invaluable.

Also at this time, James L. Thomas, then of the School of Library and Information

Sciences, North Texas State University, made his first contact with Oryx Press, beginning another remarkably fruitful relationship for the firm. Perhaps no other single individual has contributed more to the Oryx Press list of publications. In addition to librarianship, Thomas played a major role in establishing and building the Oryx Press list in the areas of serving the handicapped, education and special education, school media centers, and microcomputers, among others. For two years Oryx sponsored Thomas in a series of 28 gratis workshops entitled "Materials and Services to the Handicapped," which he presented across the United States and Canada, exposing Oryx to new readers and authors. In addition, he has compiled award-winning directories, edited collections of readings, and brought many distinguished authors to Oryx Press. He and Carol Thomas have teamed up on several publications, and the "Thomas connection" continues to be a vital source of new publications for Oryx Press.

Over the years, this network of editorial advisors has grown, and its contribution to Oryx Press is immeasurable. More individuals than can be named here have played a part, but among those who have participated are Donald D. Foos and Sanford Berman in the earlier years, and, more recently, Paul Wasserman, H. Robert Malinowsky, and Irene Glennon, among others.

The first Oryx Press catalog of publications for 1978-1979 reflected these early efforts to build a balanced list of publications. Librarianship titles predominated, and of those, the Neal-Schuman titles were prominent. One could also find in this catalog the first Cargill-Alley book, *Practical Approval Plan Management*, and the first two contributions from James L. Thomas, *Motivating Children and Young Adults to Read* and *Meeting the Needs of the Handicapped*, the first Oryx Press book for this special population. The catalog also included some of the first Oryx Press reference works: three on topics related to agriculture reflected Oryx's continuing connection with the National Agricultural Library.

YEARS OF CONSOLIDATION AND GROWTH—1980-1983

By 1980, many of what would prove to be enduring features of Oryx Press were in place. The challenge at this point was to consolidate the resources that had been developed, to continue the rapid pace of growth both in sales and in new title output, and to avoid the many stumbling blocks that young companies face at this stage of their development. For the most part, the growing staff met these challenges successfully.

Although the company had long since moved from the art gallery which had housed it in its infancy, by 1980 it had outgrown even its new offices on Camelback Road in Phoenix. Accordingly a new move was made to a suite of offices on Central Avenue north of downtown Phoenix.

The indoor-outdoor character of the new building, built around a huge inner courtyard, has had a lasting impact on the corporate culture of Oryx Press. The architecture encourages "managing by walking around," which was practiced at Oryx long before it was celebrated in the book *In Search of Excellence*. Fostering creativity and encouraging a participatory style of management seem to come naturally from the surroundings. Unfortunately, this high-tech company has outgrown the resources of the building, and still another move is planned for 1987. Finding a new home that will sustain the highly productive but informal environment that has evolved over the years on Central Avenue poses a challenge for the search committee.

The 1980 catalog announced the first Oryx Press book by Sanford Berman, *The Joy of Cataloging*, beginning a long and cordial relationship with a progressive and articulate voice for thoughtful and inclusive library cataloging. This work, which had been rejected by many major library publishers before being submitted to Oryx Press, went on to become both a commercial and critical success. The 1980 catalog also included the first announcement that the GRANTS database was accessible online through Orbit and Dialog.

Finally, 1980 witnessed the birth of *Technicalities*®, a lively, personal library monthly that reflected its editors' interests in technical services, high-technology, and innovative, progressive approaches to contemporary library issues. The Oryx Press published *Technicalities* for more than five years (until the publication was sold to M. E. Sharpe in 1986), with Jennifer Cargill and Brian Alley serving as editors for most of that time. Many new friendships, business relationships, and publications can be traced to this distinctive periodical, which played a significant part in enhancing the place of The Oryx Press in the library world.

In 1981 the number of librarianship titles listed in the catalog of publications took a quantum leap as Oryx became the exclusive North American source for most books published by the Library Association of the United Kingdom. This five-year relationship also helped enhance the position of The Oryx Press as a source of significant library literature.

The 1981 catalog also included announcements for James Thomas' award-winning *Directory of College Facilities and Services for the Handicapped* and his *Microcomputers in the Schools,* one of the first books to provide information for educators on this vital new technology. The new *Food and Nutrition Bibliography* from the National Agricultural Library was announced, extending the list of titles from that source.

In 1982 Oryx Press began a significant new undertaking that marked the beginning of a new emphasis in its publishing program for subsequent years. In November of that year the *Directory of Nursing Homes* was published; this title was the first major directory produced by Oryx from data collected entirely by the staff. It is a landmark item on the list for several reasons. The project was championed in-house by Steckler, who allayed the doubts and concerns of the staff and insisted the work be published. The project was headed by Sam Mongeau, who had directory publishing experience from the Jaques Cattell Press in Phoenix. Working from state lists, the staff attempted to identify and collect verified information from some 15,000 certified nursing homes in North America. The data collection effort was successful and the book proved to be both a commercial and critical success, being cited by ALA as one of the outstanding reference works of the year. Now in its second edition, the directory has become a permanent item on the list, and the experience in publishing it has proved invaluable. *Directory of Nursing Homes* served as the model for a number of subsequent efforts and its success encouraged Steckler and her staff to focus on other similar directories. Today Mongeau heads a growing section within the Editorial Department that is devoted to directory publishing.

Two timely and important librarianship titles highlighted the 1983 list. Frances M. Jones' *Defusing Censorship* was one of two books Oryx published on censorship in 1983, well before the problem had escalated to the heights witnessed in the past few years. *Microcomputers: A Planning and Implementation Guide for Librarians and Information Professionals* by Robert A. Walton appeared in November 1983 and became another of Oryx's all-time best-sellers. Appearing just as microcomputers were becoming essential and, eventually, ubiquitous new library tools, the book and the workshops Walton offered around the country further enhanced the image Oryx had acquired as a source of reliable information about new library technology.

Dick DeBacher joined the Oryx Press staff in March 1983 as Director of Marketing. Having worked previously at larger and much older institutions (the University of Chicago Press and the American Library Association), he was in a good position to sense that Oryx was no longer a struggling start-up company. By the close of 1983, it was becoming clear to the rest of the staff that The Oryx Press had the resources (certainly human and technical if not always financial) to enter a new stage of rapid growth as a maturing, capable, and experienced publisher of information products and services. For years, (and occasionally to this day) Oryx Press managers would relieve their anxiety when faced with a new, seemingly insurmountable task by comparing their limited resources to those of a "real" publishing firm. By the end of 1983, this old, insider's joke was heard less often. Oryx had become a *real* publishing firm with a growing list of award-winning publications and a staff in Phoenix of more than 30 individuals headed by managers with *real* publishing experience from "back East," ready to take aim at the next stage of growth.

A FULL-SERVICE INFORMATION COMPANY— 1984-PRESENT

The Oryx Press marked its tenth business year in 1984, and the staff planned a full slate of activities to build up to the February 1985 anniversary of incorporation. An expanded anniversary catalog carried the new company motto: "A Full-Service Information Company." This new motto expressed the firm's intent and ability to publish information products for diverse markets in all suitable media. A new double width exhibit booth was designed and built (just barely!) in time for the annual ALA Conference in Dallas, where it won the prize for the best multiple booth at the show.

Also in 1984, Oryx expanded its acquisitions program significantly with the hiring of Arthur H. Stickney, previously of Greenwood Press, as Director of Editorial Development. A former medical librarian, college traveler, and editor, Stickney added greatly to the professional expertise of the staff.

To ensure the highest standard of customer service, a consultant was hired to reorganize and restaff the Customer Service Department and coordinate its efforts with those of the Marketing Department. Karen H. Parry was hired to direct the department, several toll-free 800 lines were installed, and new procedures were instituted to process orders more accurately and quickly.

These were exciting times for the company. Sales were growing at a 20 percent annual rate, and, with a new emphasis on acquisitions, title output was sure to keep pace. Once again, the technical support needed shoring up to keep pace with the growth in sales and acquisitions.

To keep track of the hundreds of projects already published, in production, under contract, or being reviewed, an elaborate database program, known in-house as SCHED2, was devised. A second original computer program to help plan, administer, and evaluate the now huge Oryx Press direct mail program (more than 700,000 direct mail packages, containing more than 3,000,000 brochures, are mailed each year) was written, tested, debugged, and put to use. Both programs were difficult to write and implement, at first adding to the work load they were meant to alleviate. Today, however, it would be hard to imagine getting along without them.

Nothing added more to the excitement of the anniversary year than the list of new librarianship titles. Easily the strongest annual list yet published, it was headed by another all-time best-seller, Janette Caputo's *The Assertive Librarian*. Clearly striking a sensitive chord among many librarians, this work sparked excitement wherever it was presented, and drew special attention at conferences that year, especially at the AASL Conference in Atlanta. The directory department worked on a *National Directory of Retirement Facilities* to complement the second edition of the nursing homes directory. Finally, Oryx announced plans to convert the *Food and Nutrition Bibliography* to a quarterly index.

By 1985, an emerging new direction in the editorial program could be discerned. While continuing to publish as many as ten strong librarianship titles in the Oryx Press mold each year, the growth in new title output now would come from the second type of library literature—information products that serve librarians and other information users. These products—directories, resource guides, reference works, bibliographies, databases (online, in print, or delivered on magnetic or optical disks), and software—would serve as the growth areas in the future. Accordingly, new resources, especially the technology needed to produce these works efficiently, had to be acquired. Plans to purchase an additional, more powerful computer system to run the editorial programs and databases separately from the business, administrative, and marketing programs had to be drawn up to keep pace with the data processing load.

Mike Fields, formerly of Datagraphics, had been working with the company as a consultant on computer-based typesetting systems for many years. He, Susan Slesinger, Barbara Flaxman, Linda Archer, and the head of data processing, Debra Furlong, worked together to acquire a state-of-the-art system for compiling databases, editing data, and converting the data to camera-ready pages in-house. After months of shopping around, evaluating proposals, and testing alternatives, they decided upon a Prime 32-bit super-minicomputer, paired with Xerox's XICS electronic publishing software, driving an Autologic CRT typesetter with a companion laser proof printer. Meant to serve the company's editorial data processing needs for five years, the system has already been upgraded once to keep up with the expanding work load.

From the outset, Oryx Press has taken pride in its ability to convert carefully edited manuscripts to finished books much faster than most of its competitors. This new equipment enhanced this capability, especially when more and more manuscripts were being accepted in electronic form. Oryx encourages and supports authors who employ the latest technology to prepare their works. This encouragement is most tangibly evidenced in a royalty scheme that rewards authors willing to write, edit, and typographically encode their electronic "manuscripts" on microcomputers.

Fruits of the new technological resources began to appear in 1985. New subject directories were spun out of the rapidly growing GRANTS database. The first of these, covering grants in the biomedical sciences, was published in September of that year and is now in a second edition. Since then additional spin-offs have been produced covering the humanities and the physical sciences.

The directory department worked in 1985 with outside authors on two projects that served as prototypes for a major new undertaking. Two directories covering programs and facilities for emotionally disturbed children were published and provided models for a series of similar works now being planned in-house for drug and alcohol treatment centers and programs, and other health care and medical specialties. Also in 1985, three new reference works established a growing list on women's studies.

The librarianship list kept pace with the excitement generated by the directories and reference works, as 1985 witnessed the publication of Cargill and Alley's *Librarian in Search of a Publisher*, John Corbin's *Managing the Library Automation Project*, and a collection of Pauline Cochrane's seminal essays on improving subject access to online catalogs, *Redesign of*

Catalogs and Indexes for Improved Online Subject Access.

All business, financial, and accounting systems at Oryx Press benefited from a fresh infusion of professional acumen when Merl Waschler, formerly of the Disclosure Group and the Bureau of National Affairs, joined the firm as Vice President for Finance in 1985. The Marketing Department broadened the scope of its efforts that year by initiating a new telemarketing program under the direction of Donald DeLong, now Advertising and Promotion Manager.

Oryx added a major resource to its staff and its scope in 1986 when Dimity Berkner, formerly of UNIPUB, joined the company as Vice President for New Business and Market Development and opened a new office for the firm in New York City. Although Oryx has always taken pride in its sunbelt location, the opportunity to establish a strong ongoing presence in the Eastern corridor could not be passed up. Oryx's vital and growing links with ERIC and NAL as well as a number of other connections from Boston to Washington now can be attentively nurtured and developed by Berkner from the New York office.

Berkner's charge includes both marketing and editorial activities, and one of her first efforts was to encourage the editorial board to approve publication of the first Oryx Press microcomputer software project. *BookBrain*, a reading incentive program to be used in school and public libraries and the first interactive microcomputer database of children's book annotations, is now being written by Elizabeth Hass, with publication scheduled for mid-1987.

Oryx Press published more than 50 books for the first time in 1986, and has scheduled approximately 70 for 1987. It has just published the first volume of a new looseleaf information service covering the biotechnology industry, and the first volumes of several series of information resources under the editorial guidance of Paul Wasserman. The Oryx management is at work on a five-year strategic plan which aims to build on the strengths developed in the company's first decade.

CHARTING THE FUTURE OF AN INDEPENDENT INFORMATION COMPANY

Looking ahead, many questions and issues stand out in the minds of those charged with mapping the future for Oryx Press. While still small, even by publishing industry standards, the company has come a long way from its start as a one-person operation. There are some 40 full-time and a varying number of part-time and temporary staff members working in Phoenix alone. Advisors around the country and the new office in New York add to the communications and managerial challenge. The goal is to continue to think big without acting big. That is, The Oryx Press aims to sustain its rapid growth without succumbing to bureaucracy or the paralysis that weighs down larger corporate operations. Faced with the seemingly unlimited opportunities to build on what it does well, The Oryx Press looks to the future with confidence, knowing that the key elements of its founder's vision will sustain its growth. "Information, high-technology, and libraries" provided a solid foundation for a new company, and these factors are sure to shape the future of a now vital and mature organization.

CD-ROM in 1986*

Carol Tenopir

Databases on CD-ROM (compact disk-read only memory) were the biggest news in the database industry in 1986. During the year, many new CD products became available, others were announced as forthcoming, and some of the big names in the information industry (e.g., DIALOG and H. W. Wilson) entered the CD marketplace. It was also a year of uncertainty and flux, with Digital Equipment Corporation (DEC) entering the market in the spring only to suspend its database distribution in the fall, prices of CD products changing frequently, and the number of users not yet approaching the projected figures. The professional literature was replete with articles explaining potential benefits of databases on CD-ROM; in addition, several books on the topic were published (see "References").

CD-ROM allows database producers to distribute copies of their databases on a medium that is more durable than magnetic disks and that provides high density capacity (up to 600 megabytes per 4¾-inch disk). Libraries can offer unlimited end-user searching of these locally held databases, because they are priced on a subscription basis rather than on a connect-time basis and because the hardware, software, and database are all under local control rather than being reliant on telecommunications networks.

Although the potential for use of and impact of CD-ROM on libraries, publishers, and the online industry is expected to be profound, most experts predict a coexistence of technologies. CD is expected to be used in libraries with high volume online use of particular databases for retrospective searching by end-users, in libraries that want to budget and pay ahead for searching, and in areas where telecommunications is a problem. Online access is expected to be used for current searches, searches on less-used databases, and searching by libraries that do not want to commit themselves to the upfront subscription costs of laser discs. Print is expected to continue to coexist with online and CD and to continue as most publishers' main revenue source for many years to come.

Because laser discs are a new distribution medium for databases, there are still several unresolved problems. Different products use different software, making it difficult for a library to provide access to all the databases it wants. Laser discs are not yet standardized, so every disc cannot be played on the same disc player peripheral. Investments in multiple microcomputer workstations make start-up costs high for the library. Most laser disc updates are sent monthly, quarterly, or yearly so the information is not usually as current as corresponding online products. Finally, because the industry is so new, it is easy to get confused over who is in the business, what products are offered, and how laser discs will complement or replace online or printed products. This article discusses some of the developments in this area during 1986.

DEC BOWS OUT

The instability of CD-ROM products is demonstrated by the exit of DEC from the CD-ROM database publishing market. DEC had agreements with several large database producers including Engineering Index, NTIS, and Chemical Abstracts to produce and market subsets of their databases on CD-ROM. DEC's ambitious plans at the beginning of 1986 included future development of an entire "library" of CD-ROM databases. Instead, after only six months as database publishers, DEC decided to refocus on their traditional strengths of hardware, software, and services rather than continuing in publishing.

---

*Revised from *Library Journal*, December 1986. Published by R. R. Bowker Co., Div. of Reed Publishing, USA. Copyright © 1986 by Reed Publishing, USA, Div. of Reed Holdings, Inc. With permission.

DEC still provides private compact disc production for in-house databases or for publishers who want to market their own databases. They also sell CD-ROM players and search software. For a library this private production service could be a way to distribute the online library catalog to remote sites or it could be used as a backup to the online catalog.

Mary Berger of Engineering Index (EI), one of the database producers affected by DEC's decision, spoke at the 1986 Annual Meeting of the American Society for Information Science. Berger discussed three areas of consideration for database publishers who are contemplating CD-ROM products.

The first area is *financial/business*. EI believed one advantage of CD-ROM over online was that they would maintain more control over their database. In reality, CD-ROM products are usually joint ventures involving, in addition to the database producers, software firms, disc mastering organizations, hardware vendors, and financial backers. Publishers do get more customer data than they do with their online products, but complete control is still not in the publisher's hands. In addition, the price of CD-ROM products must be set with the online, printed, and magnetic tape products in mind so no one customer segment is alienated.

The second area mentioned by Berger is *marketing*. EI first thought that CD-ROM would be a great way to tap new end-user customers, but they found that the existing online customers were most ready to adopt the new technology. Because they are experienced searchers, these existing customers want software with search features and access speeds comparable to online.

Berger's final consideration is *product design*. CD-ROM databases are so new that no one is sure how best to package the information. EI marketed three subsets by topic, a tactic that Berger said seemed to confuse customers. It was difficult for the customers to understand what was on each disc; they would have preferred the entire database divided by publication years.

Other packaging options would be to put partial records from a complete database on a disc (e.g., everything except abstracts), to put more than one database on a disc, or to mix bibliographic information with relevant numeric or full text sources. This last option is "where we ought to be headed" according to Berger, because "we don't want CD-ROM to turn into another microfilm, a convenient storage medium."[1]

NEW PRODUCTS

Although DEC's exit has removed some databases from the market, there seems to be an almost continual offering of new CD-ROM databases. A four-part directory by Bruce Connolly in *Database* and *Online* magazines has attempted to describe and keep current with all of the laser disc databases on the market.[2]

Laser disc databases are now available for many bibliographic sources, including PsycLIT, ERIC, AV-Online, Sociofile, and Excerpta Medica, all from SilverPlatter, Inc.; Aquatic Sciences and Fisheries Abstracts, Life Sciences, and MEDLINE, all from Cambridge Scientific Abstracts; ABI/INFORM and Predicasts from Datext, Inc.; Science Citation Index from ISI; Dissertation Abstracts; Microreviews from Knowledge Access, Inc.; Government Periodicals Index, LegalTrac, InfoTrac, and Magazine Index from Information Access Company (IAC); and Wilson indexes from the H. W. Wilson Company. Source databases include Grolier Electronic Encyclopedia; Poisindex, Drugdex, Emergindex, and Identidex from Micromedex, Inc.; DISCLOSURE; full text of The Wall Street Journal from IAC; Business Research and Marquis Who's Who from Datext, Inc.; EBSCO Serials Directory and Occupational Health and Safety Information from SilverPlatter; and Books in Print and Ulrich's from R. R. Bowker.

Some of the new CD-ROM products that are of the most general interest to libraries are discussed below.

WILSONDISC

At the ALA meeting in January 1987 the H. W. Wilson Company announced the upcoming availability of their CD-ROM WILSONDISC. Twelve of the Wilson indexes are available as separate CD products. Each disc contains retrospective information corresponding to the date the index went online, providing retrospective coverage ranging from early 1981 to December 1984. Index to Legal Periodicals, for example, includes references from August 1981, Readers' Guide to Periodical Literature from January 1983, Education Index from December 1983, and Library Literature from December 1984. Each CD database is updated (and cumulated) quarterly. The annual subscription price ranges from $1,095 to $1,495 per index.

The WILSONDISC search software offers several choices for searchers with different levels of experience. Intermediary searchers may choose to use a replica of the regular WILSONLINE system or "Expert WILSONLINE" commands if they are very experienced. Less experienced searchers might opt to search WILSONDISC with the end-user WILSEARCH software or an even simpler "browse mode" system, where users rely on paging through an alphabetical list of subject headings.

With a modem and a WILSONLINE account, users of the CD-ROM database can use the same microcomputer workstation to dial-up the Wilson mainframe system. A compact disc subscription includes unlimited online searching on the corresponding online database. The subscriber pays only for the telecommunications charges. This enlightened policy will allow great flexibility for intermediaries, as they can immediately and inexpensively update a CD-ROM search with the more current materials that are only available online. The Wilson workstation acts as a combination CD-ROM system, front-end, and online system for a single subscription fee. All of the appropriate hardware and software can be purchased from the H. W. Wilson Company for a price of $4,995 for the complete workstation.

INFOTRAC II

On 15 December 1986 Information Access Company added a CD-ROM product to their twelve-inch laser disc InfoTrac product line. "InfoTrac II" covers Magazine Index citations for the current year and three back years, plus three months of current indexing for The New York Times. Subscriptions to InfoTrac II include a microcomputer workstation with built-in CD-ROM player, a printer, software, and monthly updates. The cost is $4,500 per year.

InfoTrac II search software provides the same simplified searching that comes with the InfoTrac I system. Searching is done by browsing modified LC subject headings; no free text searching or Boolean combinations are allowed.

R. R. BOWKER

R. R. Bowker Company introduced CD-ROM versions of two of their popular reference works this fall. Books in Print (BIP Plus) includes the 1986-1987 records for the entire Books in Print series (including *Books in Print, Subject Guide to Books in Print, Books in Print Supplement, Forthcoming Books*, and *Subject Guide to Forthcoming Books*). In addition, the disc contains names and addresses of publishers.

Ulrich's Plus includes records from the 1986-1987 editions of *Ulrich's International Periodicals Directory, Irregular Serials and Annuals, International Serials Database Update* plus an ISSN index and addresses of periodical publishers.

Both databases will be updated quarterly. Prices for the database with software are $895 for BIP Plus and $395 for Ulrich's Plus.

SILVERPLATTER

SilverPlatter's databases have been available for several months, but prices were revised this fall. An "ERIC CD-ROM starter kit" is available for $1,550 per year. This includes a disc with the three most recent years of ERIC records (including abstracts) which will be updated annually. The starter kit also includes a CD-ROM disc drive and the SilverPlatter retrieval software, which includes such features as Boolean combinations, truncation, and free-text searching. Libraries must have their own IBM PC computer.

Backfiles of ERIC may also be purchased on CD-ROM. Records from 1966 to 1982 for Resources in Education (RIE) are available for $1,500. Current Index to Journals in Education (CIJE) covers 1969-1982 for $750. Both archival sets (three discs) sell for $2,000. New SilverPlatter pricing options are also available for the PsycLIT database from the American Psychological Association. Both a retrospective and current disc, each including citations and abstracts to the journal literature portion of PsycINFO, are available for lease. The retrospective disc covers the period 1974-1982 and now costs $1,495 for the first year of use. Each subsequent year costs $1,195. The current disc (1981-) is updated quarterly for an annual subscription price of $3,500. There are discounts of 10 percent for subscribers to *Psychological Abstracts* in print.

DIALOG ONDISC

DIALOG announced its entry into the CD marketplace at the end of the year. The first database OnDisc is ERIC (since it is in the public domain and, appropriately, was DIALOG's first database online). ERIC OnDisc includes the entire ERIC database from 1966 to the present on a three-disc set for $3,450. The annual fee for the current disc only (1981-) is $1,950. The current disc will be updated quarterly.

The DIALOG OnDisc search software offers two search options. Experienced searchers can search using the standard DIALOG commands or novice searchers can select a simpler menu-driven version. (The OnDisc search software is more attractive than online DIALOG, making use of color and word highlighting.) As with the Wilson disc system, DIALOG OnDisc searches can be saved and uploaded to the full online system for current awareness searching.

DIALOG is planning an entire family of CD databases in the future. Six additional products will be introduced in 1987 aimed at different vertical markets.

STANDARDS

A problem for CD-ROM consumers has been the lack of standardization. The lack of a disc formatting standard means that one cannot simply purchase a CD-ROM player and assume it will work with all discs purchased. Many database producers have gotten into the business of leasing or selling CD-ROM players to ensure compatibility. A proposed ANSI standard for CD-ROM is being voted on by members of the National Information Standards Organization (NISO) in late 1986.

The "High Sierra Group," a group of computer manufacturers, developed this proposed standard. The standard deals with volume and file structures—where information is located on each disc and how that information is addressed by the computer. (Standards for things such as external labeling and bibliographic description may be separate standards developed later.) The European Computer Manufacturers Association has proposed a similar data structure standard to the International Standards Organization, so a compatible United States-international standard for CD-ROM may be forthcoming. Detailed technical explanations of the standard can be found in *CD-ROM Standards: The Book*.[3]

CD-ROM SURVEY

Sociological Abstracts included a questionnaire on CD use in its April 1986 *Note Us* newsletter. Preliminary findings (reported in the October 1986 *Note Us*) showed that 34.5 percent of the respondents felt they would have a CD-ROM search station installed in their facility between 1986 and 1988. Only 23.4 percent felt they would not; the rest either did not know or had no answer.

Respondents were divided on what should be included in a Sociological Abstracts CD-ROM product, but by far the largest number (33.9 percent) favored the entire database from 1963 onwards. The second most popular choice (17 percent) was English-language entries from 1974 onwards. Price was definitely a factor in potential use, with only 0.6 percent indicating they would be likely to subscribe to the CD-ROM product in 1986 or early 1987 if the cost was between $4,000 and $6,000 per year.

CONCLUSION

The Sociological Abstracts survey and observations made by Mary Berger of Engineering Abstracts help to summarize the current state of the CD-ROM database market. Berger's observations included the following:

- The existing online marketplace will be the first to adopt CD-ROM.
- Users need computer literacy because it is more difficult to get the CD-ROM database system up than it is to start online searching.
- Intermediaries will introduce end-users to CD-ROM.
- Database producers have a "long sell" and will not realize quick payoffs. Potential customers need many demonstrations before they are ready to purchase and much hand holding once they purchase the CD-ROM system.
- Training and hotline services are needed for CD-ROM databases just as they are for online.
- CD-ROM products should be different products or be aimed at new users rather than just replicating the online database.
- Software must be up to par in terms of access speeds and search capabilities.[4]

The following are further observations on the CD-ROM market.

- Lower cost products are needed if the CD-ROM potential is to be fully realized.
- Many users want complete databases on CD or segregation by time periods.
- Online will be used to supplement CD use for current information or seldom used databases.
- Users would like database discs to be compatible so they can use the same equipment to access multiple databases.

As is evident from this review, CD-ROM, like all new technologies, remains in its infancy. A review of progress five years from now will likely make 1986 developments look primitive indeed.

NOTES

[1] Mary Berger, "CD-ROM and Optical Publishing" (Paper delivered at the 49th Annual Meeting of the American Society for Information Science, Chicago, 28 September-30 October 1986).

[2] Bruce Connolly, "Laserdisk Directory, Part 1," *Database* 9 (June 1986): 15-26; "Part 2," *Online* 10 (July 1986): 39-49; "Part 3," *Database* 9 (August 1986): 34-39; "Part 4," *Online* 10 (September 1986): 54-58.

[3] Julie B. Schwerin, et al., *CD-ROM Standards: The Book* (Medford, N.J., Learned Information, Inc., 1986).

[4] Berger, "CD-ROM and Optical Publishing."

REFERENCES

Bowers, Richard A. *Optical/Electronic Publishing Directory*. Carmel Valley, Calif.: Information Arts, December 1985- .

Herther, Nancy K. "Access to Information: Optical Disk Solution." *Wilson Library Bulletin* 60 (May 1986): 19-21.

Herther, Nancy K. "CDROM and Information Dissemination: An Update." *Online* 11 (March 1987): 56-64.

Herther, Nancy K. "CDROM Standards Update." *Database* 9 (June 1986): 87-89.

Herther, Nancy K. "CDROM Technology: A New Era for Information Storage and Retrieval?" *Online* 9 (November 1985): 17-28.

Lambert, Steve, and Suzanne Ropiequet, eds. *CD/ROM: The New Papyrus*. Bellevue, Wash.: Microsoft Press, 1986.

McQueen, Judy, and Richard W. Boss. *Videodisc and Optical Digital Disk Technologies and Their Applications in Libraries, 1986 Update*. Chicago: American Library Association, 1986.

Miller, David C. "Running with CD-ROM." *American Libraries* 17 (November 1986): 754-56.

Murphy, Brower. "CD-ROM and Libraries." *Library Hi Tech* 10 (1985): 21-28.

Schwerin, Julie B., et al. *CD-ROM Standards: The Book*. Medford, N.J.: Learned Information, 1986.

Tenopir, Carol. "Databases on CD-ROM." *Library Journal* 111 (1 March 1986): 68-69.

Microcomputer Hardware
Current Offerings and Trends

Myke Gluck

INTRODUCTION

In 1978 the Apple microcomputer was first sold to the general public. Immediately, some librarians began experimenting with this new technology to see if any library applications could be streamlined. The answer was a loud affirmative. Today, microcomputers are commonplace in most libraries. However, librarians usually have had to become literate about microcomputers on their own, without any formal instruction. This means that there are various degrees of computer literacy in the profession as well as within a particular library staff.

The purpose of this review is both to test the reader's literacy level and to provide some leveling of knowledge concerning the current state of microcomputer technology. The article assumes that the reader has a moderate, but not advanced acquaintance with computers. A number of terms are used as the industry defines them in 1986, and the current markets of Apple and IBM (plus clones) are reviewed.

CHANGES WITHIN MICROCOMPUTERS

The most significant changes within the microcomputer itself have been the speed of the computer's brain—the central processing unit or CPU, the amount of memory that the CPU can effectively use, and the size and type of memory chips.

CPU Speed

A CPU executes instructions given by a user. These instructions come to the CPU by a rather roundabout route from the user's application programs. A critical agent in the orderly execution of instructions by the CPU is the system clock. This clock acts much like a traffic officer ensuring a smooth flow of cars through an intersection. The officer assures that all vehicles (all instructions) will get through the intersection (be executed by the CPU); and, concurrently, assures that each vehicle has sufficient time to clear the intersection before the cross traffic is allowed to enter.

Recent changes in the CPUs themselves have permitted the controlling clocks to let more instructions (vehicles) through the intersection (CPU) in less time. Readers familiar with the IBM family of microcomputers can observe this quite easily by running the same program on both an IBM PC and an IBM AT. Enhanced CPU chips often retain the capabilities of the older versions as a subset, and so older programs work with the newer CPUs. Unfortunately, manufacturers do not always attempt to maintain this upward compatibility. For example, the clock speed of the Macintosh Motorola 68000 CPU chip is higher than the Apple 6502, but since the 68000 is not an enhanced 6502 CPU chip, programs will not run on both computers without major programming changes.

Besides actual replacement of the original CPU and increased clock speed, two other means of allowing more instructions to be processed by a given CPU exist. The first is the creation of a highly compatible chip by other than the basic chip supplier for a system. A major example of this is the V20 chip that runs about 10 to 20 percent faster than the original 8086 that Intel built for the IBM PCs. The speed increment is achieved by redesigning the chip but retaining all capabilities to run software. The second means is to design chips that increase the word size, which is the basic unit of data used by the machine. (A quick refresher:

a byte is a collection of eight pieces of yes or no information with each piece called a bit. A collection of 1,024 bytes is called a kilobyte or a K and 1,024 kilobytes are called a megabyte or a meg.) The word size of the earliest microcomputers was 8 bits (1 byte). Later machines used mixed word sizes, using 16 bits (2 bytes) internally, but retaining the 8-bit word size for communicating with the older machines. The latest development is to design chips using 32-bit word size (4 bytes), such as the Intel 80386 chip.

Effective Memory Size

The memory or program storage area of a computer is usually measured in the number of bytes of data it can hold at a given time. When microcomputers first became popular, 16K or 64K of random access memory (RAM) was considered standard and quite practical. Currently, few microcomputers with a reasonable share of the market have less than 128K and many have 512K as standard. Also, many are easily enhanced to handle 640K and upwards to several meg. For example, Apple IIc, IIe, and IIGS are easily expanded to 1 meg, while the Macintosh will soon be able to accommodate 4 meg. The IBM PC/AT can accommodate 8 meg.

Many of these enhancements are at low cost per byte and are available from many competing companies that specialize in enhancements, as well as from the original computer manufacturers. In the past, limitations of the operating system software (the main program allowing other programs to be executed) prohibited the use of these large amounts of memory, but changes in operating systems and hardware technology now permit effective use of megabytes of memory. For example, the popular program AppleWorks can handle four thousand records in its database rather than fifteen hundred, and search twenty times faster.

Increased Memory Chip Size

Another significant hardware change is that memory chips themselves have been developed to hold more bytes on a single chip. The first IBM PCs came with chips that held 16K, and later models were sold with 64K chips. Chips for the IBM AT are 128K, manufacturers in this country and in Japan are making 256K chips, and 1 meg chips are not far behind. The most impressive aspect of this change is that even though the chips are capable of storing more bits, they have not increased their physical size. Increased bytes per chip may appear irrelevant to the casual user; however, the impact is tremendous because increasing the size of a machine's memory capacity is simple, and because these new chips require less electrical power. Less electrical power use means there is less heat buildup, so CPUs will last longer. It also means more power will be available for uses other than just keeping memory active.

PERIPHERALS

Computer peripherals are electronic devices which allow humans to work with computers and allow computers to communicate with each other. Broadly interpreted, peripherals include devices for data and program entry (input devices), devices for computer presentation of intermediate and final results (output devices), devices for permanent data storage and retrieval (storage/retrieval devices), and devices for sharing computer resources among users (networking and telecommunication devices). In this section peripherals available widely are discussed. Not all the devices discussed below are readily available for all microcomputers, but most can be adapted for use with all the popular brands. These device types are generic because the means of electrically connecting them to a microcomputer have been standardized. The vast majority of these devices are physically connected and electronically communicate by several different but well-known interfacing methods. These connections are often built into the microcomputer or are made available to the computer by the addition of a printed circuit card or board that inserts into a slot within the computer housing. The current state of interface standardization permits the integration of a specific device with a specific brand of computer to depend more upon the availability of software than on the compatibility of hardware.

Input Devices

There are many different devices for entering data or programs into a computer. Researchers in ergonomics and electronics are constantly seeking devices which are electronically effective but also psychologically and physiologically healthy for people to use.

Keyboards

These devices are similar to the keys of a typewriter. The user depresses a key and the symbol represented by the key is transmitted to the computer's memory for eventual processing by the CPU. The CPU usually has a copy of the typed input displayed on a special television called a monitor that permits the user to verify the typed input. Controversies have raged over the form and fit of keyboards. A major difference among popular microcomputer systems is the computer to keyboard connection: some systems have the keyboard firmly attached to the microcomputer while others have it attached by a flexible cable allowing the keyboard to be easily moved about. Users most frequently prefer detached keyboards; however, a built-in or attached keyboard is useful if the system is to be frequently moved.

Another argument has focused on the number of keys to include and their relative position on the keyboard. This is similar to the controversy over typewriter keyboard layouts. Most machines allow for reassigning the keys to different symbols than those indicated on the actual keys. However, the number of keys and their dimensions and spacing still create problems for many users. For example, the IBM PCjr's original keyboard was so poorly received by the users that later models (before discontinuation of the product) had a completely redesigned keyboard. Also, the nonphonetic languages such as Japanese and Chinese have created serious problems for engineers attempting to construct comfortable keyboards for these languages.

The actual tactile response from the keys has been another point of contention among producers and users. Some believe the keys must bounce back firmly and sound when contact is made, others consider these aspects unimportant. Often these differences are personal, so a universally acceptable keyboard does not exist. Since manufacturers have produced alternative keyboards for many of the more popular computers, the buyer often has a choice.

Most of the major manufacturers sell detachable keyboard systems for their nonportable and some of their portable models. The Apple Macintosh, IBM PC/XT/AT, Zenith 150, 248, Tandy 1000, 1200, 2000, 3000, and 6000, Commodore Amiga, and new Atari computers all have detached keyboards. This trend indicates that most new systems will have detached keyboards.

Mice

These input devices allow the user to control a pointer on the screen of the monitor (see below), allowing the user to manipulate symbols and select items from menus just by pointing. This is not a replacement for a keyboard since any user text input (word processing) would still require a keyboard. All the major brands have the means to attach a mouse. Be aware that on many devices a printed circuit card or the proper serial connection is required to physically integrate a mouse into the system, and that application programs must be specially written to take advantage of the mouse. For example, the program MacDraw on a Macintosh uses a mouse, but a similar program, Dazzle Draw for the Apple, cannot. While the Macintosh, Apple IIc, and IIGS have connections for the mouse built in, others, such as the IBM or Tandy, require separate printed circuit cards that are available with the purchase of a mouse. Also, two mechanisms exist for the mouse to "know" its location relative to a position on the monitor screen: mechanical or optical. Neither of these methods has been proven better or easier to use than the other.

Lightpens

These are input devices that allow the user to point to a location on a monitor to indicate choices from menus, or more generally to indicate a position on the screen. The interface connection for this device to a microcomputer is a standard or an inexpensive option. This device is much older than the mouse and has the same basic purpose. Again, availability of implementation software is critical. More software for serious work has been written for mice, and the mouse is the preferred pointing device since it is less tiring and more comfortable to use.

Bar Code Readers

These are devices able to read into a computer the series of varying parallel lines of the Universal Product Codes (UPC) that appear on many products on store shelves, and the special computer font numerals similar to those used on bank checks. Library circulation systems such as Follett's Circulation PLUS and OCLC's LS/2 (Dataphase ALIS2) are based on one or the other of these reading methods. The less expensive versions of this device use a lightpen-type tool to read the bar codes, while the more sophisticated systems use laser beams. Both types of hardware are currently available for use with microcomputers.

Optical Character Readers (OCRs)

These are devices that are able to scan text and graphic material and directly enter them into a computer. They are similar to copiers, except that the information goes into the computer instead of being used to make a copy. These devices are still in their infancy, mainly because they are rather slow (one page per thirty seconds is considered acceptable) and they have trouble recognizing characters from other than a narrow range of type styles or fonts. These devices are frequently used for archival purposes where documents are not edited and only need to be stored (Filenet is such a system). Major productivity gains have been made with this device, since it eliminates the need to retype the contents of a document for computer input. The major problem with these systems is not in the ability of the scanner to get the correct image input to the computer, but in the software that is used to recognize alphanumeric and special characters. The problem of correctly identifying characters such as the letter *a* in all their variations is a very difficult one.

Video Imaging

These devices use output from a video camera as input to a computer. These systems are not expensive and provide excellent opportunities for storing pictures with data. Software systems have been developed using these devices for personnel databases to include pictures of employees, for real estate databases to include pictures of homes for sale, and for online catalogs for museums to include pictures of the objects in their collections. The systems use standard VCR (video cassette recorder) cameras, a special printed circuit card, and special software. One system, called PC-EYE, by CHORUS Data Systems, Inc., sells a system for about $1,000.

Speech Systems

These are devices used to allow spoken language to be used directly as input to the computer. The problems of speech recognition by a computer are as difficult as character recognition. Like the OCR systems, these systems have been successful when vocabularies were limited and sufficient time was available to "train" the computer to recognize a given individual's speech pattern. The current systems work well but are limited. These systems are immensely valuable for the visually impaired. Systems are currently available for many popular microcomputers, but they are expensive, easily exceeding several times the cost of the computer itself.

Storage and Retrieval Devices

Floppy Disk Drives

These are devices used to read and write floppy disks — magnetically treated material in a paper or plastic sleeve. The drive spins the disk and is able to read and write on the disk's magnetic tracks. The disks are removable and provide the most common means of physically exchanging data between microcomputers. Each operating system formats or partitions the disks differently, so formatted disks are generally incompatible between dissimilar operating systems. Disks come in three sizes (8-inch, 5¼-inch, and 3½-inch) and the drives are unique to each size. Magnetic material coats both sides of the disk and so data may be stored on both sides. Drives that can read and write only one side are called single-sided; those that can read and write both sides are called double-sided. Many disks are labeled single-sided but may still be used effectively on both sides in a double-sided drive.

Much confusion exists in the terminology used to describe disk density. The best measure for accurate comparisons is the count of the number of bytes per side. Disks marked double-sided may be effectively used in a single-sided drive. The amount of information stored on each side of a disk depends upon the drive and the operating system formatting software, but ranges from about 140K to 600K per side. Newer drives of the 5¼-inch variety hold 600K per side but require special disks.

Hard Disk Drives

This term refers to drives that store data on nonflexible material that is usually not removable from the drive itself and so cannot be used interchangeably from computer to computer. Hard drives hold from 10 to over 500 megabytes (equivalent to 30 to 1,500 floppy disks). The newest hard disk drives use removable cartridges that can hold from 10 to more than 150 megabytes. These new cartridges can be exchanged between computers.

Prices for both floppy and hard disks have been dropping for the past few years. The cost of removable hard disk systems is currently greater than most of the microcomputers on the market. If the cost of hard disk storage is compared to the number of floppy disks needed for the same amount of data, hard disk storage is not expensive.

Tape Backup Systems

These are used as a quicker and less cumbersome method to provide archival copies of the contents of hard disks or floppies. A 10 meg hard disk requires at least 30 floppies to archive and is very labor intensive. Tape backups are used to quickly record the contents of a hard disk onto tape cartridges similar to cassettes. These tape cassettes hold a great deal more data than a floppy and are easy to install, use, and store. They provide a good method of data security but are rather expensive.

Compact Disks (CD)

These are laser written and read disks. They consist of polycarbonate plastic body with a clear plastic covering and are sturdier than either floppy or hard disks. The most used physical formats are the 4¾-inch and the larger 12-inch (about the size of an LP record). Each size holds upwards of 500 meg per side and often uses a Small Computer System Interface (SCSI) connection to a microcomputer. The SCSI is used since it is capable of a high data transfer rate. The Macintosh Plus now comes with a SCSI connection as standard and can be used with CD drives (or several hard disks). A printed circuit card with controller, SCSI port, and any needed software are usually bundled in the purchase of a CD drive for IBM and Tandy microcomputers.

The most common recording format is the CD-ROM (read only memory). This is analogous to 45 and 78 rpm records, since it is "stamped out" using an aluminum master (actually small pits are burned into the plastic using a high-power laser beam). The users cannot record over the CD—they can only retrieve data. The drives use low-power laser beams to read the pits burnt into the material in the duplicating process. This reading process is similar to how a needle is used to read bumps in the grooves of a 45 or 78 rpm record. These pits are seen as bits and are then transferred to the computer as data. Many reference material publishers are making their materials available in this format, so libraries are being inundated with CD materials. These drives are available with all necessary connections for under $1,000 for most microcomputers.

Even within the CD-ROM format there are several distinct data storage protocols available. A true standard or set of standards for data storage on CDs has not yet been established. The most prevalent are the Hitachi and Phillips. Unfortunately, these protocols are often incompatible with each other, so the buyer must beware. The problem is similar to that with videotapes in the Beta and VHS formats. However, some of the current application software systems such as Books in Print's BIPPLUS have software that allows use of several protocols (but not at the same time). Many of the software vendors sell the necessary hardware for their systems as an option when purchasing their software (H. W. Wilson, The Library Corporation [Bibliophile], IAC [InfoTrac], etc.).

Another recording format being exploited is the CD-I (interactive) in which text data, sound, and video images are stored on the same disk. One of the first demonstrations of this technology was the creation of a CD-I encyclopedia presenting music to be played, video images to be presented, and text details to be displayed simultaneously when a subject was retrieved. CD drives that allow the user to write disks are also available. They use a high-energy laser beam to pit blank disks (write a bit) similar to the duplicating process, and a lower-energy beam to read disks. There is no way to erase these disks once written and so they are referred to as Write-Once-Read-Many or WORM CD drives. They are expensive but are able to store massive amounts of data (500 meg to 1,200 megabytes, equivalent to 20,000 to 50,000 book pages) on a single 4¾-inch or 12-inch disk and retrieve it rapidly.

CD drives that can read and write many times are being developed. They use the principle that the magnetic properties of some materials are altered when bombarded with energy bursts from a laser and that bombarding them a second time returns them to their original magnetic state. These optomagnetic materials have been used to demonstrate multiple writes on modified CD drives. However, problems with heat affecting data integrity on the disks have been encountered, so commercially viable products are not yet available; but they will be soon.

Output Devices

Printers

These are devices for producing paper copies of computer information that are readable by people. There are two standard interfaces to printers: serial and parallel. Many printers come with either hardware connection as an option, but should a specific connection not be available from the computer manufacturer, there are devices from other vendors that can convert one interface to the other. Usually the computer end of the parallel or serial connection must be purchased separately, but more and more manufacturers are including at least one of each type as standard equipment or as part of another option. For example, the Apple IIc comes with a serial printer connection as standard, while the IBM memory expansion cards often have both multiple serial and parallel interface options.

Printers fall into four basic types: dot matrix, daisy wheel, ink jet, and laser. Dot matrix printers use a vertical column of printer pins to contact a ribbon, which makes a carbon image on paper. More pins usually means better quality output, but a printer using more pins costs more. The lower priced printers use nine pins while the more expensive use twenty-four pins. Several of these have a mode called Near-Letter-Quality (NLQ), which indicates that they can produce typewriter quality output. Dot matrix printers are also capable of reproducing computer graphic images and using multi-colored ribbons.

Daisy wheel printers are essentially typewriters connected to a computer. They produce very high quality output but they are more expensive and slower than dot matrix printers and they cannot reproduce graphics very well.

Ink jet printers shoot streams of quick drying ink onto paper. They are equivalent to dot matrix printers but are generally messier to maintain.

Laser printers use laser technology to produce outstanding output products. This technology is based on office copier technology integrated with a computer. Laser printers are the most expensive and fastest of the printers and they have graphics reproduction capability. They can use colored toner cartridges but are unable to produce multicolored output. Many laser printers are being underutilized because there is a lack of application software that exploits all their capabilities. However, this is changing rapidly as more and more software vendors see a profit in products for laser printers.

Plotters

A plotter is a very useful drawing device to make graphs, charts, and drawings on paper or acetate. Most plotters use a set of three to nine multicolored pens to draw images. They range in price from the cost of a low-priced printer to quite expensive, depending upon the size of the output sheet and their ability to distinguish between two points that are very close together (coordinate resolution). These devices are often used commercially for drawing maps, mathematical functions, and blueprints.

Monitors

These are also called CRTs (Cathode Ray Tubes), VDTs (Video Display Tubes), screens, and terminals. They are devices similar to television sets connected to a computer providing good display of both text characters and graphics symbols. They are the most common output device for all computers, since they serve well to echo keyboard inputs and display application program output.

Monitors are either monochrome or color, similar to black-and-white and color television sets. Most of the popular computer systems can use either type of display. The purchase of a monitor requires a simultaneous purchase of a circuit card to allow the computer and the display to communicate effectively unless the necessary hardware is built into the microcomputer. For example, the Macintosh and the Macintosh Plus have built-in monochrome displays, while the IBM and Tandy models have options at the time of purchase for adding hardware for a monochrome or color display. Many brands have the additional option of using rather inexpensive interface Radio Frequency (RF) converters to permit the use of a standard black-and-white or color television. The most popular brand marketed in this manner is the Radio Shack Color Computer 2. Regular television sets do not provide the same quality of display as do monitors intended for computer usage.

Resolution or quality of the monitor display is measured in picture dot elements, referred to as PELs or pixels. More pixels per square unit usually indicate a more expensive monitor and better resolution. Resolution is usually indicated by the number of pixels horizontally and by the number of pixels vertically. Good monitors are in the range of 200 by 400 or 300 by 600 pixels. The highest quality monitors, and most expensive, have 4096 by 4096 pixel resolution and are used for specific purposes such as computer-aided design, engineering, and manufacturing (CAD, CAE, and CAM). Most monitors can be made to work with most computers by acquiring the proper display printed circuit card. There are two forms of color displays: composite and RGB. Composite monitors produce slightly lower quality color than RGBs but are often less expensive. Also, a low-resolution monochrome monitor may be used with a color printed circuit card, provided it has the proper connector (but, of course, only one color is seen on the screen).

High-resolution monochrome graphics (about 720 by 340 pixels) are available for use with microcomputers; however, the amount of application software for use is slightly more limited than for the color monitors. Many of the major products do not support this type of display, or the manufacturers have to include special software to allow their products to be used with these special printed circuit cards and monitors. These special high-resolution graphics monitors and cards are referred to as TTL monitors, since they use Transistor-to-Transistor Logic to permit increased density of pixels on standard-sized screens. The Hercules card and its competitors are typical of this sort of product.

Color graphics with increased resolution and other improvements are becoming more available. These new cards and monitors allow the current base of application graphics software to work, but much current software is unable to take advantage of the special features of these systems. Typical of these is the IBM EGA (Enhanced Color Adapter) board and its competitors; however, more and more graphics software is being written to use the special features of these new and improved printed circuit cards.

Telecommunication and Networking Devices

Modems

These are devices that allow computers to talk to each other over a telephone line. Computers and telephones are clearly both electrical devices, but they speak different languages. Modem stands for modulator-demodulator, which indicates the ability of modems to translate back and forth between these two electronic languages. The most popular current types of microcomputer modems are those that communicate at 300, 1200, or 2400 bits per second, which are referred to as 300, 1200, or 2400 baud rates. All popular brands of microcomputers are able to use modems by use of a serial connection, provided that each of the two computers that are to communicate has compatible software to control the computer-to-computer conversation.

Networking

This term refers to the sharing of computer resources such as disks or printers or even software among different users of the same or different computer systems. The early microcomputer operating systems were only capable of performing one complete task after another. More modern systems allow the same computer to share its work time among several different tasks, a capability known as multitasking. Many application programs have versions that allow several users to invoke the same application at the same time—these are known as multiuser programs. The most common multiuser programs are database manager programs that allow several users to access the same stored records concurrently. An online catalog with multiple public terminals would be an example. Multiuser programs are special versions of the single-user programs that have been modified to protect the integrity of the data when accessed by multiple users. Multiuser and multitasking abilities vary widely among current microcomputers and operating systems. The IBM family and the Tandy family (to a lesser extent) have sophisticated hardware and software options to permit and promote multiuser access. IBM has developed methods that allow the computer to keep track of multiple users and their resources. Apple products are not as advanced in this capability, but some products, such as Appletalk for the Macintosh, do permit shared hardware resources.

Another major area of networking has been connecting microcomputers to large mainframe computers. The result has been access to the larger machines while still retaining the local microcomputer capabilities. There are many companies selling printed circuit cards and additional hardware to permit these connections. Again, IBM and to a lesser degree, Tandy, have been leaders in producing this mode of networking for microcomputers. IBM's aggressiveness in selling these products has been motivated by demands of the business market. Apple has been more school-oriented. However, Apple's marketing strategy will broaden as the Macintosh is improved, and so greater emphasis in networking by Apple may appear in the near future.

Also available for resource sharing are many inexpensive and unique switches that are widely marketed. These are most commonly used to connect several microcomputers to one or more different types of printers. The user must physically connect all the devices and computers to the switch and must make a manual selection of the printer and computer combination desired. These switches are highly reliable and very practical when all the equipment is in the same work area.

POPULAR MICROCOMPUTER SYSTEMS OUTLOOK

The most popular microcomputer systems are those made by Apple Computer, Inc., IBM, and producers of slight variations of these systems. The systems that are either fully or partially functionally equivalent to those of Apple and IBM are known as clones of those systems. The Apple and IBM products and their clones are discussed below. Prices given are current as of fall 1986 and do not include any educational or other special promotional discounts.

Apple

II Family

The current Apple II product line includes the Apple IIe, Apple IIc, and the IIGS. The Apple IIe was first offered in 1983 and has sold well, especially in the public schools as an educational tool. The machine now comes standard with 128K of memory, 80-column card, a 5¼-inch disk drive with controller, a 13-inch monochrome monitor, and 6 expansion slots for adding printed circuit cards to connect almost any device. It sells for approximately $1,200. The IIc comes with 128K of memory, a built-in 5¼-inch disk drive with controller, a 9-inch monochrome monitor, as well as built-in mouse, modem, second disk drive, and serial printer interfaces (not the devices themselves). The IIc sells for about $800. Both the IIe and IIc use the 65C02, which is an 8-bit CPU chip.

The latest II family member, the IIGS, is able to run most of the large base of Apple II software. It employs a new processor chip from Western Digital, 65C816 (clock rate 2.8MHz). It is capable of emulating the 65C02 chip of the current Apple IIe and IIc while providing improved speed, graphics, and networking capability. The IIGS machine comes with 265K RAM and 128K ROM as standard, expandable to 1 meg (8 meg soon), a built-in mouse, a built-in disk controller capable of working with a wide range of floppy disk formats, two serial interfaces, a jack for headphones, printer interface, an optional SCSI interface, and an optional 12-inch high-resolution color display. This new Apple also has up to seven additional slots for other peripherals. Cost for the basic configuration for the entry-level market is approximately $1,500. Apple's marketing strategy will develop over time but certainly there will be systems configured for beginning, intermediate, and professional users.[1]

Macintosh

The Macintosh comes standard with 512K of memory, a 9-inch monochrome monitor, and a 3½-inch built-in double-density disk drive and controller, and uses the Motorola 68000 (a 32-bit internal processor) chip for its CPU. The Macintosh sells for approximately $1,800. Rumors about new Apple microcomputers targeted to maintain and expand Apple's educational base of users and for Apple to become more competitive with IBM in the business world are quite prevalent. Whispers of new products to be announced by Apple in 1987 are surfacing, and they indicate that a new Macintosh with a color screen and increased networking capability using the MS-DOS operating system is in the works. This product may provide Apple with a strong product to compete with the IBM family in the business marketplace, since more and more IBM software is being modified for use on the current Macintosh.

The Apple family, from the low end Apple IIc to the powerful Macintosh, provides a range of performance and service. The availability of additional add-on memory and interfaces makes the II family excellent products for the beginning through intermediate computer user. They require minimal expertise to set up and maintain, and come with clear documentation. There is no shortage of software for these systems to allow the individual librarian to accomplish the major tasks of catalog card production, circulation, online cataloging, bibliography production, online searching, etc. The IIc and IIe have limitations compared to other systems in both speed and amount of disk storage on floppies. Add-on printed circuit boards can partially remedy these deficiencies, but at additional cost. The IIGS partially offsets these limitations, but being tied to emulating the old software does have its drawbacks. The Macintosh's more powerful 68000-chip CPU and its unique picture (icon) driven operating system eliminates most of the inherent limitations of the II family, but it currently does not have an equivalent range of convenient software for librarians. More software is being made available for the Macintosh, but it will continue to lag behind the II family for some time to come.

Several companies have attempted to produce clones for the Apple family. The most recent are the ACE 2000, 2100, and 2200 made by Franklin Computer Corporation of Pennsauken, New Jersey, that are "like" the Apple IIe. Also, the Laser 128 made by Video Technology, Ltd., of Hong Kong, and Language Arts of Portland, Oregon, is a IIc clone. The closed architecture, limited technical documentation, and aggressive pursuit of copyright infringement by Apple have limited the appearance of Apple clones in the marketplace. None of these clones claims to be 100 percent compatible with all hardware and software currently available for the real Apples. Franklin's ACE 2000 is an Apple IIe clone with 128K of memory and no disk drives, the ACE 2100 is a IIe clone with one drive, and the ACE 2200 is a IIe two-disk drive clone. The ACE family comes with a detached keyboard and looks outwardly more like an IBM PC than an Apple product. ACE also has a sixty-seven-watt power supply (IIe has thirty-five watts), a built-in fan, internal Franklin RAM memory expansion slots, color (RGB) video port, sixteen-pin joystick port, external speaker volume control, parallel printer port, and an external nine-pin joystick port, but has only two Apple-type expansion slots. Again, note that not all Apple software and hardware will work with this machine. Use extreme caution in buying such a clone if specific software or hardware products need to be used with a system. Generally, this clone runs more software and costs less than a real Apple IIe. Charles Rubin indicates that the Laser 128 is more nearly a true clone than the ACEs, since it is quieter than the ACE, is easier to set up, add to, and use than the ACE.[2] It looks like a IIc and has all the external ports of the IIe as well as a parallel printer port that the IIc does not. The estimated price for the ACE equivalent of the IIe standard is under $1,000 and the Laser 128 is under $600. These could be real bargains for the careful price-conscious shopper.

IBM

The most popular of the IBM microcomputers are the IBM PC, PC/XT, and PC/AT. The PC and PC/XT use the Intel 8088/8086, while the AT uses the improved, upward compatible 80286. All are able to add special processing chips for doing high-speed math or special input/output processing. The major differences between the PC and the PC/XT, PC/AT are that the XT and AT come with a 10 meg hard disk and three extra expansion slots for additional printed circuit cards. The PC/AT is really a different machine than the PC/XT, since it has a different processor and a higher clock speed, and requires a slightly different hard disk controller. There are no true standard configurations marketed for these machines, since each retailer markets them slightly differently; however, all come with at least one floppy disk drive besides the hard disk (hard disk optional with PC), and 256K or 512K of memory. All the interface cards and peripherals are usually priced separately since there are no built-in interfaces.

Since the IBM PC was first marketed, IBM has been very open about how the internal workings of the system were designed. This allowed many manufacturers to build and market peripherals for these machines that IBM itself would not or could not. This openness has also led to many companies creating competitive machines that are 100 percent compatible with the IBM product but at a lower price. These are true clones, but there are also several near-clones. Since the list of IBM clones and near-clones is rather large and growing, a checklist for IBM compatibility is given instead of attempting to list all manufacturers and their products, as was done with the Apple clones.[3]

IBM Compatibility Checklist

Level I is the highest level of compatibility. To get this ranking the system must:

> Use the Intel 8088 microprocessor chip for its CPU;
>
> Operate with appropriate versions of MS-DOS or PC-DOS (2.0 or higher);
>
> Read and write 5¼-inch floppy drives;
>
> Be able to support the standard IBM keyboard and its keyboard functions;
>
> Support the IBM video board's resolution and modes;
>
> Be able to support the IBM RAM standard addresses, structures, entry points, and functions;
>
> Provide identical I/O expansion slot interfaces to the IBM;
>
> Provide a clone to IBM BASIC compiler (most clones offer GW BASIC which is not capable of running all IBM BASIC programs).

(The Leading Edge computer is an example of this level of compatibility.)

Level II is a medium level of compatibility called disk compatibility. To get this ranking the system must:

> Read and write IBM formatted 5¼-inch floppy disks;
>
> Be able to run most of the programs that run on the IBM.

It may:

> Need special programs to compensate for the lack of the IBM ROM addresses, structures, entry points, and functions;
>
> Use non-IBM standard keyboards;
>
> Have a different user interface;
>
> Not be able to accept IBM interface cards and peripherals.

(Several of the Zenith and Tandy models are examples of this level of compatibility.)

Level III is a low level of compatibility called MS-DOS compatibility. To get this ranking the system must:

> Be able to run generic MS-DOS programs, but may not be able to use IBM formatted disks.

It may:

> Not use the Intel chip set and have different keyboards and interfaces. (As a result it may also use higher resolution CRTs and provide better performance, and be more comfortable to use.)

(The Sanyo 550 and Zenith 120 computers are of this level of compatibility.)[4]

IBM is about to release a new low-end microprocessor to take the place of the IBM PCjr. Another major development is a new 80386 CPU chip produced by Intel that runs even faster and is upward compatible to the current chips used in the IBM family and its clones (Compac and others have such machines on the market). However, the price tag for machines using this new 80386 chip is around $8,000 per basic machine, and they provide no new library functions. These machines serve as commercial and graphics work stations with many networking features, which is why they have relatively high price tags. Very little software is available which takes advantage of the new Intel chip, but this will change.

SUMMARY

The lower-priced microcomputer marketplace is finally settled down to some degree of standardization. Talk of an MS-DOS Macintosh, along with the demise of a number of small microcomputer manufacturers, means a more even development from a consumer's vantage point. Machines bought today will have a much longer technological and resale life provided they are close to the Apple or IBM standards. There are other manufacturers producing unorthodox machines such as the Commodore Amiga. Unfortunately, since these are so far from the standards, they appeal only to a small segment of the microcomputer market. Often these machines can do wonderful things that the others cannot, but the lack of availability of repair and of software limits their practical use in the library. Along with the standardization of the machines has come the standardization of the interfaces to peripheral devices. This second level of standardization means that generally any device may be made available for any of the standard machines. Gone are the days of the isolated hobbyist tinkering to get a machine to turn on; we are in the age of sophisticated buyers and users of machines. The machines, the users, and the marketplace have matured, and that means it is a wonderful time to be a microcomputer user.

NOTES

[1]E. Raney, "Apple Set to Release Powerful Apple II," *Infoworld* 8, no. 26 (30 June 1986): 1, 6; Julie Pitta, "Apple II Unveiled: High End Model in Apple II," *Computer System News* (15 September 1986): 1.

[2]Charles Rubin, "Send in the Clones," *A+* 4, no. 6 (June 1986): 26-44.

[3]"PC Products Compatibility Checklist," *PC Products* 3, no. 7 (July 1986): 86.

[4]Ibid.

School Library Media Program Research
Review of 1986

Daniel D. Barron

INTRODUCTION

Researchers and practitioners responsible for the intellectual foundations and management of school library media programs have a number of sources available to them which review and report the research efforts in this multifaceted area of library and information science. The purpose of this review is to provide individuals who may be approaching the literature for the first time with an overview of some research sources.

Anyone who wants to be among those at the leading edge of knowledge creation and/or innovation in the practice of the profession needs to be aware that this area, like most others in library and information science, requires a multidisciplined approach to the identification and application of relevant research. Other disciplines and areas of study such as human cognition, telecommunications, young adult and child psychology, instructional design, curriculum development, computer science, and education, to name only a few, may never include the label "school library media program" or its many synonyms, but the findings and implications reported in their literature have many implications for the successful development of school library media programs.

Time, space, and this writer's expertise do not permit a review of the proportions implied by the importance of cross-discipline research awareness and application. The reader is urged, however, to seek out annual reviews of research similar to that presented here related to the specific disciplines and areas of study mentioned.

Many of the books, articles, and speeches which have come from the recent "educational renaissance" have not included school library media programs, to the dismay of school library advocates. Perhaps those who are molding educational environments have avoided school library media practitioners because we have avoided them—especially as the knowledge bases of the cross-impacting disciplines and professions have been conceptualized and built through research.

The current literature reflects some examples of cross-fertilization in the areas of information skills—as compared to the more narrowly conceived library skills—and the impact of such skills on higher order thinking among children and young adults.[1] Also, discussions that have been published recently, to some extent as a result of the recent revision of the school library media program standards, promise that researchers will be looking at the total system in which the program and professional function. Some seem to be taking a narrow view, in which the library media professional's role is hardly distinguishable from that of the classroom teacher, while others approach this role as one in which the professional is an information manager and councilor to a unique audience.

With this caveat to the reader, the importance of drawing together, on a regular basis, the research which deals specifically with school library media programs remains critical and is the primary purpose of this article.

REVIEWS OF RESEARCH

The earliest reviews of research related to school library media programs were written by Mary Gaver in the 1960s.[2] With some overlap, but with a more broadly based approach, Jean Lowrie brought the literature review up to the 1970s.[3] Again with some overlap, but with unique inclusions, Shirley Aaron and Daniel Barron brought the reviews through the 1970s to 1982.[4] Aaron's review of doctoral dissertations was one part of two issues of *School Library Media Quarterly* and was devoted to research in this area.[5] Aaron, as coeditor of *School Library Media Annual*, completed a review of selected research studies in 1982 with the goal of presenting a more comprehensive view of the research.[6]

School Library Media Annual (*SLMA*) since 1983 has maintained an annual review of research selected by Aaron and has also included some other important reviews, such as that of Barbara Minor, which reviews research studies available through the Educational Resources Information Center (ERIC) for the period of June 1981-June 1984.[7] *SLMA* has also contained reviews of research related to specific areas of school library media programs, such as their impact on student achievement and microcomputers in the program.[8]

Other reviewers have contributed important pieces to the bibliographic puzzle by focusing their attention on specific functions or roles of the school library media program.[9] With the exception of those who are required to review the literature prior to some academic study such as a dissertation, these represent the state of the reviews to date.

1986 IN REVIEW

The reports of research included in this review were selected from searches of the ERIC, LISA, Dissertation Abstracts Online, and Education Index databases. Any report of research—an activity in which there were obvious systematic data gathering and analysis components—was considered if it appeared in a 1986 publication. Also, reports of research which were indexed for the first time during 1986 were considered for selection. Reports related to research in the areas of technology, literary analysis, and media use were included only if they were framed within the context of the school library media program.

For the purposes of presenting the review, reports are arranged in the large categories of personnel, program, materials, and general interest.

Personnel

K. K. Edwards and Isabel Schon report on a study intended to describe the continuing education and professional development activities of school library media specialists in Arizona.[10] Surveying a selected urban population, they found that district meetings, reading journals, in-services, state-level conventions, local library science courses, and professional association activity, in that order of importance, were perceived as being the most valuable. The study has implications for academic programs, professional associations, and researchers in the area of districtwide coordination. One of the implications presented in this study was the need for library education to move beyond the confines of the traditional campus.

M. Ming and G. W. MacDonald report on the Rural Library Training Project, which was begun in 1984.[11] The project's purpose is to design and deliver library education to rural librarians in Alberta. The first report indicates that the project is a success, and describes the projected activities for the remainder of the project.

The long-awaited and much debated final report of the "King Study" was reported in the literature in 1985.[12] The purpose of the study was to determine the current and future competencies required of library media professionals and others in the profession. The six-chapter report is accompanied by twelve supplementary volumes, one of which details school librarian competencies. One of the intended outcomes of the study is to help library educators develop programs which are responsive to the needs of the profession.

Certification requirements in the United States have been analyzed by C. Kosters for the time period 1950 to 1985.[13] The inclusion and influence of various technologies and media were identified in the study, along with changing role expectations of the professional related to the teaching and learning process. The researcher points out that there is little uniformity among the state requirements, and one-fifth of the states do not mention the role of the school librarian in certification requirements.

M. L. Shontz determined from a study of 760 secondary school administrators that predetermined policies, district-level supervisors, educational background in library science by the administrators, and workshop participation by the administrators were the best predictors that administrators would use an objectives-based performance appraisal of school library media specialists.[14] Years of administrative experience was not a predictor.

P. M. Turner and J. G. Coleman, Jr. report in a study of state education agencies that specific evaluation instruments and processes for school library media specialists are neither in place, nor being developed in all states.[15] They suggest that library media professionals become actively involved in the development of such instruments and processes.

In a study to determine the differences between elementary school library media programs in districts with and without coordinators, S. W. Zsiray presents some interesting conclusions.[16] The researcher suggests that district-level support did not contribute to higher levels of professional performance and that library media specialists in those districts performed professional activities on a basis equal with those who were in districts with district-level media specialists.

V. A. Cooper found little agreement among Virginia secondary school librarians concerning the nature of their perceived roles except in the most traditional functions of library administration.[17]

N. A. Van House presents information related to librarianship as a "woman's profession" and includes salary and other demographic data to describe the sociological characteristics of school library media specialists as well as others in public and academic libraries.[18]

A study dealing with similar demographics was reported by J. Bierman in which library media specialists in New Zealand were among a group of other library and information professionals studied to determine what factors account for the underrepresentation of women in senior managerial ranks.[19] Some factors identified include mobility, work continuity, attitudes toward sex roles, career commitment, and personal motivation.

Nancy Master and Lawrence Master completed a survey of the school library media specialists in Clark County, Nevada.[20] They conclude that this group perceives themselves as being not curriculum leaders, but rather support or auxiliary personnel for classroom teachers, directly involved in the reading program at all grade levels; their roles are determined to a large extent by the school principals.

Yet another in the long line of perception studies was reported by J. A. Horton.[21] Principals and teachers in four hundred small and rural Kansas schools were surveyed, and the researcher found that they generally had a positive attitude about the school library media center, with principals a bit more positive. Other conclusions in the study relate to the inadequacy of microcomputer technology in the schools and communication between teachers and librarians.

W. A. Scott found a general agreement between teachers, principals, and library media specialists concerning the perceived role of the latter.[22] All groups indicated a strong feeling that the emerging role of the media specialist as incorporating all forms of technology was appropriate, but there was disagreement as to the extent to which the media specialist should be involved in the instructional role.

Principals and media specialists in selected Michigan high schools were surveyed by R. F. C. Fitzgerald using the "Loertscher Taxonomy of Involvement in Instructional Units."[23] The researcher found that principals' expectations exceeded the actual involvement of the media specialist, highly involved media specialists had more formal education, principals with higher expectations get more written reports from media specialists, higher involvement is more frequent in larger schools, and higher involvement occurs in schools with larger budgets and higher media specialists to teacher and student ratios.

The importance of the librarian's role in a reading guidance program for fifth graders was described in a study by M. J. Mosley.[24] The researcher found that a librarian-centered reading program improved reading attitudes and habits of the students participating in the experiment and also increased their reading achievement scores on standardized tests. Similar findings were reported by R. L. Thomas.[25] This study concluded that sixth-grade children were positively influenced by the librarian-teacher collaboration in a poetry-enriched environment.

A model for optimum teacher use of audiovisual materials collections was developed by J. L. Edwards from her study of teacher-media specialist interaction.[26] She proposes that commitment on the part of the media specialist, positive interaction between the media specialist and teacher, and in-service training for teachers are the best predictors of high use of audiovisual materials by teachers.

H. T. Browne compared the roles of academic and secondary school librarians in an effort to determine the relative importance of similar tasks and time spent on those tasks by the two groups.[27] The researcher concludes that there are significant differences between the groups related to their roles as teacher, materials specialists, and professional development, and no apparent differences related to their roles as program developers and curriculum specialists.

Program

A Wisconsin study describes the interlibrary loan patterns, needs, demands, and multitype library relationships.[28] This is an update of the 1976 study which will provide the researcher in this area with some good long-term comparisons.

A districtwide study of library media programs in Calgary led the researchers to conclude that "media program use, and the instrumental importance placed upon the program used by students, was much greater in those high schools with media programs that make audiovisual materials, equipment, and media specialist services available to the students."[29] Among other things, the authors point out that audiovisual production and learning styles are positively correlated, teaching models of faculty determine basic audiovisual services, and organizational models may function as predictors of audiovisual program development.

Another districtwide study was reported by R. N. Claus and B. E. Quimbe.[30] The study of the Saginaw, Michigan school system could be valuable for the researcher interested in needs assessment as well as those studying planning models. School library media programs are included as one element of the overall needs assessment study.

A. LeClercq reports on the development and testing of a model for providing gifted high school students with library resources for research at the University of Tennessee-Knoxville.[31]

N. L. Bluemel found that gifted students who participated in a differentiated program used the library more for both leisure and school work related activities than a similar group who attended a traditional library program.[32] The students also scored higher on their standardized tests and used a wider range of materials than did traditional program students.

The findings of L. C. M. Haskell should be of interest to school library media specialists as they plan efforts to assist students who are involved in writing research papers and researchers focusing on the information gathering habits of students.[33] The author completed a "naturalistic" study of forty senior and junior high school students and four teachers from which she developed a description of their library-related research strategy.

In a comparison of Michigan schools accredited by The University of Michigan's Bureau of School Services and those accredited by the North Central Association of Colleges and Schools, M. Fisher included elements related to school library media programs.[34] His general conclusion is that there were no statistically significant differences.

Per pupil expenditure was the only significant variable related to the intellectual development of students in selected rural secondary schools in Missouri. According to the report of D. R. Burns, no other variable or combination of variables, including school library media programs meeting classification standards, was significantly related.[35]

R. H. Bailey surveyed California Media and Library Educators Association members to determine the technology needs of library media centers.[36] The researcher concludes that there is an obvious need for additional equipment, training, and software if school library media programs are to be strengthened.

Materials

S. R. Crow investigated the extent to which juvenile books which could be labeled as "controversial"—defined in terms of the subject of the book, language used, or other selected factors—were included in four periodicals identified as being the selection tools most commonly used by children and young adult librarians.[37] The number of titles included in each source, the recency of the review to the book's publication, and the treatment of the elements of controversy were included in the study. Based on her findings, the researcher concludes that these titles are in fact treated differently in review sources and school library media specialists need to be aware of that treatment if they are to read reviews knowledgeably.

Circulation records in a Hawaiian elementary school library were used to determine use patterns.[38] The researchers studied the records of a five-year period and offer conclusions about use based on sex and grade level as predictors of subjects and types of books checked out. Books about Hawaii and Asia were also considered in the use patterns.

P. L. Jeffery reports on one of the very few research projects concerned with providing materials to teachers.[39] Although set in New Zealand, the procedures, conclusions, and implications for school library media programs are universally applicable. Using "SET: Research Information for Teachers," five case studies describe the dissemination of the information related to educational research among schools of various types as well as within the schools.

Researchers developed a list of 334 science skills from resources available in selected libraries and media centers in Pennsylvania as part of a project to identify student skills perceived as being important among science teachers in secondary vocational programs.[40] The study has implications for those who are studying or implementing school library media programs in relation to specific needs identified in the school community.

Ho and Loertscher report on the field testing of a collection mapping technique to evaluate school library media collections.[41] The authors sent questionnaires to 120 schools in eleven states. In addition to describing the collections, they conclude that school library media specialists build collections which are different from those recommended by national lists, collections fall far short of the AASL standards, and collection mapping as an evaluative technique is viable and effective.

The extent to which public and school library book collections overlap was the subject of a report by C. A. Doll.[42] From a comparison of collections in two states, the researcher concludes that there is significant overlap, but also that there are enough differences to make cooperation and networking alternatives for meeting the recreational roles of these libraries possible and desirable.

S. Hall concluded from a study of high school library shelflists in Pennsylvania that there is approximately a 30 percent overlap in collections and that the shelflist may be used to generate machine readable records using the main entry and title as search keys.[43]

G. D. Funk determined that social values which are included in books written for children are related to society's increased awareness of social concerns over the past twenty-five years.[44] He suggests that educators need to be aware of these value contents if they are to develop quality literature programs.

General Interest

G. Natriello presents a review of the data collection activities of the National Center for Education Statistics with recommendations for the Center's future activity in this area.[45] Among other things, the author suggests that the Center should move beyond collecting data on schooling and consider education generally, conduct longitudinal studies of students, collect more data on school processes, organize employer sponsored student performance data, link large-scale and microlevel studies, develop pilot state level databases, and be aware of emerging data transfer technologies.

WHAT'S AHEAD?

Following is a list of the research reported as being "in progress" among doctoral students. It is taken from *School Library Media Quarterly* and the *Journal of Education for Library and Information Science.*

Evelyn Bender, "Evaluations of Selected Logic/Problem Solving Educational Microcomputer Software: A Content Analysis of Published Reviews" (Temple University).

Julie Brookhart, "The Image of the South in Realistic Fiction for Children and Young Adults, 1945-1980" (University of Chicago).

Allan A. Cuseo, "A Literary Analysis of the Homosexual in Novels Published for the Young Adult" (Columbia University).

Paul Gandel, "Field Forces as Category Determinants of Pictures" (Syracuse University).

Elspeth Goodin, "The Transferability of Library Research Skills from High School to College" (Rutgers University).

Milton G. Hathaway, "A Comparison of Male and Female Science-related Roles as Depicted in the Illustrations of Science Information Trade Books for the Middle School Student Published from 1973 through 1985: A Content Analysis" (Indiana University).

Gloria Holmes, "An Analysis of the Information-Seeking Behavior of Science Teachers in Selected Secondary Public Schools in Florida" (Florida State University).

Suzanne C. Joseph, "Cognitive Style and the Implementation Patterns of Computers in Middle Schools" (Drexel University).

Freda Kleinburd, "Literature of the Holocaust for Children and Young People" (Columbia University).

Karmidi Martoatmojo, "The Importance of Audiovisual Instruction as Perceived by the Deans and Professors in ALA Accredited Library Schools" (Florida State University).

Sarah Lewis Marxson, "Open Space Library Media Centers in Senior High Schools in the United States: Historical View" (Florida State University).

Susan K. McEnally, "The Development of the Junior Novel in America, 1870-1980" (University of North Carolina).

Carole Richards, "Perceptions of Libraries in Elementary Schools" (Rutgers University).

Susan Roman, "Popular Juvenile Fiction Series: A Study" (University of Chicago).

Elizabeth Guinan Clark Schmidt, "An Experimental Study of the Effect of Teacher Bibliographic Instruction on the Library Skills of College Bound High School Students" (Florida State University).

Margaret E. Tice, "The Plot Thickens: A Critical Study of Mystery and Detective Fiction for Children" (Columbia University).

Carol C. Young, "Huck Finn, Maisie Farange, and the Child Narrator in American Children's Literature" (Columbia University).

NOTES

[1] J. C. Mancall, S. L. Aaron, and S. A. Walker, "Educating Students to Think: The Role of the School Library Media Program," *School Library Media Quarterly* 15, no. 1 (1986): 18-27; E. R. Kulleseid, "Extending the Research Base: Schema, Theory, Cognitive Styles, and Types of Intelligence," *School Library Media Quarterly* 15, no. 1 (1986): 41-48.

[2] M. Gaver, "Research on Elementary School Libraries," *ALA Bulletin* 56, no. 2 (1962): 117-24; M. Gaver, "Is Anyone Listening? Significant Research Studies for Practicing Librarians," *Wilson Library Bulletin* 43, no. 4 (1969): 764-72.

[3] J. E. Lowrie, "A Review of Research in School Librarianship," in *Research Methods in Librarianship: Measurement and Evaluation*, ed. H. Goldhor (Urbana, Ill.: University of Illinois, 1968), 51-69.

[4] S. L. Aaron, "A Review of Selected Doctoral Dissertations about School Library Media Programs and Resources, January 1972-December 1980," *School Library Media Quarterly* 82, no. 3 (1982): 210-45; D. D. Barron, "Review of Selected Research in School Librarianship: 1972-1976," *School Media Quarterly* 5, no. 4 (1977): 271-76.

[5] Aaron, "Review of Doctoral Dissertations"; D. V. Loertscher, "An *SLMQ* Special Feature: Research and School Librarianship," *School Library Media Quarterly* 10, nos. 2 & 3 (1982).

[6] S. L. Aaron, "A Review of Selected Research Studies about School Library Media Programs, Resources, and Personnel: January 1972-June 1981," in *School Library Media Annual*, ed. S. L. Aaron and P. R. Scales (Littleton, Colo.: Libraries Unlimited, 1983), 303-67.

[7] B. B. Minor, "ERIC Research Studies Dealing with School Library Media Programs: June 1981-June 1984," in *School Library Media Annual*, ed. S. L. Aaron and P. R. Scales (Littleton, Colo.: Libraries Unlimited, 1985), 348-66.

[8] E. K. Didier, "Microcomputers in School Library Media Centers: Utilization and Research," in *School Library Media Annual*, ed. S. L. Aaron and P. R. Scales (Littleton, Colo.: Libraries Unlimited, 1985), 336-45; E. K. Didier, "Research on the Impact of School Library Media Programs on Student Achievement—Implications for School Media Professionals," in *School Library Media Annual*, ed. S. L. Aaron and P. R. Scales (Littleton, Colo.: Libraries Unlimited, 1984), 343-58.

[9] M. P. Marchant, et al., "Research into Learning Resulting from Quality School Library Media Service," *School Library Journal* 30, no. 8 (1984): 20-22; D. W. Carver, "The Changing Instructional Role of the High School Library Media Specialist: 1950-84," *School Library Media Quarterly* 14, no. 4 (1986): 183-91.

[10] K. K. Edwards and I. Schon, "Professional Development Activities as Viewed by School Library Media Specialists," *School Library Media Quarterly* 14, no. 3 (1986): 138-41.

[11] M. Ming and G. W. MacDonald, *A Cooperative Project for the Development and Delivery of Training to Rural Library Staff across Alberta. Phase Two/Three. First Interim Report* (Edmonton, Alta.: Alberta Advanced Education and Manpower, 1985). ERIC Document Reproduction Service, ED 265 869.

[12] J. Griffiths and D. W. King, *New Directions in Library and Information Science Education. Final Report* (Rockville, Md.: King Research, Inc., 1985). ERIC Document Reproduction Service, ED 265 853.

[13] C. Kosters, "A Critical Analysis of Certification Requirements for School Librarians in the Fifty States from 1950 to 1985" (Ph.D. diss., University of South Dakota, 1986).

[14] M. L. Shontz, "A Study of Middle, Junior High, and High School Administrators' Use of the Performance Appraisal by Objectives Approach in the Personnel Evaluation of School Library Media Specialists" (Ph.D. diss., The Florida State University, 1986).

[15] P. M. Turner and J. G. Coleman, Jr., "State Education Agencies and the Evaluation of School Library Media Specialists: A Report" (Paper presented at the Annual Meeting of the Association for Educational Communications and Technology, Las Vegas, Nev., 1986). ERIC Document Reproduction Service, ED 266 790.

[16] S. W. Zsiray, "A Study of the Impact of Staffing Patterns in Elementary School Library Media Centers on Program Development" (Ph.D. diss., Utah State University, 1986).

[17] V. A. Cooper, "The Role of the Secondary School Librarian in Virginia" (Ph.D. diss., University of Virginia, 1985).

[18] N. A. Van House, "Salary Determination and Occupational Segregation among Librarians," *Library Quarterly* 56, no. 2 (1986): 142-66.

[19] J. Bierman, "Career Development of Women Librarians in New Zealand," *New Zealand Libraries* 441, no. 12 (1985): 225-27.

[20] N. L. Master and L. S. Master, *Perceptions of School Librarians as Curriculum Leaders* (Clark County, Nev.: Clark County Public Schools, 1986). ERIC Document Reproduction Service, ED 271 120.

[21] J. A. Horton, "Principals' and Teachers' Attitudes toward Kansas School Media Libraries" (Paper presented at the Annual Convention of the Association for Educational Communications and Technology, Las Vegas, Nev., 1986). ERIC Document Reproduction Service, ED 267 776. For a good overview of these studies, see J. M. Pitts, "A Creative Survey of Research Concerning Role Expectations of Library Media Specialists," *School Library Media Quarterly* 11, no. 1 (1982): 167-77.

[22] W. A. Scott, "A Comparison of Role Perceptions of the School Library Media Specialist among Library Media Educators, School Library Media Specialists, Principals, and Classroom Teachers" (Ph.D. diss., George Peabody College for Teachers of Vanderbilt University, 1986).

[23] R. F. C. Fitzgerald, "Participation by the School Library Media Specialist in Curriculum Development in Selected Michigan High Schools" (Ph.D. diss., University of Pittsburgh, 1985).

[24] M. J. Mosley, "The Relationships among a Reading Guidance Program and the Reading Attitudes, Reading Achievement, and Reading Behavior of Fifth Grade Children in a North Louisiana School (Library Programs)" (Ph.D. diss., North Texas State University, 1986).

[25] R. L. Thomas, "The Influence of a Poetry-Enriched Environment on the Poetry Preferences and Responses of Sixth-Grade Children: A Librarian-Teacher Collaboration (Ph.D. diss., The Ohio State University, 1986).

[26] J. L. Edwards, "An Implementation Paradigm Applied to Selection and Utilization of Library Audiovisual Materials" (Ph.D. diss., Saint Louis University, 1985).

[27] H. T. Browne, "A Comparison of the Roles of Secondary School Librarians and Academic Librarians" (Ph.D. diss., New York University, 1986).

[28] Wisconsin State Department of Public Instruction, *Interlibrary Loan Patterns: Survey of Wisconsin*. Bulletin no. 5915 (Madison, Wis.: Wisconsin State Department of Public Instruction, 1985).

[29] Y. A. Hodges, J. Gray, and W. J. Reeves, "High School Students' Attitudes towards the Library Media Program—What Makes the Difference?" *School Library Media Quarterly* 13, nos. 3 & 4 (1985): 183-90.

[30] R. N. Claus and B. E. Quimbe, *District-Wide Comprehensive Needs Assessment Study. Elementary Level, Part I, 1984-1985* (Saginaw, Mich.: Saginaw Public Schools, Department of Evaluation Services, 1985). ERIC Document Reproduction Center, ED 263 140.

[31] A. LeClercq, "The Academic Library/High School Library Connection: Needs Assessment and Proposed Model," *Journal of Academic Librarianship* 12, no. 1 (1986): 12-18.

[32] N. L. Bluemel, "An Analysis of the Effects of a Differentiated Program on the Library Experience of Gifted Students" (Ph.D. diss., Texas Woman's University, 1985).

[33] L. C. M. Haskell, "Student Performance of a Library-Related Task" (Ph.D. diss., North Texas State University, 1986).

[34] M. Fisher, "Selected Differences among Variously Accredited Michigan Secondary Schools" (Ph.D. diss., The University of Michigan, 1986).

[35] D. R. Burns, "The Relationship of Classification Standards and Other Input Measures to the Attainment of Pupil Learning Goals in Rural Secondary Schools" (Ph.D. diss., University of Missouri-Columbia, 1985).

[36] R. H. Bailey, "High School Library Databases: An Examination of Bibliographic Data Elements" (Ph.D. diss., University of Pittsburgh, 1985).

[37] S. R. Crow, "The Reviewing of Controversial Juvenile Books: A Study," *School Library Media Quarterly* 14, no. 2 (1968): 83-86.

[38] T. B. Bard and J. E. Leide, "Library Books Selected by Elementary School Students in Hawaii as Indicated by School Library Circulation Records," *Library and Information Science Research* 7, no. 2 (1985): 115-43.

[39] P. L. Jeffery, *The Utilization of "SET: Research Information for Teachers" in Selected Educational Institutions* (Hawthorn, Australia: Australian Council for Educational Research, 1985). ERIC Document Reproduction Service, ED 266 185.

[40] E. J. Griffith and T. E. Long, *Identification of Content for a Science Skill Inventory to Be Used for Vocational Curriculum Studies. Final Report* (Mill Creek, Pa.: Huntingdon County Area Vocational-Technical School, 1985). ERIC Document Reproduction Service, ED 262 249.

[41] M. L. Ho and D. Loertscher, "Collection Mapping in School Library Media Centers" (Paper presented at the Annual Convention of the Association for Educational Communications and Technology, Las Vegas, Nev., 1986). ERIC Document Reproduction Service, ED 267 775.

[42] C. A. Doll, "A Comparison of Children's Collections in Public and Elementary School Libraries," *Collection Management* no. 1 (1985): 47-59.

[43] S. D. Hall, "High School Library Database: Examination of Bibliographic Data Elements" (Ph.D. diss., University of Pittsburgh, 1985).

[44] G. D. Funk, "An Axiological Analysis of the Predominant Values in Contemporary Children's Literature" (Ph.D. diss., Oklahoma State University, 1986).

[45] G. Natriello, *Products and Processes of the National Center for Educational Statistics: An Agenda for the Next Decade* (Washington, D.C.: National Center for Educational Statistics, 1985). ERIC Document Reproduction Service, ED 272 558.

The Research Efforts of ALA and ALISE

Ron Powell and Sharon L. Baker

Both the American Library Association (ALA) and the Association for Library and Information Science Education (ALISE) have a program to stimulate research for the profession and for introspection. This article gathers together in one listing the various research mechanisms of both organizations.

THE AMERICAN LIBRARY ASSOCIATION

ALA has a Committee on Research which was established in January 1968. This committee replaced the Advisory Committee for the Office for Research and Development, which had been concerned almost exclusively with internal research. The functions of the ALA Research Committee are to facilitate research and related activities in all units of the Association; to advise the ALA Council and Executive Board on programs, policy, and priorities regarding research; to recommend procedures to achieve expeditious consideration of all ALA unit proposals for research and related activities by the ALA Executive Board; to encourage the establishment of divisional committees for the purpose of stimulating research; to maintain liaison with all units of the Association regarding research and related activities in the units; to identify questions regarding library service which need to be answered through research and promote the conduct of research to answer those questions; and to serve as an advisory committee for the Office of Research.[1]

The 1987 chair of the ALA Research Committee is Charles R. Martell, Assistant Library Director, California State University (Sacramento, CA 95819).

In addition to the Research Committee, ALA has an Office for Research, which is directed by Mary Jo Lynch. This office carries out three functions: (1) to collect, analyze, and interpret data about the membership of ALA and users of ALA products and services on an ongoing basis for organizational decision making; (2) to collect and/or promote the collection of statistics about libraries and librarians so that ALA and other organizations will have pertinent and consistent data available to them; and (3) to monitor ongoing research related to libraries and disseminate information about such studies to the profession. In carrying out these functions, the Office for Research will provide advice regarding research and statistics to the Executive Board, Council, and other units of ALA requesting such advice.[2]

Division Research Committees

A number of ALA divisions also have research committees, each with their own charges and activities. The following are the constituted committees with their respective chairs for 1987.

American Association of School Librarians
Research Committee
Chair: David V. Loertscher
P.O. Box 266
Castle Rock, CO 80104

Association for Library Service to
    Children
Research Committee
Chair: Leslie M. Edmonds
Graduate School of Library & Information
    Science
University of Illinois
Urbana, IL 61801

Association of College and Research Libraries
Bibliographic Instruction Section, Research
 Committee
Chair: Betsy Wilson
Undergraduate Library
University of Illinois
Urbana, IL 61801

Association of College and Research Libraries
Research Committee
Chair: Thomas Kirk
Hutchins Library
Berea College
Berea, KY 40404

Association of College and Research Libraries
Research Discussion Group
Chair: Melena Rowan
BRS Information Technologies
1200 Route 7
Latham, NY 12110

Association of College and Research Libraries
Western European Specialists Section,
 Research and Planning Committee
Chair: Eva Sartori
Humanities/Social Sciences Librarian
University of Nebraska Library
Lincoln, NE 68588

Association of Specialized and Cooperative
 Library Agencies
Research Committee
Chair: Ruth M. Katz
Director of Academic Library Services
Joyner Library
East Carolina University
Greenville, NC 27834

Library Administration and Management
 Association
Statistics Section, National Data Collection
 and Use Committee
Chair: Janice Feye-Stukas
Library Development and Service, Office of
 Public Libraries
440 Capitol Square
550 Cedar Street
St. Paul, MN 55101

Library Administration and Management
 Association
Statistics Section, Using Statistics for Library
 Planning and Evaluation Committee
Chair: Stuart J. Glogoff
Circulation Department
University of Delaware Library
South College Avenue
Newark, DE 19717

Library History Round Table
Chair: Robert S. Martin
Special Collections
Hill Memorial Library
Louisiana State University
Baton Rouge, LA 70803

Library Instruction Round Table
Research Committee
Chair: Paul Vincent
Mason Library
Keene State College
229 Main Street
Keene, NH 03431

Library Research Round Table
Research Development Committee
Chair: Nancy P. Sanders
Home Economics Library
Ohio State University
325 Campbell Hall
Columbus, OH 43210

Library Research Round Table
Research Forums Committee
Chair: Robert J. Grover
School of Library and Information Management
Emporia State University
1200 Commercial Street
Emporia, KS 66801

Public Library Association
Research Committee
Chair: Joan Coachman Durrance
School of Library Science
University of Michigan
580 Union Drive
Ann Arbor, MI 48109

Resources and Technical Services Division
Planning and Research Committee
Chair: John R. James
Dartmouth College Library
Hanover, NH 03755

Resources and Technical Services Division
Cataloging and Classification Section,
 Policy and Research Committee
Chair: Ellen Siegel Kovacic
5203 Williamsburg Road, 7W
Cincinnati, OH 45215

Resources and Technical Services Division
Preservation of Library Materials Section,
    Policy and Research Committee
Chair: Carolyn Clark Morrow
National Preservation Program Office,
    LM-G07
Library of Congress
Washington, DC 20540

Resources and Technical Services Division
Reproduction of Library Materials Section,
    Policy and Research Committee
Chair: Bohdan W. Mysko
6137 North Fairhill Street
Philadelphia, PA 19120

Resources and Technical Services Division
Resources Section, Policy and Research
    Committee
Chair: Carolyn B. Fields
2011 Nautilus Street
La Jolla, CA 92037

Resources and Technical Services Division
Serials Section, Policy and Research Committee
Chair: Carolyn J. Mueller
Serials Department
University of Colorado Libraries
Campus Box 184
Boulder, CO 80309

Young Adult Services Division
Research Committee
Chair: Lesley S. J. Farmer
135 Golden Hind Passage
Corte Madera, CA 94925

Research Awards

In addition to the various committees, offices, and round tables, there are a number of awards given which promote research in the field.

1. (Carroll Preston) Baber Research Award. This annual award of $10,000 is presented to a person doing research focusing on improved library services, new uses of technology, or cooperative projects. The award is donated by Eric R. Baber and is administered by the ALA Awards Committee. For more information, write Elaine K. Wingate, staff liaison for the ALA Awards Committee, at ALA Headquarters.

2. Association of College and Research Libraries, Doctoral Dissertation Fellowship. This annual award of $1,000 is presented to a doctoral student in the field of academic librarianship whose research indicates originality, creativity, and scholarship. The award was designed to encourage the dissertation work of doctoral students who have completed all their coursework and have had their proposals accepted by their institutions. The award is donated by the Institute for Scientific Information and is administered by ACRL. For more information, write JoAn Segal, executive director of ACRL, at ALA Headquarters.

3. Frances Henne YASD/*Voice of Youth Advocates (VOYA)* Research Grant. This annual award of $500 was established to provide seed money for small-scale research projects that will have an influence on library service to young adults. Applicants must belong to YASD. Grants will not be given for research leading to a degree. The award is donated by *VOYA* and is administered by YASD. For more information, write Evelyn Shaevel, executive director of YASD, at ALA Headquarters.

4. Samuel Lazerow Fellowship for Research in Acquisitions or Technical Services. This annual award of $1,000 is given to provide librarians in acquisitions or technical services with a fellowship for research, travel, or writing. Proposals are judged on their potential significance, originality, and clarity. The award is administered by ACRL. For more information, write JoAn Segal, executive director of ACRL, at ALA Headquarters.

5. Library Research Round Table Research Award. This award is given annually for an excellent research paper. Entries are judged on definition of the research problem, application of research methods, clarity of the reporting of the research, and significance of the conclusions. The award is administered and donated by the Library Research Round Table. For more information, write Mary Jo Lynch, staff liaison for the Library Research Round Table, at ALA Headquarters.

6. Justin Winsor Prize Essay. This award of $500 is given to encourage excellence in research in library history. Essays should be original historical research on a significant subject of library history, and should be based on primary source materials and manuscripts if possible. The award is administered by the Library History Round Table. For more information, write Emily Melton, staff liaison for the Library History Round Table, at ALA Headquarters.

Research is published by ALA in a variety of ways. Some reports are published by ALA

Publishing and released as books. Most research is reported in the various journals published by the Association, either as research articles or in research columns. Journals which regularly report research findings include *School Library Media Quarterly, Top of the News,* and *Library Resources and Technical Services.*

ALISE

The Association for Library and Information Science Education (ALISE) promotes and facilitates research through a variety of activities and organizations. Within the Association are the Research Committee and the Research Interest Group. The Research Committee is the coordinating unit of the Association for all research activities. It is also responsible for reviewing any research-oriented programs planned for the annual conference and for recommending to the board of directors all awards for research-related activities. The Research Interest Group is responsible for developing research-related programs for the annual conferences. Recent conferences have also scheduled doctoral forums and "Nightcap Specials," which are opportunities for researchers to share their work informally with small groups.

ALISE annually awards one or more grants totaling $2,500 to support research broadly related to education for library and information science. The Association also sponsors an annual research paper competition. Papers may concern any aspect of librarianship or information studies. Winning papers receive honorariums of $500 and are presented at the annual conference. Recipients of these two awards must be personal members of ALISE. In addition, two outstanding doctoral dissertations completed during the preceding year are selected to be presented at the annual conference. Each winner of this competition receives a $400 award plus conference registration and a personal membership in ALISE.

The *Journal of Education for Library and Information Science* is the official publication of ALISE. Each quarterly issue regularly includes research-type articles and other scholarly papers. The journal also contains the "Research Record," a column devoted to research-related issues and listings of recently approved proposals for doctoral dissertations in library and information science. The Association continues to compile and publish its *Library and Information Science Education Statistical Report* as well.

NOTES

[1] *ALA Handbook of Organization: 1986-87.* Chicago: American Library Association, 1986.

[2] Ibid.

Part II
REVIEWS OF BOOKS

Reviews of Books

GENERAL REFERENCE WORKS

Bibliographies

1. **Best Reference Books 1981-1985: Titles of Lasting Value Selected from** *American Reference Books Annual.* Bohdan S. Wynar, ed. Littleton, Colo., Libraries Unlimited, 1986. 504p. index. $45.00. LC 86-15316. ISBN 0-87287-554-7.

Best Reference Books 1981-1985 is intended for use by new libraries building their reference collections and by existing libraries rounding out their general collections or filling in gaps in subject areas. In addition to its stated purpose, it might serve as an update for reference librarians and required reading for library science students. The 1,051 included titles were selected from the 8,316 titles reviewed in *American Reference Books Annual* (*ARBA*) from 1981 to 1985. The lengthy signed critical reviews, prepared by library educators and practicing librarians, have been updated by the *ARBA* editorial staff to reflect the latest editions and current prices.

In addition to a more readable format and double-column layout, this edition incorporates several changes from the earlier editions, all of which are improvements. It follows the latest *ARBA* arrangement of four major subject areas: (1) general reference sources, (2) social sciences, (3) humanities, and (4) science and technology. All areas are subdivided (e.g., astronomy, biochemistry, chemistry, etc.). This arrangement is convenient for readers requiring a quick overview of any given field. The two-part index, author/title and subject, is accurate and complete.

For the first time serial publications have been included. Old favorites such as *Readers' Guide to Periodical Literature*, *Social Sciences Index* and *Subject Guide to Books in Print* are reviewed. This can be a valuable feature if the serial has been substantially changed, but one wonders how many times *Ulrich's International Periodicals Directory* can be profitably reviewed. *ARBA*, for example, has been reviewed twenty-six times since 1970.

Another potential hazard in compiling a resource of this purpose is that titles filling a critical need may be included, whereas superior books in highly published areas may be excluded. However, in the specific areas checked by this reviewer—history, law, and performing arts—all selections are noteworthy and the significant titles have been included. The editor has done a careful and thorough job in selecting and arranging this work, which will be particularly useful to academic libraries unable to afford *ARBA*. [R: RQ, Winter 86, pp. 246-47; WLB, Nov 86, p. 63] Helen Carol Bennett

2. Cariou, Mavis, Sandra J. Cox, and Alvan Bregman, comps. **Canadian Selection: Books and Periodicals for Libraries.** 2d ed. Buffalo, N.Y., published for the Ontario Ministry of Citizenship and Culture and the Centre for Research in Librarianship, University of Toronto, University of Toronto Press, 1985. 501p. index. $65.00. ISBN 0-8020-4630-4.

Canadian Selection is a guide to Canadian books and periodicals for adults (no children's literature is included). It is designed, as the introduction states, "to reflect and foster the growing interest in Canadian authors, publishers, subjects, and styles of literature." The selection of material is based on the needs of small and medium-sized libraries, though it could also be useful to school and college libraries. A review of the first edition may be found in *ARBA* 79 (entry 181) and the supplement was reviewed in *ARBA* 82 (entry 156).

The book is divided into five parts. Part 1 consists of annotated bibliographies of more than five thousand books (English language only) "published in Canada, about Canada, or written by Canadians" through 1983. Entries from the first edition and the supplement are included with updated edition statements and prices. The books are grouped under subject headings and subheadings. Subjects given particular attention in this new edition are legal materials and poetry.

Part 2, a much shorter section, lists annotated bibliographies of 255 Canadian periodicals in alphabetical order by title. This information is said to be current through fall 1984.

A list of Canadian literary awards and their recipients comprises part 3. Some French titles are included here, and a current address for each granting agency is given.

Parts 4 and 5 consist of the basic author/title and subject index, respectively.

The compilers have attempted to present a balanced collection of Canadian titles, including regional writings, publications from small presses, and works with audiences of different ages and education. Approximately 180 contributors are listed, and many of the annotations are signed. Kari Sidles

3. **Recommended Reference Books for Small and Medium-sized Libraries and Media Centers 1986.** Bohdan S. Wynar, ed. Littleton, Colo., Libraries Unlimited, 1986. 262p. index. $30.00. LC 81-12394. ISBN 0-87287-540-7; ISSN 0277-5948.

This is the sixth volume in an annual series designed to help smaller libraries keep their reference collections up-to-date. Approximately one-third of the 1,786 books reviewed in *ARBA* 86 were selected for inclusion here (a total of 567 titles). The reviews are unabridged and are signed by the 258 contributors, all of them subject specialists. References to reviews published in periodicals are also included, as they are in *ARBA*.

The book is divided into four parts. A separate section on general reference works is followed by sections covering the social sciences, humanities, and science and technology. The thirty-three chapters are subdivided by form (bibliographies, dictionaries, directories) and/or topic (American history, human rights, agricultural sciences). Some variation in this pattern occurs throughout.

While not all of the reviews specifically comment on a book's suitability for the smaller library, a code system corrects this problem to some extent (C = smaller college libraries; P = public libraries; S = school media centers). The only categories of books excluded are regional guides for botany and zoology; genealogy; and reference titles in literature and art dealing with individual authors and artists.

This annual review provides a convenient and economical way for small libraries to maintain a viable reference collection.

Gary D. Barber

4. **Reference Books Bulletin 1984-1985: A Compilation of Evaluations Appearing in *Reference Books Bulletin*, September 1, 1984-August 1985.** Helen K. Wright, ed. Chicago, American Library Association, 1986. 157p. $20.00pa. LC 73-159565. ISBN 0-8389-3329-7; ISSN 8755-0962.

This is the seventeenth cumulation of *Reference Books Bulletin* (formerly *Reference and Subscription Books Review*) and the second year of its new format (see *ARBA* 86, entry 562). This volume covers reviews published between 1 September 1984 and 1 August 1985. Included in this cumulation are several bibliographical essays with subjects of various interest including science and technology reference sources, home reference books for junior and senior high school age students, and consumer health reference books. This is the first year for a feature intended as an annual inclusion, "Encyclopedia Roundup." Two indexes, a subject index and an index to type of material, complete the volume. It should be pointed out that the reviews in this edition tend to be more current than in the past.

A special note: Helen K. Wright has served as editor of *Reference Books Bulletin* for twenty-seven years and editing this cumulation concludes her service in this capacity. For this reason, a foreword, not ordinarily included in this work, has been written by Frances Neel Cheney. Anna Grace Patterson

5. Sheehy, Eugene, and others, eds. **Guide to Reference Books.** 10th ed. Chicago, American Library Association, 1986. 1560p. index. $50.00. LC 85-11208. ISBN 0-8389-0390-8.

Sheehy's *Guide to Reference Books* needs no introduction to the library profession. It is a well-respected work, introduced by most instructors in library schools to all students, with perhaps half of them purchasing the volume. This has been the case for many years, and even this fact alone may account for the tremendous popularity of the guide. Sheehy's reputation is well deserved. *Guide to Reference Books* is an adequately balanced work with an excellent bibliographic apparatus, a good index, and sufficient coverage in most areas. International in scope, *Guide to Reference Books* covers a substantial number of foreign titles—probably not as successfully as it does domestic or more precise English material, but who can do it all in one volume? Sheehy's guide is better executed than the most recent edition of its British counterpart, Walford, and is practically free of factual errors.

So what can be said about this new edition? First, some historical and descriptive notes. The previous edition, published in 1976, was reviewed at some length in *ARBA* 77 (entry 14). The first *Supplement*, published in 1980, was reviewed in *ARBA* 81 (entry 3); the *Second Supplement*, published in 1982, was reviewed in *ARBA* 83 (entry 5). On all three occasions we have said that this is a "must purchase" for libraries of all types and that Sheehy reflects some of the best practices in compiling a general bibliographic guide. We have also expressed a number of critical observations in reviewing previous editions. Annotations are very brief and primarily descriptive but not evaluative. There are some gaps in coverage and occasionally only a token coverage of foreign titles. We have also recommended omission of obsolete titles and have noted time lapses in coverage that have amounted occasionally to three or four years. These shortcomings are of only minor importance, though, and should not detract from the use of this vital work by library science professionals.

So, again, what is new in this tenth edition? Seven of Sheehy's colleagues who assisted him in this endeavor are prominently listed on the title page, as opposed to two listed in the previous edition. A significant change is that the area of "Science, Technology, and Medicine" is now covered by subject specialists outside of Columbia University Libraries. Something similar was also done by Bill Katz in his classic, *Magazines for Libraries* (R. R. Bowker, 1986), and in a work of this kind the broadened perspective can only be beneficial. The result, it seems, is that coverage of "Science, Technology, and Medicine" in the tenth edition is stronger and certainly better balanced. Moreover, this new edition includes thirty to thirty-five percent more titles. It is also more current in comparison to its predecessor. As indicated in the preface, "it was agreed at the outset that 1984 would be a relatively firm cutoff date for this edition, with selected 1985 imprints admitted when their importance seemed to warrant it. As work progressed, however, the temptation to include 1985 imprints became harder and harder to resist. As a result, those sections completed first (notably the "A" sections) show a minimal number of 1985 publications, whereas 1985 imprints appear with considerable frequency in sections which were completed last" (p. ix). In addition, many annotations include notes on forthcoming revisions or new editions, contributing to greater currency of this tenth edition in comparison to previous editions, including Winchell's volumes. This edition also has a considerable number of notes on available reprints due to use of MARC records and the RLIN database. Finally, the index, as always, is quite adequate.

Sheehy indicates in his preface that this is his final edition of the guide. The question arises as to whether the ALA will change its format to include more volumes and invite more people to participate in this important project in future editions. We will wait and see.

Pro domo sua we can indicate that there is no reference to Wynar in connection with *ARBA* (this was done in the previous edition); although, on a different note, the author's *Introduction to Cataloging and Classification* is listed in Sheehy's guide with a nice note that a new, seventh edition is scheduled for publication in 1985. Only two other titles are listed in this section—an old classic, *The Classified Catalog* by Shera and Egan (1956), and a similar classic, *Introduction to Cataloging and Classification* by Margaret Mann (1943). This is probably not enough, but this is a subjective decision the editor must make.

So again, this substantial work is highly recommended for libraries of all types, and we will be looking forward to only minimal changes in connection with the eleventh edition, that unfortunately will most likely not be prepared by Sheehy.   Bohdan S. Wynar

Biographies

6. **ARBA Guide to Biographical Dictionaries.** Bohdan S. Wynar, ed. Littleton, Colo., Libraries Unlimited, 1986. 444p. index. $40.00. LC 86-2851. ISBN 0-87287-492-3.

Of the more than 2,500 biographical sources that *ARBA* has reviewed over the past seventeen years, some 500 of the most important were selected for this volume. These reviews, written by the specialists who regularly contribute to *ARBA*, were carefully edited to make them current. In virtually all cases only those books still in print were included. Where necessary, bibliographic data were updated and prices checked against both publishers' catalogs and *Books in Print*. About 200 new entries were undertaken by the editor to accord with his stated purpose: "to offer a representative selection of biographical dictionaries and directories ... useful in the reference and information process in libraries of all types." Obviously, this valuable reference tool will also assist in the acquisition process, since in addition to critical evaluations of the 718 works adjudged worthy of inclusion it provides bibliographic descriptions and price information.

The entries are divided into two major categories. Part 1, "Universal and National Biographies," first supplies general sources not limited in their coverage to a particular topic, description, nationality or territory; and then covers those works properly subsumed under national origin, starting with the United States and moving on alphabetically through Africa, Asia, Australia, Canada, and so on. Part 2, "Biographies in Professional Fields," incorporates twenty-one subject-oriented areas; here the divisions begin with "Applied Arts," "Communications and Mass Media," "Economics and Business," and continue alphabetically down to "Science and Technology," "Social Sciences," and "Sports." Area entries reflect both publishing practices and individual disciplines. The longest section, "Literature," for example, is divided into such subjects as "General Works," "Specific Genres," and "National Literatures" — plus some thirty more such listings; so while there are over a hundred main entries in the "Literature" section, there are only five in "Geography" and three in "History." A brief introduction explains criteria employed for selection. Two detailed indexes, author/title and subject, further enhance this volume as they allow for quick cross-reference.

There is precious little to fault in this well-conceived, logically structured, and successfully executed text. In short, *ARBA Guide to Biographical Dictionaries* fulfills its stated purpose: it should prove useful not only in the largest of reference collections but even in the smallest of circulating libraries. [R: Choice, Sept 86, p. 77; JAL, Sept 86, p. 264; LJ, Aug 86, p. 134; RBB, 15 Sept 86, p. 112; WLB, Sept 86, p. 78]

G. A. Cevasco

7. Cimbala, Diane J., Jennifer Cargill, and Brian Alley. **Biographical Sources: A Guide to Dictionaries and Reference Works.** Phoenix, Ariz., Oryx Press, 1986. 146p. index. $35.00. LC 86-12805. ISBN 0-89774-136-6.

With the multitude of reference books being compiled by research librarians and academicians, there is an obvious need for guidebooks such as this. As its title indicates, this study identifies and evaluates hundreds of biographical sources. If it be objected that all the titles selected have an Anglo-American bias, it must be remembered that so do the reference collections of most university and public libraries in the United States and Canada.

While Eugene Sheehy's *Guide to Reference Books* (American Library Association, 1976) and the *Gale Biographical Index Series* (Gale, 1975) list a hefty number of the more common biographical works, an annotated access to most biographical dictionaries has heretofore been virtually nonexistent. This guide, accordingly, is meant both to aid librarians who frequently have to answer biographical questions and to assist researchers in identifying sources most likely to contain data about an individual or individuals under study. Indexed by subject and title, this useful reference tool supplies complete bibliographic information, critical remarks, a description of the arrangement, publication frequency, and method of compilation for each of its nearly seven hundred entries. Indexes provide detailed subject and author/title access.

Of additional interest: Future editions of this guide already planned will include later imprints as well as any omitted from this first effort. One interesting group of sources to be explored more fully is "vanity" biographical dictionaries. [Ed. note: At the time of writing this review, the reviewer was unaware of two recently published works by Wynar and Slocum (see entries 6 and 8).]

G. A. Cevasco

8. Slocum, Robert B., ed. **Biographical Dictionaries and Related Works: An International Bibliography of More Than 16,000 Collective Biographies, Bio-bibliographies, Collections of Epitaphs....** 2d ed. Detroit, Gale, 1986. 2v. index. $140.00/set. LC 85-8163. ISBN 0-8103-0234-8.

The first edition of this well-known work was published in 1967, with two supplements to follow in 1972 and 1978. Sally S. Small, in reviewing the *Second Supplement* (see *ARBA* 79, entry 134), indicated that it added 3,823 citations, increasing the total number of works covered in the three-volume set to 12,094 titles. This new edition includes 16,000 sources, thus updating previous editions and supplements with a net increase of approximately 4,000 titles. The arrangement and execution of this work remain the same: coverage is international in scope, each entry provides basic bibliographic information (author, title, imprint, and pagination) plus brief annotations — usually one or two sentences. All entries are arranged under numerous headings within three main categories: "Universal Biography," "National and Area Biography," and "Biography by Vocation." In addition to typical biographical sources, some related material is also included, primarily bio-bibliographies, collections of epitaphs, some genealogical works, dictionaries of anonyms and pseudonyms, historical and subject dictionaries, government and legislative manuals (with biographical material), biographies of individuals and collective biographies, biographical indexes, and selected portrait catalogs.

In a work of this magnitude some omissions or even inadequate coverage are quite common. For example, we examined a short section on Ukraine (entries 5369-5373) and found rather poor coverage. *Ukrainian Soviet Encyclopedia*, published in 1959-1965 (entry 5373), is now in its second edition, with the first volume published in 1977 and the twelfth quite recently, probably too late for inclusion. This general Soviet encyclopedia is supplemented by a number of more specialized works (e.g., encyclopedia of economy, agriculture, cybernetics, etc.). None of these multivolume sets is mentioned (a set on history being one exception). Also omitted is an excellent encyclopedic dictionary published some ten years ago in Kiev containing numerous biographical articles of Soviet Ukrainian officials. There are also two biographical dictionaries, one published in the United States and the second in Canada, that cover prominent Ukrainians in both countries. Neither of these appears in *Biographical Dictionaries and Related Works*. There is one entry (5370) covering 197 biographical sketches of "Heroes of the Soviet Union," but none for multivolume works dealing with biographies of Ukrainian scholars (published on several occasions by the Ukrainian Academy of Arts and Sciences in Kiev) or equally important biographical works covering Ukrainian figures in literature, the fine arts, science and technology, etc. The entry for *Encyclopedia of Ukrainian Studies (Entsyklopediia Ukrainoznavstva)* is incomplete in not mentioning that there are two English versions of this work that systematically update this encyclopedia: *Ukraine: A Concise Encyclopedia* (2v. University of Toronto Press, 1963-1971) and *Encyclopedia of Ukraine, Volume 1, A-F* (University of Toronto Press, 1984, in progress). To some extent, the same is true in the case of some other even better known countries, such as Poland, Czechoslovakia, or Yugoslavia. Coverage is much better balanced for German or French works and, generally speaking, is quite adequate for the United States.

The material for the United States is arranged under the following headings: "Bibliography, Indexes,, Portrait Catalogs," "General Works" and "Local (States, Cities, and Regions)." Some lapses do exist even in this section of Slocum's collection. For example, with regard to who's who type publications for Colorado, the most recent entry is for 1958. Two more works have been published since that year (e.g., *Colorado Who's Who 1984*, TY Publishing, 1984, 337p.), both reviewed in *ARBA*. Some works are no longer published (e.g., *American Directory and Who's Who in Europe* or *Community Leaders and Noteworthy Americans*). But, in general, the coverage is very good.

Slocum's *Biographical Dictionaries* is not only the most comprehensive source of this kind now available, but is also well executed and deserves to be found in all types of libraries interested in biographical research. The price, in comparison to some other Gale publications, is also very reasonable. Bohdan S. Wynar

Dictionaries and Encyclopedias

9. **ALA World Encyclopedia of Library and Information Services.** 2d ed. Robert Wedgeworth and others, eds. Chicago, American Library Association, 1986. 895p. illus. $165.00. LC 86-10894. ISBN 0-8389-0427-0.

The stated objective of this work is to establish a firm basis for the comparative study of librarianship, tracing the development of the field with historical articles, explaining and analyzing professional concepts and principles, and providing current descriptions of library and information services in countries around the world. This second edition has broadened its coverage of biographical subjects, theory and current practices in librarianship, and international organizations. This volume contains 43 percent more words than the previous edition. New or completely revised articles comprise 85 percent of the book. This edition includes approximately 470 articles, 411 contributors, and 31 editorial advisers from around the world; 350 illustrations (black-and-white); and over 150 statistical tables.

The second edition follows the same editorial plan as the first. The "Outline of Contents," which provides a detailed subject access to the alphabetically arranged work, is divided into five main categories: the library in society, from ancient times to the present; the library as an institution; theory and practice of librarianship; education and research in librarianship; and international library and information organizations and bibliographic organizations. Biographical articles are contained within these groupings. Articles vary in length from several hundred to over twenty-five thousand words; all are signed by their contributors, who were chosen for their "professional and scholarly achievements." Articles on each individual country follow a set format and include tables of statistics when available; this arrangement facilitates comparison of the various countries and aids in locating names of national library agencies. The "Parallel Index," printed in the margins of the first edition, has been replaced by a conventional index at the end of the text, which also provides references to the *ALA Yearbook of Library and Information Science*.

This is a useful reference tool, particularly for the library student, and most large libraries will want to have it. Its price will probably prohibit purchase by smaller libraries on limited budgets.
Shirley Lambert

10. **ARBA Guide to Subject Encyclopedias and Dictionaries.** Edited by Bohdan S. Wynar, with the assistance of Heather Cameron and G. Kim Dority. Littleton, Colo., Libraries Unlimited, 1986. 570p. index. $45.00. LC 86-10264. ISBN 0-87287-493-1.

This guide presents a representative selection of subject dictionaries and encyclopedias, serial and nonserial, which are considered useful in the reference and information services provided by all types of libraries. The format closely follows that of *American Reference Books Annual* (*ARBA*), from which much of the material was selected. Although the sources cited cover seventeen years of *ARBA*, only books still in print are included, except for some particularly significant out-of-print titles.

The forty-three chapters in the book are arranged alphabetically by subject; chapter subdivisions reflect both publishing practices and individual disciplines or areas. Typical entries include title; author or editor; imprint and distributor; page numbers; price; and, in most cases, LC numbers and ISBNs. The author/title index and subject index provide additional access to citations.

Like its companion volume, *ARBA Guide to Biographical Dictionaries*, this compilation will be helpful in both collection development and reference activities. Its extensive coverage will assist in locating and evaluating specialized reference tools for selection and in assessing the strengths and weaknesses of a reference collection by subject area. The editors have succeeded in separating trivial works from the esoteric, providing specialized coverage which should meet almost all reference needs. [R: Choice, Dec 86, p. 603; LJ, 15 Nov 86, p. 87; RBB, 15 Dec 86, pp. 629-30; WLB, Oct 86, p. 63]
Jay Schafer

11. **Encyclopedia of Library and Information Science. Volume 39, Supplement 4.** Allen Kent, ed. New York, Marcel Dekker, 1985. 430p. illus. $65.00. LC 68-31232. ISBN 0-8247-2039-3.

12. **Encyclopedia of Library and Information Science. Volume 40, Supplement 5.** Allen Kent, ed. New York, Marcel Dekker, 1986. 402p. illus. $65.00. LC 68-31232. ISBN 0-8247-2040-7.

13. **Encyclopedia of Library and Information Science. Volume 41, Supplement 6.** Allen Kent, ed. New York, Marcel Dekker, 1986. 368p. illus. $55.00. LC 68-31232. ISBN 0-8247-2041-5.

Allen Kent, who remains the executive editor of this set, has described the purpose of the *Encyclopedia of Library and Information Science Supplements* as follows: To update articles in the main set; to add new articles on topics currently important in the field; to include recently deceased prominent librarians; and, finally, to include articles originally commissioned for the main set but not received in time for inclusion.

The main set and first two volumes have been reviewed in *ARBA* as well as in *Library Science Annual* (see, for example, *Library Science Annual 1985*, entries 6-9). That review incorporated references to previous reviews of individual volumes and also reviewed early supplements. The *Volume 38, Supplement 3* was reviewed in *Library Science Annual 1986* (entry 7), and at that time it was concluded that an overwhelming majority of articles are on topics that might have been incorporated in the main set. On the positive side, the articles included are thorough and well documented, and the contributors are recognized authorities in their respective fields. Generally speaking, the same is true of three subsequent *Supplements.* Thus, for example, in *Volume 39* there is a very well written article by Russell Bidlack, "Accreditation of Library Education," an article by Jane Rosenberg, "Council on Library Resources, Inc.," and "Data Base Management Systems: An Introduction," by L. A. Kurtz. *Volume 40* offers extensive articles, including "National Library of Austria," "Electronic Mail," "German State Library, Berlin," and "Numeric Data Bases." (The last mentioned article was written by Peter Hernon, and is probably one of the best in the volume.) *Volume 41* offers well-researched articles on "The National Library of Medicine" and "Wales, National Library of." There are, of course, many other interesting articles, too numerous to mention.

We would like to repeat one of our previous comments in conclusion to this brief review. The impact of technology on the field of library science in the last ten years has been felt by all of us. How can this problem be resolved by using supplements? This work has taken more than one and one-half decades to produce. Do we really need to add new articles on John Baskerville or Apollonius Rhodius or Giacomio Casonova? Indeed, they are well written, but there will be no end to these supplements if we continue in this fashion. In other words, the editor and his editorial staff still have to resolve this important problem—how much to update and whom to add. Perhaps a master plan of some nature shared among the members of our profession is in order.
Bohdan S. Wynar

14. Kister, Kenneth F. **Best Encyclopedias: A Guide to General and Specialized Encyclopedias.** Phoenix, Ariz., Oryx Press, 1986. 356p. index. $39.50. LC 85-43370. ISBN 0-89774-171-4.

Kister's *Best Encyclopedias* is in its fourth edition, and has been reviewed in three previous volumes of *ARBA* (see *ARBA* 77, entry 71; *ARBA* 79, entry 74; and *ARBA* 82, entry 46). Though the first three editions were published by R. R. Bowker (the first in 1976, the second in 1978, and the third in 1981), Kister's guide is now published by Oryx Press, and has undergone several significant structural changes. The most important of these changes is that the guide has expanded in scope to include not only general encyclopedias but also reviews of special subject encyclopedias. Unfortunately, in making this change, Kister has condensed his coverage of general English-language encyclopedias dramatically. In his third edition, Kister devoted 398 pages to reviewing thirty-two general encyclopedias, whereas in this fourth edition the same section spans only 194 pages for fifty-two encyclopedias. Historically, Kister's guide has been a primary reference source for librarians and information science professionals, though this revision may place this source behind others of its kind—such as the *ARBA Guide to Subject Encyclopedias and Dictionaries* and Sheehy's *Guide to Reference Books*—as a preferred tool.

Despite this change, it is still the "General English Language Encyclopedias" section of the guide that is given the most attention. Herein he reviews encyclopedias ranging from "large multivolume sets for adults, such as the *New Encyclopaedia Britannica* and *Collier's Encyclopedia*, to small works for children, such as *Nelson's Encyclopedia for Young Readers* and *Purnell's Pictorial Encyclopedia*." These encyclopedias are listed alphabetically with each review providing basic data about the book (publisher, editor, price, number of volumes, pages, articles, words, cross-references, etc.) followed by "authoritative critical comments; comparisons to encyclopedias of similar size, price, and intended usership; sales information; and citations to reviews in other publications." An appendix follows this section and charts the information for easy comparison. As mentioned earlier, Kister has significantly reduced the information provided in this nonspecialized encyclopedia section of the guide. For example, in the third edition, Kister's profile of the *New Encyclopaedia Britannica* occupied thirty-one pages, whereas in the fourth edition he completes his profile in nine pages. In the former edition, Kister offered an extensive critical comparison between the *New Encyclopaedia Britannica* and the two other volumes of comparable quality—*Collier's Encyclopedia*, and *Encyclopedia Americana*. In fact, Kister cited these two other encyclopedia sets throughout his review of the *New Encyclopaedia Britannica* in the third edition, drawing comparisons on nearly all critical points. In the fourth edition he completes the comparison in four sentences. Further examples of the extent to which profiles have been pared down follow: *Compton's Encyclopedia* is reviewed in six and one-half pages in this edition but in ten and one-half in the third edition; the *New Illustrated Columbia Encyclopedia* is given thirteen pages in the third edition and three pages in the fourth; *Random House Encyclopedia* is given fourteen pages in the third edition and six pages in this one. It is curious that Kister made this change. The result is a much less comprehensive guide.

Following the "General English Language Encyclopedias" section is what Kister describes as an "extensive section on specialized encyclopedias," reviewing approximately 450 titles in seventy-eight pages. The encyclopedias are grouped into thirty-two subject categories. As in the previous section, these reviews provide basic data about the books followed by a critical annotation. To describe this section as "extensive" is inaccurate; these reviews are very brief, in most cases four or five lines long. For example, Kister describes *The Cambridge Guide to English Literature* in two sentences. He fails to mention that this guide to English literature includes that literature of Canada, the United States, Australia, New Zealand, Ireland, South Africa, the West Indies, and Nigeria, a fact that is disguised by the name of this publication. Moreover, he does not mention that it includes illustrations, an important criterion in selecting a reference book.

Kister's choice of entries in this section can be questioned in some cases. For example, he includes *An Encyclopedia of World History: Ancient, Medieval and Modern, Chronologically Arranged*, edited by William L. Langer (1972), but not *The New Illustrated Encyclopedia of World History*, also edited by Langer (1973). The latter work is described in *ARBA Guide to Subject Encyclopedias and Dictionaries* as identical in text to the former, but "lavishly illustrated with more than two thousand photographs, maps, charts, and drawings." It is curious that Kister did not at least append this information to his review of the *Encyclopedia of World History*. Perhaps of less importance is that a number of the titles reviewed as encyclopedias in Kister's guide are not, in fact, encyclopedias. Included in the section of "Specialized Encyclopedias" are dictionaries (e.g., *Dictionary of Irish Literature*), handbooks (e.g., *Handbook of North American Indians*), and anthologies (e.g., *Historical Atlas of Mythology*; and though many of these are encyclopedic in scope or form, that they are included renders Kister's title somewhat misleading.

Other structural changes include the deletion of the "Special Reports" section, which in the third edition included a survey of both American and Canadian librarians in which they rated encyclopedias. Further, this newest edition has not broken down the general encyclopedias into user categories, but rather lists all entries alphabetically. Finally, two appendices in the 1981 edition, "Discontinued Encyclopedias from 1960-1981" and "Almanacs and Yearbooks," have been replaced by a "General Encyclopedia Comparison Chart" and the aforementioned "Specialized Encyclopedias" section in the new edition.

The guide concludes with a brief section noting the "most important" general encyclopedias available in seven different foreign languages, followed by an annotated bibliography directing readers to selected works on encyclopedias—collections of reviews as well as information regarding editing, content, and usage. The last appendix deals with publishers and distributors of encyclopedias in North America. Finally, the index is extensively cross-referenced by title and subject, and includes both books that are reviewed and books that are cited or mentioned.

Best Encyclopedias is current to March 1, 1986, with regard to new titles, review citations, and price changes. The books reviewed are the 1984-1985 editions or the most recent editions published. Most of the titles reviewed are in print, though Kister does review a number of out-of-print encyclopedias that might appear on library shelves or that can be obtained from antiquarian booksellers and may still be important reference sources.

In conclusion, Kister's *Best Encyclopedias* remains a standard work in this area. This and future editions, which Oryx plans to publish at three-year intervals, will continue to aid librarians and other information science specialists in the selection of general encyclopedias best suited to their needs, though it is questionable whether Kister's guide will remain one of the leading sources in light of the editorial changes described here. For information on special subject encyclopedias, library and information science specialists as well as the general consumer may be well advised to consult a more comprehensive reference work such as *ARBA Guide to Subject Encyclopedias and Dictionaries* (Libraries Unlimited, 1986) or *American Reference Books Annual* for adequate coverage.

[R: BL, 15 Dec 86, p. 604; LJ, 15 Nov 86, p. 87; WLB, Nov 86, p. 63]   Ann H. Paulsen

15. Tayyeb, R., and K. Chandna, comps. **A Dictionary of Acronyms and Abbreviations in Library and Information Science.** 2d ed. Ottawa, Canadian Library Association, 1985. 279p. $20.00pa. ISBN 0-88802-195-X.

If the AAAAAA had been more active, compilers Tayyeb and Chandna would not have had to record so many widely ranging entries. For this acronym, third entry in the new edition of this dictionary, stands for Association for the Alleviation of Asinine Abbreviations and Absurd Acronyms. The new edition attempts to include as many French and Canadian abbreviations as possible. The number of abbreviations and acronyms is also expanded. Related entries range widely from reference book titles (e.g., *Grove, D.A.B.*) to such miscellaneous entries as *SIG*, "Special Interest Group" and *KISS*, "Keep it simple, Sir/Stupid." Although many of the entries will be found in other dictionaries of acronyms and abbreviations, this dictionary can be recommended for its well-searched contents, arrayed in such readable form. It will be helpful to those using the literature of library and information science.   Frances Neel Cheney

Directories

16. **Alaska Library Directory 1986: Alaska Library Network.** Compiled by the Alaska Library Association. Juneau, Alaska, Alaska Division of State Libraries and Museums, 1986. 77p. $5.00pa.

The *Alaska Library Directory 1986* contains information on public, state, and school libraries within the state of Alaska. About half the book consists of a list of all libraries, their addresses, telephone numbers, and, usually, the names of head personnel and sometimes their titles. The libraries are listed in alphabetical order under the name of the city in which they are located. The other major section of the book is composed of a list of library personnel. Information given for each person includes his or her affiliation (not mentioned in all cases), a home and/or work telephone number, and, often, a home address.

Also included in this directory are lists of Alaska Library Association commercial members and institutional members (both with addresses and telephone numbers), and names of those persons comprising the Alaska Library Association Executive Board and the State Board of Education. Names and addresses are also given for the Governor's Advisory Council on Libraries and for the Alaska Library Network Regional Centers.   Kari Sidles

17. **American Libraries 1986: U.S. and Canadian Libraries.** Munich, New York, K. G. Saur, 1986. 726p. index. $36.00pa. ISBN 0-89664-360-3; ISSN 0889-4639.

This new "telephone" directory of libraries in the United States, Canada, and U.S. possessions claims "nearly 15,000" entries for general research, governmental, university and college, public, and school libraries holding more than thirty thousand volumes, and special libraries of more than three thousand volumes. Entries are very brief, providing only name, address, main telephone number, telex number, and cable address. Information is based on K. G. Saur's "international database of libraries," which, according to the preface, is updated by questionnaires mailed to libraries. However, no indication is given whether responses were actually received within any given time frame. The United Presbyterian Church ceased to exist in 1983 with its merger with the Presbyterian Church U.S., yet it is still listed under its old name in this 1986 edition.

Entries are arranged by state, province, or possession, then by city, then alphabetically letter-by-letter, so that, for example, Newark precedes New Brunswick. An alphabetical index of names of parent units leads back to the geographically arranged entries.

American Libraries's only advantage is its convenient size, approximately 6 by 8 inches. Established library directories list many more libraries—37,148 in the 1986 *American Library Directory* (R. R. Bowker); ca. 17,500 in the 1985 *Directory of Special Libraries and Information Centers* (Gale)—and both of these provide much more information about each library, with indication of recency of update for each entry. In the future, K. G. Saur should tag all entries for which information was not confirmed within the preceding year.

James D. Anderson

18. **COSLA Directory 1986: State Library Agencies, Consultants, and Administrative Staff.** Compiled by ASCLA Headquarters Staff. Chicago, Association of Specialized and Cooperative Library Agencies, American Library Association, 1986. 32p. $5.00pa. ISBN 0-8389-7090-7.

COSLA is an acronym for the organization Chief Officers of State Library Agencies. This directory was compiled and published under an agreement between COSLA and the Association of Specialized and Cooperative Library Agencies, a division of the American Library Association. The publication was initiated five years ago.

As suggested in the title, the directory consists of a listing of state library agencies, consultants, and administrative staff. The entry for each state library agency includes the name of the agency (e.g., Indiana State Library, Library of Michigan, Oklahoma Department of Libraries), the address, and a listing of offices with the name of the incumbent and a telephone number. Following the state listing are similar registers for the U.S. Department of Education, U.S. Territorial Libraries, and Canadian Provincial Libraries.

This is a very basic directory which provides information useful to anyone needing to know whom to contact in these various agencies. The directory could be enhanced by adding a name index and improving the quality of the print and paper. However, that would likely add greater cost than benefit. As it presently stands, this publication is worth the $5.00.

P. Grady Morein

19. Dale, Doris Cruger, comp. **A Directory of Oral History Tapes of Librarians in the United States and Canada.** Chicago, Library History Round Table, American Library Association, 1986. 103p. bibliog. index. $20.00pa. LC 85-30649. ISBN 0-8389-0443-2.

Another in a series of pioneering efforts to bring the research materials of North American library history under bibliographical control, this compilation of some 205 interviews in forty repositories represents a major contribution to filling a long-lamented gap. The project took shape following the ALA Library History Round Table's program in 1980 and received reinforcement by several oral history projects that took place in the early 1980s.

Arranged by repository and then alphabetically by interviewee, each entry includes as much of the following information as available from returned questionnaires: location of brief biographical sketch, subjects covered in interview, names of other librarians discussed in interview, interviewer, date of interview, status of copyright release, length or status of audio tape, status of permission to cite or quote, status of file, and length and availability of the transcript.

The Medical Library Association has the most entries (thirty) but is the least described. Columbia University has twenty-four, SUNY Buffalo nineteen, and Utah State University, Fisk University, and University of North Carolina follow with more than a dozen. Some institutional collections are based on special research endeavors; others are more broadly based. Louis Round Wilson was the most frequently interviewed person and the leading interviewers were Carol June Bradley, Brenda Branyan-Broadbent, and Edward G. Holley.

A personal name index lists interviewees, interviewers, and other librarians mentioned in interviews. The subject index helps to identify specific topics and tie together categories, such as "music librarianship."

This economically published guide nicely complements the Round Table's *National Catalog of Sources for the History of Librarianship* (Chicago, American Library Association, 1982). It may help to ferret out other oral history tapes forgotten and unknown in various repositories or in private hands. Revised editions of both works will surely be needed in future years. Information professionals who value their heritage and the contributions of their predecessors will need access to the data in this work. [R: JAL, Sept 86, p. 245; LJ, 1 May 86, p. 98]

Donald G. Davis, Jr.

20. Jennings, Margaret S., ed. **Library and Reference Facilities in the Area of the District of Columbia.** 12th ed. White Plains, N.Y., published for the American Society for Information with Knowledge Industry, 1986. 309p. index. $43.00pa. LC 44-41159. ISBN 0-86729-151-6; ISSN 0191-2798.

Originally compiled in the Library of Congress, this was one of the first government publications turned over to the private sector and has been produced for some years by the above-named organizations. Information facilities described are in government agencies, research and development firms, national associations, international organizations, and law firms as well as academic and public libraries. Institutions range in size from the Library of Congress, where twenty-five units are described, to specialized, one-person operations. In this edition, branches of library systems are brought together and a total of 568 facilities is described. The main body of the publication is a directory of facilities arranged alphabetically by name, with cross-references used liberally to provide quick access to the proper entry. Each listing includes the address, telephone number(s), person in charge, hours, regulations showing how the facility may be consulted, the availability of interlibrary loan and photocopying services, names of online services, and, for the first time, membership in formal networks. The final portion of each entry includes a brief description of resources. Indexes of key persons, subjects, and special collections complete the volume. Because of the wealth of information resources in the Washington area, this standard reference work is a valuable tool for individuals needing information quickly. Persons and telephone numbers change quickly, but annotations can be penned in to keep information up-to-date. Several typographical errors were noted, but this is inevitable.

Overall, the entries and typography are good looking. We note, unfortunately, that the Library of Congress's hours were cited for the brief three-month period when evening and weekend service was curtailed for budgetary reasons in 1986. The regular hours of service were restored in July 1986.

Many other Washington directories are published, each to meet different needs. One of the best overall sources of information is Congressional Quarterly's *Washington Information Directory*, the latest edition of which, for 1986-1987, runs to 967 pages.

Robert W. Schaaf

21. Jones, Frances M., and Patrick L. Jarvis, eds. **Directory of Library Staff Organizations.** Phoenix, Ariz., Oryx Press, 1986. 135p. index. $37.50pa. LC 83-42747. ISBN 0-89774-080-7.

This unique reference tool provides information on 336 library staff organizations, located in public and academic libraries in the United States and Canada.

Introductory material includes information on survey methodology, results, and conclusions. Charts highlight important statistical information. The directory portion was compiled from the results of a survey conducted in cooperation with the Staff Organizations Round Table of the American Library Association and is arranged alphabetically by state or province. Each entry includes the following information: library name, address, telephone number, contact person, name of the staff organization, its purposes, names of officers, staff size, dues (if any), titles of publications, and any union affiliations. Indexes include alphabetical listing of library names; library staff organizations which do collective bargaining; library staff organizations which promote staff welfare, development, or liaison with administration; and names of publications produced by staff organizations.

Directory of Library Staff Organizations would be useful to library staff organizations; library administrators; union leaders or organizers; and library educators, especially those concerned with continuing education. [R: JAL, July 86, p. 198; LJ, 1 May 86, p. 98]

Carol J. Veitch

22. Kadec, Sarah T., and Rhoda R. Mancher. **A Guide to Information Resources Management (IRM) Associations.** Silver Spring, Md., Kadec Information Management Products, 1985. 1v. (various paging). $4.00pa.

A directory of forty-three Information Resources Management (IRM) agencies arranged in alphabetical order. Entries range from the American Society of Information Science (ASIS) and Special Libraries Association (SLA) to Council of Professional Association on Federal Statistics (COPAFS) and National Association for State Information Systems to the Independent Computer Consultants Association and the National Computer Graphics Association. Included for each organization is the name and telephone number of a contact person, extent of membership, purpose, major meetings, publications, scholarships, and awards. The volume concludes with a month-by-month calendar of major meetings for 1986 through 1987, a list of scholarships and awards, and an index which presents the forty-three associations under subject headings such as "Clearinghouses," "Decision Support Systems," "Information Education," and "Telecommunications Management." Although much of the information is included in the *Encyclopedia of Associations*, this will be a handy source for specialists in the field and for students seeking information on scholarships.

Michael Ann Moskowitz

23. **The Northwest Information Directory: A Guide to Unusual Sources and Special Collections.** Portland, Oreg., Center for Urban Education, Information Technology Institute, 1986. 238p. index. $9.50pa.

This directory is part of an ongoing effort by the Fred Meyer Charitable Trust to assist in the improvement of access to information resources in the Pacific Northwest states of Alaska, Idaho, Montana, Oregon, and Washington. In September 1985, questionnaires were sent to four thousand institutions including public, corporate, academic, government, and other special libraries in addition to museums and historical societies. The collected information was compiled into this directory, which is also available as a database and on microfiche.

This guide is arranged in five sections. The first section provides a historical view of the information industry in the Northwest, and concludes with a brief discussion on how to use the text. The second section lists contemporary information resources from arts and culture to science and technology. Section 3 lists historical resources in the Northwest. Section 4 lists appendices covering, for example, special libraries and educational libraries and associations. Section 5 comprises indexes by subject, media, collection name, institutional name, and geographic location.

Almost any library's reference collection would be well served by this excellent and affordable work. It is the most comprehensive guide to unusual and special collections in the Pacific Northwest and includes the typically known resources. [R: JAL, Nov 86, p. 329]

James M. Murray

24. Smallwood, Carol, comp. **Free Resource Builder for Librarians and Teachers.** Jefferson, N.C., McFarland, 1986. 319p. index. $15.95pa. LC 85-43591. ISBN 0-89950-221-0.

Free Resource Builder for Librarians and Teachers identifies selected agencies which provide free information on a variety of subjects in an array of formats, for example, bibliographies, maps, posters, newsletters, and curriculum materials. Among the information agencies are divisions of federal, state, and local government; businesses; and nonprofit organizations not affiliated with government. The subjects covered in this directory range from business to consumerism and travel.

A "Multi-Resource Agencies" section is largely—but not exclusively—devoted to agencies that disseminate information about health and health-related topics. "Resource Management" is a chapter devoted entirely to vertical files management; in it are suggested file headings and a list of appropriate agencies under each heading.

In the appendix is a complete listing of the federal depository libraries (regional and selective) in the United States, Guam, Puerto Rico, and the Virgin Islands. The index, which includes cross-references, is comprehensive in its coverage of subjects and organizations treated in this book.

Smallwood mentions few titles by name; rather, she alerts the reader to various types of materials which are available on selected subjects and suggests that those needing information should contact the appropriate agency or agencies. Many of the sources referred to are primary materials and should be of great interest to educators (elementary through college) and librarians (public, school, and academic). [R: WLB, Sept 86, pp. 79-80]

Dianne B. Catlett

Handbooks and Yearbooks

25. **ALA Survey of Librarian Salaries, 1986.** By Mary Jo Lynch and Margaret Myers. Chicago, Office for Research and Office for Library Personnel Resources, American Library Association, 1986. 90p. $40.00pa. ISBN 0-8389-3335-1; ISSN 0747-7201.

This work presents the results of the third nationwide salary survey of public and academic librarians conducted by ALA, assisted by the University of Illinois Library Research Center.

Included are thirty-eight tables, discussion, and seven appendices.

Salaries as of January 1, 1986 are reported for full-time librarians in each of thirteen professional positions, from entry level to director, in five classes of libraries (public, serving 25,000 to 99,999; public, serving 100,000-plus; two-year college; four-year college; and university) within four regions (North Atlantic; Great Lakes and Plains; Southeast; and West and Southwest).

Of 1,445 questionnaires mailed to a stratified random sample of libraries, 1,107 usable ones were returned, for a response rate of 77 percent, better than in 1982 or 1984, the dates of the first two ALA surveys (see *ARBA* 83, entry 219). Because the 1986 survey used practically the same methodology as earlier ones, comparative study is easy, but individual library data are not given and academic salaries based on professional rank cannot be compared to those based on job function.

Despite its shortcomings, this informative title can prove useful to library administrators, job seekers, and those studying compensation trends. [R: JAL, Nov 86, p. 333; LJ, 15 Sept 84, p. 68]

Leonard Grundt

26. **Alternative Library Literature, 1984/1985: A Biennial Anthology.** Sanford Berman and James P. Danky, eds. Jefferson, N.C., McFarland, 1986. 247p. illus. index. $35.00pa. LC 84-646841. ISBN 0-89950-234-2.

The editors of this biennial anthology are activist librarians who are committed to the thesis that librarians should be instruments of social change and social justice. Once again they have searched the literature and found articles, research reports, bibliographies, and news items that are thought-provoking and important and that deserve to reach a large audience. Among the topics considered are recruitment of Latino library professionals, pay equity for women library workers, nuclear disarmament, threatening trends in censorship, small presses, outreach, inequity in public library service, radical Right publishing, young adult resources, world literacy, and the negative effects on publishing of powerful bookstore chains. Also featured are a special section on South Africa and apartheid, an interview with Zoia Horn, memorials to Brad Chambers, and some funny—but not frivolous—examples of library humor. This time the editors have made a special effort to include more items from genuinely alternative publications. This is good, but it does present a problem. Few readers will be familiar with such publications as *Lector, VDT Newsletter, Women Library Workers Journal, Free Reader, A View from the Left,* or *New Pages.* Just as

there is a list of contributors with brief biographies, the editors should consider including a list of source publications with such information as address, sponsorship, and purpose. Also, several important news reports are too fragmentary and need augmentation, in particular the reports on the Metro Toronto library strike protesting the threats of automation, the California Library Association's Nuclear Arms Freeze Resolution, and the controversies regarding the reportedly anti-Semitic *Exiles from History.* These are very important developments, but we need to know more than the news items tell us. Even the meanings of crucial abbreviations (VDT, LNAC, COSMEP) are left unexplained. In such cases, the editors need to add a few paragraphs that establish the context and provide essential background information.

Joseph W. Palmer

27. Corry, Emmett. **Grants for Libraries: A Guide to Public and Private Funding Programs and Proposal Writing Techniques.** 2d ed. Littleton, Colo., Libraries Unlimited, 1986. 343p. bibliog. index. $22.50. LC 86-21287. ISBN 0-87287-534-2.

In response to the constantly changing nature of government funding and the trend for increased dependency on the private sector for support, Corry's second edition represents a complete revision of his earlier guide.

Updated descriptions and analyses of federal library grant programs, foundation funding, and private funding are provided for school media programs; college, university, and public libraries; and library and information science programs.

To address the shift towards funding by private sources this edition includes considerable material on where and how to gain access to these monies. To this end, chapter 6, "Foundation Funding: Finding and Applying for Grants" has been updated. A new chapter, "The Library Development Campaign," expands on the theme of attracting support from this sector through long-range planning and marketing.

Chapter 5, "Lobbying for Library Excellence," presents strategies for librarians and library patrons to lobby effectively for adequate support and financial backing of our nation's libraries. Corry presents a report that captured the attention of major New York newspapers on the woeful condition of public school libraries, "School Libraries ... No Reading Allowed," as an example.

In keeping with the original work, formats for writing effective grant proposals for both sectors are included in chapter 7. Additionally, tables, illustrations, a selective bibliography, and twelve appendices provide supplementary information on a range of programs, HEA Title II-B funding history, a directory of state contacts, how to apply for federal funding by using the *Catalog of Federal Domestic Assistance* (*CFDA*), and the text of the Atlanta-Fulton Public Library Annual Report.

This publication is recommended for all those individuals or institutions writing grant proposals and also for those who are interested in learning the skill.

Margaret E. Chisholm

28. Taylor, Richard L., and Raymond G. Roney, eds. **Job Descriptions for Library Support Personnel.** Cleveland, Ohio, Council on Library/Media Technicians, 1985. 187p. index. $25.00 spiralbound.

Librarians are fond of having collections of administrative documents from other libraries. Perhaps the longest running collection is the Association of Research Libraries' Spec-kit series covering all manner of policy issues and library activities. This is a collection of about 175 job descriptions for library support personnel. Each entry is obviously in the form used by the donating library, although no libraries are identified so there is no definitive way to know just how many libraries contributed copy. The compilers divided the material by type of library—public, college and university, and special. It is unfortunate that there are no entries for school media centers, as this class of library makes extensive use of support personnel. An index brings together classes of employees such as accounting, cataloging, and production, which allows some comparison of how the three types of libraries define a similar job function. To justify the cost of the publication at $25.00, it would seem necessary to be hiring a large number of support staff. G. Edward Evans

Periodicals and Serials

29. **Magazines for Libraries: For the General Reader and School, Junior College, College, University, and Public Libraries.** 5th ed. Bill Katz and Linda Sternberg Katz. New York, R. R. Bowker, 1986. 1057p. index. $95.00. ISBN 0-8352-2217-9; ISSN 0000-0914.

This fifth edition of *Magazines for Libraries*, like the last edition (see *ARBA* 83, entry 22) includes approximately sixty-five hundred periodicals, selected and annotated by over one hundred consultants. Included are general, non-specialist titles appealing to the layperson, the main English-language research journals, and some high-quality commercial publications. This fifth edition is a "total" revision of the fourth; every title was re-evaluated, and approximately 75 percent of those in this edition were retained from the fourth. Almost all appear in revised, updated form. Titles from the fourth edition were deleted if they (1) ceased publication; (2) changed, and are no longer suitable for libraries; or (3) were replaced by a better newer title. A title was added to this edition if it was new and considered of value, or had been overlooked in earlier editions.

Several new subject sections have been added to this edition. As before, bibliographic entries include title, beginning date, frequency, price, editor, publisher and address, illustrations, index, circulation, end date, microform, book reviews, audience, and more. Annotations describe purpose, scope, and audience; some evaluation is made in most cases. Each entry is coded to show for which type of library (school, public, academic, or special) the periodical is suited.

This compilation of information on the "best and most useful" periodical titles continues to serve as a basic selection and reference tool for its intended audience. [R: JAL, Nov 86, p. 329]

Sharon Kincaide

30. **The Serials Directory: An International Reference Book.** Susan A. Cady and others, eds. Birmingham, Ala., EBSCO Publishing, 1986. 3v. $249.00/set. ISBN 0-913956-18-X; ISSN 0886-4179.

The Serials Directory is a new, three-volume reference tool designed primarily for use by librarians and touted by the publisher as a "unique new source of bibliographic and ordering information" on more serial titles than any other printed source. It does, indeed, include an impressive number of titles (over 113,000) and an equally impressive variety of information on those titles. Data are taken from three sources: EBSCO's international title file database; the CONSER file, bibliographic records from leading U.S. libraries; and answers to direct queries to publishers. The main selection was of those titles most heavily subscribed to by librarians. Other criteria (not specified) were established for those titles not so heavily subscribed to.

The titles are arranged under 147 major subject headings, with 135 subheadings. They are then listed alphabetically. Entries include the following information (and more) when available: key title, corporate name, series statement, variant form of title, dates of publication and volume information, ISSN, type of serial, language, frequency, price, publisher name and address, telephone number, editor(s), indexes/abstracts a title is covered by, LC Classification, Dewey Classification, if book reviews are published, circulation, other formats available, and description of contents. Listed in volume 1 as an aid to the user are filing rules employed, subject headings used, and an extensive list of subject cross-references. There are also tables of currency conversions, country abbreviations, and index and abstract abbreviations.

Any new serials directory must naturally be compared to the two standard tools in this area, *Ulrich's International Periodicals Directory* (25th ed. R. R. Bowker, 1986) and *Irregular Serials & Annuals* (*ISA*) (12th ed. R. R. Bowker, 1986). Between them, *Ulrich's* and *ISA* cover some 104,300 titles, so that it may be assumed that *Serials Directory* includes titles not covered by the two standard works. Entries in *Ulrich's* and *ISA* do not include the extent of data provided by *Serials Directory*. But a random cross check of titles between these tools reveals some serious gaps in the new title. For example, for the title *Vertica*, *Serials Directory* provides no beginning date or price; yet *Ulrich's* supplies both (1977, $135.00). The same is true of *Information Economics and Policy* (1983, fl250). On the other hand, *Ecological Bulletins*, listed in *Serials Directory*, was not found in *ISA*. The conclusion must be that *Serials Directory*, ambitious as it is, does not replace *Ulrich's* and *ISA*, but rather supplements and complements them. Any library that can afford to own all three would have as comprehensive a (print) reference source on serial titles as it is possible to have. Sharon Kincaide

31. Walford, A. J., with Joan M. Harvey. **Walford's Guide to Current British Periodicals in the Humanities and Social Sciences.** London, Library Association; distr., Chicago, American Library Association, 1985. 473p. index. $55.00. ISBN 0-85365-676-2.

More than three thousand British journals in the humanities and social sciences are annotated in this edition. The aim is "to provide a selected list of current British journals in the fields concerned" and to offer a selection guide of British periodicals for serials acquisition librarians in academic and research libraries.

Journals are classified according to the Universal Decimal Classification system and listed under subject headings. Each subject heading ("Literature," "Leisure and Entertainment," "Music," "Law," "Religion," etc.) is followed by a paragraph containing a brief description of the kinds of journals included, comments on the major ones, and observations on current British publishing activity in that field. The sources that include the journals in each subject area are identified: abstracting services, indexing services, contents page, lists of periodicals, microforms, back issues and reprints, and online. The journals are then listed in alphabetical order under subject subheadings.

Information given for each journal includes the title, year it began, frequency of publication, price in pounds (and sometimes dollars), publisher, ISSN, editor, circulation, and whether or not the journal is included in the *British Humanities Index*. The annotation gives a brief description of the contents and sometimes includes representative titles of articles to illustrate the scope of the periodical. No list of abbreviations is given.

A combined subject/title index also lists sponsoring agencies and contains cross-references. All entries cite page numbers, and the subject entries include the UDC number as well.

Many of the journals cited in *Walford's* can be found in *Ulrich's International Periodicals Directory* (R. R. Bowker, 1986). A comparison of the entry for *Library Association Record* in each work illustrates that the entries contain much of the same information, though *Ulrich's* cites features in abbreviation (adv., bk. rev., bibl., etc.) and does not use annotations. Abstracting and indexing services as well as microforms, periodicals, and reprints are given for the journal in both publications. *Ulrich's* does include a fairly new journal (1983), *Library Hi Tech News*, which *Walford's* does not, but *Walford's* cites British sources not found in *Ulrich's*.

Several other discrepancies exist between the two sources. For example, *Ulrich's* lists the price for *Library Association Record* at $96.00/yr., while *Walford's* cites the correct price of $99.00/yr. In addition, *Ulrich's* incorrectly specifies R. M. Walter as the editor; *Walford's* entry citing Jane Jenkins is correct. The circulation number is also different in the two entries, *Ulrich's* giving twenty-six thousand and *Walford's*, twenty thousand.

Both *Ulrich's* and *Walford's* would be useful to librarians involved with serials acquisition, *Walford's* being the more specialized source. Kari Sidles

Quotation Books

32. **Books Are Basic: The Essential Lawrence Clark Powell.** John David Marshall, ed. Tucson, Ariz., University of Arizona Press, 1986. 95p. bibliog. $12.50. LC 85-14099. ISBN 0-8165-0952-2.

This book of quotations relates to the writings of Lawrence Clark Powell, a Librarian Emeritus of the University of California at Los Angeles, and a writer of both fiction and nonfiction, including books, articles, essays, and reviews. The editor also has included a bibliography of Powell's works. Divided into four sections—(1) books and reading, (2) libraries, librarians, and librarianship, (3) writers and writing, and (4) Lawrence Clark Powell himself—the book certainly would be a handy reference for those concerned with books, libraries, librarians, and learning. Ray Gerke

ARCHITECTURE

33. **Planning Academic and Research Library Buildings.** 2d ed. By Keyes D. Metcalf; second edition by Philip D. Leighton and David C. Weber. Chicago, American Library Association, 1986. 630p. illus. bibliog. index. $60.00. LC 85-11207. ISBN 0-8389-3320-3.

This new edition of the now classic handbook, first published in 1965, is a major revision. The purpose of the work, however, remains the same: to help librarians understand all the considerations involved in building and furnishing library buildings. This is not a primer for library administrators and architects, but a detailed account intended for those librarians who will play a major role in building planning. The authors have expanded the discussion on preparing a building program statement, and this discussion remains the heart of the book. Sample building programs are included in an appendix. The work is so complete for most topics that even the most unsophisticated user should be able to design a satisfactory building program and not be tempted to copy the examples given here or substitute another library's completed program. Practical advice is given on such topics as noise control, signage, elevators, stairways, facilities for the handicapped, and stack arrangement. The various formulas that help determine size of building, stack capacities, etc., and the tables giving suggested minimum and maximum measurements for carrels, ceiling heights, etc., are, for planning purposes, a godsend.

This edition contains better coverage than did the first edition for audiovisual areas, electrical systems and wiring, traditional library furniture, and furniture arrangement. The illustrations have not undergone the same revision as the text. Many of the floor plans pictured are from the first edition, illustrating solutions achieved in older buildings (Butler Library at Columbia, Olin Library at Cornell, Lamont Library at Harvard). The next edition should contain more illustrations and comment for major academic, college and, perhaps, public libraries completed in the late 1960s and during the 1970s.

There is some discussion of planning for library automation in the text, but not enough to make this edition the best single source for planning library buildings during the next five years, much less twenty-one years. There are no illustrations concerning arrangement of computer terminals and there is little attention given to furniture needed to accommodate computer terminals. Including a suggested layout for a machine room to house computer equipment would have been a good idea. Illustrations and discussion of a well-planned automated public catalog area would be welcome. Design ideas for the technical services department in a fully automated library should have been included in this edition.

The book is one of the most attractively produced reference books of the year. Quality paper is used and the typeface is sharp and easy to read. The typography facilitates use and adds to the attractiveness of the book. Outside margins are almost two inches, allowing ample space for marginalia. The glossary has been expanded and the index is complete (contains an estimated 3,080 entries). Included also are an "Index of Figures and Tables," a listing of equipment that might be overlooked, and an updated bibliography with annotations. Milton H. Crouch

34. Reed, Henry Hope. **The New York Public Library: Its Architecture and Decoration.** New York, W. W. Norton, 1986. 288p. illus. (part col.). index. (Classical America Series in Art and Architecture). $35.00; $16.95pa. LC 86-5394. ISBN 0-393-02317-6; 0-393-30336-5pa.

This is not really a book about a library; it is a book about a work of art that happens to be a library. There is only an occasional—very occasional—mention of use of the library, and just as rare mention of library materials. There is, to be sure, a chapter on the Catalog Room (Room 315), but only in the chapter's brief first paragraph are such commonplace items mentioned as a book catalog, computers, the information desk, and the reader who "hands in call slips." The rest of that chapter is devoted—as is practically the entire book—to exquisite descriptions of the decoration and design of the library's exterior and public areas. This reader has never seen another library—indeed, another building—described in such meticulous detail. Walls, ceilings, stairways, railings, columns, friezes, archways, domes, clocks, pedestals (to name only a few features) are described in language that is often technical, almost always affectionate, and at times matches the floridity of the design.

There are hundreds of superb illustrations—photographs (some in color), diagrams, drawings, and floor plans—that permit the reader to see the details that are described. There are also a very well done "Illustrated Glossary of Architectural and Decorative Terms" (that will be essential for most readers), and several appendices.

The book is really intended for students and scholars of the history of decoration and design. For them, it is a mine of information, well written and beautifully presented. For librarians, even those who have admired and enjoyed the NYPL as much as this reviewer has, the book has much more about the details of that library's design than one wants to know. [R: WLB, Sept 86, p. 73]

Evan Ira Farber

AUTOMATION IN LIBRARIES

General Works

35. Corbin, John. **Managing the Library Automation Project.** Phoenix, Ariz., Oryx Press, 1985. 274p. illus. bibliog. index. $35.00. LC 85-15461. ISBN 0-89774-151-X.

Given all the complexities of managing and coordinating an automation project, a project director or manager can very easily overlook some of the most basic steps. It is even more disquieting that many librarians who find themselves in the position of automation project director have had only a modicum of formal training for this role. As a result, they discover gaps in their education, some of which are embarrassing to admit.

The purpose of *Managing the Library Automation Project* "is to provide a practical handbook and guide for the librarian untrained in systems development ... who is nonetheless responsible for developing an automated library system." This book describes the step-by-step processes of planning, organizing, and managing a library automation project. It includes four major sections that parallel the major phases of an automation project: "Introductory Concepts," "Project Organization and Management," "System Procurement," and "System Installation and Operation." Four appendices, a glossary, a selected bibliography, and an index conclude the volume.

Each of the first four sections gives a good, solid, basic description of the topic covered. Of just as great value are the many examples and definitions the author gives throughout his text. In the first section, for instance, he explains the basic equipment necessary for automation and what that equipment does. The appendices include sample phases, activities, and tasks of an automation project; sample job descriptions; a list of hardware, equipment, and supplies; and a sample RFP for an integrated library system. All of this information is most useful for the automation neophyte, or even for the more experienced automation librarian who might find such a checklist reassuring.

Librarians seeking detailed specifications about individual automation components such as an online catalog, serials control, acquisitions, circulation, or a management information system should consult the works of Richard Boss, Joseph Mathews, and James Rush. *Managing the Library Automation Project* focuses on project implementation as a whole rather than on the specific components that could be automated. This book is an invaluable guide for the automation project manager and for library staff as a whole who find themselves involved in their library's automation project. [R: BL, 15 May 86, p. 1354; CLJ, Oct 86, pp. 365-66; LJ, 15 Apr 86, p. 62]

Marjorie Bloss

36. Herring, James E., and John A. Mackenzie. **Planning for Library Automation: Aberdeen City Libraries.** London, Library Association; distr., Chicago, American Library Association, 1986. 70p. (Case Studies in Library Automation). $15.00pa. ISBN 0-85365-986-9.

The work under review is part of a series whose authors "have been encouraged to develop the reasons for the decisions to commit to automation and the selection of their particular course of action; to describe the stages of implementation; and to appraise the lessons learned from their experience and the general effectiveness of the new systems." Herring and Mackenzie's book has met these goals for Aberdeen City Libraries, a large central library with seventeen branch libraries, located in northern Scotland. The process by which Aberdeen's staff concretized and eventually carried out automation plans is clearly set forth in chapters on preautomation plans, reasons for automation, choice of systems, installation, staff training, review of the present system, future developments, and lessons learned. The book also includes ten appendices that contain various documents and statistical information used in the process. An interesting feature of the book is a section in each chapter that attempts to translate the encountered decision-making problems into present-day terms. That is, it tries to determine if different decisions would have been reached if 1986 technology and knowledge were then available.

Although some of the specific problems encountered with the local municipal government will not be relevant to the United States, this book is extremely useful for any library system that is contemplating automation. The value lies more in its honest depiction of problems discovered and mistakes made, rather than in any specifics relating to hardware, software, or governmental relations.   Robert H. Burger

37. **Libraries in the Age of Automation: A Reader for the Professional Librarian.** White Plains, N.Y., Knowledge Industry, 1986. 160p. bibliog. (Professional Librarian Series). $36.50; $28.50pa. LC 86-2724. ISBN 0-86729-194-X; 0-86729-193-1pa.

This work represents a compilation of chapters which were previously published in the Professional Librarian monograph series (*The Library Manager's Guide to Automation*, 2d ed., 1984; *MARC for Library Use: Understanding the USMARC Formats*, 1984; *Data Conversion*, 1983; *The Online Catalog: Improving Public Access to Library Materials*, 1983; *Public Access Microcomputers: A Handbook for Librarians*, 1984; and *Integrated Online Library Systems: Principles, Planning and Implementation*, 1984).

Chapters include such topics as hardware and software basics, an introduction to MARC and the structure of USMARC, the purpose of data conversion, online catalogs, public access microcomputers and software, and integrated online library systems. A selected bibliography completes the work.

For libraries who have not added the source monographs to their collections, this volume can provide a useful pulling together of key points in the development of library automation. If, however, the original monographs are at hand, this reader would be of limited usefulness. In any event, the original publication dates of 1983-1984 would indicate that this material should be viewed as somewhat historical in nature, given the pace of change in the field.

Darlene E. Weingand

Reference Works

38. *Library Hi Tech* **Bibliography, Volume 1.** C. Edward Wall, ed. Ann Arbor, Mich., Pierian Press, 1986. 190p. index. $39.50pa. ISBN 0-87650-219-2.

This volume contains nineteen topical bibliographies previously submitted, but not published, in *Library Hi Tech*, a quarterly journal also issued by Pierian Press. These guides to books, serials, articles, and other resources emphasize recently published literature and have a common cut-off date of July 1985. The collection's intent is to update *Automation in Libraries: A LITA Bibliography, 1978-1982* (Pierian Press, 1983), compiled by Anne G. Adler et al.

All but the first bibliography are annotated. Most are classified and several are arranged by author. One is arranged in reverse order of chronological date of publication. Each bibliographic entry has an assigned number by which it is referred in the author and title indexes at the end of the volume.

Citations are primarily to U.S. publications with some to Canadian titles. One bibliography, "Visual Display Terminal Hazards and Ergonomic Issues," was compiled for this publication and is in the public domain. The subjects of the remaining bibliographies are: "Barcoding Library Collections," "Bibliographic Instruction: The Use of Computers," "Cable Television," "Computer Courseware Evaluation," "Disaster Preparedness," "Electronic Mail," "Inhouse Computer Systems," "Interlibrary Loan and Document Delivery," "Laserdisc Technology," "Local Area Networks," "Management Information Systems in Libraries," "Microcomputer Software," "Online Public Access Catalogs," "Retrospective Conversion," "Software Review Sources," "Telecommunication," "Turnkey Library Systems," and "Word Processing in Libraries."

This is an excellent tool for the library practitioner or student involved with advanced information technology. Its arrangement and annotations qualify it as a valuable reference source for both the reference room and the administrative office. [R: JAL, Sept 86, p. 256; LJ, 1 Nov 86, p. 50]

Danuta A. Nitecki

39. **The North American Online Directory 1985: A Directory of Information Products & Services with Names & Numbers.** New York, R. R. Bowker, 1985. 265p. bibliog. $75.00pa. ISBN 0-8352-1879-1; ISSN 0000-0841.

This new directory joins a growing number of similar guides to people, organizations, and machine-readable databases making up the information industry. With a listing of 785 database producers and 1,511 databases, Bowker's directory is nowhere near as comprehensive as others such as Martha Williams's *Computer Readable Databases: A Directory and Data Sourcebook* (American Library Association, 1985), which lists 2,805 databases, or *Directory of Online Data Bases* (Cuadra Associates, 1985), which provides detailed data on 2,764 databases. On the other hand, in addition to being less expensive, *The North American Online Directory 1985* has a wide scope and provides multiple indexes in an arrangement similar to other "Market Place" volumes from Bowker. The largest section contains an alphabetical listing of database producers and their machine-readable databases. Data about the producers consist of addresses, telephone numbers, and in some cases contact persons, number of employees, and corporate membership in professional associations. Information on databases includes coverage, type, contents, and vendors providing access. Eighteen other sections of the directory provide data on vendors, library networks, information centers, information brokers, consultants, associations, online user groups, and an extensive bibliography. A personal name/corporate name directory completes the volume. As with all such directories, the information changes rapidly. Future editions are implied but there is no mention of supplements as with some other guides. Active users of online information services may wish to supplement their other guides with this directory.

Andrew G. Torok

Data Manipulation

40. Auld, Lawrence W. S. **Electronic Spreadsheets for Libraries.** Phoenix, Ariz., Oryx Press, 1986. 168p. bibliog. index. $37.50 spiralbound. LC 85-43324. ISBN 0-89774-245-1.

Designed as a management tool for librarians, *Electronic Spreadsheets for Libraries* presents thirty-eight spreadsheet models in which data can be assembled, analyzed, and displayed. Spreadsheet samples include budget requests, book and serial fund allocations, circulation statistics, employee salary schedules, retrospective catalog conversion costs, and library standards.

Although Auld used an early-model Kaypro II microcomputer and Perfect Calc in preparing this book, use of this configuration is not necessary. The basic requirements are a microcomputer with 64K memory and two disk drives. Each template can be modified for use with another spreadsheet program (e.g., Lotus 1-2-3, VisiCalc).

This spiralbound volume is recommended only for libraries with staff already familiar with microcomputers and spreadsheets.

Janet R. Ivey

Databases

41. **Computer-Readable Databases: A Directory and Data Sourcebook.** Martha E. Williams, Laurence Lannom, and Carolyn G. Robins, eds. Chicago, American Library Association, 1985. 2v. index. $87.50pa./vol. LC 84-18577. ISBN 0-8389-0415-7.

This is one of the standard directories of databases, if not the preeminent one. In its fifth edition, it retains the essential organization and content of the fourth edition (1982), reviewed in detail by D. Raitt in *Information World Review* and reprinted in *Online Review* (vol. 10, no. 1, 1986). The sizes of the two editions do not differ greatly, and unless currency is very important, owners of the fourth edition may forego purchase of this edition. Another factor is that *C-R D* is available on DIALOG as database 230, "Database of Databases," and, according to DIALOG's latest information, the online file is reloaded quarterly. Because of its cost and online availability only libraries that consult a directory heavily will purchase this title, and then maybe only the volume that is most relevant to their needs ("Science, Technology, Medicine," or "Business, Law, Humanities, Social Sciences"). Each volume contains name, subject, producer, and processor indexes which cover both volumes. The name index lists many cross-references. The body of the directory is an alphabetical listing by title and for each database the following information is included: basic information (producer, size, update frequency, language of database, sources of online availability, and lease/license availability); brief description of subject matter and scope; brief description of indexing/coding/classification practices; and list of data elements, which is sometimes absent.

Thomas G. Kirk

42. **Essential Guide to CD-ROM.** Judith Paris Roth, ed. Westport, Conn., Meckler Publishing, 1986. 189p. illus. bibliog. index. $29.95pa. LC 85-29861. ISBN 0-88736-045-9.

The growth of CD-ROM as a tool for the information industry has been explosive, and it would be impossible to write a definitive treatise on the topic with such extensive changes occurring every month or two. This book is designed to be a guide to the basic aspects of CD-ROM technology. It is technical, yet readable for anyone with at least an introductory knowledge about computers and modern electronics. CD-ROM (Compact Disk, Read-Only Memory) is an information storage device similar in format to the audio compact disk and laser disk, but is used like a computer diskette. Its information can be extracted much in the same manner as a dial-up database (i.e., with Boolean logic) and is most commonly accessed via specially designed software on a personal computer plugged into the CD-ROM player. This book describes the preparation needed to put data into a readable format, the existing drives and players (as of early 1986), and the existing software to access these drives. It also lists corporations and reference book publishers who are providing services and information in CD-ROM format, with a description of these products. The six appendices enhance this book for reference use: (1) premastering, mastering, and manufacturing of the CD-ROM disk; (2) proposed standards for CD-ROM, and which companies and groups are involved in the standardization process. (As this review is being written, formal standards are being agreed upon. The intent is to ensure that the access software can use any brand of player to read any disk format, rather than discard all formats but one.); (3) a glossary of more than 125 terms used in this technology; (4) a directory of firms, organizations, and other groups working with CD-ROM, and what their interests or research areas are; and (5) a list of suggested readings primarily from periodicals, but also including conference proceedings and books. Trade publications and special reports are listed separately. The name index and the subject index are not particularly useful, and there is no apparent need to have them separated. On the other hand, this book is organized in such a manner that an index is not required to use its contents.

As a bonus, a CD-ROM disk (containing eighty-eight hundred public-domain and shareware programs) is included with each book. It would take 390 floppy disks to hold all these programs. The disk can be accessed with Reference Technology Company's player and software, via an IBM PC.

As a preliminary source for CD-ROM, a technology which is not even mentioned in currently published encyclopedias, this book covers an important new subject in an extensive manner, with useful illustrations, a readable text, and worthwhile reference features. [R: Choice, Sept 86, p. 160]   Gary R. Cocozzoli

43. **Essential Guide to the Library IBM PC. Volume 7: Database Management Systems.** By Jo Ann Buckley. Westport, Conn., Meckler Publishing, 1986. 211p. illus. index. $19.95 spiralbound. LC 85-10535. ISBN 0-88736-050-5.

Intended for novices, this volume describes commercially available, self-contained microcomputer database systems (DBMS). There are brief introductions to automated databases, microcomputer hardware, and DBMS software. Some 120 programs are listed. Information provided includes publishers, prices, and system characteristics. Accessory products are listed in an appendix. A few major DBMS programs are examined in more detail with evaluative comments and illustrations. There is an annotated bibliography of library applications. There are also a brief bibliography of DBMS software selection aids, a glossary, and an index. Accounting databases were deliberately and wrongfully omitted as being of little interest in libraries. Database concepts are simplified as much as possible in this volume, but true beginners will have to consult the glossary often since terms are not defined in the text. Discussions will be difficult to understand if a reader is unfamiliar with any DBMS. On the other hand, detailed descriptions of a few DBMS may assist more experienced users in making purchase decisions. The most useful part of this book is its bibliography of DBMS applications. There is enough detail in some annotations to inspire ideas for one's own library.

Margaret McKinley

44. French, James C. **IDAM File Organizations.** Ann Arbor, Mich., University Microfilms International, 1985. 157p. bibliog. index. (Computer Science. Distributed Database Systems, No. 15). $44.95. LC 85-1066. ISBN 0-8357-1631-7.

This monograph investigates the technical problem of providing a database organization that efficiently supports queries involving several search keys. The "Indexed Descriptor Access Method" (studied previously by the author's Ph.D. dissertation advisor, J. Pfaltz) is shown here to allow development of information systems that perform well with respect to query response time, multi-user service, and maintainability. The treatment of the subject is mathematical, and presumes that the reader is knowledgeable in the subject of computer data structures. This book would be useful to those building database system software or management information systems, and to researchers in data structures and databases.

Steven L. Tanimoto

Networks and Networking

45. Hafter, Ruth. **Academic Librarians and Cataloging Networks: Visibility, Quality Control, and Professional Status.** Westport, Conn., Greenwood Press, 1986. 153p. bibliog. index. (Contributions in Librarianship and Information Science, No. 57). $29.95. LC 85-24761. ISBN 0-313-24821-4.

Based on sixty-eight in-depth interviews in six academic libraries which use at least one of the three bibliographic utilities (Online Computer Library Center, Research Library Information Network, and Washington Library Network), this discussion of the effect of network technology and organizations on cataloging functions and cataloging personnel goes well beyond many similar studies. The author's discussion of the environment, from the point of view of both the library and the network, provides a context in which to consider the effect which network participation had by the time of the 1983-1984 case studies. Focusing on the relationship between network and library, the study explores the reasons for and the reality of deprofessionalization of cataloging, new patterns of control of the functions which catalogers perform, the realignment of the professional identity of catalogers, and new patterns and practices for establishing and maintaining quality control. Not a quantitative analysis of work flow, output, cost benefits, or personnel, this explanation of the ways in which networks have reshaped the function and affected the people involved is enjoyable. The author's style does justice to the research without dulling the senses. It is a worthy, readable contribution in content and presentation. [R: LJ, 15 May 86, p. 52]

JoAnn V. Rogers

46. Holligan, Patrick J. **Access to Academic Networks.** London, for the Primary Communications Research Centre, University of Leicester, by Taylor Graham, 1986. 91p. bibliog. $26.50pa. ISBN 0-947568-08-5.

This work reports the results of a study, conducted during the period January-June 1985, which surveyed the status of six universities and two polytechnics in the United Kingdom with respect to access to academic computer networks. The report also examines issues related to the reorganization of academic computer networks, in particular the establishment of the Joint Academic Network (JANET), and explicates problems encountered in attempting to expand access to networks for purposes of computer-mediated communication. The study is based on extensive interviews with a "practitioners' panel" of computing and library personnel from the eight institutions and an "expert panel" of policy level officers of networking organizations.

The study found that the use of computer networks for file transfer, software distribution, and research computing in the pure and applied sciences was well established. However, academic networks were underused for database access and for computer-mediated human communication (electronic mail and conferencing). Underlying causes for this finding seem to be low levels of computer literacy and awareness of networking capabilities for facilitating human communication, inadequate access to terminals, lack of a critical mass of users, and lack of coordination among various communities of users and potential users. Library online catalogs were found to operate independently of existing academic networks.

This is a competent, informative work, useful primarily to those interested in academic networks in the United Kingdom. There are, however, a number of potentially generalizable insights regarding the process and problems of extending access to academic networks.

Joe A. Hewitt

47. Jacob, M. E. L., ed. **Telecommunications Networks: Issues and Trends.** White Plains, N.Y., published for the American Society for Information Science by Knowledge Industry, 1986. 179p. illus. bibliog. index. $36.50; $28.50pa. LC 86-7253. ISBN 0-86729-165-6; 0-86729-166-4pa.

Edited by the vice president for library planning at OCLC, this volume contains essays written for librarians and information systems designers possessing some familiarity with and understanding of telecommunications terminology and concepts. It supplements the papers delivered at the 1985 midyear meeting of the American Society for Information Science that was devoted to telecommunications. Ten of the eleven essays in this book present material not available elsewhere. The contributors include Edwin B. Brownrigg, John Coppett, Sam Feuer, Larry L. Learn, Clifford A. Lynch, Michael J. McGill, Howard Turtle, and Stephen B. Weinstein. Their chapters describe the historical development of telecommunications networks, open systems, the UTLAS and OCLC networks, and future options in the United States and Canada. A selected bibliography follows. This work is a useful addition to the growing literature on telecommunications systems. [R: LJ, 15 Oct 86, p. 56]

Leonard Grundt

48. **Key Issues in the Networking Field Today. Proceedings of the Library of Congress Network Advisory Committee Meeting May 6-8, 1985.** Washington, D.C., Cataloging Distribution Service, Library of Congress, 1985. 88p. (Network Planning Paper, No. 12). $7.50pa. LC 85-600273. ISBN 0-8444-0518-3.

This document consists of four papers prepared for a meeting of the Library of Congress Network Advisory Committee (NAC) intended to provide direction to the National Commission on Libraries and Information Science (NCLIS) in revising the sections of the national plan which relate to networks. Included also are summaries of discussions and recommendations from the working group sessions. The four papers focus on the major decisions which determined the directions for the network development in the past and provide or limit possibilities for the future, the changing role of individuals and organizations active in networking, an overview of the present and possible future impact of evolving technology on networks, and observations on the law and legal processes which are determining the legal positions of network organizations and users. The paucity of nationwide coordinated and cooperative planning is a pervasive theme. The recommendations call for a more active role for the NAC and NCLIS. Little mention is made of the Council on Library Resources which, mainly through its Bibliographic Services Development Program, has provided support for projects which have shaped the present network environment. The issues identified here are important ones. The professional community at large needs to consider how they can be effectively addressed. [R: LJ, 1 May 86, p. 55]

JoAnn V. Rogers

49. Martin, Susan K. **Library Networks, 1986-87: Libraries in Partnership.** White Plains, N.Y., Knowledge Industry, 1986. 250p. bibliog. index. $36.50; $28.50pa. LC 86-7438. ISBN 0-86729-128-1; 0-86729-127-3pa.

Unlike the previous editions of this work, which tended to be informally descriptive about selected facets of the network scene and various organizations which participate, this volume presents a conceptualized whole of the many diverse parts which constitute networking between and among library and information agencies. It appropriately begins with a chapter on issues facing network agencies and their members, which gives the reader the opportunity to consider the subsequent chapters in light of the considerable challeges that individual libraries and their cooperative organizations face. Following is brief coverage of ideas of cooperation and factors which made possible automated networks. In terms of the utilities, two chapters focus on OCLC and RLG. Information is current, including mention of the OCLC Oxford project. There is no current similar coverage of UTLAS to compete with these. WLN is more briefly covered in the chapter on regional networks, which discusses about twenty regionals including some state networks. A well-documented chapter on network governance and behavior is a welcome addition.

Having discussed the reasons for inevitable failure of the development of a "national" network in the first chapter, the author, in chapter 8, brings together nationwide programs in a way which accurately reflects the status quo, and comments on the future. The private sector promises to continue to have considerable impact on cooperative activities among libraries in terms of automated systems, information retrieval systems, and other types of services including full-text document delivery (covered in chapter 9). Contractual issues and relationships, the linking of automated systems, and future trends complete the textual part of this volume. An appendix of about sixty pages lists twenty-two networks and members. Because of its scope and depth of treatment, particularly of the issues related to this complex and important topic, by a knowledgeable participant and long-time observer, this volume is recommended. It presents much information and gives the reader a context in which to consider the significance of the information presented.

JoAnn V. Rogers

50. Murr, Lawrence E., James B. Williams, and Ruth-Ellen Miller. **Information Highways: Mapping Information Delivery Networks in the Pacific Northwest.** Portland, Oreg., HYPERMAP, 1985. 77p. illus. maps. $25.00pa. LC 85-81728.

The introduction claims that this "atlas" offers its users a collection of "hypermaps" of visual and textual "information highways and information delivery networks in the Pacific Northwest: Alaska, Washington, Oregon, Idaho, and Montana." Intended as a guide for those who need to move information within the region, as a planning tool, and as a learning tool, the book assumes an ambitious goal in less than eighty pages. The user can proceed through sections on the technologies of information delivery, transmission, processing, electronic and electromagnetic formats, signal processing technology, video, satellite, as well as communication systems including local area networks, telephone network access, and telefacsimile. Specific details are given about library systems and networks, air routes, cable systems, and microwave systems, in each of the five states covered. The final pages of the book provide guidance for designing an information delivery capability.

Textual descriptions are generally clear though brief; factual data (e.g., statistics) are current and usually bibliographic or survey sources are cited. However, coverage is often illustrative rather than thoroughly complete (e.g., Williams's classic *Directory of Database Sources*, available in print and online, was not mentioned among references to identify databases, similarly DIALOG is featured, BRS noted, and SDC omitted in the description of electronic database vendors). Perhaps the most notable feature of this book is its unique format; composition produced on a Macintosh computer, large pages, text written in small print within delineated blocks linked with flowchart arrows, typographic bullets, boldface headings, and interspersed illustrations give this tool a workbook appearance.

The book's content offers current, high-tech info hype and basic reference data about libraries in the Northwest. The unique presentation is intriguing and inviting to read. However, as a reference tool it seems difficult to use. The absence of an index makes it impractical to retrieve specific information not fitting into the broad organization blocks of the book. The arrangement of lists is unclear in spots; the lack of pricing data precludes an evaluative comparison of delivery methods for practical application. The atlas is a fun armchair travel guide, inspiring one to take a trip, but once on the road, it may be hard to get home to the data. [R: WLB, Mar 86, p. 58]   Danuta A. Nitecki

51. **Toward a Common Vision in Library Networking. Proceedings of the Library of Congress Network Advisory Committee Meeting, December 9-11, 1985.** Washington, D.C., Cataloging Distribution Service, Library of Congress, 1986. 95p. (Network Planning Paper, No. 13). $7.50pa. LC 86-600106. ISBN 0-8444-0534-5.

At the end of a thought-provoking introduction to this report of the Network Advisory Committee meeting, Frank Grissom of SOLINET makes a relevant observation. He states that "if the network community does not find a way to effectively address ... issues and to articulate and pursue its common vision, it could be taken over by the march of events and relegated to irrelevance." It's just possible that the network community as we currently know it has more threats in common than it does visions of a future relevant to information users. This attempt to bring into focus a common vision of the future directions of networking includes papers and statement summaries from representatives of different types of library and information organizations which constitute the major "players" in the network environment. As Ronald Miller of CLASS observes in the "Overview," these players "form a loose and somewhat haphazard alliance of complementary actions which almost in spite of itself appears to be nation-wide in scope." Certain themes do emerge from the papers and group working sessions of the players representing the utilities, "national" libraries, state libraries, the private sector, local systems, and one representative user of network services. There is a need for more aggressive leadership in determining and supporting paths to development of what is variously called a nationwide, national, or emerging national network. There seems to be a continuing preference on the part of most players for a national effort not to be from the top down, and yet many express an interest in a major role for the Network Advisory Committee. Members see progress in network development as necessarily evolutionary with regard to adoption of standards and application of technological innovation. This process should be further stimulated. Barriers need to be studied and overcome. Current trends toward decentralization and distributed processes do threaten the attainment of some goals for end users and must be addressed. The end user of information needs to be given greater consideration in network planning. Some suggest that more players, such as the national professional organizations, need to be more actively involved in network planning. This report echoes themes of several previous meetings of the NAC and underlines issues which should be addressed. Not much progress is made here, however, in determining appropriate mechanisms for doing so. [R: WLB, Dec 86, p. 59]

JoAnn V. Rogers

Online Public Access Catalogs

52. Bills, Linda G. **OCLC Experimental Project: Summary and Conclusions.** Springfield, Ill., Illinois State Library, 1986. 122p. map. (Illinois Valley Library System OCLC Experimental Project Report, No. 8). free pa.

From January 1980 to December 1982, the Illinois Valley Library System and thirty-three of its participating libraries monitored an OCLC experimental project. Funded by Library Services and Construction Act (LSCA) monies, the purpose of this project was to examine the costs and benefits of using OCLC in small- and medium-sized libraries. The results of this project have been published in eight reports, covering such topics as project description, implementation, cataloging before and after OCLC, attitudes about OCLC, OCLC use in library clusters, OCLC public access, and interlibrary loan before and after OCLC.

This final report does as it says—it summarizes and concludes. The reader can't help but wonder about the techniques used to reach those conclusions. Fortunately, the other seven volumes of this work were available to me. In them are extremely detailed and analytical examinations of the impact of OCLC on the participating libraries. The writing in all reports is clear, the organization of information and its analysis superbly done. While some who already have OCLC may feel that owning these reports is a moot point, the reports are still fascinating reading. They accurately trace the impact of an online bibliographic system on a number of different library functions. For libraries just beginning to venture into an online bibliographic system, these reports are basic and essential reading. All eight reports, and not just the final one, are highly recommended.

Marjorie Bloss

53. Crawford, Walt, with Lennie Stovel and Kathleen Bales. **Bibliographic Displays in the Online Catalog.** White Plains, N.Y., Knowledge Industry, 1986. 359p. index. $30.00pa. LC 86-15348. ISBN 0-86729-198-2.

This volume presents the results of a study undertaken by the Research Libraries Group (RLG). Beginning in 1984 and continuing through 1985, the authors addressed three questions related to online public access catalogs: How should bibliographic records be displayed? How many different displays should an online catalog provide? How many bibliographic records require more than a single-screen display? In answer to the questions, they have presented a wide variety of display screen possibilities with no prescriptive solutions, maintaining that no single display would be equally suitable for all libraries.

The RLG Bibliographic Display Testbed Program (RBDISP) was developed and used to generate selected screen display designs and to produce statistics based on the displays. The book presents results of the large-scale controlled testing, which was done using current bibliographic data. Included in the text are over four hundred sample bibliographic display screens. The same eight records (print and nonprint) are used in a majority of the examples in order to allow the user to compare the appearance of the same title in different screen display formats. The RBDISP program produced examples which varied according to brief, long, or medium display; cardlike, labelled, or mixed display; narrow or wide lines; and various combinations of vertical and horizontal spacing.

Although designed for RLIN users, the RSDISP program is offered as available to other libraries who wish to test screen display designs. Library or information centers considering an online public access catalog will be able to use the examples and data presented by the authors in their planning process.

Marilyn L. Shontz

54. Manheimer, Martha L. **OCLC: An Introduction to Searching and Input.** 2d ed. New York, Neal-Schuman, 1986. 84p. $17.95pa. LC 86-060506. ISBN 0-918212-97-9.

A practical exercise workbook of value to technical service input operators or searchers during the training process and to library science students, Manheimer's work is an introduction to searching, inputting, and editing the OCLC bibliographic record. Focusing on optimum search strategies, it includes an excellent, brief introduction to OCLC and a detailed description of the derived search keys such as "Name," "Name-title," and "Title." The importance of qualifying searches with dates and/or form of material is also covered. A separate section devoted to interpreting the various tags, indicators, and subfield codes necessitates the use of OCLC documentation. Exercise 4 compares earlier cataloging to current rules and requires knowledge of the *Anglo-American Cataloguing Rules, Second Edition.* Exercise 5 on modifying the record displays only the dedicated OCLC terminal, not the newer modified IBM PC, the M-300. Other exercises focus on tagging, the name/address directory, and searching special forms of materials such as serials and audiovisual materials. If exercise 8 on the authority file had been placed earlier in the workbook following the searching exercise, it would have facilitated the learning process for those interested only in searching and not inputting. Errors in the typeface used are irritating, but overall this is a valuable aid that facilitates learning OCLC through well-developed, comprehensive exercises followed at the end of the workbook by answers. [R: JAL, Sept 86, p. 260]

Ann Allan

55. Mitev, Nathalie Nadia, Gillian M. Venner, and Stephen Walker. **Designing an Online Public Access Catalogue: Okapi, A Catalogue on a Local Area Network.** London, British Library; distr., Wolfeboro, N.H., Longwood Publishing Group, 1985. 254p. bibliog. index. (Library and Information Research Report, 39). $30.00pa. ISBN 0-7123-3058-5.

This book describes the design and construction of a prototype online public access catalog, called OKAPI, on a local area network. The catalog, with ninety thousand records, was installed and used by the public in a test mode in the Riding House Street site of the Polytechnic of Central London. Included is a brief review of the state of the art of online catalogs. Hardware used and locally developed software are described in some detail, as are creation of data files from UK MARC records, development of associated indexes, and design of a user interface with the system. The test phase of the project is analyzed. There are a bibliography, a glossary, and an index. This is a carefully organized, lucid discussion of a system for use by intelligent but unsophisticated users. One of the book's chief merits is its frank discussion of alternatives rejected, constraints, and major and minor problems. The book is worth reading as a paradigm for design and execution of a complex project. The chapters on indexing and search functions are technically oriented but, with a little patience and the use of the glossary, they are understandable. Readers interested in a review of the state of the art should be aware that it is changing rapidly and any printed works on the topic are soon outdated.

Margaret McKinley

56. **Online Catalog Screen Displays: A Series of Discussions. Report of a Conference Sponsored by the Council on Library Resources ... March 10-13, 1985.** Joan Frye Williams, ed. Washington, D.C., Council on Library Resources, 1986. 224p. illus. $7.00pa.

Reported here are the proceedings of a three-day conference on visual aspects of the online catalog. Participants represent many points of view: vendors, librarians, systems designers, and consultants. Joe Matthews reviews research on screen layout and wording. His sample screens and the discussion comments are included. Fran Spigai's paper lacks direction but does outline the significance of studying the historical development of bibliographic utilities and database vendors, or, as she calls them, reference utilities. A researcher on human/computer interaction, Kent Norman, presents a helpful analysis of appropriate screen organization and layout, necessary features in maintaining screen-to-screen consistency and compatibility. Without identifying them by name, Christine Borgman rates the online systems on display at the conference according to physical legibility, cognitive processes, command language, system metaphor, and interface ability. Alan Kay's paper is thought-provoking and startlingly futuristic. To him a good user interface tells people almost immediately what a system can and cannot do. It engages them as Kay engages the reader, making reading this volume well worth the effort. A must for technical service and advanced cataloging students, and libraries that are designing or altering online screen displays. Ann Allan

57. **Online Public Access to Library Files: Conference Proceedings. The Proceedings of a Conference Held at the University of Bath 3-5 September 1984.** Janet Kinsella, ed. New York, Elsevier Science Publishing, 1985. 202p. illus. index. $14.50pa. ISBN 0-946395-18-7.

This volume contains twelve practically oriented papers presented at a conference organized by the Center for Catalogue Research located at the University of Bath. "From Contract to Acceptance: Or Now Is the Time to Put Your Money and Your Reputation on the Line" by Bill Ainsworth is a thorough discussion of methodology for installing and implementing a computer-based system. Pauline Cochrane discusses the ideal catalog in "Subject Access—Free Text and Controlled: The Case of Papua New Guinea." Charles Hildreth reviews the state of the art in user interface with online catalogs. Paul Burton reviews hardware and software for currently available microcomputer systems. Some of the papers in these proceedings describe current technology in British libraries and are, therefore, most useful for readers interested in the state of the art in the United Kingdom. Other papers are more international in scope. All of the papers are consistent with the conference planners' aim to provide a timely forum for discussion between professionals and reflect the hard-won knowledge of seasoned professionals. In an appendix, suppliers of minicomputer systems in the United Kingdom are listed. OKAPI, an experimental online public access catalog, and several other microcomputer systems currently in use in the United Kingdom are described in a second appendix. There is a subject index. Anyone interested in online public access to library catalogs will undoubtedly find at least one paper of interest in these proceedings.

Margaret McKinley

Online Searching

58. Harter, Stephen P. **Online Information Retrieval: Concepts, Principles, and Techniques.** Orlando, Fla., Academic Press, 1986. 259p. index. (Library and Information Science). $46.00; $19.95pa. LC 85-26714. ISBN 0-12-328455-4; 0-12-328456-2pa.

This book, according to its author, can be viewed as the Boolean intersection between the discipline of information storage and retrieval and the practice of online searching. It attempts to provide to its stated audience of students, practicing librarians, and information specialists an understanding of the conceptual and intellectual framework for online information retrieval which is a prerequisite for effective and efficient online searching. In addition, the last chapter covers current trends, problems, and issues.

Following each chapter are a list of problems for students and a section of notes and references which cites publications as current as 1985. At the end of the book is a glossary of 161 terms and an index. It would have increased the book's usefulness to have had a bibliography that cumulates the end-of-chapter references as well as a more extensive, specific index. For example, to find the term "Descriptors" one has to look under "Controlled vocabulary," and with only two exceptions specific databases discussed in the text are not included in the index.

There is only one major problem in an otherwise thorough, well-written work. To the practicing searcher who tends to think more in terms of bibliographic versus nonbibliographic databases, the differentiation made between referral databases and textual-numeric databases, while theoretically sound, could be confusing. They seem more alike than different because in both types of databases some fields are numeric, and subject searching, though it sometimes takes place, is less important. Indeed, this could help account for why the Disclosure II database is listed as a textual-numeric database on page 7 and as a referral database on page 103. Anna L. DeMiller

59. Kinsock, John E. **Legal Databases Online: LEXIS and WESTLAW.** Littleton, Colo., Libraries Unlimited, 1985. 104p. index. (Advanced Online Searching Series). $28.50pa. LC 85-49. ISBN 0-87287-404-4.

This guide to effective use of the two online legal database systems is intended to supplement the vendors' manuals, emphasizing cost-effective searching; however, it is an elementary introduction not an "advanced online searching" guide as the series title implies. Descriptions of the two systems are presented separately in most instances; even the index is divided into LEXIS and WESTLAW. The WESTLAW section was out of date by the time the book was received. No recommendation of one system over the other is made, although some comparisons are given. Articles of a more advanced level comparing the two have been published in *Database*, February and April 1986.

The material in the book is clearly organized and printed in an easy-to-read format. Chapters cover the hardware and overview of both systems; preparation and execution of the online search, using one legal problem to illustrate both systems; the economics of online legal research; sample search problems; and a brief comment on trends. The lists of databases on each system are useful for comparing them but take up an inordinate amount of space.

This brief, introductory text includes practical tips on managing searching in a law office and emphasizes the use of a search strategy form to plan searches. Joyce Duncan Falk

60. **National Online Meeting. Proceedings-1985, New York, April 30-May 2, 1985.** Martha E. Williams and Thomas H. Hogan, comps. Medford, N.J., Learned Information, 1985. 521p. index. $50.00pa. ISBN 0-938734-09-1.

This is the fifth publication of proceedings of the annual National Online Meeting sponsored by *Online Review*. It contains sixty-eight of the seventy-four papers presented at the conference. While any collection of sixty-eight papers will necessarily include items of widely varying quality, the sheer number of the papers reproduced here guarantees that much valuable information will be provided. In fact, the briefness of the papers actually makes the volume very readable. One of the main values of the National Online Meetings is the up-to-date and practical discussion of current topics in the broad field of online databases. These proceedings serve a valuable purpose in making this information widely available in a timely fashion. The volume begins with an introductory overview by Martha Williams entitled "Highlights of the Online Database Field—Gateways, Front Ends and Intermediary Systems." The remaining papers cover a wide variety of topics, ranging from electronic mail to end user searching to electronic publishing to CAI to downloading. In fact, virtually any topic related to online information is covered by one or more of these brief papers. Papers are arranged in alphabetical order by author's last name. However, a detailed permuted index is included which contains all author names, affiliations, and title words. This series of annual proceedings should clearly be a part of any online service's professional collection. However, librarians and other information professionals who want to keep current in this rapidly changing field would also benefit from reading the articles in this and the earlier volumes. Greg Byerly

61. **9th International Online Information Meeting, London 3-5 December 1985.** Medford, N.J., Learned Information, 1986. 486p. index. $30.00. ISBN 0-904933-50-4.

As a reader would expect, this volume covers the state-of-the-art in the online arena. As noted in a prefatory message, papers in the 9th International Online Information Meeting encompass new developments and areas of expected growth, especially gateway or transparent systems and optical media. As in previous volumes, not all papers presented at the conference appear in this volume. Topics covered inevitably will entice any reader interested in online developments. These include the development of full-text files; use of computer-assisted instruction in online retrieval; criteria for user-friendly information retrieval systems; the potential of CD-ROM; the creation of a microcomputer database system; and major trends in the information industry. Ray Gerke

Telecommunications

62. Divilbiss, James L., ed. **Telecommunications: Making Sense of New Technology and New Legislation.** Urbana, Ill., Graduate School of Library and Information Science, University of Illinois, 1985. 114p. index. $15.00. ISBN 0-87845-072-6; ISSN 0069-4789.

This is a collection of ten papers dealing with various aspects of telecommunications presented at the 1984 Clinic on Library Applications of Data Processing, sponsored by the University of Illinois Graduate School of Library and Information Science. Only Joseph

Ford's paper, "Making Sense of New Technologies and New Legislation," deals with legislation to any meaningful degree; the remaining papers focus on new technological developments and issues related to their application in libraries. Ford's discussion focuses on the implications of AT&T divestiture; other topics treated include the selection and use of telecommunications consultants, modeling library communications traffic, telecommunications in the office, electronic mail services, packet radio, narrow band teleconferencing, and a case study of the implementation of a public library data communications network. The contributions vary greatly in quality and depth of treatment. A particularly successful paper is Richard Boss's "Telecommunications for Libraries," a tutorial on telecommunications which serves admirably as a brief, economical introduction to the terminology and basic technology of telecommunications for librarians. [R: BL, 15 May 86, p. 1376]

Joe A. Hewitt

63. Flower, Kenneth E. **Academic Libraries on the Periphery: How Telecommunications Information Policy Is Determined in Universities.** Washington, D.C., Association of Research Libraries, 1986. 43p. bibliog. (Occasional Paper, No. 11). $15.00pa. ISBN 0-918006-51-1.

The purpose of this study is "to determine how telecommunications information (TI) policy questions are resolved on university campuses and by whom." In the spring of 1985 data on TI policy were gathered from twenty-six universities. Various aspects of TI policy were included in the survey, the most important of which were the university's goals for technological development; the present status of voice, data and video communications systems; who was responsible for the formation of TI policy; and the role of the library in TI policy making.

Four key findings emerge from the study: libraries are not a sphere of authority in the formation of TI policy; libraries are generally in the least favored sphere of authority for TI policy; the libraries' involvement in TI policy committees is limited; and computing information systems do appear to be a rising sphere of authority in universities. A discussion of the survey results and a description of organizational models for determining TI policy and implementing it are also presented. Also included are appendices giving details of the status of campus wiring or wiring decision making and sample university organizational charts depicting the place of the library in the university's administrative structure.

This report is useful, for it shows the progress made on campuses in information dissemination through telecommunications and the unfortunately peripheral role of the library in this activity. [R: JAL, Nov 86, p. 328]

Robert H. Burger

CAREERS

64. Garoogian, Rhoda, and Andrew Garoogian. **Careers in Other Fields for Librarians: Successful Strategies for Finding the Job.** Chicago, American Library Association, 1985. 171p. bibliog. $12.95pa. LC 85-15800. ISBN 0-8389-0431-9.

Many who had originally intended to build lifelong careers in librarianship have found themselves leaving the profession for various reasons and starting over in other, usually cognate, fields of endeavor. Others think wistfully about making such a change at various times in their careers, yet they don't, because they lack the initiative or information about other things they could be doing with their skills and abilities. For this later group, this book should prove worthwhile.

The Garoogians supply extensive sections in which they compare "traditional" and "expanding" roles and job descriptions in the information industry. A section on images (both public perceptions and self-perceptions) makes interesting reading, but one is obliged to wade through disproportionate reams of statistics, salaries, and other numbers which fail to hold the attention and seem to be fixed in time. There follows a series of chapters on specific areas which the librarian seeking new frontiers may explore: business, government, education, and entrepreneurship, which are of value in presenting leads and ideas. Some well-aimed advice on resumes, interviews, and the like is timely but presents nothing new. A "Further Readings" section seems curiously dated, with only two sources (from over forty) having publication dates less than four years old. Finally, an occasional lapse in accuracy mars the presentation. For example, in suggesting the major newspapers which one may seek to read concerning jobs in other localities, they cite the *Miami Tribune* (p. 124).

None of these flaws, however, are fatal. The book is attractively formatted, reasonably priced, and full of good, sound, advice. As a stand-alone guide to other careers for librarians, however, it cannot take the place of Sellen's *What Else You Can Do with a Library School Degree* (Gaylord Professional Publications, 1980). [R: BL, 15 May 86, p. 1355; CLJ, Aug 86, pp. 267-68; LJ, 15 May 86, p. 52; RBB, 1 Sept 86, p. 40; RQ, Fall 86, p. 123; WLB, June 86, p. 75]

Bruce A. Shuman

65. Gurnsey, John. **The Information Professions in the Electronic Age.** London, Clive Bingley; distr., Hamden, Conn., Shoe String Press, 1985. 206p. bibliog. index. (Looking Forward in Librarianship). $25.00. ISBN 0-85157-380-0.

This is a book about electronic publishing, broadly defined to include noninteractive broadcast services (cable television), interactive services (videotext, online databases), discrete products (videodiscs, software), and electronic journals. The book focuses on marketing, use, and impact of electronic products; technical details are sparse. The analysis is set within the context of the United Kingdom, with few references to U.S. information activities. Separate chapters deal with the history and impact of each of the technologies, and a final section of three chapters discusses the impact on library education and the profession, especially the conflicting positions of the Library Association and the Institute of Information Scientists. Gurnsey is especially critical of the Library Association, which he considers to be out of touch and resistant to change. In a somewhat personal, unfocused writing style, he urges the profession to decide whether it wishes to remain tied merely to print, or whether it will play a wider role in the information industry. The point is made that no other profession knows as much about collecting, organizing, manipulating, and disseminating information, and there is no reason for librarianship to play a subordinate role.

The value of this work is that it pulls together details about the development of electronic information services in Great Britain and Europe. Even though the call for educational and professional change cuts across national boundaries, those supporting details may not be very meaningful for U.S. readers. [R: LJ, June 86, p. 54; WLB, Dec 86, pp. 58-59]
A. Neil Yerkey

66. Herrup, Steven. **Exploring Careers in Research and Information Retrieval.** New York, Rosen Publishing, 1986. 140p. bibliog. index. $9.97. LC 85-14262. ISBN 0-8239-0650-7.

Let us begin by commending Rosen for publishing a sturdy hardback volume for under $10.00 list ... a rare achievement these days. There are many other attractive features, as well. Herrup covers such topics as "Is Research for Me?," "Research as a Way of Life," and "Where the Jobs Are" in simple, forceful prose, answering quite well the important questions of who, what, where, when, and why.

There are separate chapters on business, legal, and scientific research, and all are nontechnical yet adequate in scope and coverage. He gives approximately equal coverage to the online, automated means of researching and to the more conventional methods we grew up with, since much research is still done using books and journal articles. The chapter on research methods suffers somewhat from its extreme brevity, however, and few specifics are provided.

Appendix A is a useful list of scholarships, loans, and grants, annotated and classified by field, with names, addresses (no telephone numbers), terms and conditions, requirements, and the like, while appendix B provides a select bibliography for further reading. The book suffers a bit from lack of proofreading (three typing errors show up on page 118) but the information is timely and well presented.

This is a commendable effort, as, while many books have been written on the conduct of research, few others have treated the important question of how one gets that first job in the field. All academic libraries (and library school programs) will find this book a welcome addition. Annual editions, in fact, wouldn't be a bad idea.
Bruce A. Shuman

67. Neufeld, M. Lynne, and Martha Cornog. **Abstracting and Indexing Career Guide.** 2d ed. Philadelphia, National Federation of Abstracting and Information Services, 1986. 63p. bibliog. index. $15.00pa.

Neufeld and Cornog work for the publisher, the National Federation of Abstracting and Information Services. While the cover proclaims that this is the "2nd edition, 1986," no mention anywhere in the book is made of a first edition. Even *Books in Print* doesn't list one; finally, a telephone call to Philadelphia revealed that the first edition came out in 1983. This second edition updates information the first one presented, if it could be located. The introduction never tells what is new; presumably, salary information has changed, but what else?

This book is a slender paperback, typed and photocopied, rather than printed, and stapled rather than bound. The introduction "blends" into chapter 1, with no clear line of demarcation. In fact, one wouldn't realize just where the introduction ends, had one not consulted the table of contents.

These complaints aside, the book contains some useful information. Indexers and abstractors are defined by what they do, where they do it, and what sort of education might best profit one considering going into the field. A brief chapter on the job market suggests that there are going to be more and more jobs in these related fields as time goes by, despite (maybe because of) the relentless march of automation.

Most useful, perhaps, is a sort of "yellow-pages" approach to professional societies and commercial employers in the United States and Canada who are looking for indexers and abstractors, with addresses, but not telephone numbers. A second list provides major conferences of interest to persons in, or considering, the field. The "notes" chapter consists of comments and bibliographic citations, and winds up with an "Abstracting and Indexing Services Comparison Chart," which details job titles, salary expectations, market conditions, and other information about the field in handy, tabular form. Finally, a brief index is provided, perhaps unnecessarily.

Overall, despite a rather hasty, thrown-together appearance, this book must be commended for its good advice and timely tips for people wondering what else they can do with a library school degree. One might hope, however, that future editions will give some additional thought to presentation.

Bruce A. Shuman

68. Parker, J. Stephen, ed. **Information Consultants in Action.** London, Mansell; distr., New York, H. W. Wilson, 1986. 258p. index. $56.00. LC 85-31038. ISBN 0-7201-1753-4.

This book is a collection of essays which deal with library and information consulting from an international viewpoint. The editor is an English library consultant, and contributors include English, American, Irish, Australian, Brazilian, Cyprian, and Sudanese specialists who are consultants, librarians, information specialists, and library science professors. All works in the book have been reprinted from other sources except for the last chapter. The volume is divided into five parts: "The Crosscultural Background," "The Expatriate Experience," "The Consulting Process," "Analyzing International Information Consultancy," and "Implementation in Review." The lead article contains extracts from Lester Asheim's *Librarianship in the Developing Countries* (University of Illinois Press, 1966) which discusses cultural, social, historical, and economic differences faced by consultants and persons from the host country in the 1960s, but "which continue to be relevant, in many respects, even today." The Director of the Brazilian Institute for Information on Science and Technology, Antonio A. Briquet de Lemos, presents the views of the receiver of foreign assistance in his "A Portrait of Librarianship in Developing Societies." Other chapters present problems consultants face in adapting to another country, a basic guide to library consulting, the role of international aid organizations, and implementing and analyzing recommendations made by consultants. Notes and references can be found at the end of most chapters, and an index provides quick access to specific topics.

Parker pulls together a variety of related publications which otherwise would be time-consuming and difficult to locate. His book is the latest of only five titles listed under "Library Consultants" in the *Subject Guide to Books in Print 1986-1987*, which indicates the scarcity of readily available material on the topic. Large academic, library science, and selected research libraries which are frequented by consultants will find this volume useful, but some libraries may not be able to afford the high price for it.

O. Gene Norman

69. Webb, Sylvia P. **Personal Development in Information Work.** London, Aslib; distr., Medford, N.J., Learned Information, 1986. 104p. index. $18.00pa. ISBN 0-85142-201-2.

The purpose of this slender book, as stated in the introduction, was "to define personal development in the context of information work, whilst not losing sight of the need to view it in a wider organizational setting." In attempting to fulfill such a purpose, the author discusses the role of development on the performance of the individual, information service (department), and organization. The discussion is complemented by a liberal selection of examples.

The British educational environment and organizational setting which undergird this work will be detraction enough for American readers. But on a much more serious level, the author's style of writing is frothy and inane, and her audience is not clearly established. In discussing this theme Webb switches indiscriminately between personal/individual and management/organizational perspectives. This is not a substantive work; neither is it a good "how-to" book.

Glenn R. Wittig

CATALOGING AND CLASSIFICATION

General Works

70. Hoffman, Herbert H. **Small Library Cataloging.** 2d ed. Metuchen, N.J., Scarecrow, 1986. 216p. illus. index. $18.50. LC 86-15504. ISBN 0-8108-1910-4.

Small Library Cataloging is addressed to the layperson responsible for bringing order to a small library collection. The first three chapters present the concepts of bibliographic structure, location, shelf arrangement, and classification. Chapters 4-13 cover descriptive cataloging, the assignment of subject headings, and authority control, and even offer helpful advice on filing options and serial check-in. Of course Hoffman simplifies, but the simplifications are consciously chosen and, in most cases, a reference to or explanation of the "correct" approach is provided. For example, reliance on title main entry is recommended in order to avoid getting lost in a "maze of unmanageable complications" trying to learn or apply *AACR2* chapter 21. Hoffman suggests simply accepting the latest copyright date as the date of publication, but does discuss the difference between printing, publication, and copyright dates. Hoffman does not explain the distinction between the *sa* and *xx* which appear in subject heading lists, but calls the reader's attention to these terms and wisely advises that both simply be translated into *see also* cross-references. The appendices include sample catalog cards for thirteen different types of items, a review of the sources of cataloging copy, guidance on the production of catalog cards using a microcomputer, and a list of basic library supplies and equipment. Although strictly speaking, Hoffman's terminology is correct, it does not always reflect common usage and is sometimes confusing. "Main entry," for example, is used to mean a single catalog *record* rather than a *heading*. A set of catalog cards is a "decklet." An "item" is one bibliographic unit and a "document" is one physical unit.

Hoffman's *Small Library Cataloging* is a practical approach to cataloging—a recipe book which should enable an inexperienced person to bring satisfactory organization to a small library collection. It might also be of interest to professional librarians or library school students who are interested in a clear look at cataloging basics. Jeanne Somers

71. Hunter, Eric J. **Computerized Cataloguing.** London, Clive Bingley; distr., Hamden, Conn., Shoe String Press, 1985. 215p. illus. bibliog. index. $19.50. ISBN 0-85157-377-0.

By a British author of several good programmed texts relating to cataloging, this book on the computer and its cataloging applications is a good first introduction to the basics. Beginning with an excellent, brief bibliography and a glossary of terms, Hunter goes on to discuss why the use of computers makes sense and what the objectives are for computerized cataloging. He briefly describes how a computer works and the trade-offs that occur with different types of hardware. There follows a description of the content of a bibliographic record along with an explanation of the interrelationship between MARC, UNIMARC, and ISBD. Hunter's chapter on the inputting and storage of data suffers somewhat from an American point of view, because of its British examples. Nevertheless, it is understandable and the illustrations are clear and appropriate. File structure is examined and the criteria for a good system are listed. Programming is discussed from the viewpoint of BASIC as well as the format of different outputs including the interim forms of COM, book and card, and the ultimate online form. The advantages of the online catalog are listed and examples are displayed. Searching in an online system is discussed, stressing menu, command, and free text options. Examples are plentiful and include American systems. The management chapter is weak in that it gives rather superficial treatment to only a few themes relating to management and automation. It does include a description of some in-house, turnkey, and network operations. This work is recommended for librarians who are at the beginning stages of planning for automation. It is not recommended as a library science textbook, although it could be beneficial, supplemental reading. [R: LJ, 1 Feb 86, p. 64]

Ann Allan

72. Kohl, David F. **Cataloging and Catalogs: A Handbook for Library Management.** Santa Barbara, Calif., ABC-Clio, 1986. 270p. bibliog. index. (Handbooks for Library Management, Vol. 4). $35.00. LC 85-15835. ISBN 0-87436-434-5.

This volume is one of the six volumes in ABC-Clio's Handbooks for Library Management series. At the writing of this review three other volumes of the set had been reviewed in various sources. The reviews point to the potential usefulness of the set but iterate a series of faults in the implementation, which this review reaffirms. For the six volumes in this series, Kohl has selected 807 quantitative research articles from the periodical literature published between 1960 and 1983. Because no evaluation was undertaken, many of the articles are not useful. For example, there are a number of survey articles covering topics which are no longer relevant or where the environment is so different today that the results are irrelevant. Excluded are other forms of literature (e.g., books, symposia). Of greater deficiency is the arbitrary decision to limit the selection to quantitative research articles. Managers, in the decision-making process, often look for ideas, argumentation and the experiences of others, none of which are included.

The main body of the text is a series of subject entries (listed in the table of contents, there is no subject index) which cover specific aspects of cataloging and library catalogs, such as cataloging and classification practices, automation of cataloging and the library catalog, and catalog-use studies. A summary of the findings of each original article is presented under the appropriate subject heading. Approximately one thousand paragraphs describe the 807 articles listed in the bibliography of the series, since the same paragraph may be listed under more than one subject entry. This volume, covering 116 articles, consumes a great deal of space (i.e., expense) to do very little. The apparent convenience it provides should not distract the user from serious weaknesses in the choice of material, inadequate indexing, and superfluous references. Not recommended. [R: LJ, 15 Apr 86, p. 62; RQ, Fall 86, pp. 124-25]

Thomas G. Kirk

73. **Library Systems Evaluation Guide: Cataloging. Volume 7.** Powell, Ohio, James E. Rush, 1985. 262p. bibliog. index. $64.50. LC 83-9584. ISBN 0-912803-07-X.

James E. Rush is the author of numerous papers and texts on library automation. The present volume, number 7 in his *Library Systems Evaluation Guide*, pits easy access against the arcane by describing "computer-based cataloging as it should be, not as it is" (p. 15).

To this end, the text offers a design plan encompassing expanded subject searching based on the anchor term rather than the preferred term, an image-data file, which would digitally reproduce an image of the title page and its verso, and automated ranging, which would pinpoint mathematically the exact location of the item being sought. Throughout, the text emphasizes more indexing, including table of contents information, and less redundancy. An evaluative methodology and checklist complement these innovative proposals with specific data-element descriptors and definitions. Numerical weights are assigned in table format to features and functions of prospective systems. The directory of commercially available packages is properly condensed, since this highly unstable body of information is better tracked in serial works, such as manufacturers' brochures or the *Encyclopedia of Information Systems and Services* (see *ARBA* 86, entry 586). The bibliography is marvelous and the index comprehensive. While the item is not bound well, it will probably not circulate outside the library, and it is printed so as to be easy on the eye.

In sum, this forward-looking volume does not tackle the problems of semiautomated systems, nor does it address the reference function of the catalog. Instead, Rush focuses on the creation and selection of relevant online files, alternative data entry techniques, and display formats. Intellectual catalogers everywhere will feel appreciated and challenged by this volume.

Judith M. Brugger

Cataloging-in-Publication

74. **Recommended Standards for Cataloguing-in-Publication: The CIP Data Sheet and the CIP Record in the Book.** London, IFLA International Programme for UBC, 1986. 30p. $26.00pa. ISBN 0-903043-43-2.

Recommended Standards for Cataloguing-in-Publication is the product of two IFLA working groups which included both members of CIP agencies and individuals representing publishers' concerns. Their charge was to develop a standard CIP data sheet for publishers to complete and a standard format for the CIP statement on the verso of a book's title page.

This publication provides guidelines for the CIP record, including a list of descriptive and subject elements with notes indicating whether a given element is mandatory, required if available, or optional. There are recommendations on the format of the CIP statement, with illustrative examples. A sequence of questions used in the CIP data sheet and a sample data sheet are also provided.

Jeanne Somers

Classification and Classification Schemes

75. Chan, Lois Mai. **Library of Congress Subject Headings: Principles and Application.** 2d ed. Littleton, Colo., Libraries Unlimited, 1986. 511p. bibliog. index. (Research Studies in Library Science, No. 19). $45.00. LC 85-24115. ISBN 0-87287-543-1.

Eight years ago, upon the publication of the first edition of *Library of Congress Subject Headings: Principles and Applications*, Lois Mai Chan provided a valuable service to librarians. She brought together in one volume information on the Library of Congress Subject Headings (LCSH), including history and development, philosophy, theory, and application. While the preface to *Library of Congress Subject Headings* provides a reasonable amount of information and guidance on the application of those subject headings, there is no user's manual, official or otherwise, on which librarians can rely. Chan's initial work was greeted with great enthusiasm as a volume that could fill this need. The second edition is met with no less enthusiasm.

During the past eight years, the accessibility to online catalogs by librarians and users alike has increased dramatically. The effects of the changes in our catalogs from card to machine-readable form have raised some basic questions regarding the traditional structure of subject headings. The first edition of Chan contained two major sections: "Principles, Forms, and Structure," and "Application." These two parts are brought up-to-date in the second edition, reflecting the changes found in the revisions and newer editions of *LCSH*, and the interpretations discussed in the Library of Congress's *Cataloging Service* and *Cataloging Service Bulletin*. The second edition adds a new section, "Library of Congress Subject Headings in the Online Environment," which reflects the impact of online catalogs on subject headings and anticipates further changes in the ways we access subject information. Many examples are given throughout the text. Fourteen appendices include information ranging from a glossary to the free-floating subdivisions found in *LCSH* itself, to the MARC tags for subject headings.

Chan indicates in her preface to the second edition that "this book is primarily intended for librarians and information professionals, library and information science instructors, and advanced students." As with the earlier edition, Chan has provided these users with a most valuable work made even more valuable because of the inclusion of updated and additional material. This book is a mandatory purchase for anyone working with subject headings in general and the Library of Congress Subject Headings in particular. [R: BL, 15 Sept 86, p. 99; JAL, Sept 86, p. 258]   Marjorie Bloss

76. **Classification by Broad Economic Categories.** By the Department of International Economic and Social Affairs. New York, United Nations, 1986. 68p. (Statistical Papers, Series M, No. 53, Rev. 2). $8.50pa. ISBN 92-1-161276-4. S/N E.86.XVII.24.

This classification was "originally devised mainly for use by the Statistical Office for the summarization of data on international trade.... It was designed to serve as a means for converting data ... which as it stands is not entirely suitable for analysis by end-use, to meaningful aggregates for purposes of economic analysis of the uses to which goods are put."

The Statistical Commission recommended its publication as an international classification "to serve as a guideline and ultimately as a standard with wide use ... [in order] to have a common basis for classifying the various aspects of general economic statistics, including external trade statistics."

The classification is first divided into seven broad economic categories: food and beverages, industrial supplies, fuels and lubricants, transport equipment and parts, other capital goods, consumer goods, and a general category. These categories are then divided into nineteen subcategories which are further divided into sixty-eight pages of specific headings. Each of these headings is assigned a code number from the Standard International Trade Classification.

This classification has value for the purpose for which it was structured—economic statistics. Its use as a classification scheme for a special collection of library materials is diminished by a numbering system that would not always allow items with subject content in a similar category to stand together in a logical shelf sequence.   Jean Weihs

77. Cochrane, Pauline A. **Improving LCSH for Use in Online Catalogs: Exercises for Self-Help with a Selection of Background Readings.** Littleton, Colo., Libraries Unlimited, 1986. 348p. index. $35.00pa. LC 85-23655. ISBN 0-87287-484-2.

The author tells us in her preface that the title of this book should include the phrase, "and other related subject authority files," but that it was omitted for conciseness. She disclaims any intention to improve *LCSH* (see *ARBA* 82, entry 258) as it is applied at the Library of Congress. Rather, she offers a two-part manual designed to stimulate and further the development of reliable subject authority files for online catalogs of other libraries and library networks that depend, at least in part, on LCSH.

Section 1 is organized around four perceived needs for improvement: in forms of heading and in scope notes, in cross-reference structures, in subdivision access, and in the use of classification as a subject retrieval tool. An introduction and six chapters present the problems and possibilities, with imaginative exercises and suggested additional readings. Section 2, comprising two-thirds of the bulk, offers thirty full or partial reprints of previously published papers, two by Cochrane. Most of the nineteen papers selected were first issued between 1980 and 1985, but three are from the 1970s, two from the 1960s, four from the 1950s, and two from 1946 and 1947 respectively. This shows what we all know—that good ideas have been around for a long time, but that the mills of the gods grind slowly, even in the age of computer-assisted subject retrieval. A detailed index by Robert H. Burger completes the book. Cochrane brings the wealth of her own extensive expertise to this book; it is a well-organized, attractively formatted examination of a problem that is often forgotten in the face of seemingly more solvable issues. [R: LJ, 1 Sept 86, p. 172; RQ, Fall 86, pp. 127-28]

Jeanne Osborn

78. Cochrane, Pauline Atherton. **Redesign of Catalogs and Indexes for Improved Online Subject Access: Selected Papers of Pauline A. Cochrane.** Phoenix, Ariz., Oryx Press, 1985. 484p. illus. index. $45.00. LC 85-7284. ISBN 0-89774-158-7.

This collection brings together thirty papers of an internationally recognized expert in the field of subject analysis and classification, including journal articles, conference papers, reports, and other writings. The topic is very timely and the papers, prepared between 1961 and 1984, are clearly organized under four important questions: "Where are we going in the redesign of catalogs and indexes?" "What can we do to improve subject access?" "Will classification have a use online?" and "What can be learned from subject access research?" Within this framework, the author emphasizes three major concerns—the necessity of designing catalogs and indexes specifically for online systems instead of putting manual catalogs and indexes into machine-based systems, the need to carry out useful research on subject catalog design, and the importance of making intelligent use of the results of that research. Perusal of this collection makes the user painfully aware that progress is slow and that the ideal in subject access is still in the future.

The major strength of the publication is the gathering of the papers, some of which might not otherwise be readily available. Fundamental principles of subject analysis are discussed and many of the papers are well illustrated with useful examples. Nevertheless, there are also weaknesses. Because of the twenty-five-year span, some of the early papers appear dated and are less useful than their more recent counterparts. Also some of the conference papers would benefit from more rigorous editing. Frequently, the reader is frustrated by being referred to statements of other conference speakers or participants which are not included in this volume. In spite of this, the publication has many good points. It will be read with interest by those who are concerned with the issues raised and by friends and admirers of the author and her work. Moreover it will be purchased by schools of library and information science and will provide useful supportive readings for students in classification and subject analysis. [R: C&RL, July 86, pp. 406-8; JAL, May 86, p. 100; LJ, 1 Apr 86, p. 50; RQ, Spring 86, pp. 412-13]— Nancy J. Williamson

79. **Sears List of Subject Headings.** 13th ed. Carmen Rovira and Caroline Reyes, eds. New York, H. W. Wilson, 1986. 681p. bibliog. $30.00. LC 86-7734. ISBN 0-8242-0730-0.

According to the press release, Reyes and Rovira, the new editors of *Sears List of Subject Headings*, have added some five hundred headings in the areas of computer science, high technology, children's literature, medical sciences and health care, sports and leisure activities, mathematics, business and economics, family life and relationships, social problems, and education to this standard work.

Perhaps the biggest change in this volume is in the area of computer science. Forest Press will soon be releasing the twelfth edition of *Abridged Dewey Decimal Classification and Relative Index*, and has allowed the editors to use the new classification numbers for the thirteenth edition of *Sears*. These new numbers are preceded by an asterisk (*) and appear with numbers from the eleventh edition of *Abridged Dewey Decimal Classification and Relative Index*. This provides potential for expansion in an area where growth seems to be exploding.

Another area of improvement concerns the scope notes. The number has increased significantly, and the notes provide clear and precise information. Those assigning subject headings will find them most beneficial.

For the first time, *Sears* follows *ALA Filing Rules* without modification. All headings are now interfiled ignoring punctuation. Older headings have been changed to reflect current terminology (e.g., "Space shuttles" replaces "Space vehicles, Reusable"). Cross-references seem to be adequate. The direct form of entry is being used more and more (e.g., "Employment, Temporary" is now "Temporary employment"). Progress in these areas enhances the usefulness of *Sears*.

Although the new editors have made a number of changes, they have wisely chosen to be conservative with their first-time editing of this standard work. *Sears* continues as a "required tool" for those preparing books for small to medium-sized libraries.— Anna Grace Patterson

80. **Subject and Information Analysis.** Eleanor D. Dym, ed. New York, Marcel Dekker, 1985. 498p. illus. (Books in Library and Information Science, Vol. 47). $39.50. LC 84-28611. ISBN 0-8247-7354-3.

This is an edited collection of previously published works which, with one exception, have been extracted from three publications— the *Encyclopedia of Computer Science Technology*, the *Encyclopedia of Library and Information Science*, and Martha Manheimer's *Cataloging and Classification: A Workbook*. Twenty-seven articles are organized under broad topics: "Descriptive Cataloguing," "Natural

Language Text Processing," "Indexing," "Terminology Control," "Classifying," "Abstracting," and "Extracting." The contents were selected for students and to provide reading for a course in subject analysis methodologies offered at the School of Library and Information Science, University of Pittsburgh.

The editor regards the work as introductory and she has, wisely, indicated that with the developments in research, technology, and systems design for the study of document analysis, this work should be regarded as a starting place only. Current literature should always be consulted. For the most part, the approach is fundamental, theoretical, and oriented toward information science. The text is supported by excellent illustrations and generous bibliographies, where appropriate.

While all of these articles can be found elsewhere, the volume provides a useful gathering, either for students, or for information professionals who require a starting place in seeking information on subject analysis in information organization and retrieval, and research in this area. Most importantly it brings together works by a number of recognized library and information science experts. Because of its introductory nature, it should not become quickly dated.

Nancy J. Williamson

81. **Subject Cataloging Manual: Subject Headings.** rev. ed. By the Subject Cataloging Division Processing Services. Washington, D.C., Library of Congress, 1985. 1v. (various paging). index. $30.00 looseleaf. LC 85-19854.

The widespread use of Library of Congress subject headings in North American library catalogs means that information on LC's own subject heading policies and practices is invaluable to a large number of other libraries. The present publication is one of four parts of the complete LC *Subject Cataloging Manual* and, as an internal staff document (now made available to the profession), it "addresses LC subject catalogers specifically, and describes in practical terms the procedures to follow." This is done by means of some 200 specific instruction sheets detailing certain general procedures, "References," "Name Headings as Subjects," "Geographic Headings and Subdivisions," "Free-Floating Subdivisions," "Subdivisions Controlled by Pattern Headings," and "Special Subdivisions, Materials, Themes, Etc." The instructions are those valid as of September 1985; additions and revisions since that date appear in LC's *Cataloging Service Bulletin.*

"The work is not intended to be a general introduction to subject cataloging practice. Nor is the theory of subject access its theme." It is not designed to be a "new Haykin," and consequently students and some catalogers will need to continue to use explanatory works such as Lois Chan's *Library of Congress Subject Headings* (2d ed., Libraries Unlimited, 1986) for general principles and practice and for some aspects of LC subject heading work not covered by the present instruction sheets (e.g., bracketed headings for juvenile and non-LC headings). The latter may be covered in sections of the full manual not thus far published; issuance of the "General Provisions" and "General Cataloging Procedures" no doubt would supply some of the rationale and practice which are missing in the present compilation, and the fourth (unpublished) section, "Classification," obviously would be useful for that aspect of subject cataloging.

Although even more would be desirable, this hefty publication (three and one-half inches thick, and too bulky for most looseleaf binders) provides essential information not only for operating cataloging departments but also for reference staff and other sophisticated users of the LC subject cataloging system.

C. Donald Cook

Descriptive Cataloging

82. **AACR2 Decisions and Rule Interpretations.** 3d ed. C. Donald Cook and Glenna E. Stevens, comps. Ottawa, Ont., Canadian Library Association; distr., Chicago, American Library Association, 1985. 2v. $75.00/set looseleaf with binder. ISBN 0-88802-190-9.

Evidence of the rapidity with which descriptive cataloging rules are updated can be seen from the fact that this third edition concordance follows hard on the heels of its second, 1982 edition (see *ARBA* 84, entry 145). The British Library, Joint Steering Committee for Revision of the AACR, Library of Congress, and National Libraries of Australia and Canada remain the major contributing agencies. The new cut-off date is 31 December 1983 with a few 1984 decisions included. There is a warning in the introduction that conflicts between some JSC revisions and relevant agency decisions appear. A pious assumption is voiced that revised agency interpretations will come. Ronald Hagler's *Where's That Rule?* (see *ARBA* 81, entry 233) is also utilized and credited. Perhaps the chief adjustment for users, other than the escalating cost, is that page size is no longer designed for AACR2 interleaving, but fits standard three-ring binders, which are included. Each affected AACR2 rule (see *ARBA* 80, entry 204) has its own separate page or pages. The photocopying of source passages leaves something to be desired, but the texts are for the most part legible.

Jeanne Osborn

83. **Anglo-American Cataloguing Rules, Second Edition, Revisions 1985.** By the Joint Steering Committee for Revision of AACR. Chicago, published jointly by London, The Library Association; Ottawa, Canadian Library Association; and American Library Association, 1986. 1v. (unpaged). $4.00 looseleaf. LC 85-30634. ISBN 0-8389-3324-6.

The decision to purchase this group of *AACR2* rule revisions (the third such group since *AACR2* was published in 1978) is a foregone conclusion for anyone remotely connected with standardized cataloging practices. The revisions themselves were approved at the Joint Steering Committee for Revision of *AACR* meetings of 1983 and 1984. The primary chapters of *AACR2* affected by these rule changes, additions, or deletions include chapter 1, "General Rules for Description," chapter 6, "Sound Recordings," chapter 8, "Graphic Materials," chapter 11, "Microforms" for "Description," and chapter 25, "Uniform Titles," under "Headings, Uniform Titles, and References." Rules that have changed substantially appear on separate sheets of paper that can be tipped into the main text. Each sheet is dated 1985 to distinguish it from earlier revisions.

As all catalogers know, AACR2 and its revisions are only the tip of the cataloging iceberg. Rule interpretations as published by the Library of Congress are just as essential to the cataloging process. As a result, the concept of interleaving separate sheets in with the original text is totally impractical. A revision to AACR2 which incorporates all rule revisions and which is published in looseleaf form would be greatly welcomed. The looseleaf concept is far from new. As additional rule revisions and interpretations are published, this format becomes more and more desirable. Marjorie Bloss

84. Gbala, Helen E., comp., and Edward Swanson, ed. **A Manual of AACR 2 Level 1 Examples.** 2d ed. Lake Crystal, Minn., published for the Minnesota AACR 2 Trainers by Soldier Creek Press, 1986. 42p. illus. index. $10.00pa. ISBN 0-936996-22-6.

This manual was originally compiled in 1980 for the *Anglo-American Cataloguing Rules*, second edition, (*AACR2*) training workshops. When further workshops were given in 1985, the manual was revised to reflect the rule revisions and the Library of Congress rule interpretations published to that date.

Because school libraries and small public libraries are the ones most likely to use first-level description, the materials chosen as examples are typical of their collections.

There are thirty-eight examples consisting of twenty-five books, one map, three sound recordings, one game, one laboratory kit, three realia, two computer files, and two serials. (It should be noted that because of recent rule revisions the computer file examples are no longer valid.) The examples have been chosen to illustrate certain rules in descriptive cataloging. However, pertinent *AACR2* rule numbers are also listed for access points and form of headings. Each example is given in card format and is accompanied by a picture of its chief source of information.

This manual has two handicaps. The index is only useful to a person who is knowledgeable about *AACR2* rule numbering because it indexes by rule number rather than by topic; and the forty-two pages of text and examples are held together by staples necessitating rebinding if regular use is contemplated.

Beginning catalogers or those with little training will need a book with more text and examples. This publication is recommended as an auxiliary manual. Jean Weihs

85. Olson, Nancy B. **A Manual of AACR2 Examples for Microcomputer Software.** 2d ed. Lake Crystal, Minn., published for the Minnesota AACR 2 Trainers by Soldier Creek Press, 1986. 110p. illus. $17.50 looseleaf. ISBN 0-936996-20X.

Unlike other manuals of *AACR2* examples published for the Minnesota *AACR* Trainers, this manual centers around extremely vague to nonexistent cataloging rules. Although chapter 9 of *AACR2* gives the rules for cataloging machine-readable data files, it does not specifically cover the cataloging of microcomputer software, since such software was not in existence at the time of writing. Because of the considerable amount of microcomputer software available, two groups, one from the United States, the other from the United Kingdom, felt they were unable to wait until the appropriate cataloging rules were approved by the joint steering committee for the revision of *AACR2*. As a result, cataloging guidelines for microcomputer software were formulated, based on *AACR2*'s chapter 9 and the Library of Congress's rule interpretations.

The resulting manual is, perhaps, even more valuable than its counterparts because of its attempt to formulate cataloging guidelines based on rules that do not quite apply to their subject matter. The author, in addition to relating the rules in chapter 9 to microcomputer software, explains the basis for the resulting guidelines. The examples themselves include copies of the chief sources of information, the resulting cataloging copy, and explanatory comments. While the photocopies of the chief sources are, at times, difficult to read, the overall value of this document cannot be underestimated.

Following the examples themselves are two listings: "Selected List of Computer-Related Subject Headings," based on the ninth edition of the *Library of Congress Subject Headings* and its supplements; and computer classification numbers from the Library of Congress classification schedules and their additions and changes. Similar listings of Sears headings and Dewey Decimal Classification call numbers would also have been extremely helpful.

The author indicates that the joint steering committee will complete its revision of chapter 9, which will include microcomputer software, in the fall of 1986. Although there might have been some advantage in waiting for the final rulings before issuing the second edition of this manual, international wheels turn slowly. Given the overriding necessity to standardize practices, even if they are seen as guidelines rather than rules, this manual is of major significance to any library cataloging microcomputer software.

Marjorie Bloss

86. Swanson, Edward. **A Manual of AACR 2 Examples for "In" Analytics with MARC Tagging and Coding.** Lake Crystal, Minn., published for the Minnesota AACR 2 Trainers by Soldier Creek Press, 1985. 83p. illus. $15.00pa. ISBN 0-936996-17-X.

This manual uses forty items to demonstrate the cataloging of "in" analytics. For each of these items there are an illustration of its chief sources of information and an "in" analytic presented both in card catalog format and coded and tagged for the MARC format. Many common types of "in" analytics are included, such as articles from periodicals, selections from collected works, songs from sound recordings, pictures, maps, and realia from books. A knowledge of the *Anglo-American Cataloguing Rules*, second edition (*AACR2*), and MARC coding is assumed. The four-and-one-half page introduction deals with the general purposes of the manual and the peculiarities of "in" analytic coding.

This manual is highly recommended for those familiar with AACR2 and MARC coding. However, it should be noted that, while the general principles for coding the MARC format are similar in any automated system, the particular format found here is that used by OCLC. In addition, the example on page 73 for a machine-readable data file (now called computer file) is incorrect because the cataloging rules for this type of material have changed since the manual was published.

Jean Weihs

87. Swanson, Edward. **A Manual of Advanced AACR 2 Examples.** 2d ed. Lake Crystal, Minn., Soldier Creek Press, 1985. 94p. illus. $17.50pa. ISBN 0-936996-23-4.

The first edition of this manual, which concentrated on "the application of some of the rules that may be used less frequently ... than others, and (2) on the Library of Congress rule interpretations for qualifying titles of serials and series" was published in 1982. This second edition has the same introduction and the same seventy-six examples, with the exception of those mentioned below. The examples have a picture of the sources of information, a catalog record, and the rule numbers pertaining to the main entry, descriptive cataloging, and added entries. A knowledge of the *Anglo-American Cataloguing Rules*, second edition (*AACR2*), is assumed. Minor corrections have been made; for instance, example 47 now has a missing hyphen. There are eleven new examples, and the index to rule numbers in the first edition has been omitted.

The publishers have been careless with the production of this monograph. The introduction and examples 1, 3, and 5 are given twice and out of order. Examples 2, 4, and 6 are missing, presumably unintentionally.

This manual is only recommended as a low priority purchase, partly because of the production problems and partly because the forthcoming consolidated edition of *AACR2*, scheduled for publication in 1988, and the adjustments to Library of Congress rule interpretations that will follow, will make a third edition of this manual likely.

Jean Weihs

88. Tseng, Sally C., comp. **LC Rule Interpretations of AACR2, 1978-1985.** 2d cumulated ed. Metuchen, N.J., Scarecrow, 1985. 1v. (various paging). $49.50 looseleaf. LC 85-14527. ISBN 0-8108-1834-5.

Earlier updates of this work (see *ARBA* 84, entry 153 and *LSA* 85, entries 73-74) carry cumulations of the LC *Cataloging Service Bulletin* rule interpretations through no. 21 (Summer 1983). The present eight-year review expands its coverage through no. 27 (Winter 1985), but at a substantial increase in cost. Features of these earlier versions are largely preserved or expanded here, as in the thirty-two page index which cites paginations for its 360-page first edition, as well as those in the present looseleaf volume. No binder is included, but the pages are punched for standard three-ring insertion. A similar work, C. Donald Cook's *AACR2 Decisions and Rule Interpretations* (3d ed., Ottawa, Canadian Library Association, 1985), carries data from a wider range of national cataloging agencies. For the Library of Congress specifically, it reports decisions only through *Cataloging Service Bulletin* no. 25 (Fall 1984), and does not indicate the time of decision or *CSB* appearance. Less affluent catalog departments will no doubt want to consider the comparative trade-offs available in such expensive, continually updated works.

Jeanne Osborn

Special Materials and Problems

89. Bloss, Marjorie E. **Serial Holdings Statements at the Summary Level: Recommendations.** London, IFLA International Programme for UBC, 1986. 56p. bibliog. (The IFLA International Programme for UBC Occasional Papers, No. 11). $26.00pa. ISBN 0-903043-42-4.

Librarians have an even weaker connection with magazines than regular contributors, but their desire to see things work out decently and in order is not dampened by being so low on the totem pole. Serial standardization has become proverbial in the library world. It has also become maddening in every periodicals' workroom.

But Bloss and the IFLA have combined their wits to try to resolve at least one of the difficulties regarding serials: the recommendations of standards for international periodicals holdings lists. The author admits that the work is only isagogical, introductory to the problem. But for all its "beginningness," it is a solid start. If union catalogs are a major thrust of the IFLA and the UAP (Universal Availability of Publications) and stand as the egg in this scenario, then certainly this occasional paper must come first, as the chicken. Any series of union catalogs from all over the world would mean very little if every document contained its own inner set of inner secret codes. Bloss's paper hopes to eliminate at least one of the monkey wrenches in this process.

The paper provides a statement of purpose, the background of the process, the methodology of philosophy behind the paper's guidelines, and a statement of basic concepts. There follows a definition of terms used, such as *preak, call number, chronology, display, data element*, and such like. There follows a further identification of elements on the holdings lists that are mandatory (e.g., location area, holding institution) and some others that are not required ("sublocation identifiers"). Other areas include precision codes and punctuation and symbols used. Four appendices close out this work, one of them an annotated bibliography on the subject matter at hand.

The reading of such a report is much like reading the ingredients of cereal boxes, or the FDA's percentages of certain vitamins and minerals in bullion cubes. But despite its ineluctable dry-as-dust presentation, *Serial Holdings Statements at the Summary Level: Recommendations* is a much needed first step in the long and difficult trail blazing ahead for IFLA.

Mark Y. Herring

90. **Cataloging Special Materials: Critiques and Innovations.** Sanford Berman, ed. Phoenix, Ariz., Oryx Press, 1986. 198p. index. $32.50pa. LC 86-2467. ISBN 0-89774-246-X.

This compilation of essays discusses creative approaches used by specialists in handling nine different types of special materials. They include films and videos, computer software, Spanish-language works, comic books, children's literature, serials, fine arts materials, music, and government documents. Although the materials covered have little in common in terms of cataloging, each author has found it necessary to expand upon the standard guidelines and tools for their use to account for the needs of the library user related to both the format and genre of material covered. The style of the contributors is quite varied, as is the depth of coverage of the various topics. All of the essays demonstrate firsthand knowledge of the challenges of handling the materials discussed, and most are very well documented with relevant references. Most include examples as well as discussion of the approach used. Some present illuminating historical background, which provides a context in which to consider the advisability of applying recommended methods. Larger libraries with special collections of the materials covered, as well as any library or media center which emphasizes accessibility for the patron, will find this collection interesting and useful. [R: LJ, 1 Nov 86, p. 50; WLB, Oct 86, p. 59]

JoAnn V. Rogers

91. Craven, Timothy C. **String Indexing.** Orlando, Fla., Academic Press, 1986. 246p. bibliog. index. (Library and Information Science). $29.95. LC 85-28612. ISBN 0-12-195460-9.

String indexing, the automatic production of multiple context-preserving index entries from a single "string" of index terms, has become an important alternative to traditional subject heading approaches as the computer has become the tool of choice in most indexing operations. Craven has written the first monograph on string indexing as a general approach to providing subject access to information. Most previous writing, both in article and monograph form, has treated single systems of string indexing, most notably PRECIS. Although Craven discusses many systems, including KWIC, KWOC, PANDEX, PER-MUTERM, Articulated Subject Index, KWIPSI, PRECIS, POPSI, CASIN, KWIDR, NEPHIS, LIPHIS, NETPAD, Relational Indexing, CIFT, PERMDEX, PASI, and NILS, his purpose is not to fully explicate any particular system, and in fact, his descriptions of some of these systems are so brief that they remain quite cryptic. Instead, he approaches string indexing as a general system, examining in turn the sequence of inputs, operations, and outputs and using examples from existing systems for illustration. Throughout, string indexing options are evaluated in terms of the predictability, collocation, clarity, succinctness, and eliminability (the ease with which users can recognize irrelevant entries) of the resulting index entries.

String indexing systems can be quite complex, and Craven's own clarity is occasionally threatened by intricacies too briefly explained. He is most successful, however, in providing an overall view of string indexing and providing a theoretical frame for its study. Especially helpful are brief discussions of the role of string indexing in online retrieval systems, methods for selecting and evaluating systems, and predictions of future prospects. Appendices include a glossary, a directory of organizations involved in string indexing, an extensive bibliography, an index, and more thorough treatment of Craven's own system, NEPHIS. *String Indexing* must be highly recommended to all persons and collections seriously interested in subject access systems.   James D. Anderson

92. Heynen, Jeffrey, and Julia C. Blixrud. **The CONSER Project: Recommendations for the Future.** Washington, D.C., Cataloging Distribution Service, Library of Congress, 1986. 122p. bibliog. (Network Planning Paper, No. 14). $7.50pa. LC 86-7482. ISBN 0-8444-0535-3.

To paraphrase Henriette Avram's foreword to this work, the CONSER (CONversion of SERials) Project has provided the library community with more than 625,000 high quality bibliographic and holdings records for serials, and, in so doing, has proven to be one of the profession's most successful collaborative efforts of the last decade. The present document resulted from a need to review the first twelve years of the CONSER Project, and to plan effectively for the future.

A well-conducted and unusually readable study covers the history of CONSER and presents in considerable detail its achievements, present problems, and future possibilities. The result was 102 recommendations, ranging from improvements in internal operations and management to broad questions such as the optimum degree of consistency in records, the scope of CONSER membership and participation, provision for filling in known and yet-to-be-determined gaps in coverage, and the possibility of access to the database by subject — the latter as yet largely unaddressed but much to be desired.

It is a truism, of course, that "only time will tell" how many of the recommendations can be implemented, and what the effects will be. In the meantime, this report stands as an excellent analysis of one of our major current activities, and is a credit both to its authors and to the hundreds of librarians who have made CONSER work.   C. Donald Cook

93. Holzberlein, Deanne. **Computer Software Cataloging: Techniques and Examples.** New York, Haworth Press, 1986. 83p. illus. bibliog. index. (*Cataloging & Classification Quarterly*, Vol. 6, No. 2). $22.95. LC 85-27221. ISBN 0-86656-477-2.

This short introduction provides some useful information on computer software cataloging. However, with only fourteen pages of explanation of the basic AACR2 rules, fifty pages containing approximately fifteen examples, and several pages of suggestions for shortcuts, this book does not fulfill the publisher's promise to provide "everything the professional librarian needs to know about cataloging computer software." As far as it goes, the author does give some practical guidance based on AACR2 and rule interpretations from the LC's *Cataloging Service Bulletin*. One would be better advised to purchase a more thorough treatment of the topic found in *Cataloging Microcomputer Files: A Manual of Interpretation for AACR 2* by Sue A. Dodd and Ann M. Sandberg-Fox (American Library Association, 1985) or one of the manuals covering all types of nonprint material covered by AACR2 including computer software.   JoAnn V. Rogers

94. **Notes for Serials Cataloging.** Nancy G. Thomas and Rosanna O'Neil, comps. Arlene G. Taylor, ed. Littleton, Colo., Libraries Unlimited, 1986. 123p. bibliog. $17.50. LC 86-9. ISBN 0-87287-535-0.

For serial catalogers, one of the most difficult tasks is the making of precise, clear, and readily understandable notes which describe fully the serial publications being processed. This is so because serials, in terms of their physical characteristics and the manner of publication, do undergo changes. In the absence of generally accepted rules and standards for note preparation, the book under review is of value because it provides relevant examples of notes for library science students, beginning catalogers, and other library workers who are involved in serials operation. It is also valuable in online cataloging situations, since all notes are arranged and organized according to MARC field.

There are nine chapters in the book: "500 General Note"; "515 Numbering Peculiarities Note"; "525 Supplement Note"; "530 Additional Physical Forms Available Note"; "533 Photoreproduction Note"; "546 Language Note"; "550 Issuing Bodies Note"; "555 Cumulative Index Note/Finding Aids"; "580 Linking Entry Complexity Note." Each chapter is preceded by a brief description of the scope of the field and followed by an outline that details the topical subarrangement of the notes found in the field.

A list of sources which includes the title, the Library of Congress card number, and the OCLC bibliographic record number is also provided. The list is most useful for those who are cataloging directly on OCLC, RLIN, or other bibliographic utility. The record number allows most direct access to the online database and lets the individual review the complete cataloging record and examine the context in which the note is created.

This is a useful and practical ready-reference tool for both cataloging operation and training of serials catalogers. Properly used, this work enables the catalogers to achieve greater consistency in note preparation. For better results, this should be used in conjunction with Jim Cole's *Notes Worth Noting: Notes Used in AACR2 Serials Cataloging* (Pierian Press, 1984).

Wendy Hu

95. Robl, Ernest H. **Organizing Your Photographs.** New York, Amphoto/Watson-Guptill, 1986. 191p. illus. (part col.). bibliog. index. $24.95; $15.95pa. LC 86-3654. ISBN 0-8174-5300-8; 0-8174-5301-6pa.

This guide is the first to be devoted entirely to the area of professional photography. The author uses his professional freelance photographic background and his ten years' experience as a cataloging librarian to develop a step-by-step guide to organizing the kind of filing system essential for a profitable career in photography. A valuable source for photography collection librarians, picture researchers, photo editors, photo buyers, and people with large collections of pictures to be organized.

Ernest Robl has developed an easily understood book on how to use a "library approach" to managing personal and business-oriented picture collections. The book opens with a potpourri of ideas for developing a design for cataloging a picture collection, including a candid discussion of AACR and Library of Congress subject headings. Part 1 concludes with detailed ideas for grouping photographs, designing descriptive rules, choosing subject headings, and reproducing catalog cards. Part 2 emphasizes how to store and use picture collections; part 3 shares ideas for personal computer applications; and part 4 provides strategies for growth of a picture collection.

A special feature of note is sixteen pages of award winning photographs in color. The appendices are: (1) organizations in picture librarianship, (2) an extensive glossary of terms, and (3) a useful annotated bibliography. The index is easy to use.

Thomas L. Hart

96. **The United States Newspaper Program: Cataloging Aspects.** Ruth C. Carter, ed. New York, Haworth Press, 1986. 119p. (*Cataloging & Classification Quarterly*, Vol. 6, No. 4). $22.95. LC 86-4828. ISBN 0-86656-576-0.

This collection of articles about "the most geographically extensive and most comprehensive cataloging enterprise undertaken" in the United States "which will eventually involve libraries in all 50 states and territories" has been issued in book and journal format. It begins with a summary of the history of the program, followed by a description of the task involved in coordinating this geographically distributed project. Two articles deal with the practical problems experienced by catalogers working in one of its parts, the Pennsylvania Newspaper Project.

Another two articles are devoted to cataloging rules. In the first the rules for description in *Newspaper Cataloging Manual* by Robert Harriman are compared to those found in chapters 1 and 12 of the *Anglo-American Cataloguing Rules*, second edition (*AACR2*). The second article challenges *AACR2* rules for cataloging microform reproductions as "difficult to decipher and expensive to produce and maintain." A description of the *United States Newspaper Program National Union List June 1985* includes lists of intended-audience terms, improper entry usages, and proper entry usages; charts of the top fifty nongeneral intended-audience usages; and a bibliography. Finally, there are fourteen reports about individual cataloging projects within USNP.

This publication will be most useful to USNP participants who need or wish to have a knowledge of the whole, vast program. It also contains articles of value to those who catalog newspapers in other countries. Indeed, it is rewarding reading for anyone interested in developments in the library and/or cataloging worlds.

Jean Weihs

CHILDREN'S LITERATURE

Bibliographies

97. **Books for the Teen Age 1985.** New York, The Branch Libraries, New York Public Library, 1985. 61p. index. $1.00pa.

This bibliography is revised annually, and published by the Committee on Books for Young Adults of the New York Public Library. It is composed of over twelve hundred titles, divided into seventy-three subject categories. Many entries include brief annotations, but because it lacks copyright dates, ISBNs, and other bibliographic data, it is not a selection tool. Instead, it is a reader's guide to literature judged to be of interest to teenagers. All of the books listed in the bibliography have been read by committee members, librarians who work with teenagers in the New York Public Library.

Although the entries supposedly reflect titles deemed of interest to teenagers, in some instances it might be more accurate to say that the entries reflect books which are of the appropriate reading level and format for teenage readers. Considering the teen scene today, it is unlikely that many would read *Pierced and Pretty*, a book about earrings and ear piercing. Books of a more topical nature are fewer, and buried in broader subject categories. One book about suicide is found under "Current and Changing Scene," while "Love and Sex" includes only one title on homosexuality. "Love and Sex" also includes *STD: Commonsense Guide*, but no mention is made of whether it discusses AIDS, a highly sensitive and topical issue.

No distinction is made between fiction and nonfiction, and as mentioned previously, no copyright dates are included. The print is small and difficult to read, and the annotations frequently do not adequately describe the book in question. This results in a rather generic bibliography which might be of help to the young adult casting about for something to read, but of little help to the young adult who is seriously seeking information on a particular subject, whether it be for personal edification or research purposes. Further ambiguity is seen in the choice of title. Even though areas within public libraries across the country are referred to as "YA" or "Young Adult" departments, and even though the selection committee for this bibliography uses the phrase "young adult," "teen age" is used on the cover and in the title of the bibliography.

Considering the large number of branches in the New York Public Library system, and the number of young adult patrons who are served by these branches, one can understand the need for a broad, generic bibliography, but unless a library is serving a large, metropolitan area and does not have specific, in-house bibliographies and selection tools, purchase of this bibliography is not necessary. [R: BL, 1 Sept 86, p. 53]

Barbara Sproat

98. **Children's Books in Print 1985-1986: Author Index, Title Index, Illustrator Index.** New York, R. R. Bowker, 1985. 1013p. $62.95. LC 70-101705. ISBN 0-8352-2043-5; ISSN 0069-3480.

99. **Subject Guide to Children's Books in Print 1985-1986: A Subject Index to Children's Books in 6,478 Categories.** New York, R. R. Bowker, 1985. 483p. $62.95. LC 70-101705. ISBN 0-8352-2105-9; ISSN 0000-0167.

Children's Books in Print and the *Subject Guide to Children's Books in Print* are two important resources for all librarians who work with children. These resources provide essential information for purchasing, including publisher, price, and current availability. The 1985-1986 *Children's BIP* lists more than forty-five thousand titles; the *Subject Guide* compiles them into over six thousand subject categories. The *Subject Guide* is especially useful for librarians who are expanding their collections to support new curriculum areas. In his text *Collection Development* (Holt, 1980), William A. Katz includes the children's volume of *Books in Print* and the related subject guide on his list of "Basic Bibliographies of Book-Selection Aids." These two titles provide librarians who work with children with current information necessary for the preparation of book orders.

Rebecca L. Thomas

100. Immroth, Barbara. **Texas in Children's Books: An Annotated Bibliography.** Hamden, Conn., Library Professional Publications/Shoe String Press, 1986. 187p. index. $24.50; $16.50pa. LC 86-10361. ISBN 0-208-02116-7; 0-208-02117-5pa.

This is an extremely useful annotated bibliography of children's literature (through grade eight) with a Texas focus or setting, compiled by a member of the library science faculty at the University of Texas at Austin. An exhaustive search turned up more than 1,600 potential titles, of which 654 have been selected for inclusion here. The time period spans more than a hundred years, with the earliest work, Arthur Morechamp's *Live Boys*, published in 1878, and the most recent entries published in 1984.

Popular themes and subjects include frontier and pioneer life, ranch life, cattle trails, and sports. Biographies focus on prominent Texas heroes such as Davy Crockett, Sam Houston, and Stephen Austin; on Texas politicians such as Lyndon Johnson and Barbara Jordan; on famous sports figures such as Babe Didrikson Zaharias, Lee Trevino, and A. J. Foyt; and on pop music stars such as John Denver.

Notable authors include Andy Adams, who wrote a series of cowboy stories around the turn of the century; Harold Felton, who published several collections of stories about tall-tale hero Pecos Bill; Joan Nixon, author of a series of excellent juvenile mysteries; J. R. Williams, author of a classic series of stories on the wild horse country; Carol Huff, whose *Johnny Texas* focused on the Texas Revolution; and Sybil Hancock, whose writings cover themes ranging from rodeo to oilfields. In addition, the Institute of Texas Cultures at San Antonio has published a series of excellent volumes on various Texas immigrant groups. However, the most famous of all Texas children's writers is Frederick Gipson, whose enduring classic, *Old Yeller*, written in 1956 and set in the Texas hill country of the late 1860s, became Walt Disney's first live action film blockbuster in 1957.

A title index and a subject index based on LC subject headings, plus reading level notations, combine to make this an excellent tool for school librarians, booksellers, and researchers on children's literature.

Brian E. Coutts

101. McCauley, Elfrieda. **Reading for Young People: New England.** Chicago, American Library Association, 1985. 194p. index. $17.50pa. LC 85-13368. ISBN 0-8389-0432-7.

Reading for Young People is a collection of annotations of worthy children's and young adult books which focus upon life and environment in New England. It gathers together over four hundred titles in a data-based format. The primary pattern of organization categorizes books by genre, providing bibliographic information and a key referenced to grade level appropriateness of each work. A second format reconstructs the same information by state and includes author, title, content, and age appropriateness cross-references with an internal breakout of books given by genre. A directory of regional publishers and author/title and subject indexes which also identify works by their assigned number in the genre listing complete the system of references.

Both the annotations and the system of cross-references are well suited to aiding teachers, librarians, media specialists, curriculum specialists, parents, and others who work with children and young adults in finding, selecting, and/or purchasing good materials which detail New England's social customs, history, geography, artifacts, politics, economics, folklore, and environment. In addition, the collection is designed to serve as a guide for the development of instructional units, teaching materials, courses of study, special occasion experiences, and individual or group problem-solving and inquiry activities. In that it provides a fine and broad view of materials which are more in-depth in nature than most, if not all, texts, it is a rich informational resource for study, for individual inservice teacher development, and for extended reading, and it can be used to locate materials of like content for use with groups of children or young adults whose reading skills and levels vary.

The annotations are clear, concise, and cogent. They are generally written in the style of the book review, with some references to text format and special informational or reference features given where appropriate to the needs of the adult practitioner. Each annotation is initiated by a key quote from the text or a one-sentence overview of book content, a special feature which allows the user to skim quickly for the purposes of finding specific content or materials. Many of the annotations also reflect upon the quality of the work or topic using single-word accolades. While these may elude verification, they do justifiably and appropriately, convey a strong regional pride, and do not detract from the utilitarian purposes for which the collection was designed.

Reading for Young People: New England is the eleventh and most recent book in a series of like annotated collections of regionally related works for children and young adults intended to function as educational tools. [R: VOYA, Aug/Oct 86, p. 181]

Sandra A. Rietz

102. **Notable Children's Books 1976-1980.** By The Notable Children's Books, 1976-1980, Reevaluation Committee, Association for Library Service to Children, American Library Association. Chicago, American Library Association, 1986. 70p. index. $6.95pa. LC 86-3039. ISBN 0-8389-3333-5.

Following its tradition of periodically reappraising the books on its annual lists of "Notable Children's Books," ALA's Association for Library Service to Children has produced a concise, well-organized volume that will be of use not only to librarians, but to parents and teachers, as well.

A companion volume to *Notable Children's Books, 1940-1970* (see *ARBA* 78, entry 1121) and *Notable Children's Books, 1971-75*, this annotated bibliography contains 290 entries chosen from among the books on the original

"Notable" lists and more than 150 other books published during the same time period. Each entry provides basic bibliographic information and is briefly, but clearly, annotated. The general arrangement is by age group (i.e., younger readers—preschool to grade 2, middle readers—grades 3 to 5, older readers—grades 6 to 8, and all ages) and the books are listed alphabetically by author within each subdivision. (This is a change, incidentally, from the two previous volumes in which the books are compiled into a single author list, regardless of age level.) Materials are indexed by author, title, illustrator, editor/compiler/translator/adaptor, and genre.

Introduced by a brief, well-phrased essay by Natalie Babbitt, "What Is Notable? A Personal Response," this work updates a standard children's reference source and should be welcomed by those who are building collections, weeding collections, or simply looking for a good book for a child to enjoy.

Kristin Ramsdell

103. **Popular Reading for Children II: A Collection of the *Booklist* Columns.** Chicago, American Library Association, 1986. 49p. index. $5.00pa. LC 86-3385. ISBN 0-8389-3330-0.

Booklist magazine offers a regular column which features subject area bibliographies of materials of special interest to young people. This booklet, *Popular Reading for Children II*, is a collection of these columns from 1980 to 1985. The topics are very well chosen and will be a useful addition to resources for reader guidance. Some of the topics are adventure stories, horse stories, humor, mystery, and science fiction. There are also some very helpful lists that build on the popularity of other books, such as "After Judy Blume," "After *The Borrowers*," and "After *The Incredible Journey*." The prices and availability of these titles have not been updated, which makes this useful for finding materials in existing collections but not for ordering them. Even so, school librarians and public librarians who work with children will find this a very helpful resource for making suggestions to patrons. [R: WLB, Oct 86, p. 67]

Rebecca L. Thomas

104. Povsic, Frances F. **Eastern Europe in Children's Literature: An Annotated Bibliography of English-language Books.** Westport, Conn., Greenwood Press, 1986. 200p. index. (Bibliographies and Indexes in World Literature, No. 8). $35.00. LC 86-3104. ISBN 0-313-23777-8.

This is the first bibliography of children's/young adult books to focus on Eastern Europe (Albania, Bulgaria, Czechoslovakia, Hungary, Poland, Romania, and Yugoslavia). The 315 titles included in this annotated bibliography are twentieth-century works, published in English, which reflect the lives and cultures of East Europeans and East European immigrants to the United States. Titles selected range from traditional literature to historical and modern fiction to biography and autobiography. Both out-of-print and currently available titles are included.

Entries are arranged first by country, then subdivided into the genre categories of traditional literature; historical fiction, biography, and autobiography; and other fiction. Within each subdivision, entries are alphabetical. Complete bibliographical citations are followed by annotations which frequently include comments as well as a summary of the title. Three indexes: author, translator, and illustrator; title; and subject are provided, as is a listing of sources consulted in the preparation of the bibliography.

Academic libraries, especially in institutions with schools of education or library science, would find this work useful, as will teachers of children's literature or others interested in multicultural education in children's books. Large public libraries and school systems could use the book as a collection development/curriculum enrichment aid.

Carol J. Veitch

105. Schon, Isabel. **Basic Collection of Children's Books in Spanish.** Metuchen, N.J., Scarecrow, 1986. 230p. index. $17.50. LC 86-13911. ISBN 0-8108-1904-X.

Isabel Schon has again provided an excellent source to aid in the development, support, and/or creation of collections for public and school libraries serving Spanish-speaking children.

Titles selected support the informational, recreational, and personal needs of youngsters from preschool through sixth grade levels, and were still in print as of 1986. Most books were published in Spain, Mexico, Argentina, or the United States, and a list of book dealers is provided. Arrangement follows the eleventh abridged edition of the Dewey Decimal Classification, and covers a variety of material—reference, fiction, nonfiction, essay, publishers' series, and professional books. Full entries are annotated, and include grade levels, prices, and ISBNs.

This is a valuable bibliography which will be richly embraced by all who care about the reading interests of children. Appreciation is also extended to the publisher for maintaining an affordable price.

Ilene F. Rockman

106. Shapiro, Lillian L., ed. **Fiction for Youth: A Guide to Recommended Books.** 2d

ed. New York, Neal-Schuman, 1986. 264p. index. $24.95pa. LC 85-18857. ISBN 0-918212-94-4.

The second edition of *Fiction for Youth* is a welcome update of a useful title. One hundred and twenty-five new titles have been added while ninety-four titles were deleted. Most of the deleted titles were out-of-print. As with the first edition, books included in the second edition are intended for capable young adult readers. All selections are fiction published during the twentieth century. The majority of titles are adult titles although some junior fiction by authors like Paterson and O'Dell are included.

The body of the work is an annotated bibliography arranged in alphabetical order by author. Both paperback and hardcover publishers are given in the bibliographic data for each selection. There is an "Obituaries" section annotating twenty-two titles which have gone out-of-print, but which Shapiro believes should be reborn. The book contains a title index as well as a subject index. A directory of publishers has also been provided.

This work could be used as a retrospective collection development guide. English teachers and librarians would find it very helpful when developing reading lists for high school students. Students themselves could make excellent use of it as a browsing aid when trying to find some good books to read. All in all, this book, like *Books for You* (National Council of Teachers of English, 1985), is a valuable resource for high school and public libraries. [R: RBB, 15 Mar 86, p. 1070; SLJ, May 86, p. 42; VOYA, Aug/Oct 86, p. 182] Carol J. Veitch

107. Sutherland, Zena. **The Best in Children's Books: The University of Chicago Guide to Children's Literature 1979-1984.** Chicago, University of Chicago Press, 1986. 511p. index. $35.00. LC 85-31820. ISBN 0-226-78060-0.

Sutherland continues top quality reviewing in her new edition of *The Best in Children's Books, 1979-1984*. Earlier editions of *The Best in Children's Books* covered the time periods 1973-1978 (see *ARBA* 81, entry 1254) and 1966-1972 (see *ARBA* 74, entry 1317).

The fourteen hundred titles in this third edition are again taken from *The Bulletin of the Center for Children's Books*. Each listing denotes plot, type of illustration, reading level and/or special interest reader, and identifies titles of special distinction. Arrangement is alphabetical by author, with all but the title index (which indicates author) referring the reader to the entry number.

The unique "reading level index" is arranged progressively by grades, but because of understandable overlaps of reading levels is somewhat unwieldy. Easier to use, though time consuming, are the other indexes (developmental values, curricular use, subject, and type of literature). However, until an alternate format is designed, one cannot imagine this excellent source without the indexes. It continues the high quality of its predecessors, both for reference work and collection development. [R: RBB, 1 Dec 86, p. 558] Carolynn Germann

108. Thomas, Virginia Coffin, and Betty David Miller. **Children's Literature for All God's Children.** Atlanta, Ga., John Knox Press, 1986. 107p. bibliog. index. $11.95pa. LC 85-17169. ISBN 0-8042-1690-8.

Children's Literature for All God's Children is a new resource encouraging the use of literature in religious settings. The authors recommend children's books and correlated activities for a variety of Christian worship and teaching situations.

The source first provides a rationale for incorporating children's literature in religious work, then suggests practical approaches for its use. The recommendations encompass the wide range of general children's literature, with only a few on strictly religious topics.

An annotated bibliography with 194 entries includes recommended books or series with a short summary and a "themes and values" discussion for each. Suggested grade levels are included. The themes and values portion for each book includes ideas for using the work in a religious context. Some suggestions are fresh and exciting; others are typical.

A list of the major children's book awards and a section of professional sources for leaders add to this collection. An especially useful index of themes found in the recommended books focuses on aspects of faith, belief, theology, and Christian principles. An index by genre is also included. This source is a useful, practical guide to using children's literature in Christian worship and educational settings.

Patricia Tipton Sharp

Biographies

109. **American Writers for Children since 1960: Fiction.** Glenn E. Estes, ed. Detroit, Gale, 1986. 488p. illus. bibliog. index. (Dictionary of Literary Biography, Vol. 52). $88.00. LC 86-14885. ISBN 0-8103-1730-3.

In the 1960s, social realism found its way into children's fiction as authors began to write frankly and freely about the problems not only of growing up, but also of living in a culturally diverse society. Although this realistic writing brought with it numerous attempts at censorship, many of the writers who pioneered in this field have produced works which have found a lasting place in children's literature.

The forty-four biographees included in this biographical dictionary are authors of realism as well as the writers of historical fiction and fantasy who worked in the years 1960-1986. Many of them are award winners, such as Lloyd Alexander, Judy Blume, Robert Cormier, Katherine Paterson, Judith Viorst, and Paul Zindel, to name a few.

Each biographical essay, written by a scholar or expert, depicts the author's life and work, incorporating critical quotes from published reviews wherever feasible. Supplementing each essay are bibliographies of works by and about the author. Heavily illustrated with portraits and facsimile title and text pages, the volume is attractive and readable.

An afterword by Perry Nodelman of the University of Winnipeg critically reviews the literature of the period and provides a fitting conclusion to this useful reference work. A cumulative index to the entire *Dictionary of Literary Biography* is found at the end of the volume.

Anyone interested in current trends in children's literature and biographical information on today's important authors with perceptive descriptions of their works will find this volume an invaluable resource. Sara R. Mack

110. **Something about the Author Autobiography Series. Volume 1.** Adele Sarkissian, ed. Detroit, Gale, 1986. 368p. illus. index. $50.00. ISBN 0-8103-4450-5; ISSN 0885-6842.

111. **Something about the Author Autobiography Series. Volume 2.** Adele Sarkissian, ed. Detroit, Gale, 1986. 381p. illus. index. $50.00. ISBN 0-8103-4451-3; ISSN 0885-6842.

Forty-one authors and illustrators of books for children and young adults have composed autobiographical entries specifically for these volumes. Contributors range from Betsy Byars and Nonny Hogrogian to Maureen Daly and Yuri Suhl in volume 1 and from Lois Duncan and Jean Fritz to Seon Manley and P. L. Travers in volume 2. Together, they represent authors of all types of literature for young people—fiction, nonfiction, poetry, preschool to young adult materials. An index, which will continue to cumulate the series in succeeding volumes, accesses the entries by personal names, book titles, geographical names, subjects, and essayists.

No effort was made to limit topics or provide an overall outline for these autobiographical entries, in order to provide greater artistic freedom to the authors. Surprisingly, this technique has generated a collection of readable, and often frank, informative essays of almost uniform high quality. Most entries give family background and a discussion of the author's or illustrator's work and factors which influence it. Most entries truly try to speak to young readers and project the people who create the books. Of special interest and significance are the personal and often candid photographs which accompany each entry. These provide a glimpse of the real people behind the formal publicity shots often seen on book jackets and in reference works. Some indication in the bibliography which accompanies each entry of at least the major awards and honors received by each author or illustrator would have increased the utility of this volume. A definition or discussion of the criteria used to identify "prominent" people to be invited to write their autobiographies would also be useful, especially given the wide variety of authors and illustrators included in these volumes.

In general, these are fascinating first volumes in a new series which could be valuable to children, young adults, and adults interested in children's and young adult literature, if succeeding volumes maintain or exceed the quality of the first two. [R: EL, Nov/Dec 86, p. 35; SLJ, May 86, p. 27]

Carol A. Doll

Dictionaries

112. Helbig, Alethea K., and Agnes Regan Perkins. **Dictionary of American Children's Fiction, 1859-1959: Books of Recognized Merit.** Westport, Conn., Greenwood Press, 1985. 666p. index. $49.95. LC 84-19278. ISBN 0-313-22590-7.

There is a wealth of information in this reference source. The authors have selected award-winning and notable fiction books from 1859-1959 and have provided access to them through a variety of subjects. Primarily, books are listed alphabetically by title with related entries for authors and for memorable characters. Miscellaneous entries are given for significant settings (e.g., Oz) or for other important elements. The title entry includes basic bibliographic information as well as a detailed synopsis of the work and references to specific awards the book has received. Each entry also indicates any related entries in the dictionary.

The index is especially useful with very specific entries such as adventure novels, animal novels (fantasy), animal novels (realistic), and animals (abandoned). Other index entries focus on the age of the protagonist, the time period of the novel, the setting of the novel, the ethnic customs in the story, and even specific character relationships (e.g., mother-daughter). The result is a very usable list of access points to the selected books.

The companion volume (see entry 113) will probably be more useful to librarians. However, many of the books that have been analyzed in this volume are still available and read in libraries, and this resource provides some additional assistance in using them with children. [R: Choice, June 86, pp. 1520-22; RQ, Summer 86, p. 535] — Rebecca L. Thomas

113. Helbig, Alethea K., and Agnes Regan Perkins. **Dictionary of American Children's Fiction, 1960-1984: Recent Books of Recognized Merit.** Westport, Conn., Greenwood Press, 1986. 914p. index. $65.00. LC 85-24778. ISBN 0-313-25233-5.

This dictionary is a continuation of the authors' *Dictionary of American Children's Fiction 1859-1959: Books of Recognized Merit* (see entry 112). As such, it includes 489 books (over five thousand words in length) which have been recognized as prize winners or have achieved notoriety in the field of children's literature. Picture books are not included.

For each of the titles, the authors have personally read the book, written a critical plot summary, created entries for major characters in the book, prepared a biographical entry for the author, and added miscellaneous entries of significant settings and other unique features. The descriptions of the books, authors, and principal characters are well written, concise, and include the authors' evaluative opinions. As such, the book becomes an invaluable guide to the literature for librarians, children's literature specialists, parents, and anyone else needing the information included.

The index is extensive but not complete. Themes, authors, titles, and winners of awards are included, but not all characters can be found. Book characters are included in the main section alphabetically by first name of the character, so that they will not be confused with author biographies, which are alphabetized by surname. Not all the characters can be found, however, by last name. For example, Alfred Burt from *The Alfred Summer* is entered in the "As" but cannot be found in the index under "Burt." Nevertheless, this volume is a fine addition to the reference works of children's literature and should be considered as a first purchase by those studying children's literature in-depth and in particular by those preparing booktalks.

David V. Loertscher

Directories

114. Dunhouse, Mary Beth, comp. **International Directory of Children's Literature.** New York, Facts on File, 1986. 128p. $29.95. LC 85-29372. ISBN 0-8160-1411-6.

Providing information on international children's literature publishing that previously has been either nonexistent or difficult to find in this country, *International Directory of Children's Literature* should be useful to people working in a number of children's literature areas. The juvenile publishing activities of eighty-four countries are covered (including a number from the Third World), and the information included has been obtained by direct contact with the various countries and/or from secondary sources.

The material is divided into eight sections— "Publishers," "Children's Magazines," "Children's Literature Magazines," "Children's Literature Organizations," "Children's Literature Fairs, Seminars, Conferences," "Children's Literature Prizes," "Major Children's Libraries and Special Collections," and "Statistics on Children's Books"—and the information is presented list-fashion. Organization within each section is alphabetical by country and then alphabetical by entry within the country heading. The sections do not contain explanatory introductions and the entries are not annotated. Although the contents of the entries vary with the sections, all entries in the first seven sections list name (or title) and address. (There are, however, some entries that report "address unknown.") The entries in the magazine, prize, and conference sections provide a variety of additional category-specific information including such topics as responsible organization, subjects, categories, frequency, and age levels. (Not all items are included in each section.) The statistics section lists the numbers of titles and copies of books and pamphlets produced in the various countries during one selected year (either 1979, 1980, or 1981).

Attractively formatted and sturdily bound, this easy-to-use directory collects in one volume much information that has been unavailable or is currently scattered throughout the literature. It would be a useful addition to public or academic reference collections with an emphasis in children's literature or the publishing industry in general. [R: BL, July 86, p. 1619; Choice, July/Aug 86, pp. 1652-54; RBB, 1 Sept 86, p. 44] — Kristin Ramsdell

115. Maissen, Leena, ed. **International Directory of Children's Literature Specialists.** Munich, New York, K. G. Saur, 1986. 263p. index. $49.00. ISBN 3-598-10623-8.

The International Board on Books for Young People (IBBY) has compiled for UNESCO a useful listing of specialists in children's literature throughout the world. The purpose, as stated in the introduction, was to seek people "who are able to communicate their experience and knowledge in children's literature to others, who can make a professional contribution in a seminar or a workshop." The areas in which specialists were sought included writing, translating, illustration, publishing, bookselling, libraries, school, reviewing, research, and teaching. The resulting list of 405 specialists from thirty-two countries covers a wide range of expertise. Many of the experts listed have backgrounds in library work or teaching; a somewhat smaller number are editors, translators, or writers. The entry for each individual includes information about experience and publications as well as the crucial facts of language facility. Four categories of fluency are included: mother tongue, teaching ability, ability to discuss, and ability to understand. Information about the length of time for which each individual is available for giving seminars or lectures is also included, although often in vague terms. Entries for American experts include many well-known names, but others are inexplicably missing and it is not clear exactly how the listees were chosen by the national sections of IBBY. North American librarians and educators will find this volume useful chiefly as a way of finding out about children's literature experts in countries with which they are not familiar. A subject index gives a listing of experts in particular aspects of children's literature. Although no plans for updating are mentioned, periodic revisions would be useful.

Adele M. Fasick

Handbooks

116. **The Black American in Books for Children: Readings in Racism.** 2d ed. Donnarae MacCann and Gloria Woodard, eds. Metuchen, N.J., Scarecrow, 1985. 298p. illus. index. $25.00. LC 85-10893. ISBN 0-8108-1826-4.

The second edition of this reference source updates the 1972 edition by including information about new titles and trends. Essays by specialists in children's literature, sociology, education, and history focus on topics relating to the presentation of the black experience in literature for children. Especially pertinent for librarians are the discussions within many articles on the issue of intellectual freedom.

Many award-winning books are analyzed in terms of their perspective on the black experience, including *Sounder* (Armstrong, 1969), *Words by Heart* (Sebestyen, 1979), and the *Doctor Dolittle* books (Lofting). The influence of illustrations is discussed as are the criticisms surrounding the picture books *Shadow* (Brown, 1982) and *Jake and Honeybunch Go to Heaven* (Zemach, 1982).

This is a particularly valuable collection of essays for librarians and all other individuals who work with children. It should be available as a professional resource, especially for individuals with the responsibility for reviewing and selecting materials. It should be included as a resource in library school courses in selection and acquisition. These essays provide an important perspective on the issue of the portrayal of the black experience.

Rebecca L. Thomas

117. **Children's Books: Awards & Prizes, Including Prizes and Awards for Young Adult Books.** 1985 ed. Compiled and edited by The Children's Book Council, Inc. New York, The Children's Book Council, 1986. 257p. index. $50.00. ISBN 0-933633-00-9; ISSN 0069-3472.

As in earlier editions, this title lists winners of different awards granted to authors and/or illustrators of children's and young adult books. Each entry gives a brief description of a currently extant award and then lists its winners in chronological order. The entries are grouped into four general categories—U.S. awards selected by adults, U.S. awards selected by young readers, British Commonwealth awards, and international and multinational awards. Sponsors have provided all of the information which is cumulated here.

The last edition of this work was published in 1981, and there have been some changes. Four of the awards selected by adults are no longer included. Adequate information was not available for two of these, one was discontinued, and one was outside the scope of this work. The number of awards selected by young people increased from fifteen to twenty-eight, and these now comprise the second general category. The most helpful change is the expansion of the award classification section, which provides "subject" access to awards listed by such categories as awards for poetry, awards that are for or specifically include young adult literature, and awards for manuscripts subsequently published. The title index and the person index continue to provide specific access to individual titles, authors, and illustrators.

For those libraries that need a straightforward listing of awards and prizes for children's and young adult books and which can afford the price, this could be a useful reference book. [R: RBB, 1 Nov 86, p. 394]

Carol A. Doll

118. **Children's Literature Review: Excerpts from Reviews, Criticism, and Commentary on Books for Children. Volume 9.** Gerard J. Senick and Melissa Reiff Hug, eds. Detroit, Gale, 1985. 275p. illus. index. $78.00. LC 75-34953. ISBN 0-8103-0334-5; ISSN 0362-4145.

119. **Children's Literature Review: Excerpts from Reviews, Criticism, and Commentary on Books for Children and Young People. Volume 10.** Gerard J. Senick and Melissa Reiff Hug, eds. Detroit, Gale, 1986. illus. index. $78.00. LC 75-34953. ISBN 0-8103-0342-6; ISSN 0362-4145.

120. **Children's Literature Review: Excerpts from Reviews, Criticism, and Commentary on Books for Children and Young People. Volume 11.** Gerard J. Senick and Melissa Reiff Hug, eds. Detroit, Gale, 1986. illus. index. $78.00. LC 75-34953. ISBN 0-8103-0343-4; ISSN 0362-4145.

Each volume in this series contains information on and reviews of twelve to fourteen children's authors' works (substantially fewer than earlier editions; see *ARBA* 84, entries 1120-21 and *ARBA* 77, entries 1150-51). The goal is to provide a guide for the informative selection of reading materials for children of preschool through junior high age.

Each author has his or her own section, beginning with a brief description of literary background and style, and a photograph when available. Following the author introduction are an "Author's Commentary" (not included for everyone); "General Commentary" (subdivided by reviewer's name); and reviews of individual titles, listed chronologically by publishing date. An individual title may have from two to six reviews or excerpts of reviews. Some illustrations from the books are included and, at times, candid photographs of the author.

The volumes contain a cumulative title index, an author index (which also gives cross-references to other Gale publications), and a separate author index arranged by nationality.

The organization of this book is interesting in that it can act as both a quick reference and an informative source. The reviews on specific titles offer quick access to information on a certain work. These reviews are concise and provide a variety of comments. The "Author's Commentary," on the other hand, provides an insight into a particular author's attitudes, style, and thought processes. The "General Commen-

tary" section is more scholarly and could be used in literary research.

Kari Sidles

121. Greeson, Janet, and Karen Taha. **Name That Book! Questions and Answers on Outstanding Children's Books.** Metuchen, N.J., Scarecrow, 1986. 247p. illus. index. $19.50. LC 86-10207. ISBN 0-8108-1908-2.

This unique source is a sure-fire way to encourage and stimulate excitement about reading for children in elementary through middle/junior high school. Rules for playing the game "Battle of the Books" are included along with over seventeen hundred questions (two for each title labeled by level of difficulty). A separately purchased Apple II diskette provides an additional six hundred questions. Titles reflect the best in children's literature and concentrate on post-1970 publications in all genres—folktales, fairy tales, fantasy, historical fiction, etc. Ideas apart from the game for motivating readers—bulletin boards, learning centers, lesson plans—are also provided. Perfect for classroom, school, or districtwide competitions, this practical method for bringing children and quality literature together will be welcomed by library media specialists and teachers.

Ilene F. Rockman

122. Lukens, Rebecca J. **A Critical Handbook of Children's Literature.** 3d ed. Glenview, Ill., Scott, Foresman, 1986. 278p. index. $10.95pa. LC 86-1912. ISBN 0-673-18245-2.

Using her philosophy that children's literature should be judged by the same standards as adult literature, with some small differences, as the basis of this work, Lukens has produced a handbook which, along with a wide reading of children's books, will help the reader "develop critical thinking and increase understanding of and pleasure in literature" (introduction).

The elements which are examined when literature is criticized or evaluated, such as character, plot, setting, point of view, style, tone, and theme, are carefully defined and illustrated with examples from children's books, most of which have become classics in the field. The author, in fact, suggests particular titles which should be read in conjunction with the various elements, for example: *Charlotte's Web* should be read for better understanding of character; *Tom Sawyer* for plot; *The Witch of Blackbird Pond* for setting; *The Incredible Journey* for point of view, etc.

The book is designed as a textbook for a formal course in children's literature or as a self-study manual. Each chapter concludes with suggested activities and study questions and a list of recommended books cited in the chapter. A glossary of literary terms and lists of Children's Book Awards are found at the end of the volume just preceding the index.

This third edition, although similar to the previous two (for a review of the first edition, see *ARBA* 77, entry 1158), has been updated. It contains a more complete chapter on the major genres of literature which also boasts an easy-to-use chart graphically depicting the main points. Other chapters have been updated by the addition of new titles as examples to illustrate the text.

Well written and skillfully organized, this work should be required reading for everyone who attempts to distinguish between good and poor writing for young readers. On the other hand, since no attention is given to reading levels and readers' interests, librarians who will be involved in book selection and reading guidance will need to study these areas apart from this work. [R: BL, July 86, pp. 1619-20]

Sara R. Mack

Indexes

123. Pettus, Eloise S., with Daniel D. Pettus. **Master Index to Summaries of Children's Books.** Metuchen, N.J., Scarecrow, 1985. 2v. $72.50/set. LC 85-1901. ISBN 0-8108-1795-0.

This index cites the locations of summaries of children's books found in eighty-six bibliographies, children's literature textbooks, and books of activities based on children's books. Over eighteen thousand titles published from 1974 through 1980 are found in this two-volume, three-part index. The main volume is an author listing of the books which includes author, title, illustrator, publisher, date of publication, series, grade level, and codes for books in which the children's book is summarized. Page numbers are also given for the summaries.

The second volume contains a title index of the children's books which refers by entry number to the author listing. A subject index also refers to the author listing by entry number.

The introduction to this source indicates that an index to book summaries could be a help to teachers of children's literature who are trying to keep up with the field and that the subject index could be a means of locating materials for bibliographies. However, a list of locations of plot summaries is limited in its usefulness. A compilation of the best book summaries of these eighteen thousand titles would be more helpful. Moreover, the subject index might be helpful as a beginning point in preparing a bibliography, but no evaluation is implied by inclusion in the index, so evaluative aids would be necessary to complete the selection.

The subject index is both quite specific and overly general. "Folklore" is divided by countries, areas, and people, and the divisions are definitive. Within "Folklore," "Igbo," and "Tombigbee River," for example, are cited as having one folktale each. However, the subdivision "Fiction" is not used with history materials, so one has no idea whether books are history or historical fiction.

Master Index to Summaries of Children's Books fulfills its stated purpose of providing an index to the locations of summaries of children's books; however, the source has limited usefulness. [R: Choice, Apr 86, p. 1198; EL, Sept/Oct 86, pp. 36-37; RBB, 1 Sept 86, pp. 44-45; RQ, Summer 86, pp. 539-40; WLB, Apr 86, pp. 66-67]

Patricia Tipton Sharp

124. Snow, Kathleen M., Rickey Dabbs, and Esther Gorosh, comps. **Subject Index to Canadian Poetry in English for Children and Young People.** 2d ed. Ottawa, Canadian Library Association, 1986. 307p. $25.00pa. ISBN 0-88802-202-6.

The second edition of this useful index covers 120 collections of Canadian poetry in English available in hardcover during the years 1976 to 1983. The poets represented include such well-known names as Margaret Atwood, Dennis Lee, Milton Acorn, and Leonard Cohen. Some of the anthologies analyzed are not primarily designed for children. Books which contain at least five poems which would appeal to readers between the ages of six and fourteen were selected. Subject headings seem appropriate for children's interests, ranging from puddles and teddy bears to silence and truth. It is interesting to note that, in keeping with the Canadian image, snow, rivers, lakes, and winter all have substantial listings, and as might be expected, large numbers of nonsense verses are represented. What is less predictable is that the listing for fathers (forty-five poems) is longer than that for mothers (forty-one poems) and that the lengthiest listing of all is for the subject of death—not what most people would consider a primary interest of children. There is no author or title index, although both of these would have made the listing even more valuable than it is. Nonetheless, the volume will be useful to Canadian school and public librarians who deal with children. Teachers will find it helpful in selecting poems to meet curricular needs.

Adele M. Fasick

125. Trefny, Beverly Robin, and Eileen C. Palmer. **Index to Children's Plays in Collections 1975-1984.** Metuchen, N.J., Scarecrow, 1986. 108p. bibliog. $15.00. LC 86-6418. ISBN 0-8108-1893-0.

This concise, well-organized index continues *Index to Children's Plays in Collections*, second edition, by Barbara A. Kreider (Scarecrow, 1977; see *ARBA* 78, entry 939). Kreider's work indexes collections published from 1965 to 1974 (material in the first edition, 1972 [see *ARBA* 73, entry 187], has been subsumed by the second edition); the Trefny/Palmer index covers the following decade. The same format is used by both indexes.

This most recent volume includes 540 plays from forty-eight collections and expands the scope of the earlier indexes by including pantomimes, puppetry, variety programs in play format, as well as the expected skits, monologs, and one-act plays. In all, 1,990 plays are now covered by the series.

Entries are of three types—author, title, and subject—and are listed in a single dictionary-style arrangement. The author entry serves as the main entry and provides information on the author, title, collection title and author, and number of characters in the play. The subject and title entries list author and title information. In addition to more traditional subject headings (e.g., *mice, trolls, war*), access is also provided by theme, type of play, occasion or holiday, historical period, geographical setting, famous or legendary personalities, special cast, and genre.

The index is concluded by a section providing cast analysis, a directory of publishers that provides names and addresses of publishers whose works are included, and a bibliography of collections that lists bibliographic data for the collections analyzed.

Comprehensive and easy-to-use, this index admirably updates a standard children's reference work and should prove invaluable to parents, educators, students, and librarians who have the responsibility for or an interest in children's theater. — Kristin Ramsdell

Picture Books

126. Lacy, Lyn Ellen. **Art and Design in Children's Picture Books: An Analysis of Caldecott Award-Winning Illustrations.** Chicago, American Library Association, 1986. 229p. index. $19.95. LC 86-1163. ISBN 0-8389-0446-7.

Lyn Ellen Lacy, an elementary school librarian and media specialist in the Minneapolis Public School District, provides a basic introduction to artistic elements (line, color, light and dark, shape, space, and texture) for teaching art appreciation and picture book design to children. The focus is on thirteen of the Caldecott Medal award-winning picture book titles published between 1938 and 1986. The titles selected for study are excellent examples for discussions of artistic concepts, and they include Robert McCloskey's *Make Way for Ducklings*, Maurice Sendak's *Where the Wild Things Are*, and Ezra Jack Keat's *The Snowy Day*. The reader will become knowledgeable about art and subject content standards for children's books, criteria for selection for Caldecott Medal winners, and changing tastes and societal attitudes over the decades since before World War II. Biographical and background influences on selected illustrators' works are presented in the narrative and through recommended sources for further information. The author provides a fascinating discussion of how to determine if a picture book "successfully communicates the artist's perception within the limits of its style and its conceptual intent."

This narrative guide will be of particular value when used in conjunction with the hardbound copies of picture books reviewed and with other media sources such as film and video resources on children's picture books or the authors and illustrators associated with them. [R: BL, July 86, p. 1619; SLJ, Sept 86, p. 48] — Maureen Pastine

127. Lima, Carolyn W. **A to Zoo: Subject Access to Children's Picture Books.** 2d ed. New York, R. R. Bowker, 1986. 706p. index. $39.95. LC 85-26961. ISBN 0-8352-2134-2.

When the first edition of *A to Zoo* appeared in 1982, many children's librarians recognized that it filled a long-standing need for subject access to the picture book collection. The revised and expanded second edition will be even more helpful. The 464 pages of the first edition have been expanded to 706 pages. Books listed in the first edition were those in the picture book collection of the San Diego Public Library, while this edition has been enriched by the addition of other titles chosen from reviews and literature searches. Efforts have been made to expand the scope of informational picture books, especially in science, technology, social science, and other educational areas. Also included are many board books for toddlers. In addition to the subject listing, there is a bibliographic guide arranged by author or main entry, a title index, and an illustrator index. An introductory essay gives a brief background of the development of picture books and includes suggestions for additional reading.

Some users of this book, especially those who are not trained librarians, may find the subject headings complicated. Halloween, a popular subject, is found under "Holidays—Halloween" and Africa is found under "Foreign lands—Africa." This two-step approach will be time-consuming until people become accustomed to using the book.

The clear, readable type, good design, and appealing illustrations add to the pleasure of using this book. Children's librarians will find it an indispensable tool. [R: RBB, Aug 86, p. 1671; SLMQ, Summer 86, p. 212]

Adele M. Fasick

128. McQuarrie, Jane, and Diane Dubois, comps. and eds. **Canadian Picture Books. Livres d'images canadiens.** Toronto, Reference Press, 1986. 217p. index. $25.00, $21.00 (U.S.); $20.00pa., $17.00pa. (U.S.). ISBN 0-919981-12-7; 0-919981-09-7pa.

This bilingual book is designed to provide a comprehensive listing of all picture books written or illustrated by people of Canadian origin or now residing in Canada. Because few Canadian picture books were produced until very recently, this comprehensive listing includes approximately seven hundred books.

The main listing of books is arranged alphabetically by title. Brief descriptive annotations are given for each book in the language in which it was written. Out-of-print books are noted, although other books have undoubtedly gone out-of-print since the list was compiled. The cut-off date for books included is July 1985. Books which are considered to be of superior quality are marked with a star, and roughly 25 percent of the books receive this treatment. Indexes by author and subject give additional access to individual titles or groupings.

The format and subject classification follows that used in Carolyn Lima's *A to Zoo: Subject Access to Children's Picture Books* (R. R. Bowker, 1982), a book which many children's librarians have found useful. The subject listing in this book, of course, includes both French and English headings. No listing of publishers is given, although some of them are small presses which will be difficult to locate, especially for librarians outside of Canada. Libraries with collections of Canadian picture books and those hoping to develop one will find this book helpful.

Adele M. Fasick

COLLECTION DEVELOPMENT AND SELECTION OF MATERIALS

129. **Collection Development Manual of the National Library of Medicine 1985.** Bethesda, Md., National Institutes of Health, U.S. Department of Health and Human Services, 1985. 110p. index. $12.00pa.

The National Library of Medicine (NLM) is committed to improving the delivery of biomedical information in support of medicine and health care. The institution's policy in regard to collection development influences every health science library in the country because they rely on NLM for resources and services. The library first issued its collection development manual in 1951, and the most recent edition appeared in 1977 under the title *Scope and Coverage Manual of the National Library of Medicine*. This manual was designed to serve a dual purpose: to guide NLM's staff in its selection of literature, and to explain the library's collecting practices to the staffs of other libraries. Like its predecessors, the 1985 edition defines the range of subjects to be acquired and the extent to which each of these subjects is to be covered. NLM's staff has identified over a hundred subject areas which they define and clarify with cross-references, examples, and references to the collecting policies of the National Agricultural Library (NAL). A collection level of "comprehensive," "research," or "basic information" has been designated for each of these areas.

The policy on collecting material on diagnostic imaging, medical informatics, and laboratory animals, all areas of newly growing interest, is particularly useful to practicing librarians. They may also find useful the selection guidelines by format and type of material, and the introductory comparison of the collection policies at NAL and the Library of Congress. Collection development policies are necessarily vague in reference to subject areas. Nevertheless, this manual is a serious, successful, attempt to be as specific as possible. It is complemented by NLM's fact sheet on interlibrary loan. These statements should be available to health sciences libraries of all sizes.

Margaret Norden

130. **Collection Management in Public Libraries. Proceedings of a Preconference to 1984 ALA Annual Conference June 21-22, 1984, Dallas, Texas.** Judith Serebnick, ed. Chicago, American Library Association, 1986. 95p. $3.95pa. LC 85-11196. ISBN 0-8389-3321-1.

I have long been a fan of the "slim" book, since it can normally be finished in one sitting and, because of its size, the authors have had to be concise. *Collection Management in Public Libraries* is such a book; it comprises papers presented at an ALA preconference in Dallas, Texas, on 21-22 June 1984. The papers address three related issues. The first is to "examine collection management functions, guidelines, and organizational patterns from a public library point of view." The second is to view the effect of "automation" on "collection development."

And the third is to identify "common problem areas for public library procurement." The papers include: (1) "Overview of Collection Management in the Public Library," by Linda F. Crismond; (2) "Guidelines for Collection Management," by Karen Krueger; (3) "The Role of Automation in Collection Management," by Phyllis B. Cartwright; (4) "Resource Sharing," by Hugh C. Atkinson; (5) "Management of Internal Resources," by Mary M. Bundy; (6) "An Approach to Collection Management at Providence Public Library," by Annalee M. Bundy; (7) "The Approach to Collection Management at Baltimore County Library," by Norma Rawlinson; (8) "A Minority Report on Present Book Selection Practices," by Thomas H. Ballard; and (9) "Common Threads/Questions/Challenges," by Linda D. Crowe.

As an academic librarian with experience in collection development, I found these papers interesting, and on one or two issues somewhat provocative. Collection management includes both procurement and resource sharing. The latter has been a mixed blessing in higher education, with a few "big" successes and many failures. Automation, of course, has greatly helped, as amply documented by the late Hugh Atkinson's discussion of the Illinois Library and Information Network (ILLINET), which links eighteen regional libraries "committed to interinstitutional resource sharing." He provides concrete examples of how ILLINET libraries benefit and why cooperation will become an increasing and integral part of collection management, especially in an era of shrinking financial support.

Public libraries, although responding to resource sharing, have also placed great emphasis on increased use of existing collections through user studies and by merchandising and marketing techniques borrowed from the private sector. In other words, one of the key elements of collection development is to understand use and to incorporate it as the central focus of procurement. For many public libraries, "client-centered guidelines" have become the dominant element in devising collection development statements. This, of course, differs from what is done in many academic libraries, which tend to be more "program centered" in their procurement policies. My guess is that many academic librarians will be financially compelled to adopt a more "businesslike" approach to collection development over the next few years and would, therefore, benefit from some of the suggestions contained in this collection of papers. [R: BL, 15 Sept 86, p. 99; RQ, Winter 86, pp. 261-62]

Richard H. Quay

131. **Coordinating Cooperative Collection Development: A National Perspective.** Wilson Luquire, ed. New York, Haworth Press, 1986. 253p. illus. (*Resource Sharing and Information Networks*, Vol. 2, Nos. 3/4). $39.95. LC 85-24847. ISBN 0-86656-543-4.

An unusual publication is the best way to summarize this book. It first appeared in the journal *Resource Sharing and Information Networks* (vol. 2, nos. 3 and 4, February 1986). What makes this unusual is that the articles in the journal were papers given at a conference, Coordinating Cooperative Collection Development: A National Perspective, sponsored by Eastern Illinois University and Illinois Board of Higher Education, April 1-2, 1985. Seldom are the proceedings of a conference worth publishing, and it is more rare when they are worth republishing. Although the thirteen papers are generally interesting, the text of the group discussions add little except length to the book. Furthermore, a good deal of the material has appeared in slightly different form elsewhere. (Some of the presenters, such as Paul Mosker, Karen Kruger, and Joel Rutstein, have published several articles on the topics they discussed; as a result you find almost nothing new. Note: it is not the presenters' fault that these proceedings were published and republished.) Overall, the papers were perhaps worth publishing once, but not a second time. Many people will be misled by this publication, as even the CIP data do not note the fact that the material first appeared in a journal.

G. Edward Evans

132. **Guide for the Development and Management of Test Collections: With Special Emphasis on Academic Settings.** By the Ad Hoc Subcommittee on Test Collections, Association of College and Research Libraries. Chicago, Association of College and Research Libraries, American Library Association, 1985. 34p. bibliog. $12.00 spiralbound. ISBN 0-8389-6926-7.

Compiled by a subcommittee of the Education and Behavioral Science Subsection of the Association of College and Research Libraries, this brief, spiralbound publication will provide much-needed information for librarians who must formulate policies for collections of tests used by faculty and students in education and the behavioral sciences. Two basic policy considerations identified are the security of the tests, with stipulations for use often set by the publishers, and access to the tests by faculty and students for study and research. Other aspects librarians must consider in test collection development are the types of tests to include, ranging from standardized to unpublished; the cataloging, classification and arrangement of tests; budgeting; and sources for evaluating and selecting tests for purchase. A useful chapter explains online access to information about tests, databases which are worth searching, and search strategies. There are eight short appendices, with unnumbered pages. The most useful of these are the sample test use policies, a core collection of tests, and a separate subject classification of the core collection. There is also an unannotated bibliography of major sources about tests and measurements. This concise guide will be most helpful for those academic librarians who need to establish test collections or to develop policies for collections already developed. Mary K. Biagini

133. Hall, Blaine H. **Collection Assessment Manual for College and University Libraries.** Phoenix, Ariz., Oryx Press, 1985. 212p. index. $36.50. LC 85-13694. ISBN 0-89774-148-X.

A how-to book described by the author as a "training manual," this publication on collection assessment is probably best suited for the novice or inexperienced person. There are five chapters: "Planning the Assessment Procedure," "Collection-centered Measures," "Client-centered Measures," "Assessment for Special Purposes," and "Reporting Assessment Results." The strongest sections of the book may be the third chapter, "Client-centered Measures," and the various appendices which, among other items, include a directory of accrediting groups, sample survey instruments, and the Association of College and Research Libraries' academic library standards.

However, the book seems oversimplistic in its approach to collection assessment. Rather than taking a studied universal approach to a complex subject, the author has for the most part given a step-by-step plan for one method. For example, in discussing the use of approval plan profiles in assessment, Hall, rather than surveying several plans or options, chooses one company and writes in detail concerning it. He fails to raise the complex issues that may cause problems for the assessor, such as various patterns of library organization, classification problems, particularly for libraries that have gone through various editions of Dewey and several generations of classifiers, or the multidisciplinary nature of subjects and curricula today. He takes for granted that automation provides any kind of circulation statistics necessary for assessment; this is true for some libraries but not for others.

Finally, though the author says in his introduction that the book is for professionals, he gives, among other items, such self-evident information as the need to use pencil instead of pen in checking bibliographies, the need in writing the assessment report to have a beginning, middle, and end. He says the *end* is that part where "you wrap up the report and leave the readers with a clear understanding of the results obtained from the measurements and the conclusion and recommendations you have arrived at." There are no bibliographies at the ends of chapters, and the one at the end of the text is slight, making no reference to some of the publications mentioned briefly in the body of the book. Though Hall says there is "voluminous literature on collection evaluation" he has shared only a little with his readers. The book does have a subject index.

The author has hit on a timely topic needed by the library world as it is entering more rapidly into resource sharing and cooperative collection development, but the price is high for the introduction provided. [R: CLJ, Oct 86, p. 366; JAL, May 86, pp. 56, 103; LJ, 1 May 86, p. 98; RQ, Summer 86, p. 550; WLB, June 86, p. 75] Ruth E. Bauner

134. **Selection of Library Materials in the Humanities, Social Sciences, and Sciences.** Patricia A. McClung, ed. Chicago, American Library Association, 1985. 405p. index. $49.00. LC 85-20084. ISBN 0-8389-3305-X.

The twenty-six essays here by practicing collection builders which attack selection problems in the various academic disciplines are particularly useful for their full and discriminating comments on selection tools—trade bibliographies, publishers' catalogs, review journals, etc. These are chiefly British and American, with a few foreign titles in history, philosophy, and religion (e.g., *Elenchus Bibliographicus*). The arrangement "reflects the editor's intent to examine collection building from three different perspectives: first by discussing general sources and procedures; then by looking at selection techniques specific to particular disciplines ...; and finally by analyzing the challenges associated with special formats." The latter includes microforms, machine-readable data files, and small presses, among others.

A very good index to subjects and individual titles includes twelve references each to *Library Journal* and *Choice*, only three to *Booklist*, and none to *Reference Books Bulletin*, probably because the latter two were not considered useful in academic libraries. Beginning collection builders and library science students will find it a handy compilation. [R: Choice, June 86, p. 1500; LJ, 15 Feb 86, p. 138; RQ, Summer 86, p. 556; WLB, June 86, pp. 74-75]

Frances Neel Cheney

135. Spiller, David. **Book Selection: An Introduction to Principles and Practice.** 4th ed. London, Clive Bingley; distr., Hamden, Conn., Shoe String Press, 1986. 235p. bibliog. index. $30.00. ISBN 0-85157-404-1.

This fourth edition of a work first published fifteen years ago covers most of the relevant principles and practices of the art of book selection—written policies, standards, budgeting, management, assessing user needs, book evaluation, collection assessment, weeding, interlibrary loan and cooperative acquisition, the book trade, and the unique issues of selecting periodicals, fiction, and audiovisual and other nonbook materials. Yet for all its breadth, it only introduces these subjects. It does not presume to plumb their depths. Library students and beginning professionals will find the discussions of these issues a good overview of the complexities and problems to be encountered in the practice of selecting and providing materials for users, but more experienced professionals will likely find its references and further reading suggestions of greater value. Also, public librarians will find it addresses their practices in more detail than it does those of academic libraries.

Intended for use by British librarians, the book will offer little new to many American librarians not directly interested in British librarianship. The examples, most of the research studies, as well as the social and political environments in which the selection process take place are British, with only an occasional mention of American practices. Still, its references and suggestions for further reading on the topic of each chapter provide an excellent and convenient resource to librarians anywhere interested in further study of book selection principles and applications. Blaine H. Hall

136. Stevens, Norman D. **A Guide to Collecting Librariana.** Metuchen, N.J., Scarecrow, 1986. 166p. illus. index. $19.50. LC 85-30302. ISBN 0-8103-1874-4.

The author defines librariana as any artifact that depicts any aspect of librarians, librarianship, or libraries. Examples include: autographs, badges, bookmarks, bookplates, buttons and pins, commemoratives and souvenirs, library equipment, library postcards, medals, paper clips, poetry, postage stamps, rubber stamps, shopping bags, T-shirts, and a wide assortment of other items. They are all described in great detail by Norman Stevens.

This is the first work of its kind and is written by an expert on the topic, with the bibliographic assistance of Valerie Oliver. Stevens also provides information about the acquisition, recording, preservation, and storage of a collection of librariana, and about individual and institutional collections and library museums. A comprehensive bibliography and numerous illustrations add further value to this comprehensive work.

This fascinating book should be of interest to everyone in the profession. It is also an important addition to the fields of library history and American popular culture. [R: JAL, Nov 86, p. 313; LJ, Dec 86, p. 74; RQ, Winter 86, pp. 262-63] George S. Bobinski

COLLEGE AND RESEARCH LIBRARIES

137. **ACRL University Library Statistics 1983-1984: A Compilation of Statistics from Eighty-six Non-ARL University Libraries.** Sandy Whiteley, comp. Chicago, Association of College and Research Libraries, American Library Association, 1985. 57p. $15.00pa. ISBN 0-8389-6892-9.

This publication provides descriptive information about the collections, staff size, and expenditures of eighty-six research libraries, as well as enrollment figures and numbers of Ph.D. degrees (and fields) granted by the institutions with which they are associated. Statistical data were compiled from a survey of ninety-seven libraries (89 percent response rate) which belong to ACRL (Association of College and Research Libraries, division of ALA), but which are not members of ARL (Association of Research Libraries).

The questionnaire used in this study is the same one developed by ARL for its annual survey. Thus, this report complements the annual *ARL Statistics.* The university libraries surveyed were selected from *A Classification of Institutions of Higher Education* (rev. ed. 1976), a list of Ph.D.-granting institutions prepared by the Carnegie Council on Policy Studies in Higher Education. Whiteley indicates in her introduction that this listing is not complete in terms of all the libraries that fall into this category: "We know that some universities not on the Carnegie list in 1976 now grant enough Ph.D.'s to qualify for inclusion."

The survey report begins with a list of the eighty-six libraries responding to the questionnaire and a code number which is used in data tables in place of the institution's name. The data tables provide statistical information in twenty-two categories with respect to collection, interlibrary loans, expenditures, and personnel. University median, high, and low figures are reported for each category. Selected variables are summarized. In a section titled "ACRL Library Index" rank order tables compare each library to the others, including an overview of ranges and medians for fourteen of the categories.

Footnotes to the tables, a copy of the questionnaire, and instructions for completing it conclude the work. Whiteley points out that there are no dramatic changes in this report from the previous one (1981-1982). Microforms increased the most (21 percent); serials decreased (5 percent). Interlibrary loan activity understandably increased, as had all expenditures, with the exception of binding costs.

The statistics available in this publication are of extreme interest and importance to university administrators, academic library directors, management, and other library personnel. The usefulness of this reference tool would be further enhanced if the prefatory material or introduction contained an explanation of the categories of ACRL (or non-ARL libraries) and ARL libraries, and the criteria necessary for inclusion in each group.

Lois Buttlar

138. Cummings, Martin M. **The Economics of Research Libraries.** Washington, D.C., Council on Library Resources, 1986. 216p. index. $5.00pa. LC 86-2321.

Libraries, especially research libraries, are at a crucial juncture in their development. A principal question which must quickly be answered is whether they can continue to provide the increasing diversity and improved quality of services made possible by technological advances. *The Economics of Research Libraries* attempts to answer this and several equally significant questions. Specifically, the objective of the publication is "to assist responsible institutional managers and library directors in making better use of cost information for strategic planning, budgeting, and forecasting library needs" (p. 9).

The book is addressed to university administrators, library directors, and concerned librarians. It is based on an extensive review of literature, study of deliberations conducted by a panel of experts that met three times during a two-year period, and assessment of a number of investigations on the subject of library economics funded by the Council on Library Resources.

Martin M. Cummings, Director Emeritus of the National Library of Medicine, convincingly illustrates the perplexity of evaluating cost efficiencies in libraries and persuasively documents the need to more fully understand library economics in order to implement realistic planning.

Five chapters in the book deal with the need to study library economics; library funding and user needs; cooperation and consortia; new technologies; management, performance, and evaluation; and planning for libraries in transition. The sixth chapter summarizes and draws conclusions. The four appendices include an article on economic issues and trends in academic libraries by Michael D. Cooper; a study of four universities and their libraries by Mark E. Cain; a selected annotated bibliography on user fees by Jane A. Rosenberg; and a list of the participants in the three economic seminars.

This is a publication that should be read by all librarians and institutional administrators concerned with the future of academic librarianship. The issues are complex and the questions are trying. Yet they will persist. Cummings outlines clearly and effectively what is being done and presents specific recommendations for developing a better understanding of library economics as a means of improving library performance. [R: JAL, Sept 86, pp. 234-35]

P. Grady Morein

139. Erdmann, Christine, comp. **Special Collections in College Libraries.** Chicago, Association of College and Research Libraries, American Library Association, 1986. 95p. (CLIP Notes, No. 6). $18.00 spiralbound. ISBN 0-8389-7004-4.

This work is intended to provide examples and new ideas to "librarians considering refining or expanding their special collections services" (introduction). A survey on special collections in college libraries was carried out by means of a questionnaire requesting information and soliciting documents which was sent to 148 college libraries. This volume includes the survey questionnaire (with the compiled results) followed by the reprinted documents arranged in sections on projects and activities, publicity, financial support, archives, preservation and security, and use policies. One of the reprinted documents has areas too dark to be read, but the remainder are legible. There is no index, but the table of contents lists the college documents included in each section.

Constance Mellott

140. Hardesty, Larry, Jamie Hastreiter, and David Henderson. **Mission Statements for College Libraries.** Chicago, Association of College and Research Libraries, American Library Association, 1985. 107p. $20.00 spiralbound. ISBN 0-8389-6917-8.

This 107-page paperback compiled by librarians of Eckerd College (St. Petersburg, Florida) presents the results of a survey conducted in 1984 to "gather basic data and sample documentation related to the general purposes of college libraries." Based on the responses received from a questionnaire sent to 181 college and university libraries, the survey revealed that only slightly over half the respondents (74) reported having any form of a mission statement.

The publication consists of five sections, the major one being sample mission statements which are intended to provide examples of various philosophies and objectives outlined by particular college libraries to describe their purposes and goals. Reproduced here are ten statements from private institutions with fewer than twenty-five hundred students, eleven from private institutions with more than twenty-five hundred students, one from a public institution with fewer than twenty-five hundred students, and four from public institutions with more than twenty-five hundred students. Other documents included are a copy of the questionnaire with descriptive statistics that resulted from the survey, a copy of the 1975 "Standards for College Libraries," a reprint of "The Mission of an Undergraduate Library (Model Statement)," and statements from six regional accreditation agencies concerning the college library mission.

This compilation should be very useful to college librarians wishing to develop a mission statement or to those reviewing their existing statement. [R: JAL, July 86, p. 179; RQ, Winter 86, p. 266]

Esther Jane Carrier

141. Hayes, Robert M., ed. **Universities, Information Technology, and Academic Libraries: The Next Twenty Years.** Norwood, N.J., Ablex Publishing, 1986. 178p. index. (Libraries and Information Science Series). $29.95. LC 85-22879. ISBN 0-89391-266-2.

This volume prints the papers and proceedings of the Academic Libraries Frontiers Conference held in December 1981. The Council on Library Resources brought together forty-nine academic research library directors and library educators to encourage communication and so improve the education of future academic research library managers. Six leaders in American universities (three presidents, three vice presidents) address these major issues: academic programs and structures, the economic environment, student population, information technology, and the political environment. Final sections list library issues identified by participants and briefly discuss them.

With one exception, one could imagine listening to and being stirred by the speakers. Howard Resnikoff's paper on information technology is as long as all the other papers combined and comes complete with glossary, bibliography, 189 references, and 20 figures and tables. It is obvious that Resnikoff added much to his paper following the conference, particularly since some references are to 1982 publications. Even though the words *information technology* are in the volume's title, this long article distorts the balance in the volume.

In view of the limited attendance at the conference, it is helpful to have these presentations available to a broader audience. But with such rapid changes in society, education, and technology, a volume of conference papers looking to the future should have been issued within six months at most. Nowhere does editor Hayes explain the reason for the delay. As it stands, we have a historic document that, because of its price, merits at best a place in the archival collections of research libraries. [R: C&RL, Nov 86, pp. 617-18; JAL, May 86, p. 113; WLB, May 86, p. 56]

Richard D. Johnson

142. Molyneux, Robert E. **The Gerould Statistics, 1907/08-1961/62.** Washington, D.C., Association of Research Libraries, 1986. 268p. bibliog. $25.00pa. ISBN 0-918006-11-2.

Even though librarians have long been the "keepers" of the statistical data issued by others, they have not been good recorders and caretakers of their own statistical information. It was a surprise to this reviewer to find that a moderately good time series of data does exist on research libraries in the United States. Better yet, however, it is a pleasure to see that someone has paid painstaking attention to them in terms of the key issues of reliability, validity, and comparability. Molyneux has given us a valuable resource for further historical research on academic research libraries. And through his own research use of the data, he has also called into question some of the basic assumptions that have been made about the growth of academic libraries.

The data presented here are the Gerould, or Princeton, data on the major academic research libraries in the United States from 1907 to 1962. The data were initially compiled by James T. Gerould, Librarian at Minnesota and later at Princeton. Approximately sixty different institutions are represented in the data, though not all of them for all years and all variables. The variables for which data are available are basic ones: volumes held, volumes added, materials and salary expenditures, and number of staff. The data are given in the volume in tables and graph form. Even better, however, is the fact that they are available in machine-readable form from the Association of Research Libraries (ARL). Equally useful—and indeed what sets the volume apart from similar works—is the careful attention given to the question of the comparability of the data from institution to institution and over time. Painstaking attention is paid to the data, and detailed notes are given on these processes and the changes made. One has the distinct feeling that a careful researcher provided as good a set of data as is likely ever to be available on these libraries.

Interwoven in the presentation of the institutional data is the author's analysis of the question of whether academic research libraries grow exponentially, as has been commonly stated by some writers. Molyneux shows quite clearly that they do not grow at a regular and consistent rate. This is true for groups of libraries as well as an individual library. Rapid declines and rapid advances, as a percentage increase, are much more common.

Generally, the author's two objectives of data presentation and data analysis complement each other. There are instances, however, particularly in the discussion of the results of the analysis of growth, where the interpretation gets lost in the data. The overall effect of the work, however, is one of careful attention to detail and a good hint of the possibilities open to researchers who will, it is hoped, make good use of the data in the future. (Molyneux has already done some of this in his other work, which is cited in this volume.) Administrators of academic libraries will also find the volume useful in considering the implications of growth on their libraries. Fortunately, the ARL is continuing to maintain and expand on the Gerould statistics by publishing both annual and cumulative statistical series on member libraries. Let us hope that the library associations for other types of libraries will be stimulated to similar efforts so that a greater array of data will be available for research. [R: JAL, Nov 86, p. 319]—Robert V. Williams

143. **OMS Annual Report 1985.** Washington, D.C., Office of Management Studies, Association of Research Libraries, 1985. 29p. free pa. ISSN 0278-7946.

In addition to tallying self-studies (twenty-two), training events (thirty-eight), and clients directly served (over two thousand), the Office of Management Studies's 1985 *Annual Report* provides a view of some of that year's most interesting and worthwhile activity in academic librarianship. After a brief and convenient page of 1985 highlights, the report provides both general background information and a survey of specific 1985 activities in each of the following three areas: "The Academic Library Program," "The Systems and Procedures Exchange Center," "Training and Staff Development Program." The review of these three areas features comments on several notable achievements such as the publication of *The Automation Inventory of Research Libraries* and the very well received Analytical Skills Institutes. A section on applied research and development offers updates on Preservation Planning Studies continuing under a 1984 National Endowment for the Humanities grant, the North American Collections Inventory Project supported by the Andrew W. Mellon Foundation, and the second Institute on Research Libraries for Library School Faculty. Appendices include "Staff and Program Publications," "Advisory Committees, Consultant Trainees and Project Assignments," and a financial statement. The Office of Management Studies's 1985 *Annual Report* reveals the diverse and effective ways in which the office serves ARL member institutions and, with respect to management concerns and issues, leads them.—Jeanne Somers

144. **Research Libraries: The Past 25 Years; The Next 25 Years. Papers for a Festschrift Honoring L. W. Anderson, Director of Libraries, Colorado State University.** Taylor E. Hubbard, ed. Boulder, Colo., Colorado Associated University Press, 1986. 98p. bibliog. $25.00. LC 86-2327. ISBN 0-87081-163-0.

In general, a festschrift, as a special genre, is defined as a memorial volume honoring an individual who distinguished himself or herself within a subject field and/or significantly contributed to a profession. In the case of Le Moyne (Lee) W. Anderson, retired director of libraries at Colorado State University, the festschrift is devoted to research and academic librarianship. In the foreword, Taylor Hubbard, editor of this volume, correctly states that during his thirty-seven years in academic librarianship, Anderson held a number of important professional positions including presidencies of the Association of Research Libraries (1978), the Association of College and Research Libraries (1980), and many other organizations. However, in this reviewer's opinion, his major contribution rests with the development of research/academic librarianship in Colorado. His published bibliography (pp. 95-98) is rather modest—but his contribution to academic librarianship was significant enough to warrant this festschrift.

The present volume consists of contributions by Ralph Ellsworth, Shirley Echelman, Forrest F. Carhart, Jr., Richard M. Dougherty, David H. Stam, Richard W. McCoy, and G. Edward Evans. Also, Anderson compiled a listing of his published works and entries about him, which is erroneously designated as a "bio-bibliography" since there is no autobiographical or biographical sketch of his life. The topical coverage of academic librarianship is rather sporadic, ranging from various functions of academic libraries, the role of the electronic library, collaborative collection development, and browsing in the context of an "information reliant society," to predictions on the major developments in academic librarianship after the year 2000. An especially interesting article, "Research Libraries in 2010," by G. Edward Evans, discusses several models of research librarianship in the next century. Probably the weakest feature of this publication is the absence of a comprehensive biographical study of Anderson's life and activities (the brief biographical data in the foreword are too limited). In addition, the absence of an index limits the reference value of this interesting collection of brief articles on the past, present, and future developments in academic librarianship. The price is somewhat steep for a ninety-eight-page volume.—Lubomyr R. Wynar

145. Stevens, Rolland E., and Linda C. Smith. **Reference Work in the University Library.** Littleton, Colo., Libraries Unlimited, 1986. 436p. index. $37.50. LC 86-173. ISBN 0-87287-449-4.

Reference service in academic libraries has evolved in recent years at a steady rate, especially with the use of computers and other modes of automation. *Reference Work in the University Library* is intended to provide basic instruction in reference for library school students and individuals involved in reference work in academic libraries. The book is designed as a companion to Stevens and Walton's *Reference Work in the Public Library* (see *ARBA* 84, entry 81).

The volume is divided into two major sections dealing with reference strategies and sources. Each section includes annotated listings of sources relevant to reference service. For example, section 1 on strategies consists of chapters on bibliographic, directory, biographical, and statistical information as well as a brief treatment of book reviews, bibliographic instruction, and online database searching. This last chapter is somewhat disappointing considering the impact of databases on academic libraries and librarians.

Most of the volume is taken up by the twenty-six chapters in section 2, which provide brief overviews of reference sources in subject disciplines such as history, music, economics, physics, medicine, and computer science. These chapters are not exhaustive, nor do they intend to be. The book is an updated alternative to Gates's *Guide to the Use of Libraries and Information Sources* in the fifth edition (see *ARBA* 84, entry 68) and the ninth edition of *Guide to Reference Books* (see *ARBA* 77, entry 14), and

worthy of librarians' attention. [R: JAL, Nov 86, p. 319; RQ, Fall 86, p. 117]—Boyd Childress

146. Trochim, Mary Kane, with Arthur Miller, Jr., and William M. K. Trochim. **Measuring the Book Circulation Use of a Small Academic Library Collection: A Manual.** Washington, D.C., Association of Research Libraries, 1985. 73p. bibliog. $40.00pa. ISBN 0-918006-50.

This is a practical do-it-yourself manual "intended to provide sufficient instructions for a library to carry out a book circulation use study with no, or minimal, outside assistance." The manual is based on procedures developed by the Associated Colleges of the Midwest to study collection use in small academic libraries (three hundred thousand volumes or fewer). Discussion of data collection and analysis centers on the circulation sample (completed as books are charged from the library), a stack sample (a systematic random sample of the books on the shelves) and, for those libraries wishing to take the time, a systematic random sample of the shelflist. These sampling techniques are carefully explained and sample work sheets are included. Analyzing the information to provide a basic description of collections and their use includes an examination of call number frequencies, publication year frequencies, month of last circulation, years since circulation, and percent of items never circulated.

The primary theme of the manual is the use of circulation data as a management tool for controlling the growth of library collections. The thesis is that the best predictor of future circulation is past circulation. A major fault with the method outlined here for measuring collection use is that no provision is made to ascertain use of those books removed from the shelves and used within the library. Studies show between four and six in-library uses for each circulation use. In order to make this correction, the authors suggest involving faculty members in the review process. Teaching faculty may be able to explain why certain subject areas have received less attention than other subjects. "It is evident that materials in certain disciplines are used more frequently within the library, so that information about their circulation has relevance only when combined with other sources of information." All these other sources of information are not reviewed by the manual. Relying on faculty and college administrators to correct impressions resulting from a statistical study is risky, to say the least. [R: JAL, July 86, p. 196]—Milton H. Crouch

COMPARATIVE AND INTERNATIONAL LIBRARIANSHIP

General Works

147. Anwar, Mumtaz A. **Information Services in Muslim Countries: An Annotated Bibliography....** London, Mansell; distr., New York, H. W. Wilson, 1985. 146p. index. $42.00. LC 85-17211. ISBN 0-7201-1781-X.

This specialized bibliography of consultants' reports on various aspects of library and information services in the Muslim world is intended to fill a gap in bibliographical coverage of the subject. The bibliography is introduced by two contributed articles, one on the role of the international consultant and another on the Third World perspective on information work in developing countries. The 338 entries include numerous UNESCO documents, U.S. Agency for International Development (USAID) reports, and independent surveys. Arrangement is alphabetical by author with separate indexes for subjects, titles, and joint authors. Each entry includes an annotation and/or statement of keywords, and report or document number as relevant.

As intended by the author, the bibliography does fill a gap in bibliographic coverage; however, this resource will have limited usefulness. As stated in the preface: "Access to these reports in general is limited." Many are listed as restricted and others are available only through USAID or the UNESCO Reports Division in France.

This title provides an interesting perspective on the type and scope of studies and surveys which have been completed. Individuals currently involved in library consulting or responsible for development of library and information services in Third World countries will find it particularly useful.

Because of its specialized nature, this title is recommended primarily for comprehensive collections on library and information science or the Muslim world. Consultants too will want to consider it for personal acquisition.

Ahmad Gamaluddin

148. Parker, J. Stephen. **UNESCO and Library Development Planning.** London, Library Association; distr., Phoenix, Ariz., Oryx Press, 1985. 493p. bibliog. index. $76.00. ISBN 0-85365-863-3.

This extensive study describes planning for library development in many nations, focusing on developing countries, with the support and assistance of the Carnegie Corporation of New York, the British Council, the League of Nations prior to World War II, and UNESCO (United Nations Educational, Scientific & Cultural Organization) after 1945. It is based on the author's thesis research before 1978 but updated and expanded in coverage to include the major organizational changes in UNESCO affecting archives, documentation, library, and information programs. The book is organized in four parts and eleven chapters. Part 1 reviews the origins of the concept of library development planning as evolved and disseminated in the years before the creation of UNESCO. Part 2 deals with the formation of UNESCO and with the development of its early programs, particularly in the library field. Part 3 treats UNESCO's role in the spread of library development planning through consultant missions, conferences, and meetings, culminating in the NATIS (*Nat*ional *I*nformation *S*ystem) Conference in 1974. Part 4 describes the creation of the General Information Programme of UNESCO in 1977 and its relationship to both NATIS and UNISIST (the program for the development of world science information systems initiated by UNESCO and the International Council of Scientific Unions in 1967). This part concludes with a review of UNESCO's efforts to provide guidance to member states on information policy and planning. The last one-third of the book consists of two appendices and an index. Appendix A provides a record of UNESCO Library and information consultants and their missions through 1982 and a bibliography of published and unpublished reports from these missions. Appendix B is a general bibliography of works referred to in the text.

A serious omission in the book is the neglect of the UNISIST program. For example, no mention is made of the number of UNESCO expert missions sponsored by UNISIST prior to and during the NATIS era. Neither is there any mention of the International Serials Data System supported by UNESCO under the auspices of UNISIST. Because of these omissions, the lists of UNESCO consultants and their missions in appendix A is incomplete. Many of the important mission reports sponsored by UNISIST are not included.

Despite these flaws, this book provides in sufficient detail a historical account of library development planning in many parts of the world, and thus deserves a place in all library science collections.

Hwa-Wei Lee

149. Penchansky, Mimi B., and Adam Halicki-Conrad, comps. and eds. **International and Comparative Librarianship: An Annotated Selective Bibliography. Shrinking World/Exploding Information: Developments in**

International Librarianship. New York, Library Association, City University of New York, 1986. 24p. $3.00 spiralbound (postage and handling).

The Library Association of the City University of New York (LACUNY) held its 1986 institute on the theme of international librarianship. This annotated, selective bibliography, prepared for that occasion, comprises some 170 English-language publications grouped into ten categories: "International Librarianship," "International Organizations," "International Programs," "Standards," "Library Services," "Cooperation," "Automation," "Professional Education," "Developing Libraries," "Libraries throughout the World." As is evident from their titles, these categories are so broad and vague as to be quite puzzling to the would-be user; one can hardly predict what kinds of publications will be found therein and there is no index to afford greater specificity. Though the compilers do not say so (there is in fact no prefatory statement of any kind to indicate the scope and purpose of the bibliography), one may therefore infer that this publication had merely the modest aim of offering institute participants a listing of some worthwhile readings broadly related to the subjects to be discussed. This inference is supported by the fact that the annotations are purely descriptive, not critical, and do little more than suggest the contents of the publications listed.

Nevertheless, the LACUNY bibliography may be of value to a broad audience. The subject of international librarianship interests many people but has a dauntingly large literature. It is therefore helpful to have available an identification of the more significant and readable publications. This bibliography constitutes a reasonably adequate means to that end.

Samuel Rothstein

Africa

150. Wise, Michael, comp. and ed. **Aspects of African Librarianship: A Collection of Writings.** London, Mansell; distr., New York, H. W. Wilson, 1985. 326p. index. $65.00. LC 85-15605. ISBN 0-7201-1780-1.

Post-independence governments of Africa have put much energy and resources into the development of libraries. Libraries in many African countries were created at the same time that their librarians were being trained. These librarians witnessed the rapid growth of indigenous African libraries as well as the accelerated mobilization of a cadre of library professionals. Because of the incredible demands placed upon them, many of these librarians have not been able either to record their experiences or to offer their insights in print to the broader library world. This volume attempts (and succeeds admirably) to remedy this deficit.

The volume includes twelve essays by African librarians about "librarianship in countries between the Sahara and South Africa, where English is a language of universal communication." The essays cover a broad range of topics including the development of university libraries, collection development, staff development, library education, archives, and commonalities of library and information services among several African countries. A comprehensive index is included.

Anyone interested in a series of fascinating essays on African librarianship will find a treasure in Wise's book. The essays are all well written, well documented, and well edited. The essays are a fitting monument to the triumph of librarianship over adverse social and physical conditions. [R: JAL, Sept 86, p. 245]

Robert H. Burger

Asia

151. Anuar, Hedwig. **Issues in Southeast Asian Librarianship.** Brookfield, Vt., Gower Publishing, 1985. 214p. maps. index. $38.95. ISBN 0-566-03523-5.

Libraries and librarianship in the countries participating in the Congress of Southeast Asian Librarians (CONSAL) have flourished, if not necessarily prospered, largely to the credit of outstanding librarians. The author of this collection, Hedwig Anuar, Director of the National Library of Singapore, is exemplary for her contributions to and concern for the profession and the region as well as Singapore, evident in her seminal *Blueprint for Public Library Development in Malaysia* (1968). The first eleven chapters of this collection are papers presented locally and internationally between 1972 and 1983 focusing on Singapore and the other CONSAL countries of Indonesia, Malaysia, the Philippines, and Thailand. The twelfth, "Recent Developments," is an update written especially for this volume. Each chapter has bibliographic citations, and a number include tables and bibliographic appendices, which by now are mostly of historical interest. A brief, selective index is included. The collection is divided into three sections which provide an overview of Anuar's nontechnical concerns: "National Libraries," "Public Libraries," and "Provision of Books and Readership Development." As one would expect from the public presentations of a national leader, emphasis is on description over criticism.

Particularly for libraries lacking the published CONSAL proceedings, this is a useful introduction to library development in Southeast

Asia and an excellent companion volume and update to Wijasuriya's *The Barefoot Librarian: Library Developments in Southeast Asia, with Special Reference to Malaysia* (1975), especially the chapter, "The Southeast Asian Public and the Disappearing Barefoot Librarian." The discussion and documentation of library growth in Southeast Asia afford lessons and comparisons for considering library development elsewhere in the Third World.　　　　　　K. Mulliner

152. **Areas of Cooperation in Library Development in Asian and Pacific Regions. Papers Presented at the 1983 Joint Annual Program of the Asian/Pacific American Librarians Association and Chinese-American Librarians Association June 28-29, 1983, Los Angeles, California.** Sally C. Tseng, Hwa-Wei Lee, and K. Mulliner, eds. Athens, Ohio, Chinese-American Librarians Association, 1985. 63p. $10.00pa. LC 84-71838. ISBN 0-930691-00-8.

Like many proceedings of conferences of library associations, this sixty-three-page book brings together papers which are not closely related to one another or the theme of the conference, which is "Some Aspects of Library Development in Asian and Pacific Regions." The conference was held in Los Angeles, California, 28-29 June 1983, and the proceedings were not published until 1985. Seven papers, in addition to the keynote speech and three appendices, are included in the publication. The papers vary in length and substance. Some, such as Roberts's "The Role Played by UNESCO in the Development of Library and Information Services in Asia and the Pacific Regions," Lee's "Library Internships ...," Tsuneishi's "The Library of Congress and Asian Studies," and Wang's "Library and Information Services in Taiwan ...," deal directly with Asian librarianship and the theme of the conference. Others, such as Hayes's "Cooperative Research," Lindemann's "Evaluating the Depository Library System of the World Bank," and Chen's "A Crying Need for Qualified Personnel ...," are of more general nature and not directly related to the theme of the conference.

On the whole, the slim proceedings provide for a very interesting and light reading on international librarianship in general and some aspects of library development in Asian and Pacific regions in particular.

　　　　　　　　　　Mohammed M. Aman

153. Deshpande, K. S. **University Library System in India.** New Delhi, Sterling Publishers; distr., New York, Apt Books, 1985. 153p. $22.50.

This book is a collection of essays written by K. S. Deshpande, a well-known Indian library administrator and educator. These essays on many aspects of the University Library System in India were published in various library journals of India from 1970 to 1977.

The book also includes a few papers presented by the author at various library conferences. The topics included are: "University Education and Libraries"; "Acquiring Books"; "Runaway Prices and Inelastic Budgets"; "User Oriented Libraries"; "Staff Pattern"; "Library Architecture"; "Karnatak University Library – A Model"; "Acquiring Indian Publications"; "Duties, Responsibilities and Job"; "Analysis of Sections"; "Keeping Libraries Open for Longer Hours"; "Changing Concepts"; "Library Services on a Campus"; and "University Libraries and Rural Development."

The articles are well written, but many of them do not have any references to support the facts and figures given in the articles. The library field in India has changed considerably since 1977 but the articles have not been updated. In spite of these weaknesses, the book has much to offer for students of library science, historians, and administrators of Indian academic libraries. It will certainly be a good addition for library school libraries interested in developing collections for comparative or Asian librarianship.　　　　Ravindra Nath Sharma

154. **Handbook of Libraries, Archives and Information Centers in India. Volume 1: Libraries and Archives.** B. M. Gupta and others, eds. New Delhi, Information Industry Publications; distr., Columbia, Mo., South Asia Books, 1985. 368p. index. $42.00. ISBN 0-8364-1574-4.

This volume is the first in a proposed five-volume set covering not only libraries and archives in India but information systems, services, and programs, and professional organizations as well. The present volume includes four sections, on (1) national libraries; (2) academic libraries; (3) special libraries; and (4) education, research, and manpower. Only three national libraries are treated in the first section: the National Library of India, the National Medical Library, and the Indian Agricultural Research Institute Library. Under the section on academic libraries, there are three parts, covering all of the major university libraries, the college libraries, and school libraries. Book collections, library services, finances, and staffing patterns, etc., are covered in each description. Section 3 describes ten types of special libraries, including medical, law, agricultural, and government. Each chapter is written by a representative of that type (e.g., the author of the chapter on museum libraries is the senior librarian at the National Museum in New Delhi), and each has a list of additional readings at the end.

The final section contains eight chapters on various aspects of research and manpower. There is a fairly comprehensive index which apparently will cover the whole set but was for the first volume only at the time of publication. The work gives a good overall view of libraries in India and fairly detailed accounts of some specific libraries. Particularly helpful for someone interested in the topic are the bibliographies at the ends of the chapters. The work brings together a great deal of information that might otherwise be difficult to find. — Lucille Whalen

155. Kumar, Girja. **Library Development in India.** New Delhi, Vikas Publishing House; distr., New York, Advent Books, 1986. 568p. index. $45.00. ISBN 0-7069-3023-1.

It is very difficult to deal with the development of all types of libraries of a country in one book. But an honest attempt has been made by a well-known Indian librarian, Girja Kumar, to deal with all aspects of library development in India. The book is divided into seven sections and each section deals with different aspects of Indian librarianship. "Historical Perspective," "National Library and Information," "Library Management," "Collection Development," "User Education," "Academic Colonialism," and "S. R. Ranganathan" are discussed in detail in twenty-nine chapters of the book. The credit for the development has been given to the father of Indian librarianship, S. R. Ranganathan. In fact, this is the first attempt to give a clear picture of the situation, based on the lifetime experience of a librarian and an administrator. The author has clearly mentioned the problems facing Indian libraries and has made a few good suggestions to improve the situation. Kumar is of the opinion that the introduction of modern technology will solve many problems and lead to much-needed close cooperation, sharing of resources, and birth of a new type of librarian in India.

The emphasis in this book is more on academic libraries than on special or public libraries. It is a well-written book and is recommended for all types of libraries, librarians, library educators, and others interested in Indian librarianship. [R: LJ, 1 Sept 86, p. 172] — Ravindra Nath Sharma

156. **Ranganathan's Philosophy: Assessment, Impact and Relevance. Proceedings of the International Conference....** T. S. Rajagopalan, ed. New Delhi, Vikas Publishing House; distr., New York, Advent Books, 1986. 690p. $60.00. ISBN 0-7069-3027-4.

Among those who know the history of libraries and librarianship, it is generally argued that the late S. R. Ranganathan of India, inventor of the "Colon" classification system, did more than any other individual to modernize the library and information science profession and library education in India. The proceedings of this conference include over sixty papers on all aspects of library and information science to which Ranganathan contributed, such as classification, indexing, information technology, Five Laws (which explain Ranganathan's philosophy of librarianship), library education, library movement, and reference services. Many well-known librarians and library educators from all over the world, including Derek Austin, D. J. Foskette, M. A. Gopinath, P. N. Kaula, Anis Khurshid, Girja Kumar, F. W. Lancaster, D. W. Langridge, and Peter Havard Williams presented papers included in the proceedings. The book is divided into eleven sections. Each section includes papers on one particular aspect of librarianship, such as "Law of Library Science," "Indexing Models," "Document Description," "Management of Library Information Science," "Standardization in Library and Documentations," "Reference Services," and a short biography of S. R. Ranganathan.

The majority of the papers are well written and there is a wealth of material on Ranganathan and Indian librarianship in this volume. It is recommended for all librarians, library educators, researchers, and others interested in the history of Indian libraries and S. R. Ranganathan. — Ravindra Nath Sharma

Australia

157. Cook, John. **Information, Enrichment and Delight: Public Libraries in Western Australia.** Halifax, N.S., School of Library Service, Dalhousie University, 1985. 233p. bibliog. index. (Occasional Papers Series, No. 35). $16.50 spiralbound. ISBN 0-7703-0176-2; ISSN 0318-7403.

This work is a modified version of an M.A. thesis originally submitted by John Cook to the History Department of the University of Western Australia in 1983. Cook, born in Western Australia and now working as a professional librarian in Canberra, describes the evolution of the Library Board of Western Australia from 1952 to 1976 and its tangible achievement of building a much-admired statewide system of public libraries. This history opens with a chapter on the precursors—commencing about 1850—of free public libraries in Western Australia, a period highlighted by the foundation in Perth in 1887 of the Victoria Public Library as a civic monument commemorating Queen Victoria's fifty-year reign. This is followed by a chapter on adult education, army education, and the movement toward free public libraries. Chapters 3-5 span the Library Board from 1952 to 1959, 1959 to 1971, and 1971 to 1976.

Cook's narrative is very much the story of the influence of two very strong but very different individuals, Fred Alexander and Francis Aubie Sharr. Professor Alexander taught history at the University of Western Australia from the 1920s to the 1960s. He was also director of the university's adult education service from 1941 to 1953 and officer in charge of army education in Western Australia during World War II; he was deeply involved in efforts to upgrade library services in the state. Alexander played a major role in getting legislation to establish the Library Board and has chaired it from its beginning in 1952. Sharr, formerly deputy city librarian of Manchester, was the executive officer of the Library Board from 1953 to 1976. As the introduction puts it, "He brought with him to Perth clearly thought out and firmly held views about the role and organization of libraries in modern society and as the principal library professional in the State he was able to imprint his ideas on the library system which evolved so rapidly under his leadership" (p. v). The history ends in 1976 with Sharr's retirement and the appointment of his successor, Robert Sharman, executive officer of the Library Board and state librarian.

All in all, Cook's history includes extensive use of direct quotation in the text and examination of a variety of unpublished sources (e.g., minutes of library committees and those of the Library Board of Western Australia, government agency files, University of Western Australia records, interviews), and published sources (library annual reports; books; periodicals such as *Australian Library Journal, Library Association Record, Libri*, newspapers, and so forth). The work concludes with nine appendices (members of Victoria Public Library Committee of Management, 1888-1911; members and annual expenditures of the Library Board of Western Australia, 1952-1976, etc.) and an index. Wiley J. Williams

Canada

158. **Library Systems in Alberta: Guidelines for Development. Vol. 1: Pre-Establishment.** rev. ed. Edmonton, Alta., Library Services Branch, Alberta Culture, 1985. 21p. illus. maps. bibliog. free pa. ISBN 0-919411-24-X.

Libraries considering the possibility of forming regional systems may find useful information in this careful and complete description of the process recommended for libraries in the Canadian province of Alberta. This volume deals only with the pre-establishment phase of setting up a library system; a future volume will give information about the transition and post-establishment/pre-operational phases of the process. The pre-establishment phase in volume 1 covers four stages: the informal interest group, the establishment of a steering committee, the development of a project team, and the interim board. In moving from stage to stage, the process becomes progressively more formal. Each succeeding phase is also eligible for specified consultant services and funding from the Alberta Culture Library Services Branch. Appendices include information about existing Alberta systems, examples of possible structure of the steering committee, a sample mission statement, and a copy of the legal regulations governing the establishment of library systems. A list of readings is also included. The information in this brochure deals specifically with Alberta, but the clarity of the presentation could serve as a model in other jurisdictions where comparable guidelines are not available.

Adele M. Fasick

Europe

159. Balbi, Adriano. **A Statistical Essay on the Libraries of Vienna and the World.** Jefferson, N.C., McFarland, 1986. 162p. index. $29.95. LC 84-43235. ISBN 0-89950-149-4.

This book is a translation of a work first published in 1835 by an Italian scholar, geographer, and statistician, Adriano Balbi. It is a classic work in the history of libraries, as well as in the history of statistics. The translator's preface places the work in its historical context. There is also an introduction by Balbi, which provides a flavor for the remainder of the work. In ten short chapters Balbi then describes and discusses the collections of the Imperial Library at Vienna and compares and contrasts it with other libraries in that city and in Europe. There are many tables and lists, as well as lengthy footnotes. The two appendices are of lesser importance to library historians, since they deal primarily with comparative demography. The book concludes with a chronological list of works by Balbi, and an author/title/subject index. These features enhance its usefulness. The inclusion of the original title page of the book opposite the modern one is also a valuable feature of the work. Although the book's audience is limited primarily to scholars and students of comparative and international librarianship and library history, it is nevertheless an important addition to library science collections supporting library school curricula. It is also an appropriate and valuable resource for academic and research library collections in the history of science, especially statistics. [R: WLB, May 86, p. 55]

Susan J. Freiband

160. Buzás, Ladislaus. **German Library History, 800-1945.** Jefferson, N.C., McFarland, 1986. 570p. bibliog. index. $55.00. LC 84-43197. ISBN 0-89950-175-3.

The detail and comprehensiveness of this English translation of Ladislaus Buzás's three-volume work (Wiesbaden, Ludwig Reichert Verlag, 1975-1978) is impossible to overestimate. Until this remarkable effort, students of German library history were limited to cursory accounts or brief references found in English texts and translations. If they were fluent in German, the classic *Handbuch der Bibliothekswissenschaft*, volume 3, was a valuable asset, as were other untranslated studies of German library history published prior to 1975. However, the three-volume work by Buzás was an outstanding addition to the literature in and of itself; this carefully rendered translation has made that resource accessible to all English-speaking library historians.

The translator, William Douglas Boyd, has brought his own expertise and that of other well-known historians and specialists to bear on the immense task of making the Buzás work "readable in English. At times this has meant straying from the style of the German text" (translator's preface). The organization follows the original, but has combined three separate volumes into one: "The Middle Ages" (*Deutsche Bibliotheksgeschicte des Mittalalters*; "The Early Modern Period, 1500-1800" (*Deutsche Bibliotheksgeschicte der Neuzeit*); and "The Modern Period, 1800-1945" (*Deutsche Bibliotheksgeschicte der neusten Zeit*). Of particular value are the extensive bibliographies for each volume, consisting of general works, journals, collections and series, bibliographies, etc., followed by more specific references related to the chapter topics. The full bibliography is found on pp. 483-534; there is also an excellent index (pp. 535-570).

The section on the Middle Ages is organized by two introductory/historical chapters that place German library history in its larger perspective. These are followed by individual chapters on monastery, council, university, private and other libraries, with a concluding chapter on the nature of library administration of that era. The second volume opens with an overview of the cultural history of the early modern period, reviews types of libraries (e.g., court, university, denominational, private, special), and turns to specific discussions of the contemporary library literature, the role of the librarian, collection development, arrangement, catalogs, use, binding, and the library building.

The final volume/section again provides a historical survey of the modern period and chapters on types of libraries, and concludes with discussions of library theory, the librarian, the growth of collections, arrangements, catalogs, use, binding, and the building.

This is not a work to be read casually; it is overwhelming in its details and essentially becomes a reference source of people, statistics, the culture and society, and the theory of libraries and librarianship in Germany. No issue related to libraries—whether budget, book trade, classification schemes, stack areas, even library handwriting—seems to have been omitted. It is truly a work of immeasurable value to any historian who looks to the key relationships of German history to U.S. development as well as to a basic understanding of Germany and its library development. Boyd's translation is a reflection of the original achievement of Buzás; it is "justifiably ... described as monumental, and within the field of library history these volumes are exemplary" (translator's preface). [R: LJ, May 86, p. 55]

Laurel Grotzinger

161. **Nonbibliographic Data Banks in Science & Technology: Papers Presented at a CODATA/Unesco/DFI Seminar, Stockholm, October 15-22, 1983.** Stephan Schwarz, David G. Watson, and Olov Alvfeldt, eds. Paris, ICSU Press; distr., New York, UNIPUB, 1985. 218p. illus. $39.50. LC 85-21951. ISBN 0-930357-06-X.

This is a collection of lecture texts for a course organized in 1983 in Stockholm, Sweden, by CODATA (the Committee on Data for Science and Technology of the ICSU, the International Council of Scientific Unions), UNESCO, and the Swedish Delegation for Scientific and Technical Information (DFI). Designed for information specialists in applied science and technology, the stated course objectives were "to service the current and future role of nonbibliographic data services; to describe and critically review nonbibliographic data services and services currently available to different users; to analyse the particular problems of data production, data service organization, and utilization of nonbibliographic data in science and technology; and to examine through R&D case studies problems in the application of non-bibliographic data and lessons to be drawn by data producers, by service organizations, and for user education." Course attendants came from about twenty countries.

The twenty-seven printed presentations reflect roughly (1) summary information of the course sponsors, (2) general background about scientific, nonbibliographic databases and their users, (3) descriptive examples of several data files, (4) discussion of planning, marketing, and service issues associated with the application of database management systems, and (5) reflections on the role of libraries in this emerging area. Summaries of a discussion on problems of developing countries and of a panel debate on the future of data banks in science and technology conclude the text. Listings of the program, the faculty, and the participants end the volume.

For American readers, this publication offers interesting information on what is occurring overseas, although a few U.S. presenters gave overviews. The summaries of specific databases illustrate the highly specialized content of non-bibliographic files, implying the need for a subject, technical background for effective use. The lack of a subject index and of a topical contents page significantly detracts from the reference use of the publication. However, as a textbook, it offers thought-provoking material for the student of this area of information services.

Danuta A. Nitecki

Great Britain

162. **Library and Information Plans: Report on a Feasibility Study....** Stamford, England, CPI Publications, 1986. 56p. bibliog. (British Library R&D Report, No. 5890). £9.50pa. ISBN 0-906011-32-9.

The report presented in this publication describes a study carried out in association with Cambridgeshire (England) City Council, for the British Library Research and Development Department, by Capital Planning Information. The focus of the study is on examining the feasibility of a planned approach to the provision of library and information services in a county (Cambridgeshire). The report presents the background to the study, including a profile of Cambridgeshire, its libraries, and its information services. The methodology, involving fifty interviews, is discussed, along with the interview results. There is a section on output and performance measures, and on developing an outline plan for Cambridgeshire. The final sections are devoted to conclusions and recommendations and references. Appendices include lists of contacts, initial letter, and a suggested analytical approach to planning by user need. United States developments in the area of planning for public library services are mentioned in the introductory section. The bibliography includes the *Planning Process for Public Libraries* (American Library Association, 1980) and *Output Measures for Public Libraries* (American Library Association, 1982). The introduction notes that "the difference between the present work and American efforts in this area relates to testing of the acceptability of involving *all* the main library and information services in a locality in a planned approach from the beginning" (p. 2). The report is an interesting and useful document for comparative and international studies of public librarianship. It would be an appropriate addition to library science collections, especially in schools of library and information science.

Susan J. Freiband

163. **Reader Services in Polytechnic Libraries.** John Fletcher, ed. Brookfield, Vt., COPOL, in association with Gower Publishing, 1985. 244p. index. $53.95. LC 85-10085. ISBN 0-566-03528-6.

This sourcebook in library science traces the development of polytechnical institutions in the United Kingdom, and the growth and development of libraries within these institutes of higher education. Study and comparison is made of their size, areas of specialization, and nature of services to their users. Following the introduction, or overview, of "polytechnics" and their libraries, authorities in the field discuss current library practices in the areas of the social sciences, business, management, law, art and design, and the humanities. The needs of teachers of education are discussed, followed by consideration of library services for the part-time student, online searching, and nonbook materials and services. Each section includes a bibliography of related journal and book citations to support further research. An index follows a "tailpiece," an introspective consideration by the editor of past and future progressions.

Published in association with COPOL, the Council of Polytechnical Librarians, this publication strives to assess current practices in polytechnical libraries, especially those services which relate directly to the user. The value of the book lies in the clear, concise style of writing, and the depth of coverage contributed by practitioners in the field of polytechnical librarianship. Its content is highly specific in nature, and pertains to the situation in the United Kingdom, so that purchase of the book in the United States will not be widespread. Purchase is recommended for polytechnical institutions in the United States and for research collections in international and domestic librarianship.

Barbara Sproat

164. **Student Reading Needs and Higher Education.** By David Baker. London, Library Association; distr., Chicago, American Library Association, 1986. 214p. bibliog. index. $25.00. ISBN 0-85365-926-5.

This collection of fourteen essays commissioned by the University, College and Research Section of The Library Association addresses the present problems of meeting the information and reading needs of British higher education. The contributors address such issues as the evolution of library provisions for undergraduate students; the problems and the efforts being made to meet student reading needs in different types of institutions, libraries, and individual subject areas; the relationships between libraries, booksellers, and publishers; the impact of changing teaching patterns on academic staff and the library; and likely future developments and problems relating to undergraduate teaching — all in the context of financial cutbacks, advancing technology, and the changes in the number and types of students and the structure of higher education. While these essays provide a good overview of the current status, the present problems, and the future prospects for meeting the information needs of British higher education, they are less relevant in their details to American academic librarianship, except to echo some similar problems facing higher education in the United States. We, too, have the problems of reduced book budgets, students unprepared for independent study and use of library resources, too many faculty tied to reserve reading lists and textbooks rather than exploiting the library collections, and the conflicting demands of research and curriculum support. But much of the time, the issues addressed are applicable primarily to the unique British academic structure and environment. This work will be valuable to those interested in British librarianship, but less so to others.   Blaine H. Hall

Latin America

165. McCarthy, Cavan M. **The Introduction of Automated Library and Information Services in a Newly Industrialized Country: A Case Study of the Brazilian Experience.** London, Vine Press, and Halifax, N.S., School of Library Service, Dalhousie University, 1986. 296p. bibliog. (Occasional Papers Series, No. 37). $16.50 spiralbound. ISBN 0-7703-0169-X.

McCarthy's book, a reworking of his Ph.D. thesis, is the result of a systematic survey of the thirty-one most significant automated installations in five Brazilian cities. These institutions were visited by the author. Data were gathered from other installations by means of a questionnaire.

Actually, the book contains much more than the title implies. Besides the survey and discussion of the results, approximately one-half of the book is devoted to such topics as a geopolitical description of contemporary Brazil, information on Brazilian culture, the role of libraries, the general use of computers, and automation in both industrialized and less industrialized countries. These chapters are interesting for even the general reader, for they describe the way in which the political culture in general and the bureaucracy in particular affect information use in Brazil.

The author's underlying objective for this study was "to improve the quality of library and bibliographic information systems in Brazil." In reporting the results of his survey, he makes frequent useful comparisons between automation in Brazil and automation in both the United States and Britain. The work includes a comprehensive bibliography; there is no index.

McCarthy has collected and presented a great deal of useful information. For the most part, the most interesting and valuable chapters are those that deal with Brazil and its information culture. The report of his survey results, however, is partially flawed by the lack of adequate explanation for the conclusions he draws from it and the questionable notion of his having "proven" his hypotheses (see, for example, pp. 148-49). Generally speaking, however, this work should be examined by anyone interested in automated library and automated information services in less industrialized countries.

Robert H. Burger

166. Rosenberg, Victor, and Gretchen Whitney, eds. **The Transfer of Scholarly, Scientific and Technical Information between North and South America: Proceedings of a Conference.** Metuchen, N.J., Scarecrow, 1986. 701p. index. $59.50. LC 86-15625. ISBN 0-8108-1935-X.

Conference proceedings can often make for deadly reading. Happily, this publication is an exception. The matters under discussion here are controversial and represent the first full-blown airing of a variety of views on the plight of information science in Latin America. This volume is the result of a 1983 conference held at the University of Michigan, at which twenty-one librarians and information specialists from North and South America debated matters of acquiring and distributing scientific and technical information.

The papers presented at this conference concentrate on several major areas of concern: the need for an information policy to be established in the developing nations; the rather lopsided dependence of the Latin American nations on the United States (and, to a lesser extent, on Canada) for information technology; the problem of equal access to information through bibliographic systems; the role of scholarly information; and the impact of electronic publishing. The participants identified five fundamental problems which impede the resolution of the above concerns. These problem areas include a weak national infrastructure, unresolved definitions (e.g., what is really meant by *information*), the uncertain status of information professionals, and the undetermined role of information within national development. Perhaps the most fundamental and underlying problem, however (which is evident in nearly all of the papers), is the dependent relationship between North and South America.

An array of specific concerns fills the pages of this volume. The transcripts of discussion sessions are included here, which complement the papers. However, some of the exchanges are in Spanish and are not translated (I confess here to a "northern" bias). Some examples will convey the flavor of the conference discussions: the clash of cultural values; how to decide what information to provide, and to whom; gaps in technological advances; unsatisfactory interaction with users; the intellectual development of librarians. The dialog that emerges from these sessions is intelligent, lively, and often blunt—and gives the reader some hope for progress in many of the areas under discussion. A wealth of ideas is exchanged here; there is much raw material requiring further research and investigation.

An attractive feature of this volume is its format. The major themes and conclusions of the conference are clearly set forth in the opening pages and help give the general reader a basic understanding of the issues to be discussed. In fact, the thirteen-page summary of the conference conclusions actually amounts to a kind of "Information Policy Manifesto" that can be distributed widely throughout the Third World nations. Most of the papers are published in English, with a Spanish abstract. The few Spanish papers contain an English abstract. There is a useful glossary of acronyms and abbreviations, and a brief subject index. Though quite expensive, this is a volume that belongs in most university libraries, and certainly in graduate information science collections.

Thomas A. Karel

CONSERVATION

167. Bello, Susan E. **Cooperative Preservation Efforts of Academic Libraries.** Campaign, Ill., Graduate School of Library and Information Science, University of Illinois, 1986. 52p. index. $3.00pa. ISSN 0276-1769.

One of the critical areas in librarianship which has emerged in the last few years is the preservation of printed material in our research institutions. The task is massive, quite beyond the resources of single institutions. It became imperative that regional and national plans be made and carried out if great national resources were to be preserved.

Efforts at national preservation programs, beginning in 1954 and continuing into the 1980s, are chronicled in this study. National preservation plans are studied in the three major chapters: "Early Proposals for National Plans 1954-1972," "The Preservation Program of the Research Libraries Group," "The Evolution of a National Preservation Program in the 1980s." The result is a satisfactory summary of national preservation activities over a thirty-year period and points the way to possible future action. The list of references serves as a bibliography citing the important published papers and reports on the subject, and there is an index.

Dean H. Keller

168. Morrow, Carolyn Clark, and Carole Dyal. **Conservation Treatment Procedures: A Manual of Step-by-Step Procedures for the Maintenance and Repair of Library Materials.** 2d ed. Littleton, Colo., Libraries Unlimited, 1986. 225p. illus. bibliog. $19.50pa. LC 86-20948. ISBN 0-87287-437-0.

Directed to both the preservation supervisor and the technician, this book gives seventeen step-by-step procedures for book repairs, maintenance of library materials, and protective enclosures. Morrow, a well known conservator, also includes sections on organizing and supervising a conservation workshop and deciding on appropriate treatments for various materials. Although this second edition is almost identical to the 1982 edition in format and coverage of subject matter, it exhibits a refinement of teaching technique and prose which makes it preferable to the old edition. Directions for each procedure follow a specified format and contain much detail. Since the techniques should be learned sequentially, however, they are not repeated in later instructions. The reader is referred to earlier instructions when necessary. All new photographs add to the clarity of the directions although the photograph quality is a bit grainy. Six of the procedures are completely new to the second edition, and both the bibliography and the list of suppliers have been extensively revised. As conservation departments become more prevalent in libraries, repair methods and materials are undergoing constant revision. This book reflects those changes well and thus is useful to the expert as well as to the beginner.

Linda S. Keir

169. **The Preservation of Library Materials: A CUL Handbook: Guidelines and Procedures.** New York, Preservation Department, Columbia University Libraries, 1985. 1v. (various paging). $10.00 looseleaf with binder.

Although titled a preservation handbook, this manual concentrates on procedures for binding and rebinding library materials at Columbia University. In well-organized sections it leads the reader/librarian through decisions on type of binding; labeling procedures; completing binding forms; retrieving material in process; and using an automated system for binding serials. The last quarter of the book deals with replacement of worn-out or destroyed library materials: replacement options, guidelines for microfilming, and procedures for ordering in-house microfilms. A few pages concentrate on preservation of materials by proper shelving, cleaning, and handling. Examples of forms used at Columbia, such as binding slips and the "preservation microfilming recommendation form" are included.

In fact, the whole manual is very specifically written for the Columbia University Libraries and as such may be of limited value to other institutions, especially smaller libraries. The details of specific New York area binderies, for example, will not be useful to many other readers. The value of the book lies rather in its use as a model on which others may base a similar, locally specific document, substituting individual binderies, procedures, and so on.

Before using this manual the reader should be familiar with conservation practices as explained in one of the basic manuals such as the Cunhas' *Conservation of Library Materials* (Scarecrow, 1983). — Linda S. Keir

COPYRIGHT

170. Talab, R. S. **Commonsense Copyright: A Guide to the New Technologies.** Jefferson, N.C., McFarland, 1986. 162p. bibliog. index. $14.95. LC 85-43593. ISBN 0-89950-224-5.

This is an informative little book which should be helpful to educators and librarians. The book begins with a copyright primer, then devotes nine chapters to applying the concepts to the duplication, transmission, and performance of copyrighted materials. Printed materials, music, broadcast materials, video, and computer programs are covered, and nothing seems to have been omitted. The footnotes and bibliography are extensive and excellent.

In spite of the author's diligence, there are two problems with this book. First, the author scrupulously presents the opinions of others, but rarely expresses her own position on confusing or controversial issues. Her earlier publications demonstrate her competence; her diffidence is regrettable.

Second, the book suffers terribly from bad editing. Proofreading should not be confused with editing—it is just proofreading. This author, like most authors, needed a skillful editor to help her improve sections that are unclear, need expansion, or are disconnected. In addition, the book contains factual errors that would have been eliminated through competent peer review. It is sad that this fine book suffers from such carelessness. Recommended, but hope for an improved second edition. — Jerome K. Miller

EDUCATION

171. Bobinski, George S., ed. **Current and Future Trends in Library and Information Science Education.** Champaign, Ill., Graduate School of Library and Information Science, University of Illinois, 1986. 788p. (*Library Trends*, Vol. 34, No. 4). $8.00pa. ISSN 0024-2594.

Library Trends is a quarterly journal of librarianship which is characterized as providing a medium for evaluative recapitulation of current thought and practice, searching for those ideas and procedures which hold the greatest potentialities for the future. Leigh Estabrook, dean of the University of Illinois Graduate School of Library and Information Science, serves as editor. George Bobinski, dean and professor of the School of Information and Library Studies has made an outstanding contribution, as this spring 1986 issue is impressive in content, style, and quality.

The articles in this issue represent papers presented at the Library Education Centennial Symposium held at Columbia University on 27-28 June 1986. The symposium was hosted at the Columbia University School of Library Science and was sponsored by ALISE with the financial support of the H. W. Wilson Company. Bobinski also chaired the Education Centennial Committee which planned the symposium. The purpose of the symposium was to celebrate the one hundredth anniversary of the establishment of the first library school in the United States, founded by Melvil Dewey at Columbia University in January 1887.

The topics focus on current and future trends in library information science education and cover a full range of related areas including the following: accreditation, master's and doctoral programs, faculty, students, continuing education, job market, role of the associations, the context within higher education, and education for librarianship in the next century.

The outstanding aspect of this issue is that each author is recognized as a national authority in the area in which he or she has written and each has presented provocative ideas in a stimulating manner. Of particular value are the quantitative data which have been collected and analyzed in a number of the articles. Recently library and information science education has been undergoing scrutiny and change; this issue is extremely timely and is essential reading for all library educators and all those who are concerned about the future of the profession. [R: JAL, Nov 86, pp. 315-16]

Margaret E. Chisholm

172. **Continuing Education for the Library Information Professions.** By William G. Asp and others. Hamden, Conn., Library Professional Publications/Shoe String Press, 1985. 348p. bibliog. index. $35.00; $25.00pa. LC 85-18204. ISBN 0-208-01897-2; 0-208-01898-0pa.

The authors of this work are advocates of continuing education (CE) and as they describe the contributions of various organizations and agencies to this activity, they do so with the assumption that CE is a basic responsibility. Stone provides an excellent overview of the development of education for librarianship and the role CE has played, both in the schools of library and information science and in professional associations. Although not a priority of either, CE has slowly gained ground as an important aspect of the educational continuum. Guiding principles and policies of CE are set forth, means of assessing quality are discussed, and ways to market CE are mentioned; the contributions of library associations, state library agencies, regional library systems and schools of library/information science are described. Based on surveys, the authors indicate what the providers are doing and then proceed to discuss what they should be doing. CE is seen as a responsibility by each of the provider groups surveyed. Their commitment and levels of activity vary, depending upon priorities and available resources.

The authors have provided a one-step information resource for those involved in continuing education as providers or as consumers. Past studies and current practice are summarized, thus giving a stepping-off point for further activity. Although far from unbiased, this book provides important and useful information. [R: JAL, Nov 86, p. 309; LJ, 1 Mar 86, p. 74; WLB, June 86, p. 75]

Ann E. Prentice

173. Davis, Donald G., Jr., and Phyllis Dain, eds. **History of Library and Information Science Education.** Champaign, Ill., Graduate School of Library and Information Science, University of Illinois, 1986. 1v. (various paging). (*Library Trends*, Vol. 34, No. 3). $8.00pa. ISSN 0024-2594.

Devoted to a centennial celebration of librarianship, which now includes sixty-three accredited library schools, this illuminating volume presents nine interpretive chapters of historical and sociological thought concerning library education. "Not intended to be a comprehensive or definitive treatment of the subject," several of the papers were commissioned for this issue, while others are based upon original research or theoretical speculation.

Fran Miksa provides a fascinating look at Melvil Dewey, the educator and curriculum designer; Wayne Wiegand examines the professionalization and socialization of library and information science students; Mary Niles Maack explores the changing role and status of women in library education; William Williamson discusses student trends over the past century; Laurel Grotzinger recalls how curriculum and teaching styles have evolved over the years; Philip Metzger provides an overview of teaching materials, which include textbooks, media, and periodicals; Elizabeth Stone synthesizes the growth of continuing education activities; and Michael Harris concludes with a stimulating, though critical, view of library and information science research.

All in all, this issue provides an excellent window through which to view our profession, and to enhance our understanding of its present and future directions. It will be particularly useful to graduate library education classes, and to those curious about our past. [R: JAL, Sept 86, p. 246]

Ilene F. Rockman

174. **Directory of the Association for Library and Information Science Education 1985-86.** Charles D. Patterson and Janet Phillips, eds. State College, Pa., Association for Library and Information Science Education, 1985. 129p. (*Journal of Education for Library and Information Science*, Directory Issue). $10.00pa. ISSN 0748-5786.

Directories for professional associations are basic reference sources and this title is no exception. It provides data on faculty associated with library education programs; included are sixty-four institutional (i.e., accredited); sixteen associate institutional (i.e., unaccredited), and seven international affiliate institutional library schools. Approximately eighteen hundred individuals who taught either full- or part-time during the 1984/1985 academic year are identified. The Association for Library and Information Science (ALISE), the former Association of American Library Schools (AALS), has produced its annual, separately published compilation for sixteen years. This edition provides a welcome return of its section listing faculty specializations. That section contains fifty-five teaching areas (01 "Introduction to Library and Information Science" to 55 "Publishing") with names of faculty listed under appropriate headings. The categorization is further used when examining the institutional listing that cites each faculty member, his or her rank, full- or part-time status, and specialization(s).

The directory, organized by name of the institution, has such useful information as library school addresses, telephone numbers, date of founding, major administrator(s), and faculty who can teach in a foreign language. Since it is also the handbook of ALISE, it lists the organization's officers and committee members; the goal, objectives, and 1986 priorities; and ALISE, Inc., Bylaws.

The work is clearly organized and as complete as can be expected when depending on member institutions' contributions. The closing date of the questionnaire gathering data was late 1985. As a directory, this volume is of special value to the professional in library and information science education, but is also a useful tool for individuals who need to identify subject specialists in library and information science programs, review school affiliations, and have a reference to the ALISE structure.

Laurel Grotzinger

175. **Information Technology in the Library/Information School Curriculum: An International Conference.** Chris Armstrong and Stella Keenan, eds. Brookfield, Vt., Gower Publishing, 1985. 266p. index. $53.95. LC 85-14656. ISBN 0-566-03526-X.

The papers in this book address the impact of changes in information technology on library and information education and were presented at the International Conference on Information Technology in the Library/Information School Curriculum held in London in 1983. Professionals from Australia, Poland, Netherlands, the United Kingdom, and the United States have contributed to this volume of proceedings. Although the international aspects of these papers provide an interesting look into activities in a variety of countries, their impact is somewhat limited by the severe time lag between presentation and publication (we are already more than half through the five-year range of projections) and the specific nature of some of the presentations (many deal exclusively with teaching online searching). On the other hand, several papers are noteworthy and remain important commentaries on the interrelationships between library and information school education and the changing role of the information professional. The keynote address by Blaise Cronin and the paper by Jose-Marie Griffiths make this book a worthwhile purchase, especially for those concerned with library and information education and the new technology.

Elisabeth Logan

176. Kohl, David F. **Library Education and Professional Issues: A Handbook for Library Management.** Santa Barbara, Calif., ABC-Clio, 1986. 274p. bibliog. index. (Handbooks for Library Management, Vol. 6). $35.00. LC 85-15833. ISBN 0-87436-436-1.

This final volume follows the same approach as the previous five volumes. The series as a whole summarizes 807 statistical studies, grouped under broad subjects. The summaries describe the location, date, population or survey size, response rate, and specific findings. There are, in addition, a list of journals surveyed, a bibliography of articles surveyed, and an author index.

The subjects under "Library Education" include curriculum, faculty, students, deans, etc., while under "Professional Issues" are topics like career issues, gender issues, professional organizations, and faculty status of academic librarians.

There are limitations to the value of this work. Only selected journals published in North America are included (thirty-four journals in this volume), covering the years 1960 to 1983. Only quantitative research is included. The title and subtitle are misleading since the information provided is incomplete, hard to find, and difficult to evaluate. A more exact title would be: "A Selective Guide to Quantitative Research in Library Education and Professional Issues." A much more detailed subject index is needed, as well as evaluative, summarizing comments on the significance of research done in each topic.

In summary, this is a good beginning of a needed work in our field but it should be expanded geographically, include all types of research, and provide better subject access as well as evaluative comments. A misspelled title on the title page is very disconcerting and should have been noticed before publication. [R: LJ, 1 Sept 86, p. 172; RQ, Fall 86, pp. 126-27]

George S. Bobinski

177. Rochester, Maxine K. **Foreign Students in American Library Education: Impact on**

Home Countries. Westport, Conn., Greenwood Press, 1986. 208p. bibliog. index. (Contributions in Librarianship and Information Science, No. 55). $35.00. LC 85-12675. ISBN 0-313-24201-1.

The author of this study is a senior lecturer at the Centre for Library and Information Studies, Canberra College of Advanced Education. She earned her doctorate at the University of Wisconsin in 1981 by researching American influence on librarianship in New Zealand. Her present book is a comprehensive investigation of foreign students' education in general and of library and information science study in particular.

Rochester tells us total foreign student enrollment in 1978 was only 2.3 percent of total enrollment in higher education worldwide and that library and information science students form only 0.2 percent of foreign student enrollment in the United States. However, foreign students have attended U.S. library schools since the establishment of the first library school in the English-speaking world at Columbia College in New York in 1887. Numbers of students and countries of origin, discussion of admission standards and procedures, curriculum, financial assistance available, etc., are covered. Reasons given for attending U.S. schools include lack of facilities or limited access to such facilities in the country of origin, cheaper tuition in the U.S. schools, and the high standing of American education in library and information science internationally.

Criticism of study abroad focuses on the fact that U.S. education may be too advanced for developing countries. It is important that knowledge acquired be adaptable to the home country. There is fear that Western ideas are being forced on foreign countries and, conversely, that students may not return to their country of origin. The author indicates that although brain drain is not a significant factor for the majority of foreign students, it may be more of a factor for library and information science students. The increased demand in the United States for people with information skills plus the more rewarding employment climate for women, who form the largest segment of this student population, may result in the migration of greater numbers.

Rochester concludes with an ironic commentary: while the United States is helping developing countries plan national information systems, there is at present no body in the United States to coordinate American activities relating to library and information sciences. Thoughtful analysis and clarity of presentation characterize this study. Each chapter has a list of sources cited and there is a selective bibliography of 165 references plus a useful index. [R: JAL, July 86, pp. 173-74; JAL, Sept 86, pp. 237-38; WLB, June 86, p. 75]

Virginia E. Yagello

FESTSCHRIFTEN

178. **Libraries and Information Science in the Electronic Age.** Hendrik Edelman, ed. Philadelphia, ISI Press, 1986. 177p. index. (Samuel Lazerow Memorial Lecture Series). $39.95. LC 86-3064. ISBN 0-89495-058-4.

The volume is a festschrift in honor of Samuel Lazerow, late senior vice-president at the Institute for Scientific Information (ISI). The volume contains twelve lectures presented at seven different library schools between 1983 and 1985 in a lecture series also sponsored by ISI in memory of Lazerow. This is the first volume in a projected series of future lectures. The lectures, presented in chronological order, were given by the following prominent information professionals: Frederick Kilgour, Carlos Cuadra, Richard DeGennaro, Herbert Landau, William Baker, Toni Bearman, Lillian Bradshaw, Allan Kent, Lester Asheim, Carol Nemeyer, William Paisley, and Glenn Bacon.

The common theme is the notion that change is inevitable in the electronic age. Several papers deal with information policy issues in the public and private sectors. Other papers address the education of library information professionals and their role in the future. Several of the papers contain references, and Paisley's "The Convergence of Communication and Information Science" includes numerous tables. The papers by Kilgour and DeGennaro have also been published as journal articles. A biographical sketch of the contributors and an index complete the volume. Library science students and professionals alike will find it interesting reading. [R: RQ, Winter 86, p. 263]

Andrew G. Torok

179. **Libraries in the '80s: Papers in Honor of the Late Neal L. Edgar.** Dean H. Keller, ed. New York, Haworth Press, 1985. 157p. bibliog. (*Technical Services Quarterly*, Vol. 3, Nos. 1/2). $29.95. LC 85-5862. ISBN 0-86656-459-4.

A festschrift of fourteen papers, this work presents the views of significant writers on a wide variety of aspects of librarianship. It was published in honor of Neal L. Edgar, who was associate curator of special collections at Kent State (Ohio) University Library at the time of his death, but who was better known throughout the profession for his part in devising the AACR2 cataloging rules and for his many publications dealing with serials. The authors of the papers include Bill Katz, A. Robert Rogers, James Rush, and others, and their papers reflect their fields of expertise.

Librarians, library educators, and scholars interested in library science will find this volume of value for the state-of-the-art essays on subjects as diverse as overly favorable book reviews, financing the public libraries of Ohio, the challenge of educating library and information science professionals, and subject headings for nuclear weapons and war, to name a few. A short biography of Neal L. Edgar and a bibliography of his works complete the volume.

Sara R. Mack

180. Powell, Lawrence Clark. **Life Goes On: Twenty More Years of Fortune and Friendship. Checklist of Publications: 1919-1986.** By Robert Mitchell and Betty Rosenberg. Metuchen, N.J., Scarecrow, 1986. 180p. illus. bibliog. index. $19.50. LC 86-3943. ISBN 0-8108-1890-6.

Lawrence Clark Powell's reputation as a brilliant essayist and wise commentator on the library scene is further enhanced by his latest volume, *Life Goes On*. Eric Moon, quoting from the foreword of Powell's earlier *Fortune and Friendship*, sums up the accomplishments of this remarkable man: "author, bibliographer, bookman, essayist, librarian, teacher, dean, and adroit administrator, Lawrence Clark Powell is many things. But essentially he is a magician." The volume is enhanced by Robert Mitchell and Betty Rosenberg's admirable checklist of publications, 1919-1986.

These personal essays are edifying reading for librarians long in the field as well as for those just entering, for like the calliope, they are "tooting joy, tooting hope," in this troubled world. [R: LJ, 1 Oct 86, p. 72; WLB, Oct 86, p. 58]

Frances Neel Cheney

181. **Prospects for Information Service: Essays in Honour of Daphne Clark.** Colin Harris and Peter Taylor, eds. London, Aslib; distr., Medford, N.J., Learned Information, 1985. 114p. $25.00. ISBN 0-85142-194-6.

The collection of essays contained in this book is a tribute to the late Daphne Clark, manager of Aslib's Professional Development Group from 1982 until her sudden and untimely death in September 1983. The thoughtful contributions represent a number of topics with which Daphne Clark was associated during her professional career. The seven contributions range from such topics as marketing of library services (C. Crossley) and the notion of publicly available information (R. Lester), to the interactive library picture show (N. H. Aberle) and goal definition in library and information services. The articles are written for general professional reading and not as scholarly papers or research reports. The chapter entitled "Beyond Doomsday," by D. Lewis, is designed to provoke the reader and challenge him or her to rethink the future of the profession.

The volume is a highly recommended reading for librarians and information professionals and students in graduate library and information science programs.

Mohammed M. Aman

HISTORY

182. Dickson, Paul. **The Library in America: A Celebration in Words and Pictures.** New York, Facts on File, 1986. illus. bibliog. index. 256p. $35.00. LC 86-8981. ISBN 0-8160-1365-9.

The author characterizes this photographic album as a "valentine to libraries, librarians, and patrons smitten with a passion for libraries." Dickson reveres the free public library, and considers it one of America's most noble achievements. More than four hundred photographs highlight the development of the public library in America from Benjamin Franklin to the 1980s. Heavily captioned photographs, drawn from archival repositories and publications such as *Library Journal*, are arranged into nine chapters. Each chapter and subsection is introduced by an excerpt from an article, book, or newspaper.

Visually traversing the nation, *The Library in America* offers a montage of library images: reading rooms, bookmobiles, library trains, mule-drawn libraries, libraries as portrayed in the movies, celebrities, and natural disasters. Among the themes and episodes which merit special recognition are women library workers, urban libraries, and libraries in war. Excerpts from the writings of Carl Cramer, Evelyn Geller, William Munthe, Richard Wright, and others enliven the narrative and complement the numerous photographs. A bibliography of sources and a subject index are furnished.

The volume is mistitled. It is not about all types of libraries. Rather, it is a pictorial history of the public library. Properly defined, Dickson's valentine should find many appreciative readers. [R: BL, 1 Sept 86, p. 6; Choice, Nov 86, p. 531; WLB, Sept 86, pp. 72-73]

Arthur P. Young

183. Feather, John P., and David McKitterick. **The History of Books and Libraries: Two Views.** Washington, D.C., Library of Congress, 1986. 32p. (Center for the Book Viewpoint Series, No. 16). free pa. LC 86-600073. ISBN 0-8444-0526-4.

In the spring of 1985 two British scholars presented Englehard Lectures on the Book at the Library of Congress. John Feather, senior lecturer in the Department of Library and Information Studies, Loughborough University, delivered a paper entitled "The Book in History and the History of the Book." Book history is defined as a broad canvas consisting of social, economic, and political contexts. Studies in such areas as literacy, copyright, authorship, library use, and technical production illuminate the book as a force in cultural development. According to Feather, the purely bibliographic orientation of previous scholars remains useful, but is only one element in the expansive perimeters of book history. Continuing in a similar vein, David McKitterick, rare book curator in the Cambridge University Library, presented a talk entitled "The Limits of Library History." McKitterick contends that the study of library history offers a significant perspective for the historian of scholarship and the bibliographer. Patterns of book accumulation, certification, and reader use complement many non-library areas of research. Both papers adroitly summarize the trend toward a more comprehensive, holistic definition of book history. Now is the time to move beyond conceptualization to the production of solid research which will influence the broader fields of social and cultural history. [R: WLB, Oct 86, p. 58]

Arthur P. Young

184. Howell, John Bruce. **A History of the Dublin Library Society, 1791-1881.** Halifax, N.S., School of Library Service, Dalhousie University, 1985. 33p. bibliog. (Occasional Papers Series, No. 38). $11.50pa. ISBN 0-7703-0172-X; ISSN 0318-7403.

In this brief and well-documented text, Howell chronicles the origins and development of a single scholarly subscription library, founded to serve the middle class and intellectual audiences for whom no adequate library services were being provided. Primary source material used to document the history of this nonsectarian society includes three unpublished sets of bylaws, four book catalogs of the society's collections, biographies of the society's officials, and almanacs and directories of nineteenth-century Dublin.

Members of the Dublin Library Society included some of Ireland's best known scholars and politicians; Howell takes care to indicate the relative role which individuals such as Valentine Lawless, Lord Cloncurry (1773-1853), and James Caulfield, fourth Viscount and first Earl of Charlemont (1738-99), played in the active development of the society and its collections. He also presents the consequences of the two major scandals to hit the society, under the presidencies of James O'Neill Mackle and Richard Kirwan.

Howell presents comparative information on the growth of subscription circulating libraries, placing in perspective the roles played by the Royal Dublin Society, Royal Irish Academy, Dublin Library Society, Dublin Mechanics' Institute, University Reading Society, Dublin Scientific Association, Society of Attorneys and Solicitors of Ireland, Historical and Literary Society, Library Society, and the Young Men's Christian Association (Upper Sackville Street) in such growth. Two illustrative figures, regarding membership of the Dublin Library Society and commercial circulating libraries in Dublin, are used to enhance Howell's comparisons.

A noteworthy addition to the history of libraries and librarianship, this terse essay may find its most interested audience in students and researchers of comparative and international librarianship.

Edmund F. SantaVicca

185. **Libraries, Books & Culture: Proceedings of Library History Seminar VII, 6-8 March 1985, Chapel Hill, North Carolina.** Donald G. Davis, Jr., ed. Austin, Tex., Graduate School of Library and Information Science, University of Texas, 1986. 491p. illus. index. $15.00. LC 86-14821. ISBN 0-938729-00-4.

Twenty-eight papers presented at the Library History Seminar VII held at the University of North Carolina at Chapel Hill in March 1985 make up the contents of this book. The subjects of the papers are wide ranging, providing much of interest to historians, librarians, bibliographers, and others interested in books and cultural history. Topics range from American academic library buildings 1870-1890 to the working library of Samuel Taylor Coleridge, from the historiography of Canadian library history to mosques as libraries in Islamic civilization, from the new censorship to library politics and the organization of the Bibliographical Society of America. The papers are divided among twelve categories with two papers in each category. The categories are "The Early Use of Printed Books in Europe and America," "The Formation of American Bibliothecal Institutions," "Popular Libraries in Mid-Nineteenth-Century North America," "Western Influences in the South Asian World of Books," "Circulating and Rental Libraries in the Modern United States," "The Role of the Library in Two Cultural Contexts," "The Influence of Private Libraries," "Books and Libraries in Twentieth-Century France and the Soviet Union," "Religious Literature in Two Diverse Cultures," "Women in Professional Leadership: The American South," "Research in Reading: Two

Approaches," and "Reports of Current Library Historiography Abroad." The first section of the collection contains the four papers presented in the plenary sessions. Each paper is fully documented and is prefaced by an abstract. There are a subject/title index and an author index.

This seminar was dedicated to the distinguished library historian Professor Haynes McMullen of the School of Library Science at the University of North Carolina at Chapel Hill, who retired in 1985. McMullen's accomplishments were gracefully outlined by Edward G. Holley in an opening essay.

Dean H. Keller

186. **Readings in Canadian Library History.** Peter F. McNally, ed. Ottawa, Canadian Library Association, 1986. 258p. illus. $25.00. ISBN 0-88802-196-8.

Formation of the Library History Interest Group of the Canadian Library Association in 1980 stimulated scholarly activity in this neglected area. Fourteen of the eighteen papers in this collection of readings were first read before the group between 1982 and 1984. Essays are arranged in five categories: guides to the literature, methodology, public libraries, diverse perspectives, and biography. The introductory bibliographical essays, one on mechanics' institutes and two surveys of library history literature in English and French, 1964-1984, are comprehensive treatments which should be helpful to future researchers.

Peter McNally notes that much Canadian library history is amateurish, lacks synthesis, and is not supported by graduate schools of librarianship. Some of the essays in this volume suffer from conceptual vagueness and insufficient attention to archival sources. Strong entries are by Lucile Freynet on the St. Boniface Public Library, Don Kerr on the Saskatoon Public Library, Leslie Castling on the Red River Library, and Stephen Cummings on Angus Mowat. Photographs and tabular matter accompany some of the papers. Failure to append an index is regrettable.

This volume should be considered an interim report to the library community and interested scholars in other disciplines. With the enthusiasm evident in this collection, future progress appears favorable.

Arthur P. Young

187. Wiegand, Wayne A. **The Politics of an Emerging Profession: The American Library Association, 1876-1917.** Westport, Conn., Greenwood Press, 1986. 322p. bibliog. index. (Contributions in Librarianship and Information Science, No. 56). $39.95. LC 85-12679. ISBN 0-313-25022-7.

The formative decades of the American Library Association (ALA) parallel the nation's period of dynamic library growth, and illuminate contemporary dialog about the purpose, status, and power of the library in society. Wayne Wiegand's masterful reconstruction of the founding and early development of the ALA is derived from thorough research in the secondary literature and exhaustive consultation of archival sources. Although the story unfolds within a chronological framework, analysis and interpretation are not neglected.

The ALA's struggle to forge a viable professional identity is the central focus. Along the way, there are numerous examples of geographic elitism, shifting alliances, vanity, adaptation, and reform. For several decades, suspicion between Northeast and Midwestern factions of the association derailed issues and impeded progress. In contrast to other professions, the ALA concentrated more on method than research and inquiry, a practical orientation and public perception which have lingered for a century. Committed "apostles of culture," early ALA leaders felt comfortable dispensing the best literature. Matters of efficiency and democratization, however, occasioned debate, division, and sometimes vitriol.

The contributions of such leaders as Justin Winsor, William F. Poole, Herbert Putnam, William C. Lane, and Mary E. Ahern enliven and personalize the account. Bestriding the ALA and its affairs was Melvil Dewey, entrepreneurial librarian and systematizer. While Dewey clearly advanced the ALA into a more responsive posture on some issues, he comes across as a boor and a dissembler.

Wiegand has fashioned an authoritative and readable volume which joins the few seminal works on American library history. [R: JAL, Sept 86, p. 236; LJ, July 86, p. 60; WLB, Sept 86, p. 72]

Arthur P. Young

INDEXING AND ABSTRACTING

188. Brenner, Everett H., and Tefko Saracevic. **Indexing and Searching in Perspective.** Philadelphia, National Federation of Abstracting and Information Services, 1985. 1v. (various paging). $60.00pa.

Since 1969, the National Federation of Abstracting and Information Services has offered a traveling seminar on "Perspectives in Indexing" across the United States and Canada.

Two of the seminar leaders, both long-time authorities in the design, production, and evaluation of information retrieval systems, have summarized seminar lectures in this volume. Everett Brenner, director of the American Petroleum Institute database, has written historical overviews of the development of indexing vocabularies, formats, and searching since World War II. These are well illustrated with examples, but their brevity occasionally results in confusing statements which need further elaboration. One of the newer developments in indexing—contextual string indexing such as PRECIS or the Modern Language Association's CIFT system—is omitted entirely.

To complement Brenner's treatment of system aspects, Tefko Saracevic of Rutgers University (formerly of Case Western Reserve) contributes an excellent review of factors relating to users with problems, questions, and requests as they use retrieval systems, with special attention to those aspects most affecting search results. Supplementary material describes the history of the "Perspectives" seminar as well as the more important professional associations in the world of indexing and information retrieval.

While too brief to stand alone as a textbook, Brenner's historical perspectives and Saracevic's concise review of the user system interface will serve as a valuable supplement in courses on information organization and database searching. Both the seminar on which it is based and this summary of its content are recommended for all indexers, librarians, and systems designers committed to effective information retrieval.   James D. Anderson

189. **Forms and Responses: Volume 1. Library/Acquisitions, Editorial, and Production.** Betty Unruh and Martha Cornog, eds. Philadelphia, National Federation of Abstracting and Information Services, 1986. 302p. $35.00 spiralbound.

The scope of this work is unclear from the title alone, but becomes clearer through the publisher's name. As the introduction states, "*Forms and Responses* is a series designed to help abstracting and indexing (A&I) Services [sic] and similar information publishers by acquainting them with forms and 'canned letters' used by their sister organizations." The brief introduction constitutes the only running text; the rest of this paperback, spiralbound volume contains forms employed in the acquisition and cataloging of materials by abstracting and indexing services; the worksheets used by abstractors and indexers in creating records, along with thesaurus forms (the "editorial" section); and the forms used in production, printing, and mailing of indexes. Boldface headings printed sideways on the outer margin identify the specific category of each form.

The collection is useful for managers of abstracting and indexing services, and is also relevant to researchers and educators in indexing and thesaurus design.

The flaws of this collection lie in its formal apparatus. There is no index; moreover, section headings such as "Cataloging—Miscellaneous" are useless for identifying specific types of forms. The sources of many forms are unidentified, precluding correspondence with the issuing agencies. The absence of both an ISBN and an LC card number will negatively affect sales and the speed of cataloging of this work. These omissions are inexcusable for a publisher in the information business. *The Library Forms Illustrated Handbook* (Neal-Schuman, 1984) and *A Sampler of Forms for Special Libraries* (see *ARBA* 83, entry 168) are better designed compilations of related interest.

Bella Hass Weinberg

INFORMATION TECHNOLOGY

General Works

DICTIONARIES

190. Longley, Dennis, and Michael Shain. **Dictionary of Information Technology.** 2d ed. New York, Oxford University Press, 1986. 380p. illus. $29.95. LC 86-12435. ISBN 0-19-520519-7.

This dictionary represents an exhaustive effort to compile the terms currently being used in information technology (IT). The authors have succeeded in developing a very informative lexicon for IT that will allow this burgeoning area to grow in a more orderly and informative manner. Since IT affects nearly everyone, this work will also prove useful to the layperson. There is a tendency for new areas such as IT to attract exploitative publications that capitalize on the novelty. This work is refreshing for its timeliness without sacrificing quality and will find a wide audience from among the many disciplines it addresses.

Information technology is "the acquisition, processing, storage and dissemination of vocal, pictorial, textual and numerical information by a microelectronics-based combination of computing and telecommunications" and elaboration on this definition in this 382-page dictionary continues for another 5 pages. The authors argue that IT has emerged as an independent discipline that also exploits the convergence of existing technologies, and thereby justify adding this six-thousand-plus-entry tome to facilitate communication. Neologisms abound in this arena, and aspiring information technologists will find a rich, well-illustrated array of entries in what will become a standard reference for the field. The disciplinary area originating each entry is usually identified, cross-references are useful, and extended entries for important topics give an encyclopedic flavor to the work. This volume provides a basis for understanding IT better. It will be a boon to those who have something to say and their audiences, presuming the snowflakes of interest can continue to be found in this growing blizzard of information. Marvin K. Harris

HANDBOOKS AND YEARBOOKS

191. Biggs, Penelope T., ed. **Current Research for the Information Profession 1985/86.** London, Library Association; distr., Chicago, American Library Association, 1986. 1v. (various paging). index. $75.00. ISBN 0-85365-797-1; ISSN 0268-7372.

This second yearbook of *Current Research for the Information Profession* is based on the third annual cumulation of *Current Research on Library and Information Science.* It includes "investigations, studies, surveys and evaluative innovations done or on-going in any part of the world." The purpose of the yearbook is expressed in the compiler's hope that "concerned users will find that research can provide answers to everyday problems."

The material covered is arranged by subject using the Classification Research Group's classification scheme (also used in *LISA*). Each citation includes a class number, title, the personnel involved in the project, current status, address of project, expected duration, indication of whether it has been completed or is in progress, source of funding, a brief description, and the contact person. A name index and a subject index provide access to the 1,194 items included.

The yearbook is useful for identifying current research topics, avoiding duplication of research, identifying possible gaps in the literature, and contacting relevant experts. The major limitation of this usefulness is, however, the reliance on researchers themselves for submission of information. As a result, the yearbook cannot (nor does it) claim comprehensiveness. Also generally troublesome is the scope of studies included under the rubric "information research." What are the boundaries of this field? In spite of these comments, however, the year-book is valuable and merits consultation by researcher and practitioner alike.

Robert H. Burger

192. Lesko, Matthew. **Lesko's New Tech Sourcebook: A Directory to Finding Answers in Today's Technology-oriented World.** New York, Harper & Row, 1986. 726p. index. $35.00; $18.95pa. LC 85-45209. ISBN 0-06-181509-8; 0-06-096036-1pa.

Matthew Lesko's latest encyclopedic cornucopia of resources aims at a broad audience, from researcher to "the average individual." Library patrons, though, will probably find this directory particularly useful when, eager to research the latest high-tech topics, they need a jolt of fresh sources, leads, and possibilities. *Lesko's New Tech Sourcebook* covers over five thousand resources in a dictionary arrangement of approximately 180 subjects ("Acoustics" to "Wind Energy"), with another 200 cross-references. Such high-tech topics as "Compact Discs," "Cryogenics Technology," "Electronic Funds Transfer," "Ergonomics," "Holography," "Medical Imaging," and "Supertrains" appear.

For each, numerous information sources are described: organizations and U.S. government agencies (including professional societies, trade associations, businesses, and research centers); publications, including those available free; online databases; and additional resources (companies, educational institutions, and experts willing to deal with the public). The concise, readable descriptions of each resource note purpose, services, publications (if any), costs, names, addresses, and telephone numbers.

The complete table of contents, noting every subject and cross-reference, plus a how-to-use chapter, suggested techniques for gathering information, and an extensive index add to the usefulness of the book.

On the other hand, and perhaps inevitably given the plethora of material here, typos, inconsistencies of address and odd alphabetization appear. The reader may wonder at the inclusion of some seemingly low- or non-tech topics ("Entrepreneurism," "Japan," "Legislation," "Nutrition") and the exclusion of other more applicable subjects (operating systems, for example). Cross-references though abundant, are uneven: there's no reference from "Computers" to "Microcomputers" (or vice versa) and no indication that automation is covered under "Office Automation."

Lesko, who established Washington Researchers, a company specializing in gathering information from federal bureaucrats, has also produced *Information USA* and *Getting Yours*. His *New Tech Sourcebook* can take its place beside them as an important, yet somewhat quirky, information bonanza. [R: Choice, June 86, p. 1522; LJ, Jan 86, p. 72; RBB, July 86, p. 1599]

Sayre Van Young

193. Tou, Julius T., ed. **Advances in Information Systems Science, Volume 9.** New York, Plenum Press, 1985. 340p. illus. index. $52.50. LC 69-12544. ISBN 0-306-41644-1.

Each of the five chapters in this collection of review articles is written as a tutorial that will bring the literate computer scientist up-to-date in the subject matter covered. In most cases, the author of an article is a researcher in the field, and there is therefore some bias in the detailed list of topics covered and in the attitudes expressed. This series does provide a useful set of reference materials. Most of the chapters give good bibliographies and therefore function as surveys of current and recent research in their fields. The quality of the chapters is not uniform. Some of the chapters achieve the quality of articles in the *ACM Computing Surveys*, while others, while still good, would not reach the threshold of acceptance in that meticulous journal. On the whole, however, the series would be worth acquiring for most libraries covering computer and information sciences.

Steven L. Tanimoto

INDEXES AND ABSTRACTS

194. **Information Science Abstracts. Volume 21, Number 3.** H. Allcock, ed. New York, Plenum, 1986. 1v. (various paging). index. $325.00/yr. (12 issues). ISSN 0020-0239.

Information Science Abstracts, formerly *Documentation Abstracts*, is published monthly and contains abstracts from selected books, journals, conference proceedings, reports, and patents. Journals abstracted completely are those from the sponsoring agencies: ASIS, DCI, SLA, ALA, ASI, ASIDIC, ALISE, and MLA. According to the introductory statement in each volume, more than one hundred other journals are regularly scanned for appropriate subject matter. Subject and author indexes and a list of abbreviations are included at the end of each issue, and each volume contains an index and a list of the sources abstracted.

One of the most attractive features of this publication is the clear and easily understood classification and contents statement which has appeared since 1976 at the beginning of each issue. This feature makes browsing the topics an attractive option, especially since cross-references to related areas are included when appropriate. Categories include information science and documentation; libraries and information services; information systems and applications; information generation, reproduction, and distribution; information recognition and description; information storage and retrieval; information user and usage studies; and supporting studies and techniques.

The focus is primarily on information science, but as the classification categories indicate, there is a wealth of material of interest to librarians and other information professionals.

Elisabeth Logan

195. Peniston, Silvina, comp. **Index to Information Technology.** London, Taylor Graham, 1985. 210p. $37.00pa. ISBN 0-947568-02-6.

This volume is a British publication that covers papers presented at major conferences on information technology between 1979 and 1984. The work is divided into eight index arrangements: conference volumes, papers indexed, authors, editor, geographical index, conference organizers, conference titles, and subject. The conference volume index is arranged alphabetically with each entry assigned a number. Similarly, each of the alphabetically arranged papers indexed is also assigned a number and is cross-referenced to the conference volume index. The papers indexed section entries include the author's name, title of the paper, the related volume in the conference volume index, and subject headings relating to that paper. The other indexes refer users back to either the conference volume index (as is the case with the editor index), or back to the papers indexed section (as is the case with the other indexes).

While the concept of the *Index to Information Technology* is very useful and valuable, one can't help but feel somewhat frustrated when attempting to use it. The compiler indicates that the entries are selective but never specifies the basis for selection. From a U.S. perspective, this reviewer wonders why so few American Library Association Conference papers have been included. Information on how to use this volume is sorely lacking in the introduction. The most annoying example is that there are no instructions indicating the difference in numbering between the conference volume index and that in the papers indexed section. This distinction is absolutely essential when using the other six indexes. Furthermore, there is no indication to the user which index to refer back to when using these other six indexes. Based on these major criticisms, this work is recommended in concept with the caveat of "beware of some frustrating moments when trying to use it."

Marjorie Bloss

MONOGRAPHS

196. Forester, Tom, ed. **The Information Technology Revolution.** Cambridge, Mass.,

MIT Press, 1985. 674p. illus. bibliog. index. $32.50; $14.95pa. LC 84-23422. ISBN 0-262-06095-7; 0-262-56033-Xpa.

Forester's purpose in compiling this volume is "to cover the key technological developments over the period and to track the many social changes that are following on with great rapidity." In contrast to his earlier collection, *The Microelectronics Revolution* (1981), this one is shorter on speculation and more representative of what is actually happening in this area. The work consists of forty-eight previously published articles by both U.S. and British writers that appeared in print between 1981 and 1984. The articles, culled from academic journals, books, trade magazines, general purpose magazines, and newspapers, are all of high quality. The articles are arranged under four major rubrics: "The Computer Revolution," "The Human Interface," "The Impact on Work," and "Implications for Society." Then, under each rubric, the articles are further subdivided into "chapters," each of which contains three to four articles. Guides to further reading are included at the end of each chapter and at the conclusion of the book itself. A name and subject index is provided.

Although some of the articles do contain hype, most are clearly and concisely written and serve to inform rather than to bedazzle. Forester's selection also deserves praise, for he has managed to locate articles that deal with individual topics in different and sometimes opposing ways. Because of these attributes and the book's reasonable cost in paperback, the collection would be an excellent choice either for courses in information science or the social effects of technology, as well as for the general reader who seeks to understand the various aspects of the current information technology scene.—Robert H. Burger

197. **Informatics 8: Advances in Intelligent Retrieval. Proceedings of a Conference ..., J. Wadham College, Oxford, 16-17 April 1985.** London, Aslib; distr., Medford, N.J., Learned Information, 1985. 314p. $59.00pa. ISBN 0-85142-195-4.

This, the eighth Informatics conference sponsored by the Aslib Informatics Group and the British Computer Society's Information Retrieval Specialist Group, was planned as a sequel to the seventh conference, Intelligent Information Retrieval. As such, it reflects current trends and developments in information retrieval systems, especially in the areas of database design and the representation of human knowledge within database structure of knowledge-based systems.

In his review "Ten Years of Informatics," Kevin P. Jones states that "the goal of informatics is the discovery of the optimum methods and means of representation, collection, storage, retrieval and dissemination of scholarly information" (p. 265). The fifteen presentations that comprise this volume most certainly cover this wide diversity of scope. Articles range from those dealing with cataloging, to PRECIS, to database structure and architecture for online information retrieval systems. Each article is well written and, indeed, should be savored rather than greedily consumed.

Somewhat detracting from the volume is the impression that authors were asked to submit camera-ready copy that was subsequently photocopied and bound together. As a result, typefaces differ, some of the reproductions are clearer than others, and an occasional typographical error slips in. Given the subject content, it is almost ironic that the volume has no index. Still, these features are minor when given the wealth of material in *Advances in Intelligent Retrieval*. This volume is highly recommended for all libraries concerned with information retrieval, for system users and system designers alike.—Marjorie Bloss

198. Ingwersen, Peter, Leif Kajberg, and Annelise Mark Pejtersen, eds. **Information Technology and Information Use: Towards a Unified View of Information and Information Technology.** London, Taylor Graham, 1986. 194p. $37.00pa. ISBN 0-947568-06-9.

The purpose of this collection of essays is "to outline theoretical as well as practical solutions to the problems of using information applying IT, to emphasize transfer, and to pinpoint and set in context educational and research areas." The volume comprises papers presented at the seminar on "Information Technology as a Tool for Information Use" held at the Royal School of Librarianship, Copenhagen, 8-10 May 1985.

F. W. Lancaster, in an introductory essay, warns that "efficient distribution and use of information ... is dependent much less on technology than on the existence of skilled and motivated human resources." The other papers in the volume, which repeatedly touch on this theme, are organized into three thematic groups. These are: (1) socioeconomic aspects and policy making; (2) pragmatic issues of information systems design; and (3) education for information. Each paper is preceded by an abstract and followed by a list of references. There is no index.

This group of essays is unusually rich in intelligence and ideas. In covering information technology and use from several vantage points (information brokerage, academic research, systems design, policy making) it gives the reader a multifaceted perspective on contemporary problems of IT applications and the state of information science. The volume would be especially beneficial to students in courses on information policy or information and society.

Robert H. Burger

199. Mattelart, Armand, and Hector Schmucler. **Communication and Information Technologies: Freedom of Choice for Latin America?** Norwood, N.J., Ablex Publishing, 1985. 186p. bibliog. index. $24.50. LC 85-1348. ISBN 0-89391-214-X.

Translated from *L'Ordinateur et le Tiers Monde*, this book deals with the "global challenge of the computerization of the Third World." Mattelart has written numerous books on related topics, including *International Image Markets: In Search of an Alternative Perspective* (London, Comedia, 1984) and *Transnationals and the Third World: The Struggle for Culture* (Bergin & Garvey, 1983), and this study was undertaken to "analyze the evolution of communication and information systems as a global system for the organization of power, but also as a system where various social, cultural and industrial projects confront one another." As noted in the introduction, this book is more "narrative" than many preceding studies, that is, it does not attempt to identify answers, but to "reveal unknown facts." The experiences of seven Latin American countries are used to describe the role of communication in the political, economic, cultural, and military arenas in these and other Third World countries.

The book is divided into four chapters. The first chapter reviews the evolution of the electronics industry in Latin American countries. Chapter 2 notes the interconnections between the three components of the new communication systems: audiovisual media, computers, and telecommunications. The third chapter begins with a review of the development of communications systems in Europe and then traces the evolution of computerization in various Latin American countries. Chapter 4 provides an overview of the structure of the transnational information industry and especially its impact on Latin America. This book is a passionate but theoretical discussion of the problems and potential benefits of information technologies for Third World countries. It is not intended to serve as a reference book and it cannot be recommended on that basis. However, anyone with an interest in information and its effect on various social institutions, especially in Third World countries, would find this book interesting and thought-provoking.

Greg Byerly

Information Management

200. Cortez, Edwin M., and Edward John Kazlauskas. **Managing Information Systems & Technologies: A Basic Guide for Design, Selection, Evaluation, and Use.** New York, Neal-Schuman, 1986. 179p. illus. index. $35.00pa. LC 85-32013. ISBN 0-918212-92-8.

The preface indicates that this book is "designed for librarians, information managers, consultants, records managers, management, information specialists, and students" and is "intended to provide a structure for understanding the principles and complexities involved in managing an information system." Given this proposed audience and the broadness of the topic, it should not be a surprise that the book has a basic unevenness to it. There is something of value for each of the intended audiences in this book, but in many cases the information is too briefly presented. The authors were apparently unable to decide whether they were writing a practical handbook on managing information systems or whether their goal was to present a comprehensive, but necessarily brief, overview of all aspects of information management. In some cases they succeed in providing relatively detailed information on a specific topic, but in many cases the information is so brief as to be virtually worthless. The key to any book which attempts to cover a broad range of topics is a good list of additional readings, which are referred to in the text. For example, since entire books have been written about preparing Requests for Proposals (RFPs), there is clearly no need to spend a great deal of time detailing the process in a book of this nature. Yet, this book tries to outline the process of preparing an RFP, evaluating and awarding a contract, and negotiating the system contract in eleven pages without including any relevant references in the additional reading section at the end of the chapter. This book is similar to a semester course in information technology in which the lectures are of varying quality and value, depending on the background and interest of the professor. In a similar fashion, parts of this book demonstrate an impressive understanding of a complicated topic and an ability to communicate this information clearly. Unfortunately, other sections seem much too brief and cursory and, occasionally, even inaccurate (e.g., referring to DIALOG as Lockheed or totally ignoring the potential impact of CD-ROM technology on information systems). Nevertheless, this book does represent a comprehensive outline of issues involved in managing information systems and can serve as an overall introduction to the field. Greg Byerly

201. Ein-Dor, Phillip, and Carl R. Jones. **Information Systems Management: Analytical Tools and Techniques.** New York, Elsevier Science Publishing, 1985. 230p. index. $29.95. LC 85-13013. ISBN 0-444-00957-4.

This work is designed as a textbook for information science students. The authors assume the reader has taken an introductory course in microeconomics. With this background, the user begins with an overview of information systems and resources, as well as a discussion of terminology used throughout. Further chapters cover the cost and value of information and variety of methods for looking at the economic foundations of information system management. Next, the overall structure and design of the information system, including capital budgeting, are explored. There are also chapters devoted to setting up the computer center and managing it, and software development, use, and maintenance. A variety of decision-making tools for these users and methods for using existing information systems are examined. Each chapter contains a list of references and thought-provoking exercises dealing with the material covered. The material is well written and provides a practical, informative look at setting up and managing an information system. The book concludes with a comprehensive survey of the impact of systems management on information users. Ein-Dor and Jones have produced a solid textbook.

Joanne Troutner

Information Systems

202. Belkin, Nicholas J., and Alina Vickery. **Interaction in Information Systems: A Review of Research from Document Retrieval to Knowledge-Based Systems.** London, British Library; distr., Wolfeboro, N.H., Longwood Publishing Group, 1985. 250p. bibliog. (Library and Information Research Report, 35). $30.00pa. ISBN 0-7123-3050-X.

This work reviews research judged by the authors to be relevant to the "information retrieval [IR] interaction" — the interaction of the user (including user contextual variables such as information need, cognitive style, membership in a social system, etc.) and the information system. The approach is eclectic and comprehensive. Research from a large number of disciplines and subdisciplines is reviewed for possible relevance to and/or implication for the study of the IR interaction. Areas covered include question analysis, dialog analysis, human-human interaction (the reference interview), human-computer interaction, search strategy, question-answering and expert systems, evaluation, and user satisfaction. Although the review does not succeed fully as a synthesis, the organized presentation of research results focused on the IR interaction is extremely useful and the juxtaposition of findings from disparate disciplines is often provocative. The authors' interpretative and evaluative commentaries are generally well informed and perceptive. This survey represents a successful contribution to the evolution of an integrated view of the IR interaction. Joe A. Hewitt

203. Lancaster, F. W. **Vocabulary Control for Information Retrieval.** 2d ed. Arlington, Va., Information Resources Press, 1986. 270p. bibliog. index. $27.50. LC 84-082260. ISBN 0-87815053-6.

This is a revised edition of the most comprehensive text on vocabulary control (the first edition was published in 1972), and is still one of the few monographs on the subject. Indexers and literature searchers profess love/hate feelings about controlled vocabularies. Sometimes they allow precise, effective, and efficient retrieval; other times they inhibit it. This book thoroughly examines how vocabulary decisions affect the performance of information retrieval systems and gives advice on the creation, use, and evaluation of thesauri. Unlike the first edition, there is little discussion of classification systems as vocabulary control devices. Classification is discussed only as an inherent characteristic of thesauri. While Lancaster does not ignore theory, this edition is more prescriptive. The writing has been tightened; it is terse and focused and there is less emphasis on literature review, with considerably fewer citations than the first edition. The focus of the book is on practical considerations of choosing terms, establishing relationships among them, creating effective displays, updating, and the like. Many examples and exhibits help the reader understand the concepts. Examples in Lancaster's books are usually drawn from medicine, metallurgy, and aeronautics (to the distress of students in the humanities), but it was refreshing to see here a few examples from library science and education.

The trend today is toward natural language searching because controlled vocabularies are costly and inherently resistant to change. But they will continue to play a role in information storage and retrieval. One new possibility discussed by Lancaster is the "post-controlled vocabulary" which is a stored set of successful natural language search strategies. This may add control to the advantages of natural language searching.

This is an important book for anyone creating or using thesauri. Its practical advice will help those who must develop a vocabulary, whether for a local index or an international database, and its theoretical discussion should be read by everyone involved in information storage or retrieval.   A. Neil Yerkey

204. Ostle, Judson R. **Information Systems Analysis and Design.** Riverside, N.J., Burgess Communications/Macmillan, 1985. 586p. illus. bibliog. index. price not reported. LC 85-385. ISBN 0-8087-6400-4.

Although providing extensive coverage of the subject area and containing sections on many subjects important for effective systems analysis such as information analysis and project management tools and techniques, systems analysis life cycle, and database management systems, etc., the tone of the instruction is unfortunately so elementary as to be more appropriate for a good high school text systems analysis. The general approach to illustrative facts and tables tends to be absolute rather than suggesting important circumstantial caveats, and the approaches to and definitions of information are almost exclusively those appropriate to the manufacturing business. The narrow definition of and uses for information and the elementary approach to the subject matter make this only marginally useful to the library and information sciences field, where such courses are taught at the graduate level. A better supplement to library and information science curricula would be *Management Information Systems*, by Gordon B. Davis and Margarethe H. Olsen (2d ed. McGraw-Hill, 1985) which, although somewhat narrower in focus, treats the concept of information in a more sophisticated manner.   Elisabeth Logan

Information Theories

205. Ruben, Brent D., ed. **Information and Behavior. Volume 1.** New Brunswick, N.J., Transaction Books, 1985. 521p. index. $39.95. ISBN 0-88738-007-7; ISSN 0740-5502.

The orientation of this first volume of *Information and Behavior*, edited by Brent Ruben of Rutgers University, is primarily that of information as interpreted by the disciplines of communication and social psychology. Nonetheless, there is much in this volume of interest to librarians and information scientists. The book is organized into four sections: "Information and Communication: Theoretical Issues"; "Communication and Information Processing Technology: Issues and Interpretation"; "Information Processing and Individual Behavior"; and "Social and Political Issues." Each of these sections contains at least one or two chapters of particular interest. The foreword by Alfred G. Smith points the finger at those of us in the academic world engaged in "potlatch scholarship" and "ritual evasion of significant research." Ruben's introductory chapter examines issues of the information age and makes a plea for a cross-disciplinary framework. The chapter "Computers and Computing," by Rogers and Rafaeli, gives a fascinating account of the early development of the microprocessor in Silicon Valley. In "Person-Computer Interaction: A Unique Source," Cathcart and Gumpert explore societal implications of mediated interpersonal connection between people and computers. Other chapters of particular interest include: "Indexing Systems: Extensions of the Mind's Organizing Power," by James D. Anderson; "Privatizing the Public Sector," by Herbert Schiller; and "Corporate Transborder Dataflow and National Policy in Developing Countries," by Shipley, Shipley, and Wigand.   Elisabeth Logan

206. Taylor, Robert S. **Value-Added Processes in Information Systems.** Norwood, N.J., Ablex Publishing, 1986. 257p. bibliog. index. (Communication and Information Science). $39.50. LC 85-18677. ISBN 0-89391-273-5.

This book examines information systems from the standpoint of how they add value to the usefulness of data, instead of the more traditional method of focusing on their content or technology. Organizations which produce, organize, retrieve, or disseminate information may enhance it by adding such values as ease-of-use, increased precision, and time and cost savings. The model is user-driven; the decision to adopt a new classification scheme, indexing method, or reference procedure, for example, should be analyzed in terms of how it benefits the user. Taylor evaluates libraries, indexing and abstracting services, analysis centers, and other information activities by asking three questions: What does this activity do for humans to justify its cost? Can the costs be related to the enhancements? and How much time, effort, and money must the user invest to obtain useful information?

This is an important book. It provides a unique synthesis of the value-added processes in very different information settings and presents the challenge of looking at them in a new way. It is a well-written and thorough discussion of the value-added model and its implications for administration, education, and research. [R: WLB, Nov 86, p. 58]

A. Neil Yerkey

207. **Toward Foundations of Information Science.** Laurence B. Heilprin, ed. White Plains, N.Y., published for the American Society for Information Science by Knowledge Industry, 1985. 232p. illus. $34.95. LC 85-12612. ISBN 0-86729-149-4.

This book is largely based on papers presented at four consecutive annual sessions of the Special Interest Group/Foundations of Information Science (SIG/FIS) at the annual meeting of ASIS. Papers from each year are grouped under one of four parts. The foundations of information science is a significant but difficult topic. So far there is a paucity of substantive materials. Writings on this topic tend to border on speculations and suggestions. Moreover, compilations of conference papers often suffer from uneven quality and incoherence. Unfortunately, this volume is no different. Much of the presentation is unnecessarily obscure and convoluted. This book does little to promote the study of the foundation of information science or to contribute to its basic knowledge.

The theme of part 1 is the place of information theory in information science. All four papers focus on the inadequacy of Shannon's theory as a comprehensive foundation for information science. Part 2 is devoted to the place of artificial intelligence (AI) in information science. Some interesting works in AI are presented by Rieger and by Hayes-Roth. Unfortunately, many of the papers neglect to place important aspects of AI in the larger context of information science. Parts 3 and 4 focus on the recipient and the interpretation in observation and communication. An interesting algorithm in the analysis of art objects into their aesthetic attributes is given by Stiny as an illustration of the human analytic process. The other papers represent several attempts to take various epistomological approaches to the information processing of the user/receiver. Again, most of the papers fail to define the larger framework in which these important approaches may be related.

In summary, this volume is a valiant attempt to address the problems in the foundation of our field. There is a great need to offer a clear delineation of the cognate areas of knowledge of this field, and to pose questions that need to be investigated. Unfortunately, it is difficult to discern the main points of this volume. Only clear, logical, and systematic treatment can promote interest and foster our understanding, as well as the understanding of scholars in related fields such as pattern recognition, cognitive science, and linguistics. [R: LJ, July 86, p. 60; WLB, Nov 86, p. 58]

Miranda Lee Pao

Technological Computing

GENERAL COMPUTING

General Works

208. Adams, David R., Michael J. Powers, and V. Arthur Owles. **Computer Information Systems Development: Design and Implementation.** Cincinnati, Ohio, South-Western Publishing, 1985. 623p. illus. index. $23.45. LC 83-51621. ISBN 0-538-10860-6.

This authoritative undergraduate text is a well planned and executed course for computer information system design and implementation. It is the outgrowth of a curriculum study sponsored by the Data Processing and Management Association, and its content is approved by the association. The emphasis is on business systems.

The organization of the text carries the reader through each stage of "computerization"—system design, applications, file and databases, software, testing and validation of the system, and user training. The appendix contains three detailed case studies which amplify the textual material of the volume. A useful forty-two-page glossary is also appended.

Although not a reference book in the traditional sense, this volume will be of considerable reference value to small and medium-sized public libraries, and to any library with a business clientele. The comprehensive index points to many concepts and theories likely to be of interest to patrons.

Edwin D. Posey

209. Daggett, Willard R., Kamiran S. Badrkhan, and Benedict Kruse. **Computers and Information Technology.** Cincinnati, Ohio, South-Western Publishing, 1985. 326p. illus. (part col.). index. $24.83. LC 84-51659. ISBN 0-538-04550-7.

This text is part of a set of learning materials designed to develop a complete learning program. In addition to the text these materials include a *Student Supplement*, which expands the concept in the text; a *Teacher's Manual* which provides guidelines for teaching based on the text and the supplement; and a *Test Bank*, whose answers are in the manual, and which provides a mechanism for determining student's progress. The text consists of four parts, and a total of eleven chapters, each of which starts with a set of learning objectives. The first part stresses the notion that all people process data and use information as part of their everyday lives. Using a background of history, a pattern of information need is established which leads to a discussion of the information explosion experienced in this century. The second part deals specifically with the processing of data and the development of information; and parts three and four, with the development of computer information systems, and future trends in computer technology. Well illustrated with colored photographs and diagrams, the book is an excellent introduction to computer literacy for secondary school students, grades seven through nine.

Antonio Rodriguez-Buckingham

Dictionaries

210. **Dictionary of Computing.** 2d ed. New York, Oxford University Press, 1986. 416p. $29.95. ISBN 0-19-853913-4.

The volatility and growth rate of this enormously important subject area (computing) renders any dictionary obsolete even before it is printed. However, because of the importance of "computing" to nearly every human field of endeavor, the effort to provide lexicographical guidance is extremely important.

The editors have done a good job in covering most of the important topics—languages, machines, major companies, and basic terminology. Mathematical terms, especially those relevant to computing, are also defined. The work is sparsely illustrated; most illustrations are circuit diagrams, tables, and flow diagrams. Currently "hot" topics—e.g., artificial intelligence, expert systems, parallel processing—are adequately treated.

Comparison to the *McGraw-Hill Dictionary of Electronics and Computer Technology* (1984) indicates that many more terms are defined in the present work, and the definitions are more up-to-date.

This dictionary is apt to find heavy use in most public and academic libraries, and is highly recommended. Edwin D. Posey

211. Downing, Douglas, and Michael Covington. **Dictionary of Computer Terms.** Woodbury, N.Y., Barron's Educational Series, 1986. 245p. $5.95pa. LC 85-31570. ISBN 0-8120-2905-4.

This pocket-sized paperback defines over six hundred terms that address concepts and functions in computer programming and in more than twenty specific programming languages, such as BASIC, COBOL, LISP, and PASCAL. Electronics and computer hardware and peripherals terms are also included. Many entries are more substantial than a typical dictionary definition, with some running longer than one page. Numerous examples are given via sample computer programs, flowcharts, and diagrams. The quality of definitions is uneven. Some terms which could be explained simply are unnecessarily complex, while others are made unclear by too much jargon. Despite this failing, the majority of the work is informative and direct, and covers the subject matter very well.

This work is not specifically directed toward the uninitiated beginner. The level of language used assumes that the reader has at least some knowledge of programming and computer vocabulary. For example, the sample programs which are presented to demonstrate a concept are not explained in enough detail to be understood by those who do not know how to interpret computer programs.

The numerous tables increase this book's value for reference use. At the front of the book, there is an index of tables (ASCII characters, Epson printer control codes, etc.) with the pages where they appear within the text of entries. There is also a small "subject guide," with selected terms grouped into categories (e.g., terms found in BASIC, in PASCAL; those describing hardware, operating systems, etc.). Although this reference work is very inexpensive, it is of good quality, and will be useful in any library that serves those who work with or have an interest in computers or programming. [R: Choice, July/Aug 86, p. 1652]

Gary R. Cocozzoli

212. Hipgrave, Richard. **Computing Terms and Acronyms: A Dictionary.** London, Library Association; distr., Chicago, American Library Association, 1985. 117p. $15.00. ISBN 0-85365-696-7.

Shortly after starting to count the number of computer dictionaries, directories, glossaries, handbooks, and encyclopedias reviewed in *ARBA* since 1980, I quickly ran out of fingers. The Bowker *Computer Books and Serials in Print* next assured me in 551 pages that there were nearly twelve thousand books and fifteen hundred serials on the subject as of 1984.

This particular dictionary, an English publication, is distributed exclusively in the United States by the American Library Association. It includes terms used in the United Kingdom, the United States, Europe, and Australasia, as well as many databases produced worldwide. It is a simple, straightforward dictionary, arranged from "A&I Abstracting and

Indexing" to "Zoological Record," with 117 pages and approximately twelve hundred terms in between. The definitions are purely descriptive, telling how the terms are used, not how they could, should, or may be used. Italics are used within a definition to indicate that the term is defined elsewhere in the text.

Designed for librarians, students, and the general public, and covering the subject areas of database management, networks, online cataloging and searching, videotext, and word processing, it seems a good buy for $15.00. It might well be compared, however, with the lengthier *Dictionary of Computers, Data Processing, and Telecommunications*, by J. M. Rosenberg (see *ARBA* 85, entry 1609), and the *Prentice-Hall Standard Glossary of Computer Terminology* (see *ARBA* 86, entry 1683). [R: RQ, Winter 86, pp. 248-49]—Charlotte Georgi

213. Langman, Larry. **An Illustrated Dictionary of Word Processing.** Phoenix, Ariz., Oryx Press, 1986. 289p. bibliog. $29.50pa. LC 85-43344. ISBN 0-89774-286-9.

This dictionary is a collection of over five hundred terms and concepts used in word processing. It also includes information pertaining to printers, modems, and other computer hardware that may be used in word processing. In most cases, the term is described in a good-sized paragraph, and there are *see also* references to similar or narrower terms. The author describes these references as "copious," but they are not as extensive as they should be for complete understanding of a concept. There is also a limited bibliography of a few sources for further information on word processing.

While not totally without value, it must be noted that the information in some of the definitions is potentially misleading, and in others is incorrect. Perhaps this is because different word processors use the same terminology to represent completely different operations or concepts. For this reason, computer users, especially beginners, may at times find these definitions more confusing than helpful. The author's familiarity with word processing seems to be limited to twelve best-selling programs, which are chosen for "reviews" in the appendix, but which exclude some popular titles such as Appleworks, PC-Write, WordPerfect, and Perfect Writer. In some cases, these reviews are based on the experiences of others rather than the author, and could have been more effective for comparing features if there were checklists, or more continuity in style of presentation.

It is difficult to determine the audience for this book. Its language and structure are a little too complex for beginners, but most intermediate users will be past the need for it. As an alternative, a general computer glossary or dictionary can answer many questions, and a more careful examination of the word processing manual may also be as helpful. Given its limited selection of word processors, use of this dictionary alone will not be of much help in choosing a suitable program to purchase. With the many other book and magazine sources of information about computers and programs available today, librarians should consider other items for acquisition. [R: Choice, Oct 86, p. 282; RBB, 15 Dec 86, p. 634; RQ, Fall 86, p. 114]—Gary R. Cocozzoli

214. Preston, Edward J., George W. Crawford, and Mark E. Coticchia. **CAD/CAM Dictionary.** New York, Marcel Dekker, 1985. 210p. (Mechanical Engineering, Vol. 43). $39.75. ISBN 0-8247-7524-4.

The field of CAD/CAM (computer-aided design and computer-aided manufacturing) has a large specialized vocabulary which includes acronyms. These terms are commonly used in product literature, specification sheets, and both trade and scholarly publications. The objective of this dictionary is to provide a ready-reference tool which covers general computer definitions as well as application-specific terminology.

The text of over seventeen hundred terms is arranged in straight alphabetical order, with all acronyms listed at the beginning of each letter. The definitions range from quite lengthy, as in the case of *ethernet* and *OSI Reference Model* to single sentences, as in the case of *line driver* and *incremental feed*. Terms which directly relate to CAD/CAM are generally identified as such, while general terms related to computer technology are not. For example, *flat-pattern generation* is identified as being directly related to CAD/CAM, whereas *debug* is given a basic definition. Terminology seems to be very up-to-date and includes phrases such as *tape-up* and *mask*, commonly found in the trade literature but rarely defined in current electronics or computer dictionaries.

While aimed directly at "CAD/CAM evaluation teams" in industry, the book should also be useful in any engineering or technical school library where industrial or manufacturing engineering is taught.—Susan B. Ardis

215. Sippl, Charles J. **Computer Dictionary.** 4th ed. Indianapolis, Ind., Howard W. Sams, 1985. 562p. illus. $24.95pa. LC 84-51436. ISBN 0-672-22205-1.

That a publication appears in a fourth edition must say something about its credibility as well as popularity with its users. This particular publication has had a long history, with the first, second, and third editions published in 1966, 1974 (see *ARBA* 75, entry 1774), and 1980 respectively. Charles J. Sippl was the author or coauthor for all of these editions.

The fourth edition defines more than twelve thousand terms related to all types of computers—micro, mini, and mainframe. Terms in related areas in robotics, artificial intelligence, and factory automation are also included. The definitions themselves are concise and to the point. Explanations assume some basic background in computers. No references are given for those who might like a more in-depth explanation. The fourth edition is both larger in the size of print and in the physical size of the work itself. Because of this it is somewhat easier to use than previous editions. Illustrations and pictures accompany some definitions.

Jack Carter

Directories

216. Amato, Francis. **Guide to Computer Magazines.** 1985 ed. Dallas, Tex., Steve Davis Publishing, 1985. 142p. index. $9.95pa. LC 84-91752. ISBN 0-911061-11-8.

There are scores and scores of computer magazines available today. Moreover, the computer magazine market is quite dynamic with new publications appearing and old ones disappearing every year. This book by Francis Amato provides an excellent overview of most of the available magazines. The book is divided into three sections: "Popular and General Interest Magazines," "Trade and Professional Magazines," and "Newspapers and Newsletters." In each section useful information is given about each magazine such as the intended audience, editorial focus, circulation, subscription price, and appropriate address. There is also a very useful subject/user index at the end of the book. Consequently, this book will appeal to a wide audience. Although the book has a fairly short shelf life, it is worth the price.

Curtiss Barefoot

217. **DataBase Directory. Spring 1986.** New York, Knowledge Industry, 1986. 769p. $215.00/yr. (2 issues). ISBN 0-86729-199-0; ISSN 0749-6680.

DataBase Directory, generated directly from the DataBase Directory Service online files, is issued two times per year. Access to online information is also available through BRS. The annual subscription to the printed volumes includes *DataBase Alert*, a monthly newsletter. With twenty-four hundred entries reflecting some twenty-nine hundred files, *Spring 1986* constitutes the third cumulation. Coverage is worldwide, representing all identifiable, machine-readable databases available for public access in North America and a few which are not. Full text, textual and numeric, numeric, property, bibliographic, and referral databases are included. Information was obtained from questionnaires. If producers did not respond, information was taken from the services themselves and tagged with a special symbol in the directory. New databases are also tagged with a special symbol. Entries are arranged alphabetically by name. Each entry includes database name, up to six subject categories, summary of scope and content, corresponding printed sources, subject access to database content, producer, time coverage and specific information about file content, vendor and price information, data sources, language of database, restrictions and conditions, telecommunications access, aids to database use, and indexes. In "Database Alternate Names" former names, alternate names, and acronyms are indexed. A vendor index includes databases offered, addresses, and telephone numbers. There is also a subject index. A comparable publication, *Directory of Online Databases* (Cuadra/Elsevier) appears in four issues per year, two of which are cumulative. Costing $95.00 annually, it has about the same number of entries and similar indexes, although information provided for each entry is not as complete. Choice of one directory or another could well depend on the user's need for currency and thoroughness. [R: RBB, 1 Nov 86, p. 396]

Margaret McKinley

218. **Directory of Computer Software 1985.** Springfield, Va., National Technical Information Service, 1985. 1v. (various paging). index. $40.00pa.

The NTIS is a primary component in technical publishing in the United States, as a central source for the public sale of U.S. government-sponsored research, development, and engineering reports, having almost two million titles currently in its database. This directory of computer software contains abstracts of over thirteen hundred machine-readable programs compiled in cooperation with more than one hundred federal agencies and/or their contractors. While it is a reference book, it is also a sales catalog, which is important to remember while reading the abstracts and other material.

In addition to the abstracts, there are indexes by agency, accession number, subject, hardware requirements, and computer language (where specified). Included are seven hundred new programs recently (1985) received from the National Energy Software Center (NESC). All entries are available to the public; nothing is restricted or classified. Most of these programs were created by diverse federal agencies to meet specific governmental objectives; applications to private-sector enterprise must be found. A warning: all software is provided "without installation support or maintenance service," which seems to mean *caveat emptor*, you get what you pay for and a program may require extensive modification before it can be run effectively (or at all) on your installation's computer. The items seem a bit expensive, but the NTIS is supported solely on sales and not on governmental subsidy. Paper copy is the standard format, with some magnetic tape and microfiche output for sale, as indicated.

The entries are full and complete, with extensive, highly technical abstracts and lists of keywords and related documentation. Only the most technical of engineering library environments would have need of this publication as an ordering tool. The casual browser will merely be impressed with how much the government has been up to in the way of documentation recently. Public and most academic libraries can safely give it a miss.

Bruce A. Shuman

219. **The Directory of Consultants in Computer Systems.** 3d ed. Woodbridge, Conn., Research Publications, 1985. 346p. index. $75.00. ISBN 0-89235-087-3; ISSN 8756-2685.

The *Directory of Consultants in Computer Systems* is a useful reference for locating professional consultants in the United States and Canada. In many cases, the listed consultant is an individual or the head of a very small company (two to ten people). Most of the firms program in several languages and work with various machines.

The first part of the book contains hundreds of profiles. Each profile has all of the important information about the consulting company or individual: name, address, telephone number, hardware expertise, programming languages, years in the consulting business, and fields of expertise. The second section is a very useful keyword index. Consequently, most consultants are listed in several places.

According to the information in the introduction, any professional consultant can be included in the directory simply by filling out a special application from Research Publications.

Curtiss Barefoot

Handbooks and Yearbooks

220. Blissmer, Robert H. **Computer Annual: An Introduction to Information Systems 1985-1986.** New York, John Wiley, 1985. 487p. illus. index. $20.95. ISBN 0-471-81106-8; ISSN 0271-6224.

This is a first: the automation/information field changes every day so why not an annual and a textbook, all in one? The words "1985 Computer 1986" are readily perceptible on the cover of this book, but one really has to look at the cover intently and for quite a while before seeing the word "Annual" in maroon computer graphics against a black background. Never mind: it's what's inside that counts, and what's inside is, as the young say, totally awesome!

Blissmer has over eighteen years' professional experience in the aerospace field's automation area. He believes in telling us what he's going to tell us, then telling us, then summarizing what he has told us. This, in an introductory textbook, is a boon, and makes it extremely easy, combined with an excellent back-of-the-book index, to get around in the book's many chapters. A previous edition is mentioned in the preface, but nowhere cited in the work. Presumably, there will be another one out each year, which will keep Blissmer's concepts-in-context approach timely and state-of-the-art.

Commendably, just about everything is covered, and in a lively writing style, accompanied by hundreds of small but clear black-and-white photographs, drawings, and other visual aids. A puzzlement: all pages are actually tearsheets; there are quizzes concluding chapters which may be taken by the student and turned in, but the answers are provided on the test sheets. Honor system? Don't ask.

I can't say enough good things about the clarity of the style of this book. Key concepts are highlighted in boldface, then defined. Applications (how each idea or device is used) are provided, and usually a picture of the thing itself. Chapters are introduced and summarized, for review. Lots of references and resources are presented, should the student wish to explore ideas further.

A single drawback, from the library-oriented user's point of view: Blissmer writes about what he knows: industry. His approach is not that of academic or public library information provision, but is more along the lines of a frequently occurring example: how to automate the process of building jumbo jets out of hundreds of thousands of parts, employing hundreds of people. Still, there is so much of value to the library/automation student that the book is enthusiastically recommended for libraries, with a warning that its tearsheet pagination may not survive too many circulations. But that is why it's an annual, right?

Bruce A. Shuman

Indexes

221. Computer Software Hardware Index 1985. Robert M. Bottorff, ed. Haledon, N.J., Computer Software/Hardware Index, 1986. 269p. $27.00pa.

This is a compendium of excerpts of published reviews—along with citations to those original reviews—of personal computer equipment and programs. The reviews are taken from about three dozen popular magazines. This index is a cumulation of a monthly looseleaf service, which itself was not reviewed. The computers for which equipment and programs are surveyed include the TRS-80, IBM PC and MS-DOS compatibles, Commodore 64 and 128, Apple II, and Macintosh. The program categories include educational, entertainment, and business. The book is divided into six sections: software reviews by title, citing the original publication; software reviews by subject, giving an excerpt of the original review and its citation; software reviews by computer manufacturer, citing the original publication; hardware reviews roughly by manufacturer, giving an excerpt of the original review and its citation; book reviews by author, giving a very brief description of the subject or reaction to the book; and printed programs by subject, citing the original publication. There are no table of contents, indexes, or cross-references. If one were looking for a review of a specific program, it would be difficult to locate; if one were interested in a broad subject that was an index term (the terms are not given in a thesaurus), this work would be useful. It is an ambitious undertaking that falls just short of being completely useful, particularly because of the lack of internal finding aids.

Stan Rifkin

MICROCOMPUTING

General Works

222. Falk, Howard. Personal Computers for Libraries. Medford, N.J., Learned Information, 1985. 174p. illus. $16.95. ISBN 0-938734-10-5.

Personal Computers for Libraries is an excellent and practical guide for the librarian of a small library who is investigating the possible uses of a microcomputer. The author divides the book into three parts, beginning with microcomputer applications in the library. Areas discussed include circulation, cataloging, serials management, in-house publications, index preparation, online database programs, statistical and budget management, and expanded patron services. The description of each application includes how the microcomputer is an asset, what to look for in choosing software, and examples of software currently available. A complete list of recommended software is not given.

The second and third sections of the book are basic computer literacy lessons for librarians. Software in general is discussed, with emphasis on evaluation and selection. Finally, hardware and all the peripherals are described, with practical tips for selection. Especially interesting are the discussions of office software, including databases, word processing, and spreadsheets, and a comprehensible discussion of microcomputer communications possibilities. The reader should not assume that this is a bibliography of recommendations; it is not. Nor does it include all the uses of micros in libraries; for example, card catalogs are not included. An index and a list of software discussed would have helped. Much of the information given will soon be out-of-date because of the changing technology. This should not discourage a librarian just getting into micros from using the book; it is helpful. [R: LJ, 15 Sept 86, p. 68]

Marie Zuk

223. Hayes, Jeanne, ed. Microcomputer and VCR Usage in Schools 1985-86. Denver, Colo., Quality Education Data, 1986. 203p. $39.95pa. ISBN 0-88747-217-6; ISSN 0889-0021.

Microcomputer and VCR Usage in Schools is a comprehensive, interesting, and easy-to-read report published by Quality Education Data, a division of Peterson's Guides. The report describes in text and graphs microcomputer and VCR density, distribution, and use. This information is presented state-by-state and for the nation as a whole. Comparisons are made among different socioeconomic, geographic, and ethnic groups. The interpretative narrative and projected trends are informative and thoroughly documented.

The study is useful to anyone interested in the adaptation of technology in the schools, but is even more meaningful to persons concerned about the educational impact of microcomputers and VCRs in the schools. The general conclusion is that these technologies are institutionalized and that their dramatic growth is over.

William E. Hug

224. Microcomputers for Library Decision Making: Issues, Trends, and Applications. Peter Hernon and Charles R. McClure, eds. Norwood, N.J., Ablex Publishing, 1986. 311p. bibliog. index. $29.50; $45.00 (institutions). LC 86-1043. ISBN 0-89391-376-6.

The influx of the microcomputer into library settings has been dramatic and far reaching in recent years. In most cases, this new machinery has been used to perform functions previously accomplished by typewriters and dumb terminals. While these types of microcomputer applications have enhanced many office functions, a much greater potential lies dormant. The editors of *Microcomputers for Library Decision Making* have produced a volume in which they discuss the importance to the profession of recognizing the potential for microcomputers to support decision making in libraries.

Rather than simply identifying library applications, however, they present the viewpoints of sixteen library educators, consultants, and practitioners to encourage the integration of microcomputer applications specifically for decision making purposes. "In this context, the book identifies various topics and issues related to supporting library decision making, and prepares librarians to better exploit the use of microcomputers" (p. ix).

Issues introduced in the book include the necessity for microcomputers, hardware selection, networking, in-house data collection, data transfer, and future trends. Discussions of microcomputer applications for library decision making include spreadsheets, graphics, communications, decision support systems, and more.

The book is not a "how-to" volume that purports to have all the answers. It is rather a cogent, well-written work that offers sound advice and presents a well-defined case for the use of the microcomputer in ways that will lead to more timely, more accurate, and better informed decisions in libraries. [R: WLB, Dec 86, p. 59]

John W. Collins III

Dictionaries

225. Hordeski, Michael. **The Illustrated Dictionary of Microcomputers.** 2d ed. Blue Ridge Summit, Pa., TAB Books, 1986. 352p. $24.95; $14.95pa. LC 85-27672. ISBN 0-8306-0488-X; 0-8306-2688-3pa.

The first edition of this book garnered a number of favorable reviews when it appeared in 1978 as the *Illustrated Dictionary of Microcomputer Terminology* (see *ARBA* 80, entry 1597). The new edition is double the size of its predecessor, providing brief definitions of more than eight thousand terms. That the book's scope is wider than the title indicates is shown by its Library of Congress classification of TK rather than QA. A number of terms relate to the manufacturing of computers or the use of computers in industry and the relevance of some of the entries to microcomputers is elusive (for example, *AAC:* Alaskan Air Command or *MS:* Manuscript). On the other hand, some words one might expect to find in a 1986 reference book on microcomputers are not here. There is an entry for *videodiscs* (a little out-of-date, incidentally) but not *CD-ROM, network topology* but not *local area networks*, the computer languages *BASIC* and *Fortran* but not *Pascal* or *Ada*. The reason for the title's emphasis on "illustrated" is also a little hazy. While there are 350 illustrations, these are all in the form of diagrams, many of them circuit schematics. Still, in terms of number of definitions at a reasonable cost, Hordeski's dictionary is hard to beat. [R: Choice, Nov 86, p. 454]

Robert Skinner

Directories

226. **Computer Resource Guide for Nonprofits.** 3d ed. San Francisco, Calif., Public Management Institute, 1985. 2v. index. $175.00pa./set. ISBN 0-916664-42-2; ISSN 0743-944X.

This third edition of *Computer Resource Guide for Nonprofits* is arranged in two volumes. Volume 1, subtitled "Software Directory," provides information on over three hundred software packages (an increase of 33 percent from the last edition) designed for nonprofit users. The second volume, which is subtitled "Fund Source Directory," has increased its size by 50 percent from the previous edition. It lists by corporate title over two hundred computer-related giving programs from corporations, government agencies, and foundations.

The first volume provides a checklist for assessing an organization's software and hardware needs. The answers to these questions may be applied when using the rest of the volume. Each entry is by corporate title (although the software name appears more prominently at the top of the page, creating confusion for the browser) and lists in checklist form what the package may be used for. There is also a description of the company and cost estimates for hardware and software.

The main failing of the first volume is the over-complexity of its arrangement and the lack of an index by software name. This would make the entries on, say, "School Mate" or "Telofacts" hard to locate unless one knew that Development Systems produced the former and dilithium Press the latter. The arrangement of this volume assumes one wants to look up items by company name, and its other, subject-oriented indexes are not very helpful in this regard. The indexes would have been better arranged by type of software and then by name of software, subdivided by company name. In addition, no page numbers are given. This makes volume 1 very difficult to use. Each entry seems to have been prepared separately, and the editing of the finished product lacks coherence.

Volume 2 is a more elegantly structured text. Its purpose is to list agencies that are willing to fund computer-related projects undertaken by "nonprofits" (as they are so awkwardly called here). Each entry is arranged by company name and gives relevant information about the organization, what sort of projects it funds, its monetary base, the amount of money it will give, a few examples of grants and their dollar value, and the application process. It contains several indexes that vary in usefulness from "Contributions Committee Members" to "Interests in the Field." These indexes are confusing in some respects, and use subject headings/topics that are not listed elsewhere. On the plus side, they do have page number references, unlike the first volume.

Computer Resource Guide for Nonprofits contains information, and for U.S. organizations seeking funding for computer-related projects, it appears to be quite unique. However, its poorly designed format diminishes its value, and its hefty price should make one think twice before purchasing it.

Daniel F. Phelan

227. **Directory of Microcomputer Software for Libraries.** By Robert A. Walton and Nancy Taylor. Phoenix, Ariz., Oryx Press, 1986. 564p. index. $37.00pa. LC 86-42725. ISBN 0-89774-342-3.

Librarians interested in learning about microcomputer software for librarians will find much valuable information in this well-designed and easy-to-use directory. Succinctly and explicitly, it provides answers to the following questions: How can you find out what software programs are available? What type of microcomputer equipment is required? Does the vendor provide training? What happens if the software does not work? Is a demonstration disk available?

The compilers definitely achieved their purposes. They describe in one source all identifiable microcomputer software systems for libraries. They provide informative abstracts which illustrate the basic functional capabilities and intended library audience. They profile each software program, providing the most reliable and current information available about costs, compatibility, vendor support, documentation, and order information.

It is unfortunate, however, that the authors do not provide any evaluative information about the approximately 250 software programs that they describe. Neophytes to the field of automation need to know more about the strengths and weaknesses of the many programs available. They should be offered some assistance in discriminating between programs. In this respect, librarians will be disappointed and, perhaps, misled.

Isabel Schon

228. Dyer, Hilary, and Alison Brookes, comps. **A Directory of Library and Information Retrieval Software for Microcomputers.** 2d ed. Brookfield, Vt., Gower Publishing, 1986. 145p. index. $26.95pa. ISBN 0-566-03561-8.

The second edition of *A Directory of Library and Information Retrieval Software for Microcomputers* has been updated from the recently published first edition. Its purpose is to act as a single source for details on microcomputer software for library and information work.

The directory includes software designed for acquisitions, administration, archive control, audiovisual control, cataloging, circulation, interlibrary loans, and many other library/information uses. It excludes business software used in libraries and software adapted or developed by library schools in teaching programs. No geographic limitations on country of origin have been imposed, although software from outside the United Kingdom is probably underrepresented. The alphabetically listed information has been derived from the trade literature and professional press, as well as from the suppliers themselves.

Each entry gives the name of the software package, the supplier and its address, the operating system, hardware needed to run the software, the price (in country-of-origin currency), notes on what the software is used for, references to articles in the literature discussing it (when available), and descriptors from the functions index.

The editors begin the text with a two-page discussion called "Notes on Software" which gives advice on analyzing systems to be automated, measuring needs against available software, and determining the strengths and weaknesses of a software package and its company. Following the list of software packages, there are three indexes: the function index, the hardware index, and the supplier index. Each of these refers back to the name of a software package in the alphabetical listing. There are no page numbers and no paged index.

This directory could be very useful in helping the novice sort through the vast number of library software packages on the market. It is efficiently, if rather unattractively, designed and certainly does not waste space on frills or gimmicks. It has the obvious disadvantage of being out-of-date as soon as it was printed but this is a flaw of publishing and certainly not the fault of this excellent if unexceptional listing.

Daniel F. Phelan

229. Froehlich, Robert A. **The IBM PC (and Compatibles) Free Software Catalog and Directory: The What, Where, Why, and How of Selecting, Locating, Acquiring, and Using Free Software**. Portland, Oreg., dilithium Press; distr., New York, Crown, 1986. 924p. $17.95pa. LC 85-26970. ISBN 0-517-56112-3.

This book provides PC DOS programmers and general users with a single source for obtaining over twelve thousand files and programs contained on some 625 disks. This software is part of the two major (PC-BLUE, PC-SIG) and the four smaller (CAPITAL-PC, HAL-PC, LICA PC, NEW YORK PC) free software libraries. Free software is available for an individual's use without the payment of royalties or license fees to the author. The prime sources of such software are computer user groups and bulletin boards. Although free software varies considerably in quality and usefulness, there are many data files in these libraries which will be of interest to all microcomputer users. This book catalogs and indexes the software and gives the reader sufficient information on how to acquire it.

A comprehensive introductory section defines free software, presents an overview of software libraries, supplies information on how to obtain software from bulletin boards, and gives guidelines for various applications of this type of software.

The catalog section is file-oriented. Program files are listed by library. An entry for each disk file is listed. Entries contain a unique accession or file number, file name and type, author/group source, language, title, revision or related files (if applicable), keywords, a brief summary of the file, and the hardware/software requirements. The keywords are used to describe each file's functions. These keywords are used in the directory section to allow the user to access software by file type, utility, or application.

Besides a keyword index, the directory section permits the user to identify software by language, author, title, file name, bulletin board, and computer group. The bulletin board list is arranged by telephone area code and number to allow the user to find local sources for software. The computer club/user group list presents the name of the organization in alphabetical order with address. An extremely useful index provides a listing of these groups by zip code number.

This book is an indispensable tool for anyone interested in identifying and obtaining free software for microcomputers running PC DOS. The reasonable price makes it an excellent choice for libraries as well as personal collections.

Dennis J. Phillips

230. Mason, Robert M., and Stephen C. Enniss, eds. **The Library Micro Consumer MRC's Guide to Library Software**. Atlanta, Ga., Metrics Research Corporation, 1986. 322p. index. $25.00pa. LC 85-063250. ISBN 0-932393-03-9.

This guide is organized according to traditional library divisions of labor (interlibrary loan, media management) and includes evaluations of over two hundred commercially produced library software packages. Publishers' addresses and telephone numbers, hardware requirements, and prices are included for each entry. The authors have evaluated some packages themselves and have obtained comments from named evaluators for others. The authors have developed a "FAC Chart" (features analysis and comparison) to evaluate and compare packages objectively. There are introductory sections which discuss trends, define terms, and present guidelines for selecting software. There is an annotated bibliography of current periodicals on the topic of microcomputers. Hardware selection and local area networks (LANs) are discussed in appendices. Software packages are indexed alphabetically and by hardware systems (Apple, IBM, etc.) for which they are available. There is also a software publisher index. Full of information presented in a readable, easy-to-use format, perhaps the most valuable feature of the guide is its FAC charts, which simplify comparisons among software packages. One can only hope that the authors will issue new editions from time to time. [R: LJ, 15 Oct 86, p. 56]

Margaret McKinley

231. **Micro Software Evaluations (Library Edition). Volume II: 1985**. Jeanne M. Nolan, ed. Westport, Conn., Meckler Publishing, 1986. 152p. $95.00pa. ISBN 0-88736-032-7; ISSN 8755-5794.

Evaluations of twenty-seven microcomputer software systems for library and information management applications have been contributed by library and information professionals currently using the systems.

Each evaluation contains factual information on the producer, distributor, system requirements, the setting of the installation, and an evaluation narrative. These vary in depth and content, but all are specific and most include sample screens, descriptions of use, and candid comments on size limitations, support, documentation, ease-of-use, and useful and not so useful features of the system. In addition, there is an especially useful introductory chapter containing selection guidelines for evaluating software for specific library functions: acquisitions, serials management, circulation, etc.

Since there are just twenty-nine evaluations of twenty-seven separate systems and these are in alphabetical order, the absence of an index is not a serious drawback. However, it is difficult to determine the specific functions each software system is designed to perform without reading the entire review. Furthermore, the substantial price increase reflected in this edition may preclude its purchase by smaller libraries and information centers.

Because of the nature of the rapidly changing software industry, printed evaluations of this nature are apt to contain dated factual information; however, if the reader is aware of these limitations, this volume can be a useful guide to intelligent software selection. [R: JAL, July 86, p. 184; JAL, Nov 86, p. 308; WLB, June 86, pp. 82-83]

Elisabeth Logan

232. **The Software Catalog: Microcomputers, Summer 1986.** New York, Elsevier Science Publishing, 1986. 2v. index. $105.00pa./set. ISBN 0-444-01089-0; ISSN 0736-2722.

This directory contains descriptions of 22,700 microcomputer programs. The main section is organized alphabetically by program publisher or vendor. Each entry contains the vendor's name and address, program title, description, computers and systems on which it runs, distribution medium, and price. Some entries provide additional information about versions, release dates, minimum memory, update availability, integration with other programs, and the like. Each program is assigned something called an "International Standard Program Number (ISPN)," which is a reference number used by the indexes. The synopses are generally informative but they have been supplied by the vendors and so tend to read like mini-advertisements.

The programs are indexed in about every way possible. The largest index, of subject/applications, is arranged according to a numerical scheme consisting of 8 subject categories and 127 subcategories. Each entry gives a one-sentence annotation, system requirements, and price. The ISPN refers the reader to the main entry. Other indexes are by computer system, operating system, programming language, microprocessor, and keyword/program name. Some of these indexes are further subdivided by the category scheme, but the only information provided is the ISPN. There is also a short glossary.

This is a very complete, well-indexed, and useful directory which pulls together the ever-growing and scattered information about microcomputer programs. It is part of six volumes which make up *The Software Catalog*. The others cover minicomputers, business software, science and engineering, and health professions software. They are produced from a software database called .MENU which is available for online searching (DIALOG file 232).

Several good microcomputer software directories have been published recently. Most are not as extensive as this one, but they may have other attractive features. For example, *Online Micro-Software Guide and Directory, 1983-84* (Online, Inc., 1982) describes only 730 programs but includes comparison charts and articles on evaluation criteria. *The Software Encyclopedia, 1985/86* (R. R. Bowker, 1986) covers 22,000 programs, but the short entries do not include synopses. *Software Reviews on File* (Facts on File, monthly) covers about 50 programs per month and includes abstracts of reviews.

A. Neil Yerkey

233. Van Young, Sayre. **MicroSource: Where to Find Answers to Questions about Microcomputers.** Littleton, Colo., Libraries Unlimited, 1986. 220p. index. $23.50pa. LC 85-23862. ISBN 0-87287-527-X.

Van Young's book "aims at guiding the harried librarian who is besieged by questions about microcomputers." It is very well done and up-to-date, covering basic computer literacy, buying hardware and software (directories and guides), telecommunications (including database directories), uses of microcomputers, abuses of microcomputers ("Laws and Outlaws"), technical books, computer languages and operating systems, ergonomics, history of microcomputers, software publishing, vertical file material, periodicals and indexes, and general computer/microcomputer directories, dictionaries, and encyclopedias. Annotations are thorough and include "minuses" as well as "pluses." The book ends with recommendations for a core microcomputer collection. My only quibble is that information relating to any one type of microcomputer is scattered in a variety of different chapters (there is an index, however, which directs you to all the relevant citations). Reference librarians having to field questions concerning microcomputers on a daily basis may feel that Van Young's arrangement is indeed best. In any event, this book is highly recommended, and one hopes it will be followed by timely new editions. [R: Choice, July/Aug 86, pp. 1661-62; EL, Sept/Oct 86, p. 36; WLB, June 86, pp. 82-83]

Robert Skinner

Handbooks

234. Essential Guide to the Library IBM PC. Volume 2: The Operating System: PC-DOS. By Suzana Lisanti. Westport, Conn., Meckler Publishing, 1986. 196p. $19.95 spiralbound. LC 85-10535. ISBN 0-88736-034-3.

Contrary to the title of the series in which this volume on PC-DOS is issued, this book has no particular relevance for "the library." On the other hand, it has a great deal of relevance for the novice IBM PC user no matter what the user's area of interest. If you are fortunate enough to have completely menu-driven software, you may be able to bypass understanding some of the principles of DOS, but most of us aren't so fortunate. The DOS commands which are used the most frequently by all of us are explained and illustrated in a breezy, easy-to-read style which PC manual writers everywhere would do well to emulate.

Lisanti used DOS Version 2.1 in writing this guide, but most of the notes will be useful for later versions as well. The instructions cover "essential" and "useful" commands for a PC with two floppy disk drives and for a PC-XT with one floppy drive and one hard disk drive. There is considerable repetition between the PC and PC-XT sections when Lisanti talks about the "essential" commands, but she assumes that users will not need to read both. Under each command, e.g., "DIR," there is a list of its uses, followed by the proper form, special tips, cautionary notes, add-on options, and a "hands-on session." There is a special "Introduction to Subdirectories" in the PC-XT chapter, and it is one of the best and clearest I've seen anywhere. Lisanti concludes with a good explanation of "EDLIN," the PC line-editor program, and some concrete examples of useful batch files.

Librarians who are complete novices in the PC world will find this guide extremely helpful. Those who have already learned about DOS the hard way can probably save their money, but the basics are so clearly outlined and so easy to find that even "old pros" may be glad to have this guide for quick reference. [R: BL, 15 May 86, p. 1355] Berniece M. Owen

235. Essential Guide to the Library IBM PC. Volume 3: Library Application Software. By Susan Goodrich Miles. Westport, Conn., Meckler Publishing, 1986. 196p. bibliog. index. $19.95 spiralbound. LC 85-10535. ISBN 0-88736-035-1.

This is a listing, with brief descriptions, of approximately 110 library applications software packages. The content is based solely on information provided by the producers of the software and includes only software that runs on IBM PCs or IBM-compatible hardware. The descriptions are grouped under library applications (e.g., AV management, circulation, library instruction, reference) and include the following information: title, producer's name and address, publication date, price, description (in fifty to one hundred words), availability of demonstration disk and its price, equipment requirements, illustrations of sample screens, and producer's comments. Some sample screens (white letters on a black background) are not legible. The producer's comments are sales pitches and need to be read as such. Title and producer/distributor indexes are provided.

A competing guide is the *Microuse Directory: Software* prepared by Ching-Chih Chen (Microuse Information, 1984). *Microuse Directory* is not as up-to-date and includes less information for each package. However, *Microuse* does include generic software and non-IBM-based software. The *Essential Guide* is a useful reference source for those currently shopping for library software for an IBM PC. Those who are generally surveying available software that might serve a particular library function should consult the *Microuse Directory* and write the software publishers for information.

Thomas G. Kirk

236. Flores, Ivan, and Melvyn Feuerman. The Professional Microcomputer Handbook. New York, Van Nostrand Reinhold, 1986. 881p. illus. bibliog. index. $49.50. LC 85-3139. ISBN 0-442-22497-4.

Flores's audience is the business and professional community, and he has written a detailed handbook covering hardware, operating systems, programming, and application programs on microcomputers. As is appropriate for the intended audience, emphasis is almost entirely on IBM computers, although there is a short appendix on the Macintosh, and other systems are mentioned from time to time in the text proper. Interestingly, over half of this book is devoted to application programs, including word processing, databases, graphics, and spreadsheets. The word processing examples are general; the database discussion centers on dBase II, the spreadsheet on Super Calc and later Multiplan. Both Lotus 1-2-3 and Framework and, to a lesser degree, Symphony are covered in some detail. The chapter on graphics is surprisingly detailed for a business audience. Flores writes well, although portions of the book rapidly move from simple to complex and may lose some readers (particularly in the sections on hardware). There are some curious omissions: integrated software, of course, is discussed, but you won't find this term in either the index or the glossary. Neither is there an index entry for telecommunications, and in spite of a chapter entitled "Communications," this seems comparatively to be the weakest section of the book. Considering the audience, one is surprised not to find sections on business information utilities (e.g., Dow Jones) and databases. And, unavoidably, there is the question of currency. Flores does well at this, but it is obvious that many of the most recent developments and systems, such as laser printers and the IBM AT, were not sufficiently important or well known at the time the book was being written to get the attention these now deserve. As a whole, however, this book will answer many questions that business users will have about microcomputers, and much of the book will be applicable for other professionals. In fact, although the price is rather high, it is easy to imagine this being used as a text for a course on microcomputers.

Robert Skinner

INTELLECTUAL FREEDOM AND CENSORSHIP

237. **Books on Trial: A Survey of Recent Cases.** rev. ed. 1985. New York, National Coalition Against Censorship, 1985. 27p. $5.00pa. ISSN 0749-5323.

People in the fields of publishing, education, and library services are very much aware of the work of this arm of the American Civil Liberties Union. Their ability to provide on-the-spot counseling, referral services, and background materials to those attempting to fight censorship is not as well known as it should be to those so beleaguered. This publication will help. It is revised and updated from time to time. The issue at hand deals with school book-banning litigation. There is a summary of the landmark *Island Trees* case as a basis for evaluating the current cases, a summary of other previous decisions, and most important, a list of the books that have been challenged and parenthetical notes on where the title was on trial. Fifty-one titles are included. There is a list of attorneys who have been involved in cases, arranged geographically. A brief but most relevant tool that should be on the desk of every school principal in the country, in every school library, and in all serious collections of materials on censorship. It is a unique service. Libraries will have to resort to a jiffy binding to support the stapled and very soft cover.

Gerald R. Shields

238. Burger, Robert H., ed. **Privacy, Secrecy, and National Information Policy.** Champaign, Ill., Graduate School of Library and Information Science, University of Illinois, 1986. 182p. (*Library Trends*, Vol. 35, No. 1). $8.00pa. ISSN 0024-2594.

This issue of *Library Trends* contains articles on key issues in information policy. Among them are David Linowes and Colin Bennett's "Privacy"; Stephen Gould's "Secrecy as a Part of Scientific and Technical Information Policy"; Toni Carbo Bearman's insider's view; and Robert Burger's discussion of analysis of information policy. The weight of the issue is aimed one way or another at personal privacy. Important, well informed, and timely.

Michael Rogers Rubin

239. **Censorship in the South: A Report of Four States 1980-85.** By Sissy Kegley and Gene Guerrero for the American Civil Liberties Union. New York, American Civil Liberties Union, 1986. 24p. $2.00pa.

This report was sponsored through funding from the Deer Creek Foundation and the Sapaelo Island Research Foundation, with a long list of cosponsors from library, booksellers', and English teachers' organizations. It is the result of a survey sent to every public library and school library in Georgia, Tennessee, Louisiana, and Alabama, with a 22.4 percent response. Needless to say, the results show not only an increase in challenges but also that in school libraries the loss of the material to the collection has increased over previous surveys.

Such reports can cause undue nervousness and timidity in library administrators and policy makers. However, the survey does offer encouragement on a statistical basis for the establishment of policies and procedures for the acquisition and orderly consideration of a request to remove materials. Strangely, the surveyors seemed to feel that such policies and procedures were designed to remove the threat of censorship. Practitioners in the field know that such an umbrella does not exist and have always considered the creation of policies and procedures more like an insurance policy: it won't prevent the fire but it can alleviate the damage caused when one breaks out. All collections need this kind of research, and school administrations should be bringing these statistic-based reports to the attention of layboards.

Gerald R. Shields

240. **Freedom and Equality of Access to Information: A Report to the American Library Association.** By the Commission on Freedom and Equality of Access to Information. Chicago, American Library Association, 1986.

124p. index. $10.95pa. LC 86-3655. ISBN 0-8389-3332-7.

Judging from press accounts, this report did not sit well with members of the executive board and other manifestations of the ALA establishment. In its final printed form there isn't much to feed speculation as to what upset the power base. If one wants to draw a conclusion it could well be that the interpretation of intellectual freedom developed by the commission was broader than many librarians are ready to allow. The recent changes in legal interpretations of libel are discussed as barriers to information; the control of television and cable franchises is considered; the development of a bibliographic control and access system for electronically stored information, thus allowing for effective copyright restrictions, is proposed; royalty payments to authors and publishers is advocated in the use of their materials; and among traditional concerns, censorship and government information systems are examined. It is a valuable report and should be an important springboard for much-needed discussions and consensus making. However, when it is made painfully clear in the foreword by then-ALA President Lynch that, although commissioned by ALA, the report in no way "presents the view" of the association, the pall is unleashed.

The ALA has a way of generating, from time to time, studies or policy statements that allegedly rub against the grain of the "practical" administration of libraries. These documents appear and quickly move to the shelves of the progressive literature, never to be heard again. Since nothing has happened to further the work of this commission since its report appeared, a similar fate may await this volume. This is a shame, since there are volatile issues dividing the producers of information and the disseminators of information. Those issues won't go away and this report offers a chance to open dialog, an offer seemingly too bothersome to accept. [R: BL, 15 Sept 86, p. 99; RQ, Winter 86, p. 262; WLB, Sept 86, p. 73] Gerald R. Shields

241. **Freedom of Information and Youth. Proceedings of the Twenty-third Annual Symposium Sponsored by the Alumni and Faculty, Library & Information, Rutgers School of Communication, Information and Library Studies, 13 April 1984.** Jana Varlejs, ed. Jefferson, N.C., McFarland, 1986. 92p. bibliog. $9.95pa. LC 85-43606. ISBN 0-89950-189-3.

The Twenty-third Annual Rutgers Symposium brought together a number of articulate spokespersons against censorship. The symposium's title, Freedom of Information and Youth, and the editor's preface suggest a broad approach to the issues of children's access not only to particular books and information but also to specialized services—reference, ILL, online searching, etc.

Rather than the specific exploration of youth access which the preface suggests, the speakers provide a broad framework for the problems Varlejs outlines. While there is little new in the presentations, they furnish excellent discussions of a number of aspects, including the climate of censorship, significant cases past and present, strategies for dealing with censorship, and the variety of values at work within the act of censorship. The discussions which follow each presentation help open related topics, such as religious book selection and the need to understand critics like Schlafly and Falwell.

Since most censorship issues are related to either public or public school libraries, the focus is there, with youth services librarians as a targeted audience. The fact that these proceedings provide a succinct, articulate, current, and very readable synopsis of censorship expands their usefulness to all librarians and concerned citizens. A number of appendices and a solid, annotated bibliography provide formal support mechanisms to the issues examined. These proceedings serve as a guide to the basic issues of censorship and represent a useful addition to any collection on the topic. [R: BL, July 86, p. 1607; WLB, Mar 86, p. 57]

Patricia A. Steele

242. Miller, Peggy A., and Arthur J. Levine. **The Information Executive's Guide to Intellectual Property Rights.** Washington, D.C., Information Industry Association, 1985. 1v. (various paging). $99.95 spiralbound.

The book is a layperson's guide to the practical aspects of operating a business when the product at hand is intellectual property such as books, maps, charts, phonograph records, or semiconductor chips, computer programs, and the like. The guide is divided into four chapters: (1) an overview of copyright, trade secret, trademark, and chip protection law, including practical hints presented in the form of questions and answers; (2) a general discussion of contract law, particularly as it pertains to marketing intellectual property; (3) a general discussion of other types of law, including advice on how to avoid being sued for infringing on other people's intellectual property, for harm to others caused by your business distributing inaccurate data, and so on; and (4) a discussion on how to obtain effective legal advice.

This is largely a very superficial book. It deals with complex legal matters in a very simple-minded way. For example, issues involving work for hire are covered in one and one-half double-spaced pages, enough to explain that a problem exists, but little more. Further, the book is padded with copies of a number of government forms that are easily available from the Copyright Office.

Michael Rogers Rubin

243. Mount, Ellis, and Wilda B. Newman. **Top Secret/Trade Secret: Accessing and Safeguarding Restricted Information.** New York, Neal-Schuman, 1985. 214p. index. $39.95pa. LC 85-19864. ISBN 0-918212-90-1.

This book is an attempt to address the topic of the handling of restricted information—that is, classified military information and proprietary commercial information. Included are discussions on the history of restricted information, computer technology and restricted information, and systems for handling military and commercially restricted information. Also included are tables listing the various agencies of the U.S. government, the top one hundred Defense Department contractors for FY1984, the top one hundred NASA contractors, and so on. The book is rounded out with the full text of such key pieces of law as the Freedom of Information Act, the Privacy Act, and the "Sunshine" Act.

The library community and indeed all interested citizens are in urgent need of a good book that addresses the many problems and competing pressures concerning the need to safeguard sensitive information. Unfortunately, this book is not that book. What we have here is a very simple-minded treatment of an extremely complex matter. The book starts with the internal contradiction of claiming to instruct the reader on how to both "access" and "safeguard" restricted information. The authors seem blithely oblivious to the fact that these are competing objectives. The book is then filled up with lists and lengthy reprints of easily obtained laws. [R: LJ, July 86, p. 60] Michael Rogers Rubin

INTERLIBRARY LOANS

244. **Directory of Interlibrary Loan Policies & Duplication Services in Canadian Libraries.** 4th ed. Compiled by The National Library of Canada. Ottawa, Canadian Library Association, 1986. 80p. $25.00pa. ISBN 0-88802-183-6.

The fourth edition of this directory represents the joint effort of the Interlibrary Loan Committee of the Canadian Library Association and the National Library of Canada to compile current interlibrary loan information for the library community.

Subsequent editions will be expanded to cover all libraries in the National Library of Canada's *Symbols of Canadian Libraries.* Updates will appear in their *Bibliotech* newsletter. These will update the information between editions of the directory.

The directory is divided by province (and subdivided by institution) with an initial section, "National Libraries" (Canada Institute for Scientific and Technical Information and the National Library of Canada).

In column format, each entry begins with the ILL code, institutional name, address, telephone number, and electronic mail information. This is followed by a section on interlibrary loan information: length of loan period, what formats are and are not lent, to whom materials are lent, what charges are made if any, etc. The last section on duplication services lists charges and time required for delivery for both photocopies and microfilm copies.

The directory also has a page of explanatory notes referring to some entries, an abbreviations list, and some blank pages with the aforementioned headings for inserting information on libraries not listed.

This straightforward, workmanlike publication serves its function well and is a must for all libraries lending to or borrowing from Canadian institutions. Daniel F. Phelan

LAW AND LEGISLATION

245. Coghlan, Sam, and Stephen Cummings. **Libraries and the Law: What You Need to Know about Laws Relating to Ontario Public Libraries.** Toronto, Ontario Ministry of Citizenship and Culture, 1985. 76p. $5.00pa. ISBN 0-7729-0635-1.

Public libraries in Ontario will find this compilation of laws and legal decisions which affect libraries a useful handbook. The compilers have listed federal and Ontario statutes and regulations and Canadian case law which is relevant to public libraries. Those laws and regulations which may apply indirectly to libraries are difficult to identify, but have been included whenever possible. The first part of the citator is an annotated alphabetical listing of laws, the second part is an alphabetical subject index. Appendices include lists of abbreviations, and copies of the Ontario Human Rights Code, the Municipal Conflict of Interest Act, and the Public Libraries Act. Annotations for the citations are brief and are intended only as an aid in locating the full text. Reference to a case in which the court "upheld a ruling that a theft of a book from the Cambrian College

Library ... is a trifling matter" and quashes the conviction for theft under $50.00 because "the law does not concern itself with trifling matters" raises intriguing questions for a librarian. How large must the theft be to make it more than "trifling"? Can the time and effort involved in acquiring or replacing materials be included as part of their value? Is there any recourse for libraries plagued by a series of small thefts? Clearly a lawyer would have to be consulted for advice on any of these points. Libraries in Ontario will want to have this listing available; those in other jurisdictions may hope that a similar publication will be provided for them.

Adele M. Fasick

LIBRARY HUMOR

246. Stevens, Norman D. **Archives of Library Research from The Molesworth Institute.** New York, Haworth Press, 1985. 109p. (*Technical Services Quarterly*, Vol. 3). $22.95. LC 85-16354. ISBN 0-86656-466-7.

A study of umbrellas left in the library? A computer analysis of library postcards? A cost analysis of a cost analysis? And what is the Molesworth Institute?

This book contains the ruminations of one Norman D. Stevens, who is identified on the title page as the director of the mythical Molesworth Institute, an idea which sprang from his head many years ago. The institute has taken on a life of its own since its story first appeared in the old *ALA Bulletin* in 1963.

By this time, one might well be asking, what is the function of the Molesworth Institute? It is not another foundation dedicated to glorious good works. Rather, it seems to be committed to the practice of disjunctive librarianship, a concept of the "late twentieth century," defined as follows in Stevens's *Dictionary of Libinfosci Terms* (another fictional construct). "*Disjunctive Librarianship*: The wholesome approach to librarianship ... that now dominates libinfoscience. [It] is characterized by a total disregard for analyzing the field on a rational basis."

Such terms as *libinfosci* and *libinfocenter*, it strikes me, are the natural outgrowth of the proliferating acronyms that are endemic to the practice of our profession. This is sophisticated, muted, library humor. Stevens extrapolates from present trends into the future; it is hard to tell whether or not he likes what he sees, so firmly is tongue planted in cheek. He is as deadpan as Buster Keaton when he writes of "negative library growth," or "*Oscar Gustafsen*: a tragic minor figure of American librarianship." Stevens has mastered the niceties of academic prose style. This makes his tone of mock solemnity the more effective. His book should be enjoyable reading for all of us who have ever cast a jaundiced gaze on our profession.

Randall Rafferty

LIBRARY INSTRUCTION

247. Clark, Alice S., and Kay F. Jones, eds. **Teaching Librarians to Teach: On-the-Job Training for Bibliographic Instruction Librarians.** Metuchen, N.J., Scarecrow, 1986. 232p. index. $18.50. LC 86-6598. ISBN 0-8108-1897-3.

A refreshing book on library instruction from the standpoint of academic libraries. Most of the chapters would be useful for all medium- to large-sized libraries. There is some unevenness in presentation because there are thirteen authors involved, but most of the chapters are accurate and succinct. Some references need updating, but nearly all of the important people and research studies are represented. Special surveys were also conducted specifically for this book. There were two references identified from 1985 and none from 1986. The index seems to be well done and accurate.

The individual authors have emphasized the application of theories and methodologies from the field of education to bibliographic instruction for students in higher education. The various areas covered include motivation, defining behavioral objectives, learning theory, classroom techniques, preparing teaching materials, and evaluation of results. Several chapters provide practical ideas on training staff to make the most of orientation tours, writing workbooks, evaluating the effectiveness of instruction, on-the-job training, in-house workshops, and improving the techniques of training.

Thomas L. Hart

248. Katzen, M. **Technology and Communication in the Humanities: Training and Services in Universities and Polytechnics in the U.K.** London, British Library; distr., Dover, N.H., Longwood Publishing Group, 1985. 121p. (Library and Information Research Report, No. 32). $15.00pa. ISBN 0-7123-3046-1; ISSN 0263-1709.

Katzen's study reports the results of a comprehensive survey of British universities and polytechnics in 1983 and 1984. The survey gathered data on five main areas relating to communication in the humanities: provision of bibliographic instruction; online searching of commercial databases conducted by libraries on behalf of the academic staff and students; instruction in oral and written presentation of information; provision and use of computers in humanities studies; and involvement of computer service departments in offering instruction and advice on the use of equipment and software.

The study's findings were clear. Almost all bibliographic instruction is done informally; it is not often regarded as a specialized topic in its own right or accorded a specified part in the curriculum. It is most successfully imparted when departments do recognize its importance as a specialized topic and conduct formal courses of bibliographic training in collaboration with librarians. With respect to online searching, the humanities users are shown to be much worse off than those in the sciences or social sciences; such searching is "still in its infancy" (p. 85). Training students in oral and written presentation is done mainly informally and ad hoc; more systematic attention is needed. The availability and use of computers in humanities studies is becoming much more widespread and computer service departments are providing a good deal of training.

Like all the other publications of the British Library's Research and Development Department, this report is thoroughly and competently done. For a North American audience, its chief interest will be in the comparison it offers between British and American practices and viewpoints. For those with a special interest in bibliographical instruction, there may be comfort as well as value in Katzen's study; apparently the difficulties which librarians experience in achieving recognition and attention for bibliographic instruction are so common and predictable that they should be simply taken for granted. Samuel Rothstein

249. **Library Instruction Clearinghouses 1985: A Directory.** rev. ed. By Joan Ariel with Lynn Randa. Chicago, Association of College and Research Libraries, American Library Association, 1985. 24p. $6.00pa. ISBN 0-8389-6960-7.

Intended to revise and update the 1984 directory, this product of the ACRL Bibliographic Instruction Section's Clearinghouse Committee is brief, but packed with important information.

It identifies (1) international, national, regional, state, and specialized materials and (2) directories, handbooks, newsletters, and publication columns about instructional programs; and describes (3) the scope and activities of various types of clearinghouses including founding date, funding source, goals and objectives, acquisition and loan policies, and size of collection.

Arranged by format (e.g., depository, newsletter) and subdivided by type (national, state), this typewritten source is not difficult to use because of its brevity. However, access would have been greatly improved with the addition of an introduction or statement of purpose, explanation of how the information was obtained, table of contents, and subject/geographic index.

Nonetheless, the modest price and timely information make it attractive to instruction librarians. Ilene F. Rockman

250. **Marketing Instructional Services: Applying Private Sector Techniques to Plan and Promote Bibliographic Instruction. Papers Presented at the Thirteenth Library Instruction Conference Held at Eastern Michigan University, May 3 & 4, 1984.** Carolyn A. Kirkendall, ed. Ann Arbor, Mich., published for the Center of Educational Resources, Eastern Michigan University by Pierian Press, 1986. 157p. illus. bibliog. (Library Orientation Series, No. 15). $19.50. LC 86-60025. ISBN 0-87650-201-X.

This collection of papers features six conference presentations, and seven brief "poster session abstracts." While a few of the narratives stray from a strict "marketing" focus, most present thought-provoking concepts which are a credit to their well-qualified contributors. A lengthy bibliography on library orientation and instruction rounds out this volume, while some of the most intriguing thoughts can be found in a final section featuring discussion group materials. While some of the practical suggestions for marketing bibliographic instruction (BI) may not be applicable to all environments, most readers will benefit from the plethora of extremely thoughtful theory supporting BI.

Stimulating ideas abound, not the least of which is the theory held by several authors that marketing BI can result in increased demands on sometimes already overextended library services and staff (pp. 28, 63). It was also gratifying to note at least one example of BI which included the oft-overlooked concept of "critical evaluation skills" (i.e., "locating background information on authors and publishers") and recognizing bias in books and articles (p. 61). Other nuggets include a summary of Philip Kotler's apt definition of "product orientation" versus "sales orientation," versus "marketing orientation" (p. 57), and John Berry's mind-tickling quote, "information is a resource that cannot be depleted through use" (p. 135). All in all, a stimulating compendium of ideas; recommended for professionals supervising or delivering BI. [R: JAL, July 86, pp. 181-82; JAL, Nov 86, p. 311; RQ, Winter 86, pp. 264-66]

Mary Ardeth Gaylord

251. Shih, Tian-Chu, comp. **Library Instruction: A Bibliography, 1975 through 1985.** Jefferson, N.C., McFarland, 1986. 112p. index. $14.95pa. LC 86-42607. ISBN 0-89950-236-9.

At first glance, this work seemed useful, but it didn't take very long to see that it has a number of severe shortcomings. These might have been avoided by using Deborah Lockwood's *Library Instruction: A Bibliography* (see *ARBA* 80, entry 231) as a model, but the author was apparently unaware of it. Not only is it not mentioned, but the preface states that "this field has no single-volume bibliographies in print," when actually the Lockwood volume is still available. Also, since Lockwood covers items through 1977, there's no reason for Shih to begin with 1975. Most importantly, Lockwood could have provided a fine model; her book is sensibly organized, nicely annotated, and has many cross-references. The organization of the items in Shih's bibliography, on the other hand, is much too general—the 1,065 items are listed in only four categories: "Libraries in General," "Academic Libraries," "School Libraries," and "Special Libraries." Moreover, there are no annotations; individual items in collected works (those in the annual volumes of Library Orientation/Instruction Exchange (LOEX) conference papers, for example) are not listed; and the title keyword index, which one presumes serves in lieu of more precise categories and/or a subject index, misses many items and omits or severely skimps on some important categories. (For example, "Search Strategies," has only one entry, "Teaching Methods" only two, and there are no entries at all for separate or credit courses.) There's an author index, but this is not really necessary since items are arranged by author. All these shortcomings are too bad, because a well-done, up-to-date bibliography would be welcome. One hopes this work will not discourage another compiler from doing a better job. [R: JAL, Nov 86, p. 321; RQ, Winter 86, p. 254]

Evan Ira Farber

252. **User Instruction in Academic Libraries: A Century of Selected Readings.** Larry L. Hardesty, John P. Schmitt, and John Mark Tucker, comps. Metuchen, N.J., Scarecrow, 1986. 311p. index. $29.50. LC 86-960. ISBN 0-8108-1881-7.

The rapid growth of bibliographic instruction in academic libraries over the past fifteen to twenty years may give the impression that it is a relatively recent newcomer, a midtwentieth century development in library service. Yet much of what we think of as recent innovations in user instruction was originally introduced and developed during the past century. From Justin Winsor in 1880 asserting the value of the library as a "rival and abettor" to the textbook and encouraging librarians to make themselves "indispensable" to teaching and learning, to Nancy E. Gwinn of the Council on Library Resources in 1980 assessing the results of 3 million dollars spent to encourage the development of library use instruction programs in academic libraries in the 1970s, the twenty essays in this collection have been selected to help librarians understand and appreciate their bibliographic instruction roots. Such a historical perspective as Evan Farber notes in his foreword "may remind us of our goals, our high calling, and help give us new insights and perspectives to enhance our effectiveness in working toward those goals."

Most of the significant trends and approaches to academic library user education are represented here—course-related instruction (Otis Hall Robinson, 1881), credit courses (Raymond C. Davis, 1886), the library-as-laboratory (Melvil Dewey, 1891), the faculty-librarian instructor team (Harvie Branscomb, 1940), the Library College (Louis Shores, 1968), and integrated library instruction (Kennedy, 1970). But these essays not only enhance our awareness of the trends in bibliographic instruction, they also reveal a great deal about libraries and library service in general, showing library use instruction to be only one important interrelated component of the educational process. Helpful, too, are the introductory comments to each essay by the editors that place these librarians and their views into the historical context of library instruction.

This work is highly recommended not just to all academic librarians, but to all academic administrators and faculty as well. The one principle that echoes most persistently from this collection is the need for the joint cooperative efforts of librarians, faculty, and administrators if bibliographic instruction is ever to reach its great potential. Understanding the philosophy, the theory, and the practice of instructing users in the use of libraries as iterated here by its proponents and practitioners of the past century will not only inspire us to greater efforts but provide us with a better grasp of the persistent difficulties we face. [R: LJ, 15 Sept 86, p. 68; RQ, Winter 86, pp. 267-68]

Blaine H. Hall

253. Wolf, Carolyn, and Richard Wolf. **Basic Library Skills.** 2d ed. Jefferson, N.C., McFarland, 1986. 141p. illus. index. $12.95pa. LC 85-43600. ISBN 0-89950-228-8.

There is nothing startling or original in this useful how-to manual on teaching oneself basic library research skills. The authors have written this work for college students who need to learn how to use the library. It could be used in a class or as a "self-paced instructional sequence for all students" (p. v).

Its uniform treatment, in individual chapters, of bibliographies, book reviews, general information sources, periodicals and newspapers, literature and criticism, government documents, biographies, business and consumer information, computer use, and hints for writing papers reveal a discriminating selection of titles, although many lack descriptive annotations. Each chapter includes a list of objectives, a discussion of specific topics, exercises testing comprehension of each chapter's information (with appended answers), a summary of key terms, and a bibliography of related works. The chapters are informative but basic, including, for example, a description of *Books in Print*, copies of cards from card catalogs, excerpts from *Abstracts of English Studies*, and a discussion of OCLC. A subject and title index complete this timely volume.

Frances Neel Cheney

LIBRARY RESEARCH

254. Allen, G. G., and F. C. A. Exon, eds. **Research and the Practice of Librarianship: An International Symposium.** Perth, Australia, Western Australian Institute of Technology; distr., Chicago, American Library Association, 1986. 220p. (Western Library Studies, 7). $35.00. ISBN 0-908155-61-1; ISSN 0810-5030.

This collection of eighteen papers focuses on some of the basic issues in library research, and their relevance to practicing librarians. The papers also review the experience of library researchers in particular geographical regions, including the USSR, France, Great Britain, and the Third World. The book's scope includes a consideration of library research in general (its problems, organization, support, and development), surveys of actual library research achievements, and the process of research in the library context. The authors were invited to contribute papers. They are well-known figures in the library world with impressive credentials. The stimulus for the design of the collection was the outcome of a workshop for the formulation of a National Australian Research Agenda held in 1984, sponsored by the Australian Advisory Council on Bibliographical Services. The aim was to further stimulate interest in the research process among Australian librarians.

The preface to the book provides a good introduction and overview of the papers. Each is clearly presented, well written, and well documented, including bibliographical references and footnotes. There is, however, no overall index to the book. Differences in perspectives and differing points of view on the same issues heighten the book's usefulness and interest. The compilation provides an important contribution not only to the field of library research, but also to comparative and international librarianship. It is a valuable addition to professional library science collections in schools of library and information science, as well as a useful addition to library science collections of academic and research libraries. Library educators as researchers in the field, library science students, and library practitioners all can benefit significantly from careful reading of this book.

Susan J. Freiband

LIBRARY SECURITY

255. Morris, John. **The Library Disaster Preparedness Handbook.** Chicago, American Library Association, 1986. 129p. illus. bibliog. index. $20.00pa. LC 86-1155. ISBN 0-8389-0438-6.

This handbook, written by an experienced California consultant, John Morris, contains essential, current information on safety and security for libraries. Topics discussed include building security, problem patrons, thefts and mutilation of books and materials, fire protection, water damage, planning and design for safety and security, preservation and conservation, insurance risk management, a glossary, and a bibliography.

This manual and guidebook will be extremely useful to anyone dealing with a "crisis" in a library, be it building, materials, or patrons. It analyzes problems, offers remedies, suggests options for prevention of disasters, and discusses various implementations through a series of very practical recommendations, technical advice, charts, and photographs. Rules in this book are stated clearly; in libraries, rules have to be established, defined, publicized, and posted. Librarians have to be trained and instructed to handle major and minor crises efficiently. Two important sections of the handbook are on fire protection and on water damage, two of the leading sources of library losses. In fact, according to the author, arson alone accounts for more than 85 percent of all library fires, and water incidents are some of the most common calamities for the library world. Chapter 8 constitutes one of the best concise readings on insurance, followed by appendix A, "Best's Underwriting Guide" (libraries).

Format and style of this manual are pleasing, and I would strongly recommend that this handbook be on every librarian's bookshelf in the near future.   Camille Côté

MANAGEMENT

256. **Advances in Library Administration and Organization: A Research Annual. Volume 5: 1986.** Gerard B. McCabe and Bernard Kreissman, eds. Greenwich, Conn., JAI Press, 1986. 307p. index. $40.00. ISBN 0-89232-674-3.

This volume provides a wide variety of articles ranging from "A Longitudinal Study of the Outcomes of a Management Development Program for Women in Librarianship," by Ruth Person and Eleanore Ficke, to "Three Studies of the Economics of Academic Libraries," by Paul Kantor. There is an informative study, "Volunteers in Libraries," by Rashelle Schlessinger Karp, and a scholarly presentation by Joe W. Kraus entitled "The History of Publishing as a Field of Research for Librarians and Others." The latter includes an extensive bibliography. John A. McCrossan provides a useful overview in his "Accredited Master's Degree Programs in Librarianship in the 1980's." Complementing this is an interesting study by Renee Tjoumas and Ester E. Horne, "Collection Evaluation: Practices and Methods in Libraries of ALA Accredited Graduate Library Education Programs."

Most of these articles are well written and are important contributions to our profession, though not all are research studies, as the subtitle implies. As in the previous edition, the emphasis continues to be on academic libraries. There is little of interest to public and special libraries or particularly to school libraries. The editors and publisher need to re-examine the objectives of this series and consider changing the title and subtitle. The cost of each volume remains overly high. [R: JAL, Nov 86, p. 332]
George S. Bobinski

257. Conroy, Barbara, and Barbara Schindler Jones. **Improving Communication in the Library.** Phoenix, Ariz., Oryx Press, 1986. 195p. bibliog. index. $25.00pa. LC 84-42815. ISBN 0-89774-172-2.

Management has been approached from a number of perspectives—organization, planning, finance—and in this presentation it is discussed from the perspective of communications. What role communications play in the managerial process and how one can incorporate the appropriate techniques into both organizational communication and personal communication are the authors' focus.

Theories of communication are described, as are models of communications networks and techniques for achieving optimum levels of communication within the organization and among individuals. Included within the definition of organizational communication are staff development, hiring, counseling, and numerous related activities. The manager who wishes to create a climate for interaction with and among staff will find guidelines for what to communicate, when, and through whom. Interpersonal communication relationships and skills are described. Current theories are presented as are such skills as speaking, writing, listening, reading, and developing an awareness of nonverbal communication. Communication as an integral component of change provides the manager with useful insights.

The authors have used their communications skills to present a clear, concise overview of the role of communications in management. One can dip into it for descriptions of an activity or explanations of how particular theories relate to practice. The selected bibliography lists the works of leaders in the field of communications and management. [R: BL, 15 Sept 86, p. 99; JAL, July 86, p. 197; LJ, 15 June 86, p. 54; RQ, Fall 86, p. 127]   Ann E. Prentice

258. Cronin, Blaise, ed. **Information Management: From Strategies to Action.** London, Aslib; distr., Medford, N.J., Learned Information, 1985. 189p. bibliog. $32.00. ISBN 0-85142-193-8.

This volume treats the subject of information resources management in a very lively and realistic manner. All the contributed chapters provide a wealth of information on the emergent discipline and some of the indicators that could be cited to support the arguments in favor of the new discipline. The chapters are written by British professionals for the international audience that is or should be interested in the subject. There are some provocative statements which have been expressed before by some of the authors in previous writings or speeches. For example, Dennis Lewis predicts that by "the year 2000 ... [the] librarian and information specialist will have gone the way of the brontosaurus." He advises librarians/information officers to "change—or be changed!" In his chapter "Intelligence Management," Martin White, who describes himself as a "disciple of information management," declares that information management is at least two thousand years old, and has been masquerading under the name "military intelligence." Other chapters provide good definitions for the term *information resources management* as well as practical treatment of topics such as information mapping (D. Best), the flow and management of information in organizations (A. Gilchrist), information management (P. Vickers), and education for information management (G. Bull). The list of references provides an excellent collection of select international writings on the subject of each of the chapters presented in the book. Mohammed M. Aman

259. DuMont, Rosemary Ruhig, ed. **Women and Leadership in the Library Profession.** Champaign, Ill., Graduate School of Library and Information Science, University of Illinois, 1985. 353p. (*Library Trends*, Vol. 34, No. 2). $8.00pa. ISSN 0024-2594.

That men continue to dominate the upper echelons of library management is well established. In this special issue, for example, Barbara Moran documents the meager gains achieved by top women library administrators in the first ten years of affirmative action. What remains unclear are the reasons for women's underrepresentation in library management, especially given their greater numbers in the profession as a whole. The majority of articles gathered here report on empirical research on this question.

Robert Swisher, Rosemary DuMont, and Calvin Boyer compare the "motivation to manage" in male and female MLS students and practicing librarians. Betty Jo Irvine and Joy Greiner study career and family patterns of men and women administrators in academic research libraries and public libraries, respectively. Barbara Ivy looks at resume preparation as a factor influencing differential achievement of male and female librarians. Jill Moriearty and Jane Robbins-Carter attempt to identify the effects of role models on women's careers. And Rose Knotts, Traute Danielson, and Stephen Replogle survey the personality characteristics of women who have pursued nontraditional careers. Suzanne Hildenbrand takes a dramatically different tack, looking to the history of the welfare state, professionalization, and gender relations for an understanding of women librarians' inferior status. Contemplating the future, Darlene Weingand proposes that continuing education may offer women librarians a means to strengthen their position in the profession and to influence technological change in their field. A bibliography by Katharine Phenix provides an overview of the literature from the last decade on women in libraries.

Two theories are commonly advanced to explain women's subordinate position in library management: women are either less qualified than men, or they are discriminated against. Readers will find evidence supporting both of these claims in the research reported in this volume, but no definitive resolution of the controversy. [R: JAL, July 86, p. 196; JAL, Sept 86, p. 234] Catherine R. Loeb

260. Harman, Keith, and Charles R. McClure. **Strategic Planning for Sponsored Projects Administration: The Role of Information Management.** Westport, Conn., Greenwood Press, 1985. 279p. bibliog. index. (Emerging Patterns of Work and Communications in an Information Age, No. 1). $45.00. LC 85-9881. ISBN 0-313-24931-8.

This book, written by two professionals with complementary skills in grant work and the decision-making process, represents the first in a series from Greenwood Press. While it parallels the business literature of decision making and strategic planning in essential ways, it targets a unique audience: the sponsored project administrator. Research and development administrators and grants managers are examples of individuals who could use this work as a handbook. The theoretical aspects of the book make it of interest to researchers also.

Project administrators as "people" oriented managers is a theme throughout the text. Their role is characterized as "delicate," comprising uncertainties and interdependencies. They can succeed through the efficient and effective management of the information resources in their environment. In this book the authors present a detailed plan to aid in that process.

The plan, which involves strategic planning and information management across and within the boundaries of the project and the organization, relies heavily on management theory. Steps are conceptually supported, fully defined, and explained through the text and numerous effective charts. The synthesis of relevant management theory, the multileveled approach, and the explicit detail are some of the strengths of this book. One cannot examine it without noticing the comprehensiveness of the work and the special zeal of its authors. While theorists will find the book interesting, its target audience of administrators will probably be the most receptive and best served by this excellent work.

Patricia A. Steele

261. Lindsey, Jonathan A., ed. **Performance Evaluation: A Management Basic for Librarians.** Phoenix, Ariz., Oryx Press, 1986. 222p. bibliog. index. $35.00. LC 86-42746. ISBN 0-89774-313-X.

According to the editor of this collection of journal articles and one book excerpt, the twenty "core" selections plus the thirty items in the annotated bibliography should provide a solid grasp of the most recent literature on performance appraisal both inside and outside of library settings. The selection of items is based on a five-year review of *Library Literature* and *Business Periodicals Index* as well as a perusal of *North Carolina Libraries* and Stueart and Eastlick's textbook, *Library Management*, second edition (Libraries Unlimited, 1981).

The articles focus on five broad areas: types of performance appraisal, the importance of effective communication, legal issues, performance appraisal as a management tool, and the evaluation of the effectiveness of appraisals. An index, compiled by Debbie Burnham-Kidwell, is very complete. Nine selections are from the literature of librarianship while eleven are from business and management sources. Nine articles were published in 1983 and one appeared in 1985, while the others range from 1979 to 1984. The annotated bibliography tends to provide more recent sources, with five of the items having appeared in 1985. One-half of the articles include references, and thus might be considered "scholarly." The others tend to be descriptive, opinion pieces, or how-to-do-it. As in any collection, the quality varies considerably. In each broad area, however, there is at least one substantial article.

Although this book contains considerable useful material, the editor does not provide any connecting linkages among its parts. There is, however, an implicit underlying assumption that performance appraisal is a good thing and that the editor hopes that by bringing up the issue of commitment, discussion of performance appraisal based on the items in this book will "move from process and procedure in a vacuum" to include "a sense of philosophical wholeness" (preface). Unfortunately, the total value of this book is not greater than the sum of its parts. Helen Howard

262. Panwar, B. S., and S. D. Vyas. **Library Management.** Delhi, India, B. R. Publishing; distr., New York, Apt Books, 1986. 336p. index. $37.50. ISBN 81-7018-283-2.

This monograph on library management essentially does not contribute anything new to library literature. It consists of reprints of twenty articles by library professionals from the United States, Australia, Great Britain, and India. The book is divided into six sections: library management, building and furniture, kinds of libraries, organization and management, classification schemes, and dissemination of information. Though the title of the monograph is quite broad and a wide range of topics could conceivably be included under this heading, the articles presented in this work were not selected carefully enough to give a concise view of library management. Instead, it seems that the editors were somewhat too ambitious and tried to include too many topics under the library management heading. This has resulted in very sketchy information on many topics beyond library administration and not enough information on the book's main theme.

It is unclear from the preface if the book is intended only for Indian librarianship or for librarians in general. If the first supposition is true, the monograph would have some merit because of the dearth of library literature in that country. If, however, the second purpose is intended, one must point out a number of shortcomings and inaccuracies. For example, the preface states that librarians do not have access to appropriate library literature; this would not be the case in the United States.

The reprinted articles are dated. More recent and timely literature on these topics is available in the current library literature. There are numerous typing errors and the essays written by library professionals from India include some quaint and frequently unclear phrases. More careful editing could have eliminated such inaccuracies as listing four of the U.S. contributors with wrong institutions.

This monograph could conceivably be useful to U.S. librarians who need information on librarianship in India, since ten of the reprinted essays are written by Indian librarians. In general, I would not recommend this book for purchase by any library.

Hannelore B. Rader

263. Ramsey, Inez L., and Jackson E. Ramsey. **Library Planning and Budgeting.** New York, Franklin Watts, 1986. 228p. illus. bibliog. index. $19.95. LC 86-556. ISBN 0-531-15506-4.

Inez and Jackson Ramsey are professors of library science and management respectively, and claim this book is written for the library administrator in all types of libraries. Divided into four sections, "Introduction" (planning, budgeting and costs), "Planning-Budget Cycle," "Applications to Types of Libraries," and "Other Topics" (capital budgeting, spreadsheets), the volume covers the full scope of budgeting, from the planning stages down to the specifics of accounting systems and budget categories and their definitions. Therein lies the problem with this volume: it covers too much. The general discussions of planning and budget making are too general, even superficial, to be helpful, and the details about budget structures and accounting practices may be inappropriate to the specific institution in which the administrator works. To make the volume more useful the authors included three chapters on budgeting in three types of libraries: university, public, and school. However, these are largely redundant accounts of details about budget categories, with some recognition of different emphasis but without taking into account differences in budgeting environments (e.g., dependence of public libraries on practices and structure of budgeting in local government units, public and private universities, size of libraries). This is not a helpful desk reference for the practicing administrator who has questions or seeks advice about his or her budgeting process. [R: LJ, July 86, p. 60]

Thomas G. Kirk

264. Roberts, Stephen A. **Cost Management for Library and Information Services.** Boston, Butterworths, 1985. 181p. index. $49.95. LC 84-26339. ISBN 0-408-01376-1.

In the past decade or so, three concurrent realities have impressed themselves on the library and its management; increased number of publications, need to automate, and decreased levels of funding. In order to get the maximum benefit from available money, library managers have of necessity moved toward more business-oriented practices in budgeting, accounting, costing, and performance measurement. Roberts provides us with an overview of these activities as they apply to libraries. His is a book of definitions, procedures, and applications. It is a source to which one would refer to learn how to conduct a time study or cost analysis or if a definition of *input, throughput,* or *output* was desired. The appendix includes several useful tools basic to cost management, including task description listings, library tasks and procedures, and sample data recording forms.

The author's concern that librarians lack the tools to determine cost has been answered to some degree by the publication of *Cost Finding for Public Libraries* (American Library Association, 1985) which is considerably easier to read and use. *Cost Management for Library and Information Services* would best be used as a reference source for terminology and as a retrospective guide to the literature of cost management. Although not easy to read, it is a source of much useful information and is a creditable addition to the growing number of cost management texts. [R: C&RL, Sept 86, pp. 520-22; JAL, Mar 86, p. 60; JAL, July 86, p. 168]

Ann E. Prentice

265. Schauer, Bruce P. **The Economics of Managing Library Service.** Chicago, American Library Association, 1986. 278p. index. $49.00. LC 86-14186. ISBN 0-8389-0453-X.

In the past several years considerable attention has been paid to determining the cost of library and information services. Less attention has been paid to the factors which influence service and to the ways in which one can allocate resources among the many choices and thus influence cost.

The author provides an overview of microeconomics, with its emphasis on consumer theory and the nature of production to solve the problem of how to maximize the effectiveness of limited resources. Part 2 provides examples of how to apply microeconomics and mathematical formulas to decision making. Although the focus is on the public library, models of consumer preference, discussion of library production with the ways inputs can be manipulated to vary output, and similar topics are equally applicable to any type of information service or agency. The author's emphasis is on theoretical analysis, and although a mathematical background is not necessary, a careful reading is required. Complex theories are clearly stated and examples within a library setting are given. The final chapter is an excellent overview of the economic approach to the issue of fees for service.

The suggested readings at the end of each chapter provide a comprehensive overview of what has been written about libraries and economic theory. The exercises are textbookish and may or may not be of interest. This is not an easy book to read but a careful reading is worth the effort.

Ann E. Prentice

266. Shuter, Janet, and Mike Worsam. **Librarian in the Marketplace.** Bradford, England, MCB University Press, 1985. 47p. (*Library Management*, Vol. 6, No. 4). $74.95pa. ISBN 0-86176-257-6; ISSN 0143-5124.

This very brief monograph aims to describe the "most immediately accessible and useful marketing techniques of relevance to librarians." It is actually a presentation of various pieces of material used in a three-day "course" offered by the authors. It differs from the usual text in that the authors limit commentary to a "bare minimum" and do not "explain in detail what we mean by a particular element of course material." Unfortunately, the resulting format is a sometimes disjointed and puzzling outline of course activities and content.

While the authors hope to "stimulate library managers to *think* about the various techniques and concepts presented," this jumble of time schedules and unexplained exercises does not facilitate easy learning. Although some raw marketing theory is included, it is not applied to the library setting until the three case histories in the latter half of this volume. These cases describe projects undertaken by British school librarians, and do, however, present several problem-solving and organizing techniques of potential interest to their colleagues.

Published as an issue of *Library Management*, this relatively expensive paperback does mention some thought-provoking marketing concepts, albeit with a distinct British orientation. The lack of accompanying analysis, however, may hamper a thorough understanding of such concepts by the reader.

Mary Ardeth Gaylord

267. White, Herbert S. **Library Personnel Management.** White Plains, N.Y., Knowledge Industry, 1985. 214p. bibliog. index. (Professional Librarian Series). $36.50; $28.50pa. LC 84-26146. ISBN 0-86729-136-2; 0-86729-135-4pa.

This easy-to-understand book is a good introduction to the field. It is intended to permit library managers to develop appropriate tools and judgments to help them evaluate and lead.

White, well respected dean of the School of Library and Information Science at Indiana University, covers the standard menu one would expect in a management text—communication, leadership, decision making, adapting to technological change, and goal setting. The reader is not overwhelmed by technological language or footnotes, but instead is presented with a rather brief and commonsense approach to the issues. A special feature of the work is a series of twelve case studies, or problem exercises, which challenge the reader to identify and analyze the real-life situations.

Not as detailed or scholarly as the essays included in *Personnel Administration in Libraries* (Neal-Schuman, 1981) or as interdisciplinary and comprehensive as the reprinted articles in *Management Strategies for Libraries: A Basic Reader* (Neal-Schuman, 1985), White's book, nonetheless, presents a good starting point for students, professors, and practitioners of library administration. It is not overly ambitious, and can be easily read in an afternoon.

Ilene F. Rockman

NONBOOK MATERIALS

268. Daily, Jay E. **Organizing Nonprint Materials.** 2d ed. New York, Marcel Dekker, 1986. 301p. bibliog. index. (Books in Library and Information Science, Vol. 48). $49.75. LC 86-13390. ISBN 0-8247-7504-X.

Part 1 of this book is devoted to a diversity of topics; some related to organizing nonprint materials and some not. Less than half of this section deals with two topics, materials cataloged by content and materials cataloged by identifying features. The bulk of the section is devoted to topics such as a procedural manual, defining the library and its patrons, and nonbook and nonprint materials. Part 2 of the book deals with examples of bibliographic entries and subject headings. The major portion of this section, nearly one-half of the book, is devoted to an alphabetic listing and a classified listing of subject headings devised by the author.

Although the title and the stated purpose of this book imply it will deal with nonprint materials, it only deals with five in any detail: maps, pictures, art prints, sound recordings, and video recordings. The author has devised a classification scheme using Dewey numbers, Cutter numbers, and a string of subject headings separated by semicolons similar in principal to PRECIS. The author also proposes a cataloging scheme which ignores the principles and rules found in *Anglo-American Cataloguing Rules*, second edition. This method of cataloging and classification may or may not provide easier access to a library's collection as the author espouses, but it would inhibit resource sharing and use of other libraries by library users. In addition there are minor flaws such as typographical errors, reversal of digits in Dewey numbers, and misspelled words. There are also misstatements of facts such as the statement that the classification numbers were dropped from the *Sears List* after the eighth edition. At one point the author advises the reader, "anyone who wishes to follow AACR II scrupulously is invited to skip this chapter and go on to the next." Anyone who wishes to organize nonprint materials is invited to skip this work and use the second edition of Nancy B. Olson's *Cataloging of Audiovisual Materials: A Manual Based on AACR 2.*

Donald C. Adcock

269. **Media Librarianship.** John W. Ellison, ed. New York, Neal-Schuman, 1985. 449p. index. $35.00pa. LC 84-2145. ISBN 0-918212-81-2.

Most of the thirty-five essays in this text represent the ideas of editor John Ellison, who wrote or cowrote thirteen of them, and many of his colleagues from the State University of New York at Buffalo. Other contributors are from California, Georgia, other states, and even Ontario. Their thoughts on their chosen topics are strong, almost zealous, and a few seem to be getting off their chests pet ideas and opinions on a variety of subjects.

The first chapters deal in very general terms with librarianship as a career, censorship, format discrimination, and the philosophy of librarianship. These are not especially pertinent to the stated topic "media librarianship," but then it is not adequately defined here despite a few rather limp attempts. These essays are often somewhat superficial and condescending and put forward some pretty shopworn ideas concerning censorship by omission and universal nonelitist access to information. Many are well written and all are well intentioned but these early essays deal with their subjects in only the broadest of terms.

Each essay is self-contained (in fact some are reprints from other sources) but a loose structure has been imposed upon them. The eight major sections of the book are: "The Problems," "Media Librarians," "Management of Media Services," "Selection," "Organizing Non-Print," "Productions and Presentations," "Reaching Out," and finally "Computers in Media Services." Within these divisions are essays on censorship, management, systems analysis, grant writing, cataloging, library instruction, copyright, and microcomputers.

While not specifically covering certain types of libraries, the examples are often drawn from school or especially public librarianship. While not universally true or necessarily a major problem, this bias by omission limits discussion of the unique problems of college, university, and special libraries.

Despite these shortcomings, there is much that is good here. Outstanding examples include the essays on media evaluation forms, nonprint media sources, storage and care of nonprint media, and computer applications. Some essays also discuss the controversial topic of media production within the library.

Overall, *Media Librarianship* does a creditable job of covering the field. The marginal essays can be skimmed or skipped over. The relevant essays stand out and make this collection worthwhile. [R: BL, 15 May 86, p. 1355; JAL, Mar 86, p. 48; JAL, July 86, p. 168; LJ, 15 Mar 86, p. 52; RQ, Fall 86, pp. 128-30; WLB, Mar 86, p. 59]

Daniel F. Phelan

PUBLIC LIBRARIES

270. Bolt, Nancy M., and Corinne Johnson. **Options for Small Public Libraries in Massachusetts: Recommendations and a Planning Guide.** Chicago, Public Library Association, American Library Association, 1985. 128p. $15.30 spiralbound. ISBN 0-8389-6997-6.

In 1984 the Options for Small Libraries Committee of the Massachusetts Library Association was formed to "define the needs and problems of small libraries and to develop recommendations concerning the local, state and regional support required to fulfill those roles." Nancy Bolt and Corinne Johnson were consultants to the project, the major emphasis of which is on single-manager libraries. The resulting *Planning Guide* has been made available to all public libraries in Massachusetts. The *Full Report* (the *Planning Guide* and data and discussion of the study) is the version published by the Public Library Association. The study interviews were held with the library director, a trustee, and a town official in selected towns of population under fifteen thousand. Additional surveys of all three categories were done by mail.

The central idea of the Options study is a "Role Priorization Exercise" (RPE), to be done by library directors and trustees to determine the breadth of services to be offered by a library. Choices are offered and financial implications discussed. Choices vary from closing the library (discontinue service, contract for service, merge with another library) to offering all the roles listed. Critical success factors—basic, desirable, and optional—for each role are described, and financial implications for each decision outlined. The importance of trustee awareness and involvement is stressed throughout. Recommendations for regional network and state agency assistance as well as roles of the professional associations are included.

Although appearing to be simple, and in workbook format, the *Planning Guide* offers an in-depth approach to a number of basic questions all libraries, especially small ones, must ask themselves sooner or later—including which services they can afford to offer. A library director and/or trustee working through the entire *Planning Guide* will end up with an in-depth knowledge of the role(s) played by that library.

It is too soon to judge how effective a long-range planning tool this will be. While the RPE can be done quickly, the entire planning process would take many months, especially in a small town environment. However, its approach is useful and the recommendations important. Since few libraries can afford to provide all services, the importance of determining the priorities of the roles one serves cannot be overemphasized.

Suzanne K. Gray

271. **Guidelines for Public Libraries.** 3d enl. and rev. ed. Willem R. H. Koops, ed. Munich, New York, K. G. Saur, 1986. 91p. index. (IFLA Publications, No. 36). $14.00. ISBN 3-598-21766-8.

This is the third edition of *Guidelines for Public Libraries*, issued by the International Federation of Library Associations and Institutions (IFLA). Previous editions appeared in 1973 and 1977. Arthur Jones, in his introduction to this edition, provides a description of how they may be used: "This is not a comprehensive manual of library practice, but we hope that it will be a useful tool for anyone concerned with the provision of public library services. We have tried to identify the many decisions which must be taken in establishing and managing such services, and have begun by providing a detailed checklist of services and facilities which a public library might properly consider providing." The guidelines are presented in six chapters: (1) "Public Library Services"; (2) "Media of Communication"; (3) "Staffing"; (4) "Service Points"; (5) "The Management of Public Libraries"; (6) "Networks and Support Services." The contents of each chapter are presented in succinct statements in outline form, and each statement is assigned a reference number for quick and exact citation.

In addition to the six chapters, four useful appendices are provided. They are (I) "The UNESCO Public Library Manifesto"; (II) "IFLA Standard for Public Libraries, 1973/1977"; (III) "Statistics of Selected Library Systems"; (IV) "Standards and Guidelines Relevant to Specific Aspects of Public Library Services, Issued by Specialized Groups within IFLA." The work concludes with an index.

These guidelines do not attempt to tell how to carry out the activities of librarianship, but rather suggest what might be done. A working group was appointed by the Public Libraries Section of IFLA in 1983 to revise these guidelines and the results of the group's work, published here, were presented at the IFLA General Conference in 1985.

Dean H. Keller

272. Illinois Library Statistical Report 19. Springfield, Ill., Illinois State Library, 1985. 113p. free pa.

Number 19 of the series of statistical reports conducted by the Library Research Center, Graduate School of Library and Information Science, University of Illinois at Urbana-Champaign under contract to the Illinois State Library contains four reports: "The 1984 Survey of Illinois School Library Media Centers," "A Survey of Adult Use of Public Libraries for Information," "A Review of Tax Supported Public Libraries for Information," and "Summary of Unreported Data from the 1983/84 Illinois Public Library Annual Reports." The survey of school library media centers reports information on only those schools which have centers and examines the areas of staff, collections, cataloging and processing practices, microcomputer resources and use, and financial expenditures. A telephone survey of adults eighteen years or older employed six questions to determine patterns of use of public libraries for information. The survey determined if a public library had been used for information, why the information was needed, and why the users went to a public library; if they had not gone to a public library, it determined if they found the information needed and why they had not gone to a public library. The review of public libraries established between 1971 and 1980 compares these newly established, tax-supported public libraries with those already in existence in areas such as population served, collections, staff, expenditures, hours, and circulation. The summary of unreported data briefly reports data collected by the Illinois State Library from the "Illinois Public Library Annual Report" not published elsewhere, and covers such areas as characteristics of library staff, referenda, branch libraries and bookmobiles, and nonresident borrower's cards and annual fees.

Although restricted to the study of data from Illinois libraries, school and public librarians and library schools elsewhere should find this statistical report of interest and use.

Donald C. Adcock

273. Illinois Library Statistical Report 20. Springfield, Ill., Illinois State Library, 1985. 117p. free.

Number 20 of the series of statistical reports conducted by the Library Research Center, Graduate School of Library and Information Science, University of Illinois at Urbana-Champaign under contract to the Illinois State Library contains: "A Survey of Patrons of Illinois Public Libraries ...," "The Dunn Report Revisited," and "An Index of Quality of Illinois Public Library Service 1985." Using an Apple microcomputer, selected public libraries conducted a one-day survey of patrons to determine how often they borrow books, why they come to a public library, how they find what they come for, childhood experiences with reading and public libraries, etc. The information gathered on floppy disks was then sent to the research center for analysis. The second study is a follow-up to the recommendations of a 1974 report of an Illinois House Library Finance Subcommittee regarding Illinois public library financing. The study attempts to determine what progress has been made in the intervening ten years toward implementing the recommendations of the committee. The third study utilizes surrogate patrons to determine the quality of public library service in Illinois. Surrogates (college students hired by the research center) were given specific titles and/or reference questions to locate with the assistance of librarians in public libraries in their hometowns. The ability of the library to provide the book wanted, the accuracy of the answer to the reference question, and the quality of service provided were rated to arrive at the figure for the index of quality of service.

Those wishing to conduct surveys of library patrons will find the use of microcomputers in gathering data of interest. This report does contain a section dealing with the problems encountered in this information-gathering technique and some solutions. Systems of public libraries or large library systems with branches wishing to evaluate the quality of library services to patrons may find the methodology used in the index of quality of library service of interest.

Donald C. Adcock

274. **Levels of Library Development: Re-Imagining the Realm of the Possible.** Oklahoma City, Okla., Oklahoma Library Association; distr., Chicago, Association of Specialized and Cooperative Library Agencies, American Library Association, 1985. 43p. bibliog. $10.00pa. ISBN 0-8389-7043-5.

Since the 1980 publication of Vernon Palmour's *A Planning Process for Public Libraries*, several states have attempted to modify that approach for better use by small public libraries. The Oklahoma Department of Libraries has been in the forefront of that movement. Its *Performance Measures for Oklahoma Public Libraries* (American Library Association, 1982), also produced by King Research, provides a manual for libraries to assess their current status and to plan for future improvements. *Levels of Library Development* is a concise workbook, based on *Performance Measures*, outlining the options available to local libraries, offering "financial and professional incentives towards the twin goals of long-range planning and improved quality of service to the community" while at the same time preserving local autonomy and control.

While Level I is a basic definition of public library service, Level II includes the collection of performance measures (soon to be required for qualification for state aid); Level III is attainment of certain performance standards. At Level IV, a library should have a long-range plan including some role statements. Recommendations are also included for a public library accreditation program and for funding and legislative changes necessary to implement *Levels of Library Development*. The book is concisely written with adequate examples; it should not be difficult to use. It is interesting to note that selection of a library's role, one of the Level IV activities, is one of the basic exercises around which *Options for Small Libraries in Massachusetts* (Public Library Association, 1985) is built.

Suzanne K. Gray

275. Petty, Mike. **The Albatross Inheritance: Local Studies Libraries.** Bradford, England, MCB University Press, 1985. 51p. bibliog. (*Library Management*, Vol. 6, No. 1). $74.50pa. ISBN 0-86176-227-4; ISSN 0143-5124.

This short monograph deals with the topic of local studies libraries from the perspective of the local studies librarian of the Cambridgeshire Collection, Central Library, Cambridge, England. Mike Petty is also a writer, broadcaster, and lecturer on local studies, librarianship, and local history. His basic thesis is that although "the unique comprehensive local collection has been revived, invigorated and republicized" it remains "an oddity, nonconforming to the pre-ordained management structure, an albatross inheritance." Current priorities are computer databases and community information. The work discusses briefly five aspects of local studies libraries using the Cambridgeshire Collection as the example. The chapters focus on collection development, acquisition and conservation, organization of the collection, and community relations. A listing of twenty-five references is included. The work appears in a journal format, softcover with heavy, semi-glossy paper. The price is exorbitant for the size and scope of the book, which has no illustrations. Although it would be of some interest to American local studies/public librarians, its extremely high price and totally British context limit its usefulness. Susan J. Freiband

276. **Public Libraries: Re-Appraisal and Re-Structuring, the Contribution of Research to Management and Adaptation.** Colin Harris and Brian Clifford, eds. London, Rossendale, 1985. 140p. $10.00pa. ISBN 0-946138-06-0.

These papers represent the proceedings of a 1984 seminar organized by the Library and Information Research Group to explore problems posed by retrenchment in Great Britain's public libraries. It is a companion to an earlier seminar devoted to academic library functions in times of financial difficulties.

While the topic of library responses to adverse budget climates is not new in the literature, these papers do manage to address comprehensively numerous aspects of the problem in one succinct text. The very severe cutbacks in Britain resulting from its current recession add a distinct aura of pragmatic necessity to the discussions. The presenters, who seem very well qualified for their assignments, keep this pragmatism in view throughout.

Three areas are explored: the library and its environment, the internal library environment, and the library and its user. Several themes recur as papers focus on the situation and possible responses. Among those themes are the acute need for networks and cooperatives; the need for rigorous data on comparative efficiencies in libraries; and the necessity to conduct research in order to identify user needs, to better use resources, and to operate in an informed managerial climate.

Of particular note are the papers on present British public library policy, innovations during the recession carried out by the City of Manchester libraries, and the paper by Blaise Cronin on marketing and the identification of user groups. The need to employ performance measures is well described although the territory is not unique. There is also little new for readers in the discussion of emerging technologies in public libraries.

This seminar did fulfill its mission to discuss hard answers to the difficulties of retrenchment in libraries. Even though the perspective is decidedly British, the realities are incumbent upon all librarians facing the dilemmas of service and eroding financial support.

Patricia A. Steele

277. Shavit, David. **The Politics of Public Librarianship.** Westport, Conn., Greenwood Press, 1986. 157p. bibliog. index. (New Directions in Information Management, No. 12). $29.95. LC 86-7573. ISBN 0-313-24816-8.

The author begins this book by exploding the myth that public libraries are not political institutions. Although in an earlier era an attempt was made to keep politics out of the public library, it has become increasingly clear that public librarianship has its political ramifications.

Shavit then proceeds to examine the relationship of public libraries to the three levels of government. At the local level, the author examines the structure and role of the library board and the library administration. He concludes for a variety of reasons that citizen participation plays a limited role in the administration and operation of the public library. Turning to the state level of government, the author makes clear that it is the state that has the power to authorize local governmental bodies to establish public libraries. Public libraries receive their authority to exist through state statutes. Moreover, state statutes define how public libraries are to be established, how they are to be financed, and how they are to be governed. State aid, the author points out, is an important instrument to promote interlibrary cooperation and the development of library systems. Finally, the author turns to the federal arena in relation to public libraries. It is his judgment that while the Library Services and Construction Act is the most important piece of federal library legislation enacted by Congress,

the National Library Act, introduced in 1979 but never enacted, contained the most coherent declaration of a national public library policy.

The Politics of Public Librarianship is a serious and comprehensive presentation of the relationship of the three levels of government to the development of public library service in the United States. [R: LJ, 15 Nov 86, p. 62]

Alex Ladenson

278. **Spanish-Language Books for Public Libraries.** Fabio Restrepo and others. Chicago, American Library Association, 1986. 169p. index. $9.95pa. LC 85-28940. ISBN 0-8389-0448-3.

This bibliography, authored by an ad hoc subcommittee of the RASD committee, Library Services for the Spanish-Speaking, provides a recommended list of titles on a variety of topics which are popular with Hispanic communities—especially Mexican, Puerto Rican, and Cuban. A work of literary merit had also to have wide popular appeal to be included.

Titles are arranged by Dewey Decimal Classification, with full bibliographic information and prices included. All were in print as of 1984. The short annotations are written in English. Asterisks denote titles which every library collection should include. Supplements provide a list of Spanish-language periodicals and a list of "U.S. Distributors of Spanish Materials."

The objective—to provide non-Spanish-speaking librarians with a basic list of materials with "wide popular appeal" among Hispanics—has been accomplished. Although the emphasis is on adult materials, many of the titles would be appropriate for inclusion in a high school library collection. The librarian using this bibliography to build a basic collection must realize that its scope is limited to titles/topics which are popular with Hispanics.

Patricia L. Whatley

279. **University Press Books for Public Libraries 1986.** 8th ed. New York, for the Public Library Association, American Library Association, by American University Presses, 1986. 96p. index. free pa. ISSN 0731-2857.

A project of the Small and Medium Sized Libraries section of the Public Library Association, this is a bibliography of over five hundred monographs and nineteen journals published by various members of the Association of American University Presses. A committee of public librarians from several communities has selected the titles from the 1985 offerings of these presses and arranged them in Dewey order with annotations, many quoted from sources such as *Library Journal, Choice,* and *Booklist.*

Beyond the obvious promotional benefit to the AAUP member presses whose current lists are represented here, an honest attempt has been made to bring attention to books of possible interest to the general reading public that otherwise might have been overlooked because of their scholarly origin. Recommended for the smaller library wanting guidance in selecting titles from the university press output for 1985.

Chris Albertson

PUBLIC RELATIONS

280. **Great Library Promotion Ideas II: JCD Library Public Relations Award Winners and Notables 1985.** Ann Heidbreder Eastman and Evelyn Shaevel, eds. Chicago, American Library Association, 1986. 62p. illus. index. $8.95pa. LC 86-3441. ISBN 0-8389-3331-9.

Following a format similar to *Great Library Promotion Ideas* (see *ARBA* 85, entry 193) *Great Library Promotion Ideas II* contains summaries of thirty-nine different ideas which supplement the earlier work. Seventy-four percent of the ideas come from public libraries, but the remaining twenty-six percent include ideas from school, academic, and special libraries. The John Cotton Dana (JCD) Committee selected these ideas because they "are examples of such programs that seemed fresh or especially effective or in which a discreet idea seemed noteworthy." Types of ideas include a creative program of publications, a handsome logo, a sesquicentennial celebration, a fund raising campaign, an auction of unusual items, an instrumental music festival, and a program featuring campus celebrities on a poster to promote the library.

The JCD Committee announces in the preface that the committee "plans to continue publishing *Great Library Promotion Ideas* so a large audience will be stimulated by entrants' good ideas." This should be good news for librarians searching for fresh ideas to use for public relations or for promoting library materials and services.

O. Gene Norman

281. **Library Services for Nonprofit Organizations.** rev. ed. Washington, D.C., District of Columbia Public Library, 1986. 32p. illus. map. free pa.

Those libraries wishing to provide a selective guide to fund-raising, grant-writing, and voluntarism sources will welcome this no-frills, typewritten pamphlet. Cited titles reflect the collections of the Martin Luther King, Jr., Memorial Library of the District of Columbia.

Arranged alphabetically by author, entries briefly cover title, year, call number, and location within the library. Most titles appear to have been published within the past fifteen years. No subject index is included, although subject terms follow each entry.

The booklet also describes the policies governing community use of meeting rooms; borrowing of audiovisual equipment and films; programs for children and adolescents; recreational and informational services for the elderly, disabled, or adults wishing to improve basic educational skills; and the library's community information and telephone reference services.

Although not detailed or flashy, this pamphlet meets its objectives well, and is an appropriate example for other libraries to follow.

Ilene F. Rockman

282. Liebold, Louise Condak. **Fireworks, Brass Bands, and Elephants: Promotional Events with Flair for Libraries and Other Nonprofit Organizations.** Phoenix, Ariz., Oryx Press, 1986. 135p. illus. index. $29.50pa. LC 85-43488. ISBN 0-89774-249-4.

This title offers a wealth of fine information about organizing and implementing creative programs for libraries. The author has worked in a variety of public relations jobs, including fashion publicist, newspaper reporter, and public relations account executive. She now does public relations and programming for the East Meadow (New York) Public Library.

The focus of the book is on programs for libraries; however, there are public relations examples from other agencies as well, such as the Bronx Zoo and the Mount Sinai Hospital in Miami, Florida. These nonlibrary ideas allow the author to stress some of the features that are common to all good programs: careful planning, a coordinated promotion campaign, organized implementation, publicizing success, and using themes or gimmicks.

Each chapter includes many anecdotal examples of actual programs. The author also provides helpful information on fund-raising activities and on incorporating games and contests into programs. The list of resources for each chapter includes a reference to names and addresses for more information about specific programs. For example, there are three sources for more information on planning a popcorn festival, including the coordinator of the annual festival in Valparaiso, Indiana and the address of the Popcorn Institute.

The chapter on making contact with different media resources is full of detailed, practical advice. *Fireworks, Brass Bands, and Elephants* would be a very useful resource for public libraries or for anyone involved in promoting library services. Rebecca L. Thomas

283. Liu, Grace F. **Promoting Library Awareness in Ethnic Communities.** San Jose, Calif., South Bay Cooperative Library System, 1985. 118p. illus. $8.00pa.

This book documents the experience of a one-year, federally funded outreach project, the Underserved Community Library Awareness Project, 1984-1985. The South Bay Cooperative Library System in California proposed the project, which was designed to promote library awareness to underserved ethnic communities, primarily Hispanic and Asian, and to facilitate use of library services by these groups in Santa Clara and San Benito counties. The handbook describes the different programs, cultural awareness training, and other activities undertaken by the libraries participating in the project, and includes actual project materials prepared by them. The history, background, structure, and evaluation of the project are clearly described, including identification of project staff, steering committee, and advisory board. Ten appendices include survey forms used for library staff, users, and residents; workshop and program evaluation forms; planning timetables; and an employee manual of Spanish phrases. The handbook provides many useful, practical ideas and activities for public librarians to use and/or to adapt in working with their own ethnic clienteles. One especially interesting example is the script of a slide/tape package, developed by library staff and community relations workers for ESL classes, called "A Trip to the Library." This publication, prepared by the project coordinator, extends the value of the project. It functions as an important and valuable resource tool and guide for libraries, allowing them to benefit from and build upon the successful results of the Underserved Community Library Awareness Project, a model demonstration project. It is well worth the modest price.

Susan J. Freiband

PUBLIC SERVICES

284. **Fees for Library Service: Current Practice & Future Policy.** Arthur Curley, ed. New York, Neal-Schuman, 1986. 61p. (*Collection Building*, Vol. 8, No. 1). $14.95pa. ISSN 0160-4953.

No issue has provoked such controversy within library circles as fees for user services. Whether at the local, state, or national levels, the topic incites discussion and debate about the role of a free society and the fear of the technological selling of information.

This thematic issue of *Collection Building* reprints the 1985 report of the National Commission on Libraries and Information Science (NCLIS), funded by the Council on Library Resources (CLR), "The Role of Fees in Supporting Library and Information Services in Public and Academic Libraries," and twenty-three reaction papers by distinguished members of the library and library-related communities.

The NCLIS study sought to provide "an objective statement of the pro-fee and anti-fee arguments" as a "springboard for discussion of fees with the goals of clarifying the issues and making sound policy decisions." Issues described include the public/private nature of information delivery, the rise of technology vs. the financial pressures on libraries, the costs of providing service, and the effect of charging fees.

Reaction to the report is swift and sometimes harsh. Representatives from the academic community such as Hugh Atkinson and Nancy Eaton question whether technology can triumph over budgets, and if current practices should dictate future policies. Public librarian Charles Robinson views fees as reaching into the pocketbooks of the taxpayers, while Bernard Margolis believes that there is no justifiable role for charging library fees. Library educator Leigh Estabrook raises the question of whether a library can be a socialist institution in a capitalistic society, while colleague E. J. Josey laments the influence of computerized literature searching for creating a society of "information rich" and "information poor." Library consultant Nancy Bolt questions if fees make better libraries, and Information Industry Association member David Peyton suggests that there is no such thing as "free information."

Last words are provided by former NCLIS Executive Director Toni Carbo Bearman, now Dean of the School of Library and Information Science at the University of Pittsburgh. A selective, unannotated bibliography on charging for library services compiled by NYU Social Sciences Bibliographer Marsha Suer Clark concludes the work.

The editor of *Collection Building* is to be commended for providing a forum for such provocative, lively commentaries. One only wishes that the diversity of opinions expressed made more direct connections with the practices of materials acquisition and collection development, and the effects of new technological services on the allocation of funds for monographs, serials, and other materials budgets.

A thought-provoking diversity of opinion on a timely subject.

Ilene F. Rockman

285. Glover, Peggy D. **Library Services for the Woman in the Middle.** Hamden, Conn., Library Professional Publications/Shoe String Press, 1985. 180p. bibliog. index. $22.50; $16.50pa. LC 85-15911. ISBN 0-208-02070-5; 0-208-02073-Xpa.

This book is a resource guide for women aged forty-five to sixty-five, the women in the middle. It is aimed not only at public librarians, but also at people in women's studies, in aging studies, in the media, and in governmental agencies, all of whom serve this fastest growing segment of the U.S. population. The first part of the book is a short overview of the demographic and social characteristics of the women in the middle. Part 2 discusses the kinds of library programs, services, and collections important in meeting the diverse information needs of this clientele. The scope is broad, including planning, programming, public relations, referral services, and selection. The treatment of each is necessarily short, clear, and to the point. Part 3 (the longest section of the book) is a "Quick Look-up Guide to Information Sources" arranged by topics of high interest to midlife women. The guide is intended to be a tool for these women "to identify their information needs, to provide relevant information to answer these needs, and to direct them to further resources" (p. 93). It includes books, pamphlets, and periodicals with brief, descriptive annotations. Cross-references are also included. There is an author/title index, as well as a separate subject index.

The price of $16.50 for a small paperback with fewer than two hundred pages appears somewhat high. The hardback at $6.00 more may be more reasonable. However, the information in the book will certainly be relevant and useful to public and community college librarians. The information included in the statistics and tables dates from the early 1980s, as does most of the material in the bibliography. The timeliness of the book, however, goes beyond these dates, since it represents a serious pioneering effort to call attention to midlife women and their library needs. It offers an important resource for librarians to actively respond to these needs, and thereby to effectively help these women in the middle "open windows, end isolation, raise self-esteem and lead to new careers and experiences" (p. xiii). [R: BL, 15 May 86, p. 1355]

Susan J. Freiband

PUBLISHING

286. Alley, Brian, and Jennifer Cargill. **Librarian in Search of a Publisher: How to Get Published.** Phoenix, Ariz., Oryx Press, 1986. 172p. bibliog. index. $18.50pa. LC 85-45512. ISBN 0-89774-150-1.

Getting published, traditionally a concern of teaching faculty, has increasingly become important for all types of librarians, as well. Librarians who contemplate, for the first time, sitting down and writing something—assuming that they have something interesting to say—will find this book of value to their career ladders, and it is designed to give them the determination to begin.

Alley and Cargill know plenty about publishing; one sees their names everywhere in library-related publications. They brim over with intelligent, sound advice on how other librarians can be motivated, occupied, and successful in professional writing. Their book, therefore, is a motivational don't-just-sit-there-dammit! work. Chapters on managing time, getting organized, proper equipment, and submission of book proposals to publishers are all timely and on target. While much of the advice they provide may seem to be obvious or unnecessary to those who have already written for publication, it should go a long way towards refuting reasons for procrastination to those who have meant to get into print for a long time, yet didn't seem to be able, for one reason or another, to get started.

Sections on many aspects of library-related publishing are unique and excellent: reviewing, bibliographies, word processing equipment, getting along with editors, even a section on choosing a title for one's article are to be found in this attractive, well-indexed book. Faintly amusing cartoons, featuring an extraneous but ubiquitous striped cat, accompany the text and are designed to portray some of the many frustrations and rewards of publication.

For the librarian who aspires to be a writer, this title is highly recommended and should be required reading. For librarians already published and at home with the mechanics of publication, it is less essential but still contains interesting items and some sound advice. [R: BL, 15 May 86, p. 1355; C&RL, Nov 86, pp. 628-30; LJ, 15 Oct 86, p. 56; RQ, Fall 86, p. 128; WLB, Apr 86, p. 58]

Bruce A. Shuman

287. **American Publishers 1986.** 2d ed. Marianne Albertschauser and Astrid Kramuschka, eds. New York, K. G. Saur, 1986. 3v. index. $40.00pa./set. ISBN 0-89664-375-1; ISSN 0887-9230.

This directory supplies up to eight items of information for some 54,000 U.S. publishers (vols. 1 and 2) and 7,000 Canadian publishers (vol. 3). It brings together in one alphabetical listing the name, street and cable addresses, telephone, telex and telecopier numbers, ISBN prefix and SAN number of book publishers (including small and alternative presses, associations and museums), magazine publishers, and publishers of microform, computer software and videotape materials. An index lists publishers by ISBN number. A spot check of some Chicago-based publishers against the July 1986 Chicago telephone directory revealed no errors. Many entries, however, lack a telephone number. *American Publishers* is more comprehensive, cheaper, but less detailed in the information it supplies than *Publishers Directory, 1984-1985* (Gale, 1984; see *ARBA* 85, entry 580) and *Publishers, Distributors and Wholesalers of the United States, 1985-1986* (Bowker, 1985; see *ARBA* 86, entry 613). *AP* cannot replace the more detailed and annually revised *Literary Market Place, Audio Video Market Place,* or *The International Directory of Little Magazines and Small Presses.* It is to be hoped that *AP* will be revised and updated annually and that future editions will supply a bit more information about each publisher, such as the number of titles in print, the subject specialty, and the name of the chief executive officer.

Joseph Cataio

288. Duke, Judith S. **The Technical, Scientific and Medical Publishing Market.** White Plains, N.Y., Knowledge Industry, 1985. 218p. index. (Communications Library). $34.95. LC 84-26163. ISBN 0-86729-084-6.

A guide to the tremendously growing market for technical, scientific, and medical (TSM) information, Duke's study is limited to books, newsletters and looseleaf services, magazines and journals, and database publishing, both print and online. It is directed to professionals engaged in TSM fields and examines the present state of the TSM information industry. It outlines opportunities for expansion in various types of services or products and looks ahead in a general way to the next few years.

Duke discusses the size and structure of the TSM market, as well as costs, marketing techniques, problems, and the economics of the industry. Although she acknowledges that one of the major flaws is the lack of hard statistical information, she has compiled estimates, and the book contains charts and statistical tables that compare the use of databases, the estimated revenues of various journals, data from book publishers, estimated revenues and profit margins of the ten leading TSM companies, and other data. In addition, each chapter briefly describes the individual operations of some of the leading companies in the field.

The concluding chapters include profiles of twenty-three of the major TSM publishers—these profiles discuss the various products, the markets each company dominates, and financials when available. It is in this section where the author's stated policy of considering only U.S. firms creates a notable lack of comprehensiveness. Three major TSM publishers have home offices overseas, and these companies account for a large share of the U.S. market (except in medical publishing). They are Elsevier-North Holland, Pergamon Press, and Springer Verlag. The brief mention that these companies receive (along with Longman and Masson) does not adequately address their significance. Despite this fault, the book does a good job of portraying the direction in which TSM publishing is headed. The information presented is clear and well defined. Useful for any companies involved in the TSM market, as well as a good resource for a business reference collection.

Shirley Lambert

289. **Library Publishing: Report of a Seminar Held at the British Library, 11-13 April 1983.** David Way, ed. London, British Library; distr., Dover, N.H., Longwood Publishing Group, 1985. 80p. (British Library Occasional Papers, No. 2). $5.95pa. ISBN 0-7123-0040-6.

This seminar brought together representatives of many major research libraries in several nations to discuss various aspects of library publishing and marketing. One outgrowth of the seminar was the formation of a permanent International Group of Publishing Libraries; another was the publication of this volume of proceedings. Each topic (e.g., "Production Techniques for Short-run Reference Books," "Marketing," "Retailing in On-site Bookshops," "Electronic Publishing") is covered, often all too briefly, in a paper and a couple of pages of discussion. Some papers are formal, while others and all of the discussion reports are based on the editor's notes on the informal presentations. The results, understandably, are somewhat uneven. While the volume is by no means a primer on publishing, it should be of at least limited interest to libraries and other public institutions involved in or considering publication programs.

Walter C. Allen

REFERENCE SERVICES

290. Katz, Bill, ed. **Reference and Online Services Handbook: Guidelines, Policies, and**

Procedures for Libraries. Volume II. New York, Neal-Schuman, 1986. 602p. index. $39.95. LC 81-11290. ISBN 0-918212-74-X.

Many concepts and practices in libraries are similar, and a logical first step for a library seeking to establish a policy or to evaluate an existing one is to determine what is done elsewhere. Finding information about reference collection and online policies is now extremely easy because of Bill Katz's indefatigable efforts in soliciting, selecting, organizing, and reproducing reference collection and online policies from eighty-four academic and public libraries. Volume 2 of the *Reference and Online Services Handbook* extends and augments the information about online services contained in the first volume. Included here are reference collection policies from thirty-nine libraries and online statements from forty-five, as well as sixteen online user aids, and explanations and guidelines relating to online catalogs and microcomputers. The origin of each document is clearly stated. All the policies and other statements are very lightly edited; most are reproduced verbatim and without comment. The user is expected to select or reject according to specific need. Since the user is more likely to be seeking specific information than reading a whole policy, providing access to the contents of the statements is important and so the book has an excellent, detailed index.

In his preface, Katz describes his methodology (175 libraries were approached), and analyzes his findings. He claims that in spite of much repetition in the reference collection policies, "there is enough difference ... to justify this compilation." A thoughtful summary of the rationale for the elements which go into such policies is provided by Ruth A. Fraley in a short foreword. The volume is rounded out by six articles, four of them specific to reference collection policies. These provide individual perspectives on the process of developing such items and their usefulness. [R: JAL, July 86, p. 181; JAL, Sept 86, pp. 236-37; LJ, 15 Oct 86, p. 56; RQ, Fall 86, p. 131]

Joan W. Jensen

291. Katz, Bill, and Ruth A. Fraley, eds. **Conflicts in Reference Services.** New York, Haworth Press, 1985. 236p. map. (*Reference Librarian*, No. 1). $22.95. LC 84-25147. ISBN 0-86656-385-7.

This 236-page issue of the *Reference Librarian* contains twenty-three articles on various aspects of conflict in reference services, and serves incidentally as a useful introduction to the management of such services. Bill Katz and Ruth Fraley are to be congratulated for bringing together so many aspects of the subject.

In her introduction Fraley discusses two views of conflict: as a disturbance and as a challenge. She advocates the latter view as the model for the modern, dynamic librarian. It is interesting to note that both points of view appear in the articles that follow.

John Berry sets the scene with a report of a preliminary survey of the service of reference departments to various user groups in twenty-two academic libraries. He reports that few had a reference policy or procedure manual, few kept statistics which differentiated between undergraduates, graduate students, faculty, or other users. Most libraries did not perceive any distinctions in the way they served the different groups. Drawing upon the survey and on the literature in the field, Berry underlines the lack of knowledge of the subtleties and complexities of the reference process, and advocates research to enhance knowledge and improve the service.

The majority of the papers bear out this conclusion. They discuss conflict of reference librarians with catalogers, with interlibrary loan departments, and with various types of users. They study the struggle to give optimum service with minimal funding and support. The debate on "fee vs. free," especially charging for online searching, is well reviewed. A section is devoted to bibliographic instruction and the conflict between library staff and faculty or administrators. Another section concentrates on the role of the professional, and includes relationships with nonprofessionals, a discussion of the limits of library school education for reference, and the expectations of different administrators and different users, as well as the level of help librarians should give to users and the amount of power the librarian has over the seeker of knowledge. Some resources in themselves contain a potential for conflict—at what point does the librarian providing legal or medical information overstep the bounds of his or her professional domain? How far should the librarian go in evaluating or interpreting data?

There is little new material in the volume. Authors have usually relied on the literature and on their own and others' opinions and experience. Most of the papers are well written and interesting and provide the reader with a wide variety of ideas on the subject. There is obviously some overlap from article to article and section to section, but it is not overdone. On the whole this is a useful volume for the student or practitioner of reference work.

Miriam H. Tees

292. Kohl, David F. **Reference Services and Library Instruction: A Handbook for Library Management.** Santa Barbara, Calif., ABC-Clio, 1985. 324p. bibliog. index. (Handbooks

for Library Management, Vol. 3). $35.00. LC 85-13431. ISBN 0-87436-432-9.

Like the other volumes in this series, this one summarizes original research findings that were presented in thirty-four U.S. and Canadian library periodicals from 1960 through 1983. Also like the others, "no research findings with statistical significance exceeding .05 were reported," nor were findings that had "serious problems with internal consistency and/or ambiguous and confusing text."

The two major subject areas are divided into subareas. "Reference Services" includes such items as patron use of services, online searching, and quality of tools; "Library Instruction" covers topics such as impact, prior skill level, and techniques. Each of these topics is then subdivided into applicability by type of library—general, academic, special, school, public. The research finding is summarized in a few sentences and keyed to one of the articles listed in the back of the volume. (The list includes all those cited in the six-volume series.) As one might expect, by far the greater space is given to "Reference Services"—224 pages as against 28 for "Library Instruction."

Kohl, in making such information easily available, has performed a useful service. But users ought to be aware that its limitations, both those imposed by the author and those inherent in the material, are basic. The omission of books, theses, foreign journals, and case studies excludes a significant body of findings; on the other hand, the inclusion of articles simply because they are within the book's scope gives some material unwarranted credibility. If one is aware of the limitations and looks upon the book just as a starting point (and not as "a solid basis for improving practice" as the foreword states), it can then be a useful administrative tool. [R: LJ, 1 Mar 86, p. 74; RQ, Fall 86, p. 124]   Evan Ira Farber

293. **Managing Online Reference Services.** Ethel Auster, ed. New York, Neal-Schuman, 1986. 408p. index. $35.00pa. LC 85-21542. ISBN 0-918212-93-6.

Edited works are frequently viewed with disdain, both because of the perception that the editor is nothing more than a compiler of previously published materials and because the level of quality varies widely among the articles selected for inclusion. Add to this the statement that the edited work is based on materials used in a library science course taught at the University of Toronto and expectations are quite low. Fortunately, this book demonstrates that a well-edited work can unite various disparate pieces into a whole which is of significant value. In addition, the value of a thoughtful editor who can select and organize appropriate articles is evident in this book. Twenty-six selections, published in fifteen sources between 1975 and 1984, are included. The selections are arranged into eight sections: (1) "Planning for Online Reference"; (2) "Choosing Services and Databases"; (3) "Staff Selection and Training"; (4) "Promotion and Marketing"; (5) "Financial Considerations"; (6) "Measurement and Evaluation"; (7) "Microcomputers and Online Reference"; and (8) "Impact of Online Services." Each section is prefaced by a basic summary of the issues being discussed, and a list of suggested readings is included at the end of each section. The name and subject indexes are also well done and, especially important for an edited work, allow the reader to find references to specific topics. The name index even distinguishes between an author of a selection and a name cited or mentioned. This book is set apart from other primers of online searching in that it deals strictly with the administrative aspects of establishing an online search service. It is set apart from other edited works in that it is a coherent, well-written, and well-edited whole.   Greg Byerly

294. **Personnel Issues in Reference Services.** Bill Katz and Ruth A. Fraley, eds. New York, Haworth Press, 1986. 200p. (*Reference Librarian*, No. 14). $34.95. LC 86-3063. ISBN 0-86656-523-X.

Volumes in the *Reference Librarian* provide an overview of contemporary concerns of the profession. Having determined the broad outline of a particular issue, the editors actively solicit contributions from actual practitioners in various libraries. This encourages some experienced persons who might not independently submit articles for publication to express opinions, describe programs, or evaluate specific experiences. The series thus offers a comforting reflection of reality. Fortunately, the quality of the articles—content, objectivity, variety, and writing—is reasonably high. The ultimate value of such a collection of essays depends on how well the editors select pertinent items, and how effectively they group these to develop aspects of the central theme. Bill Katz and Ruth A. Fraley perform both tasks capably, and as the series develops a rounded examination of the specialty of reference librarianship is emerging.

Fraley's introduction surveys the content of *Personnel Issues in Reference Services* and provides her own professional perspective. Sections of the anthology are "Overview," containing a single detailed survey of current issues; "Who Will Work the Reference Desk," five varied articles focusing on training for and the needs of "the front line" of service; "Administration,

Evaluation, and Staff Training," another group of five well-selected items offering insights into critical aspects of managing staff in reference departments; and "Preparation for the Job, Recruitment, Continuing Education and Other Concerns," eight items, less closely linked than those in the previous groups, but included because of the insight provided concerning provision of reference service, especially the qualifications needed by reference librarians. This volume, like the others in the series, is well worth reading and will be a good acquisition for those who can afford the relatively high price.

Joan W. Jensen

295. **Reference Services in Archives.** Lucille Whalen, ed. New York, Haworth Press, 1986. 210p. (*Reference Librarian*, No. 13). $34.95; $24.95pa. LC 85-17534. ISBN 0-86656-521-3; 0-86656-522-1pa.

Most of the articles in this collection describe reference service in a variety of archives, including women's studies, business, banking, labor and urban studies, religion, regional history, and others. Such topics as finding aids, the reference interview, rules governing use, restrictions, copyright, outreach, and evaluation of service are discussed, and most of the articles contain notes which point to additional information. Whalen sets the framework for the articles in her introduction, entitled "The Reference Process in Archives," and some of the articles, including F. W. Ratcliffe's "The Past in the Present: Reference in a British University Archival Collection" and "Expanded Access to Archival Sources," by Thomas Hickerson, have an interest beyond the more local concerns of most of the articles in the collection. The collection is valuable for the insights it provides on the reference process in archives and as a source of information on the different ways of carrying out that process. [R: JAL, Sept 86, p. 269; RQ, Winter 86, pp. 266-67]   Dean H. Keller

296. Yates, Rochelle. **A Librarian's Guide to Telephone Reference Service.** Hamden, Conn., Library Professional Publications/Shoe String Press, 1986. 136p. bibliog. index. $19.50; $14.50pa. LC 85-24113. ISBN 0-208-02082-9; 0-208-02083-7pa.

Rochelle Yates, formerly of the Brooklyn Public Library and now a librarian in a special library, has written a practical guide on telephone reference service (TRS). While primarily of interest to public library staff, the guide may be of interest to all librarians involved in TRS. It includes a description of the service, and related issues: the interview, collection, training, evaluation, and publicity. The guide reflects one person's experience with TRS and as such emphasizes some aspects (e.g., the importance of manners and proper use of the telephone), while giving less attention to others (e.g., procedures for searching). There is a tendency to say the obvious and be repetitious. Little attention is given to TRS within the context of reference service in general. The main body of text is sixty-nine pages, accompanied by endnotes, a short bibliography, and two appendices: a short list of reference sources, and the list of terms used by the Detroit Public Library for its community information and referral files. This guide may provide some practical suggestions for the practicing librarian involved in TRS. It will be of marginal interest to others. [R: LJ, 1 Apr 86, p. 50; WLB, Oct 86, p. 59]

Thomas G. Kirk

RESEARCH METHODS

297. Lutzker, Marilyn, and Eleanor Ferrall. **Criminal Justice Research in Libraries: Strategies and Resources.** Westport, Conn., Greenwood Press, 1986. 167p. index. $37.50. LC 85-17765. ISBN 0-313-24490-1.

This valuable research guide is divided into three parts. The first part, "Before You Start," provides background information, useful for both the beginner and the experienced researcher on communication and information flow, developing a master research plan, and computer and manual bibliographic searching. This part discusses formal and informal communication, primary and secondary sources, the different types of sources produced during the various stages in the flow of information, research techniques, and how to use the library and its many resources effectively. In the second part, "Locating Information," separate chapters are devoted to the following information sources in criminal justice research: encyclopedias, dictionaries, and annual reviews; newsletters, newspapers, and news broadcasts; documents, reports, and conference proceedings; indexes and abstracts; the library catalog; statistics; and printed bibliographies and guides to the literature. Each chapter has an excellent choice of titles, reflecting the interdisciplinary nature of criminal justice research, useful analytical and evaluative annotations, and additional suggestions on research techniques and using the library. The final part, "Some Special Problems," covers the following: research in legal resources, historical research of nineteenth-century America with primary sources; and resources for comparative study of criminal justice in other countries. Appendices include selected lists of Library of Congress subject headings in criminal justice; an annotated list of useful directories; and a description of selected major national commission reports in criminal justice. [R: RBB, July 86, pp. 1592-93]

LeRoy C. Schwarzkopf

298. Polette, Nancy. **The Research Almanac.** 2d ed. O'Fallon, Mo., Book Lures; distr., Metuchen, N.J., Scarecrow, 1986. 172p. illus. index. $14.95pa. ISBN 0-913839-27-2.

The profession has come to expect good work from Nancy Polette, and *The Research Almanac* is no exception. The book is an accumulation of projects, one for each day from September through May, that seek to get students involved in brief research projects. The work seeks to acquaint students with reference works that are readily available to them through "a blend of activities in technology, current events, historical subjects and current popular literature for young people." Care has been taken to balance fiction and nonfiction in a way that promotes the relationship of the two.

While the book is a series of well-designed, independent activities for young people, its value for class activities should not be discounted. Permission to duplicate up to thirty copies per year of any student activity has been granted in the book, making it an extremely attractive tool for integrating library media skills into all areas of the school curriculum. One of its major goals—to provide independent research activities for the exceptional learner— should not be overlooked, but care must be taken to make these activities meaningful to the student. This book should be purchased for its value in providing both group and independent research activities at the 4-8 grade level.

Anthony C. Schulzetenberg

SCHOOL LIBRARY MEDIA CENTERS

General Works

299. Adams, Helen R. **School Media Policy Development: A Practical Process for Small Districts.** Littleton, Colo., Libraries Unlimited, 1986. 174p. index. $23.50. LC 86-18587. ISBN 0-87287-450-8.

Adams contends that "media professionals are frequently at a loss regarding their place in policy development and the most effective way to proceed." This book is intended as a guide that will be especially useful for school media professionals who are working in small (population of one thousand or fewer students) school districts.

Her work contains twelve chapters and five appendices. After an introduction to policy making (chapters 1-2), Adams gives an overview of the policy development process (chapter 3). Chapters 4-10 elaborate on various aspects of the policy process and chapters 11-12 tie it all together. The appendices are rich in sample policies covering aspects such as copyright, resource sharing, security of audiovisual equipment, and selection of materials. Other appendices provide directories of relevant associations nationwide to which the school media professional may turn for further advice and information. The final appendix deals with job descriptions and performance evaluations. Finally, an index provides adequate access to the contents.

The book is written in a straightforward, unadorned style. Its helpful, abundant advice on matters of the policy process; its frequent suggestions concerning the information needed to implement successful policies; and the samples of forms, letters, and policies that it provides make it a useful reference source for any school media professional involved in policy formulation and implementation.

Robert H. Burger

300. **Directory of Curriculum Materials Centers.** 2d ed. Lois J. Lehman and Eva L. Kiewitt, comps. Chicago, Association of College and Research Libraries, American Library Association, 1985. 196p. $20.00 spiralbound. ISBN 0-8389-6917-8.

This much-needed guide updates the 1979 edition (available as ERIC ED 194110), and includes 170 curriculum centers representing 42 states, the District of Columbia, and 5 Canadian locations. Information is current as of 1985, and is not available in any other source.

Arrangement is alphabetical by state or province, with each entry attractively displayed on a separate page for the convenience of the user. Entries include such information as name, address, telephone number, and librarian(s); location and purpose of the center; holdings (number and types of materials); classification system; budget; number and level of staff members; loan policy; hours of service; affiliation with cooperative systems; special collections; materials deposited with the ALA Headquarters Library in Chicago, and other notes. An alphabetically arranged geographic index concludes the work.

Lehman and Kiewitt have taken the time to produce an invaluable work which will be heavily used by all who are associated with education collections, instructional materials centers, and teacher training institutes.

Ilene F. Rockman

301. **Focus on Learning: An Integrated Program Model for Alberta School Libraries.** Edmonton, Alta., Media and Technology Branch, Alberta Education, 1985. 67p. illus. bibliog. free pa.

Like many other jurisdictions, the province of Alberta has recognized that an integrated school library program is an important part of the instructional program of any school. The model suggested by the Media and Technology Branch of Alberta Education for the school library program consists of three components: instruction, development, and management. Each of these components is broken down into specific areas which need to be designed and monitored. The instruction component includes information retrieval, processing and sharing, and appreciation of knowledge and culture; development includes needs assessment, consultation and program planning, resource evaluation and selection, and inservice training; and management includes finances, personnel, technical services, facilities, and networking. This booklet suggests specific items to use in evaluating the three phases of development in each of these areas: phase 1, the minimal level; phase 2, adequate; and phase 3, the desirable level to be sought for each school library program. Appendices give information about relating thinking skills to academic curriculum, analysis forms for recording information about the school library, descriptions of key personnel roles, and the policy, guidelines, procedures, and standards for school libraries in Alberta. While the information is designed to help Albertan libraries, the clear and concise descriptions of levels of service will make this booklet useful to school districts setting up guidelines for their media services.   Adele M. Fasick

302. Hyland, Anne M. **School Library/Media Skills Test.** Littleton, Colo., Libraries Unlimited, 1986. 8p. illus. $25.00pa./set of 30. ISBN 0-87287-521-0.

303. Hyland, Anne M. **School Library/Media Skills Test: Manual.** Littleton, Colo., Libraries Unlimited, 1986. 47p. bibliog. index. $5.00pa. LC 86-7249. ISBN 0-87287-524-5.

Many school districts are assessing student progress in library media skills. In many cases, librarians are writing the assessment instrument based on the specific instructional emphasis of their program. The *School Library/Media Skills Test* and *Manual* is designed as a standardized, norm-referenced test to measure student library media ability. The test format offers fifty-three questions with multiple choices from four possible answers. The test booklet is designed to be used with a separate answer sheet, so the booklet remains unmarked and reuseable. Areas assessed include organization, selection, utilization, comprehension, and production. Specific questions are included about catalog cards, reference books, book orders for fiction and nonfiction, and types of audiovisual equipment.

The manual describes the preparation of the test instrument including pilot testing, revision, validity and reliability factors, and scoring norms. It includes four bibliographies: "Testing and Measurement," "Library Skill Development," "Library Ability Tests," and "Sources Used for Table of Specifications."

This test could be used in many library settings to assess the library media knowledge of students. As with any commercial test, specific circumstances could vary, requiring some adaptation, but in most cases the questions are general enough to fit different situations. This test and manual could also serve as a resource on library media tests for districts that are developing their own assessment instruments. [R: VOYA, Dec 86, pp. 255-56]

Rebecca L. Thomas

304. Loertscher, David V., ed. **Measures of Excellence for School Library Media Centers.** Philadelphia, College of Information Studies, Drexel University, 1985. 148p. (*Drexel Library Quarterly*, Vol. 21, No. 2). $10.00pa. LC 65-9911.

This collection of articles on evaluation in the school library media center is a welcome addition to the literature of the field. David Loertscher, who served as editor of this issue of the *Drexel Quarterly*, wrote the introduction, and in it he provides the reader with a rationale for the articles that follow. As library media professionals, he points out, we can no longer simply rely on quantitative evaluation; we must be able to evaluate what we do to show the effectiveness of our programs in learning. While the profession has developed many documents through the years to serve as quantitative guides against which to compare programs, few have been significant as tools to measure quality of programs. The articles in this issue add to the evaluative documents that have appeared in recent years which seek to provide the library media center with some methods to gauge qualitative substance. The purpose suggested in the introduction is to initiate a second step in the creation of evaluative documents. This purpose has been achieved.

The seven articles range in content from collection development to media use. Loertscher himself contributed the lead article, in which he provides the reader with an excellent method of collection mapping whereby the collection can be studied for depth and breadth. Subsequent articles show the research behind collection mapping and an application thereof. Other articles, like the one by Retta Patrick on instructional involvement, are excellent. The article by Barbara Herrin on the personality of the school librarian is interesting and indicative of the need to match personality to the job. The contributors are all either practicing school media professionals or trainers, giving the articles the tenor that school library media professionals will find of value in evaluation within their own settings. They are well written and based on sound research. — Anthony C. Schulzetenberg

305. McDonald, Margaret Marshall, ed. **Towards Excellence: Case Studies of Good School Libraries.** London, Library Association; distr., Chicago, American Library Association, 1985. 92p. illus. bibliog. $15.00. ISBN 0-85365-856-0.

The volume contains a series of ten case studies of library media service in British public schools, both elementary and secondary. Its primary audience is British educators and its stated purpose is to encourage government and public school officials to strive to attain the program recommendations outlined in the 1977 *Library Association Guidelines and Standards for School Libraries.*

The cases selected were chosen as examples of good practice, those schools which were determined to be closely following or working toward achieving the *Guidelines.* Each illustrates that it is possible for policy and practice to produce exemplary school libraries.

The information provided about each of the school library media programs is of a descriptive nature. A form for statistical data was completed by individuals from the schools. Supplemental information also provided by each school is in narrative form, following no specific outline. This lack of structure makes it difficult to compare the schools and their various accomplishments. User education, the role of the librarian, use of the library, and staff and space are topics covered in the majority of the cases. With some photos, diagrams, and floorplans, the book will have some use in comparing British to American school library media programs. — Marilyn L. Shontz

306. **School Library Media Annual 1986. Volume Four.** Shirley L. Aaron and Pat R. Scales, eds. Littleton, Colo., Libraries Unlimited, 1986. 434p. index. $40.00. ISBN 0-87287-520-2; ISSN 0739-7712.

The *School Library Media Annual 1986* is the fourth volume edited by Shirley Aaron and Pat Scales. The purpose of the annual is to discuss school library concerns, events and influences, collection development practices, current issues and future trends, and elements of an improved program. The book is well organized, including chapters written by a variety of authors, most of whom are practicing media professionals. Once again the editors have selected timely topics, such as copyright laws, online information services, critical thinking skills, and microcomputer software, as well as annually updating the reader on legislation, professional organizations, award winners, and research. This annual serves as an excellent, concise resource for all school library media specialists who need a review of up-to-date information on various issues concerning school media programs. In addition, the annual, which covers all aspects of the field, will serve as an excellent reference to be used by district study committees, state organizations, authors of articles, and students. — Marie Zuk

307. Woolls, Blanche. **Grant Proposal Writing: A Handbook for School Library Media Specialists.** Westport, Conn., Greenwood Press, 1986. 131p. bibliog. index. $29.95. LC 85-23916. ISBN 0-313-24440-5.

This book covers all the steps involved in writing and submitting a project proposal. It has been specifically written for school library media specialists, and includes many examples from the school media context. The scope of the book is broad, including the preparatory stages, the RFP, the parts of the proposal itself, personnel, budget, project evaluation, and the proposal review. There are also chapters on foundations and corporation funding, and on project management. The treatment of the many topics covered is at an introductory level (rather than in-depth); geared for the uninitiated new project proposal writer. The book is clearly written, well organized and planned, readable, and enhanced by many practical examples. There are three appendices, including two different types of RFPs and a sample PERT chart. The short but helpful selective, annotated bibliography is another valuable feature of the book.

Although the grant and proposal writing literature is large, the specific orientation of this book toward the school library media specialist gives it a unique and important niche. The author is a professor of library science at the University of Pittsburgh, a former school library media specialist, and a well-known contributor to library literature. Although the price of the book is high, it is of considerable value and interest to the school library media specialist needing assistance in the area of grant proposal writing. It is also recommended for library science students preparing for careers in the school media field. It would be a worthwhile addition to library science collections in schools of library and information science, as well as to public libraries. [R: BL, 15 May 86, p. 1356]

Susan J. Freiband

Bibliographies

308. **El-Hi Textbooks and Serials in Print 1986.** New York, R. R. Bowker, 1986. 1059p. index. $65.00. LC 70-105104. ISBN 0-8352-2169-5; ISSN 0000-0825.

Boasting eight thousand new titles and over twenty-three thousand updates, the latest edition of this standard source includes more than just textbooks. A wide range of instructional materials including professional books for teachers, programmed materials, maps, tests, periodicals, and education directories are included in an attempt to be "inclusive ... rather than selective." Arrangement is by twenty-two main categories (e.g., "Microcomputers," "Vocational Education") with additional access points by author, title, and series for books, and subject and title for serials.

Subject arrangement provides helpful *see* and *see also* references, as well as the full bibliographic information supplemented by grade, price (library binding and school), ISBN, and related teaching materials. The over forty-five thousand entries—many titles are listed in more than one subject category—are representative of 835 publishers. A key to publishers' and distributors' abbreviations concludes the work.

This is the 114th edition of this title. A 5 percent discount is offered for placing orders directly with Bowker; that will be greatly appreciated by school libraries on limited budgets.   Ilene F. Rockman

309. Stein, Morris I. **Gifted, Talented, and Creative Young People: A Guide to Theory, Teaching, and Research.** New York, Garland, 1986. 465p. index. (Garland Reference Library of Social Science, Vol. 120). $80.00. LC 81-48419. ISBN 0-8240-9392-5.

This bibliography contains summaries and annotations of books, chapters in books, and journal and newsletter articles written about gifted, talented, and creative students. The major issues, research results, and curricular and instructional programs are represented. Although a majority of the works annotated were written during the 1970s, the classics as well as a few contemporary entries from conferences and symposia can be found.

A lengthy introduction describes the state of the art and offers a look to the future. Following it are chapters arranged into three broad categories: identification and selection, education and training, and research. The topics covered are history, theory, characteristics, the disadvantaged, tests, curriculum, counseling, teachers and teaching, creativity, evaluation, parents, and programs in other countries. Within each chapter entries are grouped under brief headings according to the major theme and are generally alphabetical by author's last name. The final chapter lists agencies, periodicals, and other resources appropriate to the field.

Both author and subject indexes are provided. Although this bibliography contains a great deal of information useful to students, teachers, researchers, counselors, school administrators, parents, school board members, governmental policy makers, and lay persons, the author does not claim that it is all-inclusive. This is a monumental work and belongs in all academic libraries. [R: Choice, Dec 86, p. 610]

M. Kathy Cook

Collections

310. Beilke, Patricia F., and Frank J. Sciara. **Selecting Materials for and about Hispanic and East Asian Children and Young People.** Hamden, Conn., Library Professional Publications/Shoe String Press, 1986. 178p. bibliog. index. $24.50. LC 85-23920. ISBN 0-208-01993-6.

Librarians and teachers interested in selecting print materials for Hispanic and East Asian young readers will find much valuable information in this well-organized guide. It suggests in-service activities for school and public librarians serving immigrant or minority populations; it provides brief background descriptions, with recommended readings, for learning about several cultural groups of Hispanic-Americans and East Asian-Americans; and it examines information about the evaluation of materials related to minority and immigrant groups. There are two important deficiencies in this otherwise useful professional tool: contrary to what the title suggests, it only reviews and discusses print materials and it ignores bibliographies in languages other than English. These are crucial in serving the reading needs of many Hispanic and East Asian young readers. [R: BL, July 86, p. 1619]   Isabel Schon

311. **Children's Catalog.** 15th ed. Richard H. Isaacson, Ferne E. Hillegas, and Juliette

Yaakov, eds. New York, H. W. Wilson, 1986. 1298p. index. (Standard Catalog Series). $72.00. LC 86-15751. ISBN 0-8242-0743-2.

312. **The Elementary School Library Collection: A Guide to Books and Other Media. Phases 1-2-3.** 15th ed. Lois Winkel, ed. Williamsport, Pa., Brodart, 1986. 1067p. index. $79.95. LC 85-24287. ISBN 0-87272-091-8.

The fifteenth edition of *Children's Catalog* contains 5,715 titles, in comparison to 8,695 titles in the fifteenth edition of *Elementary School Library Collection* (*ESLC*). In addition to books, *ESLC* also lists filmstrips, videocassettes, microcomputer programs, and other forms of nonprint. Both publishers have committees active in the selection of titles for these works. The committees for both are composed of members from all parts of the country whose experience in children's librarianship is somewhat varied. Each publication points out that although these books comprise a basic collection for children's libraries, it is up to individual librarians to provide good librarianship.

The major part of each of these volumes is the classified catalog. Entries contain full bibliographic information, Dewey Decimal Classification number, the subject headings (*ESLC* from *Library of Congress Annotated Card Subject Headings for Children's Literature*; and *Children's Catalog* from *Sears List of Subject Headings*), reading level ability, and acceptable annotations. The annotations in *ESLC* are written by members of the selection committee with noted exceptions; those in *Children's Catalog* seem to be taken from reviews. *ESLC* also offers phase indications (Ph-1, Ph-2, or Ph-3) suggesting priorities for acquisition and interest level range for each title. In checking contents under "Addiction" (613.8) only seven duplications of titles were discovered. *ESLC* has eleven book titles and seven filmstrips; *Children's Catalog* has ten book titles.

Both works have indexes, but here is where the similarity ends. *ESLC* has separate author, title, and subject indexes; *Children's Catalog* contains a far superior combined alphabetical author/title/subject/analytical index. Under the subject "Blacks," *Children's Catalog* lists nine subdivisions with titles and cross-references, whereas there are only two entries under "Blacks" in *ESLC*. Although there are about the same number of entries under "Mexican-Americans," neither volume has a *see also* reference from "Hispanic Americans."

Each of these is an excellent source for basic collections: *ESLC* contains more information because of its nonprint additions; the index is considerably better in *Children's Catalog*. It would be hard to choose between them. The best choice, if possible, is both, as they complement each other.   Anna Grace Patterson

313. **Collection Management for School Library Media Centers.** Brenda H. White, ed. New York, Haworth Press, 1986. 383p. index. (*Collection Management*, Vol. 7, Nos. 3/4). $39.95; $29.95pa. LC 85-21945. ISBN 0-86656-433-0; 0-86656-416-0pa.

Originally published as numbers 3 and 4 of volume 7, *Collection Management* (*CM*), this book is to be viewed as a convenience package. Is the convenience worth $39.95? The answer is yes, if you do not subscribe to *CM* and need all twenty-seven articles; if not, you may wish to pass on this one. If you subscribe to *CM*, there is little point in purchasing the book. The book would be ineffective as a textbook, as it is too fragmented and uneven. There are five basic sections: "The Schools and Collections Development" (eleven articles); "Networking and Collection Development" (two articles); "School and Public Cooperation" (four articles); "Collections Management in Particular Areas and Formats" (eight articles); and "Intellectual Freedom and Collection Management" (two articles). Some articles are general discussions of concepts and issues, for example, Ester Dyer's "Business and Education"; others are reports of research projects, for example, Helen Williams's "Effect of Administrative Policy on the Use of School Library Media Centers and Resources"; and still others are on the order of "how I do it right," for example, David Loertscher's "The Elephant Technique of Collection Development." Almost all of the articles are reasonably written and contain a nugget or two of useful information. Nevertheless, the collection lacks consistency and a few common elements tying together everything into a unified whole. I see its primary use as a supplementary reader in a school media center course. [R: BL, 1 Oct 86, p. 221; JAL, Sept 86, pp. 247-48; VOYA, Dec 86, p. 254]   G. Edward Evans

314. **Fiction Catalog.** 11th ed. Juliette Yaakov, ed. New York, H. W. Wilson, 1986. 951p. index. (Standard Catalog Series). $80.00. LC 85-32298. ISBN 0-8242-0728-9.

The fact that this is the eleventh edition of the *Fiction Catalog* reminds us that here we have a standard reference source, one with a long history of quietly and consistently providing a valuable service to readers and libraries. As noted in the brief preface, its purpose is to update "the world of imaginative literature for the adult reader," and also to encourage maximum use of a library's collections. Titles selected for inclusion (5,131 items) were recommended by experienced public librarians. Entries that provide analysis of novelettes and composite works (2,100) extend the usefulness of the compilation. The aim is to provide a comprehensive bibliography of fiction, and not all the listed titles are still in print; for those that are, prices are included. Books in large print are identified at the entry and also under "large print books" in the index.

In the main entry section authors are listed alphabetically (in boldface type), with cross-references if necessary from variations on their names. Their works follow, cited fully enough for proper identification, including ISBNs and notes on previous editions. The annotations are substantial, almost always based on descriptive reviews, and provide a very clear impression of the books and their content to facilitate selection. The main entry section is fully analyzed in an easy-to-use index: both subject and title entries are keyed to authors in the main list, not to page numbers; subjects cover the major portion of a work and stand out in capital letters; and there are many cross-references.

A companion to the *Public Library Catalog* (H. W. Wilson, 1984), which provides access to writings about these authors, the *Fiction Catalog* continues the H. W. Wilson tradition, meeting a specific reference need in an outstanding manner. Joan W. Jensen

315. Gallo, Donald R., and the Committee on the Senior High School Booklist of the National Council of Teachers of English. **Books for You: A Booklist for Senior High Students.** new ed. Urbana, Ill., National Council of Teachers of English, 1985. 364p. index. $8.00pa. LC 85-21666. ISBN 0-8141-0363-4.

This revision is designed to supplement rather than replace earlier editions of *Books for You*. It is an annotated bibliography of approximately twelve hundred quality fiction and nonfiction titles for young adults. All of the titles included in this edition of *Books for You* were published between 1982 and 1984.

Titles are divided into forty-nine subject areas ranging from computers to easy reading to family conflicts to science fiction. An "Introduction to the Student" explains how the book is arranged, how titles were selected, and suggests ways students can use this bibliography to find titles of interest. Author and title indexes are provided. There is also a directory of publishers.

As with *Fiction for Youth* (Neal-Schuman, 1986), this work has multiple uses. It functions equally well as a retrospective collection development guide, a tool for developing high school reading lists, or as a direct resource to help students find something good to read. Recommended. [R: WLB, Mar 86, p. 78; VOYA, Aug/Oct 86, pp. 180-81] Carol J. Veitch

316. Gillespie, John T. **The Senior High School Paperback Collection.** Chicago, American Library Association, 1986. 424p. index. $30.00pa. LC 86-3401. ISBN 0-8389-0454-8.

The Senior High School Paperback Collection, published by the American Library Association, is a list of over forty-four hundred recommended titles. Although a number of selection aids were used, the author states in the preface that the final judgment was his. John Gillespie's knowledge of the field is based on a great deal of experience both as a professor of courses in children's and young adult literature and as the author of several selection tools. The lists are divided into two general areas, fiction and nonfiction, with specific subjects under each. Entries are numbered consecutively. The table of contents, giving a list of the subjects with page numbers, and the author/title index, giving the book number reference, make this resource an easy-to-use, easy-to-find selection tool. Each entry includes the author, title, publisher, series (when applicable), price, and annotation. The entries do not include references to reviews, which would have been helpful to a building media specialist and to curriculum departments selecting paperbacks for courses. Because of the titles listed and the organization of the book, this resource is definitely a necessary tool for each senior high school. Marie Zuk

317. **Good Reading: A Guide for Serious Readers.** 22d ed. Arthur Waldhorn, Olga S. Weber, and Arthur Zeiger, eds. New York, R. R. Bowker, 1985. 419p. index. $29.95. LC 85-17459. ISBN 0-8352-2100-8.

Good Reading has evolved from a pamphlet-sized publication in 1932 to a 419-page guide to selected world literature ranging in coverage from antiquity to modern times. The twenty-second edition lists and annotates twenty-seven hundred books, fitting each into one of six major sections: historical periods; regional and minority cultures; literary types; humanities and social sciences; sciences; and a special section which includes reference books for the general reader. Each section is divided into varying numbers of chapters, and each chapter begins with an essay of between five hundred and two thousand words designed to provide background information for the reader. The essays are well written but lack documentation, which would lead interested readers to further information. This edition adds several new chapters, including one devoted entirely to women's studies. As with all but the first edition, a highly selective list of titles is offered as "100 Significant Books" and carries with it the implication that no well-read person should admit to having missed a single one.

Entries in *Good Reading* include author and his or her date(s); title and publication date; short, informative, and generally critical annotation; format ("H" for hardcover and "P" for paperbound); and publisher, whose abbreviation conforms with those given in *Books in Print* and *Paperbound Books in Print*. A key to publishers is provided; their addresses, however, are omitted. An author, title, and broad subject index concludes the volume.

Good Reading is a valid compilation of worthy books, past and present. For those (young adults through adulthood) who could benefit from a list of recommended books, this volume should serve well. [R: JAL, Mar 86, p. 55; RBB, 15 May 86, p. 1378]

Dianne B. Catlett

318. Wynar, Christine Gehrt. **Guide to Reference Books for School Media Centers.** 3d ed. Littleton, Colo., Libraries Unlimited, 1986. 407p. index. $35.00. LC 86-20156. ISBN 0-87287-545-8.

The third edition of Christine Wynar's *Guide to Reference Books for School Library Media Centers* fulfills well its purpose of identifying in-print, recommended reference works "designed specifically for the juvenile and young adult market" (p. xii). Its new double-column format, typeface, and thorough indexing provide easy access to the greatly updated entries.

Although the total number of entries remains about the same (1,936 in the second edition to 2,011 in the third edition), the overall length of the annotations has increased. Also, a brief comparison of several categories from the second to the third editions revealed that 40 to 60 percent of the titles were new to the third edition, many with copyright dates of 1983-1985.

In addition to the new titles, some new categories were created and some old ones rearranged. "Database Utilities" and "Computer Software" were added as subheadings under the "Media Sources" section. Previous subheadings which became main categories in this edition include "Disabled," "Women's Studies," and "Energy," reflecting changing school curricular interests.

Since the entries are limited to those titles in-print at the time of compilation (*Books in Print 1985-86*), school library media centers with the second edition will want to keep both. Certain essential reference works are found in the second edition but not in the third, because they were out-of-print.

Elementary school library media users of this third edition will note that there is still a definite lack of recommended titles for elementary students. This is not as much a fault of this book and author as it is a problem of the juvenile publishing industry as a whole.

Marilyn L. Shontz

Media Skills and Programs

319. Carlson, Ann D. **Early Childhood Literature Sharing Programs in Libraries.** Hamden, Conn., Library Professional Publications/Shoe String Press, 1985. 119p. index. $19.50; $13.50pa. LC 85-13028. ISBN 0-208-02068-3; 0-208-02074-8pa.

Programs for children under three years of age are the fastest growing type of programming in children's services. Research in child development has shown that children's intellectual growth during these early years is as explosive as their physical growth. Against the background of these trends, Ann D. Carlson devised a research plan to investigate whether library programs for toddlers are in accordance with the practices suggested by experts in child development. To do this she developed a schema for the stages in the growth of children from birth to three years of age. The schema includes the development of verbal, motor, and social skills and the implications this development has for library programs. Having devised this schema and verified it with specialists, Carlson constructed a questionnaire for librarians who give programs for toddlers.

The results of the study are heartening. Most of the librarians showed an awareness of the needs of young children and of the way in which library programs should be organized to meet these needs. It appears that library programs are planned in ways which help young children develop to their full potential. This report of research is useful not only because it provides the results of the survey, but also because the schema, which is clear and detailed, can be used as an aid for librarians planning programs for young children. Carlson's research meets the needs of library educators and students by documenting library practices; it also meets the needs of practitioners who want practical guidance in planning programs. A most useful book. [R: JAL, Sept 86, p. 246]

Adele M. Fasick

320. Craver, Kathleen W. **The Changing Instructional Role of the High School Librarian.** Champaign, Ill., Graduate School of Library and Information Science, University of Illinois, 1986. 45p. bibliog. (Occasional Papers, No. 173). $3.00pa. ISSN 0276-1769.

Briefly and concisely, this paper reviews and examines the literature pertaining to the changing role of the school library media specialist from 1951 to 1984 to determine whether: the changes in the instructional role have been fictional or factual; the changes were those of substance or of form; the changes represented a process of growth and development in direct relationship to educational and societal evolutions; and any of the changes experienced a period of dormancy between introduction and acceptance by practitioners. In addition, selected research studies are reviewed which attempt to document the instructional status of the librarian to verify any changes.

Practitioners, researchers, and educators will definitely find much useful information about the different instructional roles of school library media specialists from 1951 to 1984 in this well-conceived publication. [R: SLJ, Nov 86, p. 50]   Isabel Schon

321. Greene, Ellin, and George Shannon. **Storytelling: A Selected Annotated Bibliography.** New York, Garland, 1986. 183p. index. (Garland Reference Library of Social Science, Vol. 302). $25.00. LC 84-48877. ISBN 0-8240-8749-6.

Storytelling is an annotated bibliography of 262 books, chapters from books, and journal articles which deepen the storyteller's understanding of the craft. Selections represent a wide variety of styles and range from the classic works of Ruth Sawyer and Marie Shedlock to contemporary storytellers like Carolyn Bauer, Jackie Torrance, and Augusta Baker.

Entries are arranged alphabetically under eight topics: "Beginnings," "Purposes and Values," "Art and Technique," "Storytelling in Special Settings or to Groups with Special Needs," "Reading Aloud," "Storytellers," "The Building of Background," "Bibliography and Indexes." Each entry includes complete bibliographic information, including additional sources if an article has appeared in more than one place. Annotations are mostly descriptive although some have a critical comment. An appendix lists some films and videotapes on the art of storytelling and a sampling of audio recordings of professional storytellers. Author, title, and subject indexes are included.

Storytelling would be especially useful in any academic library where there is a school of library science or education. It belongs in the hands of every teacher of storytelling and any public children's or school librarian who is interested in the art and craft of storytelling. [R: BL, 1 Sept 86, p. 53]   Carol J. Veitch

322. **Indicators of Quality for School Library/Media Programs.** International ed. By the Illinois Association for Media in Education and the International Association of School Librarianship. Kalamazoo, Mich., International Association of School Librarianship, 1985. 17p. $8.00pa.

Developed jointly by the Illinois Association for Media in Education and the International Association of School Librarianship, this brief paperback workbook presents international qualitative guidelines to be used in assessing local and regional school library media programs. The guide is designed to be used by library media center staff and school administrators as a tool for evaluating the quality of existing library media programs, for determining short- and long-range objectives, and for long-range planning.

Seven categories of indicators are included: library media center staff, program of services, inservice, materials and equipment, facilities, evaluation, and budget. Each indicator is to be rated on a five-point scale as to degree of acceptance ("Unacceptable" to "Endorse Completely") and degree of implementation ("Not Implemented" to "Fully Implemented"). The categories contain approximately four to ten indicators on both the local and regional levels. Care is taken by the authors to instruct the user to expand or rewrite indicators which are unacceptable or fail to meet local needs.

An appendix to these categories contains worksheets to be used to develop recommendations for local quantitative standards for print and nonprint materials and equipment. Columns provide for current inventory, number of new and replacement items needed, and estimated cost.

The guide provides a good outline of an evaluation process with general indicators which might be included. The user, however, must approach it as an outline, and not as a thoroughly defined process. Local adaptations and expansions are essential. Though not specifically international, both AECT's *Evaluating Media Programs: District & School* (1980) and Liesener's *A Systematic Process for Planning Media Programs* (American Library Association, 1976) provide more in-depth guidance to the library media center staff.

A minor problem which appears in the appendix worksheet items is the outmoded and somewhat arbitrary categories established for nonprint equipment and materials. Also, no mention is made of computer/microcomputer resources.   Marilyn L. Shontz

323. Jay, M. Ellen, and Hilda L. Jay. **Building Reference Skills in the Elementary School.** Hamden, Conn., Library Professional Publications/Shoe String Press, 1986. 187p. bibliog. index. $24.50; $16.50pa. LC 86-43. ISBN 0-208-02098-5; 0-208-02097-7pa.

This book is a well-researched, well-written, very useful tool for all elementary school librarians and media specialists. The first part includes arguments for teaching more reference and information skills, and putting more stress on the development of thinking skills. Rationale is given for the teacher and the media specialist to work as a team, sharing the instructional role as students practice thinking skills with emphasis on "higher order intellectual skills." The first part concludes with a discussion of sound instructional theories.

"Part Two: How to Use Specific Reference Titles" reviews general reference materials, as well as specific titles more appropriate for certain subjects. A short description of the contents, its useful characteristics, the skills involved, and suggested activities are included in the review of each title. This part ends with a discussion of periodicals, newspapers, and computer software.

The research process is discussed next. Again, theory and research are given in an understandable manner, followed by practical activities dealing with locating facts, bibliographies, and taking and organizing notes. In addition to outlining, two very useful but often forgotten organizational methods are explained: webbing or mapping, and flowcharting. The one area to be questioned is the discussion of the writing process as consisting of three stages: revising, editing, and proofreading. According to the National Writing Project and National Council of Teachers of English, the writing process consists of five steps: prewriting, writing, revising, editing, and rewriting/publishing. A discussion of peer conferencing and a suggested "Project Writing Checklist" conclude this section. The book ends with well-described research projects, including a social studies enrichment program, to use with students.

Hilda and Ellen Jay have organized a great deal of research and practical information and activities into a well-written, very useful book. Every elementary librarian or media specialist will find this to be an invaluable tool which should be a top priority purchase. [R: BL, July 86, p. 1619; RQ, Winter 86, pp. 260-61; SLJ, Dec 86, p. 41]

    Marie Zuk

324. Laughlin, Mildred Knight, and Letty S. Watt. **Developing Learning Skills through Children's Literature: An Idea Book for K-5 Classrooms and Libraries.** Phoenix, Ariz., Oryx Press, 1986. 270p. bibliog. index. $30.00pa. LC 86-2554. ISBN 0-89774-258-3.

Writing from the position that literature activities help children develop thinking, listening, and communication skills, the authors present sixty units. Although the "suggested ideas ... may be utilized in developing a scope and sequence of literature experiences" (p. ix), readers are encouraged to use these units to augment existing reading and language curricula.

Units focus on specific authors or illustrators. The units for the third to fifth grades also cover literary genres, themes, and nonfiction categories. Each unit includes student objectives, recommended readings (children's) with brief descriptive annotations, biographical sources, instructions for group introductory activity, and follow-up student activities. The recommended titles published in the 1970s and 1980s include out-of-print works with wide appeal. Each chapter closes with suggested culminating activities for the grade levels and a list of references.

Typically, a unit opens with the adult presenting information about the author or illustrator. The brief biographical information will help those who lack access to such recommended sources as *Something about the Author* or *Twentieth Century Children's Writers*.

Activities cover drama, art, music, poetry, listening, and writing. As an example, for *Little House in the Big Woods* children are to make a model of the house or illustrate their favorite scene. Permission is given to copy the activities. Three appendices cover biographical sources, book instruction techniques, and a directory of publishers and producers. A single index accesses authors, illustrators, titles (book, nonprint), and subjects.

    Phyllis J. Van Orden and Susan Perkins

Microcomputer Use

325. Costa, Betty, and Marie Costa. **A Micro Handbook for Small Libraries and Media Centers.** 2d ed. Littleton, Colo., Libraries Unlimited, 1986. 325p. illus. index. $23.50. LC 86-15387. ISBN 0-87287-525-3.

This second edition of Betty and Marie Costa's handbook for microcomputer applications in small libraries and media centers should put at ease those who suffer from computerphobia. Building on the previous edition, the authors have incorporated changes to reflect developments in available hardware and software. Chaptes 1, 2, and 3 present an overview of both the history and status of hardware and software; chapter 4 deals with applications; chapters 5 and 6 explore the relationship of computer applications with internal and external databases; and chapters 7 and 8 present data on choosing systems and ethics of use. Three case studies precede an excellent appendix of resource materials, ranging from glossary and bibliography to care and financing. Bibliographies, both in the appendix and at the conclusion of each chapter, are current and well selected. Copyright dates are generally between 1983 and 1986.

The book is intended as a beginner's guide, and as such, it devotes a great deal of attention to making the reader comfortable with hardware, software, and applications. The user would do well to heed the authors' suggestion that he or she read through the book completely before making decisions about microcomputers and their use in a program. The book stresses the need for analysis and preplanning, and provides the basic information necessary for application and use of microcomputers in the small library and media center. The authors have recognized the rapidly changing nature of the microcomputer world and have cited the difficulty of keeping information current. This book offers a means of doing so in presenting information that is not only basic to current use but also vital to meeting future changes. It is solid in content, clear in language, helpful in arrangement, and useful to the practitioner.

Anthony C. Schulzetenberg

326. Ho, May Lein. **Appleworks for School Librarians.** Fayetteville, Ark., Hi Willow Research and Publishing, 1985. 129p. index. $20.00 spiralbound. ISBN 0-931510-17-1.

The Apple II series of microcomputers is still the brand most often found in schools, and Appleworks is a widely used integrated word processor, database, and spreadsheet program for the Apple. Consequently, a book aimed at teaching school librarians how to use Appleworks, with examples taken from their daily routine, seems a useful enough approach. Ho's book is elementary, very gentle, and would be particularly appropriate for computerphobes or as a guide for those teaching Appleworks to school librarians. Others may find the going too slow and be put off by the in-house manual appearance of the text, which presumably was produced on a letter-quality printer. Accompanying the text and serving as the examples are fifty-one templates on a floppy disk. (Templates are prewritten forms or guides customized for a specific use.) While illustrating a wide variety of applications, including collection mapping, most are fairly simple. There are also a couple of typos on the templates (for example, *leger* for *ledger*). Librarians who are interested in templates, whether or not for Appleworks, should be aware of the Apple Template Exchange Program. See the *Apple Library Users Group Newsletter* for more details. While there are many books on Appleworks, a good choice for users with computer experience is Charles Rubin's *Command Performance Appleworks: The Microsoft Desktop Dictionary and Cross-Reference Guide* (Microsoft, 1986). [R: SLMQ, Spring 86, p. 156]   Robert Skinner

327. **The Microcomputer Facility and the School Library Media Specialist.** Blanche E. Woolls and David V. Loertscher, eds. Chicago, American Library Association, 1986. 204p. $15.00pa. LC 85-26827. ISBN 0-8389-3325-4.

This volume presents a comprehensive overview of various aspects of implementing a microcomputer facility and program in a school library situation. Included are twenty-one articles/essays by different authors. As stated in the introduction, their purpose is "to assist school library media specialists in initiating, maintaining, and expanding microcomputer use in elementary and secondary schools" (p. viii).

The book is organized into four parts. Part 1, "Planning," includes selections on selecting microcomputers and software, microcomputers in elementary schools, microcomputers in large districts, and phases in the planning process. "Operating the Facility," part 2, covers administrative uses, creating management software, cataloging software, and use of electronic mail. In part 3, "Services of the Facility," authors discuss access to electronic information, interactive videodisc technology, and teaching computer literacy in secondary schools. The final part, "Working with the Faculty," includes a review of computer-assisted instruction research, in-service planning for teachers and staff, a proposed process for planning with the faculty, developing districtwide and/or single school plans, and applications in specific curriculum areas such as social studies, music and art, English, and math and science.

While the editors can be commended for presenting a broad overview of the microcomputer facility from a variety of viewpoints, their efforts result in some unevenness in quality and redundancy. For example, Olson's "Cataloging Microcomputer Software" (p. 83), is a practical, well-written summary of the topic, immediately usable by those familiar with AACR2. Also, Flynn's "Selecting a Microcomputer" could be very helpful to those with only a beginning knowledge of types of microcomputers. On the other hand, somewhat less helpful are Loertscher's "Computer Coordinator Involvement in Instruction" (p. 152), a two-page outline of the instructional design process, and Gunderman's brief "Microcomputers in an Elementary School" (p. 54), which presents the experience of one elementary school in little detail. Redundancy is a problem in parts 1 and 4. Chapters in both parts present overlapping information on planning and the planning process in schools and/or districts.

Many of the contributing authors used a case study approach to their subjects. This emphasis on successes in individual situations does give readers practical hints and advice. While there are other books that provide a more thorough introduction to technology and its applications, this volume provides more in the way of planning steps and examples of successful school library media programs.

Marilyn L. Shontz

Toys and Games

328. Cleaver, Betty P., Barbara Chatton, and Shirley Vittum Morrison. **Creating Connections: Books, Kits and Games for Children: A Sourcebook.** New York, Garland, 1986. 417p. index. (Garland Reference Library of Social Science, Vol. 280). $27.00. LC 86-581. ISBN 0-8240-8798-4.

School librarians and teachers will be able to use this book both as a resource and as a model in developing connections between curriculum and literature. The model used is the creation of a web of topics and concepts connected with a central theme. The themes used as examples include cities, mountains, monsters, and bodies. Once a theme is chosen, the curriculum group brainstorms ideas about various aspects of the theme which could be enlarged upon for classroom use. The theme of cities covers such aspects as the cultural context, the physical world, the constructed world, people in the cities, and subtopics under each of these. After deciding upon the aspects to be included in the overall theme, the group searches for appropriate material to be used in exploring each aspect. The result is a bibliography of books and audiovisual materials suitable for classroom use. Teachers and school librarians could use this method of brainstorming for connections between almost any theme and the literature and other materials available.

In addition to suggesting a method, this book provides such bibliographies of sources for six themes. It also includes a bibliography of professional materials on children's literature, a list of subject headings, and a directory of publishers. The sources suggested under each of the themes include materials for various grade levels from kindergarten through grade 8, although the emphasis is on material for the earlier grades. A very brief annotation and bibliographic information are given for each title listed. Most of the titles are quite recent and useful. Teachers and school librarians in elementary and middle schools will find this a helpful book in planning curriculum and encouraging children to read widely. [R: RBB, 15 Oct 86, p. 334]

Adele M. Fasick

329. Sinker, Mary. **Toys for Growing: A Guide to Toys That Develop Skills.** Chicago, published for National Lekotek Center by Year Book Medical Publishers, 1986. 170p. illus. $9.95pa. ISBN 0-8151-7750-X.

Toys included in this guide were selected from the collection at the National Lekotek Center in Evanston, Illinois. Lekotek ("playlibrary") is a worldwide system of resource centers for children with special needs. These toys, however, are appropriate for all children, since developmental sequences are similar. The emphasis in this work is on toys for children from birth through age six.

The first section of *Toys for Growing* discusses the physical, social, and emotional development of children and includes the types of toys which work best for each developmental stage. The next sections discuss specific toys under the general headings of infant stimulation, fine motor/visual perception, gross motor play, auditory/musical toys, tactile toys, language play, number materials, playing games, puzzles, general toys/creative play, electronic toys and devices, and books. Most of these sections are subdivided by type of toy (e.g., "Toys to Look At," "Construction Toys," "Toys for Throwing," "Sequence Games," etc.). Each entry describes the toy and its particular play value. The manufacturer, a code for where the toy can be purchased, and a price range is also provided. Illustrations accompany at least one toy per page. Appendices give addresses for toy companies which sell directly to the public and a list of puzzle sources. The puzzle source list includes characteristics of puzzles from different manufacturers.

Toys for Growing would be a useful addition to public and school library collections as well as academic collections in institutions with teacher education or other education-related curricula. Parents and grandparents will find it a useful resource. Preschool, early elementary, and special education teachers will appreciate the evaluative descriptions. Public library children's specialists could use this tool when selecting toys for library use or a toy lending service. Carol J. Veitch

SERVICE TO DISABLED USERS

330. Craddock, Peter. **The Public Library and Blind People: A Survey and Review of Current Practice.** London, British Library; distr., Wolfeboro, N.H., Longwood Publishing Group, 1985. 106p. bibliog. (Library and Information Research Report, 36). $22.50pa. ISBN 0-7123-3051-8.

The subtitle of this work, "A Survey and Review of Current Practice," indicates that it is not simply a discussion of how the public library serves its blind users, but the report of a survey on what is actually being done. The author studied services provided to blind persons by public libraries in Great Britain during 1983-1984. Following standard research methodology, the text covers such areas as the need for the study, aims and objectives, methodology used, background, analysis of the responses to the questionnaire, and finally the conclusions and recommendations. Appendices contain information on some special projects, the Royal National Institute for the Blind, postal regulations relating to materials for the blind, a copy of the questionnaire used in the study, and a 140-item bibliography. The text is enhanced by the addition of numerous charts, giving such information as the number of libraries having subscriptions to tape services for disabled users by the sources of the services. Other aspects of service covered in the study are library holdings, reading aids and other equipment, links with other agencies, and attitudes toward service to the blind. While the study would be of greater interest to the British reader than the American reader, it would be useful in making comparison between types of services in the two countries and also perhaps serve as a model for similar studies in the United States. The addition of an index and some listing of the acronyms used—at least for the American reader—would undoubtedly make the work more useful. Lucille Whalen

331. **R Is for Reading.** Leslie Eldridge, comp. and ed. Washington, D.C., Library Service to Blind and Physically Handicapped Children, Library of Congress, 1985. 193p. free pa. LC 84-600215. ISBN 0-8444-0480-2.

Although the National Library Service for the Blind and Physically Handicapped (NLS) has become better known in recent years, it is more often thought of as a service for adults than for children. As a matter of fact, the children's component of the service did grow out of a service designed for adults. It was assumed, as the editor, Leslie Eldridge, points out, that a system that worked for adults would also work for children, but it has been found that it worked mostly for those handicapped children who already had strong support from parents and teachers. Eldridge believed the time had come to find a way to make the program work more effectively for children.

The project she undertook to realize this goal was an attempt to characterize handicapped juvenile users and nonusers and to promote new ideas for serving them through the NLS network. This was done through a series of interviews with those who come in contact with handicapped children, as it was felt that these people could provide the insights needed to revamp the program. Interviews were held with handicapped children themselves and their mothers, special education teachers and counselors, reading specialists, and librarians. Almost the entire text of the book is taken up with the interviews, most of which run three to six pages. Most of the interviewees speak frankly about the successes and frustrations they have encountered in trying to make reading important to handicapped children. Conclusions drawn from the interviews are summarized in the final pages of the book. The child counselors, for example, suggested that books should be created to appeal to senses, not just hearing; the reading specialists stressed the necessity for more communication between teachers and librarians; and parents asked for more information about the NLS program. The work should be extremely valuable for all those working with handicapped children who can take advantage of the NLS program.

Lucille Whalen

SPECIAL LIBRARIES AND COLLECTIONS

General Works

332. Ahrensfeld, Janet L., Elin B. Christianson, and David E. King. **Special Libraries: A Guide for Management.** 2d ed., rev. Washington, D.C., Special Libraries Association, 1986. 75p. illus. bibliog. index. $15.50pa. ISBN 0-87111-318-X.

The second edition of *Special Libraries* has now been revised; it still holds its place as the most useful guide for managers seeking to establish, expand, or upgrade library facilities within their organizations. Directed to a nonlibrarian audience, the book outlines the basic purposes and functions of the library and provides some guidance in determining the level of library service suitable for a particular organization. Ten chapters cover the following topics: "What Is a Special Library?" "When Is an Organization Ready for a Special Library?" "Levels of Function," "Acquisition of Materials," "Organization of Materials," "Dissemination of Materials and Information," "The Library as an Organizational Unit," "Library Staff," "Space and Equipment," "Planning the Budget." The guide is not a how-to manual for running a special library; it is intended as a planning aid for managers who have no familiarity with libraries and need to know what factors and options to consider. Library school students with an interest in special libraries will also find the guide useful. *Special Libraries* has, for the most part, maintained the same format and content since its first edition was published in 1966, with new developments (database searching, computerized cataloging, compact shelving, etc.) and updated statistics (staff salaries, average budgets and collection sizes, etc.) incorporated into each new revision. A list of graduate library school programs accredited by ALA as of 1986 and a short bibliography focusing on individual aspects of special libraries are also included.

Judy Dyki

333. Bailey, Martha J. **The Special Librarian as a Supervisor or Middle Manager.** Washington, D.C., Special Libraries Association, 1986. 158p. index. $18.95pa. LC 86-3782. ISBN 0-87111-315-5.

The first edition of this book was published in 1977 as an SLA state-of-the-art review of less than fifty pages. This greatly expanded and updated second edition serves as a review of the literature concerning librarians as managers. With a very ambitious scope, Bailey covers definitions of managers, supervision in libraries, the environment of the library, organizational structure, new functions of libraries, the status of the librarian, current management theories, computers, library education, and leadership. Each chapter briefly discusses major trends, studies, theories, and writings in each of these areas and concludes with a bibliography drawn from both library science and business literature. Although the title specifies the special librarian, the book will be of interest to academic and public librarians as well, since most of the studies cited involve these two types of libraries. Two additional bibliographies are included in the appendices: one arranged by type of activity which managers oversee, and the other by type of library. Because of the number of topics included, the treatment of each is necessarily brief. Several chapters seem cluttered and disconnected because so many areas are included. The real value of the book lies in the bibliographies, and for that reason it will be of most interest to library science students and librarians seeking a general introduction to the literature of library management.

Judy Dyki

334. Cowley, John, ed. **The Management of Polytechnic Libraries.** Brookfield, Vt., COPOL in association with Gower Publishing, 1985. 262p. index. $53.95. LC 85-9868. ISBN 0-566-03525-1.

This collection of ten essays deals with the application of major management concepts and techniques to the functioning of polytechnic libraries in England. These academic libraries are mainly, but not exclusively, technical libraries. Their managerial problems and solutions parallel closely those of some American special libraries. Present managers of polytechnic libraries view them as interactive environments, operating within the influence of local management whose policies are determined by the central administration of the total system. At the local level, each unit develops a style of operation congruent with the local environment. They are, therefore, interesting combinations of academic, special, and to some degree, public libraries. Their managerial problems, while unique, also exhibit many features that are consonant with those of the said libraries. Problems of current management concerns, short-term planning, decision making, system implementation, performance measure, multisite managing, finances, crisis management, library cooperation, and problems related to the management of information technology are the topics of the essays. This excellent book is highly recommended for practitioners and teachers of academic, special, and public library management. It is also recommended for libraries that support library science programs, especially for those with an international emphasis. Antonio Rodriguez-Buckingham

335. **SLA Triennial Salary Survey.** Washington, D.C., Special Libraries Association, 1986. 78p. $25.00pa. LC 86-1847. ISBN 0-87111-316-3.

This is the seventh salary survey of SLA members to be conducted on a triennial basis. The 1985 survey questionnaire, which was sent by first class mail along with a letter from the president to 9,691 members in the United States and Canada, resulted in a 65 percent response rate, a considerable improvement over the 36 percent achieved in 1982. Data are presented in seventy-eight tables which include mean and median salaries; historical data; and salary distribution by the following: sex, the nine geographical U.S. Census Regions and Canada, Standard Metropolitan Statistical Areas, type of institution, budget ranges, primary responsibility, supervisory responsibilities, academic background, previous experience, minority groups, age, and job title. Great care is taken in a six-page introduction to explain salary survey terminology and to provide brief summaries of the 1985 findings. The remaining seventy-two pages contain the tables, two figures, and the survey questionnaire. Careful layout and the use of boldface create very legible tables with plenty of white space. Overall this survey has met its objective of providing systematic, accurate information about salaries of special librarians and information personnel. Annual updates are being provided by sampling 25 percent of the SLA membership in 1986 and 1987. [R: LJ, 15 May 86, p. 52]

Helen Howard

336. **Who's Who in Special Libraries 1985-86.** Washington, D.C., Special Libraries Association, 1985. 196p. index. $25.00pa. ISSN 0278-842X.

The always useful directory of the members of the Special Libraries Association (SLA) — the preeminent body of special librarians in North America — was apparently a partial victim of the move of SLA's headquarters from New York to Washington, D.C. This work is less complete than last year's. Further, the paper quality seems to be newsprint only.

While a plus is the reversion from last year's experimental main listing by subject divisions with alphabetical index of member's names, and a chapter approach also, this year it is an alphabetical main (and only) listing of member's names.

Statistically, it is noted that SLA's current membership of 11,775 is concentrated with 1,386 members in the New York chapter, 856 in the Washington, D.C., chapter, and 657 in Illinois. The South Carolina Provisional Chapter is smallest at 23 members. The divisions are subject based and are important for program emphasis. Business and Finance leads with 2,366 members, Information Technology has 2,005, Library Management has 1,541, and Science Technology has 1,496. Trailing is the Physics-Mathematics Astronomy Division as the smallest at 142 members.

The usual strategy when searching for a special librarian is to look first in the newer of (1) this work or (2) the personnel index to Gale Research's *Directory of Special Libraries and Information Centers*. This year they are about equal with the Gale being distributed in October and SLA's *Who's Who* in December. Gale does have more librarians in the subspecialties, such as law, medicine, and music. Gale's ninth edition lists 28,875 names from 17,476 institutions.

E. B. Jackson

Archival Collections

337. Cook, Michael. **The Management of Information from Archives.** Brookfield, Vt., Gower Publishing, 1986. 234p. bibliog. index. $41.50. LC 85-22042. ISBN 0-566-03504-9.

The purpose of this book is "to describe in outline the nature of the management aims and systems involved in work with archive materials." Its hope is to "reassess the theory and practice of archives and records management, viewing them from the standpoint of processors and suppliers of information, as part of a developed and effective management service." As such it erases the often encountered artificial distinction between records management and archives administration.

After a brief but adequate theoretical introduction, Cook devotes chapters to the background of archives services, records management, acquisition and archival appraisal, archive arrangement, archival description and the structure of its data elements, information retrieval in archival systems, application of automation in archival management, and user services. The contents are made easily accessible by an excellent index.

As Cook notes, the problems addressed in this book will not be solved in traditional ways because the concept of the archive is now in the process of changing radically. His clearly written and concise book should help us weather this transition more easily.

Robert H. Burger

338. Phillips, C. M., and C. M. Woolgar. **Computerising Archives: Some Guidelines.** Winchester, England, Society of Archivists, 1985. 59p. (Computer Applications Committee. Occasional Papers, 1). £3.50. ISBN 0-902886-17-7.

This short, practical handbook has been designed to aid archivists in developing guidelines to help them decide what sort of computer system would best meet the cataloging and servicing requirements of the collections for which they are responsible. When choosing a computer system, archivists must consider the structure or cataloging form that will accommodate the material they must deal with; they must know if the system will handle accents, diacritics, symbols, non-Roman alphabets, etc.; they must know what the capabilities of the system are to retrieve, sort, or rearrange data, and if it would be capable of networking. This handbook provides information on these matters as well as discussions of how to choose software and hardware. An appendix contains a case study with "examples of the documentation that would be necessary on a typical computerisation project directed towards the automation of cataloguing" (p. 33). The guide concludes with a glossary of terms used in the book.

Dean H. Keller

339. Stielow, Frederick J. **The Management of Oral History Sound Archives.** Westport, Conn., Greenwood Press, 1986. 158p. illus. index. $35.00. LC 85-14716. ISBN 0-313-24442-1.

The author provides a logical and well-organized work discussing the theories behind sound archives, including processing and organizing collections, public use of the collections, and conservation management, to name a few subjects covered. The interest in oral history and the preservation of interviews on magnetic tape makes this work valuable to amateur and professional alike.

The Management of Oral History Sound Archives is well illustrated with examples of flowcharts, inventory forms, retention appraisals, folklore headings from the Library of Congress Manual, and other very helpful sample worksheets. Microcomputer applications are also discussed, and a select bibliography on database management of sound archives is included. It provides the reader with the practical information necessary for organizing and managing the collection, as well as handling the problems which may occur in making the information available for public use.

The relatively new field of oral history and sound preservation is a subject which is systematically handled by Stielow in his work. The inclusion of a bibliography at the end of each chapter provides the reader with many additional sources for continued study. The work is highly recommended to libraries and archives, and to individuals dealing with the study of oral history preservation. [R: LJ, 1 June 86, p. 100]

Carol Willsey Bell

Art Libraries

340. Jones, Lois Swan, and Sarah Scott Gibson. **Art Libraries and Information Services: Development, Organization, and Management.** Orlando, Fla., Academic Press, 1986. 343p. index. (Library and Information Science). $39.50. LC 85-28598. ISBN 0-12-389170-1.

Every library with collections of art or library science material should have a copy of *Art Libraries and Information Services.* It is an exemplary reference volume on a neglected area of librarianship and so should serve the student well. It offers up-to-date information and rational insights for the professional. It also provides clear descriptions of some of the mysterious behavior patterns of materials used by art historians, designers, and educators.

Art Libraries will serve as an excellent textbook to current practices in a variety of types of art libraries. These types, their users, and their collections are described in part 1 of the five-part volume. Part 2 focuses on collection evaluation, with sections on standards, bibliographies, and reference works, as well as good longer analyses of materials for special audiences. Those on art historians and exhibition and trade literature are excellent, revealing the special pitfalls of festschriften, AACR2, and sales indexes. Part 3 is entitled "Information Services," an umbrella title which covers bibliographic instruction, online databases, and interlibrary loan, while part 4 discusses collection development and library management. Part 4 is especially valuable as an introduction to the nitty-gritty details of library operations.

For experienced librarians, *Art Libraries* offers few totally new insights but presents a realistic appraisal of how art libraries really work. For them, the most important aspect of the volume may be the thorough and current bibliographic notes, which should inspire new interest in familiar topics. Concluding *Art Libraries* is a useful section of appendices including relevant acronyms, some database vendors, professional associations, part of a collection development policy, an annual report, part of a building program, and author, title, and subject indexes. Art historian Jones and library educator Gibson seem to have thought of everything in this well-organized and well-written work.

Stephanie C. Sigala

341. Keaveney, Sydney Starr. **Contemporary Art Documentation and Fine Arts Libraries.** Metuchen, N.J., Scarecrow, 1986. 180p. bibliog. index. $17.50. LC 85-22234. ISBN 0-8108-1859-0.

The pattern of documentation in the visual arts has always been recognized to be different than that of the sciences, but until publication of this landmark work the scope and importance of the differences have been undocumented. Keaveney's 181-page volume is a readable, but scholarly, study of the organization of information flow in the contemporary art world and the relationship of libraries to that flow. The vocabulary and methodology of information science have been applied to current materials in the fine arts and the results are striking.

Keaveney's study is divided into chapters on communications patterns, the communications network in the contemporary art world, how the various types of fine arts libraries differ in documenting contemporary art, and a summation of trends and conclusions. In her discussion, she makes the vital observation that the primary information pathway in the contemporary art world is a visual one, based on observation and exhibition of works of art. She then demonstrates that the importance of a fine arts library and the information it transmits to other members of a secondary pathway is directly related to the library's proximity to the gatekeepers, the curators and dealers, who control the primary, visual path.

The fourteen libraries studied were major art resource centers in New York and the Northeast. To document collecting patterns, forty living artists were grouped together, based on relative fame; the holdings on these artists in each library were counted and analyzed. Though such phenomena as the Matthew effect and Zipf-Trueswell distribution were found to be important, Keaveney discovered that fine arts libraries contain a far greater variety of titles than she expected and that the libraries studied had remarkably little collection overlap. While the relationship of the library to the gatekeepers of the visual path was identified as a major source of diversity in collecting paterns, institutional purpose, general lack of bibliographic control in art literature, and the treatment of ephemeral vertical file materials were also cited.

Bolstered by an impressive array of charts and appendices, *Contemporary Art Documentation* demonstrates that while a methodology based on information science can be applied to the visual arts, patterns of documentation retain a particular diversity not always easily explained by traditional hypotheses. [R: C&RL, Nov 86, pp. 622-26; LJ, 1 June 86, p. 100]

Stephanie C. Sigala

342. Markey, Karen. **Subject Access to Visual Resources Collections: A Model for Computer Construction of Thematic Catalogs.** Westport, Conn., Greenwood Press, 1986. 189p. illus. bibliog. index. (New Directions in Information Management, No. 11). $35.00. LC 86-7658. ISBN 0-313-24031-0.

A valuable contribution to the literature of picture librarianship, this volume discusses the theory of subject analysis of still visual material and proposes a methodology for providing subject access to visual resources not limited by subject content or physical format. Several chapters discuss and put into context taxonomies useful in describing and assessing current practices. The major theorist discussed is Panofsky, who identified a trilevel taxonomy describing the pre-iconographical (primary subject matter), the iconographical (secondary subject matter) and the iconographical interpretation (intrinsic meaning) levels of description. Many large, significant collections of visual materials have developed sophisticated systems of analysis and access. The discussion of the theory and various approaches to these tasks can itself be illuminating.

The unique contribution of this volume is in the suggested development of a thematic catalog of primary and secondary subject terms, which the author emphasizes requires no specialized knowledge of the sophisticated methods of specialized subject catalogers used by many collections. A thematic catalog of primary and secondary subject matter of one hundred works of art in Northern Europe, 1250-1425, is the subject of an experiment described as an example of possible application.

The approach taken by the author seems to make the assumption that the nonspecialist approach to analysis of and access to visual collections is desirable. This raises questions about the philosophy, goals, and objectives of institutions which support visual collections. These collections have been characterized by specialized interests and support. The use of computer technology to provide the type of access suggested, however, makes the suggestions feasible for many collections which may be underutilized in terms of their research and economic value to current and potential users. New storage formats for visual images also bring this work into focus. Although it reads like a dissertation, this work provides insights into limitations of current practices and suggests a way to enhance access to visual resources for research. The cost-benefit of the method remains to be investigated.

JoAnn V. Rogers

343. Viaux, Jacqueline, comp. **IFLA Directory of Art Libraries. Répertoire de bibliothèques d'art de l'IFLA. Addressbuch der Kunstbibliotheken von IFLA. Directorio de bibliotecas de arte de la IFLA.** New York, Garland, 1985. 480p. index. (Garland Reference Library of the Humanities, Vol. 510). $60.00. LC 84-48057. ISBN 0-8240-8913-8.

Compiled by art librarians of the International Federation of Library Associations (IFLA), this directory lists art libraries throughout the world *except* those in the United States and Canada. Those institutions are covered in

Directory of Art Libraries and Visual Resource Collections in North America (Neal-Schuman, 1978). This new volume describes the holdings of art libraries in forty-six countries listed in alphabetical order according to official name. An index lists all countries in each of the five official IFLA languages (English, French, German, Russian, and Spanish) with cross-references. Within each country entries are listed alphabetically first by city and then by institution.

Entries are written in one of the IFLA languages, but most are in English or French. Information in each entry includes address and telephone; access policy, hours, and holidays; loan policies; founding date; access tools; and reader services. Size of holdings by subject and type including books, slides, catalogs, periodicals, and other print and nonprint resources, is estimated according to a system explained in the front of the book. A subject index helps readers locate collections of interest.

The IFLA art librarians have compiled a useful directory which, although it will become outdated, makes a good start in providing worldwide knowledge of art library resources. Since collection information is general, most researchers will have to look further for specifics. An index of institutions would enhance the use of the next edition. In this book the reader must know an institution's location to find the entry. Despite this minor fault, the book will certainly aid researchers and scholars in finding collections in their fields of interest.

Linda S. Keir

Government Publications

344. **Directory of Foreign Document Collections.** Carol A. Turner, comp. New York, published for the Government Documents Round Table, American Library Association by UNIPUB, 1985. 148p. $20.00pa. LC 84-52793. ISBN 0-89059-045-1.

This directory identifies—by specific country—libraries in the United States and Canada which collect foreign government documents. Academic libraries comprise the majority of collections represented, but some special libraries, such as the Organization of American States' Columbus Memorial Library, are included.

Two main sections provide access to collections. The list of countries itemizes, by NUC code and collection level symbol, which collections maintain holdings for each nation. No international organizations are accessed. The "Libraries, Description of Collections" section provides names of key staff members; interlibrary loan, photocopy, and access policies; and descriptions of area and subject strengths. Publications describing or accessing the collection are also noted. While this arrangement is effective, the three-step lookup caused by using NUC codes instead of library names is awkward.

Libraries that already own the *Directory of Government Document Collections & Librarians* (see *ARBA* 85, entry 532) or the *Directory of Special Libraries and Information Centers* (9th ed., 1984) will find a great deal of duplication, but the ability to focus on a single country instead of a region or continent makes this volume valuable. The identification of collection levels using ALA definitions is particularly helpful. For example, eleven of the fifty-four institutions listed as collecting South African publications are identified as having comprehensive ("A") or research-level ("B") collections.

Lisa K. Dalton

345. Hernon, Peter, Charles R. McClure, and Gary R. Purcell. **GPO's Depository Library Program: A Descriptive Analysis.** Norwood, N.J., Ablex Publishing, 1985. 227p. bibliog. index. $32.50. LC 85-6038. ISBN 0-89391-313-8.

This book makes a significant contribution to research on the depository library program for U.S. government publications. The first of seven chapters provides an historical background of the program. The second chapter provides an excellent analysis and critique of the research literature on the program, and identifies topics which need further research. The next two chapters report the results of a nationwide mail survey which the authors conducted to obtain data to define the characteristics of depository libraries, and to compare selected types of library subgroups. The questionnaire instrument is included as an appendix. The development of the instrument and analysis of the data display excellent research techniques which are apparently intended to provide an example for the Government Printing Office (GPO) to improve its biennial survey of depository libraries. The authors used not only data from the survey, but also data from other authoritative sources, either to verify data submitted by libraries, or to avoid imposing a burden on respondents to supply information already available. The authors also used data from previous surveys to make comparisons and identify trends. The fifth chapter provides an original contribution to the literature: analysis of the results of a separate survey of the fifty-one libraries which have terminated their depository status since 1970. In chapter 6 the authors analyze GPO's design and use of the biennial survey for program decision making and planning and find them lacking in many respects. In the final chapter the authors make excellent suggestions to improve the design of the biennial survey so that the data obtained will have reliability, validity, and utility and can be used as a basis for planning, evaluation, and decision making. — LeRoy C. Schwarzkopf

346. McClure, Charles R., and Peter Hernon. **Academic Library Use of NTIS: Suggestions for Services and Core Collections.** Springfield, Va., National Technical Information Service, 1986. 60p. index. $12.00pa. ISBN 0-934213-04-6.

This manual comprises two parts. Part 1, "Promoting the Use of NTIS (National Technical Information Service) Information Services and Products," is eighteen pages in length and has cursory discussions of such topics as "Developing Collections of NTIS Materials," "Increasing Awareness of NTIS Services and Products," and "Increasing the Use of NTIS Materials." A list of references identifies titles providing more detailed discussions of topics covered in part 1.

Part 2, "NTIS Library Core Collections: A Bibliographic Guide," is twenty-eight pages in length and is intended as "a *first attempt* at identifying NTIS core titles" (preface). According to the authors, this part of the manual "is intended to help librarians, *not* just those in an academic setting, to determine which NTIS titles are significant for particular subject areas and allow them to better integrate NTIS materials into their collection" (preface). It appears that the manual achieves this more general objective; however, it is unfortunate that its title (*Academic Library Use of NTIS ...*) belies this aspect of its utility.

The manual contains two indexes (a title index and a number index). The brief paragraph explaining the title index is erroneously repeated under the number index. The purpose of the indexes, however, is obvious. There is one appendix ("Searching OCLC for NTIS Materials") which describes the OCLC EASI-Reference database, available through BRS.

Despite some minor inaccuracies or errors, this is a work that any library with a large government documents collection should find useful. Even though academic libraries/librarians are its primary audience, the identification of NTIS core collections expands its scope and utility. — Larry G. Chrisman

347. Morehead, Joe. **Essays on Public Documents and Government Policies.** New York, Haworth Press, 1986. 364p. index. (*Technical Services Quarterly*, Vol. 3, Nos. 3/4). $29.95. LC 86-9840. ISBN 0-86656-248-6.

Twenty of the thirty-four essays in this collection originally appeared in *Serials Librarian*, to which Morehead contributes a regular column. Other essays are taken from journals such as *Documents to the People* and *RQ* or from monographs. For the most part the level of government dealt with is the U.S. federal government. The last four essays, however, relate to the United Nations—its information system, serials documentation, the World Intellectual Property Organization, and the International Fund for Agricultural Development. Not surprisingly, the diversity of themes is more fully represented in the articles vis-à-vis the federal government, as mention of a few of the subjects covered will illustrate: our government as a teacher, the uses and misuses of information found in government publications, federal serials and the economic condition, the poor state of crime statistics, preserving the environment, sex themes in federal serials, a portrait of working women in government periodicals, and nonsexist language in documents.

The detailed index cites a number of government (*Appalachia, Monthly Labor Review*) and commercial (*American Statistics Index, Congressional Quarterly's Guide to Congress*) publications, the names of government figures (Hale Boggs, Margaret Thatcher) and private citizens (Theodore Bernstein, Jimmy Breslin), government agencies (Bureau of Land Management) and other organizations (American Federation of Teachers), and many specific subjects (librarians, sexual harassment).

For the record, Morehead is a professor in the School of Library and Information Science at the State University of New York, Albany. A prolific writer, he is the author of a widely used library school text on federal publications, *Introduction to United States Public Documents* (3d ed. Libraries Unlimited, 1983). In summary, this compilation is both informative and wide ranging in the topics covered.

— Wiley J. Williams

348. Schwartz, Julia. **Easy Access to Information in United States Government Documents.** Chicago, American Library Association, 1986. 49p. $12.95pa. LC 86-3393. ISBN 0-8389-0456-4.

In her efforts to provide "aid and support to those who dread documents" (p. ix), Schwartz has done an admirable job of creating a friendly, nonthreatening guide, from the bright blue cover to the preanswered exercises.

Two sections make up this manual: the first is a table, arranged by subject, which recommends an appropriate reference source for locating relevant citations or information; the second section contains concise descriptions of the sources and detailed directions for their use. Both the table and the descriptions indicate time periods covered and the types of information that can be expected from the sources, which makes it possible for infrequent documents users to quickly identify a needed tool without having to read through several pages of text.

A tutorial format is employed in the directions for using the various tools. Given the volume or section to locate, the user is encouraged to work through each exercise to see how answers have been derived. Since there are no illustrations, the user is forced to work with the reference tool actually in hand.

Schwartz has done a good job of covering the most basic documents access tools (*Monthly Catalog, American Statistics Index*, etc.), but her heavy emphasis on legal resources is puzzling. Fully half (thirteen out of twenty-five) of the sources relate to some aspect of law. In contrast, she omits several subject-specific indexes such as *Energy Research Abstracts* and the *EPA Publications Bibliography*.

While this manual is conveniently arranged and easy to use, it covers no new territory. Edward Herman's *Locating United States Government Information* (see *ARBA* 85, entry 37) is more comprehensive, and provides similar exercises for learning to use the sources. And for a direct subject approach, *Using Government Publications* by Jean L. Sears and Marilyn K. Moody (Oryx Press, 1986) is more helpful, and again, includes a broader range of sources. [R: RBB, 15 Nov 86, p. 494]   Lisa K. Dalton

349. Schwarzkopf, LeRoy C., comp. **Guide to Popular U.S. Government Publications.** Littleton, Colo., Libraries Unlimited, 1986. 432p. index. $29.50. LC 85-28444. ISBN 0-87287-452-4.

One must be intrepid indeed to venture to compile a guide of popular federal government publications, and Schwarzkopf has succeeded admirably in this daunting task. He had to address some difficult problems in selecting over two thousand titles (although there are 1,748 main entries, there are many subseries like the IRS's *Tax Information Publications*, which comprise ninety-one titles alone). The author chose to define a "popular" publication as "generally one devoted to a topic of broad interest to a large segment of the general public. Furthermore, the treatment of the subject in that publication is geared to the general reader, rather than to the professional or technician. Thus, one will find in [Schwarzkopf's] volume a number of publications on food and nutrition, gardening, health care, and recreation" (p. xvi).

Schwarzkopf mentions the utility of the quarterly *Consumer Information Catalog*, which lists pamphlets and brochures on popular subjects, free and priced, which appear in many cases in his volume. Unfortunately, as the author notes, the number of free publications has declined, one consequence of the Reagan administration's retrenchment initiatives in the reduction or elimination of government information. Despite these abridging efforts, Schwarzkopf's many entries attest to the fact that federal agencies continue to issue a wealth of general information free or at prices that are not unreasonable.

The introductory sections of the book, wherein the author sets forth purpose, definitions, scope of bibliographic citations, a recent history of the GPO pricing program, comments on the depository library program, an example of how the Superintendent of Documents classification scheme is structured, and other salient matters, are models of clarity and accuracy. The entries contain all the requisite bibliographic elements, and the annotations, though brief, are quite sufficiently descriptive. There are a guide to abbreviations, cross-references to related entries and Subject Bibliography (SB) series, an appendix of selected agency publications catalogs, and excellent subject and title indexes.

Any reader or reviewer of this compilation will find, as I did, some publications that could have been included or should have perhaps been excluded. But as Schwarzkopf acknowledges, a number of "subjective judgments" had to be made (p. xvi). I found his entries to be so thoroughly consistent with what is perceived by any reasonable person as "popular" and of general interest, that to enumerate one's own "favorites" that do not appear in this volume would be a mean-spirited exercise in gratuitous caviling. To list all the didactic and informational publications, depository and nondepository, that the federal government issues would be a futile task; this volume is the best guide assembled for this purpose, and the author in his introductory sections provides the user with those sources, like the *Consumer Information Catalog* and *U.S. Government Books*, that one can use to keep abreast of current popular issuances.

It is hoped that this estimable guide will reach the widest possible audience, including individuals and large collections, but especially the smaller, nondepository school and public libraries. A splendid achievement. [R: BL, 15 May 86, p. 1356; Choice, June 86, pp. 1524-26; JAL, May 86, p. 128; LJ, 1 May 86, p. 114; RBB, July 86, p. 1596; SLJ, 1 Apr 86, p. 19]

Joe Morehead

350. Sears, Jean L., and Marilyn K. Moody. **Using Government Publications.** Phoenix, Ariz., Oryx Press, 1985-1986. 2v. index. $67.50/vol. LC 83-43249. ISBN 0-89774-094-7(v.1); 0-89774-124-2(v.2).

Seldom have I felt such enthusiasm for a reference tool on use of government publications. With little more than a glance at the table of contents, I suspected that the authors had extensively traversed the federal documents reference scene, and my reading of the chapters confirmed their familiarity with patron needs. Volume 1 offers search strategies and basic tools for approaching questions by subject (e.g., foreign policy, federal government jobs, tax information, elections, education) and by agency. The agency section offers suggestions for accessing government grants, regulations and administrative actions and decisions, and materials on the Office of the President. Volume 2 concentrates its twenty-six chapters on finding statistics (on population, prices, defense, etc.) and on special techniques with which anyone who must deal with federal publications should be knowledgeable (legislative tracing, budget information, technical reports, translations, etc.).

Each chapter is imaginatively organized to provide a suggested search strategy, a checklist of sources, discussion of items in the checklist, sample pages, and relevant online databases, plus cross-references to other relevant chapters and to pertinent GPO Subject Bibliographies. Each volume has its own separate index by author, subject, and title. The first three chapters are repeated so that the volumes could be used independently; however, both volumes have great utility and, while they provide the clues any novice needs in getting around in federal documents, they also provide interesting and valuable review for the seasoned documents librarian.

The authors have conveniently provided us with appropriate SuDocs classification numbers and *American Statistics Index* (*ASI*) numbers. Frequent sample pages are well chosen. Finding the chapter on budget analysis delighted this reviewer; for their next edition, the authors might consider adding a chapter on social welfare policy/statistics, an area of frequent query.

Despite the expense, these volumes should be in any library having even the smallest collection of U.S. documents, and would also be very useful for referral purposes even in those libraries that do not collect them. [R: BL, 15 May 86, p. 1356; Choice, Mar 86, p. 1042; Choice, July/Aug 86, p. 1661; LJ, 15 Feb 86, p. 138; RBB, 1 Apr 86, p. 1130; RBB, 15 Oct 86, p. 339]

Mary K. Fetzer

351. Smallwood, Carol. **A Guide to Selected Federal Agency Programs and Publications for Librarians and Teachers.** Littleton, Colo., Libraries Unlimited, 1986. 321p. index. $23.50pa. LC 86-10561. ISBN 0-87287-528-8.

This is a useful book that, it is hoped, will actually get used as much as it deserves. Government publications and services are notoriously underused by the very citizens they are intended to help. At least part of that underuse, however, can be attributed to the federal government itself because of size, complexity, distance from users and, in general, a failure to adequately market its services. With the appearance of this work, librarians and teachers can no longer claim ignorance of the possibilities open to them.

Organization of the volume by agency name contributes to its usefulness. This is a simple and straightforward approach that eliminates that great guessing game of what major department a specific agency falls under. The names appear in strict A to Z order regardless of whether the organization is a subagency, office bureau, or center. Under each name the same information (if applicable) appears: objectives of the agency, curriculum applications areas, subjects (based on *Sears*), location, publications, audiovisuals available, library location and services, and special services available from the agency. A little more than two hundred agencies are covered. When an agency has state or regional offices that provide information or services, complete address and telephone numbers are given. Specific publications cited under an agency are briefly annotated and priced.

A moderately good subject index (again, using *Sears* headings) appears at the end of the volume and complements the agency entry approach well. More extensive use of subject terms and fewer entries under some headings would, however, have added to the usefulness of the work. Appendices include acronyms and abbreviations, list of federal information centers, land grant university film libraries, Sea Grant Program offices, and a list of those marvelously useful "Subject Bibliographies" from the Superintendent of Documents.

While this volume will be useful to any type of library and all educational levels, the orientation is distinctly towards school, public, and small academic libraries and teachers at the secondary level. The "selected" term in the title is definitely true, and large academic and special libraries will find it only a bare beginning point. The issue of selection of covered agencies is the only real quarrel I had with the work. The compiler owed her users some explanation of how those selections were made.

All in all, quite well done and issued at a reasonable price. While there is some degree of overlap in coverage with the two volumes of Jean L. Sears and Marilyn K. Moody's *Using Government Publications* (see entry 350) and LeRoy C. Schwarzkopf's *Guide to Popular U.S. Government Publications* (see entry 349), the approaches of all three works are sufficiently different that they complement rather than detract from each other. It is hoped the continuing availability of such works will eventually get the word out that federal government publications and services are available and useful. [R: WLB, Nov 86, pp. 65-66]

Robert V. Williams

Law Libraries

352. Kaiser, John Boynton. **Law, Legislative and Municipal Reference Libraries: An Introductory Manual and Bibliographic Guide.** Boston, Boston Book, 1914; repr., Buffalo, N.Y., William S. Hein, 1985. 467p. $37.50. index. (Legal Bibliographic and Research Reprint Series, Vol. 7). LC 85-060267. ISBN 0-89941-400-1.

This work must have been a most helpful guide for librarians working with government publications and legal materials during the early decades of this century. The author organized his sources of information by type of library; accordingly, the book is arranged, as the title suggests, in three main divisions: law, legislative reference, and municipal reference libraries. For each type a collection of basic materials, consisting of commercial sources in support of basic texts and the official documents themselves, is described, evaluated, and justified. Thus the work assumes the form of a series of bibliographic essays, in which the sources presented are exemplary rather than exhaustive.

Many traditional printed sources noted herein still comprise the knowledge base for today's practitioner. Described and annotated are such long-standing series as West's National Reporter System, slip laws, the *Statutes at Large*, the Congressional Serial Set, legal dictionaries and encyclopedias, opinions of the attorneys general, periodicals, and the like. Cataloging and classification schemes are discussed and evaluated, and a lengthy appendix provides reading lists, ordinances relating to municipal reference services, a compilation of laws establishing legislative reference bureaus for the various states, suggested class problems for library school students, and related information. The book concludes with an excellent dictionary/index with interfiled subjects, titles, and authors.

While the number of bibliographic guides to both law and government publications has grown in recent years, the major distinction in kind and not merely in degree between 1914 and 1986 is the profusion of information technology products unknown and unheralded when this guide was written. Consequently, Kaiser's work takes on an aura, perhaps undeserved, of quaint nostalgia. Nevertheless, it serves to remind us that synthesizing efforts of this kind are necessary from time to time. Recommended for the student of the history of librarianship and for larger library school collections.

Joe Morehead

353. Marke, Julius J., and Richard Sloane. **Legal Research and Law Library Management.** New York, Law Journal Seminars-Press, 1982. 468p. bibliog. index. price not reported. LC 81-19297.

354. Marke, Julius J., and Richard Sloane. **Legal Research and Law Library Management. Supplement, 1985.** New York, Law Journal Seminars-Press, 1985. 176p. price not reported. LC 81-19297.

From their long experience as law librarians, law professors, and library consultants, Marke (St. John's University School of Law, formerly at NYU School of Law) and Sloane (University of Pennsylvania School of Law) collected and updated fifty of their articles—which originally appeared in the *New York Law Journal* between 1972 and 1981—for publication in book form. The 1985 supplement, consisting of twenty-eight chapters, replaces a 1983 supplement and adds nine chapters. Material in the supplement should be examined alongside that in the 1982 volume. Chapters to which an "A," "B," or "C" is added to chapter numbers (e.g., 15A, "Index to Legal Periodicals"; 49A, "Choosing and Using a Law Library Consultant") constitute new chapters. The remaining chapters are additions to the basic ones. In addition, the supplement includes two chapters on one new topic, institutional research (chapter 51, "American Bar Foundation"; chapter 52, "American Law Institute").

The 1982 manual is organized in three parts. Part 1, an overview of legal research, discusses basic legal research methods and the role of a new specialist, the research lawyer. Part 2, "Phases of Legal Research," devotes eighteen chapters to five large subtopics: case law, statutes, administrative law, special subjects, and nonlegal research sources. The diversity of coverage in this part can be illustrated by noting that there are chapters on finding English law, federal legislative history, state legislative history, searching for federal administrative regulations, environmental law research sources, legal indexes, interdisciplinary sources for legal research, and nonlegal research resources for lawyers.

Part 3, the longest part, consists of thirty chapters on library management, such as guidelines for selecting books for a law library, technical data via online searches, law book publishing (including Federal Trade Commission guides for the law book industry), lawyers and their librarians, factors for planning a library (costs, space, contents, user comfort), legal microforms, audio cassettes and videotapes, and consultants.

In summary, this manual and its supplement provide a useful compendium of timely, practical advice on legal research and the management of law libraries.

Wiley J. Williams

Medical Libraries

355. Linton, W. D., comp. **Directory of Medical and Health Care Libraries in the United Kingdom and Republic of Ireland.** 6th ed. London, Library Association; distr., Chicago, American Library Association, 1986. 273p. index. $25.00pa. ISBN 0-85365-727-0.

This expanded and updated edition essentially follows the plan of the fifth edition (1982; see *ARBA* 84, entry 91), except that indexes now refer to any of the 604 library entry numbers rather than to pages. New appendices list nonresponding libraries dropped from the main directory, and acronyms (e.g., HATRICS) used to denote network affiliations in the entries. The index of libraries by type has been omitted, leaving indexes of personal names, institutions, counties, and special collections for use with the main directory, arranged alphabetically by locale and containing specific location and descriptive information.

Useful for health care researchers and students, professional library associations, and librarians traveling to the United Kingdom and the Republic of Ireland.

Harriette M. Cluxton

356. **Medical Librarianship in the Eighties and Beyond: A World Perspective.** Fiona Mackay Picken and Ann M. C. Kahn, eds. London, Mansell; distr., New York, H. W. Wilson, 1986. 423p. bibliog. index. $70.00. LC 85-15211. ISBN 0-7201-1776-3.

This "world perspective" is neither "rounded" nor overly biased "British-wise," but presents a "patchwork" review of medical library services, trends, and possible future developments in various countries. The book originated in a conference of librarians from twenty-five countries, held in 1983; it is acknowledged that many changes have probably occurred since then.

Contributions vary in length and quality, but in general relate to networking, uses of automation for management and information retrieval, and the medical library's role in education and research, as each author understands these in his or her own country. These case studies are supposed "to stimulate ideas and generate new approaches," regardless of the state of technology or isolation of the nation, financial and other support of the library, etc., which may be involved. Half the book concerns the experiences in the United Kingdom. "The International Experience" has articles on eight European countries. There are sections on Canada, the United States, and South America; eight scattered countries; and two major international organizations, IFLA and WHO. Each has a list of references. Biographical notes and addresses of contributors make further contacts possible. A very personal chapter, "Envoi: The Realities of International Exchange," discusses handling of foreign library visitors to Britain, and problems of serving as an overseas library consultant. Conclusions drawn about the ultimate value of new technologies and developments, particularly for the Third World, are thought provoking. Persons with special interests in international librarianship should appreciate this unique book. Overseas librarians, especially in underdeveloped situations, could find much of value in it, although cost may prevent their ever seeing it.

Harriette M. Cluxton

357. Strickland-Hodge, Barry. **How to Use *Index Medicus* and *Excerpta Medica*.** Brookfield, Vt., Gower Publishing, 1986. 60p. index. (Information Sources in the Medical Sciences, Vol. 1). $7.95 spiralbound. ISBN 0-566-03532-4.

Volume 1 of the series Information Sources in Medical Science introduces the two most widely used sources of biomedical literature, *Index Medicus* (*IM*) and *Excerpta Medica* (*EM*). Since these tools are so complicated, preliminary study does benefit the user. The items are discussed in separate chapters. For each, the history, scope, and format are followed by a description of searcher aids: MeSH, Supplementary Chemical Records, Malimet, EMCLAS, et al. Sample pages have been reproduced so that the user need not have access to the publications themselves. The editors have explained a concept as complicated as the

"Trees" in terms clear enough for a beginner, and added hints that the more experienced searcher may find useful (such as the alphabetization of chemicals with numerical prefixes). The material is designed for users of the hard copy indexes, and defers discussion of online services to a forthcoming volume in the series.

There are a few surprises here. A detailed description of annotated MeSH is irrelevant to manual searchers. It does not cover monographs "since 1976" but from 1976 to 1981. American users will wonder about the alternate English and American spellings. They would be better served by information on the cost of the tools and the procedures for ordering. These criticisms, however, are minor. The available literature focuses on the online databases, although much information can be obtained from the published tools. Familiarity with the printed aids is a prerequisite to expert computer searching. Inexperienced searchers and the information scientists who instruct them will welcome Strickland-Hodge's guide. Note the low price. — Margaret Norden

358. Wood, Sandra M., Ellen Brassil Horak, and Bonnie Snow, eds. **End User Searching in the Health Sciences.** New York, Haworth Press, 1986. 290p. bibliog. index. (*Medical Reference Services Quarterly*, Vol. 5. Supplement). $29.95. LC 86-9886. ISBN 0-86656-465-9.

Citations to the proliferating health science literature have been available through online database searching since the National Library of Medicine inaugurated MEDLINE in 1971. Heretofore, the searching has been performed by intermediary librarians or information specialists; however, direct searching by the information consumer or "end user" is the current trend. The editors of this volume have compiled articles on various aspects of this development. Among the topics discussed are the changing role of librarians, educational material, user training, library planning, commercial search programs and user friendly software, and mounting a subset of MEDLINE on a local computer. In addition, there are reports on end-user searching programs currently in operation at health science libraries at Stanford; the universities of Texas (Galveston), Minnesota, and Maryland; and Massachusetts General Hospital. These reports examine specific questions, such as how best to determine which aspects of the search process cause difficulty for inexperienced searchers.

The book's selective, annotated bibliography refers to general as well as health science literature. Although well constructed, the list lacks references to the educational literature or to sources for additional citations. Much has been published on this topic in library science, computer science, and the general literature. However, not all of it is as practical as are the articles in this compilation. Since the book is devoted to health science collections, it is handy for practitioners in this field. The articles are stimulating and informative to library educators and vendor representatives as well. Five or more copies of this book, ordered through bookstores, are available at $19.95 per copy. — Margaret Norden

Museums

359. **Museum & Archival Supplies Handbook.** 3d ed., rev. and expanded. Toronto, in association with the Getty Conservation Institute, Toronto Area Archivists Group and Ontario Museum Association, 1985. 174p. illus. bibliog. index. $20.00pa. ISBN 0-920402-05-4.

The third edition of *MASH* is an invaluable resource for museums, libraries, and individuals involved in conservation, preservation, and other archival work. The seven main sections each cover materials and equipment used in different aspects of archival processing: general materials (adhesives, paper, chemicals and solvents, etc.), materials used in the care of specific items (books, photographs, textiles, etc.), lab supplies and equipment, storage materials and cases, environment and security devices, exhibit and display units, and microfilm equipment. Each listing provides short notes on use, properties, appearance, warnings, and recommendations. Also included are names of specific suppliers (or types of stores in which the product is sold) and current prices. A directory of these suppliers, with addresses and telephone numbers, appears at the back along with a short bibliography of books, articles, and audiovisual kits on archival topics. The only drawback of the handbook is its Canadian slant; although the major U.S. suppliers are included, most of the companies are located in Canada. United States institutions will need to supplement this list with local suppliers for some of the more common items. The real value of the handbook, however, lies in its arrangement by archival function and the identification of the proper product or equipment for a specific task — this is especially useful as a quick reference for beginning archivists who are not familiar with what is available, for experienced archivists expanding into a new area, or for anyone who needs to communicate with suppliers and use the correct terminology. And anyone in search of a supplier for an elusive item will consider *MASH* a godsend! — Judy Dyki

360. **Museum Documentation Systems: Developments and Applications.** Richard B. Light, D. Andrew Roberts, and Jennifer D. Stewart, eds. Boston, Butterworths, 1986. 332p. illus. bibliog. index. $59.95. LC 85-11003. ISBN 0-408-10815-0.

Museum Documentation Systems provides a much-needed survey of the myriad systems used in museums throughout the world for controlling the information concerning their collections, with emphasis on developments in computerized systems. Over twenty-five individual museum systems and networks from twelve countries are presented and analyzed. Museums of all types are included: fine arts, natural history, military, maritime, etc. Each chapter, written by an official of the respective museum, briefly describes the history and scope of the collections, provides a thorough explanation of the documentation system used, and discusses the experience the museum has had in automating the system. Samples of forms, cards, data entry sheets, and printouts accompany each description. Several chapters cover national efforts to develop museum documentation networks, and the final chapter describes the role of international agencies, in particular the International Council of Museums (ICOM) and UNESCO, in the standardization of documentation systems and procedures. An extensive list of references, most relating to automated documentation systems, is a valuable addition to the book. As noted in the preface, most of the chapters reflect the status of the systems as of 1982 or 1983; with the lightning speed at which technology changes and develops, this is an unfortunate flaw in an otherwise excellent text. The book will be of most interest to museum libraries and to academic libraries serving museology programs.

Judy Dyki

361. **Museum Librarianship.** John C. Larsen, ed. Hamden, Conn., Library Professional Publications/Shoe String Press, 1985. 136p. bibliog. index. $18.50; $13.50pa. LC 85-10212. ISBN 0-208-01906-5; 0-208-01907-3pa.

Museum librarianship is one of the areas of the special library field that is in serious need of support literature. This short but comprehensive guide would be a helpful start to the librarian, manager, curator, or museum trustee who may be considering the establishment of a museum library. It is, therefore, a welcome addition to a fertile field. The book is intended for the management of small collections, where the librarian assumes a broad range of operational responsibilities, often requiring a background in many tasks. The underlying assumption of the book is that basic principles, activities, and procedures remain the same despite the diversity of museum subject specialization. However, while the essays are well written, informative, and general in nature, all participants are from the staff of the largest museums in the United States and Canada. Larsen has gathered eleven experts to write essays on general issues of museum library staffing; collection development; reference; cataloging; preservation; the role and services of the museum library; the relation of the library to the parent institution; and museum library facilities. Since no museum should be without a library, every museum should acquire this book. It is also recommended for large academic libraries, particularly those which support library science programs.

Antonio Rodriguez-Buckingham

National and Federal Libraries

362. **Annual Report 1985 of The Librarian of Congress: For the Fiscal Year Ending September 30, 1985.** Washington, D.C., Library of Congress, 1986. 1v. (various paging). $14.50. LC 6-6273. ISSN 0083-1565.

This hefty report provides a wealth of information about the activities of the Library of Congress for 1985. Included are reports on some exciting projects, such as the optical disk program, the mass book deacidification facility, the renovation of the Thomas Jefferson and John Adams buildings, and the ever-expanding use of technology in all departments. The report also includes summaries of the activities of the national programs, such as the American Folklife Center, the Children's Literature Center, and the National Library Service for the Blind and Physically Handicapped. Each of the major divisions—Congressional Research Service, Processing Services, Research Services, Law Library, and Copyright Office—also have their own sections, which include highlights of the year's projects. Detailed statistics are provided for the various functions of the library: acquisitions, cataloging, reader services, photoduplication, etc. Many sections of the report also have reference value, in particular a chart of current U.S. copyright relations with other independent nations of the world; officers, committees, and consultants of the library, along with an organization chart; and a list of Library of Congress publications for the year. This well-organized report is attractively bound in hardcover and includes an extensive index.

Judy Dyki

363. Maruyama, Lenore S. **The Library of Congress Network Advisory Committee: Its First Decade.** Washington, D.C., Cataloging Distribution Service, Library of Congress, 1985. 48p. (Network Planning Paper, No. 11). $7.50pa. LC 85-600214. ISBN 0-8444-0511-6.

In the foreword to this document, Henriette Avram observes of the NAC that "Its deliberations do not appear to be reaching a large segment of the profession." This may be due partly to the fact that the importance of the role of the committee in identifying, investigating, and reporting about information storage and delivery through network participation is not recognized by a large segment of the profession, even those whose services are network dependent. To some extent the work of the committee has filled a void resulting from the lack of legislated responsibility for network planning at the national level. The body of the document summarizes the activities of the committee in context and, with discussion of the context of deliberations and documents, lists the publications of the committee, and lists members and membership information.

The relatively short history of networks belies the importance of that history. This paper gives the profession a context in which to place not only the work of the committee but also other literature which relates to network development. For example, the Network Planning Paper, No. 2, *A Glossary for Library Networking*, was written with certain assumptions about a national library network which have not come to pass. To use that glossary without this understanding would be misleading.

The paper presents a history which is issue related. In a short period of time the committee has dealt with issues related to bibliographic data, governance at the national level, resource sharing from several vantage points, public and private sector relationships, telecommunications, special libraries in networks, and the information economy.

A group consisting of representatives of other organizations, this committee has broadened its base and seems interested in more segments of the population than it once appeared to be. This will make it even more important for the profession. It behooves any involved professional to understand the ways in which decisions come to be made in the field. Reading the lines and between the lines in this document should aid any librarian involved in networks (and who isn't), to understand the shape of the present and possible directions for the future. [R: WLB, May 86, p. 55]

JoAnn V. Rogers

364. Norton, Aloysius A. **A History of the United States Military Academy Library.** Wayne, N.J., Avery Publishing, 1986. 40p. illus. map. $6.95pa. LC 86-7930. ISBN 0-89529-352-8.

The United States Military Academy Library at West Point, New York, is the nation's first federal library. Early librarians and benefactors helped the Military Academy Library to amass, by the time of the Civil War, a significant collection in the areas of technology, science, government, military organization, and exploration. There were some lean years, natural calamities, and uninspired leadership at times. Exceptional direction of the Military Academy Library is credited to Edward L. Holden (1902-1914), Sidney Forman (1958-1962), and Egon Weiss (1962-). During the past twenty years, the library has occupied a new facility, automated its bibliographic records, and joined several networks. This volume is a good example of traditional library history, long on factual information and neglectful of broader conceptual matters. Future historians, for example, will no doubt examine the Military Academy Library's role in stimulating military scholarship, perhaps consolidating the experience of all military academy libraries. Produced by the Friends of the West Point Library, this modest volume is gracefully written, informative, and exceptionally well illustrated.

Arthur P. Young

Newspaper Libraries

365. Wall, Celia Jo, comp. **Newspaper Libraries: A Bibliography, 1933-1985.** Washington, D.C., Special Libraries Association, 1986. 126p. index. $12.50pa. LC 86-14604. ISBN 0-87111-319-8.

Due to the introduction of computers in newspaper libraries, the storage and retrieval of news articles is a working reality which far exceeds the capabilities of yesterday's "morgue." Before the computer can successfully solve problems, however, they must be identified and addressed. This work locates books, articles, and theses on the subject to assist the newspaper librarian in addressing the problem of computer management of this specialized library.

The work covers the topics of the history of newspaper libraries, organization and administration, classification and filing, reference materials, newspaper indexing, microforms, automation, and newspaper librarianship. Special sections cover additional sources, theses, and research papers. There are subject and author indexes. More than eight hundred references are listed.

This excellent bibliography will be applauded by librarians and is highly recommended to anyone interested in this specialized field.

Carol Willsey Bell

Science and Technology Libraries

366. Haas, Joan K., Helen Willa Samuels, and Barbara Trippel Simmons. **Appraising the Records of Modern Science and Technology: A Guide.** Cambridge, Mass., Massachusetts Institute of Technology; distr., Chicago, Society of American Archivists, 1985. 96p. illus. bibliog. index. $9.00pa.

This excellent guide is designed to lead the archivist step-by-step through the process of appraising the records of modern science and technology. While the authors of this guide realize that "absolutes" on appraisal cannot be prescribed since each institution has its own unique circumstances of mission, policy, space, staff, and resources, they do intend it to be useful in helping archivists determine if they should acquire a certain collection; in assisting in appraisal, arrangement, and description of the collection; and in helping records managers develop retention guidelines for scientific material.

The guide is divided into two major sections. The first, "Personal and Professional Activities," is relatively short and describes those activities which the archivist should consider since they may have influenced the subject's career or are an extension of his or her scientific work. The second section, "Scientific and Technological Activities," is much more extensive and is further divided into "Administration of Research and Development," "Research and Development," and "Dissemination." The focus is upon the nature of manuscript and archival records, although the importance of published books, articles, and reports as well as scientific instruments, technical models, and specimen collections as documentation is recognized. Audiovisual documents and oral histories are noted but are not dealt with in detail. The work, which is well and usefully illustrated, concludes with a list, "Scientific and Technological Discipline History Centers," a bibliography of twenty-six "Selected Readings," and an index.

Dean H. Keller

367. **Sci-Tech Libraries in Museums and Aquariums.** Ellis Mount, ed. New York, Haworth Press, 1985. 204p. (*Science & Technology Libraries*, Vol. 6, Nos. 1/2). $29.95. LC 85-16436. ISBN 0-86656-484-5.

This monograph (also published as *Science & Technology Libraries*, vol. 6, nos. 1 and 2, Fall 1985/Winter 1985/86) describes in some detail in signed essays the history, functions, holdings, services, and facilities of ten outstanding sci-tech libraries serving museums and aquariums: American Museum of Natural History, California Academy of Sciences, Deutscher Museum (Munich), Field Museum of Natural History, Museum of Comparative Zoology at Harvard, Museum of Science and Industry, National Air and Space Museum and National Museum of American History (both Smithsonian Institution libraries), Natural History Museum of Los Angeles County, and John G. Shedd Aquarium. The libraries of twenty-six other randomly selected U.S. and Canadian museums are more briefly surveyed (e.g., the museums of science in Boston and Miami, Ontario Science Centre, Franklin Institute Science Museum, and the Museum of American Textile History). According to the introduction another issue will be devoted to libraries serving botanical gardens, zoos, and other museums.

The latter half of this work consists of the regular departments of the journal: "Special Papers," "Sci-Tech Collections," "New Reference Works in Science and Technology," "Sci-Tech Online," "Sci-Tech in Review," and "Sci-Tech Notes." To be more specific with reference to this issue, the special papers are "Source Indexing in Science Journals and Indexing Services: A Survey of Current Practices" and "The Marketing Approach to Special Libraries in Industry: A Review of the Literature." The "Sci-Tech Collections" department features one paper, "Alzheimer's Disease: A Guide to Information Services." In conclusion, libraries with subscriptions to *Science & Technology Libraries* probably won't need the monograph as well.

Wiley J. Williams

368. **Weeding of Collections in Sci-Tech Libraries.** Ellis Mount, ed. New York, Haworth Press, 1986. 164p. (*Science & Technology Libraries*, Vol. 6, No. 3). $24.95. LC 85-27010. ISBN 0-86656-552-3.

Deselection is the theme of this issue. Articles on a science periodicals conversion project and sources of statistical information on malnutrition in the Third World are also included. Among the more salient topics discussed in the eight articles are space, change of mission, and condition of materials. Primary areas of teaching and research were found to be the main considerations for weeding at an IBM corporate library and M.I.T., respectively. A literature review reveals that "use" remains the most employed variable for weeding of collections. One author suggests the cancellation of some specialty journals when subscribed to specifically for a faculty member who is no longer publishing. The lack of consistent use of standardized terminology in records management creates problems for deselection. Possible considerations when weeding non-English-language journals include where the journal is indexed and its availability at other libraries.

The attempt made with AACR2 to simplify identification of periodical titles has difficulties, caused by factors inherent to serials, such as change of title name and use of different abbreviations by abstracting and indexing services. "Malnutrition and Disease in the Third World" provides a guide to materials and discusses problems of data collection on the subject.

Segal notes that models of deselection provided by the literature offer examples unique to one situation and library. Models provided by this volume are not exceptions to this pattern. This book does, however, provide a useful addition to the cumulative literature on the subject.

Robert M. Ballard

Serials

369. **Advances in Serials Management: A Research Annual. Volume 1: 1986.** Marcia Tuttle and Jean G. Cook, eds. Greenwich, Conn., JAI Press, 1986. 238p. bibliog. index. $23.75; $47.50 (institutions). ISBN 0-89232-568-2.

This volume is the first in an annual publication devoted to serials management. It is not difficult to substantiate a need for such an annual. As the editors of this volume indicate, "the significance of the serial as a form of communication has increased in the 1980s" (preface). The utility of an annual devoted to serials lies in its ability to provide relatively up-to-date, in-depth coverage of topics that is more current than similar information provided in texts and more detailed than coverage provided by journal articles.

This latter advantage is aptly substantiated by the lead article of the present volume. "Serial Agent Selection in ARL Libraries" is a forty-two page report of survey research. The length of this report allows for detailed descriptions of the research design, data analyses, and inclusion of the study's questionnaire. These are "luxuries" that are seldom found in journal reports of research projects. In general, this article on serial agent selection is an excellent example of research design and reporting.

In spite of the excellence of the lead research article, there is only one other article, out of a total of six, that justifies the annual's subtitle: "A Research Annual." There are an historical discussion of the CONSER project, three articles on organization for library serials management (one of which reports the results of a survey), and an article which studies serial prices. The volume concludes with a useful annotated bibliography of recent (1982-1985) literature on serials management. While most of these articles could meet some broad definition of *research*, the exact meaning of this concept as it is to be applied in this annual should be provided by the editors or omitted as a subtitle in future volumes.

Another issue that needs to be addressed in future volumes involves the affiliation of contributors. Of eight contributors to the present volume, all but one are affiliated with academic institutions. The preface implies that contributor affiliation will represent a wider range of institutions; future volumes should reflect this.

For the present, these criticisms are minor. The first volume of *Advances in Serials Management* is a promising beginning. It is hoped that future volumes fulfill and build on the promise of this initial effort.

Larry G. Chrisman

370. Ezzell, Joline, ed. **Issues in Serials Librarianship.** Philadelphia, Drexel University, 1986. 122p. (*Drexel Library Quarterly*, Vol. 21, No. 1). $10.00pa. LC 65-9911. ISSN 0012-6160.

An extremely valuable and welcome collection of articles for modern serials librarians. This special issue of the *Drexel Library Quarterly* contains nine articles dealing chiefly with serials automation, collection development, management, and the control of holdings information. Each article provides the readers with up-to-date information on a specific topic which the authors have chosen to address, and which is currently discussed among serials specialists. Automation is a central theme in most of the articles in this issue. Most of the libraries, especially the current users of the OCLC Serials Control System, are facing the task of conversion from an existing automated system to another, or from a manual file to an automated system. Several articles in this issue are devoted to different aspects of this major problem and provide highly useful information as well as incisive advice. Margaret McKinley compares two libraries in the transition stage from manual to automated systems, Sara Heitshu and Joan

Quinn share with the readers the experience of conversion at the University of Michigan Library, Jean Farrington describes the characteristics of stand-alone and integrated serials control devices, and Linda Sapp and Marjorie Bloss discuss the use of US MARC format for serials holdings and location information. One common feature is that they all emphasize the necessity of planning for implementation and retraining. Other pertinent issues, such as the feasibility of changes among staff assignments, workflow, and organization are also discussed. All articles are cogent, concise, and well written. The editor and contributors to this issue deserve the gratitude of all serials librarians, who will derive enormous professional benefits from its reading. Wendy Hu

371. **Projects and Procedures for Serials Administration.** Diane Stine, comp. and ed. Ann Arbor, Mich., Pierian Press, 1985. 325p. index. (Current Issues in Serials Management, No. 5). $39.50. LC 85-60593. ISBN 0-87650-190-0.

Serials seem to cause ongoing concern in all areas of a library, so much so that the phrase "serials control" is almost a contradiction in terms. This volume attempts to gain the upper hand in the battle for serials control by bringing together twenty essays, primarily on the technical services aspects of serials. A number of articles deal with work flow, and by extension, the continued debate of a serials department versus no serials department at all. Several articles focus on the problems that series cause (are they serials? monographs? both?), and give the reader a number of valid suggestions as to how best to handle them. Serials check-in is another major topic covered in this work as are cataloging, retrospective conversion, and authority work. In these cases, as with work flow and organization, the automation of serial functions serves as a unifying element.

To begin with two picayune criticisms, there are some minor typographical errors in the book. These, plus headers that begin on one page only to have the text on the next or even more pages away, are annoying. The essays themselves, however, are uniformly well written and extremely informative. The authors took their tasks seriously, resulting in very detailed (including graphic flowcharts and workforms used) explanations of procedures and processes. Unfortunately, some of the articles dealing with automation are out-of-date. This is especially true of the descriptions of OCLC's Serials Control Subsystem and to some degree, its union listing function, and to a lesser degree, Faxon's Linx System. I wish to emphasize this is through

no fault of the authors. Situations change, especially those so closely tied to automation.

There is much that is worthwhile, useful, and helpful in this work, certainly enough to warrant its cost. It unquestionably deserves a place in every library in which the many issues of serials control are confronted on an ongoing basis. [R: JAL, May 86, p. 101; LJ, 1 Apr 86, p. 50] Marjorie Bloss

372. **Serials Librarianship in Transition: Issues and Developments.** Peter Gellatly, ed. New York, Haworth Press, 1986. 305p. index. (*The Serials Librarian*, Vol. 10, Nos. 1/2). $38.95. LC 85-16439. ISBN 0-86656-497-7.

Celebrating the tenth anniversary of *The Serials Librarian*, this collection of twenty-nine essays provides a panoramic view of serials librarianship in the recent past and the near future. Topics covered include cataloging, organization, acquisitions and claiming, microforms, union listings, indexing, budgeting, subscription agencies, and government periodicals. There are an essay on education for serials librarianship and descriptions of serials librarianship in England, Australia, India, and Nigeria. One essay reviews the past decade in magazine publishing and another speculates on the future of the scholarly journal. Fleischmann and Houghton's annotated bibliography and review of serials automation deserves separate and special mention. It is well organized, thorough, and informative.

All of the essays are well written and tightly edited. Some have extensive bibliographies. While most of the articles describe the past, they should also provoke thoughtful consideration of the future of serials librarianship. Specialists in the "serials chain" and students interested in serials librarianship should give this book top priority in their professional reading lists. Other librarians will want to read many of the essays because they are replete with useful information. [R: JAL, July 86, p. 188; JAL, Sept 86, p. 238; RQ, Fall 86, pp. 131-32]

Margaret McKinley

State Libraries

373. **State Library Services and Issues: Facing Future Challenges.** Charles R. McClure, ed. Norwood, N.J., Ablex Publishing, 1986. 301p. bibliog. index. $45.00; $29.50pa. LC 85-22870. ISBN 0-89391-317-0.

This book's fifteen essays deal with some of the specific issues influencing the services of the State Library Agency (SLA). The purpose of the book is to help this organization meet the challenges of the future. The objectives are: to increase awareness among the professional community of the importance of SLA; to identify and analyze state library activities; and to recommend their improvement. The essays include a wide range of subjects. The underlying theme is that despite the crucial role SLA plays in the development of library services, new strategies are needed to meet successfully the challenges and opportunities of the future. An essay on the history of SLA shows that only recently has the agency assumed its current broad range of responsibilities for library development. Other studies deal with the funding of state library agencies; the impact of the federal government and the political role of state libraries; library development and planning for library service as the primary responsibilities of SLA; the activities of the agency as provider of services to the handicapped and institutionalized; continuing education and the success of SLA in mounting programs for librarians; the impact of resource sharing and multiple library networking; and the need to make library education consonant with the realities of state librarianship. The book should be acquired by librarians in state library agencies and by government officials. It is also recommended for large academic libraries, particularly those which support library science programs. [R: WLB, May 86, pp. 55-56]

Antonio Rodriguez-Buckingham

Theological, Church, and Synagogue Libraries

374. Burson, Lorraine E. **Recruiting and Training Volunteers for Church and Synagogue Libraries.** Bryn Mawr, Pa., Church and Synagogue Library Association, 1986. 32p. illus. bibliog. (CSLA Guide, No. 14). $5.95pa. LC 86-9682. ISBN 0-915324-24-5.

The Church and Synagogue Library Association has produced a series of fourteen guides to aid members in creating in-house libraries. Number 14, as the title suggests, deals with the training and recruitment of volunteers. This thirty-two-page paperbound publication is divided into eight chapters and includes a bibliography of related books and periodicals. Areas covered include recruitment, orientation, training methods, delegation of responsibilities, motivation, and development of teamwork.

The manual is written in a clear, straightforward manner, with frequent use of examples to illustrate certain ideas. Use is also made of black-and-white photographs, drawings, and examples of forms used in some libraries. As a staff training manual, the publication is designed to serve as an introduction to the tenets of volunteerism and librarianship. Although the manual is designed for use in larger church and synagogue libraries, the principles expounded are applicable to operations of any size. The manual is well balanced in its presentation of the various facets of librarianship and volunteerism, but makes some assumptions which might prove rather unrealistic. For example, in citing possibilities for locating volunteers, the manual identifies mothers with small children, who can type catalog cards at home, implying that these mothers would have time to complete such tasks.

Because of its specific nature, and because it is well written and informative, purchase of this manual is recommended for church and synagogue libraries, and public libraries needing specific source material to add to their library science collections. Barbara Sproat

375. Hammack, Mary L. **How to Organize Your Church Library and Resource Center.** Valley Forge, Pa., Judson Press, 1985. 128p. illus. bibliog. $8.95pa. LC 85-9863. ISBN 0-8170-1066-1.

If somebody feels called upon to get a church library started, in addition to collecting books and other resources to make available, it would be wise to acquire a book (or books) written specifically to make that job easier. Something on how to go about dealing with various church boards and committees, finding volunteers to help and how best to use their time and talents, collecting and purchasing appropriate materials to lend, funding, mending and/or processing donated materials, etc.

While this book addresses itself to many of these concerns, it seems to assume that the person reading it already knows how to function as a librarian. A nonlibrarian could read it and feel overwhelmed at the complexity of the job undertaken, and decide to find an excuse to sidestep the task entirely.

Some assumptions are made that may not be applicable in every situation: space available may be less than ideal; books available to a beginning library may not be appropriate to all age levels or needs; and some churches may prefer to have a church librarian answerable to the trustees, the pastor, a diaconate, or some other group than specifically the Christian education board or committee.

While the information in this book is very useful, it could easily discourage a church from even thinking further about starting a church library. A far preferable book, if only one can be bought to help get things going, would be

Betty McMichael's *The Church Librarian's Handbook* (Baker Book, 1984).

Judith E. H. Odiorne

376. Hannaford, Claudia. **The ABC's of Financing Church and Synagogue Libraries: Acquiring Funds, Budgeting, Cash Accounting.** Bryn Mawr, Pa., Church and Synagogue Library Association, 1985. 31p. (CSLA Guide, No. 13). $5.95pa. LC 85-13286. ISBN 0-915324-23-7.

Any church or synagogue that decides to start a library for doctrinal, spiritual, and educational purposes is going to need to deal with funding. Even once basic materials are on hand, such as books, shelving, cataloging supplies, etc., ongoing expenses will arise: additional books and/or media, promotional materials, mending supplies, etc.

This small pamphlet is worth its weight in gold in providing ideas for dealing with church and synagogue library finances. In addition to acquiring funds to begin a library, there are many ways to raise funds to continue maintaining it (several pages of fund-raising possibilities are given, above and beyond getting regular annual congregational funding).

Using funds wisely comes under the heading of stewardship, and suggestions are given about dealing with appropriate boards and committees, types of budgets and how to set them up and then stick to them, and concrete examples. Forms are even given, for reproduction, for keeping necessary records not only to expedite annual reporting, but to keep an ongoing record of multiple funds and their current status.

This is a book that belongs in every church or synagogue that might even consider having a library, and certainly in those that already make materials available to their members. It could certainly help boost both the morale and efficiency of volunteer librarians, helping them keep their books accurately. [R: JAL, Jan 86, p. 375]

Judith E. H. Odiorne

377. Slavens, Thomas P. **A Great Library through Gifts.** Munich, New York, K. G. Saur, 1986. 355p. bibliog. $40.00. ISBN 3-598-10621-1.

In this volume library educator Slavens (University of Michigan) traces the development of the Union Theological Seminary Library in New York—termed "the greatest collection of religious materials in the western hemisphere"—from its founding in 1836 to the present. The eleven chapters are arranged chronologically, each covering a specific library administration. The common theme permeating this history is found in its stated purpose—to determine "the means by which this library was developed through gifts and to demonstrate how other libraries may profit from Union's experience" (preface). This study of a well-regarded special library draws heavily upon unpublished materials (minutes of various boards and committees of the seminary, reports of the librarians, etc.), publications of the school, books and parts of books, periodicals, and newspapers. The text makes extensive use of long, direct quotations. The years since 1975 (the terms of Robert Maloy and Richard Spoor as library directors) are covered quite briefly compared to the fullness of previous administrations, whether long or short.

One final point: it is not clear to this reviewer why Slavens's 1965 dissertation from Michigan ("The Library of Union Theological Seminary in the City of New York, 1836 to the Present") is nowhere cited in the bibliography.

Wiley J. Williams

378. Smith, Ruth S. **Getting the Books Off the Shelves: Making the Most of Your Congregation's Library.** rev. ed. Bryn Mawr, Pa., Church and Synagogue Library Association, 1985. 40p. illus. bibliog. (CSLA Guide, No. 12). $6.95pa. LC 85-11650. ISBN 0-915324-22-9.

Geared to church and synagogue libraries and librarians, this volume of the Church and Synagogue Library Association Guide series deals with encouraging library use. It touches on ways to make a library worth using, building up the collection, ideal location, and good service, and then moves directly into how to promote the library.

Any library, public or private, could use good publicity. An entire chapter is devoted to publicizing the library, giving examples of techniques being used by various libraries in churches and synagogues, as well as occasionally by public libraries. A good many ideas are suggested, some of which could certainly be used by almost every library, both in the library and as outreach on behalf of the library.

Newly started church and synagogue libraries would be especially helped by some of the ways suggested to reach people and provide programs to various groups. A suggested service of library dedication is even included as one of many special events that could be sponsored by a church or synagogue library. How to report library news so that people will take an interest in a library is another topic covered, as well as ideas for displays of various kinds.

Each section is followed by bibliographic references and resources for further reading and ideas. This is a must buy for every church and synagogue library. [R: JAL, Jan 86, p. 375]

Judith E. H. Odiorne

Toy Libraries

379. Rimer, Pearl. **Toy Libraries: How to Start and Maintain a Toy Library in Your Community.** 2d rev. and enl. ed. Toronto, Canadian Association of Toy Libraries, 1986. 47p. illus. bibliog. $6.00pa. ISBN 0-919051-04-9.

Toy Libraries is a concise, practical guide for anyone who is considering establishing a toy lending library. Information ranges from users and objectives, to the benefits of a toy lending facility, to assessing community need, to legal and financial implications. Selection of toys and cataloging/circulation systems are also discussed, as are toy lending libraries for children with special needs. Bibliographies, which contain both Canadian and U.S. sources, are divided into: "Organization and Administration," "Fund Raising," "Play and Parenting," "Safety and Play Space," and "Some Useful Addresses."

While the book will probably not answer all questions a person may have about toy lending libraries, it certainly provides a good starting point. United States counterparts would be easily identifiable from the Canadian resources mentioned in the book. This work would be a valuable resource for any library which has considered adding a toy lending component. Public libraries and some special libraries would also have user groups with an interest in the information provided.   Carol J. Veitch

Women's Collections

380. **Women's Collections: Libraries, Archives, and Consciousness.** Suzanne Hildenbrand, ed. New York, Haworth Press, 1986. 194p. (*Special Collections*, Vol. 3, Nos. 3/4). $32.95. LC 84-22529. ISBN 0-86656-273-7.

A world center for women's archives: a thrilling idea, many contemporary feminists would agree. Yet how many know that such a center was first proposed in 1935, during the presumed retreat of feminism? This anthology of articles demonstrates that many of the older women's collections in the United States have their roots in the legacy of "first-wave" feminism, including the short-lived effort (1935-1940) to establish a world center for women's archives.

The eight articles in part 1 describe the history of selected women's collections in the United States, and identify their rich holdings. These range from the prestigious Sophia Smith Collection at Smith College and the equally venerable Schlesinger Library at Radcliffe, to the struggling Lesbian Herstory Archives in New York City; from the Library of Congress with its vast and broadly defined resources, to the more specifically focused National Archives for Black Women's History; from the Woman's Collection at Texas Woman's University, established in 1932, to the National Clearinghouse on Marital Rape, founded by Laura X in 1979. Following these profiles of women's collections, the three articles in part 2 raise questions about how access to resources by and about women can best be assured, critically analyzing the pros and cons of separate versus integrated collections; pinpointing thorny problems such as the interdisciplinary nature of the field and the difficulty of refining a thesaurus of subject terms; and reviewing reference works for the study of minority and Third World women. An address list of "Representative Women's Collections" completes the volume. Contributors include Sarah Pritchard, Bettye Collier-Thomas, Patricia Miller King, Susan Searing, and Beth Stafford.

There are other sources researchers can turn to for information about women's collections, such as Andrea Hinding's mammoth *Women's History Sources: A Guide to Archives and Manuscript Collections in the United States* (see *ARBA* 81, entry 810). The value of Hildenbrand's anthology lies in the overview it provides of representative collections and their fascinating history, and in the substantive issues it explores about the goals and problems of collection building. [R: RQ, Fall 86, p. 132]
                         Catherine R. Loeb

TECHNICAL STANDARDS

381. Crawford, Walt. **Technical Standards: An Introduction for Librarians.** White Plains, N.Y., Knowledge Industry, 1986. 299p. bibliog. index. (Professional Librarian Series). $36.50; $28.50pa. LC 85-23782. ISBN 0-86729-192-3; 0-86729-191-5pa.

As the author notes, "this book is a basic introduction to technical standards with particular focus on libraries and automation," although many examples from everyday life are also cited to illustrate the use of standards and the problems they create.

The book is both a textbook and a reference directory about selected standards affecting library operations and services. Together, the first six chapters offer an interwoven discussion of the history, the implications, the varieties, and the problems and dangers of technical standards, as well as a review of motives for developing formal standards. Chapter 7 examines the formal consensus standards, including a closer review of the processes required by the American National Standards Institute (ANSI) and those followed by the National Information Standards Organization (NISO) (Z39). The next chapter further reviews standards organizations with emphasis on the two in the United States most central to libraries and automation—NISO (Z39) and Accredited Standards Committee on Information Processing Systems (ASC X3). This is followed by chapter 9, "Resources for Agency Involvement," which encourages participation in all levels of the establishment of standards. The final three chapters present brief summaries of nearly one hundred standards applicable to libraries and publishers, providing data on their identification, purpose, details, and related standards. The volume concludes with two appendices, a glossary, selected bibliography, and two indexes—one to standards and a general one to names and subjects.

This is a readable, thorough examination of a topic which is an exciting passion to some and a boring necessity to others. However, the author's commitment and professional involvement embellish this useful reference source with interest and intrigue. This is a recommended volume for the technological reference shelf and for those interested in standards and their effects, particularly on the organization, storage, and communication of information. [R: JAL, Sept 86, p. 259; RBB, Aug 86, p. 116]

Danuta A. Nitecki

382. **Library Binding Institute Standard for Library Binding.** 8th ed. Paul A. Parisi and Jan Merrill-Oldham, eds. Rochester, N.Y., Library Binding Institute, 1986. 17p. illus. $5.00pa.

This, the eighth edition of standards published by the Library Binding Institute since 1935, reflects a greater need for volume flexibility as well as strength, and an increased awareness of archival standards for materials. After an introduction, the book is divided into sections on technical specifications and materials specifications. The technical specifications include standards for collation, repairs, trimming, various methods of sewing, rounding and backing the text block, making the case, and fitting the text block to the case. The material specifications deal with standards for paper, binders board, cloth, adhesives, thread, sewing tapes, and stamping foil. A glossary completes the text and is followed by a list of certified library binders. Although these are standards for the usual library materials, not rare or archival items, this standard emphasizes the need for archival-quality materials. Paper, for example, should meet the ANSI standard Z39-48-1984, which essentially eliminates acidic, woodpulp paper. This standard is clearly arranged and written in an outline form. It should be useful to binders who wish to meet library expectations and to librarians charged with the upkeep of their institution's collections. Readers interested in a fuller treatment of binding should consult the *Library Binding Manual* edited by Maurice F. Tauber (Library Binding Institute, 1972).

Linda S. Keir

Part III
REVIEWS OF PERIODICALS

Reviews of Periodicals

NATIONAL

383. **Booklist: Including Reference Books Bulletin**, Vol. 1- , No. 1- . Chicago, American Library Association, 1905- . semi-monthly (monthly, July, August). $47.00/yr.; $55.00/yr. (foreign); $3.25 (single issue). ISSN 0006-7385.

Booklist's strength is also its weakness. The precisely defined objectives which have guaranteed its survival have limited its application. Few selectors could do without the discriminating advice the journal offers and few could afford to make it their only source of reviews. From the time it began, this American Library Association publication filled a particular need—the need for library-oriented selection guidance by libraries with limited budgets. This particular need continues to exist and *Booklist* continues to fill it best. Its authority rests in its policy to publish reviews only for titles it recommends; its limitation lies in the authority it assumes.

ALA Booklist's (the journal initially included its sponsoring association's acronym in its title) first editor, Caroline H. Garland of the Dover, New Hampshire, Library, began her foreword to volume 1 with a phrase that sounded hesitant and apologetic: "To the number of book reviews already existing there would be little need of adding another...."[1] Considering the audience she addressed—an audience accustomed for thirty-three years to the brief descriptions of new books *Publishers Weekly* supplied, for fifteen years to the longer, Sunday discussions the *New York Times Book Review* provided, for three years to the scholarly essays the *Times Literary Supplement* contributed, and for almost five decades to the sagacious sense of the book trade the British *Bookseller* shared—some initial hesitancy may have been justified. The forceful conclusion that completed her introductory phrase, however, demonstrated that what seemed like apology was actually astute observation. Garland followed her nod of respectful recognition in the direction of the established sources of book reviews with a firm description of her fledgling publication's "different standpoint" and "definite purpose": uniquely, *ALA Booklist* would "embody briefly the judgment and experience of librarians for the use of librarians."[2] Backed by $100,000 of Carnegie money, the American Library Association Publishing Board could well afford to affirm the forceful half of Garland's initiatory remark. In response to an "evident need," this board voted in 1905 to issue, eight times a year at the "almost nominal subscription rate of 50 cents," a "current buying list of recent books with ... notes designed to assist librarians in selection."[3]

As if to prove the astuteness of Garland's observation and the accuracy of the ALA Publishing Board's assessment of need, *ALA Booklist* had securely established itself by the time volume 3 appeared. This third volume's foreword unapologetically and authoritatively stated that a book's appearance in its pages constituted a recommendation for purchase, and that recently published and moderately priced books were chosen purposefully for review with the selection needs of small and medium-sized public libraries in mind.[4] These same clear and unequivocal objectives, maintained without compromise over the last eighty years, have ensured *Booklist* a protected niche within the review environment.

Edna Vanek, *Booklist*'s eighth and long-time editor, included a celebratory foreword in the journal's fiftieth anniversary issue.[5] She simultaneously celebrated her publication's constancy of purpose and its ability to adapt, both to its own success and to the demands created by the exponential growth of information. The adaptations Vanek praised included an increase in both size (more pages, new features, reviews of formats other than books) and frequency (from once to twice a month). By 1955, subscriptions, rather than Carnegie, provided almost all of the publication's financial support. *Booklist* now had a staff of eleven individuals who performed the reading, final selecting, and annotating tasks, no doubt establishing a valuable consistency, a consistency gained without sacrificing the diversity of input that distinguished, and continues to distinguish, the journal as a review publication "by librarians for librarians." The old contributions system according to which librarians nationwide submitted titles annotated with brief notes stressing "servicability of format, reliability of content, and appeal" had given way to a more efficient voting system that involved the weekly solicitation of opinions from a cross-section of library book selection experts.[6]

A year and a half after Vanek celebrated the journal's fifty years of adaptive adherence to its "founders' original purpose," *Booklist* adapted again and merged with the ALA Subscription Books Committee publication, *Subscription Books Bulletin* (*SBB*). The combination of "these complementary ALA aids to book selection"[7] did not change *Booklist*'s authoritative policy of equating a review with a recommendation nor did it alter the Subscription Books Committee's practice of supplying "analytical, detailed" reviews of reference works or sets sold by subscription that included recommendations for or against purchase. It did change the frequency with which librarian readers had access to critical information concerning reference and subscription sources (*SBB* had been published quarterly); these reviews were now available on the same bimonthly basis as *Booklist*'s current and selective reviews of books, pamphlets, films, government documents, etc.

Today, as in 1905, other publications exist that function for libraries as current buying lists or selection tools, which, on first glance, appear to offer *Booklist* some serious competition. A closer examination, however, reveals that the journal, introduced, astutely, if hesitantly, by Caroline Garland eight decades ago, still maintains its "different, [unique] standpoint" and its "definite, [unduplicated] purpose." *Library Journal* (*LJ*), certainly a quintessential example of a periodical "by librarians for librarians," includes, among its feature articles, news, columns, and departments, a substantial Book Review Section, with its own editor and associate editor, and provides magazine and audiovisual reviews as well. Its issues, like *Booklist*'s, are periodically fattened by publisher's announcements. Equipped with these review components, *LJ* effectively offers selection as one of the many functions it performs.

Booklist, by comparison, devotes itself to the development of collections in small and medium-sized public libraries and in school libraries and media centers. The sense it communicates of trends in publishing, the variety of nonprint formats (e.g., films, video, and microcomputer software) it examines, the "Upfront" section it supplies of titles reviewed as far in advance as possible because of their "anticipated demand in libraries," and the short and consistently high quality reviews it provides of adult fiction and nonfiction and of books for young adults and children demonstrate an attention to materials selection, the likes of which *LJ* is not in a position to pay.

Booklist's perspective on publishing trends differs today from *Publishers Weekly*'s perspective just as it differed in 1905 when the new publication aimed at librarians dared offer itself as an alternative to the already established voice of the book trade. *Publishers Weekly*'s bestseller lists, year-in-review columns, and author interviews address the profit-oriented concerns of those who publish and sell. *Booklist*'s subject-oriented feature columns (e.g., "Vietnamese Books," "Ending Hunger: A Multimedia Resource List," "Popular Reading— Dragons," or "Contemporary Issues—Nutrition"), on the other hand, emphasize library collections as they intersect with users' informational and recreational needs.

Choice, an Association of College and Research Libraries publication, shares with *Booklist* an emphasis on collection building, selection, and user demand, but with different collections and users in mind. Approximately three thousand subject experts review books (and some nonprint items) for *Choice*, concentrating on the needs of faculty, students, and scholars; the undergraduate library, rather than the small or medium-sized public or school library, sets the context within which materials are chosen for review and evaluated. In this more academically oriented periodical, reference materials receive the same brief, critical reviews as materials in other subject categories such as photography, engineering, or philosophy.

Booklist's treatment of reference materials differs significantly from *Choice*'s treatment, and the difference epitomizes the way in which the two review publications vary. In *Booklist*, the reference review section, "Reference Books Bulletin," remains (except for the name change from "Subscription" to "Reference") as it began thirty years ago, a publication within a publication governed by its own guidelines and procedures. More than historical precedent dictates this procedural distinction. Unlike *Choice*, which presents a range of materials to its readers, some recommended, some not recommended for purchase, *Booklist* proper reviews only titles it can confidently recommend. A judgment on quality and appropriateness has already occurred before a review even appears. This policy effectively limits the journal's scope and offers libraries with stringent budgetary constraints a predefined yet eclectic universe from which selections can be made. The universe of reference books, even for small, financially constrained libraries, cannot be predefined in this same, qualitative way. Reference collections, not subject directly to the whims and vagaries of user demand, must reflect individual libraries serving the needs of particular groups of patrons and involved in particular networking situations. The long comparative and evaluative reviews (written by members of the Reference Books Bulletin Editorial Board or by guest reviewers, and revised by the board as a whole) that offer specific purchase recommendations, give public and school librarians the detailed information they need to make individual decisions concerning the purchase of expensive volumes, sets, or standing orders. The overviews of certain categories of reference materials (for example, encyclopedias, annuals, supplements, and yearbooks) featured periodically by "Reference Books Bulletin" augment the column's advisory and utilitarian function.

Review publications must be selective. *Booklist*, for example, selects the items it reviews by specifying smaller public and school libraries as its target audience, *Choice* by specifying undergraduate libraries. But *Booklist* selects according to criteria other than target audience. It chooses not to publish reviews of books, films, videos, microcomputer software packages, etc., that it cannot recommend. This choice is significant because negative reviews do not preclude purchase any more than positive reviews guarantee it. By making evaluation one of its selection criteria, *Booklist* has chosen to direct its advice toward the development of core collections. Libraries whose restricted budgets ensure that even a broad based core collection is beyond reach will profit from the ALA publication's evaluative selection policies. Libraries in more of a position to choose will prefer to evaluate on their own. However, *Booklist* demonstrates that an authoritative, core collection approach is not necessarily a narrow one. Besides providing predictable lists of Caldecott prize winners and editor's choices, the journal suggests purchases in diverse areas such as "World Cultures," "Growing Up Black," or "Intergenerational Relationships," and small press publications appear alongside the publications of presses in the mainstream.

Whether criticized for its authoritative evaluation or praised for its high quality advice, *Booklist* makes an undeniably unique contribution to the field of reviewing. Its current editor, Paul Brawley, could write today, as astutely and as confidently as Caroline Garland and Edna Vanek wrote decades ago, that his journal is "a reliable and indispensable aid to book selection, [truly] a publication by librarians and for librarians."[8]

Notes

[1] C. H. Garland, "The Editor's Foreword," *ALA Booklist* 1 (1905): 3.

[2] Ibid.

[3] *ALA Booklist* 1 (1905): 2.

[4] *ALA Booklist* 3 (1907): 4.

[5] E. Vanek, "The Booklist at Mid-Century," *Booklist* 51 (1955): 187.

[6] E. Vanek, "Memo to Subscribers," *Booklist* 53 (1956): 1-2.

[7] Ibid.

[8] E. Vanek, "The Booklist at Mid-Century."

Connie Miller

384. **British Journal of Academic Librarianship**, Vol. 1- , No. 1- . London, Taylor Graham Publishing, 1986- . 3 issues/yr. $65.00/yr. ISSN 0269-0497.

With a strong editorial board and a well-qualified editor in Colin Harris, this newest entry into the field of academic librarianship journals has an excellent chance of succeeding. According to the stated editorial policy, it is "designed as a means for the development of academic library theory and practice, in all sectors and in all countries." Although all five of the inaugural articles have a distinctly UK cast to them, they do have value to readers in most other countries. This first issue, which may not be representative of the orientation of all of volume 1, suggests that it will focus on the large research/university library rather than on the broad spectrum of academic librarianship. Final judgment on that question must wait until more issues are published.

The lead article by Maurice Line, "Survival of Academic Libraries in Hard Times," will strike a responsive chord with most university librarians who have experienced the pressures described and some of the reactions to those pressures. Susan Hawley's article outlines ten topics "worthy of research or development" as identified by a small group "convened by the British Library Research and Development Department." "User Education in Academic Libraries in the United Kingdom" is a literature review, state-of-the-art paper by Hugh Fleming. The only "research" article is Brenda Moon's "Cooperative Networks and Service to the Scholar," in which she reports the results of six case studies she conducted in a Scottish university on how scholars are currently conducting their research. Finally, M. P. Day's "Electronic Publishing and Academic Libraries" has the greatest general value, as it very nicely summarizes present activities and trends. Twenty-three of the first issue's ninety-three pages are devoted to eight book reviews; as might be expected of a British publication the reviews are detailed and generally very well done.

The journal has the potential to become a standard in the field. It must be noted with great sadness that the publisher has followed the recent British publishers' practice of charging U.S. libraries a significantly higher subscription fee. (United States customers are asked to pay $65.00, while everyone else pays £35.00, under $50.00 at the November 1986 exchange rate.)

G. Edward Evans

385. **Choice**, Vol. 1- , No. 1- . Middletown, Conn., Association of College and Research Libraries, American Library Association, 1963- . monthly (July/August, bimonthly). $110.00/yr.; $120.00/yr. (foreign); $12.00 (single issue).

The purpose of *Choice* is to inform "librarians, faculty, students, scholars and the informed public of significant current publications in terms of the relative place of the title in its subject field and in an undergraduate library collection." Just a bit past college age itself at twenty-four years old, *Choice* is published by the Association of College and Research Libraries. Its subscribers are mainly academic and large public libraries.

Choice is strictly a review journal; the only other departments are editorials, letters, and a bibliographic essay in each issue. It publishes some sixty-five hundred reviews a year; at eleven issues per year, that means a little under six hundred reviews per issue. This puts *Choice* in a very small class of really comprehensive review media, especially considering its singleminded concentration on undergraduates. *Library Journal* publishes a similar number of reviews annually, but its coverage is broader and therefore less deep in the scholarly fields.

Choice's emphasis is mainly on book reviews, but there are also reviews of nonprint media, with limited coverage of periodicals and microcomputer software. Book and nonprint reviews appear to be about 150 to 250 words in length (the journal's target length is 100-175); periodical reviews are either similarly substantive or "Short Notices" of two or three sentences. The book reviews are classed into about fifty subject headings that more or less follow Dewey.

The criterion that the reviewed item should be appropriate for an undergraduate library is stringently interpreted. Some textbooks are reviewed, but the bulk of the coverage is of monographs. More popular titles are less likely to receive coverage than more scholarly ones. The social sciences and humanities account for the bulk of the coverage (44 percent), with science and technology appreciably behind (16 percent) and other subjects taking up the remainder of space. This subject breakdown is roughly in line with percentages of undergraduate students obtaining degrees in the humanities and sciences as listed in the 1986 *Statistical Abstracts*.

Very little fiction or poetry is reviewed in *Choice* — only a few titles per issue. The journal does not review popular fiction or new novels by well-established authors, preferring to cover serious first novels or collections of poetry, especially those published by small presses. The editors also make a special attempt to cover fiction in translation, either new works or new translations.

An overall evaluation of the reviews in *Choice* can only be made in very general terms. It is possible to say, however, that reading a large number of *Choice* reviews leaves one impressed with their thoughtfulness and insight as a whole; these reviewers really know their subjects. It is probable that much of this impression is the result not only of good writing but of good editing by the *Choice* staff. (Of course, a book-minded person reading someone else's reviews will always discover a quota of "wrong" judgments of a volume's worth.)

Especially notable is the number of reviews that compare the work at hand with earlier studies; out of a random one hundred reviews chosen from a 1986 issue, thirty cited other works (not including, e.g., the author's earlier writings). This kind of comparison is frequently essential for a true evaluation of a work. Most reviewers attempt to recommend the title for a certain audience or type of collection, a practice that many librarians appreciate but that can often be misleading—especially if the reviewer, like many academics, knows little about different types of libraries.

Choice reviews books within five or six months of publication or else it will not cover them. In comparison with most scholarly journals, this is early coverage. *Choice* emphasizes this fact in its editorials, claiming that its review of an item may be the publication's first professional review. This is misleading; *Library Journal* attempts to run as many prepublication reviews as possible and uses many reviewers with equal scholarly qualifications. (*Library Journal*'s shorter reviews, however, can only cover the bare-bones facts about a book; *Choice*'s longer essays give it an advantage in usefulness.) For titles of timeless value, librarians may find that the difference of a few months may not make much difference, but on hot subjects they need the earlier notice.

Since September 1984, all reviews have been signed, breaking a twenty-year tradition of anonymity. The approximately three thousand reviewers are 90 percent faculty and 10 percent librarians, mainly at universities, colleges, or junior colleges. The January 1987 issue reported that 42 percent of reviewers had been writing for *Choice* for more than eleven years—an impressive figure and a real advantage in obtaining comparative reviews.

As for the peripheral features, the bibliographic essays are generally masterly and thorough. The subject range is wide, with room for both a broad treatment of American musical theater and an article on books about U.S. caves. Some essays help make up for the dearth of fiction reviews by surveying such genres as fiction, poetry, and plays about the Vietnam War or science fiction and fantasy titles. The editorials often give valuable statistics about publishing topics such as book prices, reviewing concerns, or *Choice*'s own procedures and editorial policies.

Choice was redesigned in September 1985, but it is still considerably stodgier in appearance than such competitors as *Booklist* and *Library Journal*. The reviews are dense—wide columns, small type (approximately eight points) with little or no extra space between lines, no color, and mundane heads. The bibliographic information for each publication reviewed is hard to read: it is all in boldface type, with authors, title, LC numbers and ISBNs, price, date, and a few other facts crammed tightly into a couple of lines. The journal's covers feature photographs of college libraries, sources of pride no doubt to the pictured institutions, but rarely including a human form. No one is reading *Choice* for its looks.

Although the journal cannot be all-sufficient for undergraduate libraries it attempts to serve—for example, no library at that level could be without a hefty fiction collection—its comprehensive coverage and especially its quality make it indispensable to its target audience.

Carol Rasmussen

386. **The Journal of Library History: Philosophy & Comparative Librarianship**, Vol. 1- , No. 1- . Austin, Tex., University of Texas Press, 1966- . quarterly. $18.00/yr.; $26.00/yr. (institutions); (add $3.00 for foreign). ISSN 0275-3650.

In 1977, the only journal that was and is devoted specifically to providing a historical perspective on books and libraries in our society was transferred from its base of origin, the School of Library and Information Studies, Florida State University, to its present home at the Graduate School of Library and Information Science, University of Texas at Austin. The early years of *JLH* were uniquely influenced by its first editor and founder, Louis Shores, who discerned and responded to the need for a publication that would be "a means of communication between historians, librarians, and the academic community at large."[1] As suggested by the title, *library history* has been the primary emphasis—especially in volumes 1 to 11, edited first by Shores and then by Harold Goldstein.

Under the able direction of Donald G. Davis, Jr., who has served as editor since the journal's move to Texas in 1977, increased attention is given to the two additional aspects of its title: philosophy and comparative librarianship. In addition to that development, library history is "construed broadly to include the history and development of the whole range of theory and practice related to library and information science."[2] The quarterly issues have been extensively enlarged in recent years through an increased number of book reviews, lengthy feature articles, "Notes," and, when possible, illustrative material. One of the major advantages of the move to Austin lies in the services of the University of Texas Press. Their expertise in cover design, layout, graphics, and typography were evident in the first issue after the transfer and have continued to date. For example, the covers of *JLH* feature "a graphically attractive bookplate or label from a significant library or book collection."[3] Each cover graphic is accompanied by a special "Note" that describes its origin, use, and meaning. Although illustrations are not prolific—nor in color—they have added to the text (e.g., "A Note on the Lost Library of the Moscow Tsars" [Summer 1983]: 304-16 has several reproductions of individuals involved in the story of the lost library and one photograph of an underground passage under the Kremlin).

The number of articles in any given issue varies from two to six. The Spring 1980 issue, for example, has only two articles: one ten pages in length, including references, and a second twenty-nine pages long including references. However, the two articles are followed by eight "Notes." The "Notes" also vary widely in depth, breadth, and intent. In the issue just cited, the "Notes" included four discussions on quite different topics: early medical librarians and their work (sixteen pages), a biographical sketch (five pages), a commentary on capitalism, liberty, and the development of the library (eleven pages), and an announcement of a new library history group that had been formed in West Germany. The next two "Notes" were review essays: "Intellectual Life in the Colonial South" (four pages) and "The Printing Press as an Agent of Change" (five pages). The "Notes" in this issue concluded with the "cover" article and biographical data on the contributors to the issue. The remainder of the issue contained twenty book reviews (one to two and one-half pages in length), one "Communication" (i.e., a letter to the editor), and the announcement of a forthcoming meeting. The total number of pages, excluding introductory material and advertisements, was over 130. Contributors included educators, librarians, and students from the United States and Canada; the authors of the book reviews reflected the same backgrounds.

The Spring 1980 issue is typical of the structure of most issues, with the "Notes" section of some length and often especially commissioned by the editor. The distinction between articles and "Notes" was clarified by Davis in the Winter 1977 issue:

> Major articles will most often consist of carefully developed papers, reports and essays based on original research and primary sources, although translations of materials not readily available in English will receive due consideration. Briefer articles and others which do not meet these general criteria may be considered for inclusion in a section of each issue devoted to scholarly notes, descriptions of source materials, news of research endeavors, and forthcoming meetings, reminiscences and summaries of oral history, and conference reports.[4]

It also needs to be noted that *JLH* has always maintained a strong advisory board and that all submissions are refereed.

One extremely valuable addition to the "Notes" section has been the one- or two-year survey of publications on American library history. Written in recent years by Wayne A. Wiegand, University of Wisconsin-Madison, the survey attempts to identify every article, monograph, and other publication that deals with some aspect of American library history. This regular offering provides an excellent supplement to *American Library History: A Bibliography*, by Michael H. Harris and Donald G. Davis, Jr. (University of Texas Press, 1978).

As already noted, book review coverage also has been expanded significantly in recent volumes. The Summer 1986 issue contains thirteen book reviews on titles that have a wide-ranging span of interest, such as rare books and special collections in the United Kingdom and Ireland, the decline of the Western empire, the *Handbook of Medieval Library History*, encyclopedias of the seventeenth and eighteenth centuries, Russian censorship of Western ideas, a centennial history of a Benedictine community and library, the first American library pioneer in India, reading the romance novel, proceedings of a library seminar, classification in the Library of Congress, etc. The reviews are signed and reflect the international basis of the journal as well as its close relationship to the academic scholarly community. Unfortunately, as with many quarterly publications, there may be considerable delay in the publication of book reviews—sometimes as much as three years. This delay is partially the result of the commitment to devote entire issues to the publication of the papers of special conferences, such as the Library History Seminar VII, Chapel Hill, March 1985, which absorbed the first and second numbers of Volume 21, Winter and Spring 1986. Other special issues have been based on the programs of the Library History Round Table, as was, for example, the Spring 1985 (Volume 20, Number 2) issue on "Library and Information Science: Historical Perspectives"—papers presented in 1984 at the Dallas convention of the American Library Association.

JLH has been consistently well edited as well as graphically attractive—even with a 1985 decision to reduce the print size in order to provide more space for text. Since the articles are refereed and carefully edited, the overall quality and accuracy of the publication have remained high. "Notes," as well as articles, are replete with documentation. The breadth of *JLH*'s coverage attracts a readership that extends beyond the library historian to other disciplines.

Although there is not yet an equal balance between international coverage and that of American library history, the journal has significant topical coverage of non-U.S. library history.

JLH has maintained a close affiliation with the Library History Round Table of the American Library Association; a member of the Round Table serves on the advisory board and *JLH* includes notices about its meetings and publications. The journal is indexed in some ten sources, including *Historical Abstracts, Library Literature,* and the *Social Sciences Citation Index.* Its own annual index is published in the fourth (Fall) number of each volume.

Unlike some areas of library and information science, this journal stands alone in its emphasis on the history of books, collections, and society. It attempts to provide its wide readership with scholarly and readable international library history and philosophy. On the whole, its audience is well served.

Notes

[1] *JLH* 12 (Winter 1977): 1.

[2] Ibid., 2.

[3] Ibid., 3.

[4] Ibid., 2.

Laurel Grotzinger

387. **Library Association Record**, Vol. 1- , No. 1- . London, Library Association, 1899- . monthly. $96.00/yr.; £43.00/yr. (United Kingdom); £52.00/yr. (all other countries). ISSN 0024-2195.

The *Library Association Record*, the British equivalent of *American Libraries*, was first published in 1899 as a monthly. It is the official journal of the Library Association and has retained its original title to the present. From 1899 to 1903 H. Guppy was the editor of the journal; from 1903 to 1922 it was edited by a publications committee of the Library Association. Arundell Esdaile was the editor from 1923 to 1935; R. D. Hilton Smith followed him, serving from 1936 to 1942; from 1943 to 1946 L. R. McColvin was editor; and W. B. Stevenson edited the journal from 1947 to 1952. A. J. Walford served as editor from 1953 to 1960, J. D. Reynolds took over as editor from 1961 to 1966; from 1967 to 1975 Edward Dudley was editor, and Roger Walter served from 1976 to 1983. Jane Jenkins has been editor since 1984.

From 1923 to 1930 the journal was published as a quarterly in a "new series." The third series ran from 1931 to 1933, and since 1934 the journal has been a monthly publication in its fourth series. The title of the serial has, however, remained the same since 1899. The volumes have been numbered consecutively each year.

The size of the journal is 8¼ by 11½ inches. It contains between forty and sixty pages per issue. Since it is not exactly the 8½-by-11½-inch popular size, it is a bit more difficult to shelve, file, or photocopy it. Each issue is bound with an attractive colored cover and illustrated abundantly with color as well as black-and-white photographs and graphics. Since 1986 the journal has been printed on somewhat heavier paper, and several changes in arrangement have improved the readability.

The *Library Association Record* is intended for the membership of the British Library Association and seems to have an annual subscription rate of eleven thousand. It includes the usual news of the organization as well as news about British libraries, and features three to five articles in each issue. Relatively short articles and news items cover all aspects of the library profession, and regular items include topics of international interest. Also included in the journal are news items about people, obituaries, a meetings calendar, a number of ads for library personnel and publishers, summaries of meetings and committee activities, and some book reviews. The content of this publication is basically that of an official news magazine for association members, with various styles of writing but consistency in coverage. Its content is abstracted in *Library and Information Science Abstracts* and indexed in *Library Literature* and *Current Index to Journals in Education.*

Most of the issues contain from two to seven medium-length reviews of monographs related to library and information science. The reviewed publications are generally published in the United Kingdom. The reviews are informative as well as evaluative.

Since the *Library Association Record* is really the British counterpart of *American Libraries*, a comparison of the two seems appropriate. It must be pointed out that the subscription price for the British publication is twice that of the American one, for U.S. subscribers. Also the size of the American journal is more manageable (8 by 11 inches) for shelving and filing. The American publication has generally twice the number of pages and a somewhat more substantial cover for better protection.

The contents of the two publications are similar. Both have revamped their appearance and content arrangement during the last two years. Both publications also are similarly attractive in appearance through the use of illustrations and photographs in color as well as black-and-white. *American Libraries* features more personnel ads than the *Library Association Record*, while the latter contains more international library news than the former. The British publication has been around for eighty-eight years, the American for eighty years. Both are very readable but not scholarly journals, and very important communication tools for respective association memberships.

The *Library Association Record* is a basic journal for library school collections and could also be useful for academic and public librarians who want to become familiar with British professional library news and concerns.

Hannelore B. Rader

388. **Library of Congress Information Bulletin**, Vol. 1- , No. 1- . Washington, D.C., Library of Congress, 1942- . weekly. free/yr. ISSN 0041-7904.

This periodical began publication 23 January 1942 with volume 1, number 1 as the *Staff Information Bulletin* of the Library of Congress as a weekly. It continued biweekly from September to November 1942, then monthly (irregular) to October 1944. The July 1943 issue was combined with the *Monthly Public Information Bulletin* of the Library of Congress and retitled *Information Bulletin*. The first retitled issue was numbered volume 4, number 1. Publication was temporarily suspended during the war years, and was resumed with the 25 July-1 August 1945 issue as a weekly publication. The reactivated periodical was intended to be a calendar of upcoming events at the Library of Congress. However, before the end of 1945, it resumed its previous characteristic of publishing new items regarding Library of Congress (LC) policies, programs, and activities and personnel. It still retains this general editorial policy.

From 1945 through 1949, the weekly issues were not numbered. Numbering was resumed with the issue of 2 January 1950 as volume 9, number 1. New volume numbers have since been assigned each calendar year. From 1952 through 1971, news items were grouped under the following section titles: "Acquisition Notes," "Notes on Publications," "Events in the Offing," "Staff Activities," "Committees and Other Meetings," "Library of Congress Publications," "Library of Congress Footnotes," "Personnel," "Notes on Other Libraries," "Exhibits," "Concerts," "Official Notices," "News of Other Organizations," "New Reference Books," and "Visitors." Those sections which appeared in a particular issue were listed in the table of contents. With the first issue of volume 31 (1972), the title was changed to *Library of Congress Information Bulletin*, the sections were eliminated, and the table of contents listed individual news items. With the first issue of volume 38 (1979), most personnel news items were consolidated in a four-page insert printed on blue paper called "Staff News," with unnumbered pages.

This newsletter contains short news items about Library of Congress policies, activities, programs, and personnel. It is intended primarily for Library of Congress staff personnel. However, the editors have long recognized that the Library of Congress is the unofficial national library of the United States, that many LC programs serve libraries nationwide, and that these libraries are affected by LC policies. In turn, the Library of Congress is interested in and affected by significant events elsewhere in the library world, both nationally and internationally. Since the late 1940s the periodical has carried reports prepared by LC staff members of the annual conferences of the American Library Association, Special Libraries Association, Association of American Law Libraries, and the International Federation of Library Associations (IFLA), and occasionally conference reports of smaller library associations. These have often been more timely and detailed than reports in the associations' official journals.

The periodical does not publish book reviews, but does publish news items or annotated lists of new LC publications. Occasionally annotated bibliographies will be published such as "The Vietnamese Conflict: A Selected List of References" (volume 44, number 30, pp. 207-12). A "Semiannual Report on Developments at the Library of Congress" provides progress reports by all major LC units for the first six months of the fiscal year. Illustrations consist primarily of photographs which began appearing in the late 1940s: usually of LC staff members who have received promotions, awards, or other honors or made significant contributions, and of distinguished visitors in connection with exhibitions, concerts, acquisitions and donations, or other special events. Occasionally, there are photographs dealing with exhibit items or library facilities.

The periodical is distributed free of charge to publicly supported libraries and research institutions, academic libraries, learned societies, and allied organizations in the United States by the LC Information Office (Washington, DC 20540). Comparable institutions and organizations in other countries may arrange to receive it on an exchange basis by applying in writing to the LC Exchange and Gift Division. The bulletin is also available to federal depository libraries (Item 785-C). Annual indexes for the years 1971-1973 and 1976 are still available and free upon request to the LC Central Services Division, Printing and Processing Section. Indexes for 1984 and 1985 volumes have been prepared by the Library of Congress Professional Association and are available for $10.00 each from the association. A 1986 index is planned. These indexes are not official government publications, and are not free or distributed to depository libraries.

An average issue contains six to eight numbered letter-sized "white pages" and four unnumbered blue pages with "Staff Notes." For example, a typical issue (22 September 1986) contained the following news items: "Consultant in Poetry Robert Penn Warren to Read at the Library," "Library Issues Policy Statement on Its Use of Print Materials in Optical Disk Format," "Fall Chamber Music Season Begins," "Library Publishes Directory of Folklife Resources," "Acquisition and Overseas Operation Directorate Holds Briefing," "Collection Development Office Holds Foreign Acquisition Seminar," "Library Receives First Volume of New Slovak Biographical Directory," "Report from a Conference on the Contemporary Ukraine," "New Cataloging Distribution Service Publications," and "New NLS/PPH Publications." The "Staff News" contained the following items: "Karen Wood Appointed Special Assistant to Deputy Librarian," "James P. Riley Is Awarded 25-Year Federal Service Pin," "Waldo H. Moore, Former Associate Register of Copyright Retires," "Staff Activities" (two items), "Staff Carpool Locator," "Personnel Changes (Appointments, Temporary Appointments, Reappointments, Resignations)." A regular feature since mid-1985 has been a list of "Meetings and Events around the Library" on the back page.

Because of budgetary restrictions, coverage of news of outside organizations and activities, including the conference reports, has been reduced. Personnel items may be found in both the white and blue pages. Editorial policy is to include the item in the white pages if the individual(s) deal with national programs. However, since many LC staff members are active in national professional library associations and the literature, interesting items of outside interest are often found in the blue pages.

LeRoy C. Schwarzkopf

389. **Quill & Quire**, Vol. 1- , No. 1- . Toronto, Key Publishers, 1935- . monthly, with supplements. $40.00/yr.; $50.00/yr. (U.S.). ISSN 0033-6491.

The absolutely best way to describe *Quill & Quire* for an American audience is to say that it is *Publishers Weekly, Weekly Record, Library Journal,* and *School Library Journal* all rolled into one, that is, all of the R. R. Bowker publications, but for the Canadian market. Its subtitle is "published since 1935 for the Canadian book trade." Physically, it is in tabloid format, web offset, with newsprint of "throwaway" quality. The layout is four columns across with small type; it averages about fifty-two pages per regular issue, more when it runs with special sections. It is now available on newsstands in Canada for $3.00, and there are microfilms of back copies and indexes available. It is indexed in the *Canadian Periodical Index* and the *Canadian Magazine Index,* and its book reviews are included in *Book Review Digest. Quill & Quire*'s circulation as of March 1986 was 6,065, mostly to libraries (3,000) and mostly in Ontario (3,600); there are only 142 subscribers in the United States.

Overall, the magazine presents straight *information* more than anything else. There are no editorials or comments and no real stands on issues, except for general support of commonsense solutions to recurring problems in the Canadian book trade (postage rate hikes, order fulfillment for acquisitions, library practices, Public Lending Right, and so forth). It lacks a focus, a crusade; it is bland, like many industry and trade magazines. Its columnists can be prickly at times, but they tend to sound off against the system as a whole. Never are there any harsh words or criticisms of any one bookstore, publisher, library, author, or reviewer. Indeed, the only feisty and really exciting section in *Quill & Quire* is the active "letters" column. The basic material in the magazine is data (news and announcements), followed by reviews and profiles of people and of businesses.

There are two book announcement issues, one in the spring and one in the fall, that list most of the new Canadian English-language books. Included with the subscription is "Forthcoming Books," a cataloging-in-publication service from the National Library of Canada, issued monthly with materials in classified order, which catalogs new Canadian English- and French-language books, as well as many government documents and conference papers (if published separately). This, of course, is useful for library acquisitions and cataloging departments, especially in Canadian studies programs throughout the world. Twice a year, *Quill & Quire* publishes *Canadian Publishers Directory,* which lists addresses for all the major publishers, and is the key to decoding the convoluted Canadian book agency business.

Other services to the book trade include information on a stream of personnel appointments and changes at publishing houses and libraries, descriptive and evaluative (but short) book reviews — maybe thirty a month that are written by librarians, academics and freelance writers—reviews of spoken-word cassettes, reports of conventions (American Library Association, Canadian Library Association, American Booksellers Association, Canadian Booksellers Association, regional meetings, and the like), and lots of gung ho material for bookstores related to Christmas shopping (displays, Christmas gift books, new books sure to sell). There are regular issues devoted to education, for textbook publishers, audiovisual producers, and teachers. But it is next to impossible to find sales figures and return rates, or even discount schedules. There is no bestseller listing either, which probably makes sense because *Quill & Quire* is a monthly, and the time lag would be enormous. Anyone who requires a bestseller list for Canada could consult the weekly issues of *Maclean's*, Canada's newsmagazine version of *Time, Newsweek*, et al.

Columns in *Quill & Quire* include Gord Graham's "Printouts," about computers and software, and Beverley Slopen's "Paperclips," about authors and publishers. Other columns that have ceased within the past year have dealt with recorded popular and classical music and with magazines. There are survey articles dealing with statistics of book sales or library circulation (usually gathered from Statistics Canada), and covering the publishing year in review or a particular segment of the trade, such as gothic novels or business book success stories.

Most of the articles are written by freelance writers, while others—such as the surveys—can be written in-house after use of the telephone. Typical articles include "Profiles": in 1986, *Quill & Quire* writers interviewed Canadian authors Walter Stewart, Alberto Manguel, Pierre Berton, Andreus Schroeder, and Matt Cohen, plus business people such as Pierre Péladeau (a Quebec media magnate) and David Kerfoot (a bookseller). These are straightforward accounts and informative biographies. Other articles in 1986 have concerned bookstore design, bookstore inventory programs, Expo 86 and British Columbia publishers, books heard on CBC Radio, an anatomy of a court case as an author sues his publisher, textbook programs, Payment for Public Use (the public lending right), bookstores in Vancouver, and the like. Very few features are directly about the library world, despite this magazine's readership. However, there is a sufficient quantity of library news and education news concerning young readers. All in all, *Quill & Quire* is a useful publication for keeping up-to-date with the Canadian book trade. The material is well written and well presented, even if it is not adventuresome and there are no editorials. It does what it says it tries to do: publishes *for* the book trade, as a service of news, notes, and reviews. And in this instance, then, it is like any other trade magazine.

Dean Tudor

390. **School Libraries in Canada**, Vol. 1- , No. 1- . Ottawa, Ont., Canadian Library Association, 1980- . quarterly. $35.00/yr. (U.S.); $35.00/yr. (Canada). ISSN 0227-3780.

School Libraries in Canada, formerly *Moccasin Telegraph*, is the journal of the Canadian Association of School Librarians, a division of the Canadian Library Association. As a journal serving a relatively small and geographically widespread constituency with all of the financial problems which that combination implies, it attempts to meet the needs of school librarians both for substantial professional articles and for news about the association and professional concerns. The news function of the journal is handled through a column written by the CASL president, reports of association meetings, and brief news items. The journal also includes two reviews of professional reading in each issue. The major portion of the journal is devoted to substantive articles on issues of concern to school librarians. Recent articles have included a valuable and thoughtful report of an investigation into censorship incidents in Manitoba libraries, a discussion of education for school librarianship in Canada and Australia, and a group of articles addressing the problem of setting standards for school libraries. While the immediate focus of most articles is Canadian, school librarians in other countries will find much of the information pertinent to their needs. Like *School Library Media Quarterly* in the United States, *School Libraries in Canada* demonstrates that school librarians are interested in solid, research-based articles which help them to cope with professional problems. The changing editorial emphases of these journals is a tribute to the increasing sophistication and professional awareness of school librarians in both countries.

Adele M. Fasick

SUBJECT-ORIENTED

391. **The American Archivist**, Vol. 1- , No. 1- . Chicago, Society of American Archivists, 1938- . 4 issues/yr. $30.00/yr. (North America); $35.00/yr. (other addresses); $9.00 (single issue); $8.00 (single issue, SAA members). ISSN 0360-9081.

The official journal of the Society of American Archivists (SAA) celebrates its fiftieth anniversary in 1988. Founded with the intention "to be as useful as possible to the members of the profession," its current role is "to reflect the thinking of archivists about trends and major issues in archival philosophy and theory." Its editorial policy has likewise shifted from an emphasis on "the concrete and practical rather than the general," to "analytical and critical expositions based on original research about subjects of broad interest."

The journal has always been a quarterly, combining the role of a scholarly and professional publication with that of a newsletter of the profession and an official record of the meetings and governance policies of the SAA. After a few years as a typical professional society publication, it was then produced from 1949 through 1981 jointly by the SAA and the National Archives, with the editor a staff member of the latter organization. This relationship was severed after the U.S. government raised concerns about its propriety (and, following the lead of President Reagan, was trying to emphasize "privatization"), leading to a rapid turnover in editors and serious financial difficulties for a couple of years. The journal now appears to be back on a firm footing, at least as firm as can be expected for the publication of a rather small professional society.

The organization of each issue has remained quite stable over the past several years. There are four to six long articles, followed by one or two shorter features. A review section consists of six to ten longer reviews, about the same number of annotations (occasionally including some evaluation), and a list of other publications received. Three kinds of books are reviewed: technical material on archival, library, and information sciences; finding aids for particular collections; and books on historical practice, business management, and other subjects, which may have relationship to the role of the archivist (e.g., works on secrecy in government and business).

In keeping with its role as an official organ, each issue of *American Archivist* (*AA*) includes minutes and reports of the Society of American Archivists. A news section tends to list important recent acquisitions of libraries and archives, but also includes brief notes on state government policy changes, recent grant awards, and other items related to state and regional archive associations. An interesting feature of this section is the annual list of major document editing projects, providing a means of contact between the projects and those who might hold material of value to them. Lacking from the news sections are any "people" items—whether advertisements for new staff, or announcements of affiliation changes—that are common features of many library-oriented journals.

Most issues also include technical notes and letters to the editor. The former range from a list of new products (with annotations apparently based on manufacturers' blurbs) to brief descriptions of preservation and other archival techniques applied in specific organizations.

An interesting change in the news items has appeared over the years, with international issues taking up less and less space over time, until there is apparently little present concern with the world outside North America. This apparent reduction in scope is most readily seen in the history of the abstract section, a feature introduced in the first number, dropped during World War II, and restored in 1960. Between 1960 and 1981, the section expanded coverage, but gradually reduced its intensity, until entire issues of foreign journals (rather than individual articles) were covered in one abstract. Then, as a result of the financial problems, the feature was dropped entirely. A related phenomenon is the gradual drop in non-American articles in general, presumably not the result of funding issues.

Many issues in the last several years have been on particular themes, as opposed to the NARS period, when such focus was rare. Current themes include the role of new formats (e.g., videotape) in archives; the impact of automation, both as producer of documents and as a management tool; collection management (with a strong emphasis on greater selectivity and a need for deaccessions); and the need for cooperation. Basic theory, in particular the question of how and why to organize the collection, continues as a popular topic, as does the issue of the image and role of archivists. Rather surprisingly, in view of librarians' concern, there are few articles on preservation, especially of paper, although many of the advertisements tend to be on this topic. A tendency of many articles to draw on library experience and theory suggests that closer cooperation of archivists with librarians is a reality.

A comparison of the nature of the articles with professional library and information science journals is quite enlightening. The mix of article types is quite surprising, especially in view of the current editorial policy: the majority of articles (not only the shorter features) tend to be "how-we-do-it-good," or even "how-you-should-do-it-good," descriptions of local practice. Other than the occasional survey, the only research method in evidence is the literature review. For all practical purposes, there is no use of quantification in any form at all. While there has been (at least to this reviewer) an overemphasis on numbers in much of the library and information science literature, there is certainly a place in any field for exact (or nearly so) measurement. Thus far, at least as far as this journal is concerned, the archival profession appears to have avoided it.

The irony in this situation is quite strong, since there has been a tendency in the archival profession to look down upon librarians as "mere technicians." Few major journals in the library field have presented material on the elementary level sometimes found in *AA* in a long time. Given the general lack of formal training in archival work (a rather high percentage of archivists learned all they know on the job, having been trained as historians), there is undoubtedly a need for such instruction for many SAA members, thus explaining its presence here. On the other hand, too many of the more theoretical pieces tend to rely heavily on the personal impressions of their authors, with little reference to any empirical evidence for their validity. Since both the historians and the librarians have adopted techniques and principles of the more exact sciences, it is a little surprising that those who have so much in common with both have yet to do so.

This is not to criticize the journal—it is an accurate reflection of the concerns, needs, and methods of its readers, the members of the SAA. Maintaining a triple role of newsletter, official organ, and professional journal is not easy. After some hard times in the last few years, *American Archivist* continues to perform well in all three areas. It remains, for archivists, record managers, and those with interest in their concerns, the most important tool currently available. James H. Sweetland

392. **Aslib Information**, Vol. 1- , No. 1- . London, Association for Information Management, 1973- . 10 issues/yr. £30.00; £25.00 with membership; £25.00 (U.K.); £15.00 with membership (U.K.). ISSN 0305-0033.

Aslib Information is the house organ of Aslib—The Association for Information Management (formerly the Association of Special Libraries and Information Bureaux). The publication is primarily a regional periodical covering Aslib activities. Aslib might be best described as the British equivalent of the Special Libraries Association (SLA) in the United States, except that Aslib is more directly involved in sponsoring and conducting research. The broader scope of Aslib is reflected in the contents of *Aslib Information*. Unlike SLA's newsletter *Specialist*, which contains fewer pages and is more limited in scope, production aspects and content of Aslib's publication approach those of the news magazine *Bulletin* published by the American Society for Information Science (ASIS). In addition to being the main news publication for the ASIS, the *Bulletin* contains as standard fare brief articles of long-term interest to the information profession. *Aslib Information* also presents occasional signed articles dealing with current issues and new applications of information technologies, but to a lesser extent than the *Bulletin*. It should be pointed out that all three associations also publish journals that are outlets for scholarly articles, and that various specialized groups within these associations may also have newsletters.

Professionally printed by Abington Press Ltd. (Northampton, Great Britain), an average issue of *Aslib Information* consists of twenty-five pages containing a nominal mix of black-and-white advertisements, illustrations, and photographs. Standard sections include a column from Aslib's director, a column on information technology, general news about Aslib, and information about activities within specialized groups. Other sections include letters to the editor, occasional job notices, and professional development activities sponsored by Aslib. Items of interest to non-Aslib members include book reviews and a calendar of events. The book reviews are well done but are too few to provide a constant source of information. The calendar of events is more comprehensive and provides data on conferences several months in advance. There are sufficient numbers of meetings listed to allow foreign professionals to plan trips to England in conjunction with other activities. For the most part, *Aslib Information* is a good example of what a house organ should be, no more, no less.

Andrew G. Torok

393. **The Bottom Line: A Financial Magazine for Librarians**, Vol. 1- , No. 1- . New York, Neal-Schuman, 1986- . quarterly. $36.00/yr.; $45.00/yr. (institutions); $60.00/yr. (foreign). ISSN 0888-0454.

Pressure on librarians to be more knowledgeable about financial matters has been steadily increasing; the appearance of this publication indicates that one publisher believes the pressure is strong enough to sustain yet another specialized library journal. According to the "Charter Issue" editorial statement, the journal's purpose is to provide "clear, understandable, and practical information about library applications of financial tools and techniques" for academic, public, and special libraries. The twenty-one member editorial board reflects the interests of all three types of libraries. The editor, Betty J. Turock, is a faculty member of the School of Communication, Information and Library Studies at Rutgers University. With only one issue it is impossible to judge how good the journal will be but the content of the present issue suggests it will be a worthwhile publication, if the same quality is maintained. The format apparently will be two or three "feature" articles and eight regular columns.

The four inaugural feature articles indicate the range of topics to be covered. "Financing Library Automation," by Murry Martin, contains practical advice, while Alice Gertzog's "Gathering Grants" is a more general article on the advantages and disadvantages of using grant monies to operate a library. Catherine Reilly's "Productivity Measurement for Fiscal Control" is a how-we-did-it article rather than a review, as the title might suggest. Finally, "Employee Benefits: Emerging Trends for Librarians," by Marjorie Watson, is a good overview of what is taking place in one area of librarian compensation. Columns included are "On Account," "Alternative Funding Sources," "The Micro Edge," "Library Investing," "Economics," "Cutting Costs," "Personal Finance," and "Book Reviews." This first issue generally contained good information, but the journal will need to stay *very* current. For example, the "Personal Finance" column dealt with IRA information that is significantly modified by the 1986 Tax Reform Act. This is very much an American publication; some things will be of worldwide interest, but most of this issue's content specifically addresses American practices and needs.   G. Edward Evans

394. **The Indexer: Journal of the Society of Indexers and of the Affiliated American and Australian and Canadian Societies**, Vol. 1- , No. 1- . London, England, Society of Indexers, 1958- . semi-annual. $15.00/yr. ISSN 0019-4131. [Note: Also available with membership in the American Society of Indexers.]

Information on the history and purpose of *The Indexer* can be gleaned from the preface to the compilation *Indexers on Indexing*, a selection of articles from the journal under review, published in 1978.[1] The journal began as the organ of the [British] Society of Indexers (the first society of its kind), and is still "the only publication in England dealing solely with indexing."[2] As the editor of this compilation—a former editor of the journal—the late Leonard Montague Harrod stated, "the main objective of *The Indexer* through the years has not been to provide basic instruction.... Instead, *The Indexer* has dealt with some of the debatable problems that challenge even experienced back-of-the-book indexers."[3]

These statements of scope are examined in greater detail below, but at this point, it may be useful to indicate the difference between education and certification of indexers in the United States and England, which may explain the focus of *The Indexer*. In America, many indexers study their craft in schools of library and information science, while others are self-taught (generally book indexers) or trained on the job by serial indexing and abstracting services. In England, indexers may be *registered* after their work has been scrutinized by the Board of Assessors of the Society of Indexers, which offers a correspondence course in collaboration with the Rapid Results College. Thus, indexing is a recognized profession in Great Britain, and it is not surprising that the practitioners discuss their concerns in a specialized journal.

The subtitle of *The Indexer* has changed over the years, to reflect the affiliation of additional indexing societies with the Society of Indexers. Although ostensibly an international journal today, representing the American Society of Indexers (from volume 8, 1972), the Australian Society of Indexers (from volume 10, number 4, 1977), and the Indexing and Abstracting Society of Canada (from volume 11, number 3, 1979), the "flavor" of the journal is still decidedly British, with the majority of contributions emanating from Great Britain and relating to indexing practice in that country. This point is easily documented from the table of contents of the April 1986 issue, which includes the following articles: "The Indexing of Welsh Place Names," "Victorian and Edwardian Periodicals for Children: Some Bibliographical Problems," "A Shavian Index," and "Indexes Past: *Lady's Magazine*." Furthermore, the "Notes for Contributors" suggest the *Oxford English Dictionary* as a spelling authority and refer to a British Standard for proof correction.

The Indexer has always appeared semi-annually, but each volume includes four issues, spanning two years. The dating of issues changed from "Spring" and "Autumn" to "April" and "October" with volume 8 in 1972. There have been four editors-in-chief in the twenty-nine years of the journal's publication, the first two of short tenure: Harold Smith, 1958-1959, and John L. Thornton, 1959-1963. L. M. Harrod served from 1964 to 1978, and Hazel Bell has continued editing *The Indexer* to date.

The current statement of scope of the journal is simple: "We welcome reports of research or personal experience in indexing, and comments on indexes."[4] The reports of personal experience greatly outnumber the research reports in the periodical, however. The intended audience is the practicing indexer rather than the researcher in library or information science. Harrod's statement cited above notwithstanding, the journal and his compilation do include articles for the beginner (e.g., "Introduction to Book Indexing" and "Indexing Hints for

Beginners"). In a more recent issue, we find "What You Make It: Freelancing for the Beginner." Although the majority of subscribers are believed to be back-of-the-book indexers, the journal also includes descriptions of indexing practice for single journals; secondary (I&A) services; and other formats, such as newspapers, encyclopedias, and photograph collections. In recent volumes, there are numerous papers on computer-assisted indexing, consistent with the periodical's emphasis on techniques. Indexes in all disciplines, from the humanities to the sciences, are well represented in the pages of *The Indexer*.

Editorials in *The Indexer* often discuss the multifaceted nature of indexing and express concern that the journal may not be meeting the needs of all segments of the profession. J. D. Lee, a guest editorial writer, noted that "the first object of the Society of Indexers is to 'promote improved standards and techniques of all forms of indexing, whether of books and periodicals and other publications or of other information storage and retrieval systems.' "[5]

The periodical includes numerous book reviews, covering not only works about indexing, indexes, and thesauri, but many reference works and general library/information/computer science books as well. The last two groups sometimes get "biased" reviews — from the point of view of an indexer. For example, Hazel Bell devotes half of her review of *The Writer and the Word Processor* (April 1986) to a discussion of the three pages on indexing software in the book and a critique of its three-page index. *The Indexer*'s list of "Publications Received and Publications Noted" also includes useful annotations.

The journal has several very entertaining feature columns: "Indexers in Fiction," "Indexes Past," and "Indexes Reviewed." The latter includes excerpts from book reviews that comment on indexes, classified into three groups — "Indexes Praised," "Indexes Censured," and Indexes Omitted" — with each subarranged by publisher of the work reviewed. This column was recently mentioned in an article on the importance of indexes that appeared in a journal for publishers.[6]

Other recurring features are "Conference Reports," summarizing the highlights of various information science meetings, and "Technical Forum," which poses indexing issues and solicits opinions from readers. "Letters to the Editor" include comments on prior articles, giving authors an opportunity to respond to criticisms, as well as observations on the status of indexers and indexing. Editorials frequently address the professional concerns of indexers as well. As the journal of four societies, *The Indexer* also includes annual reports of their activities. A new feature beginning with volume 15, number 1 is "Indexing and Abstracting: A Current Awareness Bibliography" by Hans H. Wellisch, supplementing his book-length compilations.[7] The 1986 edition covers 1984 publications.

The style and quality of writing in the pages of *The Indexer* is uneven. Many papers are in the first person, including texts of speeches given to various indexing societies, as well as the "How I Index Good" articles which dominate the pages of the journal. The informal style of writing is not pointed out for criticism; it is indicative, however, of the nature and quality of the articles. They report much interesting and useful information, but very little of it is synthesized or integrated with earlier literature. As a professor of indexing and information science, this reviewer selects many articles from *The Indexer* to illustrate methods of indexing various formats (e.g., letters and encyclopedias); theoretical papers and research reports are found more often in the *Journal of Documentation, Journal of the American Society for Information Science,* and *International Classification*. Wellisch's current awareness bibliography, cited above, serves to highlight the scatter of the indexing literature. Whereas there are information theoreticians who believe that indexing is the same process as classification, most contributors to *The Indexer* associate indexing with alphabetic arrangement; the scope of the term is thus more limited in the journal under review than in general information science periodicals.

The papers in *The Indexer* feature numerous interesting ideas and pronouncements about indexing. Ironically, despite the rather detailed volume indexes, these are difficult to retrieve. A reader desirous of recalling these would have to develop a personal index. Coverage of the journal by indexing and abstracting services is impressive. As might be expected, it is indexed by *Library Literature, Information Science Abstracts,* and *Library and Information Science Abstracts.* The inside front cover of the current issue of *The Indexer* lists, in addition, coverage by *Chemical Abstracts* and INSPEC. The MARC (machine-readable cataloging) record for this serial also notes coverage by *Book Review Index.*

The journal fills a niche in the library and information science literature — serving primarily the freelance back-of-the-book indexer, with much useful material for indexers of other materials and for students and teachers of indexing. It should find a place in all library science collections and in the personal collections of professional indexers and indexing researchers and educators.

As an indicator of the value of the journal, we may cite the results of a survey conducted by the American Society of Indexers indicating that "readership interest level in *The Indexer* is high among ASI members" and that most feel that the portion of ASI dues spent on *The Indexer* is reasonable.[8] It is, in this reviewer's opinion, a highly readable and, in some ways, quaint journal that is unique in library literature—technical, but without the mathematics and Greek letters found in the more scientific journals; well focused, ensuring that most of its content will be relevant to its readers; and a lively forum on highly specific questions representing a concern for *good indexing*—a goal that should be of interest to all practitioners of library and information science.

Notes

[1] *Indexers on Indexing: A Selection of Articles Published in The Indexer*, edited by Leonard Montague Harrod for the Society of Indexers (New York: R. R. Bowker, 1978).

[2] *Indexers on Indexing*, ix.

[3] Ibid.

[4] *The Indexer* 15 (April 1986): 64.

[5] J. D. Lee, "Editorial," *The Indexer* 13 (October 1983): 217.

[6] Nancy Mulvany, "In Praise of Indexing: How to Make It Better," *Small Press* 4 (September/October 1986): 66-69.

[7] Hans H. Wellisch, *Indexing and Abstracting: An International Bibliography; Indexing and Abstracting, 1977-1981* (Santa Barbara, Calif.: ABC-Clio, 1980-1984).

[8] "*The Indexer* Survey," *ASI* [American Society of Indexers] *Newsletter* 7 (March/April 1985): 18.

Bella Hass Weinberg

395. **Information and Referral: The Journal of the Alliance of Information and Referral Systems**, Vol. 1- , No. 1- . Indianapolis, Ind., Alliance of Information and Referral Systems, 1979- . semi-annual. $20.00/yr.; $10.00/yr. (individual members of AIRS); (free with AIRS agency membership); $30.00/yr. (institutions); $7.50 (single issue). ISSN 0278-2383.

Information and Referral (*I&R*) began publication in the spring of 1979, under the auspices of the Alliance of Information and Referral Systems, Inc. (AIRS), a confederation of help groups concerned with the delivery of human services. AIRS, founded in 1973, is now a network of over 450 members, agency and individual, throughout the United States and Canada. It attempts to offer a professional "umbrella" for information and referral providers. *I&R* comes out twice a year, edited by Michael P. Speciale, of Middletown, Connecticut, and published in Indianapolis, where the AIRS national office is located. Membership may be individual or agency, and belonging to AIRS gives one a 50 percent break on the subscription cost. The AIRS editorial review board consists of eleven librarians, educators, and social workers who read all manuscripts.

The journal claims to be "concerned with practical and theoretical issues related to the impact of information and referral on the design and delivery of human services." This includes consumer concerns, such as access to information, unmet needs, grievances, and the like. The format consists of a brief editorial, which is more an introductory than declamatory or opinion statement, followed by four papers (each preceded by an abstract), a book review section and a section of "media reviews," actually an annotated bibliography. Articles are more narrative than polemic or philosophical, seemingly a means of describing successful information and referral experiences and a source of encouragement to those seeking funding, recognition, or pointers on achieving their missions. Each article provides a selective list of references for further reading. As the articles are contributed by different writers and cover different topics, there is some variation in quality, but all in the issue reviewed (vol. 7, no. 2, 1985) are packed with sound advice and lists which may be used as core collections.

Overall, this journal is a boon to all libraries, voluntary action centers, neighborhood and senior citizen centers, employee assistance programs, and other agencies, public and private, dealing with the unmet needs of groups and individuals whose voices are too seldom heard in modern society. Recommended.

Bruce A. Shuman

396. **International Review of Children's Literature and Librarianship**, Vol. 1- , No. 1- . London, Taylor Graham Publishing, 1986- . 3 issues/yr. $55.00/yr. ISSN 0269-0500.

This journal is published in Great Britain through the Department of Library and Information Studies at Loughborough University. The editorial board has an international representation of librarians and educators. The journal is "designed to explore the range of issues of current concern to those working in the field of children's literature around the world: the management of library services to children and adolescents; educational issues affecting library services; information technology; user education and the promotion of services; staff education and training; collection development and management; critical assessments of children's and adolescent literature; book and media selection; research in literature and library services for children and adolescents" (editorial statement, vol. 1, no. 1).

The first issue (Spring 1986) includes articles on in-service training, the future of children's services and school librarianship, and an examination of the changing state of childhood. The article on in-service training focuses on some specific studies and developments in the United Kingdom and their impact on the educational needs of librarians. An overview of some possible teaching strategies for in-service meetings is included. The two articles on the future of children's services and school librarianship examine the trends and attitudes that have influenced these youth services areas; they focus primarily on the situation in the United Kingdom. The article on childhood discusses the relationship between children's literature and the changing attitudes about children. This issue also includes in-depth reviews of ten books.

While the focus of this issue is decidedly British, future issues should provide a more international perspective. This journal would provide very valuable information for library school programs. The international emphasis would aid in making a comparative analysis of services to children. The articles and reviews are scholarly and would effectively meet the research needs of library school students.

Rebecca L. Thomas

397. **Journal of Documentation**, Vol. 1- , No. 1- . London, Aslib, 1945- . quarterly. £50.00 (United Kingdom); £65.00 (foreign orders). ISSN 0022-0418.

In 1945 the *Journal of Documentation* first appeared in its austere gray cover which served to identify it as a member of the society of serious scholarly journals of that time. While many journals have adopted attractive covers or jauntier titles, the *Journal of Documentation* has remained unchanged. Just as the somewhat ambiguous name and drab cover still remain, even more important, the *Journal of Documentation* continues to provide its readers with well-researched and understandable articles concerning "the recording, organization and dissemination of specialized knowledge."[1]

Aslib, a British association of special librarians and information scientists, founded the *Journal of Documentation* in 1945 at the prompting of Theodore Besterman, who then became its first editor. According to Besterman, "anything in which knowledge is recorded is a document, and documentation is any process which serves to make a document available to the seeker after knowledge."[2] This definition and its study formed the chief concern of the *Journal of Documentation* from its beginning.

Besterman's tenure as editor was brief due to his receiving the appointment of Counsellor, Bibliographical and Library Centre for UNESCO in 1946. He concluded his work as editor with the completion of volume 2 of the journal. Initially E. M. R. Ditmas, then director of Aslib, served as acting editor, with the assistance of an Aslib-appointed editorial board, from June to December 1947.[3] After that the Aslib council decided to retain the editorial board permanently and to make Ditmas managing editor, which office she continued to hold until her retirement in 1962. Succeeding managing editors of the *Journal of Documentation* have been well-known and accomplished British librarians and information scientists: Barbara Kyle (1962-1965), Herbert Coblans (1966-1977), K. Spark Jones (1978-1980), Peter J. Taylor (1981-1983), and Richard Kimber (1984-present).

The scope of the *Journal of Documentation* is far broader than might be expected from a journal that is sponsored by an association of special librarians. Although the traditional concerns of special librarians with medical, business, and technical materials frequently form the subjects of its articles, other topics also abound. Research appearing in the *Journal of Documentation* can just as frequently deal with materials of the pure sciences, social sciences, humanities, and general knowledge. Articles on classification, cataloging, indexing, and circulation are based on research in a wide variety of subjects, formats, and library settings. In addition, analyses of institutional organization and publishing patterns, discussions of developments and practices in education for librarianship and information science, and considerations about the very nature of what constitutes knowledge and information appear on the pages of this publication. Finally, the applications of the research coming out of this journal can be theoretical, practical, or both. Thus, in the tradition of Sir Francis Bacon, the *Journal of Documentation* makes all knowledge its province. As a result of this broad scope, the *Journal of Documentation* is of interest to a wide range of librarians — special, public, and academic — along with library educators.

To the first-time examiner of the *Journal of Documentation*, its contents present a formidable appearance. Arcane formulas, crowded tables, and complex graphs seem to dominate its pages. Appearances, however, are deceiving. The three or four articles that appear in each quarterly issue of the *Journal of Documentation* are written with both specialists and nonspecialists in mind. Every article is preceded by a straightforward and concise abstract. Most articles are organized as scientific papers with clear and understandable introductions to the problem and conclusions that are comprehensible to a general librarian readership. The middle of each article presents the data and complex methodologies of interest to specialist readers, as do appendices when they are appropriate. Recent issues have included articles dealing with the validity of the 80/20 rule for the circulation of library materials, trends in library and information science training, and classification using back-of-the-book indexes.

The *Journal of Documentation* also contains approximately ten to twelve signed book reviews in every issue. Generally the book reviews are five hundred to seven hundred words in length and are written by competent experts. The books reviewed cover numerous topics of librarianship from preservation and classification to library history or the sociology of knowledge.

The *Journal of Documentation* is a rare commodity in the world of library literature. It combines scholarly depth, clear writing, and a broad range of interests in a way that continues to stand out even though the general quality of research and writing on library and information science has been steadily improving. Although Theodore Besterman only spent two brief years getting the *Journal of Documentation* started, he established a tradition of fine scholarship and editing that his successors have maintained ever since.

Notes

[1] Masthead, *Journal of Documentation*.

[2] Theodore Besterman, "Introductory Note," *Journal of Documentation* 1 (June 1945): 1.

[3] C. Le Maistre, "The Editor Resigns," *Journal of Documentation* 3 (June 1947): 1-2; G. Woledge, "The Managing Editor," *Journal of Documentation* 18 (June 1962): 41.

Ronald H. Fritze

398. **Journal of the American Society for Information Science**, Vol. 1- , No. 1- . New York, John Wiley, 1949- . bimonthly. $110.00/vol.; (foreign, add postage: $27.00 surface; $82.00 airmail). ISSN 0002-8231.

The *Journal of the American Society for Information Science* (*JASIS*) is considerably more than a house organ of the society. The broad scope of the journal includes the wide, fairly traditional subject areas of information systems, information science, and all aspects of library science. Even more specifically, these fields can be narrowed down into the theory of information science; communication, management, economics, and the marketing of information; applied information science; and the social and legal aspects of information. Recently, articles have begun to appear that bring the previously defined scope even more up-to-date by including articles on artificial intelligence and information technology.

JASIS prides itself on the fact that it is a single, blind refereed journal; in other words, the author of a paper does not know the referee, but the author's name is not hidden from the reviewer. Papers are received or solicited on either theoretical or applied aspects of the subjects listed above. In addition to these articles, opinion papers can be found in the "Perspectives" section, which focuses on a different topic each time the section is published. Other sections of the journal include "Letters to the Editor" that can voice differing opinions on previously written articles, "Brief Communications," a section including short articles on important and timely topics, and a book review section.

There are a number of journals with which *JASIS* can be compared. The ones that come immediately to this reviewer's mind are *Information Technology and Libraries* (*ITAL*), *Library Resources & Technical Services* (*LRTS*), both publications issued by divisions of the American Library Association, and Haworth Press's *Technical Services Quarterly* representing the technical services and technology perspectives; and *College & Research Libraries*, another ALA divisional publication, representing the public services point of view. *JASIS* provides much broader coverage of a wider variety of subjects than does any one of the other journals cited. Furthermore, *JASIS* contains more articles focusing on pure research (in the sense that statistics are used) than do the other journals. This does not mean to say that articles of a research nature do not appear in *ITAL, LRTS, Technical Services Quarterly* or *College & Research Libraries*, nor does it mean that *JASIS* avoids articles of a descriptive nature. This is simply one aspect to consider when deciding whether or not to subscribe to *JASIS*.

Of course, the bottom line is, does *JASIS* bring an original perspective to the field of information science, or do other journals make *JASIS* superfluous? Without a doubt the money spent for a subscription to *JASIS* is well spent. The subjects covered are broader than those found in the journals previously mentioned, and give the reader a good choice in subject matter. The authors come from a wide variety of libraries or information centers. While the articles are occasionally obtuse, they offer the reader a different view of the subject matter than can be found elsewhere. A subscription to *JASIS* is essential to any library attempting to stay abreast of the ever-changing field of information science. Marjorie Bloss

399. Judaica Librarianship: A Publication of the Association of Jewish Libraries, Vol. 1- , No. 1- . New York, Association of Jewish Libraries, 1983- . semi-annual. $25.00/yr.; $18.00/yr. (students and retirees). ISSN 0739-5086.

The Judaica or Hebraica library has long been the province of the rabbi and/or scholar knowledgeable about the content of sacred books. However, this traditional librarian-scholar is no longer in adequate supply, nor necessarily suited, to serve the numerous and varied collections stimulated by increased Jewish publications, communal institutions, and courses of study. A need has arisen for professional librarians who specialize in a subject area that includes many facets: Jewish sociology and history, Jewish life in America, Israeli affairs, religion, and philosophy. The Association of Jewish Librarians (AJL), the organization that publishes the *Index to Jewish Periodicals*, inaugurated *Judaica Librarianship* (*JL*) to address the concerns of this new breed of librarian. Membership in AJL includes a subscription to *JL*; however, the journal may also be purchased separately. The editorial board includes a few names recognizable to the layperson (Dr. Schmelzer of New York's Theological Seminary and Dr. Greenbaum from the University of Haifa), but most editors will be known only to their professional colleagues. Devoted to the principles of library science, networking, automation, and international publication as they relate to material of Jewish interest, *JL* includes regular columns on childrens' literature, important special collections, library classification and cataloging, and reference tools and services. Unlike other journals of this genre, *JL* does not routinely include book reviews. Recent issues feature author and subject bibliographies (Isaac Bashevis Singer, Jewish art, the Jews in Poland and Russia), acquisitions tools, and a discussion of the day school library. These articles, which are experiential rather than research oriented, are consistently well written and practical in content. An annual index appears in the second, and final issue of each year. *JL* is indexed in the *Index to Jewish Periodicals, Index of Articles on Jewish Studies, Information Science Abstracts*, and *Library and Information Science Abstracts*. Such extensive coverage guarantees that material in the journal will be sought by library users. Librarians of appropriate collections will welcome this excellent periodical.

Margaret Norden

400. Library Currents: Your Source for Current Library Information, Vol. 1- , No. 1- . Grass Valley, Calif., Practical Perspectives, 1984- . monthly. $36.00/yr.; (add $12.00 for foreign orders); $4.00 (single issue). ISSN 0741-4188.

Published monthly in an attractive eight-page looseleaf format, *Library Currents* aims to "review and summarize library and management literature on a regular basis, to provide library managers with useful and timely information." Consequently, rather than excerpting articles and books, the editors provide the essential ideas or concepts advanced by writers in professional publications. Most items average one hundred to two hundred words in length, separated by topical headlines and ending with complete bibliographic citation and subscription information (or price).

Focus of the publication is on current topics, and current articles and books. In this, it succeeds: items selected for inclusion are written in an interesting and concise manner, keeping the perspectives of the library administrator in mind. In addition to well-rounded coverage, each issue classes together items of departmental or functional interest, for example, online catalogs, serials, public services, online searching, and so on.

At a time when time itself is at a premium, *Library Currents* offers a digest of current thought and perspectives that cuts across the many specialized areas of librarianship, presenting the reader with an overview of topics too easily missed by the limits of specialty professional journals. Another distinct advantage of subscribing to the publication is coverage of business and other professional journals that are relevant to administration in libraries. Recommended especially for those libraries where budgets preclude subscription to many professional journals; the publication has relevance to all levels of library administration.

Edmund F. SantaVicca

401. **The Reference Librarian**, Vol. 1- , No. 1- . New York, Haworth Press, 1981- . quarterly. $36.00/yr.; $75.00/yr. (institutions); (for foreign, add $10.00). ISSN 0276-3877.

When editor Bill Katz discussed his hopes for *The Reference Librarian* in its premier issue, he spoke of quality, new approaches, and new ideas. A journal which would carve out a unique niche for itself by examining specific reference problems to an extent impossible in other established titles was the goal. A perusal of the series to date gives assurance that goal has been met.

The Reference Librarian continues to approach reference concerns in single-theme issues. Broad overviews of the topics are presented while expressions of a controversial nature are not inhibited. The twenty or so articles in each issue are generally contributed by librarians from all types of libraries. Students and laypersons share their perspectives when appropriate. The emphasis is on a *unique* view tempered with experience and practicality. The prominent editorial board helps assure the expertise of the authors, who submit manuscripts by invitation only.

The flexibility to examine problems in a concentrated manner and from a variety of perspectives distinguishes *The Reference Librarian* from valued periodicals such as *RQ* and *RSR: Reference Services Review*. *RQ*'s broad range of articles and reviews on topics related to user-oriented library services and *RSR*'s topical bibliographies, reviews, and articles are not supplanted by *The Reference Librarian*; rather, its purpose and design tend to expand beyond what those journals accomplish, covering new, yet appropriate ground. In some instances the topics examined are refreshingly unique. The issue on evaluation was particularly noteworthy in filling a void. The subject of reference services for children and young adults had rarely been covered with such completeness. In most cases the themes chosen have represented problematic and challenging areas of the reference field. A quick review of upcoming issues indicates continued viability for the journal.

While the guaranteed brilliance of every article in every issue of such a monographic series is an impossibility, *The Reference Librarian* has managed to make a valuable contribution to the field of reference librarianship. The writing is of even quality and themes are thoroughly explored. The responsiveness of editors and the perceptivity of its contributing authors assures a place in the library literature for this title. As long as reference continues to challenge and change, librarians, students, and educators will find such a series useful and indeed welcome.

Patricia A. Steele

402. **School Library Media Activities Monthly**, Vol. 1- , No. 1- . Baltimore, Md., LMS Associates, 1984- . monthly (except for July and August). $40.00/yr.; $50.00/yr. (foreign). ISSN 0889-9371.

School Library Media Activities Monthly has been published since 1984, with the stated purpose of serving as a vehicle for the sharing of creative ideas used by media specialists for the teaching of library media skills. Content Editor Paula Montgomery and Managing Editor H. Thomas Walker are successful authors and editors of a number of books on the teaching of library media skills. Their experience comes through in the content of their journal. It is well edited and presents many useful ideas in an accessible format. The journal permits the photocopying of material for instructional use by the original subscriber, which is a tremendous help for busy media specialists, who may well want copies of the calendars, activities, and clip art.

Articles are brief and informative, contributed by practicing media specialists. They focus on important issues and frequently provide a cornucopia of practical activities. Regular features include the "Activities Almanac," a day-by-day calendar of the month complete with notable events, birthdays, or holidays. Brief notes on activities that can be planned around some of these events are included. "Into the Curriculum" outlines activities in more detail that can be planned together with the classroom teacher for specific curriculum units. "Sharing Skills" is just what it sounds like – a column for readers to share ideas about the teaching of specific library media skills. "Catalyst" provides a forum for outside commentary about "major philosophical issues related to teaching library media skills." "Keeping Current" reviews important materials in the field. And finally, "Computer Cache" presents articles which address new developments in the use of computers in the media center. Generally, the activities are appropriate for the K-8 age group.

The format is an easy one to use; logos identify each section, and the layout is pleasing. Covers are bright and eye catching; the interior stock is good quality and glossy. This reviewer has only one criticism concerning presentation: the open sans serif typeface is difficult to read, even in the double-column format. It works fine in the calendar, but the articles would be much more readable in a more traditional serif face.

This is a truly useful publication, particularly for the elementary media specialist. Not indexed in *Library Literature*.

Shirley Lambert

403. **Science and Technology Libraries**, Vol. 1- , No. 1- . New York, Haworth Press, 1980- . quarterly. $36.00/yr.; $72.00/yr. (institutions and libraries); (Canadian/Mexican, add $7.00; other foreign orders, add $10.00). ISSN 0194-262X.

This journal was launched, according to the editor, "simply because until now there has never been a periodical devoted entirely to science and technology libraries and information centers regardless of their type of sponsorship and regardless of the fields of science or technology with which they may be involved." Each issue focuses on a specific theme, with the articles varying in number, length, and depth of coverage. On the whole, the articles describe particular situations and do not produce a cohesive overview. Themes covered include sci-tech libraries in museums and aquariums, weeding of collections, role of computers, serving and users, fee-based services, role of serials, collection development, role of translations, role of parents, and role of technical reports.

According to the editorial policy presented in volume 1, number 1, each issue was to include an introduction written by an expert on the subject of that issue. This feature has appeared only sporadically, being replaced by an editorial or an introduction by the editor. Each issue was to provide also four special features: "Sci-Tech Online," "New Reference Works in Science & Technology," "Sci-Tech Notes," consisting of short communications, and "Letters to the Editor." The first two of these features are appearing regularly. "Sci-Tech Notes" has appeared sporadically, and only one letter has been published (Spring 1983). Two new sections have been added: "Sci-Tech in Review" was introduced in the Fall 1983 issue with the purpose of providing an annotated current awareness service; "Sci-Tech Collections," which appeared first in the Fall 1984 issue, provides "descriptions of the key literature on certain sci-tech topics of current interest." From time to time a "special paper" on some topic of special concern is also included. The editor and most of the members of the editorial board have remained unchanged. The format changed in Fall 1981 from an 8½-by-11-inch size to a more compact one. There has been a trend toward issues with more pages, with the major growth being in the "New Reference Works in Science and Technology" section.

This reviewer finds the issues dealing with the role of particular types or forms of literature specific to sci-tech collections and services more useful than broader topics which could be discussed in a variety of disciplinary settings. The special features are valuable, especially the reviews of new reference works and the guides to the literature of specific fields or topics. The editor has, on the whole, met his objectives. The question is, however, whether there are still enough themes specific to sci-tech libraries and enough authors capable of producing articles of high quality to warrant continued publication in the long term.

Helen Howard

404. **Special Collections**, Vol. 1- , No. 1- . New York, Haworth Press, 1981- . biannual. $45.00/yr.; $105.00/yr. (institutions and libraries); (add 20 percent for foreign orders). ISSN 0270-3157.

Special Collections aims to present a thorough and skillful description and current analysis of library resources, more than is available through the standard guides to special collections. The issues are theme oriented, each focusing on U.S. and Canadian collections in the arts, the sciences, the social sciences, and the humanities. These terms are interpreted broadly, so the scope of the journal encompasses a wide variety of topics including, for example, ballet and dance, aeronautics, science fiction, biochemistry, and banking and finance. Each issue describes major and unusual collections in a single field. The articles are written by authoritative contributors who cover the history, content, and unusual resources of important special collections in that field. In addition, the Library of Congress holdings in the field are reviewed, if significant. Guides to subject holdings in other U.S. and Canadian collections are noted. State-of-the-art articles and those focusing on the bibliographic control of the subject are included. Directories of other collections of the same subject are another important feature. Frequently articles by private specialist collectors, antiquarian dealers, and specialist publishers are included.

Each issue has a short foreword written by the general editor, as well as an over-all introduction to the field and to the individual issue, presented by the guest editor. Issues also include a book review section featuring books relating to the subject, and an essay-type review article covering publications of interest to special collections librarians and their users. The specialist guest editors and the Board of Advisors represent authoritative, distinguished scholars in the special collections field. The general editor, Lee Ash, is also a recognized, well-known figure in this field. Articles are scholarly, well written, clearly organized, and of high quality. Occasional black-and-white illustrations, including photographs, facsimiles, tables, and charts are included. Generous use of footnotes enhances the periodical's usefulness.

Special Collections is intended to attract not only librarians, but also "collectors and antiquarians of all kinds, as well as publishers and scholars." The wide scope and perspective of the articles achieve this end. This periodical fills a clearly defined need. It serves to strengthen and enhance scholarship and learning in the area of special collections, as well as to foster coordination of similar subject collections, and to improve methods and techniques for cooperative acquisitions by library networks and systems.

Susan J. Freiband

REGIONAL

405. **Alabama Librarian**, Vol. 1- , No. 1- . University, Ala., Tuscaloosa News, 1949- . monthly. $15.00/yr.; $5.00/yr. (Alabama Library Association members). ISSN 0002-4295.

This is the official publication of the Alabama Library Association. Currently a monthly twelve- to twenty-page tabloid-format publication, the *Alabama Librarian* was created by order of the association's Executive Council in May 1949. At that time, Mabel Willoughby was appointed the first editor. The first issue appeared in December 1949 with the charge of informing members about news of the association. During the 1970s the publication contained more research and general information articles than it previously included. The major intent, however, has remained that of reporting news of members and the organization.

In 1982, the *Alabama Librarian* assumed its current tabloid format and more rigid structure. Each division has an editor responsible for disseminating news of that division through the general newsletter. Within the *Alabama Librarian*, then, are the "College, University and Special Libraries" pages, the "Paraprofessional Roundtable" pages, etc. Most articles are short news items; scholarly articles, when they appear, generally take the form of annotated bibliographies. Members of each division contribute articles pertinent to specific divisions. Articles of general interest or announcing conferences, awards, appointments, or timely information are usually included on the first pages. One issue is a membership directory, and one is devoted almost entirely to the annual Alabama Library Association conference.

The *Alabama Librarian* has not been indexed in *Library Literature* recently; most likely this is due to its nonscholarly, reporting service function. As a newsletter, it adequately serves its purposes of keeping members informed about issues relating to Alabama libraries and librarians.

Jean Parker

406. **Bay State Librarian**, Vol. 1- , No. 1- . Nahant, Mass., Massachusetts Library Association, 1910- . semi-annual. $15.00/yr. ISSN 0005-6944.

407. **Media Forum**, Vol. 1- , No. 1- . Hanover, Mass., Massachusetts Association for Educational Media, 1977- . quarterly. $15.00/yr.

The *Bay State Librarian*, published twice a year by the Massachusetts Library Association, reflects the interests of the association membership, primarily public librarians. Each issue contains articles of philosophical substance, as well as announcements and suggestions from the Public Relations Committee. Occasional interviews, such as that with Arthur Curley, newly appointed director of the Boston Public Library, also appear. A companion publication, the *Bay State Letter*, released eight times a year, contains many more meeting notices and short articles that provide a better understanding of the scope and range of the concerns and activities of MLA members.

The *Media Forum*, the official publication of the Massachusetts Association for Educational Media, is published quarterly. Ranging in length from four to twelve pages, this newsletter offers information about meetings and institutes relevant to elementary and secondary school library media specialists. In addition, it contains numerous short notices about media-related legislation on the national as well as the state level; the broadcast schedule for educational television; an occasional listing of "quick and pithy reviews" that unfortunately omit a good deal of information necessary to make even a quick judgment about the value of the described media. Despite this last weakness, the newsletter is a useful mechanism for the membership: regular reading will provide subscribers with a succinct overview of the interests, concerns, and activities of school media specialists.

Susan S. Baughman

408. **Catalyst (Des Moines)**, Vol. 1- , No. 1- . Des Moines, Iowa, Iowa Library Association, 1948- . bimonthly. $24.00/yr.; free with membership. ISSN 0730-711X.

Catalyst is the organ of the Iowa Library Association (ILA), which has a current membership of 1,515. The circulation of *Catalyst* is around 1,800, and it is published six times yearly. The current editor is Naomi Stovall, executive assistant to the executive board of the

Iowa Library Association. There is an editorial committee but articles are not refereed, nor is *Catalyst* indexed either internally or externally.

Catalyst is the professional communication source for libraries and librarians throughout the state of Iowa and associated contiguous states. It includes information of major significance; editorials; and articles by librarians, trustees, friends, and others associated with the profession. There are classified ads from vendors, libraries, and boards as well. Typical contents include ILA news of all kinds; announcements and news from organizations, institutions, and libraries from around the state; and infrequent very brief essays, editorials, or articles. Although some older *Catalysts* included book reviews, this practice has more recently been abandoned. Most issues are between twelve and sixteen pages long.

The quality of writing and layout is good. Information is clear and to the point. Most photographs are of adequate quality but are primarily head-shots of people in the news. There is a dearth of graphics or visual creativity. As a brief, well-produced newsletter, *Catalyst* makes an indispensable contribution to its constituency.   James Rice

409. CMLEA Journal: The Official Publication of the California Media and Library Educators Association, Vol. 1- , No. 1- . Burlingame, Calif., California Media and Library Educators Association, 1977- . semi-annual (minimum). $15.00/yr.; free with membership; $15.50/yr. (Canada and Mexico); $16.00/yr. (other foreign). ISSN 0196-3309.

CMLEA Journal is the official publication of the California Media and Library Educators Association, and shares its birthdate with its sponsoring organization. Its frequency has changed from quarterly to semi-annual in the course of its ten-year existence but this is a minor change, indeed, for any publication of a new organization. A subscription to the journal is included as a benefit of membership in the association. The journal addresses current issues of concern to librarians and media specialists working in educational institutions in California. *CMLEA Journal* has editorials in each issue on topics of interest to library and media educators in California. It usually features substantial and practical articles which address various aspects of a current educational or political issue in which the editors make an explicit effort to represent various points of view. Other articles summarize and interpret current research in educational theory. Still others describe successful methodologies employed in library or media centers.

Illustrative material is sparse but the editorial staff pays careful attention to typography and layout and has created an attractive magazine. It is clear that the editors have also set high standards for the quality and type of article published. They have, moreover, successfully maintained those standards throughout the journal's existence. While *CMLEA Journal* is an official publication of a California library and educational organization, it frequently contains articles which are sufficiently general to interest library educators in other states. For example, "Worthy of Note," a column in each issue, is a selected, annotated bibliography of recent ERIC publications related to library and media education. Although it is the official publication of a highly specialized organization, librarians in other specializations may well find topics of interest in many issues of *CMLEA Journal*. It goes far beyond the simple reporting of organizational activities to which similar publications limit themselves. Its political commentary is feisty and cogent. It is a fine example of a regional professional journal.

Margaret McKinley

410. Connecticut Libraries, Vol. 1- , No. 1- . Hartford, Conn., Connecticut Library Association, 1958- . 11 issues/yr. $25.00/yr. ISSN 0010-616X.

After years of change and some struggle, *Connecticut Libraries*, the "official newsletter of the Connecticut Library Association," has evolved into a publication that seems to have found its place and its most effective format and style.

Begun in 1958, the magazine has a circulation of about 850 and charges $25.00 per year for nonmember subscriptions. It is a monthly (eleven times a year), is not indexed in *Library Literature*, is illustrated with three to four photographs/drawings per issue, accepts advertisements (usually two to four per issue), and is well edited by David Kapp, a long-time senior library administrator at the University of Connecticut. The newsletter contains articles of interest to Connecticut libraries and librarians, but nowhere mentions its precise policies and goals. The state library issues its own publication, the *Connecticut State Library Newsletter*.

Connecticut Libraries used to be a small quarterly issue, fifty pages long. In the early 1980s it became taller and "snappier" in appearance, but remained quarterly and fairly "quiet," and was still sent via slow third class mail. In August 1982, in order to more quickly and clearly inform its readers, the Connecticut Library Association decided to merge *Connecticut Libraries* with CLA's small, amateurish-looking monthly, *CLA Memo*. In March 1985, *Connecticut Libraries* added glossy paper, appealing crisp headlines and layout, and a striking purple masthead on the top of page 1. This now very attractive, slim newsletter is distributed via first class mail. Issues are usually eight to twelve pages long, although longer issues come out at CLA election and conference times.

A typical eight-page issue is arranged in the following format: first page, feature story; second page, an "Opinion" or "The Gadfly" column discussing a current/controversial issue; third page, "The President's Column," an article by the current CLA president; fourth page, "Around the State," on grants and workshops; fifth page, "ALA News & Notes" column together with "People" column, or perhaps four one-paragraph news items; sixth and seventh pages, a second feature article and the rest of the page 1 feature, or else a page of conference/meeting boxes to be clipped/mailed in; eighth page, calendar of events and CLA membership blank form.

Recent feature articles included one on the children's literature collection at the University of Connecticut; one on problems with medical reference; another on problems with legal reference; "The Cost of Shortchanging Children's Librarianship"; one on the pros and cons of the new statewide automation networks; "Research Instruction in Connecticut's Academic Libraries" (a survey on bibliographic instruction); and "Literacy Volunteers in Connecticut."

Starting with the September 1984 issue, *Connecticut Libraries* became much more controversial. At that time, CLA President Michael Simonds began a column, "Simonds Says," that attempted to goad various Connecticut library institutions into renewal and action. Simonds did not inaugurate his column timidly—he "attacked" the only ALA-accredited library school in the state. These critical articles enhanced the newsletter's image and have "inspired" Connecticut librarians to read the newsletter much more than in past decades.

Connecticut Libraries is attractive, quick and easy to read, and answers everything a Connecticut librarian needs to know to be informed. There are two criticisms one might voice: there are very few scholarly articles in the publication (one or none in each issue), and those that do appear are often written by a small "inbred" group of CLA regulars. The inbreeding is a fact with nearly all U.S. state library association publications—it is always the same few who are willing to work and think. The lack of scholarly articles is probably due to CLA's choosing to "go newsletter" rather than "journal" in the publication's scope. Although this was indeed the correct choice, CLA might eventually aim to stretch this newsletter to a twelve- or sixteen-page issue length to "force" the inclusion of more feature articles.

As it now exists, *Connecticut Libraries* is an excellent publication that meets its unstated purpose in excellent form. It should serve as a model to all state library associations on how to produce a cheap and short but very attractive and effective monthly library publication.

Thomas C. Clarie

411. **Florida Media Quarterly**, Vol. 1- , No. 1- . Tallahassee, Fla., Florida Association for Media in Education, 1974- . quarterly. $20.00/yr.

Florida Media Quarterly, the official publication of the Florida Association for Media in Education, has been published quarterly since 1974, when the organization was first formed by uniting three separate groups, the Florida Association for School Librarians, Florida Audiovisual Association, and Florida Educational Television Association. *FMQ* is included with membership in FAME, but many subscriptions are held by others at the rate of $20.00 per year. *FMQ* contains articles of interest to those involved in the broad field of media in education, including school library media specialists, media technicians, instructional designers, instructional media personnel at all levels, and those involved in the training of media professionals. The content of the journal reflects the current needs and activities of the members of FAME, and its focus has continued to change as the organization has grown and the profession has changed.

Articles are usually submitted by members or solicited from the membership of FAME and are practical and creative rather than philosophical or scholarly. Several issues each year are "theme related" while others have a broad range of articles. Notable past issues have included these themes: personal and professional development, media and exceptional education, video production and applications, computers in the media center, media and vocational education, and highlights of annual conferences. The periodical also provides members with each year's legislative platform, scholarship applications, nomination forms for FAME offices, minutes of the executive board meetings, and a column by the president of the association. *FMQ* has no book reviews.

Florida Media Quarterly is a slick, impressive looking publication. It is 8½ by 11 inches in size and well illustrated with line drawings and occasional photographs. The periodical has won several awards from the Florida Magazine Association. One of the best state journals in educational media, *FMQ* serves its members and subscribers well.

Donna Toler Baumbach

412. **HASL Newsletter**. Honolulu, Hawaii Hawaii Association of School Librarians, 1960- . irregular. free with membership.

The *HASL Newsletter*, published by the Hawaii Association of School Librarians, is primarily designed to inform members of the activities and concerns of this exceptionally active organization. The circulation is approximately 270 copies. Since timeliness is of primary importance for such a mission, it is published irregularly in a photocopied and stapled format which mixes various typescripts and dot matrix prints. Despite this combination, it is an attractive publication, often livened with computer-output graphics. Each issue contains a calendar of events for HASL members, conference details, and news items of interest to Hawaii's school librarians.

It complements, rather than competes with, the Hawaii Library Association's *HLA Newsletter*. Its intended audience is confined to school librarians, and since it is designed to keep this group up-to-date on their organization and the educational milieu in which they function, it is generally of minimal interest to librarians outside the school environment and in areas other than Hawaii. It does, however, maintain good editorial standards and sometimes contains editorials, comments, and observations which would be of interest to school librarians throughout the United States.

Larry N. Osborne

413. **Hawaii Library Association Journal**, Vol. 1- , No. 1- . Honolulu, Hawaii, Hawaii Library Association, 1944- . annual. free with membership. ISSN 0017-8586.

Like most state library association publications, the *HLA Journal* has varied over the years, both in content and in style, depending upon funds, membership interest, and skills of the editors. Quality has generally been good, however, and despite being the official organ of the Hawaii Library Association, it has never succumbed to the temptation to be a gossip sheet for the organization. Instead, each annual edition has between five and ten usually well-written articles. Most of these deal with librarianship from a Hawaiian perspective (e.g., "The Impact of AACR2 on Hawaiian Place and Corporate Names"), but many are only loosely connected to library practice. Past issues have included historical studies, genealogical works, biographical sketches, and oral history materials covering Hawaii and the Pacific region. These are often written by long-time residents with access to unique collections of local materials.

While such materials do not make up the majority of each issue, they do provide a very attractive spice, and could easily justify a subscription for any non-Hawaiian library with interest in the area. The coverage of *HLA Journal* is wider than the state proper; it also publishes articles describing libraries and library practice in other Pacific Rim countries, as well as Asia, U.S. possessions, and the Pacific Islands. At least twice in the past it has attempted to compile comprehensive lists of library and information centers in Hawaii and the Pacific Islands.

The *HLA Journal* is indexed in *Library Literature* and *Library and Information Science Abstracts*. It is issued in a stapled 5½-by-10-inch two-color format, and in recent years has often included photographs.

For librarians in Hawaii the *HLA Journal* is a must. Elsewhere, it is primarily of interest to those who are professionally tied to the Pacific region, or who simply have a longing to practice their profession in the tropics and tradewinds.

Larry N. Osborne

414. **Hawaii Library Association Newsletter**, Vol. 1- , No. 1- . Honolulu, Hawaii, Hawaii Library Association, May 1958- . quarterly. free with membership.

An attractive, two-color publication in an 8½-by-11-inch format, the *Hawaii Library Association Newsletter* is primarily designed to communicate association interests and policy to its membership, which includes librarians representing all types of libraries.

Most of the content of the *Newsletter* is made up of calendar items and reports of the activities of various sections of the Hawaii Library Association: "Children and Youth," "College and University," "Federal," "Hawaiiana," "Special and Reference," and "Technical and General Services." Each issue also includes an editorial from the association's president and a feature, "In the Spotlight," which often profiles a local librarian, and always includes short summaries of the activities of selected librarians. Extensive coverage is provided of the issues and events of the association's twice-yearly conferences, including full coverage of the often nationally known major speakers' addresses.

While having no pretensions of being a scholarly journal, the *HLA Newsletter* does include reviews of books and other materials of interest to Hawaii's librarians as well as information about the national context in which Hawaii's concerns and issues exist. It is more general in scope than the Hawaii Association of School Librarians' *HASL Newsletter* (see entry 412), and defers publication of article-length items to the association's *HLA Journal* (see entry 413).

The *Newsletter* has recently switched from mimeograph reproduction to offset, and, coupled with attractive typesetting and layout, this produces an exceptionally attractive publication. This shift has also permitted increased use of high-quality photographs, and allows it to compare favorably with other state organizations' publications of the newsletter type.

Larry N. Osborne

415. **IAME News for You**, Vol. 1- , No. 1- . Chicago, Illinois Association for Media in Education, 1956- . quarterly. free with membership.

416. **ILA Reporter**, Vol. 1- , No. 1- . Chicago, Illinois Library Association, 1962- . bimonthly. free with membership. ISSN 0018-9979.

417. **Illinois Libraries**, Vol. 1- , No. 1- . Springfield, Ill., State Library, 1919- . monthly. free. ISSN 0019-2104.

News for You, the official newsletter of the Illinois Association for Media in Education, a section of the Illinois Library Association, is issued in the fall, winter, spring, and summer. This well-done publication varies in length from twelve to sixteen pages as it strives to meet its purposes of informing members of the association's programs and activities and of trends and developments within the school library media field in Illinois, and of serving as a medium for the exchange of ideas and viewpoints.

ILA Reporter, the newsletter of the Illinois Library Association, is scheduled to be published every other month but appears intermittently throughout the year. Consisting of eight pages printed on newsprint, this utilitarian publication attempts to keep members informed about the activities of the association and its sections.

Illinois Libraries, the respected publication of the Illinois State Library, is published monthly except July and August. Each year issues are dedicated to reports of the Illinois library systems, public library statistics, reports of the Illinois Library Association, and a miscellaneous issue which provides articles on a variety of unrelated topics. The remaining issues are devoted to single topics covering a wide variety of subjects. Past issues have dealt with such topics as genealogical collections, school library media services, library law, and technical services. Articles tend to be reflective or retrospective, suitable for reference rather than news.

Donald C. Adcock

418. **Indiana Media Journal**, Vol. 1- , No. 1- . Terre Haute, Ind., Association for Indiana Media Educators, 1978- . quarterly. $10.00/yr.; free with membership. ISSN 0164-7660.

This quarterly journal is the official publication of the Association for Indiana Media Educators. Publication began in the fall of 1978. *IMJ* succeeds *Hoosier School Libraries*, which began publication in 1961. Contributions are encouraged from AIME members and other practicing school library media personnel. Attempts are made to have several articles each year written by someone outside of Indiana. *Indiana Media Journal* provides practicing school library media personnel with an opportunity to publish, provides practical information on current trends in the field, and exposes the readers to new ideas or different points of view. The magazine provides a variety of informational, how-to-do-it articles, news items about events affecting school librarians, and association news. The quality of the writing is consistently good throughout the issues. The editors do an excellent job of providing worthwhile, usable information and ideas. *Indiana Media Journal* is an exemplary periodical in the category of state publications. The publication is indexed in *Library Literature*.

Joanne Troutner

419. **Iowa Media Message**, Vol. 1- , No. 1- . Ames, Iowa, Iowa Educational Media Association, 1972- . 4 issues/yr. $15.00/yr. (with membership).

The *Iowa Media Message* (*IMM*) is the official instrument of the Iowa Educational Media Association (IEMA), formerly the Iowa Association of School Librarians. The current membership of IEMA is 553 and the current editor of *IMM* is Don Rieck of the Media Resources Center of Iowa State University, Ames, Iowa. The current circulation is around 600.

IMM is much like many state media association organs. Most issues are about twenty pages long with occasional inserts of conference announcements, letters from the president, or news updates. Typical contents include items such as conference information, president's and officers' reports, committee and task force reports, news announcements, minutes from important meetings, awards, editorials, book reviews, articles written by practitioners, and a good deal of advertising.

The quality of writing and editing is high. News items as well as articles are to the point, readable, and informative. Cartoons, photographs, tables, and a variety of other graphics frequent the pages. Key information such as dates, places, and contact people are well highlighted and the format is attractive.

As a brief professional newsletter, there is no internal or external index but even so, this journal makes an indispensable contribution to its constituency. James Rice

420. **Kentucky Libraries**, Vol. 1- , No. 1- . Paducah, Ky., Kentucky Library Association, 1933- . quarterly. $12.00/yr. ISSN 0732-5452.

Kentucky Libraries, which began publication in 1933 as *KLA Bulletin*, has been published under its current title since 1980. Although its name has changed, its purpose and coverage have remained essentially the same. *Kentucky Libraries* is the official publication of the Kentucky Library Association (KLA), and as such exists primarily as a source of news and information of concern to members. The news items commonly report on state conferences, activities of the various divisions and committees of the association, and library programs and people in the state. Although the association is made up of members from all types of libraries, *Kentucky Libraries* has in the past appealed generally to an audience of public and school librarians. In recent years, this emphasis has shifted somewhat, and currently issues of interest to special and academic librarians receive greater coverage than they did previously.

A typical issue contains a report from the KLA president, two or three short feature articles, conference previews or highlights, news of association and member business, and a calendar of events. Personnel news and book reviews are also standard features; a recent recurring column is "Kentucky Kaleidoscope," which reviews books about the state. Another standard inclusion is an annual membership manual and directory, which is published concurrently with the summer issue.

Contributors are encouraged to include graphics with their submissions, and photographs are commonplace in *Kentucky Libraries*. It is a small journal; the issues average thirty pages in length and generally contain more pages of news than of feature articles. The articles, which average about three pages, are usually written by Kentucky librarians and tend to be of a general rather than a scholarly, specialized, or technical nature. Examples of typical articles are tributes, reports of innovative programs in member libraries, and articles discussing applications of new technologies. The latter are not always on the cutting edge; for example, a 1986 article states that online searching is the key to grappling with the information explosion, going on to explain what bibliographic databases are and how information is retrieved from them. Occasionally research articles appear, such as a recent report on a regional survey of children's reading interests. *Kentucky Libraries*'s feature articles are of some interest, serving as an excellent source of practical ideas and information for KLA members. The majority of articles provides examples of successful solutions to common problems. However, this journal is most valuable for its local and regional news and its coverage of the Kentucky Library Association itself. *Kentucky Libraries* has a circulation of twelve hundred and is indexed in *Library Literature*. Emily L. Werrell

421. **LLA Bulletin**, Vol. 1- , No. 1- . Baton Rouge, La., Louisiana Library Association, 1937- . quarterly. free with membership; $10.00/yr. (out-of-state). ISSN 0024-6867.

The *LLA Bulletin* served originally as a newsletter with some articles. It has since expanded into a full journal, but maintains some of the functions of a newsletter. Its quarterly format precludes its use as a "news" conveyer, but does allow for some in-depth articles on a variety of topics designed to appeal to anyone with an interest in librarianship, especially Louisiana librarianship. It contains official statements of the Louisiana Library Association, rosters of committees and divisions, and a directory of membership. In addition, information provided by the association president, executive director, ALA councilor, and other officers is sometimes included. Articles are descriptive and tend to be scholarly. Trusteeship and school librarianship are generally overlooked. Excellent coverage of political and economic aspects of public librarianship and of academic and special library topics is provided.

The *Bulletin* also includes lengthy reviews of items which are of interest to Louisianians, especially items not likely to be reviewed elsewhere. Selection of materials to be reviewed is through the Louisiana Literary Award Committee. The quality of the writing is good. Because reviews are long, there are only a few in each issue.

The *Bulletin* has added columns which are of consistently high quality. Two theme issues per year have addressed such topics as literacy in Louisiana, funding Louisiana libraries, and oral history in Louisiana libraries.

The format is professional; quality of the photographs varies. *LLA Bulletin* compares favorably with other state vehicles, and occasionally rises above most professional journals.

Linda Leveque Bennett

422. **Maine Memo**, Vol. 1- , No. 1- . Augusta, Maine, Maine Library Association, 1979- . monthly. free with membership.

Maine Memo is the newsletter of the Maine Library Association. Although it is scheduled to be published monthly, in the past few years it has appeared approximately seven times a year at intervals of one to two months. It should not be confused with the association's more substantial quarterly, *Down East Libraries*. Each issue of the *Memo* consists of a single, legal-sized sheet of photocopied text. With the exception of occasional "printers' devices" there are no illustrations. The publication schedule varies and there have been errors in the numbering scheme. The May 1986 and June 1986 issues are both labeled Volume 8, Number 3.

The major purpose of the *Memo* is to report on current Maine library news and the statewide impact of national library developments. The *Memo* meets this goal. Typical issues note upcoming special events, list job vacancies, report on positions recently filled, describe duplicate or unwanted materials offered to other libraries, comment on library-related news from the state government, and digest announcements from the Maine Library Association and area libraries. Maine libraries of all types are represented. Information is presented in the form of brief announcements rather than lengthy articles. The *Memo* is short, easy-to-read, and unpretentious. Together with *Down East Libraries*, it should be required reading for anyone interested in keeping up with the Maine library scene.

Thomas H. Patterson

423. **The Newsletter, California Library Association**, Vol. XXI- , No. 10- . Sacramento, Calif., California Library Association, 1979- . monthly. free with membership. ISSN 0199-1299.

This newsletter is popularly called *CLA Newsletter*. To be accurate, however, it held this title from volume 3, number 2, in 1961 to volume 13, number 5, in 1971. It is now called *The Newsletter, California Library Association*. It began publication as *Current Library Affairs* in March 1959, carrying this title through volume 3, number 1, in 1961. In addition to its title changes, it has also undergone a number of frequency changes. Presently issued monthly, with combined July/August issues, there have been as few as four issues per year in the past. In 1959, as *Current Library Affairs*, the newsletter was mimeographed, its frequency was irregular, and it was intended to serve as a means of communication with the association's membership. Editorial matter included association news; miscellaneous news items about the members themselves; reports of meetings; news about relevant legislative activities; noteworthy acquisitions by California libraries; and announcements of job vacancies, scholarships, and internships available as well as association news. By 1965, the newsletter was printed on an offset press and had acquired a more professional look. By 1968, news items about individual members had vanished and there was more emphasis on association and legislative news. News items frequently included analyses or more descriptive details. At present, *The Newsletter* is the chief means by which association business is communicated to its members, so that reports of association business, news notes, and meeting announcements form the bulk of the editorial matter. In addition, it disseminates current information about California libraries and legislation. There are brief notes describing recent publications as well as a few occasional special features.

In the past two years, there have been explicit efforts to revitalize what had become a prosaic newsletter. Recent additions include "CSL Research Roundup," which highlights California-based library research and is written by the Chair of the California Society of Librarians Research Committee. Separately numbered "occasional papers," which are thoughtful discussions of library trends in California, have also appeared. The newsletter is now, as always, an 8½-by-11-inch newsletter-style publication whose illustrative material is limited to line drawings, graphs, and charts. In view of the fact that its editorial turnover is high, its prose style has been consistently good over the past ten years. Throughout its publication history, *The Newsletter* has taken the initiative in informing its readers about major legislative and public issues related to libraries in California. Skimming issues for the past twenty-six years or so, one is able to review California legislative history for this period as it applies to libraries, books, and publishing. *The Newsletter* serves a vital function in California, informing librarians in California about their libraries and related public issues.

Margaret McKinley

Part IV
ABSTRACTS OF LIBRARY SCIENCE DISSERTATIONS

Abstracts of Library Science Dissertations

Gail A. Schlachter

INTRODUCTION

Unlike the commercially produced monographs, reference books, and journals described elsewhere in this edition of *Library Science and Information Annual*, doctoral dissertations are cloaked by fragmented and sluggish bibliographic announcements and distribution channels. While it is possible to contact library schools at the end of each year to identify dissertations completed there during that year, the only way to learn about dissertations dealing with library and library-related topics that were prepared outside of library schools is to wait until they are listed in *Dissertation Abstracts International* (*DAI*). However, dissertations completed in the third and fourth quarter of one year are frequently not included in *DAI* until the third or fourth quarter of the next year. As a result, it was impossible to review dissertations completed in 1986 and meet the manuscript submission date for this edition of *LISCA*. Thus, this volume provides a review of the 1985 dissertations and, similarly, each subsequent volume will cover dissertations completed in a previous year.

To date, 83 library, information, and related dissertations completed in 1985 have been identified. To place those doctoral studies in perspective, the following quantitative profile is modeled after the statistical analysis provided in Schlachter and Thomison's *Library Science Dissertations, 1925-1972: An Annotated Bibliography* (Libraries Unlimited, 1974) and *Library Science Dissertations, 1973-1981: An Annotated Bibliography* (Libraries Unlimited, 1982).

Completion Data

On the average, 14 dissertations were completed each year between 1925 and 1972. From 1973 through 1981, the yearly average increased 800 percent, to 111 dissertations per year. The number of dissertations completed in 1985 (83) was down substantially from both the 1972 to 1981 yearly average and the totals reported in the previous two editions of *Library Science Annual*: 102 in 1984 and 120 in 1985.

Sponsoring Schools

The 83 dissertations reviewed for this edition of the *Annual* were completed at 37 private and public institutions of higher learning in the United States and Canada, less than one-third the number of schools involved in the total production of library and library-related dissertations between 1973 and 1981. The six "top" producing universities, responsible for over 50 percent of the doctoral studies reviewed for 1985, are Case Western Reserve University (14 percent), University of Pittsburgh (14 percent), Indiana University (8 percent), Florida State University (5 percent), University of Illinois (5 percent), and Texas Woman's University (5 percent). Only Case Western Reserve University, University of Illinois, and University of Pittsburgh were also listed as top producers in this section of the *Library Science Annual* analysis last year.

Degrees Received

Following the pattern set between 1925 and 1981, the Ph.D. remained the most commonly earned degree (83 percent) in 1985, followed by the Ed.D. (14 percent), and the D.B.A. (3 percent). Although in past years other degrees (e.g., D.L.A., D.Ed.) were also represented in the dissertations reviewed, to date none have been reported for studies completed in 1985.

Methodology Employed

As in the analyses reported by Schlachter and Thomison in the two volumes of *Library Science Dissertations*, each of the 83 dissertations completed in 1985 was placed into one of seven research categories: citation/content analysis, experimental design, theoretical treatment, operations research (systems analysis and all forms of information storage and retrieval), survey research (case studies, mailed questionnaires, interviews), historical analysis (including biographies and bibliographies), and other (including those dissertations for which insufficient information was available to determine methodology employed). The ranking of research methodologies employed in the 83 dissertations completed during 1985, from most to least used, is survey research (57 percent), citation/content analysis (15 percent), operations research (13 percent), experimental design (7 percent), historical analysis (6 percent), theoretical treatment (1 percent), and other (1 percent). This ranking of methodologies is almost identical to the rankings (as well as the percentages) reported in this section of *Library Science Annual* last year. The only real difference noted was in the area of citation/content analysis, which increased from 10 percent to 15 percent of the dissertations reported for 1985.

Sex

Although women have consistently constituted the majority of practicing librarians, they authored only a minority of library, information, and related dissertations from 1925 to 1979. It was not until 1980 (and again in 1981) that women were responsible for over half of the dissertations completed. In 1983, however, this situation was reversed; only 45 percent of the dissertations reviewed for that year were written by women. The trend continued in 1984 and 1985, when 46 percent and 47 percent of the doctorates earned, respectively, went to women.

Summary

Using the results of this quantitative analysis, it is possible to develop a profile of the library and information science dissertations completed in 1985. As in the preceding 50-year period, the typical dissertation continued to be written for the Ph.D. degree by a male using survey research methods at one of a handful of major universities in the United States.

Because of space limitations, it is not possible to describe each of the 83 dissertations covering library, information, and related topics that was completed in 1985. Instead, 40 of these dissertations—chosen because of their quality, interest, relevance, or representativeness—are abstracted below.

ABSTRACTS

424. Bailey, Robert H. (Ed.D., Brigham Young University, 1985). **Computer Technology in California School Library Media Centers: An Assessment of Needs and Applications, 1984.** 323p. Order no. DA8603363.

PURPOSE: The purpose of this study was to determine the difference between media center librarians' anticipated and actual use of computers.

PROCEDURE: Looking at literature published primarily since 1980, Bailey reviewed the development and current status of automation in library media centers. He also surveyed a random sample of 1983-1984 members of the California Media and Library Educators Association to assess their views on the need for computers to handle library operations (e.g., acquisitions, inventory, cataloging, reference) and their ranking of the value of sources of information on automation.

FINDINGS: Computer assistance is helpful for such general library service functions as acquisitions, inventory, cataloging, reference, networking, managerial support, and computer-based education.

CONCLUSIONS: Although there is a definite need for automation to strengthen school library media centers, applications are still in their formative stages.

RECOMMENDATIONS: Bailey presented a number of recommendations for in-service education and intersegmental development of more advanced integrated library systems for schools (involving the computer industry, educational agencies, and library media centers).

425. Baker, Sharon Lynn (Ph.D., University of Illinois, 1985). **An Exploration into Factors**

Causing the Increased Circulation of Displayed Books. 261p. Order no. DA8500119.

PURPOSE: In an attempt to determine why book displays result in increased usage, Baker compared the circulation of fiction titles labeled "recommended" with those in prime display areas, in nonstrategically placed display areas, and on the regular shelves.

PROCEDURE: A standard pretest/posttest experimental design was used at two small public libraries in Illinois. Baker also interviewed by telephone patrons checking out titles being studied.

FINDINGS: Prime display location, resulting in increased accessibility and visibility, was shown to be a causal element. The "recommended" label was not.

CONCLUSIONS: Libraries interested in increased circulation should establish book displays in high traffic locations, so that the titles will be accessible and visible to large numbers of patrons.

RECOMMENDATIONS: Labeling "recommended" titles to narrow the browser's choice of materials may work better in a large library than in the small libraries surveyed in this study; therefore, Baker recommended that this approach be studied further.

426. Boals, David Michael (Ph.D., University of Southern California, 1985). **Levels of Work and Responsibility in Public Libraries.** (Copies available exclusively from Micrographics Department, Doheny Library, University of Southern California, Los Angeles, CA 90089-0182).

PURPOSE: The operational definitions for time span of discretion (TSD) and felt fair pay (FFP) developed by Jacques were used in this study to identify and measure the levels of work and responsibility that exist in public library jobs.

PROCEDURE: Public libraries in Southern California serving various population sizes formed the study population. Interviews were conducted to collect data on TSD (80 cases) and FFP (55 cases). Frequency distributions and correlation coefficients were used to analyze the data.

FINDINGS: The longest assigned task for most of the public library job holders interviewed (94 percent) was one year or less. Similarly, most professional employees (87 percent) operated within the first baseline strata of professional responsibility (from three months to one year in their longest assignments). TSD and FFP strongly correlated (.90).

CONCLUSIONS: The finding that public library job holders generally operated within the first baseline strata of responsibility should be taken into account when library management and library educators develop models for planning, organization, evaluation, and career progression. FFP and TSD can provide objective bases for measuring levels of responsibility and corresponding fair payment levels, not only in public libraries but in other bureaucratic organizations as well.

427. Broadway, Marsha Denise (Ph.D., Florida State University, 1985). **Self-Directed Instruction in Query Formation and Presentation for College Students.** 205p. Order no. DA 8524597.

PURPOSE: This study examined the relationship between self-directed instruction and the quality of query formation/presentation among college students.

PROCEDURE: Broadway employed a quasiexperimental method, based on a pretest/posttest design. Students enrolled in a library-sponsored undergraduate bibliographic instruction course at one academic institution were the subjects. They were divided into a control group (receiving no instruction in query formation/presentation) and an experimental group (receiving a self-directed instructional text on query formation/presentation). Pretest scores were used as covariates; posttest scores were submitted to analyses of covariance. A follow-up evaluation was conducted ten weeks after the posttest with five members of the experimental group.

FINDINGS: The following hypothesis was supported at the .10 level of significance: College students receiving instruction in query formation/presentation would be more able than students not receiving instruction to distinguish between ready reference and research queries, to generate ready reference queries that match information needs, to generate research queries that match information needs, to generate research queries that contain presentation elements, and to state reference librarians' major functions in assisting information seekers.

CONCLUSIONS: Query formation/presentation can be taught through self-directed instruction. This instruction can effectively improve students' abilities in query formation/presentation and can clarify the role of librarians attempting to assist information seekers.

428. Casey, James Benjamin (Ph.D., Case Western Reserve University, 1985). **Assessment of Quality in Book Selection: An Evaluation of the Effectiveness of Opinions Rendered by Peer Reviews in American History Journals.** 215p. Order no. DA8525259.

PURPOSE: It was the purpose of this study to examine the relationship between the evaluations offered of American history books (in the book reviews presented in American history journals between 1970 and 1975) and the actual acceptance of these books by historians and librarians during subsequent years.

PROCEDURE: Casey examined the reviews of one hundred American history books published between 1970 and 1975 in American history journals. He measured the correlation between the earliest dated review opinion and the consensus of all history journal review opinions, and he compared the number of positive and negative review opinions with quantifiable measures of acceptance.

FINDINGS: The correlation between the earliest dated review opinion and the consensus of all history journal review opinions in this study was .546. Relatively weak correlations were found between overall review opinions and evidence of "use-success." The first qualitative assessment offered in a review journal (such as *Choice*) was found to be more helpful than the first history journal review opinion in reflecting subsequent frequency of use. History journal review opinions tended to be more positive than negative (82 to 18 ratio).

CONCLUSIONS: The earliest assessment of a history book can offer a fair indication of subsequent review opinion. Review opinions of new American history books, however, are not especially helpful as predictors of the future use of those books. The overwhelmingly positive nature of book reviews in American history journals is in keeping with the findings of book reviewing practices in other fields. The predominance of positive reviews could be a major factor in reducing the importance of qualitative assessments in the selection process.

429. Caswell, Jerry Vaughn (Ph.D., University of Wisconsin, 1985). **Factors Governing the Amount of Duplication in Content Derived Keys.** 144p. Order no. DA8501573.

PURPOSE: While past literature on truncated search keys has focused on the retrieval performance of a limited number of formulas, this dissertation examined the characteristics governing duplication in content derived keys.

PROCEDURE: A number of different formulas were tested on both small files (one thousand author and title records) and one large file (eighty thousand records).

FINDINGS: The rate of duplication for a given formula increased with file size; as the length of a key decreased, the number of duplicates increased. Component position (especially the first component) had some effect in reducing duplication. Duplication was also reduced as the number of components in the key was increased. There were considerable differences between straight duplication and weighted duplication (where an increasingly severe penalty was assigned for every succeeding degree of duplication) when formulas of one, two, three, and four components were used. Formulas with five components produced exact correspondence between the two duplication scales. The most effective eight-character formula for reducing duplication (no formula completely eliminated duplication) was 4,1,1,1,1.

CONCLUSIONS: The findings can be used in the development of logical or primary record keys for bibliographic files with relational database management systems on small computers in libraries.

430. Ciliberti, Anne C. (Ph.D., Rutgers University, 1985). **The Development and Methodological Study of an Instrument for Measuring Material Availability in Libraries.** 224p. Order no. DA8604810.

PURPOSE: In order to determine academic library patrons' purposes, motivations, and satisfaction in subject card catalog searches, Ciliberti developed an instrument to measure material availability, and measured the usefulness of the instrument in both obtrusive and unobtrusive measurement situations.

PROCEDURE: Ciliberti expanded the branching technique for known-item search outcomes developed by Kantor and others by adding a second branch for subject search outcomes in her measurement instrument. She then calculated separate performance measures for known-item and subject search outcomes from the products of the success probabilities for each of the branches and created a single performance measure for the known-item and subject search measures. The instrument was tested in an academic library setting.

FINDINGS: While there was no significant difference between the measures from Kantor's original instrument and from Ciliberti's instrument (even though Ciliberti had added the subject search branch), there was a significant difference between the measures derived from obtrusively observed searches (they were lower) and measures derived from unobtrusively observed searches. When the instrument was tested, Ciliberti found that the purposes of patrons' subject searches were either to find factual information or to pursue general reading interests, the motivations were to complete class assignments or to conduct personal research, and the satisfaction levels with the amount and content of the materials were generally high.

CONCLUSIONS: Ciliberti offered two major conclusions: material availability measurement instruments are not strengthened by the addition of subject search outcomes, and patrons' self-reporting may not be valid.

431. Cooper, Veronica Anne (Ed.D., University of Virginia, 1985). **The Role of the Secondary School Librarian in Virginia.** 120p. Order no. DA8615533.

PURPOSE: In an attempt to identify the appropriate role for secondary school librarians in Virginia, Cooper studied the amount of agreement and disagreement among Virginia school librarians about the actual and preferred frequencies of performance of thirty-two selected library activities.

PROCEDURE: Questionnaires were sent to 25 percent (127) of the total number of secondary school libraries in Virginia; responses were received from 71 percent of the sample. T-tests were used to analyze the data collected.

FINDINGS: While there were six areas of agreement among the respondents (e.g., organization of materials through a classification system, provision of a card catalog, maintenance of financial records), there was disagreement over a majority (twenty-six) of the activities studied. In addition to the thirty-two activities examined, respondents proposed twenty-eight more activities to be considered in defining their role.

CONCLUSIONS: There is a lack of role definition among secondary school librarians in Virginia.

432. Das-Gupta, Padmini (Ph.D., Syracuse University, 1985). **An Investigation into the Two-Poisson Model of Automatic Indexing.** 169p. Order no. DA8524409.

PURPOSE: It was the purpose of this study to examine document indexing (the representation of documents) within the framework of the Two-Poisson model of automatic indexing.

PROCEDURE: The Two-Poisson model was examined with two objectives in mind: (1) to test ways of improving the model and (2) to compare the Two-Poisson model with other automatic indexing models.

FINDINGS: Das-Gupta found that modifications to the Two-Poisson model of automatic indexing only moderately improved its performance and that its performance proved to be similar to that of the other models tested.

433. Desjarlais-Lueth, Christine (Ed.D., University of Illinois at Urbana-Champaign, 1985). **Brown University and Its Library: A Study of the Beginnings of an Academic Library.** 212p. Order no. DA8521753.

PURPOSE: In this historical study, the author attempted to provide some insight into the development of an academic library in an institutional context and the people who helped to define the future of academic libraries, librarianship, and higher education in general.

PROCEDURE: To collect data for this study, Desjarlais-Lueth examined primary documents and reviewed relevant secondary sources.

FINDINGS: In 1785, Brown University formed a committee to oversee the library. Fifty years later, under Francis Wayland, a Permanent Library Fund was created, and the library became actively involved in its own development. The country's first full-time professional librarian, Charles Coffin Jewett, was hired at Brown in 1842. By 1850, Brown's faculty were involved in the library's collection development activities. A two-fold selection policy was followed: any work required to support instruction was viewed as an indispensable instrument for research and was added to the collection; any title that represented ultimate authority in the field had intrinsic value and it was acquired.

CONCLUSIONS: Under Wayland's tenure (1827 through 1855), the colonial college library transformed itself into the academic library of today. While neither Brown University nor its library has been viewed as a premier institution, the data presented in this study led the author to conclude that the library deserves recognition as a pace setter in the historical development of academic libraries.

434. Durand, Joyce Jenkins (Ph.D., Georgia State University, 1985). **A Bibliometric Study of Student Use of Periodicals for Independent Research Projects in High School Libraries with Implications for Resource Sharing.** 140p. Order no. DA8521698.

PURPOSE: This study was conducted to examine the ways in which high school students use library resources in independent research projects.

PROCEDURE: To study the students' use of library resources, Durand analyzed the bibliographies they compiled as part of their research projects and interviewed the participating students, their teachers, and their librarians.

FINDINGS: While the surveyed students used a wide variety of materials, books were the dominant form. On the average, the students used three books, one periodical, and two other types of resources (e.g., newspapers, reference books, encyclopedias) to prepare their papers. The periodicals used by the students—which conformed to Bradford's law of literature scatter—were mainly recent issues, were generally housed in their school libraries, and tended to be indexed by the *Readers' Guide to Periodical Literature*. To locate information, the students typically used the card catalog first, looked in *Readers' Guide* next, and then consulted an encyclopedia. In addition, most students used a public or college library to do their papers, as well as their school library.

CONCLUSIONS: The information-seeking behavior displayed in this study was influenced by the instruction the students received from their teachers and librarians as well as by the resources that were available in their school libraries. Thus, Durand concluded, information use for this group could be expanded by providing more comprehensive instruction and by resource sharing with local libraries.

435. Edwards, Janet Lane (Ph.D., Saint Louis University, 1985). **An Implementation Paradigm Applied to Selection and Utilization of Library Audiovisual Materials.** 215p. Order no. DA 8604374.

PURPOSE: This study explored librarian-teacher cooperation in the selection and use of audiovisual materials.

PROCEDURE: A questionnaire containing ninety Likert-type items and a number of demographic questions was sent to librarians in Missouri elementary schools. The questions focused on six specific areas: librarians' commitment to the unified media concept, feedback mechanisms for librarian-teacher information exchange, teacher participation in decision making, resource support, in-service activities offered by the librarians to the teachers, and librarians' estimates of audiovisual materials used by teachers. The data collected were analyzed using Pearson product moment correlation, step-wise regression, and one-way analysis of variance.

FINDINGS: Edwards found the following correlations: feedback mechanisms with in-service activities and with resource support, librarians' commitment with the other non-demographic variables (except teacher participation), librarians' commitment to feedback mechanisms with in-service activities, high use estimates with presence of adult paid library assistants, and per pupil expenditure for audiovisual materials and all nondemographic variables except teacher participation in decision making (but these correlations were slight).

CONCLUSIONS: Based on her findings, Edwards offered the following model of fostering maximal teacher use of the library's audiovisual collection: "committed elementary school library media specialists who use certain strategies such as giving feedback to and seeking feedback from teachers and offering in-service training on the selection and use of audiovisual materials, perceived high use of them by teachers in classroom settings."

436. Emdad, Ali (Ph.D., Case Western Reserve University, 1985). **Self-Direction in Scientific Research: A Selective Analysis of the Elite and Ultra-Elite in American High Energy Physics.** 127p. Order no. DA8510120.

PURPOSE: Drawing on the assertions made by Merton and Zuckerman, Emdad tested the theory that Nobel prize winners are self-directed investigators.

PROCEDURE: For the purposes of this study, "ultra-elites" were defined as American Nobel prize winners and "elites" were defined as members of the National Academy of Sciences in the field of high-energy physics. Emdad employed bibliometric analysis to measure communication attributes in the subject literature. Comprehensive bibliographies of the physicists were prepared to represent the subject knowledge related to high-energy physics. Citation analysis was used to identify communication patterns among the scientists. In addition, information on the physicists was collected from standard biographical sources.

FINDINGS: Citation analysis revealed that the ultra-elite in the study used their own research to a greater extent than did the elite study group. Recognition of the physicists in the study seemed to relate to self-direction, but name-ordering of the scientists in their journal publications, collaboration rate, and productivity did not.

CONCLUSIONS: This type of study can help to explain the communication systems of the ultra-elite and the elite. Further, information about self-citations may be helpful in the creation of more efficient citation indexes.

437. Friedrich, Adele E. (Ph.D., University of Pittsburgh, 1985). **Competencies for the Information Professional in the Coming Decade: A Delphi Study.** 169p. Order no. DA8524099.

PURPOSE: Interested in developing a core curriculum responsive to the needs of information practitioners and students, Friedrich asked a panel of librarians and information scientists to identify the competencies considered most important for future information professionals.

PROCEDURE: Friedrich first reviewed the library and information science literature to identify competencies that would be generic to the profession rather than specific to a job. These competencies were submitted to a panel of "experts" (librarians and information professionals who were active participants or award winners in four professional associations), using a two-round Delphi technique. Over half of the original panel (51 percent) completed both rounds.

FINDINGS: Interdisciplinary and job "generic" (versus job "specific") competencies were rated most highly by the panel. These included management competencies, especially the ability to communicate in both written and spoken forms. Computer programming skills were considered least important by the respondents. There was a high level of agreement in the rankings of these competencies among all the participants, whether they identified themselves as information professionals or as librarians.

438. Glasco, Ingrid T. M. (Ph.D., University of Pittsburgh, 1985). **The Impact of the OCLC Interlibrary Loan Subsystem on ARL Libraries.** 194p. Order no. DA8617156.

PURPOSE: In this study, Glasco investigated the impact of OCLC's Interlibrary Loan Subsystem (ILL Subsystem) on five areas of interlibrary loan activity at research libraries: patterns of interlibrary lending and borrowing, productivity, attitudes toward OCLC and its ILL Subsystem, use of the OCLC Online Union Catalog, and organization and staffing.

PROCEDURE: To collect information for the study, Glasco sent questionnaires to seventy-seven members of the Association of Research Libraries (ARL) who were participating in the OCLC ILL Subsystem as of February 1984 (sixty-eight responses) and conducted interviews with the directors and interlibrary loan librarians in three of these libraries.

FINDINGS: The data indicated (1) increased borrowing and lending between the surveyed ARL libraries and small and medium-sized academic libraries, public libraries, and special libraries; (2) a 21-percent increase in productivity (defined as the number of lending/borrowing transactions handled per staff hour); (3) a 35-percent increase in the total volume of lending/borrowing transactions; (4) a 12-percent increase in staff hours; (5) an increased use of student assistants in interlibrary loan services (an average increase of eleven hours per week); (6) a positive attitude toward OCLC that predated the libraries' use of OCLC's ILL Subsystem; (7) a perception on the part of the surveyed librarians that OCLC's ILL Subsystem had resulted in improved interlibrary loan service to patrons as well as in increased levels of interlibrary loan lending; and (8) that participants viewed OCLC's Online Catalog as the most important bibliographic tool in interlibrary loan services, even though it had not fully replaced printed catalogs in the surveyed ARL libraries.

439. Goldstein, Eileen Sara (Ph.D., University of California, Los Angeles, 1985). **The Use of Technical Information by Engineers of the Electrical Sector in Mexico.** 412p. Order no. DA 8513113.

PURPOSE: In this exploratory study, Goldstein examined the information-seeking behavior of engineers employed in Mexico's electrical sector.

PROCEDURE: Goldstein sent questionnaires to researchers in the Instituto de Investigaciones Electricas (IIE) and to practitioners in the Comision Federal de Electricidad (CFE) in Mexico; she received responses from 328 researchers (82 percent response rate) and 690 practitioners (42 percent response rate). Data were collected on frequently used information sources, amount of time spent reading and communicating, types of people consulted, problems encountered, and coping mechanisms used. Potential relationships were examined between (1) information use and language ability, technical area, work specialty, project phase, work location, distance from major information centers, and perceived accessibility; and (2) information use behaviors and type of employee (researcher or practitioner).

FINDINGS: As a group, the surveyed engineers tended to read more than they communicated, to obtain written information sources in personal files, to consult with colleagues in their own organizations, and to encounter problems in document delivery. Practitioners differed from research engineers in a number of ways: they used formal written information sources more, used current information more, and demonstrated a greater need for translations than did the researchers.

440. Grunberger, Michael W. (Ph.D., Rutgers University, 1985). **Textual Analysis and the Assignment of Index Entries for Social Science and Humanities Monographs.** 136p. Order no. DA8520363.

PURPOSE: Grunberger focused on the results of indexing—the index entry and its relation to indexed text—to examine the process indexers follow in selecting index entries.

PROCEDURE: Using descriptive and inferential techniques, Grunberger analyzed a sample of index entries taken from humanities and social science monographs to test the relationship of indexability with two variables: term location within paragraphs and term frequency on cited pages.

FINDINGS: Indexability was not found to correlate with either term location within paragraphs or term frequency on cited pages. The analysis revealed that indexed terms were distributed evenly within paragraphs of the sampled monographs; they did not cluster in discrete segments or paragraphs. Further, non-indexed terms were also distributed evenly within the surveyed paragraphs. Indexed term frequencies on posted pages concentrated in the low-to-medium frequency ranges, while on non-posted pages they concentrated in the low frequency range.

CONCLUSIONS: When it comes to full-text units, it appears the naturalist approach to indexing (i.e., that term frequency and location relate to indexability) does not apply.

RECOMMENDATIONS: The findings of computational linguistics, cognitive theory, and artificial intelligence should be incorporated into any future research conducted to examine the ways indexers determine indexability.

441. Hamshari, Omar Ahmad Mohammad (Ph.D., University of Michigan, 1985). **Job Satisfaction of Professional Librarians: A Comparative Study of Technical and Public Service Departments in Academic Libraries in Jordan.** 161p. Order no. DA8600448.

PURPOSE: Focusing on academic libraries in Jordan, Hamshari compared the job satisfaction of librarians in technical and public service departments and examined the relationships of motivator factors (satisfiers) and hygiene factors (dissatisfiers) with job satisfaction.

PROCEDURE: Questionnaires were sent to public and technical service librarians in eight university and twelve community college libraries in the East and West Banks of Jordan. Responses were received from 109 librarians: 74 working in technical services and 35 working in public services. The data were submitted to one-way analysis of variance and multiple regression analysis.

FINDINGS: Statistically significant differences were found between participants on the bases of sex, marital status, ability utilization, achievement, activity, authority, coworkers, creativity, independence, human, supervision-technical, comfort, communications, variety, challenge, and career satisfaction.

CONCLUSIONS: Technical service librarians in Jordan are more satisfied with their work than are public service librarians. Both motivator and hygiene factors contributed to the overall satisfaction of the two occupational groups. The data partially supported Herzberg's theory of job satisfaction.

442. Ikpaahindi, Linus Nguhwar (Ph.D., University of Pittsburgh, 1985). **The Relationship between the Needs for Achievement, Affiliation and Power and Frequency of Use of Information Sources and Scientific Productivity among Nigerian Veterinary Surgeons.** 128p. Order no. DA8617157.

PURPOSE: While earlier studies of information needs and information-seeking behavior have examined a number of environmental factors (e.g., subject area, work place) and demographic variables (e.g., experience, status), this is the first piece of doctoral research to consider personality as a possible explanation for the fact that some individuals obtain and use information sources more frequently than others.

PROCEDURE: This study measured the possible relationship between social/psychological needs (achievement, affiliation, and power) and (1) frequency of information use and (2) scientific productivity among Nigerian veterinary surgeons. The data on needs were collected using Edwards Personal Preference Schedule and were analyzed using both Pearson product moment correlation and multiple regression.

FINDINGS: While need for achievement and scientific productivity are positively correlated, there appears to be no relationship between the other needs and either productivity or frequency of information use.

CONCLUSIONS: Personality has only limited value in the explanation of differential use of resources or productivity.

443. Jackson, Joseph Abram (Ed.D., Vanderbilt University, 1985). **A Documentation and Analysis of Status and Employment Variables in Job Descriptions among Academic Librarians.** 132p. Order no. DA8517417.

PURPOSE: Interested in studying the current status and range of variability in academic librarians' job opportunities, Jackson reviewed published job advertisements to identify the rank, tenure, faculty duties, and benefits available to academic librarians.

PROCEDURE: The study group consisted of published advertisements in the *Chronicle of Higher Education* offering job opportunities for librarians in academic institutions. The data collected were analyzed using the Statistical

Package for the Social Sciences, which generated frequency distributions, cross-tabular tables, and other related statistical tests.

FINDINGS: Most of the advertised positions offered academic librarians faculty rank and tenure (68 percent) but a twelve-month appointment (78 percent), one month's vacation, and twelve days of sick leave. Applicants were required to have earned at least a master's degree, although a number of positions required an advanced degree (27 percent) and at least two years of experience (59 percent). Most of the vacancies were in the north central, southern, and middle states regions; in private institutions; in the areas of public service and technical processing; and advertised in June and December.

CONCLUSIONS: The minimum standards established for academic librarians during the past two decades have not yet been achieved, although significant improvements are apparent from the data analyzed in this study.

444. Karp, Rashelle Schlessinger (Ph.D., Florida State University, 1985). **Unions and Public Librarians' Attitudes toward Unionization and the Profession of Librarianship.** 294p. Order no. DA8513380.

PURPOSE: In this study, Karp explored the impact of public library unionization on librarians' attitudes toward unions and librarianship as a profession. In particular, she examined the possible relationship between type of union and attitudes held.

PROCEDURE: Questionnaires were sent to 2,317 librarians employed in (unionized or nonunionized) public libraries serving populations of 100,000 or more. T-tests and multiple stepwise regression were used to analyze the data collected.

FINDINGS: Respondents with favorable attitudes toward unionization tended to work in unionized libraries, belong to the union, work in the larger libraries, have fewer years of professional work experience, earn less money, be politically liberal, have little to do with administrative duties, and work in libraries without staff associations. Union members generally held less favorable attitudes toward service than did nonunionized librarians.

445. Kasper, Barbara (Ph.D., Indiana University, 1985). **A Comparative Analysis of Public Library Service to Children in Indiana during the 1970s.** 188p. Order no. DA8527014.

PURPOSE: This dissertation represents the first attempt to assess library services to children in Indiana.

PROCEDURE: Using selected standards for children issued by the American Library Association in 1964, Kasper collected data from 238 public library directors in Indiana in 1979. The questionnaires she sent requested information on 1978 children's services (87 percent response rate). She also gathered 1978 data on adult library services and 1970 socioeconomic data from the 1970 U.S. Census publications. These three groups of data were reported as ordinal, and were analyzed using descriptive statistics (for the library data) and Pearson product moment correlations (for the socioeconomic data).

FINDINGS: Public libraries with professional staff serving children conducted almost twice as many programs and nationally recommended activities as the statewide mean. The data revealed a positive correlation between levels of children's services and levels of adult services. Library services to children also related significantly to community education and income level.

CONCLUSIONS: The findings demonstrate the importance of professional librarians in the provision of quality library service to children.

446. Lowry, Glenn Richard (Ph.D., Rutgers University, 1985). **A Profile and Functional Job Analysis of Key Staff Positions Found in U.S. Online Database Production Organizations.** 283p. Order no. DA8520380.

PURPOSE: In this study, Lowry investigated the staffing patterns and organizational structure of online database production organizations in the United States.

PROCEDURE: The author surveyed all U.S. online database producers to determine the number of staff in eleven employment categories and to examine the policy formulation, managerial, and decision-making techniques used by the study group. An in-depth analysis was made of the staff positions and organizational structures of three of the production firms. Functional job analysis was used, based on the U.S. Department of Labor's methodology for the *Dictionary of Occupational Titles.*

FINDINGS: Staffing patterns were not based on organizational sponsorship. Few people were employed in any one staffing category. Between 1982 and 1984, there was a decrease in the number of abstractors and indexers employed; during the same period, there was a rapid increase in the number employed in the "other" category (reflecting increased staffing in the areas of marketing, customer service, and user education). Using organization and process flow charts, Lowry illustrated the relationships of staff employed in one of the large production firms studied.

RECOMMENDATIONS: Educational programs for students interested in careers in the online industry should reflect the changes in staffing patterns reported for 1982 through 1984. Indexing language and thesaurus construction should be taught as an elective, since controlled vocabularies have been developed in-house by most of the database producers studied. Library and information science core curricula should be supplemented with substantial study in another discipline.

447. Mustafa, Suleiman Hussein (Ph.D., University of Pittsburgh, 1985). **Microcomputer-Based Information Storage and Retrieval Systems: An Exploratory Study on the Use of Microcomputers in University Libraries.** 244p. Order no. DA8603905.

PURPOSE: In this exploratory study, Mustafa attempted to determine if microcomputerization in academic libraries could be accounted for by one or more of the following six factors: the degree of available computerization, the planning approach to automation adopted, the level of control over computing power, the data processing method used, the degree of reliance on network and database services, and the degree of reliance on commercial applications software.

PROCEDURE: The study population consisted of 195 library systems affiliated with universities granting doctoral-level degrees. The data were collected by questionnaire in the fall of 1984 (116 responses). In addition, interviews were conducted with representatives from twenty-five of the surveyed libraries. For the purposes of this study, Mustafa measured the extent of microcomputerization on the basis of the number of micros acquired, the degree of their contribution to computer-based systems, and the level of policy support for micros.

FINDINGS: On the average, each library system had 10 microcomputers (although the largest number reported was 126). Most of these machines were 16-bit IBMs and were used for management applications and online information retrieval. Most of the respondents supported the use of micros (80 percent) and were satisfied with the performance-effectiveness and cost-effectiveness of their micro-based systems. Little relationship was found between the extent of microcomputerization and the six independent variables under study.

CONCLUSIONS: Based on the data reported in this study, Mustafa concluded that the two most promising areas for further research into factors relating to the extent of microcomputerization in university libraries are the degree of control over computing resources and the level of computerization available.

448. Olevnik, Peter Paul (Ph.D., State University of New York at Buffalo, 1985). **A Study of the Organizational Implications of Faculty Status for Librarians in the College Library.** 293p. Order no. DA8509142.

PURPOSE: Focusing on four-year colleges, Olevnik studied library directors' perceptions of the relationship between faculty status for academic librarians and the library's organization/governance structure.

PROCEDURE: To collect the data used in the study, Olevnik conducted a literature review, consulted with selected academic library directors and staff members, pretested the survey instrument on selected academic library directors, and mailed the final instrument to library directors at three hundred colleges lacking or having extremely limited doctoral programs (68 percent useable response rate).

FINDINGS: The data revealed a positive correlation between librarians' status and library organization as well as between librarians' status and their participation in decision making. However, the level of association ranged from extremely slight to only moderate.

CONCLUSIONS: Neither providing nor denying faculty status for academic librarians had high levels of association when examined by forms of participation, regardless of decision-making area.

449. Overmier, Judith Ann (Ph.D., University of Minnesota, 1985). **Scientific Rare Book Collections in Academic and Research Libraries in Twentieth Century America.** 257p. Order no. DA8528830.

PURPOSE: This study was designed to answer three research questions: (1) Is scientific rare book collecting a twentieth-century phenomenon? (2) Does this type of collecting follow traditional rare book acquisitions practice? (3) Does it reflect general trends in rare book collecting?

PROCEDURE: Overmier surveyed scientific rare book collecting in the twentieth century by reviewing the published literature (including rare book dealers' catalogs and exhibition catalogs) and interviewing librarians, private collectors, and rare book dealers. She then surveyed eighty-one collections, selected thirty-six scientific rare book collections to identify and briefly describe, and examined three of these collections in-depth: the Burndy Library, the Dibner Library of the History of Science and Technology at the Smithsonian Institution, and the DeGolyer Collection in the History of Science and Technology at the University of Oklahoma (using on-site visits to the collections, interviews with collectors and the librarians, comparisons of holdings against checklists, and analyses of acquisitions records).

FINDINGS: Based on her data, Overmier found that scientific rare book collecting has been a phenomenon of this century and that this type of collecting follows both traditional rare book trends and acquisitions procedures.

450. Palmer, Pamela Rae (Ed.D., Memphis State University, 1985). **Graduate Education of Academic Librarians.** 183p. Order no. DA 8519707.

PURPOSE: This study focused on the status of graduate education among librarians employed at academic institutions in the southeastern states with enrollments of at least 1,000 graduate students.

PROCEDURE: Questionnaires were sent to approximately fifty directors of academic institutions in southeastern states (88 percent response rate). The data were analyzed using raw figures and percentages.

FINDINGS: The only graduate degree earned by the majority (approximately 67 percent) of the librarians employed at the institutions in the study was the master's degree in library science; this was true of librarians hired either before or after 1980. If an additional graduate degree had been earned, it tended to be a master's degree in a subject or professional area. Most of the institutions in the study group supported additional graduate degree work through policies and practices. While the presence of an additional graduate degree related to salary at the time of hiring, it seemed to have little relationship to the amount awarded in the periodic salary increases that followed. Library directors supported additional degree work, but there was no consensus on whether or not an additional graduate degree should constitute the terminal professional credential for academic librarians. However, almost all of the surveyed library directors (over 90 percent) believed additional degree work contributed to academic librarians' competencies.

451. Paskewitz, Barbara U. (Ph.D., University of Pittsburgh, 1985). **A Study of the Relationship between Learning Styles and Attitudes toward Computer Programming of Middle School Gifted Students.** 99p. Order no. DA 8603902.

PURPOSE: This study examined the relationship between middle school gifted students' attitudes toward computer programming and (1) sex, (2) grade, and (3) learning style (defined by Paskewitz as including preference for formal or informal design, motivation source, responsibility level, persistence level, need for structure or flexibility, perceptual strengths/weaknesses, need for mobility, preference for learning situation, and right brain/left brain orientation).

PROCEDURE: The study population consisted of 107 gifted students in grades six through eight. Data were collected using Dunn, Dunn, and Price's *Learning Style Inventory*, Torrance's *Your Style of Learning and Thinking*, form B, and Rusnock's *Attitude toward Computer Programming Survey*. To analyze the data, Paskewitz used Pearson product moment correlation and analysis of variance.

FINDINGS: When it came to learning style, the students generally favored an informal design, were self-motivated and persistent, preferred flexibility over structure, liked to learn on their own, had perceptual strengths, and desired mobility. However, none of these factors, nor the fact that they demonstrated an integrated brain hemispheric approach to thinking and learning, related to the students' attitudes toward computer programming. The only factor that correlated with attitude was sex; boys scored significantly higher in all of the grade levels studied than did girls.

RECOMMENDATIONS: Paskewitz proposed as topics for additional study a further examination of the relationship between sex and attitudes and an exploration of the possible relationship between cognitive style and attitudes toward computer programming.

452. Pugliese, Paul James (Ph.D., University of Pittsburgh, 1985). **The Nature of Managerial Work: The Extent Mintzberg's Roles Are Required by the Chief Executives in Academic and Public Libraries.** 173p. Order no. DA8503906.

PURPOSE: The four-fold purpose of this study was (1) to determine the managerial roles and role groups found for academic and public library directors; (2) to assess the applicability of Mintzberg's managerial role model to this group; (3) to describe the job assignments of this group in terms of job content, managerial roles, and role groups; and (4) to identify any similarities or differences between the two population groups (academic and public library directors).

PROCEDURE: In order to tie job-activity questions to the managerial role model developed by Henry Mintzberg, Pugliese sent a questionnaire to a selected group of public library and academic library directors.

FINDINGS: Academic and public library directors were similar in their ratings of job activities and managerial roles, of Mintzberg's role groups (interpersonal, informational, and decisional), and of Alexander's grouping of material roles (strategic management, operational management, external interfacing, and internal interfacing).

CONCLUSIONS: Managerial job activities and managerial roles performed by the two groups were similar and were independent of library setting or specific environment. When these findings were compared to other studies of public/private sector executives, Pugliese found similar ratings.

453. Rapp, Barbara Ann (Ph.D., Drexel University, 1985). **A Comparison of Document Clusters Derived from Co-Cited References and Co-Assigned Index Terms.** 229p. Order no. DA 8513956.

PURPOSE: Interested in the database partitioning effects of two fundamentally different indexing systems, Rapp examined how similarly co-cited references and co-assigned MeSH terms structure a set of documents.

PROCEDURE: First, Rapp selected a matched dataset of more than 8,500 documents taken from the MEDLINE database, the Institute for Scientific Information's citation database, and twenty cardiology journals published from 1975 to 1977. Then, she used single-link clustering to partition the data set in three ways: (1) co-citation clustering for reference relationships; (2) term clustering for MeSH index terms; and (3) document clustering for MeSH index terms. To measure similarity of document placement, the results of the cluster analyses were compared pairwise. Overlap between cluster systems was measured by computing an asymmetric measure of percent overlap between all cluster pairs in the two systems and by tracing member papers in each of the cluster systems. If papers mapped to several clusters, intercluster relationships were also examined.

FINDINGS: There was extremely low overlap between the three cluster systems. However, clusters within each system were cohesive in subject content.

CONCLUSIONS: The three cluster systems studied appear to organize a database in very different ways. This most likely occurred because the systems are based on different intellectual structures. These results parallel the low overlap found in comparative retrieval studies and suggest that the methods of representing document content are complementary.

454. Ro, Jung Soon (Ph.D., Indiana University, 1985). **An Evaluation of the Applicability of Ranking Algorithms to Improving the Effectiveness of Full Text Retrieval.** 224p. Order no. DA8607438.

PURPOSE: Questioning the assumption that information retrieval based on full text of documents results in higher recall and lower precision than does retrieval based on paragraphs, abstracts, or controlled vocabularies, Ro compared the effect of the various retrieval techniques on precision and recall.

PROCEDURE: Using a subset of records from the January 1979 through August 1983 *Harvard Business Review* and nine search questions, Ro compared the effectiveness of full-text retrieval with other retrieval techniques. The author also developed twenty-nine weighting algorithms for automatic extractive indexing in an attempt to improve the prevision of full-text retrieval.

FINDINGS: Paragraph, abstract, and controlled vocabulary searching achieved statistically lower recall and higher precision than did full-text retrieval. Each of the twenty-nine algorithms developed by Ro improved the precision of full-text retrieval, although there was no significant difference between the algorithms.

CONCLUSIONS: While the performance of algorithms did not vary much at high levels of recall, the algorithms did well at low levels of recall.

455. Rolando, Margaret Kernan (Ed.D., Montana State University, 1985). **An Investigation of Children's Perceptions of Story Content as Elicited by Three Modes of Presentation: The Storyteller, the Reader, the Sound Slide Show.** 182p. DA8512030.

PURPOSE: In this exploratory study, Rolando developed the first existing pencil and paper instrument that measured children's perception of story content in order to identify the relationship between different modes of presenting a story—storyteller, book and reader, and sound slide show—and content emphasized.

PROCEDURE: During 1984, ninety third graders from three schools in Butte, Montana were presented the fairy tale "The Wild Swans" in one of the three modes under study. After the presentation, the students responded to a paper and pencil instrument that measured their perceptions of three different types of content from the story: factual, affective, and inference.

FINDINGS: The data indicated there was no statistical relationship between the media used and the type of content perceived by the study group. However, the research process revealed that students were more actively involved with book and reader and sound slide presentations than with the storyteller.

RECOMMENDATIONS: Rolando suggested a number of cross-media research areas for further study: influence of the format of sound slide illustrations, possible interchangeability of sound slide show and book and reader presentations, continued development of suitable paper and pencil instruments, possible differences in the information potential of different media, factors related to learning style, longitudinal assessment of the effects of the different presentation modes, and delineation of specific media attributes.

456. Rubinyi, Robert Michael (Ph.D., University of Wisconsin, 1985). **The Effects of the Introduction of Microcomputers on the Communication and Information Behavior of Community Based Nonprofit Organizations.** 383p. Order no. DA8601560.

PURPOSE: Because financial pressures make it impossible to accept administrative inefficiency and duplication of services within nonprofit organizations, Rubinyi examined the possible beneficial effects of the introduction of microcomputer systems into this environment.

PROCEDURE: The study group consisted of seventy-two nonrandomly selected small-to-moderate-sized community-based nonprofit organizations that had participated in a computer grant program. As part of the grant, these recipients had agreed to work together in "networks" of three to five agencies each, to share computer-developed databases and information resources. Each of the organizations was surveyed five times, beginning with the point at which it received the new microcomputer system and concluding after a nine-month period had passed. The survey instrument contained open-ended qualitative questions, which were structured to obtain anecdotal comments and descriptive information from the respondents.

FINDINGS: During the first nine months following installation, computers were used more for functions that improve organizational efficiency or effectiveness (e.g., word processing, database management) than for networking. While most organizations had underestimated the time required to learn a computer system, there were no other signs of computer-induced organizational disruption.

CONCLUSIONS: Community-based nonprofit organizations can benefit from the use of microcomputers, particularly for increasing internal efficiency and external effectiveness (e.g., improving client communications).

RECOMMENDATIONS: Telecommunications applications could also be useful for groups with specifically defined needs and should be supported by the public and private sectors in the same manner as computer systems are now being supported.

457. Siitonen, Leena Marjktta (Ph.D., University of Pittsburgh, 1985). **Online Searching: Relations between Online End Users' Search Behavior, Their Search Results and Their Satisfaction with Search Results.** 222p. Order no. DA8603903.

PURPOSE: Siitonen defined "end users" as "professionals who, without being information specialists, conduct online searches on bibliographic data bases for their own work" and investigated their behavior in an industrial setting.

PROCEDURE: The author found end users in seven companies and collected data from the users in one large industrial corporation. Several research techniques were used: a questionnaire and two queries to be searched on selected topics in the INSPEC database (through BRS) were sent to ninety-two end users and completed by 21 percent of them; an interview schedule was completed by fifteen end users; and the case study method based on an adaptation by Fidel for online searching was employed.

FINDINGS: End user searching in an industrial environment is a relatively new development (averaging two years). End users tended to be self-taught, both for computer operations and online searching. While some relationship was discovered between computer experience and number of searches conducted, no relationship was found between computer experience and search results. Individual performance varied greatly. End users were generally more satisfied with overall results than with the individual characteristics of the results.

CONCLUSIONS: The characteristics of query formulation fundamentally affect practically every aspect of search performance.

RECOMMENDATIONS: The methodologies and instruments developed for this study of mediated online searching should be tested and revised to analyze nonmediated searching. In particular, the case study method should be modified to analyze searches conducted by end users on their own queries based on their individual information needs.

458. Spencer, Albert Franklin (Ph.D., Florida State University, 1985). **A Perception Study of the Accomplishment of the Goals for Indian Library and Information Service in Native American Education Institutions.** 197p. Order no. DA8522753.

PURPOSE: In this study, Spencer attempted to determine if selected groups (administrators, librarians, native American and non-native American educators, and school and college respondents) had different perceptions about the extent to which the *Goals for Indian Library and Information Service*—established in 1973 by the National Indian Education Association and the American Library Association—have been implemented.

PROCEDURE: Librarians and administrators employed in 124 native American schools and colleges were asked to complete a survey questionnaire that contained Likert-type questions relating to the implementation of six goal areas: cultural needs, native American materials, programming, native American personnel, native American representation, and funding. Responses were received from 133 individuals at 73 percent of the surveyed institutions.

FINDINGS: At the .05 level, no significant difference in perception was found between librarians and administrators or between native American and non-native American respondents. However, a significant difference was discovered between school and college educators on the accomplishment of four of the six goals studied: college librarians/administrators generally held a more positive assessment (in the areas of cultural needs, materials, programming, and personnel) than did their school colleagues.

CONCLUSIONS: The respondents were conservative in their view of the accomplishment of the *Goals for Indian Library and Information Service*. Active support was not reported for two of the six goals: employment of native American library personnel and provision of native American materials reflecting cultural awareness. There is a relationship between availability of continuous funding and perceptions of the achievement of the goals.

459. Stocking, Sandra (Ph.D., University of Pittsburgh, 1985). **Language Teaching and Library Instruction: Using Target Language Resources to Support the Undergraduate Curriculum.** 191p. Order no. DA8617158.

PURPOSE: The purpose of this study was to demonstrate how instruction in target language reading skills can be integrated with the library research process.

PROCEDURE: After analyzing the language used in six English-language library instruction workbooks, applying Relational Mapping (a text analysis method) to the six workbooks' presentation of resources basic to undergraduate research (the card catalog, encyclopedias, and serial indexes), and identifying a set of core concepts common to all six workbooks, Stocking designed a library instruction workbook in Spanish. The workbook, which was prepared to focus on popular music, was then submitted for review to a panel composed of members representing foreign-language education, linguistics, Spanish, and library instruction. Panel members were asked to rate each workbook by using a scaled evaluation form.

FINDINGS: The panel members endorsed both the idea and the specific development of a library instruction workbook in a target language (in this case, in Spanish).

CONCLUSIONS: Library instruction workbooks in target languages can contribute to the goals of both language and library instruction.

460. Walden, Winston Allen (Ph.D., Southern Illinois University at Carbondale, 1985). **Academic Status of Librarians in State-Supported Nondoctorate-Granting, Four-Year Colleges and Universities.** 471p. Order no. DA 8610609.

PURPOSE: This study was designed to answer two questions related to academic status: (1) Do academic librarians have the type of faculty status defined by the Association of College and Research Libraries' *Standards*? and (2) Are librarians employed in institutions that grant faculty rank more likely to have the type of faculty status defined by the *Standards* than those working without faculty rank?

PROCEDURE: Walden sent questionnaires to libraries in state-supported nondoctorate-granting four-year colleges and universities; 284 libraries responded (88 percent). He collected data on the number of academic institutions that met each or all of the nine components that make up the Association of College and Research Libraries' *Standards* for faculty status.

FINDINGS: The data showed that the standards most frequently met by the surveyed institutions were: academic freedom (86 percent), research funding (85 percent), paid leaves (80 percent), university governance (78 percent), library governance (60 percent), and tenure (59 percent). Fewer libraries met the requirements for professional autonomy (34 percent), promotion (24 percent), or compensation (10 percent).

CONCLUSIONS: Few libraries met all nine of the standards; librarians in institutions granting faculty rank met the standards more frequently than librarians in institutions that did not; most librarians had many of the same rights and responsibilities as did the faculty in their institutions.

461. Waldo, Michael J. (Ph.D., Indiana University, 1985). **A Comparative Analysis of Nineteenth-Century Academic and Literary Society Library Collections in the Midwest.** 235p. Order no. DA8527040.

PURPOSE: The purpose of this study was to examine and compare the library collections of midwestern colleges and literary societies in the nineteenth century.

PROCEDURE: Waldo examined the library collections of ten college and thirteen literary societies located at twelve midwestern college campuses. Among the characteristics compared were: subject composition, relationship between the collection and the college curriculum, the number of popular titles held, and the number of titles held in common in some of the collections. In addition, publication dates for the titles in two of the college libraries were studied.

FINDINGS: Holdings in the areas of literature and religion were substantially different in the two types of library collections, but the holdings in many of the remaining subject areas were generally similar. College collections usually contained as large a variety of well-represented subjects as did literary society collections. A large number of titles were held in common by the two types of libraries located on the same campus. Both types of collections contained a number of popular titles. In the two college collections examined for publication date, a sizeable proportion of "recent" books was recorded.

CONCLUSIONS: The data do not support the commonly held assumptions that nineteenth-century college and literary society library collections were substantially different or that college collections were inferior.

462. Wallace, Danny Paul (Ph.D., University of Illinois, 1985). **The Relationship between Journal Productivity and Obsolescence in a Subject Literature.** 142p. Order no. DA8511688.

PURPOSE: This study represents the first attempt to examine the relationship between journal productivity and journal obsolescence for a single subject literature (in this case, articles dealing with desalination).

PROCEDURE: For the purposes of this study, Wallace measured journal productivity by the number of references to a particular journal in a database of references from articles dealing with desalination. Obsolescence was measured by the median age of the references to a particular journal. The author hypothesized that there would be an inverse relationship between journal productivity and journal obsolescence.

FINDINGS: The data did not support the hypothesized relationship; Wallace found that there was only a tendency for highly productive journals to have low median citation ages, or for high journal median citation ages to associate with "unproductive" journals. Similarly, only a weak relationship was discovered between the subject orientation of a sample of articles and the Price's index values of the same sample with journal productivity and median citation age.

CONCLUSIONS: The findings did not support the expectation that the research front phenomenon would explain the observed relationship between journal productivity and journal median citation age.

463. Wiggins, Gary Dorman (Ph.D., Indiana University, 1985). **Factors Which Influence the Choice of Document Delivery Mechanisms for Serials by Selected Scientific and Technical Special Librarians.** 276p. Order no. DA8516632.

PURPOSE: The purpose of this study was to determine the extent to which scientific and technical libraries needing to obtain copies of journal articles have access to the full range of document delivery options.

PROCEDURE: For the purposes of this study, the document delivery options considered were interlibrary loan, commercial document delivery suppliers, informal exchange, and reprint requests. Questionnaires were sent to four hundred librarians, two hundred in academic special libraries and two hundred in for-profit special libraries (50 percent response rate). The data collected were analyzed using the Statistical Package for the Social Sciences.

FINDINGS: There was no difference in the way the two types of special libraries (academic and for-profit) used the free interlibrary loan option. However, when a charge was associated with the interlibrary loan request, more academic libraries (66 percent) than for-profit libraries (37 percent) passed the charge along to the user. Both groups were less concerned with the cost of a document delivery mechanism than with its speed, although this element was more important to for-profit than it was to academic special librarians. For-profit librarians were less likely to conduct bibliographic checking and verification before submitting a request, were less likely to belong to a network, and were less likely to have access to online union lists of serials. Academic librarians (76 percent) were more likely to transmit interlibrary loan requests by electronic means than were for-profit librarians (44 percent).

CONCLUSIONS: Different types of scientific and technical special libraries make different use of the various types of document delivery options.

Author/Title Index

Unless otherwise indicated, reference is to entry number. References to authors or titles mentioned only in an annotation are identified by an *n* following the entry number (e.g., 102n). References to page number are identified by a *p* (e.g., p. 4).

A to Zoo: Subject Access to Children's Picture Books, 2d ed., 127
AACR2 Decisions and Rule Interpretations, 3d ed., 82, 88n
Aaron, Shirley L., p.37; 306
ABC's of Financing Church and Synagogue Libraries, 376
ABI/INFORM, p.22
Abridged Dewey Decimal Classification and Relative Index, 12th ed., 79n
Abstracting and Indexing Career Guide, 2d ed., 67
Academic Librarians and Cataloging Networks, 45
Academic Libraries on the Periphery, 63
Academic Library Use of NTIS, 346
Academic Status of Librarians in State-Supported Nondoctorate-Granting, Four-Year Colleges and Universities, 460
Access to Academic Networks, 46
ACRL University Library Statistics 1983-1984, 137
Adams, David R., 208
Adams, Helen R., 299
Adler, Anne G., 38n
Advances in Information Systems Science, Vol. 9, 193
Advances in Library Administration and Organization ... Volume 5, 256
Advances in Serials Management, 369
Agricola, p.15
Ahrensfeld, Janet L., 332
ALA Survey of Librarian Salaries, 1986, 25
ALA World Encyclopedia of Library and Information Services, 2d ed., 9
Alabama Librarian, 405
Alaska Library Association, 16
Alaska Library Directory 1986, 16

Albatross Inheritance: Local Studies Libraries, 275
Albertschauser, Marianne, 287
Allcock, H., 194
Allen, G. G., 254
Alley, Brian, 7, 286
Alternative Library Literature, 1984/1985, 26
Alvfeldt, Olov, 161
Amato, Francis, 216
American Archivist, 391
American Libraries 1986: U.S. and Canadian Libraries, 17
American Library Association, Association for Library Service to Children, 102
American Library Directory, 17n
American Publishers 1986, 287
American Reference Books Annual, 1n, 3n, 6n, 10n, 14n
American Writers for Children since 1960: Fiction, 109
Anglo-American Cataloguing Rules, Second Edition, 54n, 84n, 85n, 86n, 87n
Anglo-American Cataloguing Rules, Second Edition, Revisions 1985, 83
Annual Report 1985 of The Librarian of Congress, 362
Anuar, Hedwig, 151
Anwar, Mumtaz A., 147
Appleworks for School Librarians, 326
Appraising the Records of Modern Science and Technology, 366
Aquatic Sciences and Fisheries Abstracts, p.22
ARBA Guide to Biographical Dictionaries, 6, 10n
ARBA Guide to Subject Encyclopedias and Dictionaries, 10, 14n
Archives of Library Research from The Molesworth Institute, 246

Areas of Cooperation in Library Development in Asian and Pacific Regions, 152
Ariel, Joan, 249
Armstrong, Chris, 175
Art and Design in Children's Picture Books, 126
Art Libraries and Information Services, 340
ASCLA Headquarters Staff, 18
Aslib Information, 392
Asp, William G., 172
Aspects of African Librarianship, 150
Assessment of Quality in Book Selection, 428
Association of College and Research Libraries, Ad Hod Subcommittee on Test Collections, 132
Audio Video Market Place, 287n
Auld, Lawrence W. S., 40
Auster, Ethel, 293
Automation in Libraries ... 1978-1982, 38n
AV-Online, p.22

Badrkhan, Kamiran S., 209
Bailey, Martha J., 333
Bailey, Robert H., 424
Baker, David, 164
Baker, Sharon Lynn, 425
Balbi, Adriano, 159
Bales, Kathleen, 53
Barefoot Librarian, 151n
Basic Collection of Children's Books in Spanish, 105
Basic Library Skills, 2d ed., 253
Bay State Librarian, 406
Beilke, Patricia F., 310
Belkin, Nicholas J., 202
Bello, Susan E., 167
Berman, Sanford, 26, 90
Best Encyclopedias, 14
Best in Children's Books, 107
Best Reference Books 1981-1985, 1
Bibliographic Displays in the Online Catalog, 53
Bibliometric Study of Student Use of Periodicals for Independent Research Projects in High School Libraries with Implications for Resource Sharing, 434
Biggs, Penelope T., 191
Bills, Linda G., 52
Biographical Dictionaries and Related Works, 2d ed., 8
Biographical Sources, 7
BIP Plus. *See* Books in Print PLUS
Black American in Books for Children, 2d ed., 116
Blissmer, Robert H., 220
Blixrud, Julia C., 92
Bloss, Marjorie E., 89
Boals, David Michael, 426
Bobinski, George S., 171
Bolt, Nancy M., 270

Book Selection, 4th ed., 135
Booklist, 383
Books Are Basic: The Essential Lawrence Clark Powell, 32
Books for the Teen Age, 1985, 97
Books for You: A Booklist for Senior High Students, 106n, 315
Books in Print, p.13; 6n, 67n
Books in Print PLUS (BIP Plus), pp.22-23, p.30
Books on Trial, rev. ed., 237
Bottom Line: A Financial Magazine for Librarians, 393
Bottorff, Robert M., 221
Bregman, Alvan, 2
Brenner, Everett H., 188
British Journal of Academic Librarianship, 384
Broadway, Marsha Denise, 427
Brookes, Alison, 228
Brown University and Its Library, 433
Buckley, Jo Ann, 43
Building Reference Skills in the Elementary School, 323
Burger, Robert H., 238
Burson, Lorraine E., 374
Business Research, p.22
Buzás, Ladislaus, 160

CAD/CAM Dictionary, 214
Cady, Susan A., 30
Cambridge Scientific Abstracts, p.22
Cameron, Heather, 10
Canadian Picture Books, 128
Canadian Selection, 2d ed., 2
Careers in Other Fields for Librarians, 64
Cargill, Jennifer, 7, 286
Cariou, Mavis, 2
Carlson, Ann D., 319
Carter, Ruth C., 96
Casey, James Benjamin, 428
Caswell, Jerry Vaughn, 429
Cataloging and Catalogs, 72
Cataloging Microcomputer Files, 93n
Cataloging of Audiovisual Materials, 2d ed., 268n
Cataloging Special Materials, 90
Catalyst (Des Moines), 408
Censorship in the South, 239
Chan, Lois Mai, 75, 81n
Chandna, K., 15
Changing Instructional Role of the High School Librarian, 320
Chatton, Barbara, 328
Chemical Abstracts, p.21
Chen, Ching-Chih, 235n
Children's Book Council, 117
Children's Books: Awards & Prizes, Including Prizes and Awards for Young Adult Books, 1985 ed., 117

Children's Books in Print 1985-1986, 98
Children's Catalog, 15th ed., 311
Children's Literature for All God's Children, 108
Children's Literature Review, 118-20
Choice, 385
Christianson, Elin B., 332
Church Librarian's Handbook, 375n
CIJE. *See* Current Index to Journals in Education
Ciliberti, Anne C., 430
Cimbala, Diane J., 7
Clark, Alice S., 247
Classification by Broad Economic Categories, 76
Cleaver, Betty P., 328
Clifford, Brian, 276
CMLEA Journal, 409
Cochrane, Pauline Atherton, 77-78
Coghlan, Sam, 245
Cole, Jim, 94n
Collection Assessment Manual for College and University Libraries, 133
Collection Development Manual of the National Library of Medicine 1985, 129
Collection Management for School Library Media Centers, 313
Collection Management in Public Libraries, 130
Commission on Freedom and Equality of Access to Information, 240
Commonsense Copyright, 170
Communication and Information Technologies, 199
Comparative Analysis of Nineteenth-Century Academic and Literary Society Library Collections in the Midwest, 461
Comparative Analysis of Public Library Service to Children in Indiana during the 1970s, 445
Comparison of Document Clusters Derived from Co-Cited References and Co-Assigned Index Terms, 453
Competencies for the Information Professional in the Coming Decade, 437
Computer Annual ... 1985-1986, 220
Computer Books and Serials in Print, 212n
Computer Dictionary, 4th ed., 215
Computer Information Systems Development, 208
Computer Resource Guide for Nonprofits, 3d ed., 226
Computer Software Cataloging, 93
Computer Software Hardware Index 1985, 221
Computer Technology in California School Library Media Centers, 424
Computerising Archives, 338
Computerized Cataloguing, 71
Computer-Readable Databases, 39n, 41
Computers and Information Technology, 209

Computing Terms and Acronyms, 212
Conflict in Reference Services, 291
Connecticut Libraries, 410
Conroy, Barbara, 257
CONSER Project, 92
Conservation of Library Materials, 169n
Conservation Treatment Procedures, 2d ed., 168
Contemporary Art Documentation and Fine Arts Libraries, 341
Continuing Education for the Library Information Professions, 172
Cook, C. Donald, 82, 88n
Cook, Jean G., 369
Cook, John, 157
Cook, Michael, 337
Cooper, Veronica Anne, 431
Cooperative Preservation Efforts of Academic Libraries, 167
Coordinating Cooperative Collection Development, 131
Corbin, John, 35
Cornog, Martha, 67, 189
Corry, Emmett, 27
Cortez, Edwin M., 200
COSLA Directory 1986, 18
Cost Finding for Public Libraries, 264n
Cost Management for Library and Information Services, 264
Costa, Betty, 325
Costa, Marie, 325
Coticchia, Mark E., 214
Covington, Michael, 211
Cowley, John, 334
Cox, Sandra J., 2
Craddock, Peter, 330
Craven, Timothy C., 91
Craver, Kathleen W., 320
Crawford, George W., 214
Crawford, Walt, 53, 381
Creating Connections: Books, Kits and Games for Children, 328
Criminal Justice Research in Libraries, 297
Critical Handbook of Children's Literature, 3d ed., 122
Cronin, Blaise, 258
Cummings, Martin M., 138
Cummings, Stephen, 245
Cunha, Dorothy G., 169n
Cunha, George M., 169n
Curley, Arthur, 284
Current and Future Trends in Library and Information Science Education, 171
Current Index to Journals in Education (CIJE), p.23
Current Research for the Information Profession 1985/86, 191

Dabbs, Rickey, 124
Daggett, Willard R., 209
DAI. See Dissertation Abstracts International
Daily, Jay E., 268
Dain, Phyllis, 173
Dale, Doris Cruger, 19
Danky, James P., 26
Das-Gupta, Padmini, 432
Database Directory. Spring 1986, 217
Database, p.22
Datex, Inc., p.22
Davis, Donald G., Jr., 173, 185
Davis, Gordon B., 204n
Dazzle Draw, p.28
Descriptive Guide to Development of the Collection, p.9
Deshpande, K. S., 153
Designing an Online Public Access Catalogue, 55
Desjarlais-Lueth, Christine, 433
Developing Learning Skills through Children's Literature, 324
Development and Methodological Study of an Instrument for Measuring Material Availability in Libraries, 430
DIALOG, p.14, p.17, p.21
DIALOG OnDisc, pp.23-24
Dickson, Paul, 182
Dictionary of Acronyms and Abbreviations in Library and Information Science, 2d ed., 15
Dictionary of American Children's Fiction, 1859-1959, 112
Dictionary of American Children's Fiction 1960-1984, 113
Dictionary of Computer Terms, 211
Dictionary of Computers, Data Processing, and Telecommunications, 212n
Dictionary of Computing, 2d ed., 210
Dictionary of Information Technology, 2d ed., 190
Directory of Art Libraries and Visual Resource Collections in North America, 343n
Directory of Computer Software, 1985, 218
Directory of Consultants in Computer Systems, 3d ed., 219
Directory of Curriculum Materials Centers, 2d ed., 300
Directory of Foreign Document Collections, 344
Directory of Government Document Collections & Librarians, 344n
Directory of Interlibrary Loan Policies & Duplication Services in Canadian Libraries, 4th ed., 244
Directory of Library and Information Retrieval Software for Microcomputers, 2d ed., 228
Directory of Library Staff Organizations, 21
Directory of Medical and Health Care Libraries in the United Kingdom and Republic of Ireland, 6th ed., 355
Directory of Microcomputer Software for Libraries, 227
Directory of Online Databases, 217n
Directory of Oral History Tapes of Librarians in the United States and Canada, 19
Directory of Special Libraries and Information Centers, 17n, 344n
Directory of the Association for Library and Information Science Education 1985-86, 174
DISCLOSURE, p.22
Dissertation Abstracts database, p.22
Dissertation Abstracts International (DAI), p.229
Divilbiss, James L., 62
Documentation and Analysis of Status and Employment Variables in Job Descriptions among Academic Librarians, 443
Dodd, Sue A., 93n
Dority, G. Kim, 10
Downing, Douglas, 211
Drugdex, p.22
Dubois, Diane, 128
Duke, Judith S., 288
DuMont, Rosemary Ruhig, 259
Dunhouse, Mary Beth, 114
Durand, Joyce Jenkins, 434
Dyal, Carole, 168
Dyer, Hilary, 228
Dym, Eleanor D., 80

Early Childhood Literature Sharing Programs in Libraries, 319
Eastern Europe in Children's Literature, 104
Eastman, Ann Heidbreder, 280
Easy Access to Information in United States Government Documents, 348
EBSCO Serials Directory, p.22
Economics of Managing Library Service, 265
Economics of Research Libraries, 138
Edelman, Hendrik, 178
Educational Resources Information Center (ERIC) databases, p.16, pp.22-23
Edwards, Janet Lane, 435
Effects of the Introduction of Microcomputers on the Communication and Information Behavior of Community Based Nonprofit Organizations, 456
EI. *See* Engineering Index
Ein-Dor, Phillip, 201
Eldridge, Leslie, 331
Electronic Spreadsheets for Libraries, 40
Elementary School Library Collection, 15th ed., 312

El-Hi Textbooks and Serials in Print 1986, 308
Ellison, John W., 269
Emdad, Ali, 436
Emergindex, p.22
Encyclopedia of Information Systems and Services, 73n
Encyclopedia of Library and Information Science. Vol. 39, Supplement 4, 11
Encyclopedia of Library and Information Science. Vol. 40, Supplement 5, 12
Encyclopedia of Library and Information Science. Vol. 41, Supplement 6, 13
End User Searching in the Health Sciences, 358
Engineering Index (EI), pp.21-22
Enniss, Stephen C., 230
Erdmann, Christine, 139
ERIC databases. *See* Educational Resources Information Center databases
Essays on Public Documents and Government Policies, 347
Essential Guide to CD-ROM, 42
Essential Guide to the Library IBM PC. Vol. 2: The Operating System: PC DOS, 234
Essential Guide to the Library IBM PC. Vol. 3: Library Application Software, 235
Essential Guide to the Library IBM PC. Vol. 7: Database Management Systems, 43
Estes, Glenn E., 109
Evaluating Media Programs, 322n
Evaluation of the Applicability of Ranking Algorithms to Improving the Effectiveness of Full Text Retrieval, 454
Excerpta Medica, p.22. *See also How to Use "Index Medicus" and "Excerpta Medica"*
Exon, F.C.A., 254
Exploration into Factors Causing the Increased Circulation of Displayed Books, 425
Exploring Careers in Research and Information Retrieval, 66
Ezzell, Joline, 370

Factors Governing the Amount of Duplication in Content Derived Keys, 429
Factors Which Influence the Choice of Document Delivery Mechanisms for Serials by Selected Scientific and Technical Special Librarians, 463
Falk, Howard, 222
Feather, John P., 183
Fees for Library Service, 284
Ferrall, Eleanor, 297
Feuerman, Melvyn, 236
Fiction Catalog, 11th ed., 314
Fiction for Youth, 2d ed., 106, 315n
Finguson, Ronald L., p.4
Fireworks, Brass Bands, and Elephants: Promotional Events with Flair for Libraries and Other Nonprofit Organizations, 282

Fletcher, John, 163
Flores, Ivan, 236
Florida Media Quarterly, 411
Flower, Kenneth E., 63
Focus on Learning, 301
Foreign Students in American Library Education, 177
Forester, Tom, 196
Forms and Responses, 189
Fraley, Ruth A., 291, 294
Free Resource Builder for Librarians and Teachers, 24
Freedom and Equality of Access to Information, 240
Freedom of Information and Youth, 241
French, James C., 44
Friedrich, Adele E., 437
Froehlich, Robert A., 229

Gale Biographical Index Series, 7n
Gallo, Donald R., 315
Garoogian, Andrew, 64
Garoogian, Rhoda, 64
Gates, Jean Key, 145n
Gbala, Helen E., 84
Gellatly, Peter, 372
German Library History, 800-1945, 160
Gerould Statistics, 1907/08-1961/62, 142
Getting the Books Off the Shelves, rev. ed., 378
Gibson, Sarah Scott, 340
Gifted, Talented, and Creative Young People, 309
Gillespie, John T., 316
Glasco, Ingrid T. M., 438
Glover, Peggy D., 285
Goldstein, Eileen Sara, 439
Good Reading, 26th ed., 317
Gorosh, Esther, 124
Government Periodicals Index, p.22
GPO's Depository Library Program, 345
Graduate Education of Academic Librarians, 450
Grant Proposal Writing, 307
Grants for Libraries, 2d ed., 27
GRANTS, p.14, p.17, p.19
Great Library Promotion Ideas II, 280
Great Library through Gifts, 377
Greene, Ellin, 321
Greeson, Janet, 121
Grolier Electronic Encyclopedia, p.22
Grunberger, Michael W., 440
Guerrero, Gene, 239
Guide for the Development and Management of Test Collections, 132
Guide to Collecting Librariana, 136
Guide to Computer Magazines, 1985 ed., 216
Guide to Information Resources Management (IRM) Associations, 22

Guide to Popular U.S. Government Publications, 349, 351n
Guide to Reference Books, 10th ed., 5, 14n
Guide to Reference Books for School Media Centers, 3d ed., 318
Guide to Selected Federal Agency Programs and Publications for Librarians and Teachers, 351
Guide to the Use of Libraries and Information Sources, 5th ed., 145n
Guidelines for Public Libraries, 3d ed., 271
Gupta, B. M., 154
Gurnsey, John, 65

Haas, Joan K., 366
Hafter, Ruth, 45
Halicki-Conrad, Adam, 149
Hall, Blaine H., 133
Hammack, Mary L., 375
Hamshari, Omar Ahmad Mohammad, 441
Handbook of Libraries, Archives and Information Centers in India, Volume 1, 154
Hannaford, Claudia, 376
Hardesty, Larry L., 140, 252
Harman, Keith, 260
Harris, Colin, 181, 276
Harter, Stephen P., 58
Harvey, Joan M., 31
HASL Newsletter, 412
Hastreiter, Jamie, 140
Hawaii Library Association Journal, 413
Hawaii Library Association Newsletter, 414
Hayes, Jeanne, 223
Hayes, Robert M., 141
Heilprin, Laurence B., 207
Helbig, Alethea K., 112-13
Henderson, David, 140
Herman, Edward, 348n
Hernon, Peter, 224, 345-46
Herring, James E., 36
Herrup, Steven, 66
Heynen, Jeffrey, 92
Hildenbrand, Suzanne, 380
Hillegas, Ferne E., 311
Hinding, Andrea, 380n
Hipgrave, Richard, 212
History of Books and Libraries, 183
History of Library and Information Science Education, 173
History of the Dublin Library Society, 1791-1881, 184
History of the United States Military Academy Library, 364
Ho, May Lein, 326
Hoffman, Herbert H., 70
Hogan, Thomas H., 60
Holligan, Patrick J., 46
Holzberlein, Deanne, 93

Horak, Ellen Brassil, 358
Hordeski, Michael, 225
How to Organize Your Church Library and Resource Center, 375
How to Use "Index Medicus" and "Excerpta Medica," 357
Howell, John Bruce, 184
Hubbard, Taylor E., 144
Hug, Melissa Reiff, 118-20
Hunter, Eric J., 71
Hyland, Anne M., 302-3

IAME News for You, 415
IBM PC (and Compatibles) Free Software Catalog and Directory, 229
IDAM File Organizations, 44
Identidex, p.22
IFLA Directory of Art Libraries, 343
Ikpaahindi, Linus Nguhwar, 442
ILA Reporter, 416
Illinois Association for Media in Education, 322
Illinois Libraries, 417
Illinois Library Statistical Report 19, 272
Illinois Library Statistical Report 20, 273
Illustrated Dictionary of Microcomputers, 2d ed., 225
Illustrated Dictionary of Word Processing, 213
Immroth, Barbara, 100
Impact of the OCLC Interlibrary Loan Subsystem on ARL Libraries, 438
Implementation Paradigm Applied to Selection and Utilization of Library Audiovisual Materials, 435
Improving Communication in the Library, 257
Improving LCSH for Use in Online Catalogs, 77
Index Medicus. See *How to Use "Index Medicus" and "Excerpta Medica"*
Index to Children's Plays in Collections, 2d ed., 125n
Index to Children's Plays in Collections 1975-1984, 125
Index to Information Technology, 195
Indexer, 394
Indexing and Searching in Perspective, 188
Indiana Media Journal, 418
Indicators of Quality for School Library/Media Programs, 322
Informatics 8, 197
Information and Behavior, Volume 1, 205
Information and Referral, 395
Information Consultants in Action, 68
Information, Enrichment and Delight: Public Libraries in Western Australia, 157
Information Executive's Guide to Intellectual Property Rights, 242

Information Highways: Mapping Information Delivery Networks in the Pacific Northwest, 50
Information Management, 258
Information Professions in the Electronic Age, 65
Information Science Abstracts. Vol. 21, Number 3, 194
Information Services in Muslim Countries, 147
Information Systems Analysis and Design, 204
Information Systems Management, 201
Information Technology and Information Use, 198
Information Technology in the Library/ Information School Curriculum, 175
Information Technology Revolution, 196
InfoTrac, pp.22-23
InfoTrac II, p. 23
Ingwersten, Peter, 198
Interaction in Information Systems, 202
International and Comparative Librarianship, 149
International Association of School Librarianship, 322
International Directory of Children's Literature, 114
International Directory of Children's Literature Specialists, 115
International Directory of Little Magazines and Small Presses, 287n
International Review of Children's Literature and Librarianship, 396
Introduction of Automated Library and Information Services in a Newly Industrialized Country, 165
Investigation into the Two-Poisson Model of Automatic Indexing, 432
Investigation of Children's Perceptions of Story Content as Elicited by Three Modes of Presentation, 455
Iowa Media Message, 419
Irregular Serials and Annuals, 12th ed., 30n
Isaacson, Richard H., 311
Issues in Serials Librarianship, 370
Issues in Southeast Asian Librarianship, 151

Jackson, Joseph Abram, 443
Jacob, M.E.L., 47
Jarvis, Patrick L., 21
Jay, Hilda L., 323
Jay, M. Ellen, 323
Jennings, Margaret S., 20
Job Descriptions for Library Support Personnel, 28
Job Satisfaction of Professional Librarians, 441
Johnson, Corinne, 270
Joint Steering Committee for Revision of AACR, 83
Jones, Carl R., 201

Jones, Frances M., 21
Jones, Kay F., 247
Jones, Lois Swan, 340
Journal of Documentation, 397
Journal of Education for Librarianship, p.4
Journal of Education for Library and Information Science, p.47
Journal of Library History, 386
Journal of the American Society for Information Science, 398
Judaica Librarianship, 399

Kadec, Sarah T., 22
Kahn, Ann M. C., 356
Kaiser, John Boynton, 352
Kajberg, Leif, 198
Karp, Rashelle Schlessinger, 444
Kaser, David, p.4
Kasper, Barbara, 445
Katz, Bill, 29, 290-91, 294
Katz, Linda Sternberg, 29
Katzen, M., 248
Kazlauskas, Edward John, 200
Keaveney, Sydney Starr, 341
Keenan, Stella, 175
Kegley, Sissy, 239
Keller, Dean H., 179
Kent, Allen, 11-13
Kentucky Libraries, 420
Key Issues in the Networking Field Today, 48
Kiewitt, Eva L., p.4; 300
King, David E., 332
Kinsella, Janet, 57
Kinsock, John E., 59
Kirkendall, Carolyn A., 250
Kister, Kenneth F., 14
Kohl, David F., 72, 176, 292
Koops, Willem R. H., 271
Kramuschka, Astrid, 287
Kreider, Barbara A., 125n
Kreissman, Bernard, 256
Kruse, Benedict, 209
Kumar, Girja, 155

Lacy, Lyn Ellen, 126
Lancaster, F. W., 203
Langman, Larry, 213
Language Teaching and Library Instruction, 459
Lannom, Laurence, 41
Larsen, John C., 361
Laughlin, Mildred Knight, 324
Law, Legislative and Municipal Reference Libraries, 352
LC Rule Interpretations of AACR2, 1978-1985, 2d ed., 88
Lee, Hwa-Wei, 152
Legal Databases Online, 59

Legal Research and Law Library Management, 353
Legal Research and Law Library Management. Supplement, 1985, 354
LegalTrac, p.22
Lehman, Lois J., 300
Leighton, Philip D., 33
Lesko, Matthew, 192
Lesko's New Tech Sourcebook, 192
Levels of Library Development, 274
Levels of Work and Responsibility in Public Libraries, 426
Levine, Arthur J., 242
LEXIS. *See* Legal Databases Online
Librarian in Search of a Publisher, 286
Librarian in the Marketplace, 266
Librarian's Guide to Telephone Reference Service, 296
Libraries and Information Science in the Electronic Age, 178
Libraries and the Law, 245
Libraries, Books & Culture, 185
Libraries in the Age of Automation, 37
Libraries in the '80s, 179
Library and Information Plans, 162
Library and Information Science Education Statistical Report, p.47
Library and Reference Facilities in the Area of the District of Columbia, 12th ed., 20
Library Association Record, 387
Library Binding Institute Standard for Library Binding, 8th ed., 382
Library Binding Manual, 382n
Library Currents, 400
Library Development in India, 155
Library Disaster Preparedness Handbook, 255
Library Education and Professional Issues, 176
Library Forms Illustrated Handbook, 189n
Library Hi Tech Bibliography, 38
Library in America, 182
Library Instruction, 251
Library Instruction Clearinghouse 1985, 249
Library Management, 262
Library Micro Consumer MRC's Guide to Library Software, 230
Library Networks, 1986-87, 49
Library of Congress Information Bulletin, 388
Library of Congress Network Advisory Committee, 363
Library of Congress Subject Headings: Principles and Application, 2d ed., 75, 81n
Library Personnel Management, 267
Library Planning and Budgeting, 263
Library Publishing, 289
Library Resources and Technical Services, p.47
Library Science Dissertations, p.229
Library Services for Nonprofit Organizations, rev. ed., 281
Library Services for the Woman in the Middle, 285
Library Systems Evaluation Guide, 73
Library Systems in Alberta, 158
Liebold, Louise Condak, 282
Life Goes On: Twenty More Years of Fortune and Friendship. Checklist of Publications: 1919-1986, 180
Life Sciences, p.22
Light, Richard B., 360
Lima, Carolyn W., 127
Lindsey, Jonathan A., 261
Linton, W. D., 355
Lisanti, Suzana, 234
Literary Market Place, 287
Liu, Grace F., 283
LLA Bulletin, 421
Locating United States Government Information, 348n
Loertscher, David V., 304, 327
Longley, Dennis, 190
Lowry, Glenn Richard, 446
Lukens, Rebecca J., 122
Luquire, Wilson, 131
Lutzker, Marilyn, 297
Lynch, Mary Jo, 25

MacCann, Donnarae, 116
MacDraw, p.28
Mackenzie, John A., 36
Magazine Index, p.22
Magazines for Libraries, 5th ed., 5n, 29
Maine Memo, 422
Maissen, Leena, 115
Management Information Systems, 2d ed., 204n
Management of Information from Archives, 337
Management of Oral History Sound Archives, 339
Management of Polytechnic Libraries, 334
Management Strategies for Libraries, 267n
Managing Information Systems & Technologies, 200
Managing Online Reference Services, 293
Managing the Library Automation Project, 35
Mancher, Rhoda R., 22
Manheimer, Martha L., 54
Manual of AACR 2 Examples for "In" Analytics with MARC Tagging and Coding, 86
Manual of AACR 2 Examples for Microcomputer Software, 2d ed., 85
Manual of AACR 2 Level 1 Examples, 84
Manual of Advanced AACR 2 Examples, 2d ed., 87
Marke, Julius J., 353-54
Marketing Instructional Services, 250
Markey, Karen, 342

Marquis Who's Who, p.22
Marshall, John David, 32
Martin, Susan K., 49
Maruyama, Lenore S., 363
Mason, Robert M., 230
Master Index to Summaries of Children's Books, 123
Mattelart, Armand, 199
McCabe, Gerard B., 256
McCarthy, Cavan M., 165
McCauley, Elfrieda, 101
McClung, Patricia A., 134
McClure, Charles R., 224, 260, 345-46, 373
McDonald, Margaret Marshall, 305
McKitterick, David, 183
McMichael, Betty, 375n
McNally, Peter F., 186
McQuarrie, Jane, 128
Measures of Excellence for School Library Media Centers, 304
Measuring the Book Circulation Use of a Small Academic Library Collection, 146
Media Forum, 407
Media Librarianship, 269
Medical Librarianship in the Eighties and Beyond, 356
MEDLINE, p.22
Merrill-Oldham, Jan, 382
Metcalf, Keyes D., 33
Micro Handobok for Small Libraries and Media Centers, 2d ed., 325
Micro Software Evaluations (Library Edition). Vol. II, 231
Microcomputer and VCR Usage in Schools 1985-86, 223
Microcomputer Facility and the School Library Media Specialist, 327
Microcomputer-Based Information Storage and Retrieval Systems, 447
Microcomputers for Library Decision Making, 224
Microreviews, p.22
MicroSource, 233
Microuse Directory, 235n
Miles, Susan Goodrich, 235
Miller, Arthur, Jr., 146
Miller, Betty David, 108
Miller, Peggy A., 242
Miller, Ruth-Ellen, 50
Mission Statements for College Libraries, 140
Mitchell, Robert, 180
Mitev, Nathalie Nadia, 55
Molyneux, Robert E., 142
Moody, Marilyn K., 348n, 350, 351n
Morehead, Joe, 347
Morris, John, 255
Morrison, Shirley Vittum, 328
Morrow, Carolyn Clark, 168
Mount, Ellis, 243, 367-68
Mulliner, K., 152

Murr, Lawrence E., 50
Museum & Archival Supplies Handbook, 3d ed., 359
Museum Documentation Systems, 360
Museum Librarianship, 361
Mustafa, Suleiman Hussein, 447
Myers, Margaret, 25

Name That Book! Questions and Answers on Outstanding Children's Books, 121
National Catalog of Sources for the History of Librarianship, 19n
National Council of Teachers of English, Committee on the Senior High School Booklist, 315
National Library of Canada, 244
National Online Meeting, 60
National Technical Information Service (NTIS) database, p.21
Nature of Managerial Work, 452
Neufeld, M. Lynne, 67
New York Public Library, 34
Newman, Wilda B., 243
Newsletter, California Library Association, 423
Newspaper Libraries, 365
9th International Online Information Meeting, 61
Nolan, Jeanne M., 231
Nonbibliographic Data Banks in Science & Technology, 161
North American Online Directory 1985, 39
Northwest Information Directory, 23
Norton, Aloysius, 364
Notable Children's Books 1976-1980, 102
Note Us, p.24
Notes for Serials Cataloging, 94
Notes Worth Noting, 94n
NTIS databases. *See* National Technical Information Service database

Occupational Health and Safety Information, p.22
OCLC: An Introduction to Searching and Input, 2d ed., 54
OCLC Experimental Project, 52
Olevnik, Peter Paul, 448
Olsen, Margarethe H., 204n
Olson, Nancy B., 85, 268n
OMS Annual Report 1985, 143
O'Neil, Rosanna, 94
Online Catalog Screen Displays, 56
Online Information Retrieval, 58
Online, p.22
Online Micro-Software Guide and Directory, 1983-84, 232n
Online Public Access to Library Files, 57
Online Searching, 457

Options for Small Public Libraries in Massachusetts, 270
Orbit, p.17
Organizing Nonprint Materials, 2d ed., 268
Organizing Your Photographs, 95
Ostle, Judson R., 204
Overmier, Judith Ann, 449
Owles, V. Arthur, 208

Palmer, Eileen C., 125
Palmer, Pamela Rae, 450
Panwar, B. S., 262
Parisi, Paul A., 382
Parker, J. Stephen, 68, 148
Paskewitz, Barbara, 451
Patterson, Charles D., 174
Pejtersen, Annelise Mark, 198
Penchansky, Mimi B., 149
Peniston, Silvina, 195
Perception Study of the Accomplishment of the Goals for Indian Library and Information Service in Native American Education Institutions, 458
Performance Evaluation, 261
Perkins, Agnes Regan, 112-13
Personal Computers for Libraries, 222
Personal Development in Information Work, 69
Personnel Administration in Libraries, 267n
Personnel Issues in Reference Services, 294
Pettus, Daniel D., 123
Pettus, Eloise S., 123
Petty, Mike, 275
Phillips, C. M., 338
Phillips, Janet, 174
Picken, Fiona Mackay, 356
Planning Academic and Research Library Buildings, 2d ed., 33
Planning for Library Automation, 36
Poisindex, p.22
Polette, Nancy, 298
Politics of an Emerging Profession, 187
Politics of Public Librarianship, 277
Popular Reading for Children II, 103
Povsic, Frances F., 104
Powell, Lawrence Clark, 180
Powers, Michael J., 208
Prentice-Hall Standard Glossary of Computer Terminology, 212n
Preservation of Library Materials, 169
Preston, Edward J., 214
Privacy, Secrecy, and National Information Policy, 238
Professional Microcomputer Handbook, 236
Profile and Functional Job Analysis of Key Staff Positions Found in U.S. Online Database Production Organizations, 446
Projects and Procedures for Serials Administration, 371

Promoting Library Awareness in Ethnic Communities, 283
Prospects for Information Service, 181
Psychological Abstracts, p.23
PsycINFO, p.23
PsycLIT, pp.22-23
Public Libraries, 276
Public Library and Blind People, 330
Public Library Catalog, 314n
Publishers Directory, 1984-1985, 287n
Publishers, Distributors and Wholesalers of the United States, 1985-1986, 287n
Pugliese, Paul James, 452
Purcell, Gary R., 345

Quill & Quire, 389

R Is for Reading, 331
Rajagopalan, T. S., 156
Ramsey, Inez L., 263
Ramsey, Jackson E., 263
Randa, Lynn, 249
Ranganathan's Philosophy, 156
Rapp, Barbara Ann, 453
Reader Services in Polytechnic Libraries, 163
Reading for Young People: New England, 101
Readings in Canadian Library History, 186
Recommended Reference Books for Small and Medium-sized Libraries and Media Centers 1986, 3
Recommended Standards for Cataloguing-in-Publication, 74
Recruiting and Training Volunteers for Church Synagogue Libraries, 374
Redesign of Catalogs and Indexes for Improved Online Subject Access, 78
Reed, Henry Hope, 34
Reference and Online Services Handbook ... Volume II, 290
Reference Books Bulletin, 4n
Reference Books Bulletin 1984-1985, 4
Reference Librarian, 401
Reference Services and Library Instruction, 292
Reference Services in Archives, 295
Reference Work in the Public Library, 145n
Reference Work in the University Library, 145
Relationship between Journal Productivity and Obsolescence in a Subject Literature, 462
Relationship between the Needs for Achievement, Affiliation and Power and Frequency of Use of Information Sources and Scientific Productivity among Nigerian Veterinary Surgeons, 442
Research Almanac, 2d ed., 298
Research and the Practice of Librarianship, 254

Research Libraries, 144
Resources in Education, p.23
Restrepo, Fabio, 278
Reyes, Caroline, 79
RIE. *See* Resources in Education
Rimer, Pearl, 379
Ro, Jung Soon, 454
Roberts, D. Andrew, 360
Roberts, Stephen A., 264
Robins, Carolyn G., 41
Robl, Ernest H., 95
Rochester, Maxine K., 177
Rolando, Margaret Kernan, 455
Role of the Secondary School Librarian in Virginia, 431
Roney, Raymond G., 28
Rosenberg, Betty, 180
Rosenberg, J. M., 212n
Rosenberg, Victor, 166
Roth, Judith Paris, 42
Rovira, Carmen, 79
Ruben, Brent D., 205
Rubinyi, Robert Michael, 456
Rush, James E., 73

Sampler of Forms for Special Libraries, 189n
Samuels, Helen Willa, 366
Sandberg-Fox, Ann M., 93n
Saracevic, Tefko, 188
Sarkissian, Adele, 110-11
Scales, Pat R., 306
Schauer, Bruce P., 265
Schindler, Barbara, 257
Schlachter, Gail A., p.229
Schmitt, John P., 252
Schmucler, Hector, 199
Schon, Isabel, 105
School Libraries in Canada, 390
School Library Media Activities Monthly, 402
School Library Media Annual, p.37
School Library Media Annual 1986, 306
School Library Media Quarterly, p.37, p.47
School Library/Media Skills Test and *Manual*, 302-3
School Media Policy Development, 299
Schwartz, Julia, 348
Schwarz, Stephan, 161
Schwarzkopf, LeRoy, 349, 351n
Sciara, Frank J., 310
Science and Technology Libraries, 403
Science Citation Index, p.22
Scientific Rare Book Collections in Academic and Research Libraries in Twentieth Century America, 449
Sci-Tech Libraries in Museums and Aquariums, 367
Sears, Jean L., 348n, 350, 351n
Sears List of Subject Headings, 13th ed., 79

Selecting Materials for and about Hispanic and East Asian Children and Young People, 310
Selection of Library Materials in the Humanities, Social Sciences, and Sciences, 134
Self-Directed Instruction in Query Formation and Presentation for College Students, 427
Self-Direction in Scientific Research, 436
Sellen, Betty-Carol, 64n
Senick, Gerard J., 118-20
Senior High School Paperback Collection, 316
Serebnick, Judith, 130
Serial Holdings Statements at the Summary Level, 89
Serials Directory, 30
Serials Librarianship in Transition, 372
Shaevel, Evelyn, 280
Shain, Michael, 190
Shannon, George, 321
Shapiro, Lillian L., 106
Shavit, David, 277
Sheegy, Eugene, 5
Shih, Tian-Chu, 251
Shuter, Janet, 266
Siitonen, Leena Marjktta, 457
SilverPlatter, pp.22-23
Simmons, Barbara Trippel, 366
Sinker, Mary, 329
Sippl, Charles J., 215
SLA Triennial Salary Survey, 335
Slavens, Thomas P., 377
Sloane, Richard, 353-54
Slocum, Robert B., 8
Small Library Cataloging, 2d ed., 70
Smallwood, Carol, 24, 351
Smith, Linda C., 145
Smith, Ruth S., 378
Snow, Bonnie, 358
Snow, Kathleen M., 124
Sociofile, p.22
Sociological Abstracts, p.24
Software Catalog, 232
Software Encyclopedia, 1985/86, 232n
Software Reviews on File, 232n
Something about the Author Autobiography Series. Vol. 1, 110
Something about the Author Autobiography Series. Vol. 2, 111
Spanish-Language Books for Public Libraries, 278
Special Collections, 404
Special Collections in College Libraries, 139
Special Librarian as a Supervisor or Middle Manager, 333
Special Libraries, 2d ed., 332
Spencer, Albert Franklin, 458
Spiller, David, 135
State Library Services and Issues, 373

Statistical Essay on the Libraries of Vienna and the World, 159
Stein, Morris I., 309
Stevens, Glenna E., 82
Stevens, Norman D., 136, 246
Stevens, Rolland E., 145
Stewart, Jennifer D., 360
Stielow, Frederick J., 339
Stine, Diane, 371
Stocking, Sandra, 459
Storytelling: A Selected Annotated Bibliography, 321
Stovel, Lennie, 53
Strategic Planning for Sponsored Projects Administration, 260
Strickland-Hodge, Barry, 357
String Indexing, 91
Student Reading Needs and Higher Education, 164
Study of the Organizational Implications of Faculty Status for Librarians in the College Library, 448
Study of the Relationship between Learning Styles and Attitudes toward Computer Programming of Middle School Gifted Students, 451
Subject Access to Visual Resources Collections, 342
Subject and Information Analysis, 80
Subject Cataloging Division Processing Services, 81
Subject Cataloging Manual, rev. ed., 81
Subject Guide to Children's Books in Print 1985-1986, 99
Subject Index to Canadian Poetry in English for Children and Young People, 2d ed., 124
Sutherland, Zena, 107
Swanson, Edward, 84, 86-87
Systematic Process for Planning Media Programs, 322n

Taha, Karen, 121
Talab, R. S., 170
Tauber, Maurice F., 382n
Taylor, Arlene G., 94
Taylor, Nancy, 227
Taylor, Peter, 181
Taylor, Richard L., 28
Taylor, Robert S., 206
Tayyeb, R., 15
Teaching Librarians to Teach, 247
Technical, Scientific and Medical Publishing Market, 288
Technical Standards, 381
Technology and Communication in the Humanities, 248
Telecommunications, 62
Telecommunications Networks, 47

Texas in Children's Books, 100
Textual Analysis and the Assignment of Index Entries for Social Science and Humanities Monographs, 440
Thomas, Nancy G., 94
Thomas, Virginia Coffin, 108
Thomison, Dennis, p.229
Top of the News, p.47
Top Secret/Trade Secret, 243
Tou, Julius T., 193
Toward a Common Vision in Library Networking, 51
Toward Foundations of Information Science, 207
Towards Excellence, 305
Toy Libraries, 2d ed., 379
Toys for Growing, 329
Transfer of Scholarly, Scientific and Technical Information between North and South America, 166
Trefny, Beverly Robin, 125
Trochim, Mary Kane, 146
Trochim, William M. K., 146
Tseng, Sally C., 88, 152
Tucker, John Mark, 252
Turner, Carol A., 344
Tuttle, Marcia, 369

Ulrich's International Periodicals Directory, 25th ed., 30n, 31n
Ulrich's Plus, pp.22-23
UNESCO and Library Development Planning, 148
Unions and Public Librarians' Attitudes toward Unionization and the Profession of Librarianship, 444
United Nations Department of International Economic and Social Affairs, 76
United States Newspaper Program, 96
Universities, Information Technology, and Academic Libraries, 141
University Library System in India, 153
University Press Books for Public Libraries 1986, 279
Unruh, Betty, 189
Use of Technical Information by Engineers of the Electrical Sector in Mexico, 439
User Instruction in Academic Libraries, 252
Using Government Publications, 348n, 350, 351n

Value-Added Processes in Information Systems, 206
Van Young, Sayre, 233
Varlejs, Jana, 241
Venner, Gillian M., 55
Viaux, Jacqueline, 343
Vickery, Alina, 202

Vocabulary Control for Information Retrieval, 2d ed., 203
Vyas, S. D., 262

Walden, Winston Allen, 460
Waldhorn, Arthur, 317
Waldo, Michael J., 461
Walford, A. J., 31
Walford's Guide to Current British Periodicals in the Humanities and Social Sciences, 31
Walker, Stephen, 55
Wall, C. Edward, 38
Wall, Celia Jo, 365
Wall Street Journal database, p.22
Wallace, Danny Paul, 462
Walton, Joan M., 145n
Walton, Robert A., 227
Washington Information Directory, 20n
Watson, David G., 161
Watt, Letty S., 324
Way, David, 289
Webb, Sylvia P., 69
Weber, David C., 33
Weber, Olga S., 317
Wedgeworth, Robert, 9
Weeding of Collections in Sci-Tech Libraries, 368
WESTLAW. *See* Legal Databases Online
Whalen, Lucille, 295
What Else You Can Do with a Library School Degree, 64n
White, Brenda H., 313

White, Herbert S., 267
Whiteley, Sandy, 137
Whitney, Gretchen, 166
Who's Who in Special Libraries 1985-86, 336
Wiegand, Wayne A., 187
Wiggins, Gary Dorman, 463
Williams, James B., 50
Williams, Joan Frye, 56
Williams, Martha E., 39n, 41, 60
WILSONDISC, pp.22-23
Winkel, Lois, 312
Wise, Michael, 150
Wolf, Carolyn, 253
Wolf, Richard, 253
Women and Leadership in the Library Profession, 259
Women's Collections, 380
Women's History Sources, 380n
Wood, Sandra M., 358
Woodard, Gloria, 116
Woolgar, C. M., 338
Woolls, Blanche E., 307, 327
Worsam, Mike, 266
Wright, Helen K., 4
Wynar, Bohdan S., 1, 3, 6, 10
Wynar, Christine Gehrt, 318

Yaakov, Juliette, 311, 314
Yates, Rochelle, 296

Zeiger, Arthur, 317

Subject Index

Unless otherwise indicated, reference is to entry number. References to page number are identified by a *p* (e.g., p.4).

AACR 2. *See* Anglo-American Cataloguing Rules, second edition
Aaron, Shirley, p.37
Abstracts and abstracting, 188-89, 194. *See also* Indexes and indexing
   career guide, 67
Academic libraries. *See* College and research libraries
ACRL. *See* Association of College and Research Libraries
Acronyms and abbreviations, 15
   computing terms, 212
Africa, 150
ALA. *See* American Library Association
Alabama, censorship, 239
Alaska, 16, 23, 50
Alberta, Canada, p.37; 158, 301
ALISE. *See* Association for Library and Information Science Education
Alley, Brian, pp.16-17
American Library Association (ALA), pp.3-4
   on censorship, 240
   history, 187
   research awards and programs, pp.44-47
Anderson, L. S., 144
Anglo-American Cataloguing Rules, second edition (AACR2), 82-88
Apple microcomputers, pp.26-28, p.30, p.32; 326
   compatibles, pp.33-35
Aquariums, science and technology collections, 367
Archer, Linda, p.15, p.19
Architecture, 33-34
Archival collections, 295, 337-39, 359, 380
Arizona, school library media centers, p.37
Art libraries, 340-43
Asia, p.39; 151-56
Association for Library and Information Science Education (ALISE), research programs, p.47

Association of College and Research Libraries (ACRL)
   doctoral fellowship assistance, p.46
   statistics, 137
Atari microcomputers, keyboards, p.28
Australia, 157
Automation in libraries, 35-37, 178. *See also* Microcomputer use and microcomputing; Online public access catalogs; Online searching
   bibliography, 38
   in Brazil, 165
   for cataloging, 71, 77-78
   data and databases, 40-51
   directory, 39
   school library media centers, 424
   special collections, 338, 342
   technical standards, 381
   telecommunications, 62-63
Awards and prizes
   children's literature, 117, 126
   library and information science research, pp.46-47
   library public relations, 280

Baber Research Award, p.46
Bailey, R. H., p.39
Bar code readers (microcomputer input device), p.28
Barron, Daniel, p.37
Berger, Mary, p.22, p.24
Berkner, Dimity, p.20
Berman, Sanford, p.17
Berry, John, p.14
Bibliography, 1-5
   children's literature, 97-108
   comparative and international librarianship, 149
   library instruction, 251
   newspaper libraries, 365
   school library media centers, 308-9

Bierman, J., p.38
Biography, 6-8, 109-11, 336
Bits, p.27
Blacks. See under Ethnic populations
Bluemel, N. L., p.39
Book industries and trade. See Publishers and publishing
Books, 183, 185, 382. See also Children's literature; General reference works; Rare books
Brazil, 165
Brown University Library, 433
Browne, H. T., p.38
Burns, D. R., p.39
Bytes, p.27

CAD/CAE/CAM. See Computer aided-design, -engineering, and -manufacturing
Caldecott Awards, 126
California, p.39
Canada, 2, 17, 158, 186, 245
  children's literature, 124, 128
  school library media centers, p.37; 301
Careers for librarians, 64-69
Cargill, Jennifer, pp.16-17
Cataloging and classification, 45, 70, 72-73, 82-88
  online systems, 71, 77-78
  special materials, 89-96, 268, 342
Catalogs. See Online public access catalogs
Cataloging-in-Publication standards, 74
Cathode Ray Tubes (CRT). See Monitors
CD. See Compact disks
CD-I. See Compact disk-interactive
CD-ROM. See Compact disk-read only memory
Censorship. See Intellectual freedom and censorship
Central processing unit (CPU), pp.26-27
Chief Officers of State Library Agencies (COSLA), 18
Children's and young adult services, 298, 445, 455. See also School library media centers
  gifted programs, p.39; 309, 451
Children's literature, pp.39-40; 90, 455. See also School library media centers: collections
  bibliography, 97-108
  biography, 109-11
  dictionaries, 112-13
  directories, 114-15
  handbooks, 116-22
  indexes, 123-25
  picture books, 126-28
Church libraries. See Theological collections and church and synagogue libraries
Circulation systems, p.28, p.39; 146, 425
Classification. See Cataloging and classification
Claus, R. N., p.39

Coleman, J. G., Jr., p.38
Collection development, 129-36, 377, 428
  for library school libraries, pp.3-11
  school library media centers, pp.39-40; 310-18
  weeding, pp.7-8; 368
College and research libraries, 138-41, 143-46, 433, 452
  automation, 45-46, 63, 447
  collections and collection development, pp.3-11; 130-33, 449, 461
  conservation efforts, 167
  faculty status for librarians, 448, 460
  government publication use, 346
  India, 153
  interlibrary loan, 438
  job opportunities, 443
  library instruction, 252, 427
  statistics, 137, 142
Columbia University, p.3, pp.5-7; 169
Comic books, cataloging, 90
Commodore Amiga microcomputers, keyboards, p.28
Compact disk-interactive (CD-I), p.30
Compact disk-read only memory (CD-ROM), pp.21-25, p.30; 42
Compact disks (CD), p.30
Comparative and international librarianship, 147-66, 254, 262, 356. See also individual countries
Computer aided-design, -engineering, and -manufacturing (CAD/CAE/CAM), p.31
  dictionary, 214
Computers. See Microcomputer use and microcomputing
Computing Information Services, Inc., p.16
Congress of Southeast Asian Librarians (CONSAL), 151
Connolly, Bruce, p.22
CONSAL. See Congress of Southeast Asian Librarians
CONSER. See CONversion of SERials
Conservation, 167-69
Consultant careers, 68, 219
CONversion of SERials (CONSER), 92
Cooper, V. A., p.38
Copyright, 170
COSLA. See Chief Officers of State Library Agencies
CPU. See Central processing unit
Criminal justice, research methods, 297
Crow, S. R., p.39
Curriculum materials centers, 300

Data manipulation, 40
Database producers and services, 41-44, 161, 217, 446. See also Compact disk-read only memory
Datagraphics, pp.14-15, p.19

Subject Index

DeBacher, Dick, p.18
DEC. *See* Digital Equipment Corporation
DeLong, Donald, p.20
Descriptive cataloging, 82-88
Dewey, Melvil, p.3
Dictionaries and encyclopedias, 9-15
   biographical works, 7-8
   children's literature, 112-13
   computers and information technology, 190, 210-15
Digital Equipment Corporation (DEC), pp.21-22
Directories, 16-24
   children's literature, 114-15
Disabled users, p.17; 330-31
Disaster preparedness in libraries, 255
Disk drives, p.29
Doctoral dissertations, pp.229-30. *See also* American Library Association: research awards and programs; Association of College and Research Libraries: doctoral fellowship assistance
Doll, C. A., p.40
Drama and theater for children and young adults, 125
Dublin Library Society, 184

Economics
   classification schemes for, 76
   of library management, 138, 265
Education for library and information science. *See* Libraries and information science: education
Educational Resources Information Center (ERIC), research reviews, p.37
Edwards, J. L., p.38
Edwards, K. K., p.37
Electronic publishing, 65
Emory University, library collection development, pp.7-8
Encyclopedias. *See* Dictionaries and encyclopedias
ERIC. *See* Educational Resources Information Center
Ethnic populations, 283, 310
   blacks, 116
   native Americans, 458
Europe, 65, 104, 159-61
European Computer Manufacturers Association, p.24

Fee-based services, 284
Festschriften, 144, 178-81
Fiction, 314
Fields, Mike, p.15, p.19
Fisher, M., p.39
Fitzgerald, R. F. C., p.38
Flaxman, Barbara, p.16, p.19

Follett Circulation PLUS, p.28
Foos, Donald D., p.17
Frances Henne YASD/*Voice of Youth Advocates (VOYA)* Research Grant, p.46
Franklin Computer Corporation, p.33
Free information resources, 24
Funding sources for church and synagogue libraries, 376. *See also* Grants and grant proposal writing
Funk, G. D., p.40
Furlong, Debra, p.19

Gaver, Mary, p.37
General reference works
   bibliographies, 1-5, 97-108, 149, 251, 308-9, 365
   biographies, 6-8, 109-11, 336
   dictionaries and encyclopedias, 9-15, 112-13, 190, 210-15
   directories, 16-24, 114-15, 216-19
   handbooks and yearbooks, 25-28
   for microcomputing, 35-39, 208-24
   periodicals and serials, 29-31, 308, 462-63
   quotation books, 32
Georgia, censorship, 239
Germany, library history, 160
Gerould, James T., 142
Gifted students, p.39; 309, 451
Glennon, Irene, p.17
Government publications, 90, 344-52
Grants and grant proposal writing, 27, 307
Great Britain, 162, 164, 258
   cataloging and catalogs, 55, 57, 71
   disabled users services, 163
   library careers, 69, 266
   periodicals, 31
   polytechnic libraries, 248, 330, 334
   public libraries, 275-76
   publishing, p.17; 65

Hall, S., p.40
Handbooks and yearbooks, 25-28
   children's literature, 116-22
   information technology, 191-93
Hardware. *See* Microcomputer hardware
Haskell, L. C. M., p.39
Hawaii, school library media centers, p.39
High Sierra Group, p.24
History of librarianship. *See* Libraries and information science: history
Hitachi compact disks, p.30
Ho, M. L., p.40
Horton, J. A., p.38
Humanities, 31, 134, 248, 440
Humor for libraries, 246
H. W. Wilson Company, pp.21-22

IAC. *See* Information Access Company
IBM microcomputers, p.23, pp.26-28, pp.30-35, p.43
  operating system (PC-DOS), 234
  software, 229, 235
Idaho, 23, 50
IDAM. *See* Indexed Descriptor Access Method
Illinois, public libraries, 272-73
Indexed Descriptor Access Method (IDAM), 44
Indexes and indexing, 91, 188-89, 440, 453. *See also* Abstracts and abstracting
  automatic models, 194-95, 432
  career guide, 67
  to children's literature, 123-25
  vocabulary control, 203
India, 153-56
Indiana, children's services, 445
Information Access Company (IAC), pp.22-23
Information management. *See* Information technology: management
Information Resources Management (IRM), directory, 22
Information science. *See* Libraries and information science
Information technology, 190-99, 248. *See also* Automation in libraries
  computing, 208-21
  management, 200-201, 258, 260
  and publishing, pp.13-14
  systems, 202-4
  theories, 205-7
Institute for Scientific Information (ISI), p.22
Intellectual freedom and censorship, 237, 239-42
  restricted information, 238, 243
Interlibrary loan, 244, 438
International librarianship. *See* Comparative and international librarianship
Ireland, medical libraries, 355
IRM. *See* Information Resources Management
ISI. *See* Institute for Scientific Information

Jaques Cattell Press, p.15, p.18
Jeffery, P. L., p.39
Jordan, 441
Journals. *See* Periodicals and serials
Justin Winsor Prize Essay, p.46
Juvenile books. *See* Children's literature

Kansas, p.38
Keyboards (microcomputer input device), pp.27-28
Kilobytes, p.27
"King Study," p.37
Knowledge Access, Inc., p.22
Kollin, Richard, p.13
Kosters, C., p.37

Language Arts microcomputers, p.33
Laser 128 microcomputers, p.33
Laser discs, pp.21-22
Latin America, 165-66, 199
Law and legislation for libraries, 245
Law libraries, 59, 352-54
Leading Edge microcomputers, p.34
LeClercq, A., p.39
Lee, Robert, p.4
Librarians, 28, 426, 437, 441, 443-44. *See also* Libraries and information science; Library support staff; Management
  career options, 64-69
  education, 171-77, 450
  faculty status, 448, 460
  and publishing, pp.13-15; 65, 286
  salary survey, 25, 335
  school library media centers, pp.37-38
Libraries and information science, 32, 136, 171-77, 245-46, 255, 450. *See also* College and research libraries; Library of Congress; Public libraries; Special libraries and collections
  acronyms and abbreviations, 15
  alternative literature, 26
  architecture, 33-34
  education, pp.3-10; 171-77, 450
  history, 168, 182-87, 433
  and publishing, pp.13-15; 289
  staff organizations directory, 21
Library Association of the United Kingdom, p.17
Library instruction, 247-48, 250-53, 292, 427
  clearinghouse directory, 249
  and language reading skills, 459
  school library media centers, 298, 303, 319-24, 434
Library of Congress, 48, 51, 362-63
  classification scheme, 75, 77, 88
Library research. *See* Research and research methods
Library Research Round Table Research Award, p.46
Library school libraries, collection development, pp.3-10
Library support staff, 28, 426
Library technology. *See* Information technology
Lightpens (microcomputer input device), p.28
Loertscher, D., p.40
Louisiana, censorship, 239
Lowrie, Jean, p.37
Lynch, Mary Jo, p.44

MacDonald, G. W., p.37
Machine-readable cataloging (MARC), 86
Macintosh microcomputers, pp.27-28, pp.30-31, pp.33-35. *See also* Apple microcomputers

Malinowsky, H. Robert, p.17
Management, pp.37-38; 256-62, 266. *See also* Personnel management
  archival collections, 337
  budgeting, 263-65
  college and research libraries, 452
  law libraries, 353-54
  public libraries, 452
  serials collections, 369, 371
  special libraries, 332-34
MARC. *See* Machine-readable cataloging
Martell, Charles R., p.44
Massachusetts, public libraries, 270
Master, Lawrence, p.38
Master, Nancy, p.38
Medical libraries, 355-58
Medical publishing, 288
Megabytes, p.27
Melcher, Daniel, p.13
Mexico, 439
Mice (microcomputer input device), p.28
Michigan, pp.38-39
Microcomputer hardware, pp.26-35
  index to, 221
Microcomputer software
  cataloging, 85, 90, 93
  for CD-ROM, pp.21-23; p.30
  directories, 218, 227-30
  evaluations, 231-32
  indexes, 221
Microcomputer use and microcomputing, p.28, pp.30-32, p.35; 222-24, 325-27, 447, 451, 456. *See also* Automation in libraries; Microcomputer hardware; Microcomputer software; Technological computing
  dictionary, 225
  directories, 226-33
  general reference works, 35-39, 208-21
  handbooks, 234-36
Micromedex, Inc., p.22
Military libraries, 364
Ming, M., p.37
Minor, Barbara, p.37
Missouri, p.39
Modems, p.32
Mongeau, Sam, p.18
Monitors (microcomputer output device), pp.31-32
Monographs on information technology, 196-99
Montana, 23, 50
Mosley, M. J., p.38
Museums, 359-61, 367
Muslim countries, 147

NAL. *See* National Agricultural Library
National Agricultural Library (NAL), pp.17-18, p.20

National and federal libraries, 362-64. *See also* Library of Congress
National Center for Education Statistics, p.40
National Information Standards Organization (NISO), p.24
National Library of Medicine, collection development, 129
Native Americans. *See under* Ethnic populations
Natriello, G., p.40
Neal, Jack, p.15
Network Advisory Committee of the Library of Congress, 48, 51, 363
Networks and networking, p.32; 45-51
Nevada, p.38
New England, children's literature, 101
New York State Library at Albany, p.3
New York State University at Fredonia, p.14
New Zealand, pp.38-39
Newspapers and newspaper libraries, 96, 365
Nigeria, 442
NISO. *See* National Information Standards Organization
Nonbook materials, 269
  cataloging and classification, 89-96, 268, 342
  copyright, 170
  selection procedures, 435
Norton, Jeffrey, p.13

OCLC. *See* Online Computer Library Center
OCRs. *See* Optical character readers
Office of Management Studies (OMS), 143
OKAPI (online public access catalog), 55
OMS. *See* Office of Management Studies
Online Computer Library Center (OCLC), 52
  bar code readers, p.28
  college and research libraries, 438
  input and search strategies, 54
Online public access catalogs, 52, 54-55, 57
  bibliographic display, 53, 56
  and CD-ROM, p.22
Online searching, 58-61, 290, 293, 429
  and CD-ROM, p.21, p.24
  directory, 39
  medical libraries, 357-58
  retrieval methods, 454
  user satisfaction, 457
  vocabulary control, 203
Ontario, Canada, library law, 245
Optical character readers (OCRs), pp.28-29
Oral history collections, 19, 339
Oregon, 23, 50
Oryx Press, pp.13-20

Parry, Karen H., p.18
Pennsylvania, pp.39-40

Periodicals and serials, 29-31, 369-72, 434, 462-63
  bibliography, 308
  cataloging and classification, 89-90, 92, 94
  national, 383-90
  regional, 405-23
  subject-oriented, 216, 391-404
Peripherals for microcomputer hardware, pp.27-32
Personnel management, pp.37-38; 267, 294, 426
Phillips compact disks, p.30
Photographs, cataloging, 95
Pickett, Doyle, p.16
Picture books. *See under* Children's literature
Plotters (microcomputer output device), p.31
Poetry for children and young adults, 124
Powell, Lawrence Clark, 32
Printers (microcomputer output device), pp.30-31
Privacy and restricted information. *See* Intellectual freedom and censorship: restricted information
Public libraries, 270-79
  Australia, 157
  children's services, 445
  collection development, 130
  history, 182
  management, 426, 452
Public relations, 280-83
Public services, 284-85. *See also* Reference services
Publishers and publishing, 286-89. *See also* Electronic publishing; Oryx Press

Quimbe, B. E., p.39
Quotation books, 32

Radio Frequency (RF) converters, p.31
Radio Shack microcomputers, p.31
RAM. *See* Random access memory
Random access memory (RAM), p.27
Rare books, 449, 461
Reading programs, p.38
Reed, Kaye, pp.15-16
Reference services, 145, 290-96. *See also* Public services
Religion, children's literature, 108
Research and research methods, 66, 254, 297-98, 430. *See also* American Library Association: research awards and programs; Association for Library and Information Science Education, research programs
  and personality factors, 442
  school library media centers, pp.36-41, 434
  science and technology, 436, 439
RF. *See* Radio Frequency converters

Richter, Anne J., p.13
R. R. Bowker Company, pp.13-15, pp.22-23
Rural Library Training Project, p.37

Salary surveys, 25, 335
Samuel Lazerow Fellowship for Research in Acquisitions or Technical Services, p.46
Sanyo microcomputers, p.35
Schon, Isabel, p.37
School library media centers, p.17, p.37; 298-307, 319-24, 431, 434
  automation, 325-27, 424
  bibliographies, 308-9
  collections, pp.39-40; 310-18, 328-29, 435
  policy development, 299
  program evaluation, pp.38-39; 322
  research, pp.36-41
  skills and programs, 319-24
Schuman, Patricia, p.15
Science and technology information and libraries, 366-68
  collection development, 134
  document delivery, 463
  international information transfer, 166
  nonbibliographic data banks, 161
  publishers and publishing, 288
  rare book collections, 449
  research methods, pp.39-40; 436, 439, 442
Scotland, automation in libraries, 36
Scott, W. A., p.38
SCSI. *See* Small Computer System Interface
Security in libraries, 255
Serials. *See* Periodicals and serials
Sharpe, M. E., p.17
Shontz, M. L., p.37
SilverPlatter, Inc., pp.22-23
Slesinger, Henry, p.15
Slesinger, Susan, p.16, p.19
Slesinger, Yaranoff and Associates, p.15
Small Computer System Interface (SCSI), p.30
Social sciences, 31, 134, 440
Software. *See* Microcomputer software
Spanish-language materials, 278, 459
  cataloging, 90
  children's literature, 105
Special libraries and collections, 139, 332-36. *See also* Archival collections; Art libraries; Law libraries; Medical libraries; Military libraries; Museums; National and federal libraries; Newspapers and newspaper libraries; Oral history collections; Rare books; Science and technology information and libraries; State libraries; Theological collections and church and synagogue libraries; Toy libraries; Women: special collections

Subject Index

academic tests, 132
document delivery, 463
government publications, 344-51
salary surveys, 335
serials, 89, 92, 94, 369-72
Speech systems (microcomputer input device), p.29
State libraries, 18, 373
Steckler, Phyllis B., pp.13-16, p.18
Stickney, Arthur H., p.18
Storytelling, 321
String indexing, 91. See also Indexes and indexing
Subject headings, 75, 77, 79, 81
Synagogue libraries. See Theological collections and church and synagogue libraries

Tandy microcomputers, p.28, pp.30-32
Tape backup systems (microcomputer storage and retrieval device), pp.29-30
Technical services, 71. See also Automation in libraries; Cataloging and classification
Technical standards, 381-82
Technological computing, 208-9. See also Microcomputer use and microcomputing
dictionaries, 210-15
directories, 216-19
handbooks and yearbooks, 220
indexes, 221
Telecommunications, p.21, p.32; 47, 62-63
Telephone reference service, 296
Tennessee, censorship, 239
Texas in children's literature, 100
Theological collections and church and synagogue libraries, 374-78
Thomas, Carol, p.17
Thomas, James L., pp.16-17
Thomas, R. L., p.38
Thompson, Anne, p.16
Toy libraries, 379
and collections, 328-29
Turner, P. M., p.38
Two-Poisson model of automatic indexing, 432

UNESCO. See United Nations Educational, Scientific and Cultural Organization

Unions in librarianship, 444
United Kingdom. See Great Britain
United Nations Educational, Scientific and Cultural Organization (UNESCO), library development planning, 148
United States, library directories, 16-21
University of Tennessee, library collection development, pp.8-10

Van House, N. A., p.38
Video Display Tubes (VDT). See Monitors
Video technology, 223
microcomputer imaging, p.29
Video Technology, Ltd., p.33
Vienna, Austria, 159
Virginia, school library media centers, p.38; 431
Volunteers, 374

Waschler, Merl, p.20
Washington (state), 23, 50
Wasserman, Paul, p.17
Weeding. See under Collection development
Wilson, William K., p.14
Wisconsin, school library media centers, pp.38-39
Women
in library administration, 259
library services to, 285
school library media centers, p.38
special collections, 380
WORM. See Write-Once-Read-Many
Write-Once-Read-Many (WORM) CD drive, p.30

Yaranoff, Chris, p.15
Yearbooks. See Handbooks and yearbooks
Young adults. See Children's and young adult services; Children's literature

Zenith microcomputers, p.28, p.35
Zsiray, S. W., p.38

AUG 1 3 1987,